# KANO

## ENVIRONMENT, SOCIETY AND DEVELOPMENT

Published by

Adonis & Abbey Publishers Ltd

**United Kingdom**
Southbank House
Black Prince Road
London
SE1 7SJ
United Kingdom
Emails: editor@adonis-abbey.com,
Tel: 0845 388 7248

**Nigeria**
No.3 Akanu Ibiam Street,
Aso-villa, Asokoro.
P.O. Box 10546
Abuja
Tel: +234 (0) 8165970458, 07066997765

Year of Publication 2014

British Library Cataloguing-in-Publication Data
A catalogue record for this book is available from the British Library

ISBN: 9781909112391(Paper Back)
       9781909112407(Hard Cover)

A.I. Tanko and S.B. Momale (Eds.)
*Kano: Environment, Society and Development*
London & Abuja, Adonis & Abbey Publishers

ii

# KANO

## ENVIRONMENT, SOCIETY AND DEVELOPMENT

**A. I. Tanko and S. B. Momale**

Adonis & Abbey Publishers Ltd

# TABLE OF CONTENTS

Table of
Contents

A.I. Tanko and S.B. Momale (Eds.)
*Kano: Environment, Society and Development*
London & Abuja, Adonis & Abbey Publishers

iv

## PART III: RESOURCE UTILISATION AND MANAGEMENT

Table of    A.I. Tanko and S.B. Momale (Eds.)
Contents     *Kano: Environment, Society and Development*
          London & Abuja, Adonis & Abbey Publishers

# PART IV: ISSUES IN DEVELOPMENT: CASE STUDIES

| Table of Contents | A.I. Tanko and S.B. Momale (Eds.)<br>*Kano: Environment, Society and Development*<br>London & Abuja, Adonis & Abbey Publishers |
| --- | --- |

vi

# Preface

*Kano: Environment, Society and Development* has been planned to be a compendium on the Kano Region. *The Kano Region* has been taught and studied around some universities and colleges especially in Africa for more than three decades without a standard book. Although there were some attempts at different times that published *Some Aspects of the Physical Geography of the Kano Region, and Related Human Responses (Olofin, 1987)* and *Laboratory of Areal Differentiation: Metropolitan Kano in Geographical Perspectives (Olofin and Tanko, 2002)* these were of limited coverage and dimensions, for which therefore, they were narrowly used.

It is important to state though that the Region has been widely studied and most of these were variously documented by different experts and students on the Region. This book is an attempt to bring together their works together in the forms of chapter contributions. The book describes, discusses and analyses the different perspectives on the Region. It uses language understandable to those with limited understanding of any typical environment in the Africa's Savanna and is essentially useful to those with some basic understanding of the Kano Region in particular and other similar regions in Africa under similar geographical settings. The book is subdivided into four Parts (I - IV) each containing different chapters. On the whole, there are thirty one Chapters.

Part One which is essentially the description of the (physical) *Kano Environment* has five Chapters (1-5) starting with Professor Emmanuel Ajayi Olofin's that describes the location, relief and landforms of the Region. The six landform types that characterise the Region are identified, comprising the dissected hilly highlands, high plains with grouped hills, pediplains, sandy plains, dune fields and alluvial channel complexes. The geographical location of the Region within the semi-arid tropics influences the climatic characteristics while the landforms have significant influence on the drainage, hydrology and water resources management.

In Chapter Two, Maryam Liman, Halima Abdulkadir Idris and Ummi Khalthum Mohammed describe the weather and climate focusing on the factors that control the climatic characteristics of the Kano Region. The four seasons as experienced in the Region are

Preface | A.I. Tanko and S.B. Momale (Eds.)
*Kano: Environment, Society and Development*
London & Abuja, Adonis & Abbey Publishers

**vii**

identified, characterised and explained. These are followed by a detailed description of the rainfall characteristics. The Chapter concludes that the rainfall regime influences the drainage and hydrology of the Region.

Chapter Three by Adnan Abdulhamid focuses on drainage, hydrology and water resources of the Region. The Chapter delves into the available surface water resources from rainfall, ground water resources, major river systems and water supply. It also highlights some issues arising due to water resource management in the Region. According to the Chapter water resource distribution and moisture availability is important to agriculture particularly where the soils are fertile for crops production.

In Chapter Four, Essiet Unanaowo Essiet describes and analyses the soils of the Region. The relationship between the soils and the geological formations, the physical and chemical properties of the soils and their agricultural potentials is explained. Soils stability and nutrients status is influence by vegetation which is variable and continuously changing within the Region.

The focus of Chapter Five by Murtala Muhammad Badamasi is on vegetation. After defining vegetation, the Chapter describes the five key factors determining the nature and pattern of vegetation. The vegetation types in the Region are explained and the major tree species are identified. The Forest Reserves and the Community Forest Areas of the Region are also described. The impact of human activities on vegetation and forestry resources is assessed and recommendations offered for the sustainable management of the vegetation resources of the Region. Invariably, the vegetation resources of the Region have been significantly affected by the urban growth of Metropolitan Kano.

Part Two is on the sub-theme of *the Kano People* and has eight Chapters (6-13). It begins with Bello Gambo's Chapter Six on the Origin and Growth of Kano City. The Chapter examines the political, economic and social capitals of the Region based on a number of theoretical foundations. The author traces the origin and growth of urban Kano from around the 6th and the 7th Centuries to date. In order to achieve a temporal analysis of the growth, the author classifies happenings during the pre-colonial, colonial and post Independence periods. The major social, economic and political factors, associated with major historical periods are examined. The author highlights the

Preface | A.I. Tanko and S.B. Momale (Eds.)
*Kano: Environment, Society and Development*
London & Abuja, Adonis & Abbey Publishers

implications of the spatial and temporal growth of the city on the factors highlighted. The Chapter concludes with a reflection on the rapid population growth witnessed in the Region over the past Century.

Chapter Seven by Ahmed Maigari Ibrahim explores population growth in the Kano Region, which according to the Chapter expanded from 2.4 million in 1931 to about 13.7 million in 2006. The implications of the rate of growth on the population to land ratio as well as the structural characteristics of the Region population on socio-economic development are examined, including its prospects, prosperity and posterity. This population is spatially distributed, forming unique landscapes such as the Kano Emir's Palace as well as the religious and cultural landscapes within Metropolitan Kano.

Within the Kano Metropolis, a unique landscape with immense social, political, religious and historical significance is the Kano Emir's Palace. Aliyu Salisu Barau's Chapter Eight assesses the geographic landscapes and their functions using the case in the Kano Palace. The Chapter describes the population in the Palace and its ecosystem and how it pairs with sustainability index and demands of the paradigm of new urbanism. According to the Chapter, compared to the Kano city, the Emir's Palace demonstrates the practicability and possibility of harmonious coexistence between human population, land use and ecosystem security and therefore ranks high in the sustainability index.

Chapter Nine by Adamu Tanko and Halima Idris is about trade, commerce and industry. These were traced back in history to the periods of the trans-Saharan trades. Following this, the circumstances and the impact of the trading activities were examined following three periods of pre-colonial, colonial and post Independence, similar to the scale used in Chapter Six. In this way Kano was shown to have favourably participated in long- and short-distances trade establishing links through complex networks of routes in today's West Africa. Contemporary economic and political events have been shown to have affected these activities.

Abdallah Uba Adamu's Chapter Ten traces the cartography of Arab migrations from North Africa and the Middle East to Northern Nigeria in general and Kano in particular, and the various ways they influence, but are not influenced by, the culture and society of Kano. It

Preface | A.I. Tanko and S.B. Momale (Eds.)
*Kano: Environment, Society and Development*
London & Abuja, Adonis & Abbey Publishers

ix

traces the long history of migration and settlement and the consolidation of the North African community in Kano. The social organisation, the commercial activities, the political leadership and their influence on Sufism was examined. The British occupation and the emergence of Lebanese communities in Kano are explained. The Yemenite arrival in Kano associated with British colonialism was explored. Finally, the intergroup contact, migrations and community formation in Kano was evaluated, and this has influences on the landscapes of Metropolitan Kano.

In Chapter Eleven, Ibrahim Badamasi Lambu describes the cultural landscapes of Metropolitan Kano with specific focus on religious landscapes. It presents the Geography of Religion in the City, showing areas of religious culture. It traces and describes the origin and influence of the two major religions, Islam and Christianity and the proliferation of cultural religious landmarks. The influence of this on the multi-cultural and multi-ethnic composition of the population in the Kano City was highlighted.

In addition, to cultural and religious landscapes, the book examines the economic landscapes as exemplified by the rural markets as focused in Chapter Twelve by Ishaq Aliyu Abdulkarim. The concept of rural markets is defined and its relevance to the social and economic wellbeing of rural populations is described. The evolution, types and characteristics of rural markets in the Region is explained, and the contribution of the markets to the economy of the Region is examined. The potential contributions of rural markets, if improved and developed is highlighted to address the challenges of poverty facing the Region as expatiated in Chapter thirteen.

Chapter Thirteen by Julius Afolabi Falola closes Part two of the book. The Chapter describes and addresses the definition of poverty and its different issues and perspectives. It describes its nature within the Kano Region describing its four measures (being education, housing, facilities in houses and waste disposal). The reasons for poverty are explained and the strategies for addressing the problems emanating from it are proffered. Such strategies include improvement in agriculture, where soil fertility management is essential.

Part Three is on *Resource Utilization and Management in the Region*. It has nine Chapters (14-22). Maharazu Alhaji Yusuf's Chapter Fourteen explores issues in soil fertility management, with

Preface | A.I. Tanko and S.B. Momale (Eds.)
*Kano: Environment, Society and Development*
London & Abuja, Adonis & Abbey Publishers

x

emphasis on smallholder farmers who are the major agricultural producers in the Kano Region. Three farming systems are identified and described and the nature of soil fertility management (fallowing, manuring/fertilization, agronomic methods, cultivation methods, residue management) was described. The effectiveness of soil fertility management to improving agricultural yields is closely associated with efficient utilisation and management of water resources.

Chapter Fifteen by Adamu Idris Tanko addresses Water Resource Development and Management in the Kano Region. It highlights these within the broad Hadejia-Jama'are-Komadugu-Yobe Basin, covering sub-themes including surface and groundwater resources development, water uses and the challenges of sustainable water resource management as reflected in increasing population, non-availability and the non-usability of basic meteorological data, limited knowledge about available water, nature and magnitude of water demands, and conflicts between and among cultivators and herders over shared resources among others. Poor land and water management practices, unutilised development potentials, inadequate maintenance of existing water infrastructure, changes in river ecologies and socio-economic conditions are among the major challenges. The drive towards integrated water resource management is examined, including the need for biodiversity management within the entire Region and beyond.

In Chapter Sixteen, Salisu Mohammed focuses the biodiversity and wild foods. After defining the multi-disciplinary perspectives of biodiversity, the Chapter examines biodiversity in the Region, using two case study villages of Tumbau and Dagaceri. The diversity in flora and fauna are determined and the uses of the plant and animals species for various purposes like medicine, ornaments, foods and ecological conservation which are highly important for the sustainable management of the Kano Region. The relevance of biodiversity management to diverse livelihoods in the Region, such as pastoralism that depends on favourable ecological conditions is buttressed in the Chapter. The challenges of conserving biodiversity using Gene Banks and other techniques are examined.

Pastoralism as a livestock breeding system in the Kano Region is the concern of Chapter Seventeen by Saleh Bashayi Momale. The type of livestock breeding practices, the forms of mobility, the distribution of pastoralists and the contributions of livestock breeding to the

Preface | A.I. Tanko and S.B. Momale (Eds.)
*Kano: Environment, Society and Development*
London & Abuja, Adonis & Abbey Publishers

xi

economy of the Region is explained. The problems facing the pastoralists and the challenges of inadequate grazing areas and pastoralists - farmers' conflicts are analysed. Education and social enlightenment as well as the need for promotion of improved livestock breeding techniques are among the strategies identified for addressing some of these challenges.

Chapter Eighteen by Nuratu Mohammed dwells on education and educational development in the Region. The Chapter emphasises the relevance of education for the sustainable development of societies and as an important indicator of Human Development. The forms (western and Islamic) and the stages (primary secondary and tertiary) are discussed, tracing the historical development of these forms and levels of the education. The progress recorded, the challenges facing educational service delivery and the strategies for addressing these challenges are also discussed.

Muhammad Abubakar Liman and Isa Umar Farouk's Chapter nineteen is on Passenger Travel Services. The centrality of transport in defining the patterns of urban and rural interactions is explained, including pattern, forms and dynamics of inter-urban transport service in the Region and the intra-urban transport within Kano Metropolis. The roles of the private and public sectors are evaluated, including some perspectives on commercial motorcycle operators (*Achaba*) and Tricycles (*A Daidata Sahu*). Policy suggestions are proffered, noting that the dynamic nature of societies requires continuous review in response to social, economic and technological changes.

Transition to the Information Era is therefore the central concern of Chapter Twenty by Muhammad Abubakar Liman. Tracing the major "revolutions" in human history, the Chapter asserts that the intimate union of the computer and telecommunications marks the on-set of the information era. It analyses the distribution of the TCMs being the spatial materiality supporting the space of flows in the Kano Region. It finally assesses the factors that influence the pattern of distribution.

The contemporary challenge of Gender and Gender Mainstreaming is the focus of Mairo Haruna's Chapter Twenty One. Gender is defined, noting that it is influenced by social, cultural and religious processes and norms. Central gender issues including women productive and reproductive roles, women and education (both Islamic

Preface | A.I. Tanko and S.B. Momale (Eds.)
*Kano: Environment, Society and Development*
London & Abuja, Adonis & Abbey Publishers

xii

and Western), women and governance and women access to resources were described and analysed. According to the Chapter, the prospect for enhancing the role of women is an important matter that needs to be vigorously pursued because of its enormous implications on maternal health, quality of family life and sustainable social and economic development.

Chapter Twenty Two by Yusuf Muhammad Adamu on Maternal Health in Rural Kano deal with one of the most contemporary challenges of the Region. Situating the Chapter within the concepts of Medical Geography, it presents global, regional and local (using Kausani village as a case study) trends in maternal mortality and morbidity, noting that the Kano Region has one of the highest rates of maternal mortality in the world. Antenatal and Obstetric Care Services in the rural Kano is discussed and the causative factors for mortality is explained, including the role of cultural factors. The role of Traditional Birth Attendants (TBAs) is assessed and suggestions for reversing the current trend are provided.

Part Four is captioned *Issues in Development: Case Studies* also has nine Chapters (23-31) beginning with Aliyu Danshehu Maiwada's Chapter Twenty three, Urban Planning in the context of Rapid Growth of Urban Kano. The city, one of the leading commercial and industrial centres experiencing rapid growth rate, the institutional and administrative framework for planning during the colonial and post colonial period is examined. The existing organisational framework for planning in Metropolitan Kano and the urban planning and development in practice is evaluated. Recommendations are offered including the need to develop multiple growth centres within the Region in order to reduce pressure on Metropolitan Kano, where health and other services are rapidly developing.

The distribution of Primary Health Care Facilities within the Kano Metropolis has enormous implications on health care delivery as described in Chapter Twenty Four by Mohammed Ahmed. After defining the concept of Primary Health Care services (PHCs) and its roles towards Sustainable Development, the Chapter traces the development of health care facilities in the Region and examines the functions and spatial distribution of PHCs within the Metropolis. It reveals that the Metropolitan areas occupied by the Higher Class segment of the society are better served.

Preface | A.I. Tanko and S.B. Momale (Eds.)
*Kano: Environment, Society and Development*
London & Abuja, Adonis & Abbey Publishers

Oyelayo Abike Adekiya's Chapter Twenty Five deals with Human Excreta Management in the Kano Metropolis. The Chapter contextualises the discourse on the effects of poor personal and domestic hygiene in the transmission of many infectious diseases and examines the practice of excreta disposal and personal hygiene among residents in two residential districts: the Kano Municipal Council and the Sabon Gari in the Fagge Local Government Council. Strategic recommendations are proffered to address the challenge of ineffective and poor management of human excreta and personal hygiene in the Metropolis.

The issues and challenges of Urban Pressure and Tree Cover Change are addressed by Roy Maconachie's Chapter Twenty Six. It addresses the concept of land degradation and the notion of vegetation loss in the Kano Closed-Settled Zone drawing findings from case study areas within the Zone. It explores local knowledge of vegetation and perceptions of vegetation change. Woodfuel demand and utilisation in the Region is described within the context of prevailing economic factors. Conflicting land use patterns amidst climatic and other influences and its implications on woodland degradation is examined. According to the Chapter, this influences not only sustainable resource management within the Region, but also on domestic household energy choices.

Chapter Twenty Seven by Ibrahim Baba Yakubu on Household Energy discusses the household energy situation in the Region. It examines the importance of energy at household level and its impact on the socioeconomic well-being of the people. Different concepts and practices relating to woodfuel as a major household energy source, urban energy demand and supply, the sources of woodfuel and the household energy transition in Kano are explained, all in the context of the ongoing challenges of rapid population growth and climate change.

Focusing on one of the most contemporary debates is Luka Fitto Buba's Chapter Twenty Eight, the Climate Change in the Kano Region. Supporting the claim of an ongoing climate change at the global level, the Chapter presents and analyses the long term climatic and meteorological data of the Kano Region, including the seasonal and annual distribution of temperature and rainfall. Time series and other spatial and temporal analyses of the records were used to provide evidence of climate change in the Region. He concludes that the

Preface | A.I. Tanko and S.B. Momale (Eds.)
*Kano: Environment, Society and Development*
London & Abuja, Adonis & Abbey Publishers

challenges of adapting to climate change in a Region prone to droughts and desertification calls for reflection and informed planning to guarantee sustainable management of the natural resources.

Chapter Twenty Nine by Ahmed Maigari Ibrahim on Drought and Desertification describes the three types of droughts including meteorological, hydrological and agricultural droughts. Desertification is described as a process of degradation of ecosystem in arid and semi-arid regions. The perception, causes and consequences of drought and desertification is discussed, including the human response adopted in the Kano Region. Erosion and land control mechanisms is among the human responses since the soils of the Region are prone to erosion hazards.

Chapter Thirty by Kabiru Ahmed addresses occurrences of Erosion Hazards in the Kano Region. The relationship between land use intensification and accelerated erosion as an aspect of landform studies is described. Erosion hazard is found to have been associated with the three tier landscape units in the Region (i.e. the highland, upland, and lowland). The relationship between vegetation and erosion is described and control mechanisms are examined. Recommendations for effective management of erosion hazards are provided.

Mahmud Muhammad Lawan's Chapter Thirty One deals with Democratization and Governance in Kano State within the framework of the universal crave for good democratic government. The Chapter conceptualizes democracy, democratization and governance and reviews the geographical and socio-economic background of Kano as well as the dynamics and challenges of democratization. Recommendations are offered for the enthronement of an effective and sustainable democratic system that will strengthen good governance essential for the peaceful, progressive and sustainable development of Kano State in particular, the Region and Nigeria at large.

Upon all these, we as Editors of the different Chapters (and the very many other submissions that could not go through) would like to express our sincere gratitudes to the authors who contributed to the book, and especially for their zeal and determination in addressing issues raised in their write-ups despite the tight schedules even as we continue to work in an environment of uncertainties.

Finally, we want to thank the Mac Arthur Foundation and the Mac Arthur Grant Implementation Committee (MAGIC) at Bayero

Preface | A.I. Tanko and S.B. Momale (Eds.)
*Kano: Environment, Society and Development*
London & Abuja, Adonis & Abbey Publishers

XV

University Kano for providing the grant for the book project. In this case, we must mention the names of Dr. Ado Dan'Isa (the Grant Liaison Officer, GLO, at BUK), the Immediate Past Vice Chancellor of Bayero University, Kano Professor Attahiru M. Jega, OFR, his successor, Professor Abubakar Adamu Rasheed, *mni*, MFR; Professor Kabiru Ahmed, Professor Muhammad Yahuza Bello all for their support in accessing the Grant.

Other people worthy of mention are Professor M.J. Mortimore, Professor E.A. Olofin, Professor J.Afolabi Falola, Dr. Reginald Cline Cole, Professor Tony Binns, Dr. Roy Maconachie, Dr. Kenny Lynch, Dr. Simon Milligan and all teachers and students of the Kano Region especially at Bayero University, Kano, all for their immense support on this project and similar other projects that provided better understanding of the Region.

Finally, we wish to express appreciation to both Abdulkadir Sani and Abdullahi Rabiu, both of Geography Department, Bayero University, Kano who assisted with the cartographic works.

Preface | A.I. Tanko and S.B. Momale (Eds.)
*Kano: Environment, Society and Development*
London & Abuja, Adonis & Abbey Publishers

xvi

# Foreword

Reginald Cline-Cole
*Centre of West African Studies, University of Birmingham, UK*

Although starting life as a Greek proverb, the observation that there is always something new out of Africa (*semper aliquid novi Africam adferre* in Latin) is widely credited to Aristotle, but has in reality come down to us in the present via a tortuous historical, philosophical and ideological route, partly courtesy of the much quoted rendition of Pliny the Elder and/or Erasmus: *ex Africa semper aliquid novi* (Feinberg and Solodow, 2002). The saying is apposite on at least three counts.

First, there *is* always something new in and from that part of Africa that is the Kano Region requiring close observation, examination, documentation, analysis and explanation. 'New' here is understood as 'different', even 'admirable', rather than as 'strange', possibly 'undesirable', as in early usage of the proverb. The need for, and appearance of, this collection of essays on the region's changing geography/ies therefore represent both a reflection of, and response to, what is a contemporary and positive interpretation of the proverb.

Second, in its various forms -- as discipline, practice and object/subject of study -- Geography epitomises *both* heterogeneity *and* hybridity, and well beyond the 'natural' realm highlighted in and by early Greek and Roman usage of the proverb. Indeed, the range of themes, approaches and coverage making up this collection demonstrate this beyond all reasonable doubt. Here, too, then, the current usage represents a more modern and optimistic twist on an old proverb, whose early deployment can be traced to attempts to both capture and reflect what was perceived as the ('bizarre' or 'exotic') diversity and ('monstrous') hybridity characterising African wildlife and, albeit more rarely, its humans (Feinberg and Solodow, 2002; Knowles, 2005).

Third, and finally, adopted as motto of the South African Museum to reflect that institution's role in knowledge production and dissemination, the original Aristotelian version of the proverb (*semper aliquid novi Africa affert*) was reportedly preferred, with its implied

Foreword | Reginald Cline-Cole, in
A.I. Tanko and S.B. Momale (Eds.)
*Kano: Environment, Society and Development*
London & Abuja, Adonis & Abbey Publishers

suggestion that the museum was being charged with responsibility for 'bringing forth' or 'contributing' *new* knowledge about Africa, including via publishing (van den Heever, undated). As in the preceding cases, this favoured interpretation of the age-old saying is a far cry from the latter's original proverbial sentiments. Of more direct relevance for us, however, is that, once again, it is an understanding which chimes with the aim and objectives of the considerable professional undertaking which the volume represents.

In short, *The Geography of the Kano Region* sets out not only to demonstrate how and why geography matters in the specific context of this part of (northern) Nigeria, but also to contribute to an understanding of nature and society in Africa more widely, and to do so in a 'nuanced, contextualised and balanced' way (Bates, 2012). It is, literally, something new out of Africa.

## References

Bates, R. (2012), 'History of Africa through western eyes', *The Guardian* Newspaper, Thursday 1 November, http://www.guardian .co.uk/world/2012/nov/01/africa-history-western-eyes (Accessed 5 April 2013)

Harvey M. Feinberg, H.M. and Solodow, J.B. (2002), 'Out of Africa', *Journal of African History*, 43, 255-61

Knowles, E. (ed)(2005). *The Oxford Dictionary of Phrase and Fable*. Oxford University Press

van den Heever, J. A. (undated), 'Out of Africa there's always something new' http://academic.sun.ac.za/botzoo/paleo/africa.htm (Accessed on 2 April 2013).

Foreword | Reginald Cline-Cole, in
A.I. Tanko and S.B. Momale (Eds.)
*Kano: Environment, Society and Development*
London & Abuja, Adonis & Abbey Publishers

# List of Contributors

ABDULHAMID, Adnan, PhD (BUK), is a Lecturer in the Department of Geography, Bayero University, Kano. His academic interests are in the fields of hydrology, water resource management and vegetation studies.

ABDULKARIM, Ishaq Aliyu, is a Lecturer in the Department of Geography, Bayero University, Kano. He is a Doctoral candidate at Bayero University. His teaching and research interests are in the fields of rural geography, agricultural geography and medical geography.

ADAMU, Abdallah Uba, PhD (Sussex), is a Professor of Media and Cultural Communication in the Department of Mass Communication, Bayero University, Kano. He was formerly the Head of Science Education Department in the University before he was academically repackaged to transfer to Mass Communication. His current research interests are in the fields of Popular Media and Culture.

ADAMU, Yusuf Muhammad, PhD (BUK), is a Professor of Medical Geography in the Department of Geography, Bayero University, Kano. His academic interest is the fields of Medical Geography, Cultural Geography and Social Geography.

ADEKIYA, Oyelawo Abike, PhD (UI), was formerly a Lecturer in the Department of Geography, Bayero University Kano, and now with the Department of Geography and Regional Planning, Olabisi Onabanjo University, Ago-Iwoye, Ogun State. Her teaching and research interests are in the fields of Urban and Regional Planning as well as Waste Management.

AHMED, Kabiru is a Professor of Geography in the Department of Geography, Bayero University, Kano. His teaching and research interests are in the fields of land resource survey techniques, EIA and community based natural resource management.

AHMED, Mohammed is a Cartographer in the Department of Geography, Bayero University, Kano undergoing postgraduate studies

List of Contributors | A.I. Tanko and S.B. Momale (Eds.)
*Kano: Environment, Society and Development*
London & Abuja, Adonis & Abbey Publishers

xix

in GIS at Ahmadu Bello University, Zaria. His research interests are in the fields of Cartography, Remote Sensing and GIS.

BADAMASI, Ibrahim Lambu is a Lecturer in the Department of Geography, Kano State University of Science and Technology, Wudil. He is currently a PhD candidate at Bayero University Kano working on Religious Places. His teaching and research interests are in the fields of culture and environment, EIA, research techniques and other related aspects of Human Geography.

BADAMASI, Murtala Muhammad is a Lecturer in the Department of Geography, Bayero University, Kano. He is a Doctoral candidate in the Department of Geography, Usmanu Danfodiyo University, Sokoto. His teaching and research interests are in the fields of Vegetation Change Analysis, Water Resource Evaluation, Waste Management and Remote Sensing and GIS.

BARAU, Aliyu Salisu, a PhD researcher in GIS/Urban Sustainability, Faculty of Built Environment, Universiti Teknologi, Sukudai, Johor, Malaysia. His academic interests are in the field of Social and Cultural Geography, and Environmental Management.

BUBA, Luka Fitto, PhD (BUK), is a Senior Lecturer in the Department of Geography, Bayero University, Kano. His academic interests are in the fields of climatology, climate change and agricultural meteorology, research and analytical techniques.

ESSIET, Unanaowo Essiet, PhD (Aberdeen), is a Professor of Soil Science in the Department of Soil Science, Bayero University, Kano. His academic interests include soil fertility management, soil conservation and sustainability of agricultural soils.

FALOLA, Julius Afolabi, PhD (Ibadan), is a Professor of Geography in the Department of Geography, Bayero University, Kano. Some of his academic interests cover the diverse fields of rural geography, development geography, agricultural development and research and analytical techniques.

| List of contributors | A.I. Tanko and S.B. Momale (Eds.)<br>*Kano: Environment, Society and Development*<br>London & Abuja, Adonis & Abbey Publishers |
| --- | --- |

xx

FAROUK, Isa Umar, PhD (BUK), is a Lecturer in the Department of Geography, Bayero University, Kano. His academic interests are in the fields of transport and logistics planning and management, urban geography and urban planning and regional development.

GAMBO, Bello, PhD (BUK), is a Lecturer in the Department of Geography, Bayero University, Kano. His teaching and research interests are in the fields of rural and urban development agricultural geography and geographic thought.

HARUNA, Mairo, is a Lecturer in the Department of Geography, Bayero University, Kano. She is a Doctoral candidate in the Department of Geography, BUK. Her teaching and research interests are in the fields of gender and development, agricultural geography and GIS.

IBRAHIM, Ahmed Maigari, PhD (BUK), is a Senior Lecturer in the Department of Geography, Bayero University, Kano. His teaching and research interests are in the fields of environmental science, EIA, livelihoods and natural resource management.

IDRIS, Halima Abdulkadir, is an Assistant Lecturer in the Department of Geography, Bayero University, Kano. She has just concluded an M.Sc. in Lannd Resources (Development) at Bayero. Her academic interests are in the fields of climatology and climate change.

LAWAN, Mahmoud Muhammad, PhD (BUK), is an Associate Professor of Political Science in the Department of Political Science, Bayero University, Kano. He is currently the Chairman, Academic Staff Union of Universities (ASUU), Bayero University Chapter. His academic interests are in the fields of democracy and development, poverty, corruption and development and public policy reforms.

LIMAN, Maryam, is an Assistant Lecturer in the Department of Geography, Bayero University, Kano. She is a Doctoral candidate in the Department of Geography, BUK. Her teaching and research interests are in the fields of climatology and climate change.

| List of contributors | A.I. Tanko and S.B. Momale (Eds.)<br>*Kano: Environment, Society and Development*<br>London & Abuja, Adonis & Abbey Publishers |

xxi

LIMAN, Muhammad Abubakar is a Senior Lecturer in the Department of Geography, Bayero University, Kano. He is a Doctoral candidate in the Department of Geography, ABU. His teaching and research interests are in the fields off urban geography, urban infrastructural management, urban growth and urban transportation systems.

MACONACHIE, Roy, PhD (Sussex), is a Lecturer in the Department of Social and Policy Sciences, University of Bath, the United Kingdom. His academic interests are in the fields of development geography and international development studies.

MAIWADA, Aliyu Danshehu, is a Senior Lecturer in the Department of Geography, Bayero University, Kano. His teaching and research interests are in the field of urban planning systems, urbanisation, development control, sustainable management of urban landscapes and environmental education.

MOHAMMED, Nuratu, PhD (BUK), is a Senior Lecturer in the Department of Geography, Bayero University, Kano. Her academic interests are in the fields of gender and development, rural geography, tourism and environmental education.

MOHAMMED, Salisu, PhD (BUK), is a Senior Lecturer in the Department of Geography, Bayero University, Kano. His teaching and research interests are in the field of plants biodiversity, biogeography and management of Sahelian environmental resources.

MOHAMMED, Ummi-Kalthum is a Graduate Assistant in the Department of Geography, Bayero University, Kano. She is working for her M.Sc. at the Department of Geography, Bayero University. Her teaching and research interests are in the fields of geomorphology and land use management.

MOMALE, Saleh Bashayi is a Lecturer in the Department of Geography and a Researcher at the Centre for Dryland Agriculture, Bayero University, Kano. He is a Doctoral candidate in the Department of Geography, Bayero University. His teaching and research interests are in the fields of natural resource management,

List of contributors | A.I. Tanko and S.B. Momale (Eds.)
*Kano: Environment, Society and Development*
London & Abuja, Adonis & Abbey Publishers

xxii

pastoralism, climate change, participatory development and remote sensing.

OLOFIN, Emmanuel Ajayi, PhD (ABU), is a Professor of Geography in the Department of Geography, Bayero University, Kano and a leading scholar in the Kano Region. He is the author of the first book on the Kano Region: "*Some Aspects of the Physical Geography of the Kano Region, and Related Human Responses, Departmental Lecture Series 1*", published in 1987.

TANKO, Adamu Idris, PhD (BUK), is a Professor of Geography in the Department of Geography, Bayero University, Kano. He is currently, the Dean, Faculty of Social and Management Sciences, Bayero University, Kano. His teaching and research interests are in the fields of geomorphology, Water Resource Evaluation, Irrigation Management, Environmental Impact Assessment (EIA) and Climate Change.

YAKUBU, Ibrahim Baba, PhD (BUK), is an Associate Professor of Geography in the Department of Geography, Bayero University, Kano. His academic interests are in the fields of land use conservation, biodiversity, forestry resource inventory and management and energy.

YUSUF, Maharazu Alhaji, PhD (BUK) is an Associate Professor and Head of Geography at the Department of Geography, Bayero University, Kano. His academic interests are in the fields of soils management and fertility, soil survey, smallholder tropical farming system and agroforestry.

List of contributors | A.I. Tanko and S.B. Momale (Eds.)
*Kano: Environment, Society and Development*
London & Abuja, Adonis & Abbey Publishers

**xxiii**

# Part I
# The Kano Environment

# Chapter One

## LOCATION, RELIEF AND LANDFORMS

Emmanuel Ajayi Olofin

### Location

The Kano Region occupies the southwestern rim of the Chad depression. It shares physiographic divides with the Niger and Benue River Systems to the south and southeast, with the Niger System to the southwest and west, including the Chad-Sokoto Divide. The elevation of the Region above mean sea level ranges from about 400 metres (m) at the northeast margin to over 1000m at the highest southern tip. The Region, except for the section east of the Hydro-Geological Divide, is part of the popular High Plains of Hausaland. The rock structure, relief and landforms of the Region are closely linked. This Chapter describes the relief and landforms in the Region.

### Relief Regions

The relief of the Region can be described under three types which are found in three zones respectively. These are: the south and south-eastern highlands, the middle and western high plains and the north-eastern low Chad Plains. The first two types are part of the High Plains of Hausaland and the third is a part of the Chad Plains.

The Highlands occupy a relatively small area to the south and constitute part of the foot slopes of the Jos Plateau which lies further south. The elevation is generally above 650m and reaches well over 1000m around the Rishi Hills. Most of the rocky outcrops in this zone are of Younger Granites, and the local relief is up to 300m.

The High Plains occupy more than 50% of the surface area of the Kano Region and lie on elevations ranging between 450m and 650m. The high plains consist of areas of low relief, usually less than 20m and areas of grouped hills where the hills may rise higher than 100m above the plains. The plains are developed on rocks of the Basement Complex and outcrops of these rocks constitute most of the hills, both grouped and ungrouped.

Chapter 1 | Emmanuel A. Olofin, in
A.I. Tanko and S.B. Momale (Eds.)
*Kano: Environment, Society and Development*
London & Abuja, Adonis & Abbey Publishers

The Low Chad Plains occupy the section of the Region east of the Hydro-Geological Divide. The elevation of this zone is about 420m, with a local relief of about 20m. The beds of the alluvial channels which are prominent in this zone lie at elevations of about 10 to 20 metres lower than the average given above.

## Typical Landform Units

Six landform types can be identified as follows: dissected hilly highlands, high plains with grouped hills, pediplains, sandy plains, dune fields and alluvial channel complexes (Figure 1.1).

The Dissected Hilly Highlands consist of the Rishi Hills and constitute the most rugged topography in the Region. The Rishi Hills are part of the foothills of the Jos Plateau which lies south of the Region. The hills are massive, bare rocky outcrops, mostly of the Younger Granites and are highly dissected. The mean foothill elevation is between 700m and 800m but most of the peaks are higher than 1000m. The maximum elevation is put at 1230m, with a dominant slope angle of about 20 degrees. Hill slopes steeper than 30 degrees are common. The hilly highlands are surrounded by one of the plains with grouped hills: the Dadi Plains.

The High Plains and grouped Hills are next to the Rishi Hills in ruggedness. The general elevation of the plains is higher than 550m, except for the Dakwat Plains which lie at about 470m. The most distinct ones are the Dadi, the Garanga and the Dakwat Plains. The Dadi Plains are essentially footslopes to the Rishi Hills to which they are next in ruggedness. The mean elevation is about 700m, but the summits of many of the bare rocky outcrops (of older Granites) rise up to 200m above the plains. The dominant slope angle is put at 13 degrees and hill slopes are steeper than 30 degrees.

The Garanga Plains occupy an extensive area, starting from Rano in the north and extending to the south-central boundaries of the Region where they merge with the Ningi Piedmont (outside the Region). The mean elevation is about 550m, but rocky hills (Older Granites) which rise up to 150m above the plains dominates the scenery. The plains are undulating. Dominant slope angle is between 3 and 5 degrees but hill slopes steeper than 20 degrees are quite common. The Dakwat Plains are found north of the Gari Plains. But

| Chapter 1 | Emmanuel A. Olofin, in |
| | A.I. Tanko and S.B. Momale (Eds.) |
| | *Kano: Environment, Society and Development* |
| | London & Abuja, Adonis & Abbey Publishers |

2

for the Kazaure quartzite ridges these plains could have been part of the Gari Plains. The mean elevation of the flattish plains is about 470m, but the quartzite ridges, which trend NNE-SSW, rise up to 120m above the plains. Hill slopes are steeper than 20 degrees, but the plains slope at a mean angle of 2 degrees.

The Pediplains are developed over the rocks of the Basement Complex and constitute part of the High Plains identified under relief zones above. The following units can be identified: the Kano, the Gaya, the Zala, the Iggi, the Daura, the Sokoto and the Kaduna Plains. Of these plains, the ones fully within the Chad Drainage System and constituting about half of the Kano Region are the Kano, the Gaya and the Iggi Plains. The very limited section of the Kaduna plains in the most southern part of the region and the minute sections of the Sokoto and Dara Plains to the northwest are part of the Niger Drainage System while the Zala Plain in the southeast drains into the Benue System through River Gongola.

The Kano Plains are made up of many distinct sections, prominent among which are: the Gari, the Jakara, the Chalawa, the Kamanda and the Basara Plains. Most of these pediplains has been covered by a layer of wind drift material which could be up to 2.5m thick, except in sections where the mean elevation is above 520m and the slope is greater than 2 degrees. Where the wind drift is present the pediplains slope at characteristic depositional angles ranging from zero to two degrees (e.g. Gari: 0.5° Gaya: 0.5° Jakara: 1.0° and Iggi: 1.5°). Such plains are called drift plains here (but called "loess" or pedisediment" by some writers).

A typical drift plain, such as the Kano Plain, consists of the following morphological units: an upland plain, two river terraces and wide channel beds, all sloping at angles less than 2 degrees. Others are inter-unit scarps sloping at angles steeper than 60 degrees and isolated residual hills ranging in height from 10m to 50m above the plains. Consequently, NEDECO(1974) has recognized the following landform units in the area: a storm channel (also called "floodplain") which is flanked by a low terrace which rises steeply from the channel, a high terrace separated from the low terrace by a steep wall, and an upland plain, also separated from the high terrace by a steep wall. Thus from the upland plain to the river channel, there are three steep units. 3 to 4 metres high and up to 60° steep which encourage rapid

Chapter 1 | Emmanuel A. Olofin, in
A.I. Tanko and S.B. Momale (Eds.)
*Kano: Environment, Society and Development*
London & Abuja, Adonis & Abbey Publishers

runoff, in spite of the gentle slopes ($1°$ to $2°$) on the terraces and upland plain (Figure 1.2). Ahmed (1987) has illustrated certain unique characteristics of drift plain as shown in Table 1.1.

The residual hills, usually located on the upland plain, are of two types: a granite outcrop which can occur anywhere in the landscape (e.g. the Tamburawa rock) and a regolith hill, usually capped by laterites, which occurs usually at the interfluves (e.g. Goron Dutse and Dala Hill in Metropolitan Kano). Hill slopes are generally steeper than 20 degrees. In areas where the drift material is absent and true pediplains occur (e.g. Kamanda and Basara sections of the Kano Plains), the mean elevation is higher than 550m (e.g. Basara 590m, Kamanda 690m) and dominant slopes are in the range 3 to 5 degrees. The occurrence of rocky outcrops is more frequent in such areas and the local relief is greater than 30m.

The Sandy Plains are great sand sheets occupying the north and central parts of the low Chad Plains. They are characterized by very gentle slopes, low relief (usually less than 15m) and disappearing stream channels. Occasional sand dunes and swampy depressions break the otherwise monotonous flattish landscape. The Gumel and the Hadejia Sand Plains are two main examples.

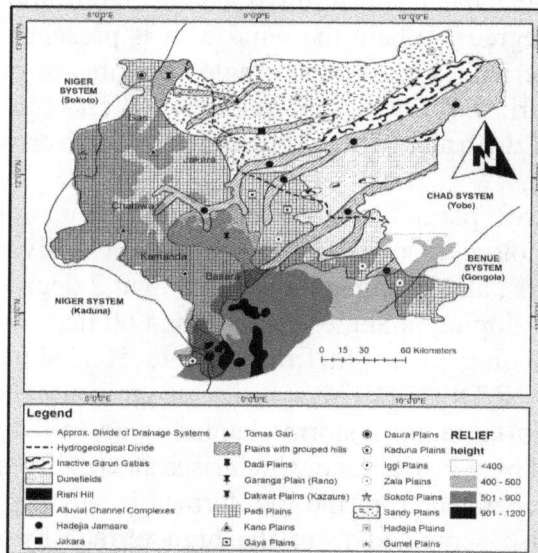

**Figure 1.1: Relief and Landforms of Kano Region**
*Source: Modified from Olofin (1987)*

Chapter 1 | Emmanuel A. Olofin, in
A.I. Tanko and S.B. Momale (Eds.)
*Kano: Environment, Society and Development*
London & Abuja, Adonis & Abbey Publishers

**4**

The Dune Fields occupy the rest of the low Chad Plains not utilized by rivers. They lie to the south of the sandy plains and are traceable to Latitude 11° N where they are believed to mark the southern margin of an extensive desert during the time of their formation. They are a combination of longitudinal (ridge-like along wind direction) dunes and transverse (across wind direction) ones at different stages of conversion into longitudinal types. Satellite images show them to be multi-linear and aligned NNE-SSW. The Latenwa Dunefields in the Kano Region mark the western margin of the dunes on the Chad Plains. They are now stabilized and constitute part of the fossil landforms in this part of the country. The local relief in the dune fields is up to 30 m. The Jahun Dunes and those near Kiyawa are extensions of these dunes.

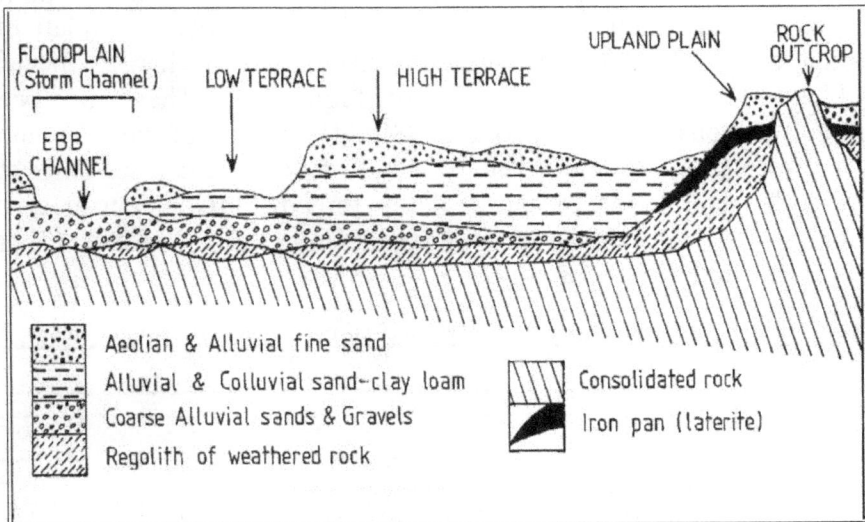

**Figure 1.2: The Landform Units of the Kano Plains**
*Source: Olofin (1980)*

The Alluvial Channel Complexes are created by the major river systems such as the Hadejia and the Jama'are and consist of both old (inactive) and current (active) flats. Individual streams of the northern sandy plains (Tomas-Gari and Jakara) also create alluvial channels of considerable width. The old alluvial flats are abandoned floodplains and back swamps originating from the migration of the rivers over

Chapter 1 | Emmanuel A. Olofin, in
A.I. Tanko and S.B. Momale (Eds.)
*Kano: Environment, Society and Development*
London & Abuja, Adonis & Abbey Publishers

very extensive channel-cum-floodplains. Active channels are sandy, flat-bedded and steep-walled. Upper headstreams such as the Challawa and the Kano develop alluvial channels in excess of 250m wide while bigger rivers such as the Hadejia develop complexes which are kilometres in width. The storm channels and their associated low terrace gully in the upper reaches such as River Kano and River Challawa deserve special mention. The mean elevation of the channels in these reaches is about 450m decreasing to a mean of about 400m in the lower reaches. The natural storm channel is a very wide sandy alluvial channel (Figure 1.3) designed to evacuate the flash flow of the wet season. Hence, it is usually larger than the mean annual flow associated with it. For example, the pre-dam Kano channel between Tiga and its confluence with Challawa had a mean with of 240 metres and a mean depth of 2 metres, giving a cross sectional area of 480m$^2$, for only a mean annual discharge of 37m$^3$/sec. The bed was relatively regular except for slight narrow depressions that discharged the last trickles of flow as the channel dried off Figure 1.3). These have been termed "ebb channels" by Olofin (1980). The mouth of the associated low terrace gully "hung" over the edge of the channel, as observed during the dry season, because of the forced alluvial deposit at its mouth at the height of the storm channel flow during the wet season. This is illustrated in Figure 1.4

**Table 1.1: Slope Characteristics in the Basement Complex Zone of the Kano Region**

| Slope Category | Surface Material | Land Use | Dominant Erosion Process | Land Segment | Average Slope |
|---|---|---|---|---|---|
| UPPER SLOPES | | | | | |
| Laterite cap or granitic rock | Rock or Regolith hill | Surface mining | Mass movement | *Tsauni* | 15° or more |
| Boulder slopes | Boulders or iron stones | None | Gully | *Tsauni* | 7 - 15° |
| Interfluve or alluvial fan | Sand to loam | Cultivation – rainfed | Slope wash | *Tudu* | 0.5 to 1.5° |
| MID SLOPES | | | | | |
| Rubble slope | Laterite or granite rubble | Grazing | Gully or creep | *Tsauni* | 4 - 7° |
| Upper valley slope or upper terrace | Sand to loam | Cultivation - rainfed | Slope wash | *Tudu* | 2 - 4° |
| LOWER SLOPES | | | | | |
| Lower valley slope or lower terrace | Sand to loam | Cultivation - rainfed, some irrigation | Slope wash | *Tudu* | 1 - 3° |
| Floodplain, or alluvial fan | Loam to hydromorphic | Irrigation, market gardening | Essentially depositional | *Kwari,* or *fadama* | 0.5 - 1.0° |

**Source:** *Ahmed (1987), modified*

Chapter 1 | Emmanuel A. Olofin, in
A.I. Tanko and S.B. Momale (Eds.)
*Kano: Environment, Society and Development*
London & Abuja, Adonis & Abbey Publishers

Dam and reservoir construction in the region modified alluvial channels downstream of such dams to produce new terraces and or narrower active channels, depending on the type of reservoir management. A large portion of the pre-dam alluvial channels has been rendered inactive because of large decreases in river discharges downstream of the dams. Where the downstream discharge is appropriately regulated, some reaches of the affected channel have been completely metamorphosed into a very narrow channel, flanked by new muddy terraces or floodplains which now support fadama cultivation. A good example is the River Kano channel from the outlet of the Tiga Dam to its confluence with River Challawa.

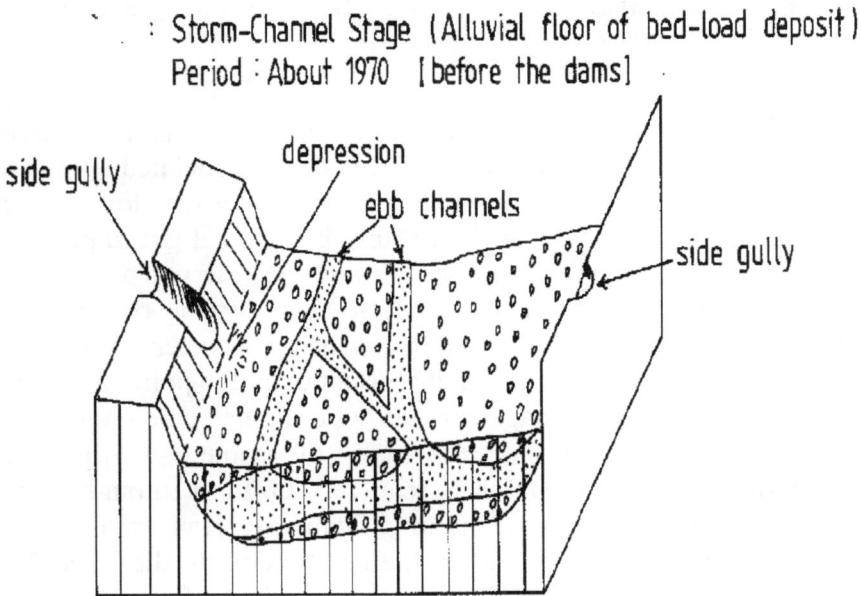

**Figure 1.3: Sand alluvial Storm Channel of Kano River before Tiga Dam**
*Source: Olofin (1980)*

Emmanuel A. Olofin, in
A.I. Tanko and S.B. Momale (Eds.)
*Kano: Environment, Society and Development*
London & Abuja, Adonis & Abbey Publishers

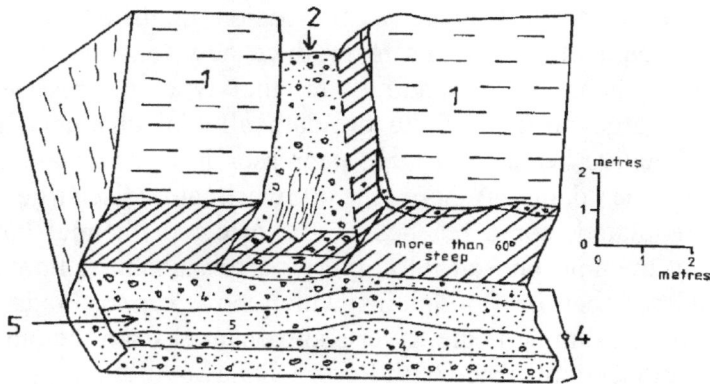

**Figure 1.4: Low Terrace Gully Morphology before Dam Construction**
Key: 1 = Low terrace surface; 2 = Gully floor; 3 = Hanging gully mouth; 4 = Storm channel and 5 = Ebb channel
*Source: Olofin (1980)*

As hinted above the pre-dam Kano channel was an alluvial channel, approximately 240m wide and 2m deep, associated with deep sand accumulation on the bed which is reshaped by the flow of each year. After the construction of Tiga Dam, the channel got impounded upstream of the dam to form a reservoir and the reservoir water level becomes the new base level of operation for inflowing rivers. Thus, channels upstream remain virtually unchanged except for slight aggrading near the reservoir and delta formation at the point of inflow.

The Tiga Reservoir management allows a regulated perennial flow in the natural channel as a result of some socio-political considerations. This flow which is relatively uniform throughout the year has directed the nature of the modification of Kano channel and its associated low terrace gullies in the reach between the Tiga Dam and the Challawa River confluence. The regulated flow initiates a smaller channel suitable for the reduced mean and uniform flow. This channel is incised into the former wide storm channel. The average width of the channel is currently less than 20m (less than 10% of the pre-dam width) and it is incised about 1.40m into the pre-dam channel, creating a channel-in-channel morphology (Figure 1.5). That is, an artificial river terrace has been developed that is about 90% of the width of the former storm channel, supporting various degrees of vegetation density and/or cultivation. The sandy material eroded as a

Chapter 1 | Emmanuel A. Olofin, in
A.I. Tanko and S.B. Momale (Eds.)
*Kano: Environment, Society and Development*
London & Abuja, Adonis & Abbey Publishers

result of the incision during the time of formation had implications for channel responses further downstream in the Hadejia system where it blocked some secondary channels. However, the abandoned silt + clay material on the new terrace enhanced plant growth and is still supporting cultivation.

The associated low terrace gully has also been modified to produce a gully in gully morphology with an extension incised into the new terrace to reach the new active channel as illustrated in Figure 1.6. The new gully terrace is also vegetated.

Where water is not regulated on a perennial basis downstream of the dams, the channels have marginal modification in that they are slightly narrower than the pre-dam width but incised into the pre-dam alluvial sediments. Such channels are believed to be in a state of perpetual erosion. The Watari downstream of the Bagwai Dam is affected this way.

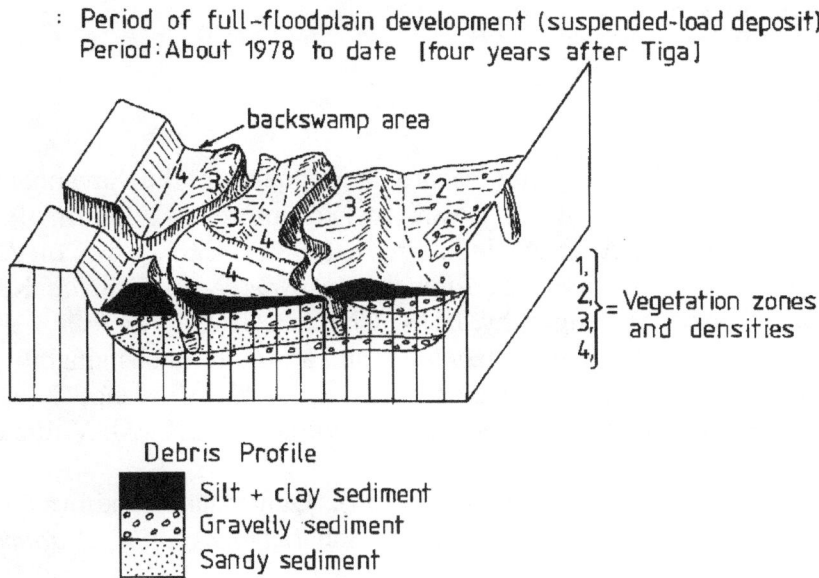

: Period of full-floodplain development (suspended-load deposit). Period: About 1978 to date [four years after Tiga]

backswamp area

1.
2.
3.  } = Vegetation zones and densities
4.

Debris Profile

Silt + clay sediment
Gravelly sediment
Sandy sediment

**Figure 1.5: Modified Kano Channel after the Construction of Tiga Dam**
Note: Vegetation zones are in order of increasing densities from 1 to 4
*Source: Olofin (1980)*

Chapter 1 | Emmanuel A. Olofin, in
A.I. Tanko and S.B. Momale (Eds.)
*Kano: Environment, Society and Development*
London & Abuja, Adonis & Abbey Publishers

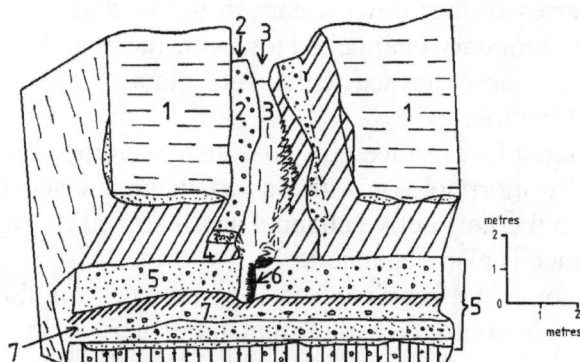

**Figure 1.6: Modified Low Terrace Gully Morphology after the Construction of Tiga Dam**
**Key:** 1 = Low terrace surface; 2 = Remnant of the former gully floor; 3 = New incised gully-in-gully; 4 = Remnant of former hanging gully mouth; 5 Terrace of modified storm channel; 6 = Extension of incised gully into new river terrace and 7 = Incised active river channel
*Source: Olofin (1980)*

# References

Ahmed, K. (1987) Erosion hazard assessment in the Savanna: the Hadejia-Jama'are River Basin, In Mortimore, M., Olofin, E. A, Cline-Cole R. A. & Abdulkadir, A. (1987) *Perspectives on Land Adminstration and Development in Northern Nigeria*, Kano, Department of Geography, BUK, Chapter 23: 234 - 247

Essiet, E. U. (1995) Soil management and agricultural sustainability in the small-holder farming system in northern Kano, Nigeria, *Journal of Social and Management Studies (JOSAMS)*, Volume 2: 37 - 46

Grove, A. T. and Warren, A. (1968), Quaternary landforms and climate on the south side of the Sahara, *Geographical Journal*, 134: 194 - 208

Olofin, E. A. (1978) Effects of gully processes on farmlands in the Savanna areas of Nigeria - Challawa Basin case study. *Kano Studies, NS1 (3)*: 74 - 83

Chapter 1 | Emmanuel A. Olofin, in
A.I. Tanko and S.B. Momale (Eds.)
*Kano: Environment, Society and Development*
London & Abuja, Adonis & Abbey Publishers

Olofin, E. A. (1980), *Some Effects of Tiga Dam on the Environment Downstream in the Kano River Basin,* unpublished PhD Thesis, Ahmadu Bello University, Zaria, 266 A4 pp

Olofin, E. A. (1985) Climatic constraints to water resource development in the Sudano-Sahelian zone of Nigeria, Water International, Vol. 10, No. 1: 29 - 37

Olofin, E. A. (1987) *Some Aspects of the Physical Geography of the Kano Region, and Related Human Responses, Departmental Lecture Series 1*: Kano, Dept, of Geog, BUK. 50 pp

Olofin, E. A. (1996) Dam-induced failure of the Hadejia-Nguru Wetlands, northern Nigeria, and its implication for the fauna; In Beilfus, R. D. et al, eds. *Proceedings 1993 African Crane and Wetland Training Workshop,* Baraboo: International Crane Foundation: 141 - 146

Olofin, E. A. (2000) *The Gains and Pains of Putting a Waterlook on the Face of the Drylands of Nigeria,* First Inaugural Lecture Presented in 1992, Kano: Bayero University

Umar, A.; Ben-Musa, S.; Idris, M, and five others (1985) *Groundwater Monitoring and Imbalance in Kano State,* Kano, WRECA

World Resources Institute (WRI) and IIED (1988) *World Resources 1988 - 89.* New York, Basic Books

Chapter 1 | Emmanuel A. Olofin, in
A.I. Tanko and S.B. Momale (Eds.)
*Kano: Environment, Society and Development*
London & Abuja, Adonis & Abbey Publishers

11

# Chapter Two

## WEATHER AND CLIMATE

Maryam Liman, Halima Abdulkadir Idris and Ummi Khalthum
Mohammed

### Introduction

The Kano Region is characterised with marked wet and dry seasons. It
has been described as one of the most economically vibrant parts of
Nigeria making huge contributions in agricultural production. The
climate of the Region has the dominant influence over most of the
agricultural activities. Generally, the Region has a semi-arid climate,
with a mean daily temperature of 30°C. The months of December to
February are colder, with the lowest temperature recorded around
20°C. The rainfall regime is characterized by two seasons, namely, the
rainy season from May to October and the dry season from November
to April. The average annual rainfall is about 884mm increasing from
north to south. In the extreme south, it could reach 1200mm per
annum around Riruwai and Doguwa.

### Climate

The climate is the tropical wet and dry type coded as AW based on the
Koppen's classification of climate. Temperature is a very critical
element in this area. Temperature in the Region ranges from 21°C in
the coldest months (December/January) to 31°c in the hottest months
(April/March). Four distinct seasons are experienced, which are the
dry and cool, dry and hot, wet and warm, and dry and warm seasons
(Olofin, 1987).

The seasons are determined by the movement of two air masses, a
moist cool southerly mass known as south-westerlies and a hot and dry
northern mass called the north-easterlies. The moist southern air forms
a wedge under the lighter dry air and the region where the two air
masses meet is primarily an area of pronounced moisture gradient. The
humidity gradient is called the intertropical discontinuity (ITD).

Chapter 2 | Maryam Liman, Halima A. Idris & Ummi K. Mohammed, in
A.I. Tanko and S.B. Momale (Eds.)
*Kano: Environment, Society and Development*
London & Abuja, Adonis & Abbey Publishers

The annual motion of the ITD is northwards between February and August and southwards between September and January. The north-south movement of the ITD influences weather pattern. Maximum rainfall is recorded in an area of considerable disturbance (air movement) $8^{\circ}$ to $9^{\circ}$ southwards of the ITD. However, when disturbance is limited or when the northward movement of the ITD is restricted, drought is recorded. The level of disturbance and the northward movement of the ITD are influenced by the global pattern of pressure and winds as well as the interaction of the surface air and the upper air mass (the jetstreams). When the ITD is southwards, the Region is under the influence of the north easterlies. The weather changes arising from the movement of the ITD gives the four seasons.

### a. *Hot and Dry Season (Rani)*

The ITD starts its southward movement in February and between March and May it has no considerable influence in the Region and the weather is hot and dry during the *rani* season. The mean temperature is 28°c to 30°c while this is the season when the "false" start of the rain is recorded in May. A few rainfall instances are recorded in May and rain days are separated by days of dry spell and less than 1% of the annual rainfall is recorded in May.

### b. *Warm and Wet Season (Damina)*

The ITD has by now made considerable advance northward and rainfall is recorded in the Region. Heavy rains are recorded mainly in the evenings for one to three hours, with high intensity in the first forty minutes of the rainfall occurrence. Over 90% of the annual rainfall in the Region is recorded in this season. This is the humid period when surface runoff is available for stream flow and soil moisture in sufficient for plant growth. *Damina* is the crop growing season when grains and legume are grown. Temperature drops to an average of 24°C to 29°C while evaporation is lower because of the higher relative humidity of the moist south westerlies air. This is why the runoff-coefficient is highest during this season.

Chapter 2 | Maryam Liman, Halima A. Idris & Ummi K. Mohammed, in
A.I. Tanko and S.B. Momale (Eds.)
*Kano: Environment, Society and Development*
London & Abuja, Adonis & Abbey Publishers

## c. *Warm and dry season (Kaka)*

The ITD is now in its southward retreat and only a few showers may be recorded in October accounting for less than 8% of the annual rainfall. This is the harvest season between October and November when farmers are busy harvesting crops and traders are buying what is offered. Average temperature is $28^{\circ}$-$29^{\circ}$c and this is a dry season as evaporation is in excess of rainfall. This is a season when soil moisture is depleted and stream flow recedes.

## d. *Cool and dry season (Bazara)*

The ITD reaches its southern limit during this season and the Region is under the influence of the northeasterly winds which brings a cool and dusty weather called 'Harmattan". From December to February, the dry air from the north brings no rainfall but transported harmattan dusts are deposited to replenish soil nutrient. The depth of the windrift material varies from an average of 1m to 2m. This is the cool season when temperature is $25^{\circ}$ to $27^{\circ}C$.

In terms of rainfall distribution, the Kano Region is divided into three zones (MARDITECH, 2011). The northernmost is "rainfall zone 1" with 110 to 130 rainy days a year. The second is rainfall zone 2" which lies south of the first with 120 to 130 rainy days a year. The southernmost is "rainfall zone 3" that has 130 to 150 rainy days per year.

With some instances of "missing data", monthly rainfall distribution for Kano State can be studied from "Monthly Rainfall Data" collected by Land Management Unit, Technical Services Department, KNARDA, for various Local Government Areas (LGAs) in the Region from 1987 to 2006 (Tables 2.1 and 2.2).

**Table 2.1: Average Annual Rainfall (mm) in the Three Zones in the Kano Region**

| Year | Zone 1 | Zone 2 | Zone 3 |
|------|--------|--------|--------|
| 1999 | 848.7 | 758.0 | 774.6 |
| 2002 | 746.0 | 607.3 | 647.5 |
| 2003 | 1036.2 | 836.6 | 920.4 |

Chapter 2 | Maryam Liman, Halima A. Idris & Ummi K. Mohammed, in
A.I. Tanko and S.B. Momale (Eds.)
*Kano: Environment, Society and Development*
London & Abuja, Adonis & Abbey Publishers

The monthly data consistently show that the rainfall reaches a peak in July and August, suggesting that erosion processes are most active in these two months. June is probably a period when soils are continuously being wetted. With this wetting, soil aggregates are dispersed into individual particles. July and August would be the time when transport from field to river and from river to reservoir occurs.

Further analysis of the monthly rainfall distribution for selected years (Tables 2.2a-c) suggests a high concentration of rainstorms in two months, July and August. For the selected areas and years, more than 55 % of the annual rainfall occurs within the 62 days in these two months. If the annual rainfall is 1000mm, 60% falls in July and August, and half of the days are rainy, the average daily rainfall would be 600/31 mm = 19mm. However, there will most likely be rainstorms of various sizes in any one period, implying that some storms will be much larger than 19mm. According to a study by Haskoning (1981), the one-day total precipitation with a return period of 1 in 5 years is about 90mm for Kano.

**Tables 2.2a-c: Rainfall in the wettest months, July and August, in selected Local Government Areas (LGA) in Kano State**

**(a)  Kano Northwest**

| Years | LGA | Annual Rainfall (mm) | July Rainfall (mm) | August Rainfall (mm) | July +August Rainfall (mm) | July + August Rainfall (%) |
|-------|-----|---------|---------|---------|---------|---------|
| 1985 | Dawakin Tofa | 559.2 | 151.1 | 183.5 | 334.6 | 59.8 |
| 1986 | Dawakin Tofa | 602.5 | 166.0 | 163.0 | 329.0 | 54.6 |
| 1988 | Dawakin Tofa | 705.0 | 184.0 | 345.0 | 529.0 | 75.0 |
| 1990 | Dawakin Tofa | 450.0 | 201.0 | 128.0 | 329.0 | 73.1 |
| 1991 | Dawakin Tofa | 800.0 | 252.0 | 318.0 | 570 | 71.3 |
| 1993 | Dawakin Tofa | 1018.0 | 303.8 | 295.0 | 598.8 | 58.8 |
| 1994 | Dawakin Tofa | 716.0 | 110.9 | 288.8 | 399.7 | 55.8 |
| 1996 | Dawakin Tofa | 1029.4 | 206.0 | 386.0 | 592.0 | 57.5 |
| 1997 | Dawakin Tofa | 750.4 | 145.8 | 269.8 | 415.6 | 55.4 |
| 1999 | Dawakin Tofa | 864.4 | 268.2 | 335.8 | 604.0 | 69.9 |
| 2000 | Dawakin Tofa | 678.9 | 77.7 | 194.3 | 272.0 | 40.1 |
| 2001 | Dawakin Tofa | 843.0 | 103.0 | 437.0 | 540.0 | 64.1 |
| 2002 | Dawakin Tofa | 734.0 | 178.0 | 207.0 | 385.0 | 52.5 |
| 2003 | Dawakin Tofa | 644.0 | 187.0 | 253.0 | 440.0 | 68.3 |

Chapter 2 | Maryam Liman, Halima A. Idris & Ummi K. Mohammed, in
A.I. Tanko and S.B. Momale (Eds.)
*Kano: Environment, Society and Development*
London & Abuja, Adonis & Abbey Publishers

## (b) Kano South East

| Years | LGA | Annual Rainfall (mm) | July Rainfall (mm) | August Rainfall (mm) | July +August Rainfall (mm) | July + August Rainfall (%) |
|---|---|---|---|---|---|---|
| 1986 | Sumaila | 939.7 | 274.1 | 295.2 | 569.3 | 60.6 |
| 1988 | Sumaila | 980.5 | 206.9 | 463.7 | 670.6 | 68.4 |
| 1990 | Sumaila | 565.3 | 207.4 | 161.5 | 368.9 | 65.3 |
| 1991 | Sumaila | 1206.7 | 435.4 | 465.4 | 900.8 | 74.6 |
| 1994 | Sumaila | 929.5 | 223.3 | 416.3 | 639.6 | 68.8 |
| 1996 | Sumaila | 752.0 | 137.7 | 263.4 | 401.1 | 53.3 |
| 1999 | Sumaila | 877.5 | 264.7 | 314.6 | 579.3 | 66.0 |
| 2000 | Sumaila | 700.9 | 150.3 | 192.1 | 342.4 | 49.0 |
| 2001 | Sumaila | 910.0 | 213.0 | 344.0 | 557.0 | 61.2 |
| 2002 | Sumaila | 766.0 | 122.0 | 263.0 | 385.0 | 50.3 |
| 2003 | Sumaila | 942.0 | 225.0 | 384.0 | 609.0 | 64.6 |

## (c) Kano Southwest

| Years | LGA | Annual Rainfall (mm) | July Rainfall (mm) | August Rainfall (mm) | July +August Rainfall (mm) | July + August Rainfall (%) |
|---|---|---|---|---|---|---|
| 1985 | Karaye | 1042 | 220.2 | 284.6 | 504.8 | 48.4 |
| | Gwarzo | 702 | 158.0 | 200.0 | 358.0 | 51.0 |
| 1986 | Karaye | 902.9 | 239.1 | 265.1 | 504.2 | 55.8 |
| | Gwarzo | 797.6 | 219.2 | 243.1 | 462.3 | 58.0 |
| 1988 | Karaye | 1245.3 | 167.2 | 553.0 | 720.2 | 57.8 |
| | Gwarzo | 897.2 | 187.4 | 117.7 | 305.1 | 34.1 |
| 1989 | Karaye | 806.4 | 247.6 | 227 | 474.6 | 58.9 |
| | Gwarzo | 449 | 117.6 | 134.8 | 252.4 | 56.2 |
| 1990 | Karaye | 894.4 | 398.7 | 209.1 | 607.8 | 68.0 |
| | Gwarzo | 579.6 | 171.0 | 126.2 | 297.2 | 51.3 |
| 1991 | Karaye | 880.0 | 234.3 | 330.4 | 564.7 | 64.2 |
| | Gwarzo | 823.3 | 186.9 | 370.0 | 556.9 | 67.6 |
| 1993 | Karaye | 1019.0 | 293.0 | 347.3 | 640.3 | 62.8 |
| | Gwarzo | 623.0 | 203.3 | 161.4 | 364.7 | 58.5 |
| 1994 | Karaye | 1035.0 | 138.2 | 363.0 | 501.2 | 48.4 |
| | Gwarzo | 786.0 | 178.0 | 238.0 | 416.0 | 52.9 |
| 1996 | Karaye | | 190.0 | 276.4 | 466.4 | |
| | Gwarzo | 584.0 | 142.9 | 274.2 | 417.1 | 71.4 |
| 1997 | Karaye | 819.2 | 135.8 | 235.0 | 370.8 | 45.3 |
| | Gwarzo | 1064.9 | 492.0 | 187.2 | 679.2 | 63.8 |
| 1999 | Karaye | 892.2 | 248.0 | 369.0 | 617.0 | 69.2 |
| | Gwarzo | 823.4 | 280.2 | 310.7 | 590.9 | 71.8 |
| 2000 | Karaye | 865.2 | 182.0 | 256.0 | 438.0 | 50.6 |
| | Gwarzo | 780.8 | 176.0 | 209.0 | 385.0 | 49.3 |
| 2001 | Karaye | 1157 | 184.0 | 429.0 | 632.0 | 54.6 |
| | Gwarzo | 903.0 | 214.0 | 324.0 | 508.0 | 56.3 |
| 2002 | Karaye | 731.0 | 132.0 | 279.0 | 493.0 | 67.4 |
| | Gwarzo | 617.0 | 240.0 | 222.0 | 354.0 | 57.4 |
| 2003 | Karaye | 1010.0 | 221.0 | 416.0 | 656.0 | 49.8 |
| | Gwarzo | 906.0 | | 328.0 | 549.0 | 60.6 |

*Source: MARDITECH (2011)*

Chapter 2 | Maryam Liman, Halima A. Idris & Ummi K. Mohammed, in
A.I. Tanko and S.B. Momale (Eds.)
*Kano: Environment, Society and Development*
London & Abuja, Adonis & Abbey Publishers

From daily rainfall recorded at the Bayero University Meteorological Station (Table 2.3) the number of rainstorms per month is relatively low, implying that the average rainstorm is relatively large.

Table 2.3: A summary of daily rainfall during wet season at Bayero University Kano

| Year | June No. of rain-storms | June Large rainstorms (mm)* | July No. of rain-storms | July Large rainstorms (mm) | August No. of rain-storms | August Large rainstorms (mm) | September No. of rain-storms | September Large rainstorms (mm) |
|---|---|---|---|---|---|---|---|---|
| 1999 | 3 | 39.6 | 5 | 77.0; 64.0; 48.8 | 9 | 60.0; 54.0; 34.0 | 9 | 55.6 |
| 2000 | 10 | 32.0; 30.0 | 7 | 31.5; 55.4 | 13 | 31.6 | 9 | 41.9; 36.3 |
| 2001 | 6 | 32.2; 40.9; 32.8 | 8 | 30.3; 32.8 | 13 | 30.5; 50.0 | 8 | 34.3; 34.9 |
| 2002 | 6 | 55.4; 80.4 | 7 | 39.5; 32.3 | 11 | 70.0; 35.8; 37.0; 42.0; 48.0 | 7 | 42.9; 31.0; 34.3 |
| 2003 | 8 | 32.8 | 9 | 32.2; 33.6; 41.2; 54.8 | 11 | 40.0; 47.5; 100.5; 40.6 | 8 | 70.9; 55.4; 30.0 |
| 2004 | 8 | 51.4; 51.2; 37.4; 33.5 | 9 | 47.0; 45.0; 47.0; 60.0 | 9 | 55.0; 42.0; 60.0; 80.0 | 8 | 80.4; 41.0; 50.0; 48.0; 61.2; 70.0 |
| 2005 | 10 | 48.7; 40.1; 74.3 | 9 | 53.4 | 15 | 60.7; 70.0; 54.0; 60.7; 50.3; 49.0; 70.4; 66.5; 30.6; 45.0; 36.0; 33.0 | 6 | 32.2 |
| 2007 | 5 | | 7 | 30.0; 33.2; 46.0; 48.0 | 8 | 40.0; 33.9; 42.0; 80.0; 51.0; 50.0; 49.8 | 7 | 30.0; 34.0; 46.0; 39.8; 44.0 |
| 2008 | 5 | 30.0; 32.0 | 8 | 48.0; 31.0; 49.6; 55.0; 46.0; 70.0; 63.0 | 9 | 43.0; 52.0; 35.2; 84.0; 77.0; 80.0 | 10 | 31.0; 45.7; 34.8; 49.6; 58.2; 78 |

*Rainstorms = 30.0mm or greater
*Source: MARDITECH (2011)*

From rainfall records at Bayero University Meteorological Station (1999 to 2008), some insight into transport of sediments during the wet season can be gained. The number of storms per month, on average, is highest in August. However, the total number of storms is not as important as the number of large storms (>30.0mm) since large storms are normally associated with high intensity. The month with the most erosive rainfall, i.e. the month with the greatest number of

Chapter 2 | Maryam Liman, Halima A. Idris & Ummi K. Mohammed, in
A.I. Tanko and S.B. Momale (Eds.)
*Kano: Environment, Society and Development*
London & Abuja, Adonis & Abbey Publishers

large rainstorms, varies from year to year. In years such as 2005 and 2008 when the number of large rainstorms was high, there was most likely to be substantial sediment transport. In some months, rainstorms of 70mm, 80mm (such as August 2003) or even 100mm (like in August 2008) were recorded.

## Conclusion

Located in the Semi-arid climatic zone of Nigeria, the Kano Region experiences four distinct seasons, *Rani, Damina, Kaka* and *Bazara* closely associated with the movement of the ITD. The mean annual Rainfall is about 884mm varying greatly from the northern and southern parts of the Region. On the average, the wettest month is August where the highest number of rainstorms and sediment transport are recorded.

The weather and climate of the Kano Region play a great role on the agricultural practices and are favourable to large scale cultivation of cereals, groundnuts, beans and vegetables. The socioeconomic activities of the people are also closely linked with the seasons, with crop production dominating during the wet season and off-farm activities (*ci rani*) dominating during the dry season.

## References

Haskoning Engineering Consultants (1981), Watari River Project Reconnaissance Study, Ministry of Agriculture and Natural Resources, Kano State, Nigeria

MARDITECH (2011), Development of a GIDS-Based Soil Suitability Classification for Rice Production in Kano State, Nigeria, Unpublished Interim Report submitted to the Kano State Government, MARDITECH, Kualar Lumpur, Malaysia

Olofin, E.A. (1987): *Some Aspects of physical Geography of Kano Region and Related Human Responses*. Department of Geography, Bayero University, Kano (BUK), Debis Standard Printers, Kano

| Chapter 2 | Maryam Liman, Halima A. Idris & Ummi K. Mohammed, in |
|---|---|
| | A.I. Tanko and S.B. Momale (Eds.) |
| | *Kano: Environment, Society and Development* |
| | London & Abuja, Adonis & Abbey Publishers |

# Chapter Three

## DRAINAGE, HYDROLOGY AND WATER RESOURCES

Adnan Abdulhamid

## Introduction

The availability of freshwater is of immense significance to the people of the Kano Region affecting their lives in many ways. The rapid growth of population in the area coupled with the steady increase in water demand for domestic, agricultural and industrial development have imposed severe stress on the available freshwater resources in terms of both the quantity and quality, requiring consistent and careful assessment and management for sustainable development.

The first benchmark on some aspects of drainage and hydrology of the Region was provided by Olofin (1987). Although there were earlier works by Bennet, et al (1978), it is important to point out that the work dealt with the subject in too general form, since they focused on the central Nigeria and the Kano Region was seen only as a unit in several units discussed, therefore many issues were left untouched. One reason why such subject needs to be reviewed in the present-day Kano Region is the human signatures that are increasingly pinned on the physical landscape particularly in the last two decades when Jigawa State was, in 1991, curved out of the then Kano State.

Human population expansion and changes in the level of technology in the use of water for example drilling of boreholes instead of digging traditional shallow wells, construction of new earth dams even in Jigawa State (which previous policy indicated that it was not feasible for earth dams), the use of water pumps for irrigation in place of traditional shaduff, and creation of mega water plant across the major rivers to mention a few, are some of the anthropogenic processes that upset the river drainage pattern and levels of water availability for different uses in nearly all parts of the Region.

It is argued that "climatic harshness is the major component that can distort geomorphic system and water resource of a place" (WMO, 2002:3). According to the same source, climatic harshness also

Chapter 3 | Adnan Abdulhamid, in
A.I. Tanko and S.B. Momale (Eds.)
*Kano: Environment, Society and Development*
London & Abuja, Adonis & Abbey Publishers

manifest on vegetation depletion as well. Investigation by Food Agricultural Organization (FAO) in 2004 has shown decline of 2.6% annually of the forest cover from 1990-2000 in the Region. The trends in temperature anomalies is a reflection of the slight increase in temperature above normal in the region with +0.48$^0$C and satellite data indicate that recent warmest year were 1998, 2002, 2003, 2001 and 1995 in decreasing order (WMO, 2004).

More complex combinations of variables that make the hydrology, drainage and water management in the Kano Region are possible if the geology is considered (Szentes, 1974). This Chapter reviews some theoretical concepts and principles of hydrology and drainage systems and the management strategy for water resource development within the Region.

Despite the importance of hydrology in the understanding and utilization of water resources, the number of gauging stations in the Region is drastically reducing in number over the years. The functional ones no longer provides reliable hydrological data required for predicting flooding, sediment yields by rivers and streams as well as predicting drought.

## Available Water Resource from Rainfall

Meteorologists recognize the relationship between rainfall amount and available water resource in any given area. Chapter Two has given the climatic characteristics in the the Region which by way of summary reflect decreasing rain-days from about 150 days in the south to as low as about 100 days in the north. Similarly, total amount of rainfall received reflects decreasing pattern as one leaves the southern part of the Region to the north. For example, in the 2006, the total precipitation in the Kano south (as measured around the Tiga area) was 1200mm, at central Kano it was 855mm, while it was assumed to be around 650mm around Maigatari and 578mm at Birniwa towards the Sahelian part of the Region. Figure 3.1 shows the pattern of rainfall with the isohyets running from 1200mm in the south to 500mm in the north (WARDROP, 2000).

It is clear that the total water supply in the Region is dependent upon rainfall on yearly basis with the mean value of 850 mm (0.85m) from the isohyets running west-east, and dissecting the region into two

Chapter 3 | Adnan Abdulhamid, in
A.I. Tanko and S.B. Momale (Eds.)
*Kano: Environment, Society and Development*
London & Abuja, Adonis & Abbey Publishers

equal parts. Considering the total land area of $43,000km^2$ ($43,000,000,000 M^2$), the total annual water harvested through rainfall amounts to $3.7 \times 10^{10}$ cubic meters ($4.3 \times 10^{10}m^2 \times 0.85m$). Some of the water is lost into the atmosphere through evapotranspiration, while some flow in Hadejia-Jama'are River system into the Lake Chad while others seep underground forming the groundwater resource. Various factors affect this resource, the most important being the rock structure. It is generally believed that groundwater availability is much higher in the Chad formation than in the Basement Complex.

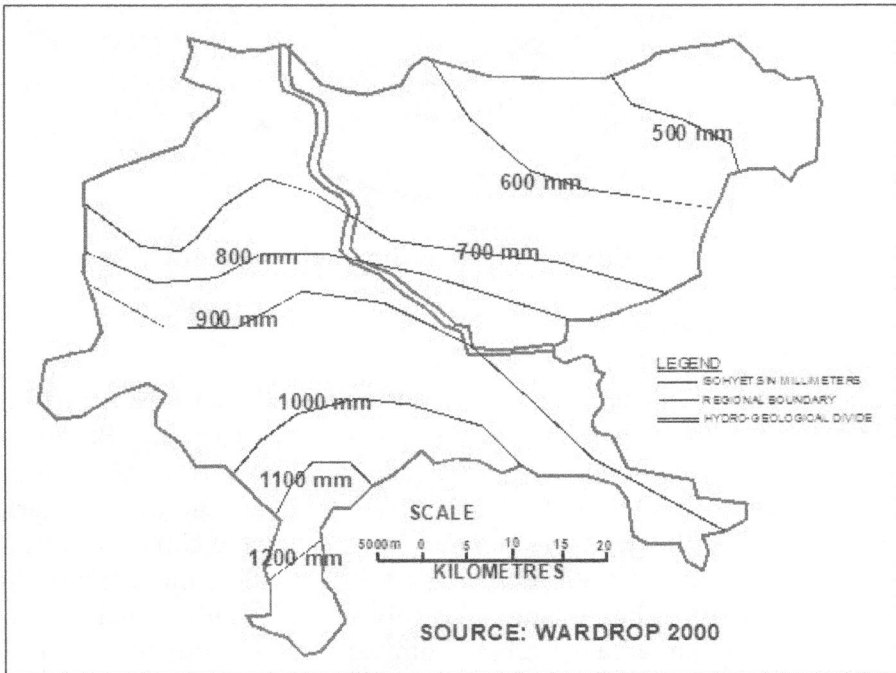

**Fig. 3.1 Mean Annual Rainfall of the Kano Region**

It was estimated through hydrogeological calculation that a loss of water to regional annual groundwater flow amounts to $50 \times 10^7 m^3$ (Schultz, 1976). This value is not compatible, considering the uncertainties in estimating groundwater. However, the effect of increasing evapotransipiration rate can invariably reduce the value to the minimum directly from the groundwater table considering high rate of evapotransipiration in the Region.

Chapter 3 | Adnan Abdulhamid, in
A.I. Tanko and S.B. Momale (Eds.)
*Kano: Environment, Society and Development*
London & Abuja, Adonis & Abbey Publishers

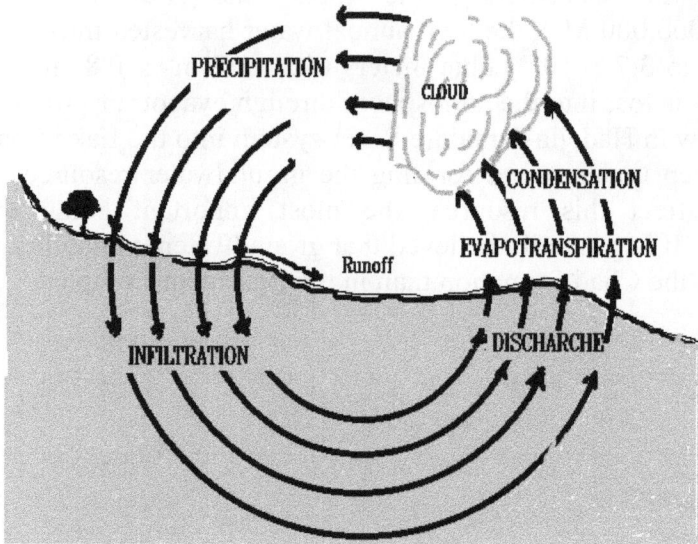

**Figure 3.2: Environment in the Hydrological Cycle**

### *Groundwater Resource*

Groundwater volumes have been measured at eleven locations from Birniwa (on the Chad formation) to Zarewa (on the Basement Complex). The volume of groundwater decreases from the North-eastern side of the Region to the south-western part and this is clearly associated with the geology. The measurements were carried out from spot heights (Table 3.1) for each point selected where the depth of the aquifer was used. For example, Birniwa with aquifer thickness of 30.5m within an area of 28,372.6m$^3$ and with porosity of 0.33, generated a capacity volume of 9,363.0m$^3$ (i.e. 30.5m x 30.5m x30.5m x 0.33).

From the calculation of the porous media (Table 3.1), it is indicated that the volume of water increased with increasing depth of the aquifer though, this is not always the case. But since the relative volume in the Chad Formation and the Basement Complex are realistically different (as there is higher groundwater resource in the former than in the latter), permeability and transmissibility are equally not the same as observed from the two contrasting grounds.

Chapter 3    Adnan Abdulhamid, in
A.I. Tanko and S.B. Momale (Eds.)
*Kano: Environment, Society and Development*
London & Abuja, Adonis & Abbey Publishers

24

**Table 3.1: Volume of Cross-sections of Porous Media at Eleven Sample Locations**

| Location | Aquifer Thickness (m) | Aquifer volume($m^3$) | Porosity of the Aquifer | Porous media volumes ($m^3$) |
|---|---|---|---|---|
| Birniwa | 30.5 | 28,372.6 | 0.33 | 9,363.0 |
| Garun-Gabas | 74.9 | 31,472,212.2 | 0.33 | 1,038,583.0 |
| Jahun | 48.0 | 110,392.0 | 0.60 | 66,355.2 |
| Kaugama | 50.7 | 130,323.8 | 0.29 | 37,793.9 |
| Kichau | 20.7 | 8,869.7 | 0.02 | 177.4 |
| Kogo | 30.0 | 27,000.0 | 0.03 | 810.0 |
| Shafar | 39.4 | 61,163.0 | 0.11 | 6,727.9 |
| Yandutse | 24.0 | 13,824.0 | 0.05 | 691.2 |
| Yankatsari | 23.0 | 12,167.0 | 0.04 | 486.7 |
| Zara | 13.0 | 28,561.0 | 0.05 | 1,428.1 |
| Zarewa | 10.7 | 1,225.0 | 0.04 | 49.0 |

*Source: Calculated Values (2007)*

The human responses as per water-demand and the hydrogeological characteristics of the Kano Region have been evaluated. The Basement Complex and the Chad Formation geologies have their own peculiar problems emanating from their infiltrography, lithography and stratigraphy. Their responses to same treatment need good management strategies.

## Drainage

The Hadejia River system constitutes the main drainage which contributes about 80% of the historic flow of the river system (Figure 3.2). The mean annual flow at Wudil was calculated at $1.890m^3 \times 10^6$ (Schultz, 1976; WRECA, 1985) which comes from three main tributaries: Kano, Challawa and Watari. The remaining 20% of the River discharge comes through the Jakara system which disappears underground in the Chad Formation.

This Zone has been described as having characterized by high rural population, with the combination of drainage basins of Rivers Hadejia, Katagum and Jama'are entering the Yobe system (Olofin, 1987). The main rivers in the area which get their water from rainfall are Rivers

Chapter 3    Adnan Abdulhamid, in
A.I. Tanko and S.B. Momale (Eds.)
*Kano: Environment, Society and Development*
London & Abuja, Adonis & Abbey Publishers

**25**

Gari, Thomas (also called River Tomar), Jakara, Challawa-Kano-Hadejia, Gaya and Katagum. All the river systems evolve within the Region.

Along the main river channel numerous tributaries emerge to make dendritic patterns; criss-crossing the Basement Complex surface, leaving the Chad formation with few of the tributaries due to its porous nature and heavy sediments. The different systems are described as follows:

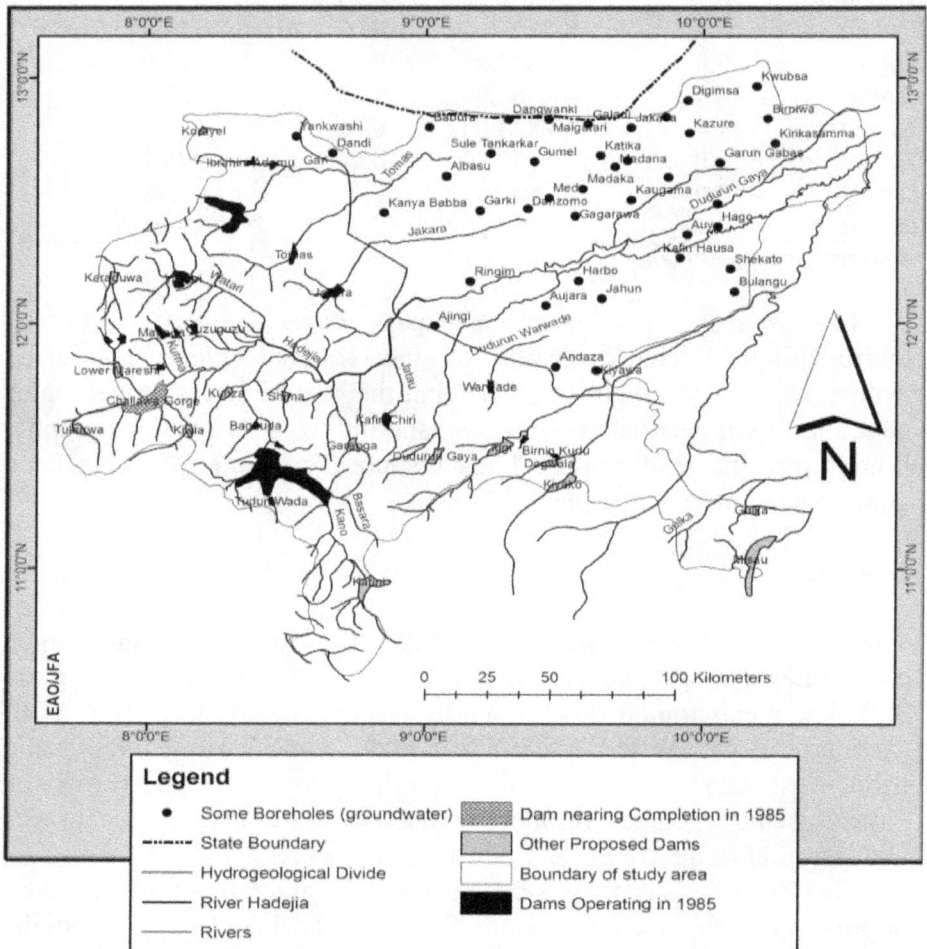

**Figure 3.3: Drainage System of the Kano Region**

Chapter 3 | Adnan Abdulhamid, in
A.I. Tanko and S.B. Momale (Eds.)
*Kano: Environment, Society and Development*
London & Abuja, Adonis & Abbey Publishers

## The Kano River System

The system emerges from the foothills of the Jos Plateau. As it flows it first runs vertically towards the north, until it reaches the confluence with the Challawa River. Together they flow in the eastern direction. At the first entry point (to the Region) the dense vegetation cover of the Falgore Game Reserve (at the southern part) protects the flow of the River yielding very low sediments. The Reserve therefore serves as a filter to the Tiga Reservoir. However, human intervention on the forest resources is making the reserve vulnerable. In addition to this, the Kano system is the main source of water for human consumption, particularly for urban Kano and the settlements along the course of the River, raising issues of water quality especially as it receives most of the effluents from the Sharada and Challawa Industrial Estates through the Salanta-Tatsawarki streams in the Metropolitan Kano.

## The Jakara River System

The first source of the River is traced into the Kano city (i.e. the Jakara/Rafin Mallam) and the second source is the Bompai Industrial Estate (i.e. the Getsi). For this, the quality of the water is very low and not suitable for many uses. The River was dammed at Wasai in Minjibir Local Government for the last three and a half decades without proper utilization. Before the dam, this flow disappeared into Yadai and Yukana sand dunes (in the north eastern part of the Region) and which still forms the only longitudinal dune fields in the present Kano State. Other rivers that joined the Jakara at Chedi in Minjibir Local Government are the Agalawa, Gwagwata and Fagwalawa Rivers from the north. The Agalawa floodplain has been one of the most important *Fadama* that was put to intensive cultivation in the Region (before the Dam).

## The Watari River System

Watari River gets its sources from numerous tributaries west of Shanono and Gwarzo. The river passes through Bagwai where it was dammed. Downstream, the river flow through Janguza and joined the Challawa. The Bagwai (i.e. Watari) Dam is one of the most productive

Chapter 3    Adnan Abdulhamid, in
A.I. Tanko and S.B. Momale (Eds.)
*Kano: Environment, Society and Development*
London & Abuja, Adonis & Abbey Publishers

dams in the Region that is utilised for variety of purposes, particularly dry season irrigation providing livelihoods to thousands of the rural populace.

## The Magaga River System

Magaga and Watari Rivers in mythology of *Hausawan-Kano* have spiritual influences in battle of great rivalry. Any passerby of any of the two Rivers who, according to the myth, wished for an end of the rivalry (through conveyance of greetings/well wishes from the other to the one he was crossing) would be drowned by the one he was crossing. This myth came up from the ancient religion of river worshiping in *Maguzanci*. The Magaga River is dammed at Gude and planned to supply water to many areas along Gwarzo Road, including Garo, Rimin Gado and many other smaller towns around it. The river runs south eastwards, and is one of the tributaries of the Challawa River.

## The Guzu-Guzu River System

This River is part of the Challawa system but dammed at Kanya in the northern part of Kabo. The River is not fully utilised as little irrigation is carried out with fishing carried out only by local fishermen. The reservoir is in its full capacity, capable of supporting the entire area in the west central parts of the Region but its potentials are yet not fully exploited.

## The Gari River System

In the western extreme of the Region, the Gari system takes its source from Kaduna and Katsina States in the Katsina Highlands around Malumfashi, which also serves as one of the headwaters of the Challawa River System which creates dendritic networks moving eastward. Some of its major tributaries include Koganya, Kwakwa, Jare and Marashi all of which join the Challawa River. The last three tributaries meet at Damagari in Tudun-Kaya, Karaye Local Government. Koganya flows into Challawa at the upstream of the Gorge Dam in Rogo Local Government area. This area, unlike many

Chapter 3 | Adnan Abdulhamid, in
A.I. Tanko and S.B. Momale (Eds.)
*Kano: Environment, Society and Development*
London & Abuja, Adonis & Abbey Publishers

areas of the Basement Bomplex, has groundwater potentials with various drainages cutting across. This River system was dammed at Karaye and is called the Challawa Gorge Dam which is currently the largest earth dam in the Kano Region.

Other Rivers from this axis that joined the Challawa are Kumanda, Kariya, Bagwari and Bargi. Also part of the system is the Kusalla River, which runs south through Kurugu where it was dammed. Initially this was the source of water for Karaye and Gwarzo towns before the construction of the Challawa Gorge Dam.

## The Tagwami River System

Takwami is the main river flowing through Dabar Kwari north of Kumurya to the south of Dawakin Kudu to form a confluence with the Gulu River. Both flow into the Chalawa River. As one moves into Warawa Local Government, the density of the network reduces with Waya and Sinanfi streams draining in sub-dendritic pattern into the *Kogin* Wudil. Another River in this system is the Kwazari that runs from the north to flow into the Hadejia River through Zakirai.

## The Dudduru River System

This is a subsystem of the Hadejia River which flows from Adarau and Katafila Rivers. At this stage the density of the drainage network lowers as the systems enter the Chad formation. Dudduru shows its resilience only in the rainy season as it disappears into the sand dunes in the dry season. In the rainy season, the channel of the River widens extensively before it eventually flows into the main Hadejia River by the eastern side of Ringim town. The widened channels break into two major channels (Duddurun-Gaya and Duddurun Mallam Jatau) forming good alluvial fans of *fadamas*. The two channels supply high amount of discharge into the Hadejia River.

## The Iggi River System

This is a subsystem of Yobe system. The substantial additional water the Region gets from outside is through this system. The streams in the system run west ward into the Challawa River and the Hadejia Valley.

Chapter 3 | Adnan Abdulhamid, in
A.I. Tanko and S.B. Momale (Eds.)
*Kano: Environment, Society and Development*
London & Abuja, Adonis & Abbey Publishers

Iggi and Dudduru are the main river systems in the Chad Formation with wide channels and supply substantially into the Hadejia.

## The Tukuikuyi River System

Other Rivers in the Region that can be reckoned with are the Tukuikuyi, Seleri and Kakori. Tukuikuyi is said to have ceased to discharge its water until recently in 2010 when the river discharges up to the fringes of Birniwa town.

## The Tomar River System

Tomar sometimes called Tomas/Thomas is one of the disappearing streams in the Jigawa sand dunes. The River sources its water from Tsanyawa and Makoda area. It is dammed forming a reservoir at Shankere village close to Wailare a few kilometres from Danbatta town. Despite the large volume of water in the reservoir little utilization of the water is made by the farmers through irrigation in the neighbouring villages. This river has few tributaries.

### Issues in Water Resource Supply in the Region

A major challenge facing the future development of water in Kano Region must overcome three major complex issues. First, is the 'migration' of groundwater from the areas underlain by the Basement Complex to those underlain by the Chad Formation. The migration is due to seepage to Chad formation, which is more porous in geological formation, containing large carrying capacity of sizeable aquifer. The location of Chad formation at the lower elevation and the high abstraction from the Chad aquifer by the rural populace, where groundwater is the major option to the people is of great concern to water management in the present day Kano State.

WRECA (1985) had earlier suggested interregional water transfer to Chad formation. The transfer should be sought otherwise to include basement complex parts of the region. How to go about the transfer cannot easily be described by simple spatial scope of the Kano Region but could perhaps include the entire area surrounding the mega-Chad, which involved several states; hence within the mandate of the Federal

Chapter 3 | Adnan Abdulhamid, in
A.I. Tanko and S.B. Momale (Eds.)
*Kano: Environment, Society and Development*
London & Abuja, Adonis & Abbey Publishers

Government. The challenge of interregional water transfer still remains with more complex challenges of politics, policy design and implementation. It is hoped that water transfer might be possible in the future.

Another challenge for the future development of groundwater of the Kano Region has to do with the rising demand of water by an ever increasing population. The Region has the highest population in northern Nigeria with over 14 million people. The increasing demand for water by the urban and rural dwellers calls for research to ascertain the per capita intakes of the population as well as water needs of other diverse domestic, institutional and industrial uses. The inadequacy of electricity over the last 10 years has incapacitated the water pumping agencies in Kano and Jigawa States, which increasingly put much pressure on groundwater leaving surface water bodies withering. This has led to serious dewatering of aquifers to such an extent that water is now mined in the dry season in Kano city and other sizeable towns. Population-water ratio is becoming a serious problem in Kano that needs urgent solution.

Another major challenge for the future is to integrate in every description and or predictive analysis a quantitative assessment of uncertainty arising from the underlying conceptual mathematical model and to integrate human-water demand pattern with climatic variability. From the historical data of annual rainfall of the Region, a mean annual rainfall for 10 years indicated serious drought in the 1980s. Since then there were gradual increase in the rainfall which indicate probability of affecting the groundwater potentiality. But still rainfall data of 2007 showed a sharp decrease, which to a larger extent affect the groundwater condition from practical point of view. The issue of climatic variability is a reality, but its relation to groundwater in this area is scantly established.

## Proposal towards Proper Water Resource Management

To address the issues of sustainable water resource development, proven and sound management strategies must be developed. Any management strategy must integrate the environment (both physical and social) with a sound management information system that checks and guards environmental degradation through good policy that

Chapter 3 | Adnan Abdulhamid, in
A.I. Tanko and S.B. Momale (Eds.)
*Kano: Environment, Society and Development*
London & Abuja, Adonis & Abbey Publishers

guarantees supply of water. Three tier management strategies are hereby proposed (Fig. 3.4). This should start from the management of water at the local level, to state or regional level and then to the national level. The strategy must also consider the identified problem at each specific location, recognise the intervention measures and take into account the available local technology.

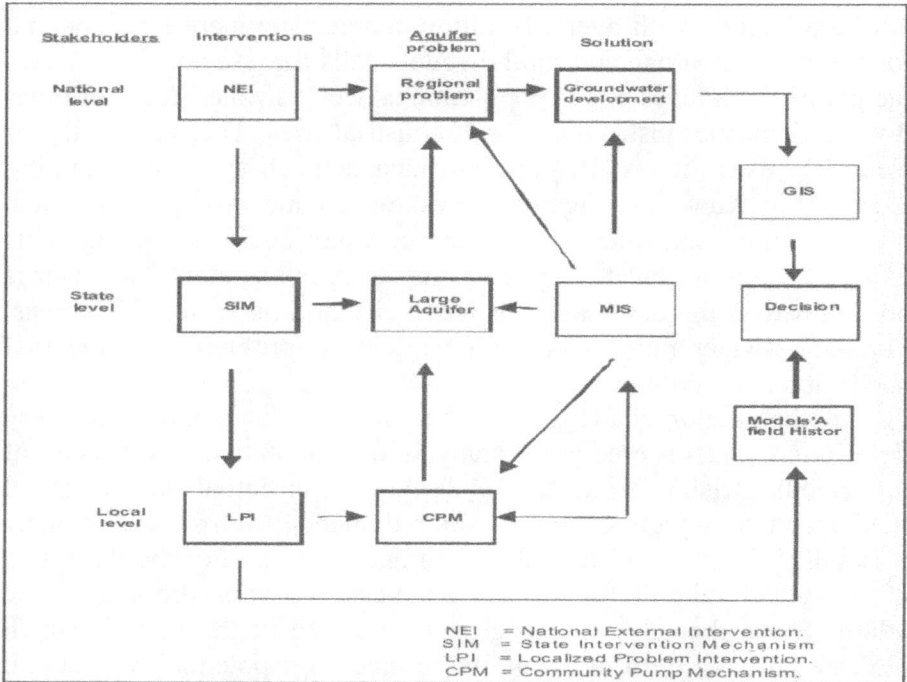

**Figure 3.4**: **The Three-tier Management Strategy**

## Conclusion

The Kano Region has witnessed substantial increase in the level of demand and consumption of water for various uses, particularly for agricultural, industrial and domestic uses over the last few decades. This development is described as a "Silent Revolution" often with no planning or control on the part of government authorities (Llamas and Martínez-Santos 2010). The popularization of the submersible pumps and irrigation pumps has made this possible; enabling more people to exploit available water resources, whether on the surface or

Chapter 3 | Adnan Abdulhamid, in
A.I. Tanko and S.B. Momale (Eds.)
*Kano: Environment, Society and Development*
London & Abuja, Adonis & Abbey Publishers

underground. Kano is also facing higher challenges from climatic vulnerability and ground water 'migration'. River systems in the Region are continuously depleted with several constructed dams on the Basement Complex being contaminated from domestic and industrial effluents without proper utilization. Again there has been a rapid rise in the indiscriminate drilling of boreholes by individuals, governments and corporate organisations that is not regulated or coordinated. Three-tier management strategy has been proposed. This should start from the management of water from the local to state or regional down to the national levels. The proposed three tier strategy will facilitate adequate diagnosis of water demand, supply and consumption, proper analysis of water needs for specific locations and evolution of interventions and strategies that will guarantee quality water use planning, taking cognisance of local technologies and sustainable management of the surface and underground water resources of the Kano Region.

## References

Abdulhamid, A. (2010): *An Assessment of Aquifer Potentials in the Kano Region.* PhD. Thesis   submitted to the Department of Geography, Bayero University Kano-Nigeria.

Bennett, J.G., A.A. Hutcheon, J. Ibanga, W.J. Rackham, and J. Valette (1978): Environmental Aspects of Kano Plains: *Land Resources of Central Nigeria.* Vol.2. Ministry of Overseas Development. England.

FAO (2004). *Global Forest Resources Assessment 2000: Main Report.* FAO forestry Paper 140. Food and Agricultural Organization of United Nation

Hanche-Olsen, H. (2004): Buckingham's $p_i$ theorem. Paper in *TMA4195 Mathematical Modeling* from Hanchen @ math.ntnu.no retrieved on 1st October, 2006.

IUCN, 2005: Pre-water audit for the Komadugu-Yobe River Basin, noethern Nigeria and Southern Niger. The World Conservation Union, Federal Ministry of Water Resources and Nigerian Conservation Foundation, Kano- Nigeria.

Chapter 3 | Adnan Abdulhamid, in
A.I. Tanko and S.B. Momale (Eds.)
*Kano: Environment, Society and Development*
London & Abuja, Adonis & Abbey Publishers

Kano State (2005): Tamburawa Water Works. A publication of Research and Documentation Directorate. Edited by Ado-Kurawa, I.

Llamas, M. R. and Martínez-Santos, P (2010): *Intensive Groundwater Use: Silent Revolution and Potential Source of Social Conflicts.* Editorial, *Hydrogeol. J.* Royal Academy of Sciences, Spain. And Complutense Univ. of Madrid, Spain

Macdonald and Partners (1986): Rural Water Supplies. Final Report, Vol. 1, *Main Report* KNARDA, December House Station Road, Cambridge, England

Olofin, E.A. (1987): *Some Aspects of physical Geography of Kano Region and Related Human Responses.* BUK, Debis Standard Printers, Kano.

Schultz International Limited (1976): Hadejia River Basin Study. Volume E. *Water Resources.* Published by the Can International Development Agency.

Szentes, G. (1974) - *Hydro-geological Data of North-East Kano State.* Water Resources and Engineering Construction Agency (WRECA), Kano State.

WARDROP Engineering Inc. (1990): *Final Report-Rural Water Supply Project*, Volume II. Kano State Agricultural and Rural Development Authority (KNARDA), Kano, Nigeria.

WMO (2002): the convention to combat desertification (NNCCD) in *weather and climate: the variability and change.* Sustainable development beyond 2002. World Meteorological Organization. Geneva, Switzerland.

World Bank, 2008: National Action Plan (NAP) - Towards Implementation of IWRN in the Lake Chad Basin of Nigeria. Draft Final Report. World Bank, UNDP and UNEP, Nigeria.

WRECA (1985): *Groundwater Monitoring and Imbalance in Kano State.* Water Resource Engineering and Construction Agency (WRECA), Kano, Nigeria

Chapter 3 | Adnan Abdulhamid, in
A.I. Tanko and S.B. Momale (Eds.)
*Kano: Environment, Society and Development*
London & Abuja, Adonis & Abbey Publishers

# Chapter Four

## SOILS

Essiet Unanaowo Essiet

### Introduction

The soils of the Kano Region are derived from the two main geological formations; the Basement Complex and the Chad Formation. The Basement Complex rocks are quite variable in size and composition and include schists, shales and granites among others. The soils formed over the Basement Complex rocks are relatively well structured and posses sufficient depth to permit the cultivation of most staple crops. The soils on the Chad Formation, on the other hand, are poorly structured and excessively drained. They are derived mostly from the Aeolian parent materials. However, in view of the prolonged influence of the Sahara dusts in the area, all surface soils in the Kano Region contain Aeolian materials. The soils are generally free of stones. A common feature of soils in the Basement Complex area is the occurrence of plinthite or ferruginous hard pans with depth. Such occurrence restricts roots and water distribution and so reduces agricultural potential of the soils. In some cases, the ferruginous hard pans may be exposed at the surface through denudation; and in such cases affected soils would be put out of agricultural production.

### Physical Properties

#### Texture

Most of the soils in the Region are sandy, at least in the surface horizon (0-30cm). Soils formed over Aeolian materials are sandy than those formed over Basement Complex Rocks. The sand fractions often exceed 70 percent in most surfaces except for hydromorphic soils found in river valleys where the proportion of sand is much lesser. The surface textures range from sandy to sandy loam.

In cultivated soils, the clay content of surface soils range from 2 to 10 percent (Essiet 1990, 1995) with lowest values being recorded in

Chapter 4 | Essiet U. Essiet, in
A.I. Tanko and S.B. Momale (Eds.)
*Kano: Environment, Society and Development*
London & Abuja, Adonis & Abbey Publishers

the profile of soils developed over Aeolian deposits. In soils over the Basement Complex, the clay content increases with depth and could reach between 25 and 40 percent in the 45 - 75cm depth.

The sandy nature of the top soils in the Kano Region has several implications for agricultural land use. For one, nutrients added as fertilizers would be loosely held and so easily lost through leaching. Secondly, infiltration will be high thus resulting in poor moisture retention capacity. Finally, such soils would be easily eroded by either wind or water with the associated soil management problems.

## Available Water Holding Capacity (AWHC)

Two soil components are responsible for the retention of moisture, i.e. clay and organic matter. Incidentally, both components are low to very-low in the soils especially with the economic use of irrigation water. One problem associated with decrease in soil moisture in the Region is the hardening of soils. The exact mechanism of this phenomenon is not understood but it makes land preparation after rainy season extremely difficult. This means that farm operations have to be suspended till the following rainy season when the soils would be moistened by the first rains. Available Water Holding Capacity ranges from 41 percent to about 56 percent in cultivated and uncultivated soils respectively (Essiet 2001).

## Structural Stability and Resistance to Erosion

Soil structure refers to the way and manner the individual soil particles are arranged into units called aggregates to form a porous medium. The soil structure determines retention of moisture and circulation of air and water, infiltration of water, penetration and expansion of the root system and ease of cultivation.

The soils of the Kano Region have weak aggregates which are quickly lost on cultivation. This renders them very susceptible to erosion by water. After a few rains, the little fine particles are lost, the soils tend to be powdery and single grained in structure and so is easily eroded by winds. The observation above underscores the need to avoid the use of heavy land preparation equipment on arable land in the Region. These equipment cause smearing and compaction both of

Chapter 4 | Essiet U. Essiet, in
A.I. Tanko and S.B. Momale (Eds.)
*Kano: Environment, Society and Development*
London & Abuja, Adonis & Abbey Publishers

which tend to intensify soil erosion. In irrigation schemes, after initial levelling of the land to assist the application of irrigation water, subsequent land preparation will be limited to the use of less destructive equipment such as chisel ploughs and harrows (Essiet 1990, 2001).

## Chemical Properties

### Nutrient Content

The most deficient nutrient elements in soils of the Kano Region are nitrogen, phosphorus, potassium and sulphur. This fact is reflected in the formulation of chemical fertilizers whereby one or more of the nutrients are supplied either as single or mixed fertilizers. In addition, some micro-nutrients such as boron, zinc and molybdenum are also deficient. The micronutrients are often supplied as additives to major fertilizers.

### Nitrogen

In tropical soils as a whole, the organic component of the soil supplies almost the entire natural nitrogen present. Small amounts are also supplied through rainfall, rhizophere fixation and dust. It follows therefore that the nitrogen status of soil is closely linked to its organic matter content and variability. Total nitrogen content of cultivated topsoils in the Kano Region ranges from $0.2kg\ ha^{-1}$ to $0.6kg\ ha^{-1}$ (Essiet, 1995, 1998, 2001) with the lower values being recorded in soils that have been cultivated for a long period without any amendment with fertilizers. Nitrogen is a critical element in crop production in the Kano Region. This is so because the main staple crops are made up of grains which require more of nitrogen than any other element to give economic yield.

The most significant avenue of nitrogen loss in the Region is the burning of residues from crops and fallows (Kowal and Kassam, 1978). Such losses have been estimated at between 20 and 40 $kgN\ ha^{-1}$ per annum (Nye and Greenland, 1960). Other losses come through leaching, immobilization, denitrification and the 'export' of produce.

Chapter 4 | Essiet U. Essiet, in
A.I. Tanko and S.B. Momale (Eds.)
*Kano: Environment, Society and Development*
London & Abuja, Adonis & Abbey Publishers

Significant increases in crop yields in the Kano Region would exert great demands on nitrogen supply from the soils. This increased demand is unlikely to be met by soil native nitrogen ($NH4^+$ and $No3^-$ nitrogen and nitrogen from organic matter mineralization) since these sources of nitrogen are closely related to the soil organic matter level which is generally low in the Region. It therefore follows that any increase in nitrogen availability to crops must come from biologically fixed nitrogen and chemical fertilizers. These two forms of nitrogen should be used in a complementary manner to ensure the sustainability of soil and environmental quality.

## *Phosphorus*

The amount of total P in cultivated soils in the Kano Region is generally low with ranges from 65.0ppm to 280.0ppm (Essiet, 1990, 1995, 1998). This low amount indicates that widespread P deficiencies are likely in the Region even though total P levels are not a good indication of P availability to crops. This is due largely to the tendency of soluble phosphorus to reach with soil components (mostly silicate clays) to form relatively insoluble compounds which are unavailable to plants. This phenomenon called phosphorus fixation is encouraged by low soil pH. Phosphorus deficiency in soils of the Region could be corrected by the application of phosphate fertilizers, usually single or triple superphosphate. Such an application should, however be carried out with care to avoid nutrient imbalance due to the 'residual effect' of phosphorus. The latter is caused by the 'trapping1 of phosphorus molecules in non-exchangeable position by silicate clays. The trapped phosphorus is however released slowly to plants as the phosphate concentration in the labile pool drops.

## *Potassium*

Few K deficiencies exist in cultivated soils in the Kano Region. This is due to the fact that, unlike the case of phosphorus, most of the potassium taken up by crops accumulates in the residue. Thus the return of crop residues to the soil ensures reasonable levels of soil potassium. Total content of potassium in soils of the Region is

Chapter 4 | Essiet U. Essiet, in
A.I. Tanko and S.B. Momale (Eds.)
*Kano: Environment, Society and Development*
London & Abuja, Adonis & Abbey Publishers

determined by the nature of the parent material and varies from 0.2g/kg to 0.4g/kg (Essiet, 2002, 2003).

Unlike phosphorus, much of the total potassium in soils of the Region is in available form. It is readily available to crops although in soils that have been intensively cropped without amendment with fertilizers available potassium levels would drop significantly.

Crop removal constitutes the largest avenue of loss of soil potassium especially when most of the produce is 'exported'. Kowal and Kassam (1978) estimate that a crop of 9400kg/ha maize would remove 39kgK in grain and 157kg in the residue. Other avenues of loss include leaching, soil erosion and surface run-off.

## Calcium and Magnesium

These are dominant cations (over 80%) in the Kano Region soils and they are moderately taken up by plants. Thus very few deficiencies have been reported. Meredith (1965) reported deficiency of calcium in groundnuts resulting in 'blind' nuts and low shelling percentages. Total contents of soils in the Region range between 2.0 and 20.0kg/ha and 3.0 and 30.0kg/ha for magnesium and calcium respectively (Kowal and Kassam, 1978). Of these amounts, about 60 percent would be in exchangeable form.

## Sulphur

This nutrient element is widely deficient in soils of the Region and such deficiencies have been reported in groundnuts (Brand, 1969). Most of the sulphur found in surface soils in the Region is derived from organic matter decomposition and since most of the soils in the Kano Region are low in organic matter, the sulphur content would be correspondingly low. A mean content of 45ppm was reported by Goldsworthy and Heathcote (1963) for northern Nigeria. In view of the strong relationship between soil sulphur content and organic matter, the burning of surface litter and crop residues would result in substantial losses of sulphur.

Chapter 4 | Essiet U. Essiet, in
A.I. Tanko and S.B. Momale (Eds.)
*Kano: Environment, Society and Development*
London & Abuja, Adonis & Abbey Publishers

## *Micronutrients*

Information is scanty on the deficiency of micronutrients in soils of the Kano Region. Soils derived from sandy parent materials are usually poorer in micronutrient content than those formed over less sandy materials, e.g. crystalline and metamorphic rocks. Thus soils in the Kano Region with their predominantly sandy texture would be expected to be widely deficient in micronutrients.

The micronutrients most deficient in the Kano Region are molybdenum and zinc. They are supplied as additives to major fertilizers. The main problem associated with correction for micronutrients deficiency is that the borderline between sufficient and toxic amounts is very thin. This is especially true with molybdenum. This problem is further complicated by the fact that in the case of molybdenum, soil organic matter which is the component that moderates toxic amounts is very low.

## Conclusion

Generally, the agricultural potential of soils in the Kano Region is rated as low to marginal. The exceptions to this are the hydromorphic soils found in valley bottoms and flood plains of rivers (*fadama*) in the Region. The poor nutrient status of soils in the Region is largely responsible for this low agricultural potential. Efforts at raising the agricultural potential of the soils must aim at increasing their fertility levels. This could be achieved by the application of fertilizers (both organic and inorganic in a complementary manner) and soil management practices aimed at soil conservation.

## References

Braund, M. (1969), Sulphur fertiliation in Cotton in tropical Africa, *Sulphur Institute*, 5, 3-5

Essiet, E.U. (1990), A composition of soil degradation under smallholder farming and large-scale Irrigation Land Use in Kano, Northern Nigeria. *Land Degradation and Rehabilitation*, Vol. 2, 209-214.

Chapter 4 | Essiet U. Essiet, in
A.I. Tanko and S.B. Momale (Eds.)
*Kano: Environment, Society and Development*
London & Abuja, Adonis & Abbey Publishers

40

Essiet, E.U. (1995), Soil Management and Agricultural Sustainability in the Smallholder Farming System in Northern Nigeria, *Journal of Social and Management Studies*, Vol. 2, 37-46.

Essiet, E.U. (1998), Farming Techniques and Soil Quality in the Drylands of Northern Nigeria in: Ukpong, I.E. (ed.) *Geography and Nigerian Environment*. The Nigerian Geographical Association, 252-257.

Essiet, E.U. (2001), Agricultural Sustainability Under Small-holder Farming in Kano, northern Nigeria. *Journal of Aid Environments*, 48, 1-7.

Essiet, E.U. (2003), Managing Soil Resources for Sustainable Agricultural Production in the Semi-Arid Northeastern Nigeria (SANEN) in: Onokala, P.C. et al (eds.) *Environment and Poverty in Nigeria*. Jamoe Enterprise, 74-85.

Goldsworthy, P.R. and Heathcote, R.G. (1963), Fertilizer trials with groundnuts in northern Nigeria. *Empirical Journal of Experimental Agriculture*, 31, 351-366.

Kowal, J.M. and Kassam, A.H. (1978), *Agricultural Ecology of Savanna*: A study of West Africa. Clarendon, Press, Oxford.

Meredith, R.M. (1965), A Review of the Responses to Fertilizers of the Crops in Northern Nigeria. *Samaru Miscellaneous Paper*, No 4, IAR, Samaru, Nigeria.

Nye, P. And Greenland, D. J. (1960), The soil under shifting cultivation. *Tech. Com.* No. 51. Commonwealth Bureau of Soil, Herpenden.

Chapter 4 | Essiet U. Essiet, in
A.I. Tanko and S.B. Momale (Eds.)
*Kano: Environment, Society and Development*
London & Abuja, Adonis & Abbey Publishers

**41**

# Chapter Five

## VEGETATION AND FORESTRY

Murtala Muhammad Badamasi

### Introduction

Vegetation refers to the plant community found in any given area (Iloeje, 1981). In other words, it could be described as all the plants which grow together in any area. Hence, it is the community of different species of plants growing together in a particular habitat or environment and possessing a certain general physical appearance. The physical appearance is viewed from the relative proportions of the different species as well as their spatial distribution in space (both horizontal and vertical), i.e. the way in which the different species of plants are arranged in space.

The occurrence and the resulting nature and pattern of vegetation that emerges in any given area reflect the inter-play that exists between five different factors. These factors are climate, soils (edaphic), physiographic, biotic (flora and fauna) and anthropogenic (man). Vegetation may be natural when it grows and has remained without interference by man; derived when it is a re-growth after the original plant cover has been destroyed; or artificial or what Olofin (1987) termed "*cultural*" when it has been planted by man.

Natural vegetation is a plant community that is completely unaffected by human activities whether directly or indirectly. According to Olofin (1987) this kind of vegetation hardly exists in the Kano Region (earlier defined adequately in chapter one) due to the rising population and increasing agricultural land intensification. The derived vegetation is the type that has been influenced, to varying degrees, by human activities including pockets of forest plantation and cultivated lands that constitute majority of the Kano landscape. This Chapter describes the distribution, utilization and management of vegetation resources in the Kano Region.

The Chapter is organized into three parts. The first part which consists of the next three sections, describes the ideal and current status of vegetation cover in the Region. A second part provides a

Chapter 5 | Murtala M. Badamasi, in
A.I. Tanko and S.B. Momale (Eds.)
*Kano: Environment, Society and Development*
London & Abuja, Adonis & Abbey Publishers

prelude into the efforts towards conserving and developing forests and forestry. The emerging foot print of man in and around the region that has hitherto impacted upon the Region is discussed in the third part. Finally, a conclusion is drawn, noting that sustainable forestry resource development is needed to adequately protect and empower the Region.

## Natural Vegetation

Stable vegetation communities which are in equilibrium with climatic and soil conditions are referred to as the climatic climax vegetation, and they form part of an ecosystem in steady-state equilibrium (Lockwood, 1976). Since climate varies considerably over the surface of the earth, with many regions of restricted water or energy supply, several types of climatic climax vegetation are to be expected. Thus, the coastal areas in Nigeria for instance where the rainfall is relatively high and persistent are characterized by dense, tropical rain forest, or swamp forest. Further inland such as the Kano Region with limited supply of water at a continental scale (sub-humid) is typified by the *Savanna* as climatic climax vegetation. Savanna is simply described as closed grass or other predominantly herbaceous vegetation with scattered or widely spaced woody plants. Three types of Savanna could be identified in the Region which responds to variation in the amount of rainfall received that decreases from south to north. Towards the southern tip of the Region where the amount of rainfall is high, the northern *Guinea* Savanna is the climatic climax vegetation and in the extreme northern part with low rainfall, the *Sahel* is the climatic climax vegetation. While much of the interior part of the Region is characterized by the *Sudan* Savanna, it is important to note that the major controlling factor influencing this local variation in climatic climax vegetation distribution is water supply rather than energy supply[1].

---

[1] Kano Region being part of the tropical environment means that energy supply is surplus and thus has little contribution to local variation in the distribution of climatic climax vegetation.

| Chapter 5 | Murtala M. Badamasi, in |
| | A.I. Tanko and S.B. Momale (Eds.) |
| | *Kano: Environment, Society and Development* |
| | London & Abuja, Adonis & Abbey Publishers |

## Guinea Savanna

The northern Guinea Savanna is a woodland or bush land with grasses shorter than in the southern guinea where grasses are 1.5m to 3m tall. The area receives high rainfall and forms the part of major watersheds in the entire Region. It covers locations south of Tudun Wada, particularly around the hilly areas of Dadi Plains and Rishi Hills and some tip of Gwaram and Birnin Kudu to the southeast (Olofin, 1987). Much of the area is now derived (re-growth) Savanna woodland with the gallery woodland found on the bank of River Kano dissecting the Falgore Game Reserve and other rivers (Figure 5.1). Floristic composition has declined owing to human utilization of forest resources (Table 5.1).

## Sudan Savanna

According to Olofin (1987), the Sudan Savanna can be said to be the typical vegetation of the Kano Region. It has scattered trees in open grassland with short grass species (under 1.2m tall) which co-dominates. The trees are usually characterized by broad canopies and they are seldom taller than 20 meters. The trees are well adapted to the environment. Water in form of rainfall is available for a few months in this region, as such majority of the species are deciduous and only few are evergreen (e.g *Tamarindus indica*).

## Sahel Savanna

The vegetation is characterized by scrubland of semi-desert type. It is made up of thorny tree species, regenerating shrubs and perennial or annual grasses and forbs with dry patches of bare sandy or stony ground intervening. Except in the natural depressions, river valleys and around seasonal ponds where larger trees benefit from shallow groundwater and form small areas of dense woodland. The number of woodland and grassland species identified in the region is reported to be >400 (Mortimore, *et al.*, 2008).

In addition, even during the wet season, complete ground cover is never achieved (Olofin, 1987). It is important to note that Sahel

Chapter 5 | Murtala M. Badamasi, in
A.I. Tanko and S.B. Momale (Eds.)
*Kano: Environment, Society and Development*
London & Abuja, Adonis & Abbey Publishers

vegetation in this Region is of recent intrusion, as land use practices are changing.

## *Derived Savanna*

Ahmed (2006) has earlier noted that the natural vegetation covers less than 5% of the land area and even then it is largely degraded except for the Falgore Reserve which also suffers from encroachment (Table 5.2). The over-riding human influence means that most tree species are common to both northern Guinea and the Sudan Savanna. In fact it has been argued that the division of the Savanna vegetation of Nigeria into zones is in any case of doubtful validity (Davis, 1982). This development has given rise to what most authors refer to as derived or secondary re-growth Savanna vegetation. Four distinct types of sub division could be observed here: woodland, Savanna woodland/tree Savanna, shrub Savanna, and the gallery woodland.

Woodland has a closed canopy of medium-sized trees of 10-15m height, but at some spot within the reserve tree height may be up to 25 -30m. Tree diversity and density are high with limited number of shrubs forming a light canopy except for pockets of degraded areas. The woodlands are mostly found within the forest/game reserve such as the Falgore, but high grazing density and other form of exploitation have turned the reserve into what could be described as Savanna woodland. The Savanna woodland is characterized by open stands of medium-sized trees 8 -10 meters and occasionally greater in height; with a more or less closed canopy under which small trees and shrubs grow. They are mostly found along the river floodplains especially on river Hadejia in the north-eastern part of the region.

The gallery woodland or what some authors refer to riverine woodland is a complex formation combining riparian forest, and co-exist with the woodland. They occupy the floodplains of major rivers, an example could be found within the Falgore Game Reserve where River Kano dissects the reserve in a southeast-north direction. Even then, the gallery is seriously threatened as it is highly fragmented owing to fire and browsing by cattle. The natural gallery no longer exists in the Sudan Savanna. It has been removed by man.

Chapter 5 | Murtala M. Badamasi, in
A.I. Tanko and S.B. Momale (Eds.)
*Kano: Environment, Society and Development*
London & Abuja, Adonis & Abbey Publishers

Shrub Savanna vegetation comprises only scrubs of varying density with very few occasional trees. It is found usually adjoining the Savanna woodlands.

## Cultural Vegetation

The anthropogenic activity of man has transformed the climax vegetation over the years through the influence of fire, grazing, cultivation and wood cutting; it has been replaced by the 'cultural vegetation' that presently characterizes the landscape (Yusuf, 2001). The cultural mosaic of vegetation is now often referred to as 'farmed parkland' (Pullan, 1974), a sustainable agro-forestry strategy where certain trees are protected and integrated into the farming system (Maconachie, 2007). It is a farmland characterized by scattered small trees and shrubs which are more common on fallow land where regeneration may take place. About 75% of the land is cultivated parkland with average tree densities of less than 25 per hectare (Ahmed, 2006). Olofin (1987) identified three plant associations:

- Cropped land;
- Parkland fallow; and
- Afforested land.

It is important to note however that, all the categories shown in Figure 5.1 can be further sub-divided. The trust is that the Kano Region like other parts of northern Nigeria is a dynamic mosaic of vegetation stages, or types, whose pattern of distribution is largely influenced by human activity, though other factors may assume local importance. As further needs are pursued, more detailed explanation of the complex relationships involved in the establishment of new vegetation will become possible (Davis, 1982). Figure 5.2 provides a typical complex vegetation distribution found around Hadejia, northeastern corner of the Region where the Hadejia River drains into the Hadejia-Nguru wetlands.

| Chapter 5 | Murtala M. Badamasi, in
A.I. Tanko and S.B. Momale (Eds.)
*Kano: Environment, Society and Development*
London & Abuja, Adonis & Abbey Publishers |

## Forestry and Forest Reserves

These may be seen as the science of planning and caring for large areas of trees. Areas where the land cover is dominated by trees are regarded as forest vegetation. They include close canopy forest and open woodland where some leaves and twigs of adjacent trees overlap. It is worth noting that forestry in the Kano Region like elsewhere in northern Nigeria predates the establishment of a regional forestry department in 1910, whose initial agents for local intervention were based on the work of Elliott (a Forest Officer) in 1904. Earlier attempts by the British administrators to develop the Region consist of the creation of forest reserves. The series of poor rainfall years in northern Nigeria, which coincided with the beginning of the colonial century, and more generally with an empire-wide preoccupation with nature preservation and conservation, forms the rationale for concern over state-perceived links between environmental degradation and the exploitation of land and forestry products.

Cline-Cole (2000) provides a detailed historical perspective of forestry in Kano and noted that the establishment of forest policy at first aimed at self-sufficiency in forestry and this in turn was influence by intervention practices that promoted "restriction" to the use of forest products. During the World War II, the dimension metamorphosed to a process of further consolidating and legitimizing British colonial state through an indirect rule. However, this has raised important questions concerning ownership of and control over land and forest resources and perhaps the issues surrounding who regulates access to these forests and woodlands. Locally, redefining the ownership and control of forest and the resources therein has implications for livelihood diversity and security which were different from those associated with forest or woodland reservation (Cline-Cole, 2000).

There are two types of ownership of forest in the Kano Region - private (individual) plantation and Government plantations and reserves (forest/game reserves, community forest reserves [CFR], shelterbelt, and afforestation sites). The private plantations are found mostly around homesteads and sometimes on the boundaries of farmlands (Ayuba, 2009) and recently around poultry farms. The

Chapter 5 | Murtala M. Badamasi, in
A.I. Tanko and S.B. Momale (Eds.)
*Kano: Environment, Society and Development*
London & Abuja, Adonis & Abbey Publishers

major tree species planted are Neem, *Eucalyptus, Accacia*, and other economic trees.

Government plantations include CFR and forest/game reserves. Most of the forest reserves were established by the colonial administration and is controlled and managed by the State Forestry Department (Table 5.2) except for the Falgore game reserve which was (still is) managed and controlled by the Kano State Zoological and Wildlife Management Agency (KAZOWMA). The forest reserves are under strict protection (tree felling and hunting activities are strictly prohibited therein). As part of the effort by the British administration to preserve natural vegetation, CFR were established and supervised by the then Native Authorities (N.A). Here community members were allowed into the forest occasionally to extract products. The dry and matured trees are normally cut down for house construction, fuelwood and other purposes. Other products derived from such reserves include honey, fruits and medicine (from parts of tree). Majority of the CFR are natural while a few are plantations (Table 5.3). Following the post independence administrative reforms, the management of the CFRs by the N.A. was taken over by respective State Departments of Forestry.

Both the CFRs and the Forest reserves were treated as 'common pool' since the policy does not really spell out in clear terms ownership, and as such community members fell trees indiscriminately, while grazing intensity is quite high. This could be rooted to a supposition community member's hold that their forefathers were alienated from their lands by the then British administration (see Cline-Cole, 2000), and now that they are off, they could regain their access right to use even though it is not legally recognised. The overall result has hitherto culminated into serious encroachment into the protected areas. Currently, only reminiscence of such reserves exists, except for a very few.

## *Forestry Development*

Natural vegetation covers less than 5% of the land area of the Kano Region and is largely degraded except for some protected areas. The Global Standard for a sustainable and safe land is 20% vegetal cover. In Nigeria, the natural vegetation covers about 10%, therefore the Federal Government settled for 10% as the minimum vegetation cover

Chapter 5 | Murtala M. Badamasi, in
A.I. Tanko and S.B. Momale (Eds.)
*Kano: Environment, Society and Development*
London & Abuja, Adonis & Abbey Publishers

as standard for Nigeria.Thus, the Kano Region is far below the Nigerian standard coupled and this increases its susceptibility to the threat of desertification especially along the frontline local governments in the extreme northern parts of the Region (Fig. 5.4). Efforts to sustainably manage the vegetation resources of the region witness the development of different forestry programmes with the following overall objectives:

i.   Control of desert encroachment (through stabilization of sand dunes, restoring productivity of agricultural lands);
ii.  Preventive measures (wind breakers) against heavy winds;
iii. Provision of forest resource requirement to the populace (energy, medicinal, industrial); and
iv.  Maintaining biological diversity, among others.

### *Seedling and Seed Bank*

Seed banks are critical to sustainable forestry development. Seeds are either sourced from government owned plantations (good mother seed that have succeeded) or sister organization such as the National Botanical Garden in Getso town. The garden has a multitude of about 100 indigenous species. The seeds are collected and stored in the office until they are ready for distribution to the multiplication centres. Exotic species account for 60% in terms of composition, while indigenous species account for 20% and the remaining 20% are fruit seedlings (Table 5.4).

| Chapter 5 | Murtala M. Badamasi, in |
| | A.I. Tanko and S.B. Momale (Eds.) |
| | *Kano: Environment, Society and Development* |
| | London & Abuja, Adonis & Abbey Publishers |

**Table 5.1: Major Tree species in the Kano Region** (*Source: Aliyu (2006); Ahmed (2006); Fieldwork, 2010*

| Plant species | Hausa name | Type | Height | Major uses | Location |
|---|---|---|---|---|---|
| Anogeissus Leiocarpus | Marke | Tree | 30m | Firewood, fodder, carvings, Laxative | Guinea |
| Khaya segalensis | Madaci | Tree | 30m | Firewood, fodder, timber, medicine | Guinea |
| Parkia clappertoniana | Dorawa | Tree | | Firewood, fruit, seasoning | Guinea |
| Terminalia avicennioides | Baushe | Tree | 10meter | Firewood, fodder, medicine | Guinea |
| Acacia polyacantha | Farcen shirwa | Tree | 15-23m | Firewood, fodder, beverage, medicine (snake bite) | Guinea (Falgore forest) |
| Percopsis laxiflora | Farin Makarho | Tree | 7-14m | Firewood, fodder | Guinea (Falgore forest) |
| Vitellaria paradoxa | Kadanya | Tree | 10-15m | Firewood, Shea butter | Guinea (Falgore forest) |
| Adansonia digitata | Kuka | Tree | 10meter | Food (edible fruits and leaves), medicine | Guinea/ Sudan |
| Diospyros mespiliformis | Kanya | Tree | 12 -15m | Firewood, fodder, edible fruits | Guinea/ Sudan |
| Moringa oleifera | zogale | Shrub | 8m | Food, medicine | Guinea/ Sudan |
| Tamarindus indica | Tsamiya | Tree | 25 -30m | Firewood, beverage, laxative | Guinea/ Sudan |
| Vitex domiana | Dinya | Tree | 10 -15m | Firewood, food , medicine | Guinea/ Sudan |
| Sclerocarya birrea | Danya | Tree | 10 - 15m | Firewood, food (edible fruits), medicine | Guinea/ Sudan |
| Acacia albida | Gawo | Tree | 15 - 25m | Firewood, fodder, food, gum, medicine | Sudan |
| Acacia Seyal | Dushe | Tree | 17m | Firewood, fodder, food, gum, medicine | Sudan |
| Borrasus aethiopum | Giginya | Tree | 30- 35m | Timber, food (edible fruits), craft, building | Sudan |
| Hyphaene the baica | Goriba | Tree | | Firewood, fodder, food (edible fruits) | Sudan |
| Piliostigma thonningii | Kalgo | Shrub | | Firewood, fodder | Sudan |
| Ziziphus Spina-Christi | kurna | Shrub/ Tree | 20m | Food (edible fruits), medicine | Sudan |
| Acacia nilotica | Bagaruwa | Tree | up to 20m | Firewood, fodder, food, medicine | Sudan/ Sahel |
| Acacia Senegal | Dakwara | Shrub/ Tree | 2 - 6m | Firewood, fodder | Sudan/ Sahel |
| Acacia sieberiana | Farar kaya | Tree | 25m | Firewood, fodder | Sudan/ Sahel |
| Balanites aegyptiaca | Aduwa | Tree | 6- 10m | Firewood, edible fruits | Sudan/ Sahel |
| Guiera senegalensis | Sabara | Shrub | | fodder , firewood | Sudan/ Sahel |
| Phoenix dactylifera | Dabino | Tree | 15 - 20 (30) | Food | Sudan/ Sahel |

Chapter 5 | Murtala M. Badamasi, in
A.I. Tanko and S.B. Momale (Eds.)
*Kano: Environment, Society and Development*
London & Abuja, Adonis & Abbey Publishers

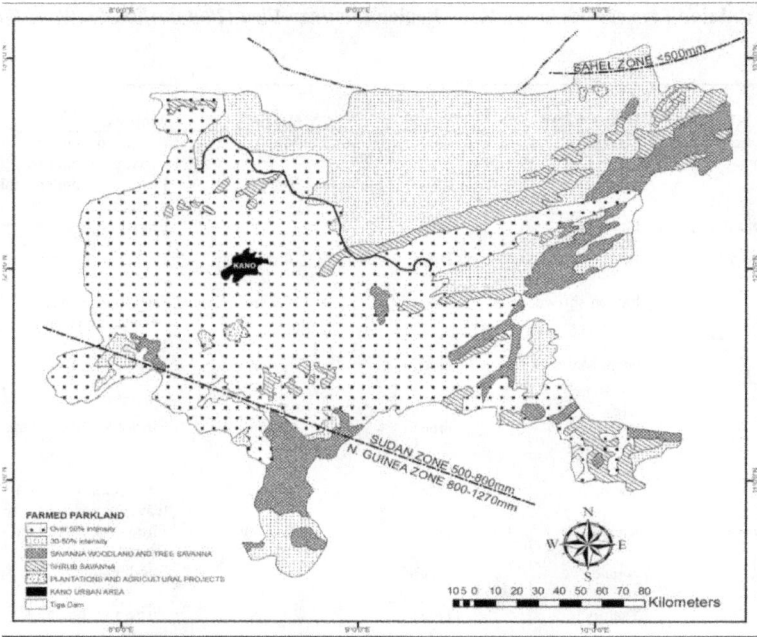

**Figure 5.1 Distribution of Vegetation in the Kano Region**

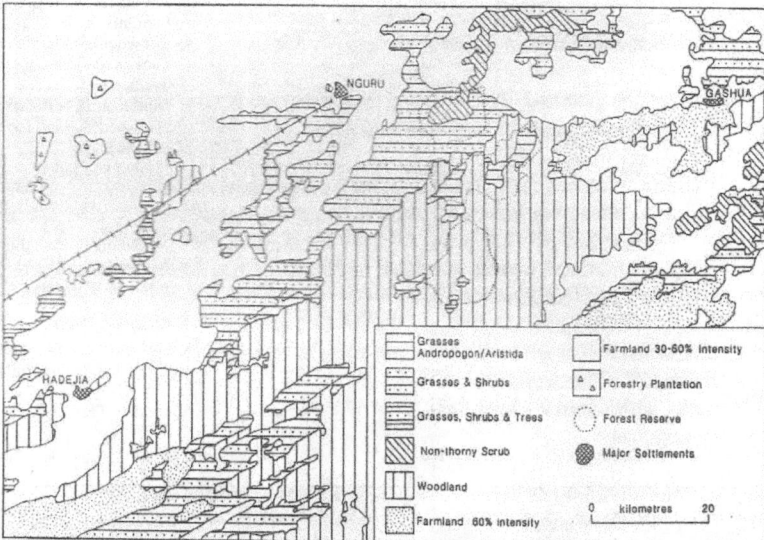

**Figure 5.2: Vegetation of the Hadejia-Nguru Wetlands (after Parry and Trevett, 1979)**

Chapter 5 | Murtala M. Badamasi, in
A.I. Tanko and S.B. Momale (Eds.)
*Kano: Environment, Society and Development*
London & Abuja, Adonis & Abbey Publishers

## Table 5.2: The Major Forests in the Kano Region

| Name | LGA | Extent (hectare) | Veg. type | Type of Plantation | Gazette No. | Management Objective | Threat |
|------|-----|------------------|-----------|--------------------|-------------|----------------------|--------|
| Kogin Kano | Doguwa | 57130.15 | N/Guinea | Natural forest | 5 | Protection/ Game reserve | Enchroachment |
| Dansoshiya | Kiru | 3862.32 | N/Guinea | Natural forest | 1 | Protection | Enchroachment |
| Maje | Bebeji | 726 | Sudan | Natural forest | 6 | Protection | Enchroachment |
| Duddurun Gaya | Gaya | 24438 | Sudan | Natural forest | | Protection | Seroius Enchroachment |
| Karamarini | Makoda | 700 | Sudan | Natural forest | | Protection | Seroius Enchroachment |
| Gasaltani | Dambatta | 198 | Sudan | Natural forest | 4 | Protection | Ilegal tree felling |
| Jekarade | Dambatta | 95 | Sudan | Plantation | 8 | Protection | Ilegal tree felling |
| Gafan | Bunkure | 1490 | Sudan | Natural forest | | Protection | Ilegal tree felling & encroachment |
| Kyarana | Kiru | 27.75 | Sudan | Natural forest | 7 | Protection | Ilegal tree felling & encroachment |
| Iggi | Dutse/ Kiyawa/ Birnin Kudu/ Buji | na | Sudan | Natural forest | | Protection | Ilegal tree felling & encroachment |
| Gurmina | Birnin Kudu | na | N/Guinea | Natural forest | | Protection | Ilegal tree felling & encroachment |
| Farin Dutse | Gwaram | na | N/Guinea | Natural forest | | Protection | Ilegal tree felling & encroachment |
| Rabadi | Gwaram | na | N/Guinea | Natural forest | | Protection | Ilegal tree felling & encroachment |
| Warwade | Gwaram | na | N/Guinea | Natural forest | | Protection | Ilegal tree felling & encroachment |
| Godiya | Guri | na | Sudan | Natural forest | | Protection | Ilegal tree felling & encroachment |

*Source: Kano State Afforestation Programme (2010); Fieldwork, 2010*

Chapter 5 | Murtala M. Badamasi, in
A.I. Tanko and S.B. Momale (Eds.)
*Kano: Environment, Society and Development*
London & Abuja, Adonis & Abbey Publishers

## Table 5.3: Some Community Forest Areas (CFA) in Kano State

| Name | LGA | Extent (hectare) | Veg. Type | Type of Plantation |
|------|-----|------------------|-----------|--------------------|
| Mahuwa | Makoda | 307.2 | Sudan | Natural |
| Tsoho | Bichi | 173.8 | Sudan | Natural |
| Yola | Bichi | 50 | Sudan | Natural |
| Jabirawa | Gwazo | 17 | Sudan | Natural |
| Dundun Bature | Karaye | 98 | Sudan | Natural |
| Dutsen Kure | Kiru | 27.75 | Sudan | Natural |
| Kurun ken Sani | Kumbotso | 130 | Sudan | Natural |
| Dangado | Rano | 168.96 | Sudan | Natural |
| Fancha | Kibiya | 211.48 | Sudan | Natural |
| Ruwan Madofa | Shanono | 50 | Sudan | Natural |
| Zaura Babba | Ungogo | 25.2 | Sudan | Natural |
| Katata | Gwarzo | 140 | Sudan | Natural |
| Tumuku north | Tsanyawa | 96 | Sudan | Natural |
| Tumuku south | Tsanyawa | 210.6 | Sudan | Natural |
| Karoman minjibir | Minjibir | 28 | Sudan | Natural |
| Falla | D/Tofa | 20 | Sudan | Natural |
| Dunawa | D/Tofa | 60 | Sudan | Natural |
| Falungo | Bunkure | 14.6 | Sudan | Plantation |
| Matan fada | Bichi | 73.6 | Sudan | Natural |
| Danzabuwa | Bichi | 50 | Sudan | Natural |
| Dajin ganji | Dambatta | 61.9 | Sudan | Natural |
| Dawan kumbo | Gabasawa | 244 | Sudan | Natural |
| Dajin Gabasawa | Gabasawa | 191.8 | Sudan | Natural |
| Jinju | D/Tofa | 128 | Sudan | Natural |
| Yan Bewa east | D/Kudu | 12.8 | Sudan | Plantation |
| Yan Bewa west | D/Kudu | 62 | Sudan | Plantation |
| Fanisau | Ungogo | 147 | Sudan | Plantation |
| Yanmata | Ungogo | 97.2 | Sudan | Plantation |
| Maimeka | Gezawa | Na | Sudan | Plantation |
| Jido | D/Kudu | Na | Sudan | Plantation |
| Abudakaya | Minjibir | Na | Sudan | Plantation |
| Dan Dake | Minjibir | Na | Sudan | Plantation |

*Source: Kano State Afforestation Programme (2010)*

Chapter 5 | Murtala M. Badamasi, in
A.I. Tanko and S.B. Momale (Eds.)
*Kano: Environment, Society and Development*
London & Abuja, Adonis & Abbey Publishers

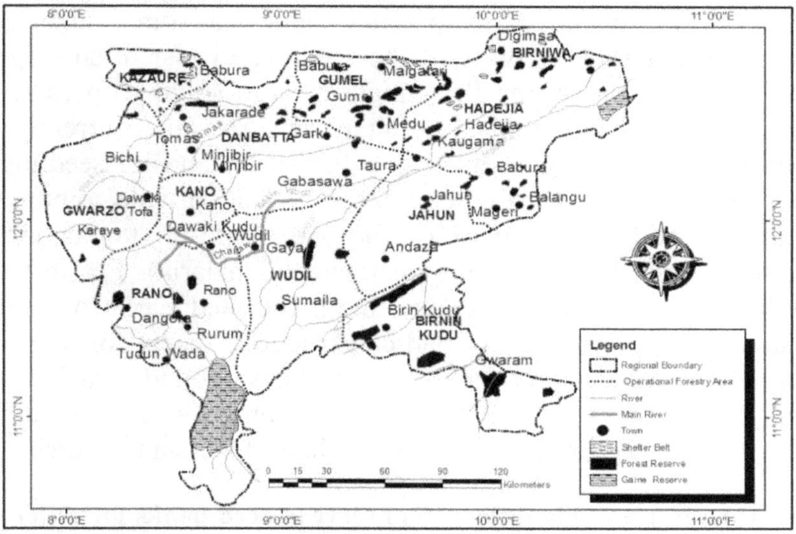

**Figure 5.3: Protected Areas in the Kano Region**

**Figure 5.4: Desert prone areas in the Kano Region**

| Chapter 5 | Murtala M. Badamasi, in |
| | A.I. Tanko and S.B. Momale (Eds.) |
| | *Kano: Environment, Society and Development* |
| | London & Abuja, Adonis & Abbey Publishers |

Seed bank are expensive to maintain because it requires adequate insect control, regulated temperature and moisture, and good packaging to keep the viability of the seed. The insistent shortage of electricity in the region and the nation at large could jeopardize the existence of the bank. Owing to numerous reasons, currently the Forestry department cannot meet up with the demand for seedling by Local Government Areas, institutions and private/commercial nurseries. In addition, sources of the seedlings are threatened by development and debarking (for treatment of malaria). For instance, the author observed that Mahogany that had dotted Zaria road in the past had already given way to road construction, except for 64 stands that could be noticed between Kwanar Dawaki and Karfi towns. Recent development of filling stations along Gezawa road had continued to further threaten the only available Mahogany source.

**Table 5.4: Example of Plantations that serve as seed banks for different trees species**

| Tree Specie | Location of Plantation | Local Government Area |
|---|---|---|
| *Eucaliptus* | Yanbawa shelter belt | Dambatta/Makoda |
| *Azadirachta indica* (neem) | Minjibir | Minjibir |
| Gum Arabic | Dawan Adam | Gezawa/Gabasawa |
| Teak/*Gmelina* | Dansoshiya | Kiru axis |
| Fruits (Guava, Castor) | Yaryasa | Tudun Wada |
| *Cassia* | Marken Kakuri | Bunkure |
| Mahogany | Gezawa | Gezawa |

*Source: Author's work*

## Nurseries

Four different categories of nurseries can be recognized across the Kano Region: government owned; private commercial owned; individual non-commercial; and non-governmental organization. By far the government owned nurseries provides more than 85 to 90 percent of the seedling produced annually. For instance, Kano State

Chapter 5 | Murtala M. Badamasi, in
A.I. Tanko and S.B. Momale (Eds.)
*Kano: Environment, Society and Development*
London & Abuja, Adonis & Abbey Publishers

has a total of 36 nurseries with a cumulative capacity of 5 million seedlings per annum[2]. However, this figure is hardly met.

More than 350 private commercial nurseries dot the urban landscape in the Region, and their production is very low owing to low capital base. They have been organized under   body known as *Association of Gardeners.* Through the association government provide them with technical support and little incentives to boost their production.

Individual non-commercial and non-governmental organizations have equally contributed tremendously towards nursery development. A typical example is a botanical garden developed by Professor Fatima B. Muktar near the Dawakin Kudu town. The Garden has more than 100 species of trees (exotic and indigenous) and a host of ornamental flowers.

## *Afforestation Projects*

The overall objective of afforestation project in the Region is to combat the desertification process and its associated impacts. Part of this effort was the establishment of shelterbelt and afforestation projects across the Region. The major species used for this purpose include neem and eucalyptus (Table 5.5). Both species are very resilient and coppice very well. Their growth rate is high and seed mortality is low. These characteristics make them well adaptable and good for afforestation. However, both species have tendencies of dominating other species found within their vicinity due to their high acidity.

Apart from preventing accelerated soil erosion and providing shade, both species are good sources of firewood, and they have been used for medicinal purpose such as curing malaria. Oil extracted from neem tree has equally generated income to household practicing such activity. In recent time individuals have taken the advantage of pollarding ability of eucalyptus species, they plant and nurture it to maturity level and sell them off as electric poles or fuelwood. The

---

[2] In a personal interview with the Kano State Director of Forestry and Ecology, Ministry of Environment, he said the reality is that the production was just 300,000 seedlings in the year 2009; and 500,000 in 2010.

Chapter 5    Murtala M. Badamasi, in
A.I. Tanko and S.B. Momale (Eds.)
*Kano: Environment, Society and Development*
London & Abuja, Adonis & Abbey Publishers

wide spread Gum Arabic production in Jigawa State is a welcome idea for forestry resource development. The species are highly resilient to desert condition and the harvested product (gum) yield high return on investment.

As substantial part of the Region falls within the frontline of desert prone areas, NGOs such as Fight Against Desert Encroachment (FADE) are assisting in establishing woodlots in villages and schools. Other NGOs involved in forestry include the Nigerian Environmental Society (NES) and the Nigerian Conservation Society. Some schools in Kano such as the Benny International have made concerted efforts to plant and maintain trees of 1km long along the Eastern Bye-pass. Lafiya Surgery and Criss Path Marketing Solutions have been involved in philanthropic activities towards combating desertification.

### Table 5.5: Some established afforestation projects

| Location | Year of establishment | No. of belt | No of rows of tree per belt | length in Km | Type of species |
|----------|----------------------|-------------|-----------------------------|--------------|-----------------|
| Yan kameye | 1989 | 4 | 8 | 6 | Eucalyptus, cashew, Neem |
| Kore | 1990 | 5 | 8 | 10 | Neem & Eucalyptus |
| Kabani | 1991 | 5 | 8 | 10 | Neem & Eucalyptus |
| Ruwan Tsa | 1991 | 5 | 8 | 10 | Neem & Eucalyptus |
| Tinki | 1992 | 4 | 8 | 7.5 | Neem |
| Tattarawa | 1992 | 5 | 8 | 5 | Neem & Eucalyptus |
| Saye | 1992 | 5 | 8 | 5 | Neem |
| Marke | 1992 | 5 | 8 | 10 | Neem & Eucalyptus |
| Gezawa | 1992 | 5 | 8 | 5 | Neem & Eucalyptus |
| Fagwalo | 1993 | 8 | 8 | 16 | Neem & Eucalyptus |
| Yan gwanda | 1993 | 5 | 8 | 10 | Neem |
| Zangon Mata | 1993 | 5 | 8 | 5 | Neem |
| Kiyawa | 1993 | 5 | 8 | 5 | Neem & Eucalyptus |
| S/G Gezo | 1993 | 5 | 8 | 5 | Neem & Eucalyptus |
| Gafasa | 1993 | 5 | 8 | 10 | Neem & Eucalyptus |
| Barya | 1993 | 5 | 8 | 5 | Neem |
| Fardachi | 1993 | 5 | 8 | 5 | Neem & Eucalyptus |
| Fagwalawa | 1993 | 5 | 8 | 10 | Neem |
| Dan madaki | 1993 | 5 | 8 | 10 | Neem |
| Romi | 1994 | 5 | 8 | 8 | Neem & Eucalyptus |
| Kwaski | 1994 | 4 | 8 | 12 | Neem |
| Dinya Madiga | 1994 | 5 | 8 | 10 | Neem |
| Zakiran Kafi | 1994 | 5 | 8 | 10 | Neem |
| Dumma | 1994 | 5 | 8 | 10 | Neem |

*Source:* Fieldwork (2010)

| Chapter 5 | Murtala M. Badamasi, in<br>A.I. Tanko and S.B. Momale (Eds.)<br>*Kano: Environment, Society and Development*<br>London & Abuja, Adonis & Abbey Publishers |

## Human Impact on Forest Resources

Deforestation in all its ramifications (e.g urbanization and fuel wood extraction) has been identified as one major cause of forest cover change in addition to climate change (Mocanachie, 2004; 2007; Mortimore, 1989; 2002).Despite the fact that literatures focusing on social forestry in the Region suggests that farmers and land managers could continue to support sustainable tree resource use for many years to come, even in times of increasing competition' (e.g. see Cline-Cole et al., 1990), others have suggested that pressure from land use change/intensification could halt the system (Maconachie, 2007, Maconachie, et al., 2009). The latter assumption might be gaining ground.

A study by Herrmann *et al.* (2005), focusing on the temporal and spatial patterns of vegetation greenness and rainfall variability in the Sahel from the 1982 to 2000 using remote sensing techniques demonstrated that 'only parts of northern Nigeria and Sudan show areas where human impact hypothetically inhibited a greening trend in order of magnitude expected from the positive trend in rainfall conditions' across the Sahel. They concluded that, 'the neglect of good land use practices due to civil strife and conflict' might be a cause. Of course there are evidences to show that pockets of vegetation degradation rather than deforestation have occurred in the Region (Uchua, 1999; Riruwai, 2006; Badamasi and Yelwa, 2010) and much literature have documented the links between vegetation modification and fuelwood production and consumption (Cline-Cole, et al., 1990; Maconachie, 2004). For instance, Badamasi and Yelwa (2010) using Remote Sensing techniques observed series of change in the hitherto protected area of the Falgore Game Reserve between 1975 and 2000, and noted that *dense woodland* have already turned to *very open woodland* within three decades. This has implications for both wildlife habitat and erosion. This has been attributed to grazing, fire and, recently, woodcutting.

As earlier noted, by far cultivation is the most visible activity that manifests its impact on vegetation change in the Region. Large scale irrigation schemes and opening up of vast fadama lands for cultivation that were previously utilized for grazing purposes have continued to reduce the available shrublands and protected areas to host high

Chapter 5 | Murtala M. Badamasi, in
A.I. Tanko and S.B. Momale (Eds.)
*Kano: Environment, Society and Development*
London & Abuja, Adonis & Abbey Publishers

grazing intensity. Available literature focusing on pastoralism have pointed out the impact these land use change has on the available shrinking pasture and water especially within the project areas (Baba, 1989; Binns and Mortimore, 1989; Adams, 1993; Tanko, 2001), and therefore the pastoralists are tempted to encroach on the forest reserves. It would appear that these concerns have great bearing on the discussions concerning vegetation, since extraction of forest resources (forest products and water) for grazing and high stocking density can accelerate the rate of vegetal depletion, especially where protection is relaxed. Addressing the issues bordering access to, and right over, grazing area is crucial to the sustainability of forest in the Region.

One of the ongoing debates on the impact of dam construction in the Region is the appearance of *Typha* weed - aquatic plant species that has dotted the landscape especially along River Hadejia and within the waterlogged project areas which is fast growing. This impedes the flow of water along the river channels and in irrigation canals, and is expected to modify the ecology, thus creating new vegetation colony if not adequately controlled.

Over a decade ago several authors have pointed out the ever increasing off-farm activities as an alternative livelihood option amongst poor grassroots actors in the Sub-Saharan Africa, (El-Bashir, 1997); and particularly in the northern Nigerian context (Cline-Cole, 1995; Meagher and Mustapha, 1997). 'There is a danger that [these] off-farm activities could extract too much natural capital from the resource base and threaten the sustainability of resource management systems' like never before. It is therefore not surprising that the sale of fuelwood, economic tree products and even grasses and shrubs is becoming an increasingly common method of generating income. This has earlier been observed by Mortimore (1989), that despite intricate and robust adaptations to seasonal and inter-annual drought, farmers and other producers in such places were marginalized by the environment and the political economy.

This has been collaborated with the recent field-based evidence suggesting the supposition that the changing world economy especially in form of increase in oil prices may manifest itself in environmental change especially vegetal loss. According to the study, Maconachie, et al., (2009) submitted that:

| Chapter 5 | Murtala M. Badamasi, in
A.I. Tanko and S.B. Momale (Eds.)
*Kano: Environment, Society and Development*
London & Abuja, Adonis & Abbey Publishers |

...the rising prices of kerosene and other petroleum-based domestic fuels...are making fuel wood a much more attractive alternative as a domestic fuel choice. ...the poorest and most disadvantaged households may find it increasingly challenging to meet their basic energy needs (Maconachie, et al., 2009 p1090).

The essence of the above prelude is neither to downplay other causes of vegetation change nor to over flog the fuelwood-vegetation change nexus but to stress the basic fact that it is gaining momentum as never before. The feeling is therefore to promote sustainable use of vegetation resource as its depletion may in turn translate into another poverty cycle.

## Conclusion

The Chapter describes the expected climax vegetation and some of the indicators reflecting the dynamic status of vegetation within the Region. The ever increasing demand on the limited forest resources and the reduced carrying capacity of the fragile forest ecosystems' response could trigger real environmental degradation. This further reiterated the fact that environment and development are not exclusive of one another but are complementary and inter-dependent, and this explain the rationale behind the concept of sustainable development.

It is therefore important that government evolve a sustainable forest resource management framework and policy that will incorporates all stakeholders including the indigenous people and their needs. Efforts should be made to create job opportunities, encourage research and development especially in the field of solar energy. There is the need for continuous monitoring of biomass and development of commercial forestry on a large scale within the Region. The likely influence of political economy both at micro and macro levels on environmental degradation should not be neglected. To this end the adoption and/or modification of Sustainable Livelihood Framework of DFID is advocated.

Chapter 5 | Murtala M. Badamasi, in
A.I. Tanko and S.B. Momale (Eds.)
*Kano: Environment, Society and Development*
London & Abuja, Adonis & Abbey Publishers

# Acknowledgement

The author appreciates the contribution of Alhaji Bashir Umar, the Director Forestry and Ecology of the Kano State Ministry of Environment in providing support and data for this Chapter.

# References

Adams, W. M. (1993) Agriculture, Grazing and Forestry. In: Hollis, G. E., W. M. Adams and Aminu-Kano, M. (eds.), *The Hadejia-Nguru Wetlands: Environment, Economy and Sustainable Development of a Sahelian Floodplain Wetland*. International Union for Conservation of Nature (IUCN), pp. 89-96.

Ahmed, K. (2006) The Physical Environment of Kano State, *www.kanostate.net/physicalenvironment.html*.

Aliyu, B. S. (2006) *Some Ethnomedicinal Plants of the Savanna regions of West Africa: Description and Phytochemicals*. Vol. I & II, Triumph Publishing Company Limited, Kano.

Ayuba, H. K. (2009) Prospects for Sustainable Management of Forest Resources. In: Waziri, M., Kagu, A. and Monguno, A. K. (eds.) *Issues in the Geography of Borno State*. Adamu Joji Publishers, Kano: p62-69.

Baba, J. M. (1989) The Problems of Rural Inequalities on the Kano River Project, Nigeria. In: Swindell, K., Baba, J. M. and Mortimore, M. J. (eds.), *Inequality and Development: Case Studies from Third World*. Macmillan Publishers, pp. 140-157.

Badamasi, M. M. and Yelwa, S. A. (2010) Change Detection and Classification of Land Cover at Falgore Game Reserve: A Preliminary Assessment. *Biological and Environmental Sciences Journal for the Tropics*, 7 (1): 75-83.

Binns, J. A. and Mortimore, J. M. (1989) Ecology, Time and Development in Kano State, Nigeria. In: Swindell, K., Baba, J. M. and Mortimore, M. J. (eds.), *Inequality and Development: Case Studies from Third World*. Macmillan Publishers, pp. 359-380.

Cline-Cole, R. (1995) Livelihoods, sustainable development and indigenous forestry in dryland Nigeria. In: Binns, T. (ed.), *People and Environment in Africa*. John Wiley and Sons, hichester, pp. 171-185.

Chapter 5 | Murtala M. Badamasi, in
A.I. Tanko and S.B. Momale (Eds.)
*Kano: Environment, Society and Development*
London & Abuja, Adonis & Abbey Publishers

62

Cline-Cole, R., 2000. Redefining forestry space and threatening livelihoods in colonial northern Nigeria. In: Cline-Cole, R., and Madge, C. (eds.), *Contesting Forestry in West Africa*. Ashgate Publishing Limited, Aldershot, pp. 36-63.

Cline-Cole, R., Main, H. and Nichol, J. (1990). On fuelwood consumption, population dynamics and deforestation in Africa. *World Development* 18 (4), 513-527.

Davis, G. (1982) Vegetation. In: Swindell, K. (ed.) *Sokoto State in Maps*. University Press Limited, Ibadan, p12-13.

El Bashir, H. (1997) Coping with famine and poverty: the dynamics of non-agricultural rural employment in Darfur, Sudan. In: Bryceson, D.F., Jamal, V. (eds.), *Farewell to Farms: De-Agrarianisation and Employment in Africa*. African Studies Centre Research Series, Leiden. Ashgate, Aldershot, pp. 23-40.

Herrmann, S. M., Anyamba, A. and Tucker, C. J. (2005) Recent Trends in Vegetation Dynamics in African Sahel and their Relationship to Climate, *Global Environmental Change*. 15: 394-404.

Iloeje, N. P. (1981) *A New Geography of Nigeria*. Fifth edition. Longman, Ikeja. pp65.

Lockwood, J. G. (1976) *The Physical Geography of the Tropics: An Introduction*. Kuala Lumpur, Oxford University Press, pp. 162.

Maconachie, R. (2004) Sustainability Under Threat?: Urban Pressure and Land Degradation in Kano Close-Settled Zone, Nigeria, Unpublished DPhil Thesis, Department of Geography, University of Sussex.

Maconachie, R., Tanko, A. I. and Zakariya, M. (2009) Decending the Energy Ladder? Oil price shocks and domestic fuel chaoices in Kano, Nigeria. *Land Use Policy*, 26: p1090-1099.

Meagher, K. and Mustapha, A.R. (1997) Not by farming alone: the role of non-farm incomes in rural Hausaland. In: Bryceson, D.F., Jamal, V. (eds.), *Farewell to Farms: De-Agrarianisation and Employment in Africa*. African Studies Centre Research Series, Leiden, Ashgate, Aldershot, pp. 63-84.

Maconachie, R. (2007) *Urban Growth and Land Degradation in Developing Cities: Change and Challenges in Kano, Nigeria*. Ashgate, Aldershot: 194p.

Chapter 5 | Murtala M. Badamasi, in
A.I. Tanko and S.B. Momale (Eds.)
*Kano: Environment, Society and Development*
London & Abuja, Adonis & Abbey Publishers

63

Mortimore, M. (1989) *Adapting to Drought: famines and Desertification in West Africa.* Cambridge University Press, Cambridge.

Mortimore, M. (2002) Development and Change in Sahelian Dryland Agriculture, in Belshaw, D. and Livingstone, I. (eds.) *Renewing Development in Sub-Saharan Africa: Policy, Performance and Prospects,* London and New York: Routledge, pp. 135-152.

Mortimore, M., Ariyo, J., Bouzou, I. M., Mohammed, S. and Yamba, B. (2008) A dryland case study of local natural resource management in the Maradi-Kano Region of Niger and Nigeria. In: Gill Shepherd (ed.) *The Ecosystem Approach: Learning from Experience.* Gland, Switzerland: IUCN, p 23-58.

Nichol, J. (1990) The ecology of wood fuel. In: Cline-Cole, R., Falola, J., Main, H., Mortimore, M., Nichol, J., and O'Reilly, F. (eds.), *Wood fuel in Kano.* United Nations Press, Tokyo.

Olofin, E. A. (1987) *Some Aspects of the Physical Geography of the Kano Region and Related Human Responses,* Departmental Lecture note series No. 1, Department of Geography, Bayero University, Kano. 50p.

Parry, D. E. and Trevett, J. W. (1979) Mapping Nigeria's Vegetation from Radar. *Geographical Journal,* 145: 265-281.

Pullan, R.A. (1974) Farmed parkland inWest Africa, *Savanna 3 (2),* 119-152

Riruwai, A. S. (2006) Socio-economic Variables Affecting Falgore Game Reserve in Doguwa Local Government Area, Unpublished Masters in Environmental Management Thesis, Department of Geography, Bayero University Kano.

Tanko, A. I. (2001) The Disadvantaged Community: Pastoralist in the Land Project Areas of Northern Nigeria. In: Shitu, M. B. and Adamu, Y. M. (eds.) *Studies on Inequality in Nigeria: A Multi-Disciplinary Perspective.* FSMS, p285-296.

Uchua, K. A. (1999) Application of Photographic Remote Sensing Techniques in Studying Land Use and Land Cover of Karaye Area of Kano State, Unpublished MSc Thesis, Department of Geography, Bayero University, Kano.

Yusuf, M. A. (2001) Soil assessment and indigenous soil management strategies in semi-arid North Eastern Nigeria. Unpublished PhD Thesis, Department of Geography, Bayero University, Kano.

Chapter 5    Murtala M. Badamasi, in
A.I. Tanko and S.B. Momale (Eds.)
*Kano: Environment, Society and Development*
London & Abuja, Adonis & Abbey Publishers

# Part II
# The Kano People

# Chapter Six

## ORIGIN AND GROWTH OF URBAN KANO

Bello Gambo

### Introduction

Studies in the origin and expansion of urban centres have attracted the attention of scholars in different disciplines, each category with particuliar emphasis - geographers, historians, sociologists, political scientists and economists, among others. Urban Kano is not left out in the studies by the different scholars. This multi-disciplinary contribution would yield a more comprehensive exposition of the evolution of an urban area.

In Nigeria, pattern of urban growth has occured in three stages: pre-colonial, colonial and post-indipendence. These stages provide a convinient framework for understanding the processes of urbanisation in the country (Ayeni,1998; Abumere, 2002).

Kano, cutting across these stages, has a long history of urbanisation, infrastructural development and articulated economy. Infact, it has been the largest city in the savannah belt of Africa south of the Sahara (Shea, 2003). The purpose of this chapter is to examine the evolution and expansion of urban Kano so as to see the development in urbanisation and infrastructure.

### Theoretical Basis

Three theoretical perspectives, among others, provide guidelines in urban studies (Ayeni, 1998). First, is the functional specialisation theory of urbanisation (Mabogunje, 1968). Specialisation of production among individuals has led to greater efficiency and increased productivity. The activities of specialist producers coupled with the administrative coordination, with changing sophistication, could provide explanatory framework for the emergence and expansion of urban areas.

Secondly, in the social sciences, there are three guiding concepts in the study of urban geography in Nigeria: behavioral, structural and

Chapter 6 | Bello Gambo, in
A.I. Tanko and S.B. Momale (Eds.)
*Kano: Environment, Society and Development*
London & Abuja, Adonis & Abbey Publishers

demographic. Behavioral process of urbanisation is concerned with the changes in experience which individuals pass through over time, and the associated patterns of behaviour. Structural process, which is related to the activities of the whole population and the changes in the economic structure, views increasing economic specialisation and advancing technology as the factors that induce movement of people out of agricultural communities into other larger non-agricultural communities. Demographic process of urbanisation suggests that the process of population concentration in a given environment is a way of ordering a population to attain a certain level of subsistence.

Thirdly, geographers in particular have emphasized the cencept of spatial analysis in the study of urbanisation, studies of the spatial patterns and consequencies of urban systems. Specifically it would involve aspects of location, distribution, differences and similarities, strucutre, and expansion.

## Origin Of Urban Kano

The evolution of urban Kano has attracted the attention of many scholars (for example, Barkindo,1983; Adamu, 1999; Falola, 2002; Olofin and Tanko, 2002). The first people to establish Kano community were iron-smelters from Gaya, now the headquarters of Gaya Local Government Area in the present Kano State, around 6th to 7th century. These people were in search of iron ore (tama) which they used to manufacture farm implementts, and they found it in large quantity at the laterite cap of Dala hill. The name of the leader of these people was Kano from whom the area got its name.

The availability of the needed resource coupled with the defensive advantage provided by the hill attracted the migrants to settle there permanently, producing hunting implements. Soon, this community of blacksmiths attracted people from other places. These migrants had different skills, and this led to the establishment of other industries, like weaving, dyeing and tanning.

The establishment of these occupational groups provided this early Kano settlement an urban setting. Scholars have confirmed that big settlements in Nigeria and Hausaland in particular were cities right from their early stage in pre-colonial time as they were central places (Ayeni, 1998; Liman and Adamu, 2003).

| Chapter 6 | Bello Gambo, in |
| | A.I. Tanko and S.B. Momale (Eds.) |
| | *Kano: Environment, Society and Development* |
| | London & Abuja, Adonis & Abbey Publishers |

## Expansion In Urbanisation And Infrastructure

Waugh (1995:384) defined urbanisation "as the process whereby an increasing proportion of the world's, a nation's or a regions's population lives in urban areas". Thus, it could be seen as the process by which people move to an urban area and settle in large numbers. With this conceptual foundation, one could trace the process and develoment of urbanisation to the early Kano settlement, together with the associated infrastructural development.

### *Pre-colonial Period*

In this period "urbanisation was traced to the empires and kingdoms that appeared in the West African Sudan. For Kano, the first was produced by the first wave of migrants probably of Eastern Sudanic Negroid stock. The influx of these migrants induced expansion of the settlement beyond Dala hill to other neighbouring hills - Gwauron Dutse, Fanisau, Tanagar, Santolo and Magwan (Adamu, 1999).

One of the prominent migrants was Dala from whom Dala hill derived its name. He suppressed the earlier worshipping of bakin ruwa (dark pool) of river Jakara and replaced it with a more organised and sophisticated form of worship, that of *Tsumburbura*. He introduced a buiding, a four-cornered room for his idol at the bottom of Dala hill. In this way, he established the Kano religious dynasty. His great grandson, Barbushe perfected it and became the leader of the *Tsumburbura* pagan priesthood. Thus, religion contributed to the expansion of urban Kano. Barbushe was also engaged in hunting at Kurmi hunting grove, where the present Kurmi market is situated (Olofin and Tanko, 2002).

A second set of migrants were hunters from Gaya who later turned to farming because they discovered that Kano had a fertile land, around 9th century. Thus, they introduced farming skills, leading to production of surplus food. That coincided with outbreak of famine elsewhere in West Africa. This situation attracted and induced migration of people from the famine striken areas of West African sub-region (Kebbi, Borno, Katsina, etc) to Kano. This led to the establishment of a new agricultural community, Madatai Community.

Chapter 6 | Bello Gambo, in
A.I. Tanko and S.B. Momale (Eds.)
*Kano: Environment, Society and Development*
London & Abuja, Adonis & Abbey Publishers

The Dala and Madatai communities existed side-by-side in the early Kano, consisting of amalgamation of hunters, blacksmiths and other artisans, traders, worshippers and farmers. The urbanisation experienced in this period led to the development of infrastructure (politically, economically and educationally).

Politically, the economic buoyancy of Kano coupled with lack of military formation and leadership, exposed it to attacks by envious communities. Thus, Kano solicited for help from Queen of Daura, who had a strong and organised Kingdom. She sent her son, Bagauda, to organise protection for Kano, who later became the king around 999AD. After Bagauda's death, his son Warisi (1063 - 1095) took over as the second king of Kano. When Warisi died, his son Giji-masu (1095-1134) became the third king and started the construction of the city wall in the 11th centuary, which was finished in the 12th century during Yusa, the fifth emir. The wall then housed Dala and Gwauron Dutse hills, the seat of power established by Gijimasu at Gazarzawa close to Dala hill, the settled area from the centre to the southeast and parts of Jakara River (Figure 6.1).

The building and subsequent extensions of the Kano city wall was an inducement of urbanisation (Liman and Adamu, 2003). The extension of the wall took place in three stages (Barkindo, 1983). The first extension was in the 15th century when *Sarki* Muhammadu Rumfa (1463-1499) found it necessary to extend the wall southeastward to house his newly built palace. The second stage of the extension was in the 16th centuary, done inorder to further strengthen the former fortification against constant attacks from Katsina and Kwararrafa. The last extension was in the 17th century by *Sarki* Muhammadu Nazaki (1618-1623), necessitated by the inadequacy of the latest extensions to withstand attacks. The extensions of the city wall attracted expansion of the built-up area, used for residential, commercial and industrial purposes. Table 6.1 shows these spatial expansions.

Chapter 6 | Bello Gambo, in
A.I. Tanko and S.B. Momale (Eds.)
*Kano: Environment, Society and Development*
London & Abuja, Adonis & Abbey Publishers

## Table 6.1: Spatial Expansion of Kano City

| PERIOD | BUILT-UP AREA | WALLED AREA |
|---|---|---|
| 12th Century Extent | 4.5 squire km | 9.4 squire km |
| 15th Century Extent | 7.0 squire km | 14.5 squire km |
| 16th Century Extent | 7.5 squire km | 15.5 squire km |
| 17th Century Extent | 8.5 squire km | 17.5 squire km |

*Source: Liman and Adamu (2003:147)*

Gates were constructed at different periods for the following reasons (Barkindo, 1983:12-13; Olofin and Tanko, 2002):

I.   to allow the movement of people in and out of the city.
II.  to check unwanted elements, like known thieves or robbers and spies; and
III. the gates (including the city wall) were the most important criteria for differentiating the city from the villages.

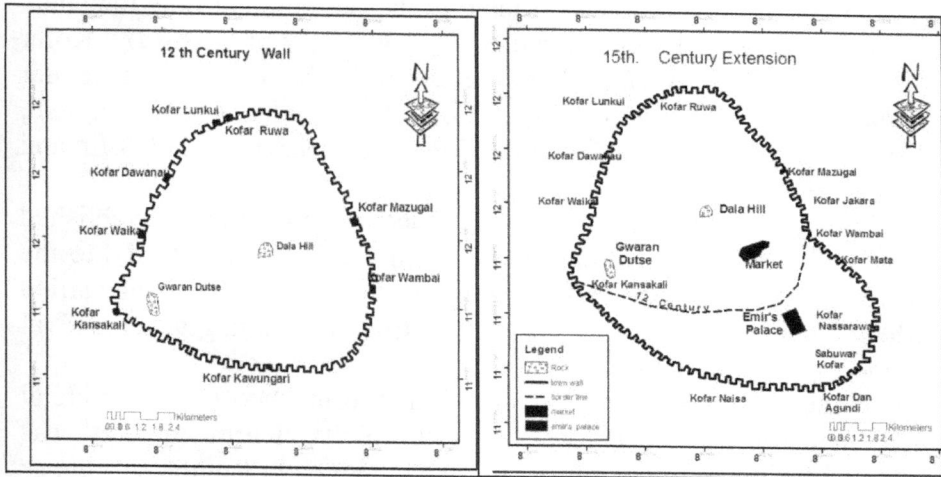

| Chapter 6 | Bello Gambo, in<br>A.I. Tanko and S.B. Momale (Eds.)<br>*Kano: Environment, Society and Development*<br>London & Abuja, Adonis & Abbey Publishers |
|---|---|

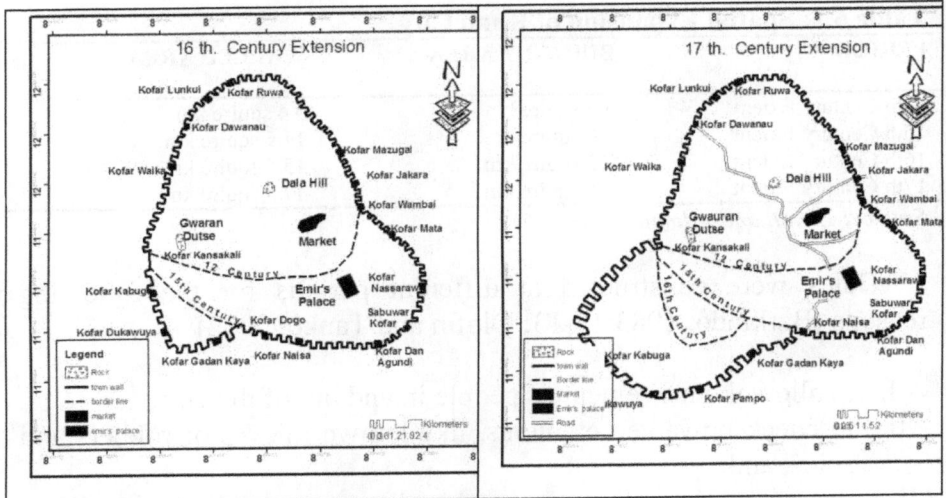

**Figure 6.1 the Development of Walls around Kano City**

The Gates that were constructed in the pre-colonial time included: Kofar Wambai, Kofar Mazugal, Kofar Lunkui (Ruwa), Kofar Dawanau, Kofar Waika, Kofar Kansakali, Kofar Kabuga, Kofar Dukawuya, Kofar Gadon Kaya, Kofar Na'isa, Kofar Dan Agundi, Kofar Nassarawa and Kofar Mata (Barkindo, 1983:12 - 13; Olofin and Tanko, 2002).

For administration of justice, Muhammadu Rumfa established courts. The Jihad of Uthman bn Fodio in the 19th centuary led to the reorganisation of the administrative machinery and intensified educational, economic and social infrastructure, leading to the arrival of more people into Kano city.

In the economic arena, urbanisation in Kano boosted commercial and industrial infrastructure (Adamu, 1999). Kurmi market was established in the 15th century during Muhammadu Rumfa, serving as a terminus and distribution centre for the foreign and internal commodities. The most notable industries were the dyeing and leather ones, all producing goods for the Arabs. Other industries were blacksmithery, calabash decoration and carpentry. In fact, "from the 15th Century onwards, Kano city developed into one of the major commercial and manufacturing centres in the West African Sudan" (Hambolu, 2002).

Chapter 6 | Bello Gambo, in
A.I. Tanko and S.B. Momale (Eds.)
*Kano: Environment, Society and Development*
London & Abuja, Adonis & Abbey Publishers

Educational infrastructure started to be established during the reign of *Sarki* Ali Yaji Dan Tsamiya (1349 - 1358), when the first and famous school of Jurispuridence (Figh) was established at Madabo, which could get the definition of a University (Adamu, 1999), divided into faculties (Tsangayu). Then, Quranic schools were established in different wards. This consequently led to the development of advanced scholarship and high influx of lecturers and students from different places.

The factors that contributed to urbanisation and consequent infrastructural expansion in pre-colonial urban Kano were the folllowing (Hambolu, 2003: 2; Shea, 2003: 105; Mabogunje, 1968: 47):

i) *Geographical Location*: Kano city is situated at the apex of long distance trade routes running along north-south and east-west axes.

ii) *Fertile soil, sudan grassland and favourable rainfall*: These encouraged complex agricultural system which produced foodstuff, raw materials for home industries and surplus for international trade.

iii) *Relative peace and stability:* Peaceful and stable condition encouraged industrial and commercial activities in the region.

iv) *Ahigh groundwater table*. This supported such a cosmopolitan city, and the economic and political structures.

## Colonial Period

British colonial rule started in Kano on 3rd February 1903, when Abbas bn Abdullah (1903 to 1919) was appointed as the eight emir, after the Jihad (Saeed, 2003). Urbanisation was facilitated and infrastructure expanded by the activities of colonial masters, so that by the end of the colonial rule, Kano had developed into a dual city, the walled (old) city and the new city (outside) (see Figure 6.2).

Chapter 6    Bello Gambo, in
A.I. Tanko and S.B. Momale (Eds.)
*Kano: Environment, Society and Development*
London & Abuja, Adonis & Abbey Publishers

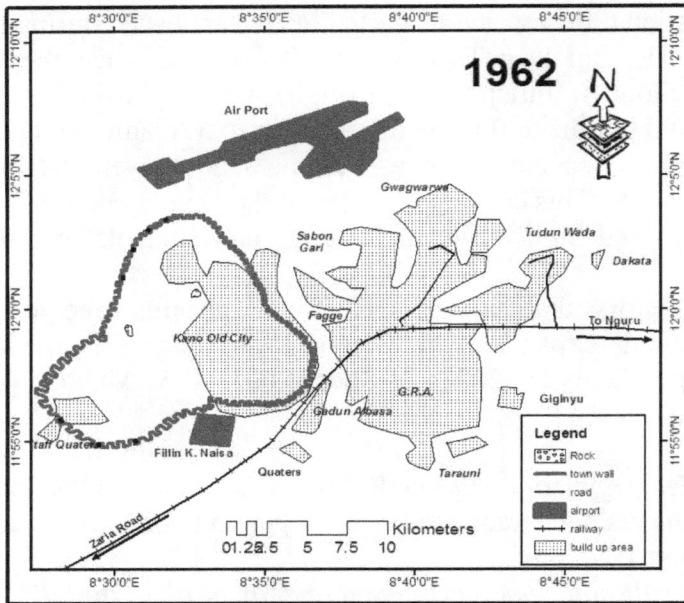

**Figure 6.2: Kano Metropolitan Growth (1962)**

In 1903, residential area of Nassarawa was established for the colonial administrators. In 1904, residential area for colonial army and police officers at Bompai was created (formerly called Geiza). Sabon Gari was created in 1912 for migrants from southern Nigeria. Tudun Wada was created in 1914 for migrants from elsewhere in Northern Nigeria. Lebanese Quarters for Lebanese and Syrians was created in 1915 at Fagge-ta-Kudu. Gwagwarwa (Brigate) was created in 1945 (in Gabari Village) for the natives in the colonial force. Relocation areas were established after the establishment of Bompai industrial estate: Ja'oji, Tarauni, Giginyu and Dakata.

The urbanization during this period was also associated with the development of economic infrastructure. The London and Kano company was opened in 1907. By 1915, Kano Metropolis had fifteen European trading companies, and four Syrian, three African non-indigenous and thirty-five Arab firms, all engaged in import and export of goods. Sabon Gari market was established in 1914 at the outskirts of the Sabon Gari Township and moved to its present area in 1918. The Central Business District (CBD) was created in 1918. The Nigeria's first ever textile mill was established in Kano in 1950. Between 1954-1961, many private Lebanese companies were formed. Bompai Industrial estate was established towards the end of the colonial administration (1955 - 1958).

| Chapter 6 | Bello Gambo, in |
| | A.I. Tanko and S.B. Momale (Eds.) |
| | *Kano: Environment, Society and Development* |
| | London & Abuja, Adonis & Abbey Publishers |

74

In the educational context, many infrastructure were developed. For example, in 1909, Hans Vischer (popularly called Dan-Hausa) established an experimental government school at Nassarawa which was of different categories, which attracted students and teachers, not only from within but from outside. These were the school for the sons of chiefs and other influential people, an Elementary vernacular School and the Teacher Training School.

Kano Middle School was established in 1927 during the reign of Emir Abdullahi Bayero (1926 - 1953). Kano Judicial School was created in 1929, which gave birth to Kano Law School in 1934 and later transformed to the School for Arabic Studies. In 1940, a school for the blind was established by Sudan Interior Mission (SIM) for teaching reading and writing, and crafts and other trades. Also, SIM created a Junior Secondary School in 1944 for training Juvenile boys of different tribal parentage. The first Secondary School was opened by the Catholic Mission in 1949. Also, Catholic Mission established St. Louis Girls Primary School and Boys Primary School in 1958.

Politically, as part of indirect rule, the colonial government established Native Authority (N.A.), which was a system that incorporated the local people in the administration of the area.

Many infrastructure were established in the colonial era. Railway began operation in Kano in January 1912. Motorable roads started in 1925. Provision of electricity and water supply started in 1925. Hospitals and Clinics were built. For example, Kano General Hospital (now Murtala Muhammad Hospital) and Nassarawa European Hospital were built in 1927. Kano International Airport was established in 1935. Recreational places for the British colonialists were made such as the European catering rest house (now Central Hotel) and the European club (now Kano Club).

## Post-Independence Period

Two important developments greatly contributed to urbanization and infrastructural development in Kano at the begining of this period: creation of Kano State (1967) and local governments (1975). These attracted more migrants. Consequently, by 1980, Kano had spatially expanded beyond the colonial extent (Figure 6.3).

Chapter 6 | Bello Gambo, in
A.I. Tanko and S.B. Momale (Eds.)
*Kano: Environment, Society and Development*
London & Abuja, Adonis & Abbey Publishers

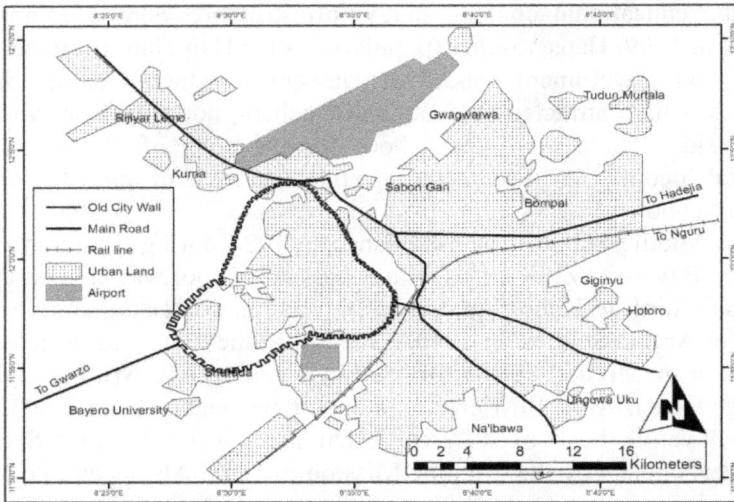

**Figure 6.3: Kano Metropolitan Growth (1981)**

Residential infrastructure were expanded. For example, housing estates were created - Kundila, Ja'oji, Zoo Road, Gwammaja and Sabo Garba (popularly called Jan Bulo) housing estates. The surrounding villages became fully incorprated into the Kano urban setting by the end of the 1980s. These include Gandun Albasa, Gyadi-Gyadi, Yan Kaba, Rijiyar Lemo, Unguwa Uku, Na'ibawa and Dorayi, among others.

In commerce, Kurmi and other pre-existing markets were expanded and modernized. Also, "additional markets were built at Sharada, Kofar Wambai, Tudun Wada and Kofar Ruwa among others" (Mustapha and Yakudima, 2008: 47). The specialized markets for agricultural food products came into being. Before they were part of all-purpose markets (Falola, 2002; Liman and Adamu, 2003). Three additional industrial estates were established at Sharada, Chalawa and Gunduwawa/Hadejia Road, in addition to the small scale industries that dot the city centre. By around early 2000, large scale departmental stores have come up outside the Central Business District, which include Country Mall, Jifatu, Jujin Labu, Sahad and many others. There are numerous shopping complexes and consultancy services providing wide range of services in the fields of education, law, health, estate management and property development.

Chapter 6 | Bello Gambo, in
A.I. Tanko and S.B. Momale (Eds.)
*Kano: Environment, Society and Development*
London & Abuja, Adonis & Abbey Publishers

76

The colonial educational infrastructure were expanded and new ones established. Primary and post primary schools increased in number. Tertiary institutions and educational boards were established. Table 6.2 provides the higher institutions established in Kano State, and majority of them are in urban Kano. The boards and agencies established are provided in Table 6.3.

There are institutions for trainning health personnel run by State Governments (Dakata, 2008), but majority are outside urban Kano. These are the Schools of Health Technology at Kano and Jahun, the Schools of Nursing at Kano and Birnin Kudu, the Schools of Clinical Assistants at Danbatta and Hadejia, the School of Hygiene in Kano and the School of Midwifery at Danbatta.

In addition, there are military and paramilitary training institutions such as the Flying Training School (Nigeria Air Force), the Nigeria Police Academy, the Custom Training School, the Immigration Training School and the Fire Service Training School.

**Table 6.2: Higher Institutions of Learning in Kano State**

| Institutions | Year of Establishment |
|---|---|
| Bayero University, Kano (initially Abdullahi Bayero College) | 1973 |
| Federal College of Education, Kano | 1961 |
| Kano State College of Arts, Science and Remedial Studies | 1972 |
| Aminu Kano College of Islamic Legal Studies | 1976 |
| Audu Bako College of Agriculture | 1977 |
| Sa'adatu Rimi College of Education (formally Kano State College of Education) | 1981 |
| Kano State Polytechnic | 1987 |
| Federal College of Education (Technical), Bichi | 1987 |
| Kano University of Technology, Wudil | 2001 |

*Source: Danyaro (2006)*

Chapter 6 | Bello Gambo, in
A.I. Tanko and S.B. Momale (Eds.)
*Kano: Environment, Society and Development*
London & Abuja, Adonis & Abbey Publishers

77

**Table 6.3: Educational Boards and Agencies in Kano State**

| Boards and Agencies | Year of Establishment |
|---|---|
| Kano State Educational Resource Department | 1967 |
| Kano State Scholarships Board | 1968 |
| Kano State Library Board | 1968 |
| Kano State Universal Basic (formally Primary) Education Board | 1976 |
| Kano State Agency for Mass Education | 1980 |
| Science and Technical Schools Board | 1982 |
| Kano State Teachers' Service Board | 2003 |

*Source: Danyaro (2006)*

In the post-Independence, social infrastructures included those of information, youths, trasport, housing, water supply, sports and culture (Danyaro, 2006). The Kano Printing Press and the Triumph Publishing Company were established in 1980, the Kano Television Corporation in 1982, History and Culture Bureau in 1987, the Kano State Censorship Board in 2001, the Kano State Transport Authority (Kano Line) in 1988, the Kano State Zoological and Wildlife Management Agency in 1999, the Kano State Housing Corporation in 1980, the Dala Building Society in 2000 and the Water Resources and Engineering Construction Agency (WRECA) in 1973 among others.

Politically, infrastructure were set to strenthen government activities (Danyaro, 2006). Ministries, Departments and Agencies (MDAs) were created for this purpose. Examples are the Ministry of Local Government (1967), Ministry of Justice (1967), Ministry of Planning and Budget (1967), Ministry of Agriculture and Natural Resources (1967), Ministry of Environment (1999), Ministry of Land and Physical Planning (1999), Kano State Urban Planning and Development Authority (1962), Kano State Pension Board (1967), Kano State Pilgrims Welfare Board (1968), among others. By the end of the 20th century, Urban Kano had expanded to about 60 km$^2$ out of which 48 km$^2$ was built-up (Falola, 2002) (Figure 6.4).

Chapter 6 | Bello Gambo, in
A.I. Tanko and S.B. Momale (Eds.)
*Kano: Environment, Society and Development*
London & Abuja, Adonis & Abbey Publishers

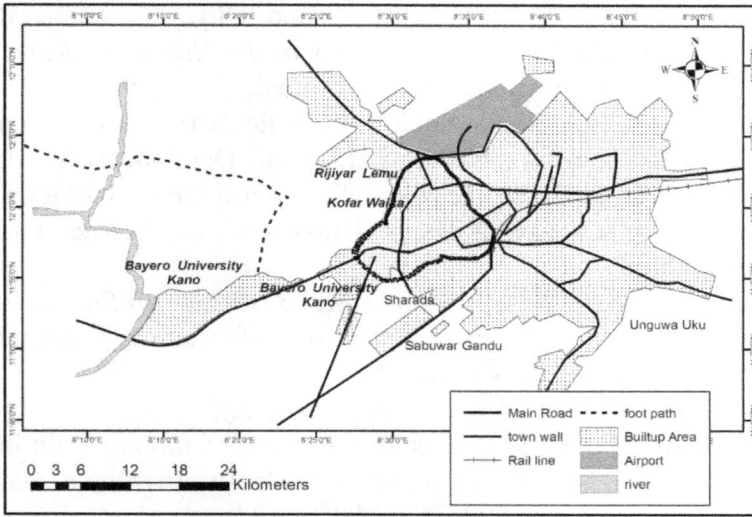

**Figure 6.4: Kano Metropolitan Growth (1991)**

## Conclusion

In the growth of urban Kano, expansion in urbanization contributed to development in infrastructure and vice-versa. Urbanization in Kano was a process that occurred throughout its three phases of historical development. Indeed, Kano today is still among the largest urban centres in Sub-Saharan Africa, second to only Lagos in terms of population and spatial extent.

## References

Abumere, S. L. (2002) *Urbanization*. In Africa Atlases (Nigeria)

Adamu, M. U. (1999) *Confluences and Influences: The Emergence of Kano as a City-State*. Kano: Munawwar Books Foundations.

Ado-Kurawa, I. (2003) "The Reign of Sarkin Kano Abdullahi Bayero 1926-1953". In Hambolu, M. O. (ed.) *Perspectives on Kano-British Relations*. Kano State: Gidan Makama Muzeum.

Ayeni, B. (1998) "Urban Geography". In In Areola, O. and Okafor, S. I. (eds.): *50 years of_Geography in Nigeria: The Ibadan Story*. Ibadan: University Press.

Chapter 6 | Bello Gambo, in
A.I. Tanko and S.B. Momale (Eds.)
*Kano: Environment, Society and Development*
London & Abuja, Adonis & Abbey Publishers

Barkindo, B. M. (1983) "The Gates of Kano City: A Historical Susvey". In Barkindo, B. M. (ed.) *Studies in the History of Kano*. Nigeria: Heiemann Educational Books Limited.

Dakata, F. A. G. (2008) "Some Socio-Economic Services in Kano Region". In Olofin, E. A., Nabegu, A.B. and Dambazau, A. M. (eds.) *Wudil Within Kano Region: A Geographical Synthesis*. Department of Geography, Kano University of Sciene and Technology Wudil.

Danyaro, M. M. (Ed.) (2006) *Kano State 3 Years of Shekarau Administration*. Kano State: Ministry of Information, Internal Affairs, Youths, Sports and Culture.

Falola, J. A. (2002) *Kano*. In Africa Atlases (Nigeria).

Hambolu, M. O. (2003) "Perspectives on the British Colonial Rule in Kano 1903-1960". In Hambolu, M. O. (ed.) *Perspectives on Kano-British Relations*. Kano State: Gidan Makama Muzeum.

Liman, M. A. and Adamu, Y. M. (2003) "Kano in Time and Space: from a City to a Metropolis". In Hambolu, M. O. (ed.) *Perspectives on Kano-British Relations*. Kano State: Gidan Makama Muzeum.

Mabogunje, A. L. (1968) *Urbanization in Nigeria*. London: University of London Ltd.

Mustapha, A. and Yakudima, I. (2008) "Population and Settlement". In Olofin, E. A., Nabegu, A. B. and Dambazau, A. M. (eds.) *Wudil Within Kano Region: A Geographical Synthesis*. Department of Geography, Kano University of Sciene and Technology Wudil.

Olofin, E. A. and Tanko, A. I. (2002) *Laboratory of Areal Differentiation: Metropolitan Kano in Geographical Perspectives*. Department of Geography, Bayero University, Kano.

Saeed, A. G. (2003) "The Establishment of British Colonial Rule in Kano During the Reign of Emir Abbas bn Abdullah 1903-1919". In Hambolu, M. O. (ed.) *Perspectives on Kano-British Relations*. Kano State: Gidan Makama Muzeum.

Shea, P. J. (2003) "The establishment of the Colonial Economy in Kano". In Hambolu, M. O. (ed.) *Perspectives on Kano-British Relations*. Kano State: Gidan Makama Muzeum.

Waugh, D. (1995) *Geography: An Integrated Approach*. United Kingdom: Thomas Nelson and sons Ltd.

Chapter 6 | Bello Gambo, in
A.I. Tanko and S.B. Momale (Eds.)
*Kano: Environment, Society and Development*
London & Abuja, Adonis & Abbey Publishers

# Chapter Seven

## POPULATION GROWTH IN THE KANO REGION

Ahmed Maigari Ibrahim

### Introduction

Population does not only represent the total number of human inhabitant in a particular area, but also its means of livelihoods, prospect, prosperity, and posterity. The phenomenal increase in human numbers in relation to the finite supply of basic life supporting resources, economic development and environmental quality makes the scenario a growing born of contention among both scholars and policy makers. This is because the population saga is bedeviled with both issues and challenges. The focus of this work, therefore is to evaluate these issues and challenges in the Kano region; being among the most populous region in Nigeria and also in Africa South of the Sahara.

### The Population Growth Rate

The Kano Region as a geographical entity can stand as one of the epicenters of rapid population growth with a dynamic population size, composition and distribution that evolved along the history and culture of the Region. Although the demographic profile of the Region dating back to the pre-colonial times was not adequately documented, the population history of that period is quite relevant in terms of comparative analysis. Population growth then was relatively low with less than one percent annual growth rate and a density of about 1 to 4 persons per $Km^2$. From the 1930s to date however, population grew exponential with little variation around the 'Kano Closed-settled Zone', moderate in the southwards and wide variation in northwards, especially in the Northeastern parts of the Region such as Gumel and Hadejia Emirates. From 1931 to 1952, for example, the annual growth rate was 1.5 to 2%, and increased to 2.0 to 2.5% from 1952 to 1991

Chapter 7 | Ahmed M. Ibrahim, in
A.I. Tanko and S.B. Momale (Eds.)
*Kano: Environment, Society and Development*
London & Abuja, Adonis & Abbey Publishers

and 15 years later (from 1991 to 2006) it increased by over 5% (Table 7.1).

**Table 7.1: Population Growth in Kano Region, 1931 - 2006**

| Census Year | Total Pop. | Growth Rate | Density/Km$^2$ |
|---|---|---|---|
| 1931 | 2,438,844 | 1.5 | 53.3 |
| 1952 | 3,396,350 | 2.0 | 74.2 |
| 1962 | 4,832,609 | 2.4 | 105.5 |
| 1991 | 8,685,995 | 2.5 | 189.7 |
| 2006 | 13,732,331 | 3.6 | 299.9 |

*Source: Census Data*

From Table 7.1, the population of the Kano Region has grown far above what Thomas Malthus (1766 - 1834) predicted that '... population would double itself after every 25 years...'. Over a period of 75 years the population of the Kano Region increased from 2.4 million in 1931 to about 13.7 million in 2006. This has not only confirmed Malthus (1798) prediction, but also lowers the extent of re-multiplication to about 13 years and further magnifies the power of population in terms of growth rate.

Another amazing issue is the population - land ratio which has been the focus of many scholars such as David Ricardo, Karl-Marx, Neo-Malthusian scholars, and Boserup (1965) and environmentalist. With a total land area of 45,792.5Km$^2$, the Kano Region had an average density of 53.3 persons per square kilometer in 1931 but by 2006, the density had increased by about 5.6 times (over 500%) with a density of about 300 persons/km$^2$.

## The Prospect

The age and sex structure of population in the Kano Region portrays the unique outlook of the region. About 47% of the population are aged 0 - 14years, 48% are aged 15 to 59years, while the remaining 5% are aged 60years and above. This shows not only the youthful nature of the population but also its vulnerability to rapid growth. Moreover, the sex ratio is moving concurrently between male and female with a slight difference of 1.6% in 1991 and about 2.5% in 2006 (Table 7.2). Thus the sex distribution index (number of males per 100 females), depicts an inconsiderable excess of males in the Region.

Chapter 7 | Ahmed M. Ibrahim, in
A.I. Tanko and S.B. Momale (Eds.)
*Kano: Environment, Society and Development*
London & Abuja, Adonis & Abbey Publishers

Another important characteristic of the population in the Kano Region is the spatial distribution of people. The population is unevenly distributed with great variation between urban and rural areas and also between the northern and southern parts of the Region. The highest number of the people are concentrated within Kano Metropolis which comprises Municipal, Dala, Gwale, Nasarawa and Tarauni LGAs, followed by what Tiffen (2001) described as the inner areas (immediately adjacent to the city; Kumbotso and Ungoggo). The density, as well thins out from the Central parts of the Region (such as Dawakin Kudu, Gezawa and Gaya) to the Outer areas such as Dutse, Karaye, Kiyawa, Rano and Bichi. The northern part which includes Hadejia, Kazaure, Gumel, Danbatta, and Jahun are areas with relatively lower population density.

**Table 7.2: Population Structure in Kano Region by Sex and Age: 1991 and 2006**

| State | 1991 Census | | | | | 2006 Census | | | | |
|---|---|---|---|---|---|---|---|---|---|---|
| | T. Pop. | Male | % | Female | % | T. Pop. | Male | % | Female | % |
| Jigawa | 2,875,525 | 1,455,780 | 50.6 | 1,419,745 | 49.4 | 4,348,649 | 2,215,907 | 51.0 | 2,132,742 | 49.0 |
| Kano | 5,810,470 | 2,958,736 | 50.9 | 2,851,734 | 49.1 | 9,383,682 | 4,844,128 | 51.6 | 4,539,554 | 48.4 |
| Region | 8,685,995 | 4,414,516 | 50.8 | 4,271,479 | 49.2 | 13,732,331 | 7,060,035 | 51.2 | 6,672,296 | 48.8 |

| Age | 1991 Census | | | 2006 Census | | |
|---|---|---|---|---|---|---|
| | T. % | Male % | Female % | T. % | Male % | Female % |
| 0 – 14 | 42.8 | 22.1 | 20.7 | 47 | 25.1 | 21.9 |
| 15- 59 | 50.8 | 26.5 | 24.3 | 48 | 24.8 | 23.2 |
| 60+ | 6.4 | 3.9 | 2.5 | 5 | 2.7 | 2.3 |
| Total | 100 | 52.5 | 47.5 | 100 | 52.6 | 47.4 |

*Source: 1991 & 2006 Census Data*

This observed pattern of distribution showcase three main issues. First is level at which rural urban migration is going on in the Region. Kano being the centre of commerce, acts as a 'central place' which according to Von-Thunen's Theory of Central Place, growth, density and development starts from the central places and diminishes towards the hinterland. Table 7.3 highlights some of these observations. Secondly, the distribution pattern further portrays the index of carrying capacity in the Kano Region. Thirdly it seemingly suggests the magnitude of the challenges facing the entire region.

Chapter 7    Ahmed M. Ibrahim, in
A.I. Tanko and S.B. Momale (Eds.)
*Kano: Environment, Society and Development*
London & Abuja, Adonis & Abbey Publishers

**Table 7.3: Spatial and Temporal Distribution of Population Density in Kano Region**

| Sectors | 1931 | 1952 | 1962 | 1991 | 2006 |
|---|---|---|---|---|---|
| Kano Metro | 2459 | - | - | 2481 | 19,200 |
| Inner District | 146 | 230 | 275 | 972 | 1,763 |
| Central District | 123 | 205 | 245 | 313 | 551 |
| Outer District | 47 | 72 | 84 | 156 | 204 |
| Northern District | 51 | 83 | 107 | 148 | 168 |

*Source: Census Data*

## The Prosperity

Educational attainment and productive labour force are the basic indices that highlight the affluence level of people or community as they stimulate innovation and economic growth and development. The level of educational attainment in the Kano Region is the reincarnation of that of Northern Nigeria. Formal Western education is generally low in contrast to Islamic education which is generally high in most Muslims dominant communities. The 1952 Census indicated that less than one percent (0.8%) of the population aged seven years and above was literate in Roman Scripts. In 1991 the situation greatly improved with about 43% of males and 38% of females aged 12 - 14 years attaining primary level of education. The gross primary schools enrolment was 67.4% and 16.7% for secondary schools. The 2006 Census shows school enrolment in the region has further improved; about 51.4% of the population aged 6 years and above attained school from nursery to higher levels with a significant difference between Males (29.3%) and Females (22.1%). The detail is presented in Tables 7.4a&b.

## Table 7.4a: Distribution of Educational Attainment: 6 Years and Above (2006)

| State | None | | | Nursery and Above | | |
|---|---|---|---|---|---|---|
| | Male % | Female % | Total % | Male % | Female % | Total % |
| **Kano** | 21.4 | 24.6 | 46 | 31.5 | 22.5 | 54 |
| **Jigawa** | 23.8 | 30.5 | 54.3 | 26 | 19.7 | 45.7 |
| **Regional** | 22.1 | 26.5 | 48.6 | 29.3 | 22.1 | 51.4 |

*Source: Census, 2006*

Chapter 7 | Ahmed M. Ibrahim, in
A.I. Tanko and S.B. Momale (Eds.)
*Kano: Environment, Society and Development*
London & Abuja, Adonis & Abbey Publishers

**Table 7.4b: Enrolment in Schools: Nursery to Postgraduate Levels**

| ex | Total | None | Nur-sery | Pri-mary | JSS /Mo-dern School | SSS/ SEC /TTC | OND /NCE | Uni-versity Gra-duate/ HND | Post Gra-duate | Other |
|---|---|---|---|---|---|---|---|---|---|---|
| | | | | | **Kano** | | | | | |
| Male | 3,815,650 | 1,543,189 | 540,642 | 433,963 | 312,085 | 636,338 | 155,635 | 89,424 | 28,363 | 76,011 |
| emale | 3,398,298 | 1,778,064 | 444,000 | 377,417 | 208,016 | 447,414 | 54,525 | 24,803 | 7,230 | 56,829 |
| otal | 7,213,948 | 3,321,253 | 984,642 | 811,380 | 520,101 | 1,083,752 | 210,160 | 114,227 | 35,593 | 132,840 |
| | | | | | **Jigawa** | | | | | |
| Male | 1,647,742 | 786,861 | 209,882 | 170,201 | 104,607 | 228,617 | 58,342 | 28,631 | 7,565 | 53,036 |
| emale | 1,658,573 | 1,008,850 | 179,231 | 151,275 | 73,495 | 178,467 | 17,609 | 6,429 | 1,866 | 41,351 |
| otal | 3,306,315 | 1,795,711 | 389,113 | 321,476 | 178,102 | 407,084 | 75,951 | 35,060 | 9,431 | 94,387 |
| | | | | | **Regional** | | | | | |
| otal | 10,520,263 | 5,116,964 | 1,373,755 | 1,132,856 | 698,203 | 1,490,836 | 286,111 | 149,287 | 45,024 | 227,227 |

*Source:* Census, 2006

Though there is still high level of illiteracy in western education, it is evident that the trend of educational development in the region is increasing and this will surely deliver a sound labour force in the near future. Currently there is adequate supply of skilled and non-skill labour in the labour market of the Region, with the exception of medical professionals, which the region depends on other parts of the country. In Kano metropolis, for example, there is excess supply of non-skill labour which invariably affects its wages. The cost of a day man-work (8 hours; 8.00am to 4.00pm) is generally cheap ranging from N500.00 to N2,000.00, while wages and salaries of casual workers range from N6,000.00 to N20,000.00 per month.

## The Posterity

The posterity of population in Kano Region cannot be separated from the issues and challenges discussed above. Going by the conventional Malthusian and Boserupian literatures, the Kano Region by now would have been cut in the vicious circle of ecological degradation. However, with proper and adequate management of these issues and challenges, it has now been established that smooth transition to posterity in the region and around Kano Close-Settled Zone in particular is ensured. In response to rapid population growth that characterized the Region, people and communities pursue two main adjustment mechanism; agricultural intensification and economic diversification. These to say the least raised land productivity, sustain

Chapter 7    Ahmed M. Ibrahim, in
A.I. Tanko and S.B. Momale (Eds.)
*Kano: Environment, Society and Development*
London & Abuja, Adonis & Abbey Publishers

and boost small holder agriculture, sustain large families and avoided degradation scenario.

Agricultural intensification simply refers to the intensive use of land in Agro-pastoral production for maximum output to meet the demand of teaming population under careful management, which is both economically and ecologically sustainable (Robert et. al., 1993). A study by Mortimore (1993) in the Kano Close-settled Zone from 1964 to 1984 revealed that 'the Kano triple system of crop, livestock and tree husbandry has survived intact the pressure of urbanization... that the functional relationships between these three elements are stable ecologically and economically, and that rather than damage the sustainability of the system, the increasing dense population has chosen to diversify out of primary production'. Similarly tree density has been stable over a decade at about 15/ha as against what was obtained in the 1960s; about 0.8/ha (Cline-Cole et al., 1990). Integration of trees into the farming system in form of farm forestry has been the main reason. Farmers in the Kano Closed-settled Zone, in particular, owned and invest in trees, thus every tree on farmland has its owner; who either plants it, nurses it, inherits or purchased it. Thus tempering with farmland trees is considered as an act of trespass and punishable in the court of law.

Moreover, it has been demonstrated that increasing population density in the Region has affected land positively as increasing scarcity of land in the Region promotes investment both in conservation and yield-enhancing improvements (Mortimore and Tiffen, 1995). Maigari (1998) observed that farmers in the Kano Region and indeed Northern Nigeria perceived land as a precious resource which provides the source of family livelihoods, a prestigious commodity and an asset material that form linkage from one generation to another. As such they invest on their landholding to transmit it in good condition to their future generation.

To reduce pressure off agricultural land the able work force in the Region had diversified income sources through pursuing numerous livelihood options at household level. A study by Maigari (1998) revealed that by combining crop production, livestock rearing and numerous off-farm activities (an average of 6 options per household unit), households in rural areas of Gezawa and Birniwa achieved a sustainable livelihood. Usually the income generated from off-farm

Chapter 7    Ahmed M. Ibrahim, in
A.I. Tanko and S.B. Momale (Eds.)
*Kano: Environment, Society and Development*
London & Abuja, Adonis & Abbey Publishers

activities are either spent on food or re-invested in farming input or livestock, so also the income from livestock is reinvested on the other economic activities if food security is guaranteed.

## Conclusion

Analysis of the population dynamics in the Kano Region has shown that its growth and distribution pattern have demonstrated that the relationship between land and human resources could be sustained under careful management. As postulated by Adam Smith (1723-1790), the size and structure of population are indicators of prosperity of a country, thus the population growth in the Kano Region stands as a path way to the healthy economy of the region. Thus, the assertion of Adam Smith (1776) that 'if people are prosperous they will have more children and real wages would increase as the demand for labour increases' could be valid in the Kano Region for two main reasons. First the teeming population in the Region provides adequate market for goods and services produced in the Region and beyond. It has facilitates numerous opportunities for trade and specialisation, and stimulates surplus production and economies of scale in infrastructural development.

Secondly, it has yielded enough labour force for the take off of all developmental activities in the Region and the nation at large. Currently, over 70% of the people within Kano metropolis draw their livelihoods off agricultural production. The high population has stimulated investments in health, housing, transport, and education. The growing proliferation of private hospitals and clinics, rental houses and private schools in Kano metropolis alone is a testimony to the multiplier effect of population growth in the Region.

Therefore it is worth noting that high population growth with a corresponding change in technology and means of production and sound population and environmental policies could lead to sustainable development. Thus, to fully realise the good benefits accompanying high population growth in the Region and beyond, it is important to improve adaptation mechanisms through appropriate policies and programmes and effectively implement them. Failure to address issues and challenges associated with population pressure or growth would lead to a precarious situation. As it has been established in some

Chapter 7 | Ahmed M. Ibrahim, in
A.I. Tanko and S.B. Momale (Eds.)
*Kano: Environment, Society and Development*
London & Abuja, Adonis & Abbey Publishers

communities in Africa and Asia where population growth failed to keep pace with fundamental changes in economic organisation such as technology, investment and markets, leading to backwardness and under development. One-third of the countries in Sub-Saharan Africa are heading towards such gloomier future (Barnes, 1990; Hansen, 1990; Montgomery and Brown, 1990).

## References

Adam, Smith (1776), *The Wealth of Nations*. Microsoft ® Encarta ® 2009. © 1993-2008 Microsoft Corporation. All rights reserved.

Barnes, F. Douglas (1990),"Population Growth, Wood Fuel, and Resources Problems" Acsadi, T. F. George, Johnson-Acsadi, G. and Bulatao, A. Rodolfo (Eds): *Population Growth and Reproduction in Sub-Saharan Africa, Technical Analysis of Fertility and its Consequences*, World Bank Symposium.

Boserup, E. (1965) *The Condition of Agricultural Growth*. Allen and Unwin, London. (Reprinted in 1993 by Earthscan, London)

Cline-Cole, R. A., Falola J. A. Main R. C., Mortimore M. J. Nicchol J. E. and O'Reilly F. D. (1990) *Woodfuel in Kano*. Tokyo United Nation Press.

Hansen, Stein (1990) "Absorbing a Rapid Growing Labour Force" in Acsadi T. F. George, Johnson-Acsadi, G. and Bulatao, A. Rodolfo (Eds): *Population Growth and Reproduction in Sub-Saharan Africa, Technical Analysis of Fertility and its Consequences*, World Bank Symposium.

Maigari, Ahmed Ibrahim (1998) Livelihood Options Under Intensifying Aridity in Northeastern Nigeria. Unpublished PhD. Thesis, Department of Geography, Bayero University, Kano, Nigeria.

Malthus, Thomas R., (1798) *Essay on the Principle of Population*. Microsoft ® Encarta ® 2009. © 1993-2008 Microsoft Corporation. All rights reserved.

Mortimore, M. (1993) The Intensification of Pre-Urban Agriculture: The Kano Close-Settled Zone, 1964 - 1986. In B. L. Turner II, Goran Hyden, and Robert Kates Eds. *Population Growth and Agricultural Change in Africa*, University Press Florida.

Chapter 7 | Ahmed M. Ibrahim, in
A.I. Tanko and S.B. Momale (Eds.)
*Kano: Environment, Society and Development*
London & Abuja, Adonis & Abbey Publishers

Mortimore, M. and Tiffen, Mary (1995) Population and Environment in Time Perspective: The Machakos Story, in Tony Binns Ed. *People and Environment in Africa*. John Wiley and Sons

Montgomery, R. Mark and Brown, K. Edward (1990) Accommodating Urban Growth in Sub-Sahara Africa; in Acsadi T. F. George, Johnson-Acsadi, G. and Bulatao, A. Rodolfo (Eds): *Population Growth and Reproduction in Sub-Saharan Africa, Technical Analysis of Fertility and its Consequences*, World Bank Symposium.

National Population Commission (2010) Federal Republic of Nigeria 2006 Population and Housing Census, Priority Tables Vol. VII Population Distribution by Age, Sex, and Educational Attainment, State and Local Government Area, NPC, Abuja Nigeria

Nigeria, (1955) *Population Census of the Northern Region of Nigeria*, 1952 -1953 Census Superintendent Lagos.

Nigeria, NPC (1992) *Census News, 3/1*. National Population Commission Lagos.

Nigeria, NPC (1998) *1991 Population Census of the Federal Republic of Nigeria*. Analytical Report at the National Level. National Population Commission Lagos.

Robert, W. Kates, Goran Hyden, and B. L. Turner II (1993) Theory, Evidence, Study Design, in. B. L. Turner II, Goran Hyden, and Robert Kates Eds. *Population Growth and Agricultural Change in Africa*, University Press Florida.

Tiffen, Mary (2001) Profile of Demographic Change in the Kano-Maradi Region, 1960-2000. *Drylands Research Working Paper 24*

Chapter 7  Ahmed M. Ibrahim, in
A.I. Tanko and S.B. Momale (Eds.)
*Kano: Environment, Society and Development*
London & Abuja, Adonis & Abbey Publishers

# Chapter Eight

## THE KANO EMIR'S PALACE

Aliyu Salisu Barau

### Introduction

A universally acceptable definition of sustainability is elusive. According to Kluvankova-Oravaska and Chobotova (2007) sustainability is *maintaining* the capacity of ecological systems to support social and economic systems. In another view, it refers to *transforming* ways of living to maximize the chances that environmental and social conditions indefinitely support human security and wellbeing (McMichael, *et al* 2003). In African context, Mabogunje (2004) suggests that sustainability represents a modern version of a traditional concept of "usufruct" whereby every generation is seen as trustee with rights of beneficial use (or usufruct) of resources it inherited from its ancestors and has duty to pass it to posterity as much as possible unimpaired by mismanagement. It is axiomatic that the planet Earth is literally filled with ecological challenges driven by development activities. Nigeria belongs to class of low sustainability countries. It ranks No.153 in the Global Environmental Performance Index with a score of 40.2 points towards the bottom of the list (Emerson et al 2010). It is important to explore the state of environmental sustainability at smaller spatial and administrative regions in Nigeria. In this situation, landscapes are important environmental systems that can provide diverse insights and perspectives.

Landscape sustainability studies on the Kano region particularly in the past have illustrated a tradition of sustainable resource use despite increasing aridity and population intensity. Soils, trees, cultivars, moisture, domestic animals and human livelihoods are managed jointly and sustainably. Most of such studies focussed on rural and peri-urban agro-ecological landscapes. This can be seen in Mortimore (1989; 1993); Mortimore *et al.* (2005); Mortimore and Adams (1999); Harris (undated, 1998); Ahmed (1998, 2000); Tanko (2001); and Marshal *et al* (2009) to mention a few. Above works focus on

Chapter 8 | Aliyu S. Barau, in
A.I. Tanko and S.B. Momale (Eds.)
*Kano: Environment, Society and Development*
London & Abuja, Adonis & Abbey Publishers

91

agricultural landscapes of the Kano Close-Settled Zone (KCSZ), an area that is largely rural and partly peri-urban. It is possible that the entrenched heritage of sustainability in the Kano region may extend beyond rural and peri-urban areas to the core urban spaces. As such, this Chapter focuses on Gidan Rumfa (The Kano Emir's Palace) which is an ancient landscape of continuous traditional authority in sub-Saharan Africa. This chapter is interested in exploring the landscapes of the Kano Palace with a view to understanding the location of the landscapes and their functions, the strategies that govern the palace population and its ecosystem and how does Gidan Rumfa pair with sustainability index and demands of the paradigm of new urbanism.

**Gidan Rumfa, Kano City and Sustainability**

Gidan Rumfa (the House of Rumfa) was constructed by the innovative Sarki Muhammadu Rumfa (ruled 1463-1499). Rumfa is noted as one of the 50 greatest Africans in history (Walker 2006). According to Barau (2007a) the Kano palace was constructed in the years 1479 to 1482 and ranks as the largest traditional palace in sub-Saharan Africa (Nast 1996), as well as the oldest continuous sit of traditional authority in Nigeria (Ado-Kurawa 2008). Ibrahim (2001) points out that the palace was retained by the Fulani jihadist who took over Kano in the 19th century. The British colonialists as well assented for it to continue with its historically established functions. Like the Kano Close-Settled Zone (KCSZ), Gidan Rumfa attracts attention of researchers from different research backgrounds. Some of such studies focus on its architecture (Sa'ad, 1981; 1989; Dmochowski, 1990; Carroll, 1992). For its historical values, there are works like those of Rufa'i (1995), Smith (1997), and Khalil (2007). While Nast (1992) is interested on gender and space in the Kano Palace; Barau (2010a) investigated the palace biodiversity and Khalil and Bayero (forthcoming) are interested on the palace linguistics and etiquettes. With such a diverse and interesting research attractions, Gidan Rumfa is also considered as a diplomatic landscape that hosts global political, religious and business leaders from around the world (see Barau 2007a). Most of the studies noted above portray myriad of interesting aspects of Gidan Rumfa as a unique landscape in the Kano Region.

Chapter 8 | Aliyu S. Barau, in
A.I. Tanko and S.B. Momale (Eds.)
*Kano: Environment, Society and Development*
London & Abuja, Adonis & Abbey Publishers

Gidan Rumfa popularly called *Gidan Sarki* (literally Emir's House) is clichéd: *Gidan Sarki Gari Guda Ne* (meaning: The Emir's Palace is a town). This cliché may arise from the size and awesome grandeur of the ancient palace. According to Khalil and Bayero (2004) the Kano Palace is a *ward* because of its numerous houses, a *town* due to its collection of wards, infrastructure, hierarchy of authority and dialect. Gidan Rumfa is strategically located in the ancient walled city of Kano. The ancient city of Kano developed its form and spatial organisation through the influences of the principles of Sharia which are embedded with elements of sustainability (Barau 2010b). The influence of Islam on spatial form of Kano city and Gidan Rumfa is through its location, functions and structural orientation (Nast 1996, Naniya 2007). It is assumed that development of city walls made Kano a full city around 11th century (Liman and Adamu 2003). The said development radiates from its gated walls covering 18 miles radius which made Kano a compact city (Olofin and Tanko 2002). During the 16th Century, Kano ranks as the third largest city in Africa after the North African cities of Cairo and Fez (Dan Asabe 1996). Kano then might look as a truly sustainable city, as only about 1,800 acres out of its total landmass of 5,400 acres were built up (Frishman 1977). This spatial form looks every inch eco-friendly because of the numerous ponds, open spaces and scrublands found within and around the city. Institutionalisation of sustainability is further consolidated in Kano and other towns through the 19th century land use policies for range lands and built up areas in the Sokoto caliphate (Zahradeen 1990, Hakim and Zubair 2006).

Generally speaking, one cannot disconnect the landscape of the Kano Palace from the city, hence the need to understand the current sustainability status of the Kano city. The city is now a strained landscape inundated by massive development challenges. Population explosion and mass urbanisation degrade the quality of Kano urban landscapes. Virtually all the major open spaces, ponds and scrublands known three decades ago have disappeared (Maiwada 2000; Barau 2007b; Barau 2010b). In the past, influence of Sharia and traditions induce the city's landscape quality. However, since the colonial and post colonial eras, urban land management in Kano is governed by provisions of the *Town and Country Planning Laws of 1946, Land Use Act of 1978* and the *Nigerian Urban and Regional Planning Law,*

Chapter 8 | Aliyu S. Barau, in
A.I. Tanko and S.B. Momale (Eds.)
*Kano: Environment, Society and Development*
London & Abuja, Adonis & Abbey Publishers

*Decree No 88 of 1992* which underpin the policies and institutions of urban planning and land management. Corruption, lack of defined policy and framework for urban land, institutional conflicts, high level of subsidy in land allocation, and inadequate manpower constitute the cog wheel to sustainable land management in Kano (Garba 1993). The need to appreciate sustainability situation of Kano may stem from the fact that Kano sustains a lead as the top city of northern Nigeria, a region known with a fewer urban centres as compared with more urbanised southern Nigeria (Polese and Denis-Jacob 2009). So far, the major effort to put the city on the track of sustainability is through the Sustainable Kano Project (SKP) initiated in 1996 in collaboration with the UN Habitat. The project aimed at building the necessary institutional and human resource capacity for engendering urban sustainability (Alkali 2005, UN Habitat/UNEP 2008). Unfortunately, in the opinion of Olujimi (2009), the SKP fails to achieve its objectives in Kano because its foundation was laid on a skeletal ground. Therefore, sustainability in contemporary urban development in Kano is elusive. The problem may arise from the apparent apathy towards implementation of the development plans as well as legal and other institutional weaknesses that characterise the wider national development planning in Nigeria (Dung-Gwom 2010; Kaltho 2010; Owei 2010).

Concluding on the palace and city perspectives, it is clear that palaces affect and are in turn affected by problems of environmental changes. For instance, in Saudi Arabia, urbanisation, modernisation and land use change pose serious threats to ancient palaces, citadels and castles which cause displacements and overcrowding around them (Al-Sheikh 2010). Elsewhere, palaces themselves respond to the challenges. In the United Kingdom new initiatives to uphold sustainability are introduced at the Buckingham, Balmoral, Sandringham, Kensington, Marlboro House and other palaces through energy saving, biodiversity protection and promotion, recycling and noise reduction mechanisms (*The Royal Household* 2008/2009).

Chapter 8 | Aliyu S. Barau, in
A.I. Tanko and S.B. Momale (Eds.)
*Kano: Environment, Society and Development*
London & Abuja, Adonis & Abbey Publishers

94

## The Geography of Gidan Rumfa

Built within the 15th century, Gidan Rumfa is located between latitude 11°59'32.67N and Longitude 8°31'06.02E. It approximately covers 33 acres surrounded by walls of 20-30 feet high from outside and average of 15 feet from within the palace complex (Archnet 2010). From its north and south Gidan Rumfa is flanked by fields that almost equal the size of its walled area. The palace southern outer walls are oriented towards *al-qibla* (the direction of Ka'aba in Mecca). Nast (1996) reveals that, the United States' National Aeronautics and Space Agency (NASA) confirms this assertion not only as correct but precise. Gidan Rumfa was constructed on open plains with no vicissitudes or any form of rock outcrops. Geologically it lies on basement complex of the older granite just as some other parts of Kano city (Olofin and Tanko 2002). The soils of uncovered surface especially the *Sheka* (gardens/parks) areas are organic due to high content of leaf fall which in some measurements averaged depth of 6cm that form a sticky peat (measured by author). The vegetation of the palace is a derived Sudan savanna which is now upgraded into the like of gallery forest with a well-defined canopy, under growth, and epiphytes. Its floral species composition is diverse and comprises indigenous and exotic species (Table 8.1). It also has a bulk population of various faunal species. The gardens of the palace cover about two third of the palace land mass (Barau 2010a). The spatial organisation and high tree density of Gidan Rumfa develops a diurnal range of microclimate which always falls averagely by 2°C below the diurnal temperature readings of urban spaces few metres away from the palace.

The population of *Cikin Gida* (Emir's private quarters) is estimated to be around 200 persons (including the Emir, his wives, concubines, children and domestic servants). This is revealed in personal communications with Mallam Ibrahim Muhammad (Emir's Palace ward head) held at Kofar Kwaru (August 22, 2010). In the same pers comm., it was established that there are 579 households in the Palace (excluding the Emir's and deceased family heads whose houses are still occupied by their families). With an average of 8 persons per house, the population of Emir's Palace is around 4,000 persons. The Kano Emir's Palace is a centripetal point and it has the

| Chapter 8 | Aliyu S. Barau, in |
| | A.I. Tanko and S.B. Momale (Eds.) |
| | *Kano: Environment, Society and Development* |
| | London & Abuja, Adonis & Abbey Publishers |

spatial capacity of holding close to a tens of thousands people within and around its sides. The palace receives visitors on daily basis and occasionally during ceremonies and the number of such visitors may also run to tens of thousands per year.

**Table 8.1: Flora and Fauna composition in Gidan Rumfa**

| Floral Composition | | Faunal Composition | | |
|---|---|---|---|---|
| Local Species | Exotic Species | Birds | Animals | Insects |
| *Balanites aegyptiaca (desert date)* | *Azadirachta indica (*neem) | Cattle egret | | Beetle |
| *Ficus thonningii* | *Mangifera indica (*mango) | | Vesper Bat | Ants |
| *Adansonia digitata (baobab)* | *Psidium guajava* (guava) | Ostrich | Tortoise | Earthworm |
| *Tamarindus indica (tamarind)* | *Carica papaya (*pawpaw) | Crow | Rats | Grasshopper |
| *Khaya senegalensis (*mahogany) | *Vitis xx (*grape) | Peacock | Snails | Bee |
| *Luffa aegyptiaca* (loofah gourd) | Flamboyant | | | Scorpion |
| mushroom spp. | *Citrus sinensis* (orange) | | | Firefly |
| *Borassus aethiopum* (deleb palm) | | | | |
| *Lawsonia inermis* (henna) | | | | |
| *Acacia nilotica* (Egyptian Mimosa) | | | | |

*Source: Fieldwork, 2010*

Chapter 8 | Aliyu S. Barau, in
A.I. Tanko and S.B. Momale (Eds.)
*Kano: Environment, Society and Development*
London & Abuja, Adonis & Abbey Publishers

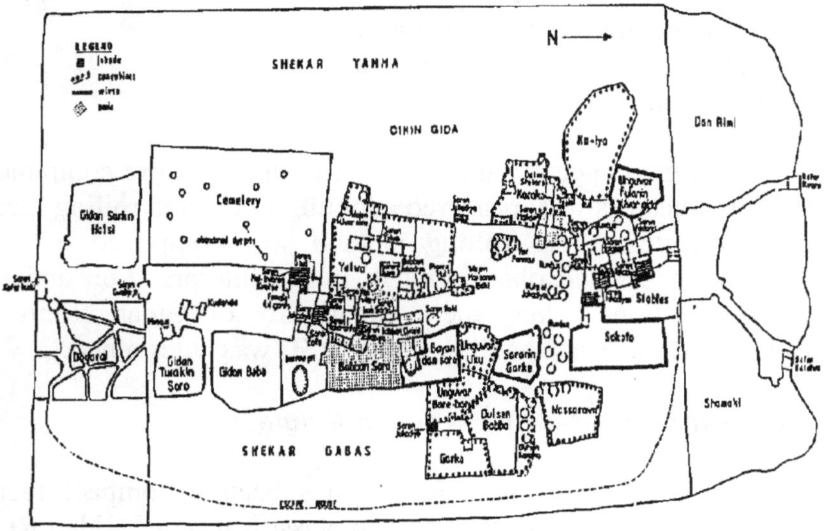

**Figure 8.1: Map of Gidan Rumfa adapted from Nast 1992**

Tourism and heritage are but one of the leading values of Gidan Rumfa. Its architecture, the events it hosts as well as its tangible and intangible heritage are important tourism assets. Based on its outstanding cultural value, Gidan Rumfa along with other monuments within Kano city were accepted on the UNESCO Tentative List of World Heritage Sites since 2007 (UNESCO 2010).

*Sustainability Performance*

In order to ascertain sustainability performance of Gidan Rumfa the Environmental Sustainability Index (ESI) model was adopted. This model was developed by the World Economic Forum's Environment Task Force, the Yale University Center for Environmental Law and Policy, and the Centre for International Earth Science Information Network of Columbia University (de Sherbinin 2003; Kates, Parris, and Leiserowitz 2005). The building blocks of ESI are five core components subdivided into 20 indicators and 68 variables. The five core components are:

Chapter 8 | Aliyu S. Barau, in
A.I. Tanko and S.B. Momale (Eds.)
*Kano: Environment, Society and Development*
London & Abuja, Adonis & Abbey Publishers

a. Environmental Systems,
b. Reducing Stresses,
c. Reducing Human Vulnerability,
d. Social and Institutional Capacity, and
e. Global Stewardship.

The compliance of Gidan Rumfa to the five core components and the 20 indicators was measured adopting integrated rolling method for data collection. This rolling method was comprised of fieldwork (measurements and observations), image interpretation and personal communications. Thus, the compatibility of Gidan Rumfa to the Environmental Sustainability Index (ESI) was determined.

## Landscape Classification in Gidan Rumfa

Since 15th century Gidan Rumfa has been a compact rectangular building. The three main landscape classification of Gidan Rumfa are namely; built-up areas, open spaces and green areas (Table 8.2). This classification is visualised in figures 8.2 and 8.3 which show the landscape divisions. The green landscapes (*Sheka*) located in the east and west respectively constitute about 40% of the total palace area, the built up landscapes cover roughly 35% of the palace while the open spaces represent about 25% of the total palace landscape. This could be interpreted as an ecologically sound balance in the palace land use system. As noted by Nast (1992) the palace landscape morphology undergoes transformations as reigns and dynasties evolve. Open spaces are still fairly distributed even within the built up areas and the palace is a whole. The palace seems to be the largest biodiversity sink within urban and peri-urban Kano as image of wider city areas show (Figure 8.1). The species compositions of palace green areas are listed in Table 8.1. The Palace green sites serve as niche and colonies particularly for two species of fauna namely *cattle, egret* and *bats*. There are numerous other species of birds observed and believed to have made the palace their safe havens.

| Chapter 8 | Aliyu S. Barau, in |
|---|---|
| | A.I. Tanko and S.B. Momale (Eds.) |
| | *Kano: Environment, Society and Development* |
| | London & Abuja, Adonis & Abbey Publishers |

## Table 8.2: Landscapes of Gidan Rumfa

| Landscape Classification | Approximate % of palace area | Location Identifiers |
|---|---|---|
| Built-up Areas | 40% | Kofar Kudu (Sothern gate) Administrative offices, school, parking lots, mosque, boys quarters, residences, Private Secretary's office, 8 royal courtrooms, garages, Soron Ingila, Soron Chafe. Cikin Gida (Emir's Private Quarters) Rumfar Kasa, Babban soro, Soron baki, wives and concubines areas, clinic, Shamaki (royal horses' park). Cikin Gida wards: Ka-iya, Nassarawa, Sokoto, Yelwa, Garko, Unguwar Fulanin Uwar-gida, Unguwa Uku, Unguwar Bare-bari, Kofar Arewa (Fatalwa/Kwaru) Unguwar Shamaki, Unguwar Dan Rimi, Lokon Kwaru |
| Green Areas | 35% | Shekar Yamma (western garden); Shekar Gabas (eastern garden); Filin Tambari green round |
| Open Spaces | 25% | Filin Kofar Kudu (southern gate), Filin Tambari (Kofar Arewa), Sararin Garke (cikin gida) Filin fadancin dare |

*Source: Fieldwork 2010*

**Figure 8.2: Google Earth image of Gidan Rumfa**

Chapter 8 | Aliyu S. Barau, in
A.I. Tanko and S.B. Momale (Eds.)
*Kano: Environment, Society and Development*
London & Abuja, Adonis & Abbey Publishers

**Figure 8.3: A closer view of Gidan Rumfa land cover and land use**

*Contemporary Spatial Functions and Services of Gidan Rumfa*

The activities identified above are what the Millennium Ecosystem Assessment (2003) referred to as *provisioning*, *regulating* and *supporting* ecosystem services. Gidan Rumfa sustains its position as a landscape of traditional authority in Kano Region for over 500 years. Then it is possible to see that the palace landscapes offer the fourth ecosystem services namely *cultural*. Over time, changes have been witnessed in the palace spaces due to reconstructions or expansions and addition of structures. In general, the core traditional functions of major palace landscapes like *Cikin Gida* and *Kofar Arewa* (Northern gate) remain as from the inception of the palace. In addition to the traditional space uses, the palace landscapes have acquired new functions which can be attributed to the emergence of republic governance in Nigeria as well as new patterns that emerged with creation of Kano Province/State during colonial and post colonial periods. Such developments create new uses for the palace landscapes (Table 8.3).

Chapter 8 | Aliyu S. Barau, in
A.I. Tanko and S.B. Momale (Eds.)
*Kano: Environment, Society and Development*
London & Abuja, Adonis & Abbey Publishers

**Table 8.3: Landscapes and Services at Gidan Rumfa**

| Functions | Highlights | Locations |
|---|---|---|
| Residential | For Emir's first family and slave officials | *Cikin Gida, Kwaru, Fatalwa and Kofar Kudu* |
| Leadership | Emir is No.1 traditional ruler in Kano State | *10 different Royal Courtrooms* located in the palace |
| International Diplomacy | Gidan Rumfa hosts over 30 world political leaders from colonial to postcolonial Nigeria. It also hosts many business and opinion leaders. | *Soron Ingila* (English hall) hosted Queen Elizabeth II, President Carter, Ghaddafi, Bill Gates among many others. Durbar is organised for heads of State/Government at *Filin Kofar Kudu* |
| Peacekeeping | From political, sectional or religious crises the Emir holds reconciliation talks between communities, government, labour etc | Emir preaches peace from the *10 royal courtrooms* or at *Kwaru* during Sallah speeches |
| Heritage & Tourism | Gidan Rumfa is potential World Heritage Site. Kano Durbar is first and best of its kind | *Gidan Rumfa (as a whole)* |
| Research | Resourceful for academic and all forms of research from different fields of interest | *Gidan Rumfa (as a whole)* |
| Education | There is 1 primary school, 1 junior secondary school, 1 Islamiyya school, 1 Quranic school | *Kofar Kudu, Kwaru* |
| Spiritual Development | Annual Ramadan Tafsir, Ashafa recitation, Maulud and Annual Tijjaniyya Zikr, | *Kofar Kudu* |
| Funerary Services | Cemetery; Funeral prayers for Kano important personalities | *Kofar Kudu royal cemetery, Filin Kofar Kudu* |
| Public gathering | Launching of government programmes, appeal funds, book launch, and other ceremonies | *Filin Kofar Kudu & Kofar Kwaru* |
| Entertainment/Recreation | Praise singers, the royal musical band ('Yan Bindiga) and royal drummers ('Yan Tambari) entertain the royalty. Inside women play *Wasan Tashe*, and *Wasan Gauta* to entertain themselves and the Emir. In the past concubines relax at sheka; now the eastern sheka is relaxation ground for the Emir. | *Sararin Kofar Kudu, Filin Tamabari, Sararin Garke, Sheka* |

*Source: Fieldwork 2010*

## *Population Dynamics and Adaptive Strategies in Gidan Rumfa*

With an estimated population of about 4,000 inhabitants and a compact area of approximately 50 acres (palace central gate open space included) Gidan Rumfa has a high population density. This could be one of the overwhelming population densities in Africa. This contrasts rather sharply the population density of Kano Close Settled Zone which is put at around 500 people/km$^2$ (Mortimore (1993) or that of 441 persons per square kilometre outlined by National Population Commission for Kano State in the 2006 census. This steep density is tremendously tasking for this relatively small space. Thus some adaptation strategies for curtailing population pressure on

| Chapter 8 | Aliyu S. Barau, in<br>A.I. Tanko and S.B. Momale (Eds.)<br>*Kano: Environment, Society and Development*<br>London & Abuja, Adonis & Abbey Publishers |

environmental systems of the palace are being adopted. The strategies vary from *Cikin Gida* to *Kofar Arewa* or slave residential section of the palace. Though expectedly the Emir has a very large family, however most of the princes and princesses are raised outside Gidan Rumfa (at home of other royalties). The palace uses non-resident labourers for some services. Prisoners are the main outsourced labourers.

Both within *Cikin Gida* and *Kofar Arewa* there is phenomenon of densification (building intensification vertically and horizontally) through construction of more houses for the family members of the Emir and slave title holders. Generally there is restricted access to some spaces. *Cikin Gida* is mainly women's domain, male domestic servants and Emir's close relations. The royal gardens (*sheka*) are inaccessible even to palace residents. For occasions such as funerals, royal title installations, or wedding ceremonies that attract hundreds of thousands of people there are defined places for such gatherings and people disperse immediately after such occasions. Crowd is controlled through creation of batches or appointments for homage making visits to the Emir.

Several other mini Palaces like Gidan Nassarawa, Babban Daki (royal residence of the Emir's mother located few metres away from Gidan Rumfa), as well as royal farm houses at Fanisau, Dorayi, Wudil, Takai and others help in reducing pressure on Gidan Rumfa.

### Gidan Rumfa and Compliance to Environmental Sustainability

Gidan Rumfa has appropriately demonstrated positive compliance to the ESI criteria (Table 8.4). The Palace as an institution and as a landscape is maintained on the principles of sustainability. The dozens of Emirs that ruled Kano from the stable of Gidan Rumfa across varying ages and dynasties sustained the heritage of the palace landscapes and pass it to the future generation in spite of changing physical, social and political circumstances.

| Chapter 8 | Aliyu S. Barau, in |
|---|---|
| | A.I. Tanko and S.B. Momale (Eds.) |
| | *Kano: Environment, Society and Development* |
| | London & Abuja, Adonis & Abbey Publishers |

## Table 8.4 ESI Performance by Gidan Rumfa

| Components | Indicators | Compliance by Gidan Rumfa |
|---|---|---|
| Environmental Systems | Air Quality | Vehicle access to Cikin Gida is restricted. Parking close to Soron Giwa is only for Emir's limousines. |
| | Water Quality | Pipe borne water/boreholes |
| | Biodiversity | Largest biodiversity sink in urban and per-urban Kano |
| | Land | Compact land with fair distribution of green built and open spaces. |
| Reducing Stress | Reducing Air Pollution | Use of horses, restricted access to motorised vehicles. |
| | Reducing Water Stress | Not all houses are connected to mains |
| | Reducing Ecosystem Stress | No poaching or tree felling allowed |
| | Reducing waste and consumption pressure | Most of the waste tonnage generated in the palace is organic and biodegradable. |
| | Reducing population growth | Densification, depopulation of palace children and outsourcing of hard labour |
| Reducing Human Vulnerability | Basic human sustenance | Basic infrastructure available |
| | Environmental health | Palace clinic, immunisation programmes observed routinely |
| Social and Institutional capacity | Science and Technology | There are schools in the palace |
| | Environmental governance | Cleanliness of the palace is through hierarchies - cleaners, inspectors and Sarkin Tsafta (King of Hygiene) |
| | Eco efficiency | Solar energy cell panels observed at eastern Sheka, predominance of mud structures, low noise |
| | Private sector | Business community and many professionals are fairly represented in the Emir's Council. |
| Global Stewardship | Participation in international collaborative efforts | Participating in tree planting campaigns, hosting of global environmental NGOs. Emir is patron of FADE a leading global NGO fighting desertification. |
| | Green house emissions | No industry sited at palace, use of horses and manual instruments as well as use of solar panels at eastern Sheka |
| | Reducing transboundary environmental pressures | Information sharing from ward, village and district head levels to the Emir, Government and public |

*Source: Fieldwork, 2010*

## Conclusion

Gidan Rumfa is an exclusive urban landscape in the Kano Region. It is a city within a city. Though, it constitutes a tiny percentage of total size of the ancient walled city of Kano, the palace proves to be a sustainability hub because its landscapes reflect the earliest sustainability heritage of the Kano city during the pre-colonial era when it was replete with open spaces, scrublands and ponds. This means the journey towards achieving sustainability could and should start from smaller landscapes. The paradigm of sustainable urbanism calls for compact city as against sprawl. The concept calls for cities

Chapter 8 | Aliyu S. Barau, in
A.I. Tanko and S.B. Momale (Eds.)
*Kano: Environment, Society and Development*
London & Abuja, Adonis & Abbey Publishers

with green architecture, low carbon emission, and low resource consumption. In Gidan Rumfa these features are clearly discernible through its mud dominated architecture, green and open spaces, densification and compactness, commitment to the traditional values, sacredness and aesthetics of the palace landscapes. Compared to the Kano city, Gidan Rumfa demonstrates the practicability and possibility of harmonious coexistence between human population, land use and ecosystem security.

The overall conclusion drawn by this Chapter is that sustainability thrusts on the traditions and value systems of the people of Kano region. Sustainable agricultural practices in the KCSZ and Gidan Rumfa are satisfactory *mainly* because of synthesis of the human-land heritage systems that are passed from generation to generation. In the Kano Region, the traditional sustainable practices in either rural or urban landscapes are administered through local skills, experiences and informal knowledge systems. It is apparent that concepts and practices of sustainable development introduced through modern scientific and technological channels and institutions have rarely advanced the course of sustainability in critical sectors like urban development, agriculture, water resources development, infrastructure, and environmental management despite the huge funds expended, time spent and efforts made. It is suggested that all professionals and policymakers working on the theme of sustainable development in the Kano region should explore and integrate local practices and practitioners to build framework of sustainability for their projects and programmes.

**Acknowledgements**

I wish to thank Nasiru Wada Khalil for crucial role he played throughout the conduct of the research that contributed data for this Chapter.

Chapter 8 — Aliyu S. Barau, in
A.I. Tanko and S.B. Momale (Eds.)
*Kano: Environment, Society and Development*
London & Abuja, Adonis & Abbey Publishers

# References

Ahmed, K. (1998) "Soil Moisture Relationships in Dagaceri" in: *Soils, Cultivars, Livelihood and Nutrient Dynamics in Semi Arid Northern Nigeria*. Department of International Development (DFID), London

Ahmed, K. (2000) "Management of Agricultural Landscapes in the Kano Region" in Falola, J.A; Ahmed, K; Liman, M.A; Maiwada, A. (eds.) *Issues in Land Administration and Development in Northern Nigeria*, Department of Geography, Bayero University, Kano.

Ado-Kurawa, I. (2008) *About Kano*. Research and Documentation Directorate, Government House, Kano. p. 24.

Alkali, J.L.S. (2005) Planning Sustainable Urban Growth in Nigeria: Challenges and Strategies. Paper presented at the Conference on Planning Sustainable Urban Growth and Sustainable Architecture, held at the ECOSOC Chambers, United Nations Headquarters, New York, on 6th June 2005

Al-Sheikh, A.H. (2010) *Architectural Heritage of the Kingdom of Saudi Arabia*. Second Edition. Ministry of Municipal and Rural Affairs,Riyadh Archnet(2010)Emir's Palace at Kano.<http://archn et.org/library/sites/one-site.jsp?site_id=7730> accessed on 16th August 2010.

Barau, A.S. (2007a) *The Great Attractions of Kano*. Research and Documentation Directorate, Government House, Kano.

Barau, A.S. (2007b) Ecological Cost of City Growth- The Experience of Kano in Nigeria. Paper presented at the 5th African Population Conference, organized by the Union for African Population Studies, Arusha Tanzania

Barau, A.S. (2010a) Biodiversity Security in the Kano Emir's Palace: Explanations on Variety, Mystery and Reality. Paper Summary prepared for *Colloque International BiodiverCities: Enjeux et stratégies de gestion durable des aires protégées urbaines et périurbaines au Nord et au Sud. International Conference* organised by Urban Protected Areas Network/Institut Libertas/Uni versite de Paris Ouest Nanterre September 2010.

Barau, A. S. (2010b) "Islamic Instruments for Sustainable Urban Spatial Planning and Management" in: Lehmann, S.; Al Waer, H.;

Chapter 8 | Aliyu S. Barau, in
A.I. Tanko and S.B. Momale (Eds.)
*Kano: Environment, Society and Development*
London & Abuja, Adonis & Abbey Publishers

105

Al-Qawasmi, J. (eds) *Sustainable Architecture and Urban Development.* Centre for the Study of Architecture in the Arab Region, Amman p.355

Carroll, K. (1992) *Architectures of Nigeria: Architectures of the Hausa and Yoruba peoples and of the Many people's between Tradition and Modernisation.*Society of African Missions/Ethnogr aphica/Lester Crook Academic Publishing, London

Dan Asabe, A. (1996). Kano Labour and the Kano Poor 1930-1990. Unpublished Ph.D thesis submitted to History Department, Bayero University, Kano.

De Sherbinin, A. (2003) The Role of Sustainability Indicators as a Tool      for Assessing Territorial Environmental Competitiveness. Presented at the International Forum for Rural  Development  4-6 November 2003 at Hotel Grand Bittar, Brasilia, Brazil

Dmochowski, Z. R. (1990) *An Introduction to Nigerian Traditional Architecture, Volume1.* London: Ethnographica Ltd. 4.5, 5.20-5.25.

Dung-Gwom, J.Y. (2010) Concept Notes on the Nigerian National Physical Development   Plan. Being a Paper Presented at the Sensitization Meeting on the Preparation of      the NPDP organized by the Federal Ministry of Lands, Housing and Urban Development held at Royal Tropicana Hotel, Kano August 19th 2010.

Emerson, J., D. C. Esty, M.A. Levy, C.H. Kim, V. Mara, A. de Sherbinin, T. Srebotnjak.
(2010). *2010 Environmental Performance Index.* New Haven: Yale Center for   Environmental Law and Policy

Frishman, A. (1977). The Spatial Growth and Residential Location of Kano. A PhD Dissertation submitted to Northwestern University.

Garba, S.B. (1993) Urban Land Management Problems and Low Income Housing: Case    Study of the Kano Metropolitan Area. Paper presented at DEMO 93, The Canadian      International Agency   Sponsored   International   Conference   on   Nigerian Indigenous Building Materials, Kongo Conference Hotel, Zaria

Harris, F. (1998) *Indigenous Intensification of Agriculture: The Kano Close-settled Zone.*      Seminar   on   Local   Knowledge   in Tropical Agricultural Research and Development.      Organised by   Tropical   Agricultural   Association.   September,   26,   1998.

| Chapter 8 | Aliyu S. Barau, in |
|---|---|
| | A.I. Tanko and S.B. Momale (Eds.) |
| | *Kano: Environment, Society and Development* |
| | London & Abuja, Adonis & Abbey Publishers |

University of Durham. www.taa.org.uk/Harrisdone.htm accessed on 12th April 2008.

Harris, F. (undated) *Intensification of Agriculture in the Semi Arid Areas: Lessons from Kano Close-Settled Area, Nigeria.* International Institute for Environment and Development-Sustainable Agriculture and Rural Livelihoods Programme. Gatekeeper Series No.59

Ibrahim, O. F. (2001) *Prince of Times: Ado Bayero and the Transformation of Emiral Authority in Kano.* Africa World Press, Inc. New Jersey

Kaltho, J. B. (2010) The National Physical Development Plan: A Veritable Tool for Sustainable Growth and Development in Nigeria. Being a Paper presented at the Sensitization Meeting on the Preparation of the NPDP organized by the Federal Ministry of Lands, Housing and Urban Development held at Royal Tropicana Hotel, Kano August 19th 2010.

Kates, R. W.; Parris, T. M.; Leiserowitz, A. A. ( 2005) "What is Sustainable Development? Goals, Indicators, Values and Practice." *Environment: Science and Policy for Sustainable Development* 47(3) 8-21

Khalil, N. W; Bayero, S. A. (2004) Nishadin Matan Kulle: Tsokaci akan Wasannin Cikin Gidan Sarki. Paper presented at the 6th International Conference on Language, Literature, and Hausa Tradition organised by Centre for Study of Nigerian Languages Bayero University Kano

Khalil, N. W. (2007) *Bayi a Gidan Dabo.* Gidan Dabino Publishers, Nigeria

Khalil, N. W.; Bayero, S. A. (Forthcoming) Language and Etiquettes of the Kano Palace

Liman, M.A.; Adamu, Y.M. (2003) "Kano in Time and Space: From City to a Metropolis." In Hambolu, M.A (Ed.) *Perspectives of Kano British Relations.* Gidan Makama Museum, Kano.

Mabogunje, A. L. (2004) "Framing the Fundamental Issues of Sustainable Development in Sub-Saharan Africa." *CID Working Paper No. 104.* Cambridge, MA: Sustainable Development Program, Center for International Development, Harvard University

Chapter 8 | Aliyu S. Barau, in
A.I. Tanko and S.B. Momale (Eds.)
*Kano: Environment, Society and Development*
London & Abuja, Adonis & Abbey Publishers

**107**

Maiwada, A.D. (2000) "Disappearing Open Spaces in Kano Metropolis" in Falola, J.A; Ahmed, K; Liman, M.A; Maiwada, A. (eds.) *Issues in Land Administration and Development in Northern Nigeria*, Department of Geography, Bayero University, Kano.

Marshall, F., Waldman, L., MacGregor, H., Mehta, L.; Randhawa, P. (2009) *On the Edge of Sustainability: Perspectives on Peri-urban Dynamics,* STEPS Working Paper 35, Brighton: STEPS Centre

McMichael, A.J.; Butler, C.D.; Folke, C. (2003) New Visions for Addressing Sustainability. *Science* 302, 1919; DOI 0.1126/science. 1090001

Millennium Ecosystem Assessment (2003) Millennium ecosystem assessment, ecosystems and human wellbeing: A framework for assessment. Island Press, Washington, DC

Mortimore, M. (1989) *Adapting to Drought- Farmers, Famine and Desertification in West Africa.* Cambridge University Press.

Mortimore, M. (1993) "The Intensification of Peri-urban Agriculture: The Kano Close- Settled Zone, 1964 - 1986." In: Turner, B.L., Kates, R.W. and Hyden, G. (eds) *Population Growth and Agricultural Change in Africa.* University Press of Florida.

Mortimore, M.; Adams, W.M. (1999) *Working the Sahel-Environment and Society in Northern Nigeria.* Rutledge, Research Global Environmental Change, London.

Mortimore, M.; Ba, M.; Mahamane, A.; Rostom, R.S.; Serra del Pozo, P.; Turner, B. (2005) "Changing Systems and Changing Landscapes: Measuring and Interpreting Land Use Transformation in African Drylands" *Geografisk Tidsskrift, Danish Journal of Geography 105(1):101-118*

Naniya, T. (2007) "An introduction." In Adamu, A.U. (Ed.) *Chieftaincy and Security in Nigeria - Past, Present and Future.* Research and Documentation Directorate, Government House Kano.

Nast, H. (1992) *Space, History and Power: Stories of Spatial and Social Change in the Palace of Kano, Northern Nigeria, circa 1500-1990.* Ph.D Thesis Department of Geography, McGill University, Montreal, Quebec.

Chapter 8 | Aliyu S. Barau, in
A.I. Tanko and S.B. Momale (Eds.)
*Kano: Environment, Society and Development*
London & Abuja, Adonis & Abbey Publishers

**108**

Nast, H. (1996) Islam, Gender, and Slavery in West Africa circa 1500: A Spatial Archaeology of the Kano Palace, Northern Nigeria. *Annals of the Association of American Geographers* 86 (1) 44-77

Olofin, E.A.; Tanko, A.I. (2002) *Laboratory of Areal Differentiation: Metropolitan Kano in Geographic Perspective*. Department of Geography, BUK, Field Studies Series 1.

Olujimi, J. (2009) Evolving a Planning Strategy for Managing Urban Sprawl in Nigeria. *Journal of Human Ecology*, 25(3) 201-208

Oravska, T.K; Chobotova, V. (2007) "Institutional Analysis of Sustainability Problems" in Oravska, T.K.; Chobotova, V.; Sauer, P. (eds) *Institutional Analysis of Sustainability Problems- Emerging Theories and Methods in Sustainability Research Book of Proceedings.*Institute for Forecasting, Slovak Academy of Sciences p.8-20

Owei, O. B. (2010) Shortfall in Past National Development Initiatives in Nigeria. Being a Paper Presented at the Sensitization Meeting on the Preparation of the NPDP organised by the Federal Ministry of Lands, Housing and Urban Development held at Royal Tropicana Hotel, Kano August 19th 2010.

Polèse, M.; Denis-Jacob, J. (2009) *Staying on the Top. Why Cities Move Up (or Down) the Urban Hierarchy: an International Comparison over a Hundred Years*. INEDITS Working papers No 2, 2009, Montreal

Rufa'i, R. A. (1995) *Gidan Rumfa: The Kano Palace*. Triumph Publishing Company, Gidan Saadu Zungur, Kano

Sa'ad, H.T. (1989) "Continuity and Change in Kano Traditional Architecture" in *Kano and Some of Her Neighbours*. Barkindo, B.M. (Ed.) Department of History, Bayero University, Kano, Ahmadu Bello University Press Limited, Zaria

Saad, H. T. (1981) Between Myth and Reality: The Aesthetics of Traditional Architecture in Hausaland. Ann Arbor: University Microfilms International, 233-235, 351.

Tanko, A. I. (2001) "Some Physical and Chemical Changes in Soils, and their Agricultural Implications under Large-Scale Irrigation in the Kano Region, Northern Nigeria". *Proceedings of Faculty Seminar Series*, Vol.1, FSMS, Bayero University Kano

Smith, M.G. (1997) *Government in Kano 1350-1950*, Westview Press, Minneapolis

| Chapter 8 | Aliyu S. Barau, in |
| | A.I. Tanko and S.B. Momale (Eds.) |
| | *Kano: Environment, Society and Development* |
| | London & Abuja, Adonis & Abbey Publishers |

**109**

The Royal Household (2008/2009) *The Royal Household and the Environment*. Accessed on www.royal.gov.uk viewed August 16th 2010.

UN Habitat/UNEP (2008) *The Sustainable Cities Nigeria Programme (1994-2006): Building Platforms for Environmentally Sustainable Urbanisation*. SCP Documentation Series, Volume 7. UN-Habitat/UNEP Nairobi.

UNESCO (2010) *Ancient Kano City Walls and Associated Sites*. Accessed on <www.unesco.org/en/tentativelists/state=ng> viewed on August 16th.

Walker, R. (2006) *When We Ruled*. Every Generation Media, London

Zahradeen, M. S. (1990) "The Acquisition of Land and its Administration in the Sokoto Caliphate as Provided in Abdullahi Danfodiyo's *'Ta'alim-'al-Aradi'* in *State and Society in the Sokoto Caliphate*. Kani, A.M.; Gandi, A.K. (eds) Usmanu Danfodiyo University Series 1, Sokoto pp. 193-206

Chapter 8 | Aliyu S. Barau, in
A.I. Tanko and S.B. Momale (Eds.)
*Kano: Environment, Society and Development*
London & Abuja, Adonis & Abbey Publishers

# Chapter Nine

## TRADE, COMMERCE AND INDUSTRIES

Adamu Idris Tanko and Halima Abdulkadir Idris

### Introduction

Population maps of tropical Africa have been used as far back as the 1930s to show how they could draw attention and curiosity to urban Kano. From the maps, it was obvious that Kano varied significantly especially in terms of population density. This was what Mortimore (1967; 1975) used in conceiving his idea of the Kano Close-Settled Zone (KCSZ) hence defined it as an area around Kano city with population density of over 250-300 people per square kilometers. Peace and tranquility and outright acceptance by the *Kanawas* of other people of different cultures and beliefs enhanced the status of the city as a great trading, commercial and later industrial centre. These attributes (of peace and tranquility) can be traced to the original *Abagayawa*. The apparent tranquility in the society impressed so many neighboring communities that they began to migrate and settle among the *Abagayawa*. Among those that settled very early was the belligerent group led by Bagauda who shortly after the 999AD raised and established himself as a nominal chief.

Many rulers came after Bagauda, and it was noted that the rulers (at different periods) all perceived the wisdom of a sort of neutrality, which helped immensely in developing Kano in many respects, and particularly it provided the peace needed for trade, commerce and later industry to develop. For instance, in the 17th Century when Mai Idris Alooma expelled all the influence of the Kwararafa he strengthened and extended the influence of the Bornu over the entire [northern] region, Kano quickly acknowledged the overload ship of the Bornu. Moreover, Kano had, before the Islamic Jihad of the 19th Century, been one of the three southern termini of the trans-Saharan trade routes. The Kano route was the central and the weakest of the three - the Katsina to the west and the Bornu to the east. But with the Jihad, Kano quickly acknowledged the primacy of the Sultan, while Katsina vehemently resisted until it was eventually conquered and the Emir

Chapter 9 | Adamu I. Tanko & Halima A. Idris, in
A.I. Tanko and S.B. Momale (Eds.)
*Kano: Environment, Society and Development*
London & Abuja, Adonis & Abbey Publishers

**111**

relocated to Maradi (in today's Niger Republic). This further stabilized and strengthened the central Kano route and it became the busiest. Moreover, after the Jihad, Kano was quick to accept the Europeans with comparatively little resistance. Despite the fact that today, the importance of the trans-Saharan trade was eroded; Kano as an *entrepot*, a market and an industrial centre, it naturally, attracted commerce from all directions. The discussion in the Chapter is based on the theme of the evolution and development of trade, commerce and industry in Kano and how these happened over time and space.

## Pre-Colonial and Colonial Activities in Kano

This section is intended to present and review early trading, commercial and industrial activities in the pre-colonial and colonial Kano, tracing the origin of all the three activities to the establishment of the Jihad government in Hausaland.

### *Early Trade and Commerce in Kano*

For several centuries, a profitable and extensive network of cross-lands had been established by the various African States which started first, between Morocco and Ghana. Since that time onwards, a complex network of caravan routes crossing the Sahara was established over which the volume of trade increased. The trade became concentrated on several trade routes; the first of these was the North-south trade route which began in Tripoli with a branch from Morocco passing through Ghademes and the oasis of Air to the Hausa States of Katsina and Kano after passing through Agadez and Zinder (Fig. 9.1). Through this route, the Arab traders from North Africa brought items such as carpets, silk, spices, perfumes, cowry shells (the currency of western Sudan), shoes, weapons and religious manuscripts which were in great demand in Hausaland. While the Tuaregs from Azbin and Agadez brought commodities into Kano and Hausaland such as red and white salts from Takedda, potash or Naron, Henna, Horse (which were highly favoured in Hausaland referred to as *Dan-Asbin*), camels, slaves and date-palms which they exchanged for products such as grains, cotton garments and dyed clothes which were in great demand in the Sahara. Other product which Kano exported to

| Chapter 9 | Adamu I. Tanko & Halima A. Idris, in |
| | A.I. Tanko and S.B. Momale (Eds.) |
| | *Kano: Environment, Society and Development* |
| | London & Abuja, Adonis & Abbey Publishers |

North Africa and the Ghat included; sandals, tanned hides and skins, leather products etc.

The Emir of Kano Abdullahi Burja (1435-1452 A.D) was said to be the first ruler to have acquired camels in the Hausaland which may well suggest the first direct Kano's participation in the trade. Certainly by this time, a caravan route from Kano to the Ghat had been opened. This was the period when Asbenawa (Tuaregs) started to frequent Hausaland for transactions in salts and cotton. During the reign of his successor Yakubu Dan-Burja (1452-1463 AD), the trade increased even further, that salts came from Abzin and Arabs and Kanuri merchants also came to settle in Kano. By the 15th and 16th centuries the trans-Saharan trade reached its peak and by the death of Muhammad Rumfa (1463-1499 A.D) the system of termini had become obsolete. Thus, the North African merchants were going through Kano and further into the other parts of the Sudan and Kano merchants were also sending caravans in all directions.

By the 1850s Kano was noted to have had a powerful merchant class that maintained extensive external links through the trans-Saharan trade for which Kano served as a major entrepot (Shea, 1975; Lovejoy, 1973). It was in a way, a trade centre for the very populous district that comes to be known as the Close-Settled Zone (Mortimore, 1967). This Zone was already fairly densely populated by the period. It is clear that at that date, and probably as late as the 1890s, the area was a net exporter of grains, though by - the later date - is seems that the gains was mainly from the salt caravans coming primarily from Taghaza. There was also a large local trade in cloth of the cheaper varieties. There was production of very large export of textiles, relatively to the size of the population, Kano was considerably more productive than it is today in grain and other foodstuffs; it was already an importer of cotton. Foodstuffs were cheap in Kano: a whole family could live at ease, including every expense, including clothing, for 50,000 to 60,000 cowries, 20 to 24 dollars, a year, Kano was described as one of the most fertile spots on earth.

From 1891, Kano came to be a well known participant in the trans-Saharan trade. Generally, the development of the trade began after the Muslim Arabs invasion of North Africa in about the seventh century A.D.

Chapter 9    Adamu I. Tanko & Halima A. Idris, in
A.I. Tanko and S.B. Momale (Eds.)
*Kano: Environment, Society and Development*
London & Abuja, Adonis & Abbey Publishers

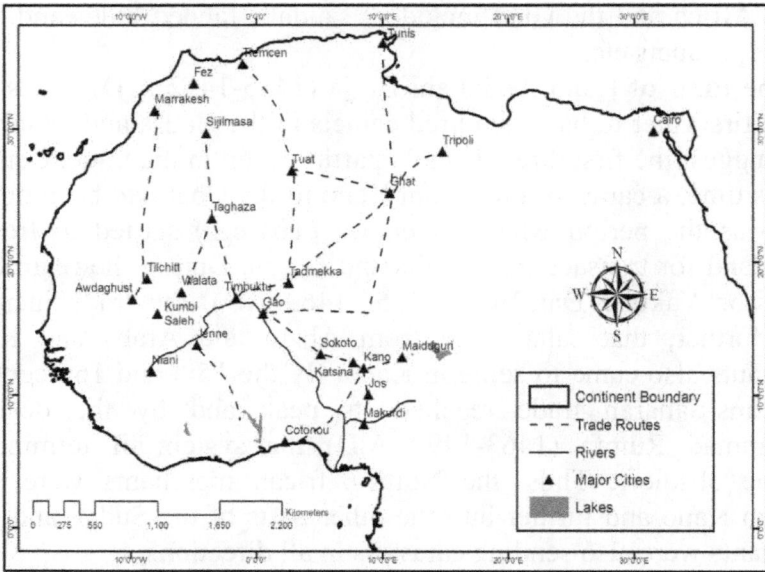

**Figure 9.1: The Trans-Saharan Trade Routes**

Some of the identifiable routes which sprang up included the Kano-Katsina-Sokoto and continuing from there to Niamey, Timbuktu and beyond (Fig. 9.1). There was also the Kano - Zaria route leading to the cotton belt area down to Nupe and thereafter to Minna, in today's Niger State. Another well known track ran from Kano through Zaria and crossed the Niger at Bussa, thence ran on through Dahomey and Togo before continuing to Salaga and Kumasi in Ghana (Gwanja). Kano had concentrated on the trade to the south, for which two routes dominated through Zaria to the Jos Plateau and the Benue valley. The major commodities exported by Kano over these routes were cotton clothes, horses and beads, while on the Zaria route, Kano imported European goods coming up the Niger and high quality locally produced iron. But on the Benue route, Kano imported salt, antimony and slaves in return the merchant took textiles and leather goods, horses as well as military equipment. Kano also imported ivory, iron, wood and slaves which were vital for the development and continuation of Kano's craft and industrial productions.

On the Kano-Bornu routes, especially in the 18th and 19th centuries when the volume of trade between the two states grew, the exchange

Chapter 9 | Adamu I. Tanko & Halima A. Idris, in
A.I. Tanko and S.B. Momale (Eds.)
*Kano: Environment, Society and Development*
London & Abuja, Adonis & Abbey Publishers

commodities from Bornu were acacia gum, iron, ostrich feathers and other goods of luxury which were referred to in Kano as "*Kayan Gabas*" (eastern stuffs) which had received the attention and support of Kano ruling class. In return, Kano sent commodities such as pepper, locust bean, agricultural goods as well as the usual textile cotton clothes and leather products.

Apart from the exchanges of tradable goods, some tribes of the desert were known to come and settle in Kano. For example, the Tuaregs (also referred to in Hausaland as Azbinawa, Agadasawa, Bugaje and Agalawa) were known to have migrated and settled in Kano (especially the Fagge area where most of them became *Fatomas* and brokers). They engaged in a variety of economic activities such as agricultural productions, textile productions, distribution and the provisions of commercial infrastructure including urban community of brokers, financiers, landlords as well as construction of warehouses for the storage of goods for their customers. They were also known to have practiced some craft occupations in Fagge such as weaving and sewing. The efforts by Kano in making the trade route safer and expanding the economy during the Jihad period attracted many merchants, scholars and artisans from Bornu and 'Wangara' to settle in Kano.

The City and Emirate of Kano in the nineteenth century were deeply involved in trade of many kinds, from the purely local trade in foodstuffs and other necessities, to long distance trade which extended over a great area of West Africa, the Sahara, and beyond. Its prosperity depended on markets and supplies of raw material far beyond its direct control. Dependency on the economic situation in places so remote from its control is the lot of any trading centre, and, indeed, of any economy which has escaped from the stagnation of total self-subsistence. Since such dependency is necessarily a two-way affair, buyers being as much dependent on remote sellers as sellers on remote buyers , it is hard to follow the argument that such dependency is necessarily harmful in itself; the more important issue is the terms on which trade takes place - who gets the best of the bargain.

Upon all these, Kano's participation in the trans-Saharan trade was estimated to account for only one-fifth of the total trades involving it at the time. The Saharan trade was primarily in the hands of North African merchants, who shared the profits with the Saharan caravan leaders. The Kano end of the trade was handled by their resident

| Chapter 9 | Adamu I. Tanko & Halima A. Idris, in |
|---|---|
| | A.I. Tanko and S.B. Momale (Eds.) |
| | *Kano: Environment, Society and Development* |
| | London & Abuja, Adonis & Abbey Publishers |

**115**

agents, most of whom intended to repatriate their profits in the long run. The profit to Kano consisted in such taxes as could be collected (including 'gifts' from visiting merchants) and the profits on goods sold to the North Africans. Profits on the desert trade seem to have been estimated at some 200% to 300%; they might be divided equally between the merchant who put up the capital and the caravaneer or the merchant might ensure 100% return by invoicing the goods at double their cost price, the caravan leader gaining whatever profit he could after this had been paid. The trade to Borno has been described by Denham in the 1820s, and appears to have been about as profitable; a camel-load of merchandise would be bought in Tripoli for $150 (about 250% above prime cost), and brought in a return of $500 after paying expenses; one man was put in charge of three camel loads who received one third of the profits remaining. This was, of course, if all went well. To some extent these apparent high profits may have resulted from the monopoly over the desert trade which the Ghadamsi and other North African merchants and their Tuareg allies were able to maintain. But the fact that many other merchants were able to enter the trade during the feather boom suggests that it was only when profits were even higher that they did much more than cover the risks of the trade.

The arrival of many migrant elements brought about a boom in external trade and exchange, through the establishment of various industries as ethnic groups came with their skills, in various fields of endeavor, to sell in exchange for their needs. As result of this prosperity, a bourgeoisie class started to emerge. They accumulated wealth, slaves and other properties like horses. The establishment of a mercantile mentality sowed the seeds of emerging capitalism in Kano as far back as 12th century.

## *Emergence of Industries in Kano*

Kano is unique among the leading industrial centers of Nigeria in that industrialization emerged from within an urban society with a comparatively advanced pre-colonial handicraft and mercantile capitalist tradition (Bashir, 1983). Historically, the advanced pre-colonial economy encouraged dense peasant settlements in the peri-urban areas surrounding the city. Both of these factors, an advanced

| Chapter 9 | Adamu I. Tanko & Halima A. Idris, in |
| | A.I. Tanko and S.B. Momale (Eds.) |
| | *Kano: Environment, Society and Development* |
| | London & Abuja, Adonis & Abbey Publishers |

pre-colonial economy and dense peasant settlements, continue to exert influence on the structure, consciousness and action of Kano's fledgling industrial working class (Lubeck, 1987).

In discussing Kano as an emerging industrial city, it is relevant to make the connection of its rapid population increase through in-migration with the salient aspects of urban cultural forms which grew up in the neighborhoods that housed the newly urbanized labor. Ethnic and racial ties often provided the links for migration chains, and they helped recent migrants find jobs, housing, and friendship in a new environment. These ties often resulted in ethnically segregated urban neighborhoods among the working class. This was how the Kano Sabon Gari, Fagge, and other peri-urban settlement clusters came into being. It may be argued, however, that since Kano is not an industrial city per se, the characteristics of density clusters reflect more of a diversified economy centered around commodity utilization from the factories, rather than large scale industrial production. Despite everything, Kano's urban cultural role fit well with the capitalist economic order that came to dominate all other social institutions. Capitalism depended on the production of commodities through wage labor in the interests of capital accumulation. The city became a center of such production processes and the location for the industrial factories in which this production most typically took place. It was also the residence for the other "commodity" necessary to its productivity, wage laborers. Ancillary urban functions-banking, wholesale and retail trade, transportation and communications nodality grew up to expedite the factory production or the provision of the labor force.

The Arabs' industrial patronage stimulated the growth of industries in Kano (Adamu, 1999). They financed local craftsmen by giving them advanced payments which enabled them to produce the desired commodities for the Arabs (read Chapter 10).

| Chapter 9 | Adamu I. Tanko & Halima A. Idris, in |
| | A.I. Tanko and S.B. Momale (Eds.) |
| | *Kano: Environment, Society and Development* |
| | London & Abuja, Adonis & Abbey Publishers |

## Post Colonial Trade, Commerce, Industries in Kano

In contemporary Northern Nigeria, Kano is one of the most important and largest commercial centres. The City has over four million people (over 10 million in Kano State) and provides a stable and continuous market for both manufactured and semi-processed goods. The volume of trading activities conducted on daily basis in the markets, notably Muhammadu Abubakar Rimi Market (Sabon-Gari), Kwanar Singer, Kantin Kwari, Kurmi and Dawanau signify not only its great potentials, but its eminence as a market for various products.

In addition to the large and specialized markets, Kano is also known for various kinds of agricultural products which provide huge raw materials for Agro-Allied industries. Agricultural products like maize, Guinea Corn (sorghum), rice, cotton and groundnut are readily available to serve as raw materials for oil milling, flour and textile industries. Other agro-based raw materials are Gum Arabic, livestock, Hides and Skin, Cowpeas, and Citrus fruits. Currently, Kano is approved by the Federal Government of Nigeria as the second Export Processing Zone (EPZ) in the country and the State Government is making efforts for its actualization. The EPZ is expected to provide additional impetus to both local and foreign investors. Furthermore, the State is one of the three States in the Northern part of the country that serve as a dry port and Inland Container Depot (ICD) to serve the import/export activities of the hinterland shippers.

The EPZ is located at two places, namely Panisau near the Mallam Aminu Kano International Airport and Kanye village in Kabo Local Government Area. The Zone is to provide appropriate enabling environment that will encourage development and growth of export oriented industries particularly those relating to the non-oil sector of the economy. It is also to attract local and foreign investors, ensure maximum utilization of the abundant raw materials available in the state, encourage diversification of the State's and Nigeria's revenue base and provide opportunities for employment. Infrastructural facilities like the International Airport (Mallam Aminu Kano International Airport - MAKIA), second only to the Lagos Murtala Muhammad International Airport in importance within the country, the road and Railway links to other parts of the country as well as the

Chapter 9 | Adamu I. Tanko & Halima A. Idris, in
A.I. Tanko and S.B. Momale (Eds.)
*Kano: Environment, Society and Development*
London & Abuja, Adonis & Abbey Publishers

excellent road network within and outside the State provide opportunities for the steady growth of commercial activities.

Today, Kano is the second largest industrial centre in Nigeria and the largest in Northern Nigeria. There are at present over 400 privately owned large, medium and small scale industrial factories producing various products such as textile, tanned leather, foot wears, cosmetics, plastics, enamelware, pharmaceuticals, ceramics, furniture and bicycles. Others include agricultural implements, soft drinks, food and beverages, dairy products, vegetable oil, groundnut oil, animal feeds, etc. Evidently, it serves as the terminus for two conflicting processes emanating from the capitalist character of the wider society: capitalist investment in urban property for profit making on one hand, and class conflict on the other. The former process subjects the human and natural environment to the interests of capital accumulation; the latter makes for the formation of urban neighborhood associations, ethnic associations, and other sorts of class alliances that organize local resistance to profit taking. Kano City now becomes a battleground for these opposing forces.

The strategy to boost the growth of industries by the governments in Kano was to provide, in addition to the Bompai, other large industrial estates such as the three phases (Phases 1, II, and III) of the Sharada Industrial Areas, the Challawa Industrial Area and Tokarawa Industrial Layout. These areas had several manufacturing industries. More of such industrial estates were being envisaged in the future with programmes aimed at maintaining very close ties with the organized private sector to establish a variety of industries. This was offering opportunities for joint venture in the existing state owned enterprises such as the multi-million Naira Magwan Water Restaurant and Daula Hotel etc. Indigenization decrees of the 1970s helped to promote indigenous entrepreneurship, which in the 1980s became well-entrenched in the sub-sectors of food, beverages, vegetable oil, metal and wooden furniture products, and soap, perfumes, toiletries and cosmetics (Olukoshi, 1996). The light consumer goods sub-sectors, where much of the indigenous and Levantine capital is concentrated, registered very high rates of return in the 1970s and 1980s - no doubt aided by the existence of an oil boom-induced mass market for such goods.

Despite this positive outlook came the general economic malaise in the late 1980s, and Austerity Measures and Structural Adjustment

Chapter 9    Adamu I. Tanko & Halima A. Idris, in
A.I. Tanko and S.B. Momale (Eds.)
Kano: Environment, Society and Development
London & Abuja, Adonis & Abbey Publishers

Programmes (SAP) were introduced in the economy. By the early 1990s the government made the drive towards accessing a loan from the International Monetary Fund (IMF) of World Bank. As most of the industries established in Nigeria during the 1960s and 1970s (i.e. essentially the oil boom era) were import substitution-based, with the fall in oil prices, the value of naira crashed. With this development most of the industries collapsed because they relied on imported raw materials and especially spare parts and machineries (Olukoshi, 1991; Forrest, 1993). The worst affected were those in the North especially Kano. Olukoshi (1996) has given the impact of the crisis on the Kano manufacturing sector (as on the rest of the national economy) which was immediate and drastic. He gives an estimate that between 1982 and 1985, between 50 and 75 percent of all manufacturing establishments in Kano had to cease production for varying periods of time, ranging from two weeks to one year, because of the acute shortage of raw materials and spare parts. He further shares the results of a survey covering 34 companies in six subsectors of manufacturing in Kano, and with ownership spreading among foreign, indigenous, and Levantine manufacturers, the Kano Branch of the Manufacturers Association of Nigeria (MAN) confirmed the devastating effects of the crisis on industry. The survey, spanning the period from January to October 1984, found that the seven textile companies it covered were all, on average, utilizing only about 14 percent of their installed capacity. They had also retrenched over 2,000 workers and the foreign exchange allocation which they received through import licenses issued by the federal government in 1984 could only meet only 20 per cent of their total requirements.

As a prelude towards the problems for Kano, governments at both the regional and federal levels had failed to support the zeal of local and private investors towards industrial development in Kano. Most of the industries in Kano were established by private investors. According to Olukoshi (1996) manufacturers in Kano are made up of three main sub-groups: foreign corporate investors/managers who have established subsidiaries that are run by professional staff and answerable to head offices overseas; their indigenous Nigerian counterparts (investors as well as managers); and a large number of Levantine/Asian business people, some with a long history of association with the Kano area. The regional government in Nigeria,

Chapter 9 | Adamu I. Tanko & Halima A. Idris, in
A.I. Tanko and S.B. Momale (Eds.)
*Kano: Environment, Society and Development*
London & Abuja, Adonis & Abbey Publishers

during the First Republic (1960 - 1966), did not establish any industry in around Kano as it did in Kaduna and Sokoto, which hosted the textile and cement industries respectively. The Federal Government established only one industry in Kano, the National Truck Manufacturers (NTM), a commercial vehicle assembly plant that was never viable because of its precarious foundation and it was closed and later privatized. But in Kaduna, the federal government established a fertilizer plant, a motor assembly plant and a refinery. The last two are all functioning and the refinery is perhaps the most important industry in northern Nigeria.

Contemporary efforts by manufacturers in Kano have been noted to focus the twin issues of the sourcing of local raw materials and production for export, and from which a complicated picture has emerged (Olukoshi, 1996).

> At a certain level, all the Kano manufacturers displayed an awareness of the need to source inputs locally wherever possible. Some of the manufacturers were in fact using local substitute raw materials in their production process. But those firms that remained import-dependent-and they were many, ranging from the soft drinks factories to those producing chemical products -simply mobilized funds locally and obtained foreign exchange in order to import the required inputs-taking full advantage of trade liberalization. Interestingly, trade liberalization also exposed the manufacturers to vigorous competition from cheap imports consisting of new and used (second-hand) commodities, a development which served to reinforce their problems of production and marketing. Indeed, as cheap imports of consumer goods flowed into the national economy, particularly from East Asia, many Nigerian manufacturers were to protest vigorously about the dumping of goods on the local market by foreign business interests (Olukoshi, 1996; 44).

Today industrial production in Kano primarily remains in the tanning industry which processes hides-and-skins that are transported to countries of the world know for leather manufactures. Generally, at Kano's three industrial estates - Bompai, Challawa, and Sharada - industrial sludge and liquid waste are routinely deposited in open drains, sewer systems and water courses without treatment. The waste treatment facilities that do exist are either inadequate or not functioning, and very little enforcement takes place. The environmental implications of these include high level of both air and water pollution reported in and around Kano (Tanko and Ahmed,

Chapter 9 | Adamu I. Tanko & Halima A. Idris, in
A.I. Tanko and S.B. Momale (Eds.)
*Kano: Environment, Society and Development*
London & Abuja, Adonis & Abbey Publishers

1994; Ahmed and Tanko, 2000). Many farmers were also able to make a connection between the poor quality waters and the degradation of the soils, that irrigated plots apparently often developed a 'crust' on their surface, and would not allow water or air to infiltrate (Binns et al 2006).

## Conclusion

Kano has been bastion of trade and commerce in the Sub-Saharan Africa for many centuries. It prospered as the southernmost nodal point of the trans-Saharan trade during the pre-colonial times. At the wake of colonialism Kano retained its vigour for trade and commerce, that the growth of the industry was given an impetus. This has been improved upon in the post colonial period when its products were taken far and wide that it got connected to the trans-Atlantic trade and partaking in global trade and manufacturing. For both trade of the old and new routes Kano is the premier point exercising commercial influences over its adjacent locations. It was not until the 1990s when Nigeria's economic melt-down affected the activities. Trade, commerce and the industry are now struggling. Despite the resilience and forward looking of the entrepreneurial *Kanawas*, contemporary activities are far from being the desired.

## Reference

Adamu, M. U. (1999), the Emergence of Kano as a City State, Munawwara Book Foundation, Kano

Ahmed, K. and A. I. Tanko (2000), "Assessment of Water Quality Changes for Irrigation in the River Hadejia Catchment". *Journal of Arid Agriculture* 10, 89 - 94.

Bashir, I.L. (1983), the Politics of Industrialisation in Kano: Industries, Incentives, and Indigenous Entrepreneurs, Ph.D. Thesis, Boston University, Boston, Massachusetts.

Binns, J. A. (Tony), R.A. Maconachie and A. I. Tanko (2003), "Water, Land and Health in Peri-urban Food Production: The Case of Kano, Nigeria". *J. Land Degradation and Development*. (2003) 14: 43-444.

Chapter 9 | Adamu I. Tanko & Halima A. Idris, in
A.I. Tanko and S.B. Momale (Eds.)
*Kano: Environment, Society and Development*
London & Abuja, Adonis & Abbey Publishers

Forrest, T. (1993), Politics and Economic Development in Nigeria, Westview, Boulder, Colorado

Lovejoy, Paul (1973), The Hausa Kola Trade 1700-1960: A Commercial System in the Continental Exchange of West Africa, Ph. D. Thesis, University of Wisconsin, Madison.

Lubeck, P. (1987) Islamic Protest and Oil-Based Capitalism: Agriculture, Rural Linkages, and Urban Popular Movements in Northern Nigeria. In: Watts, M. (ed.) *State, Oil, and Agriculture in Nigeria*. Berkeley: Institute of International Studies, University of California, Berkeley, pp. 268-290.

Mortimore, M. (1967) Land and population pressure in the Kano Close-Settled Zone, Northern Nigeria. *The Advancement of Science*, 23, pp. 677-88.

Mortimore, M. (1975), Peri-urban pressures In: Moss, R.P., and R.J.A.R. Rathbone (eds.) *The population factor in African Studies*. University of London Press Ltd., London, pp. 188-197.

Olukoshi, A. (1991), An Assessment of the Economic Recovery Programme of the Nigerian

Olukoshi, A. (1996), *Economic Crisis, Structural Adjustment and the Coping Strategies of Manufacturers in Kano, Nigeria,* United Nations Research Institute For Social Development, Document No. DP 77

Shea, Phillip (1975), The Development of an Export-Oriented Dyed Cloth Industry in Kano Emirate in the 19th Century, Ph.D. Thesis, University of Wisconsin, Madison

Tanko, A. I. and K. Ahmed (1994), "Quality Hazards in Water for Irrigation at the Kano River Project Phase 1 (KRP 1)". *Journal of Social & Management Studies (JOSAMS)*, BUK. Vol. 1 (1994): 47-59.

Chapter 9 | Adamu I. Tanko & Halima A. Idris, in
A.I. Tanko and S.B. Momale (Eds.)
*Kano: Environment, Society and Development*
London & Abuja, Adonis & Abbey Publishers

Brokensha, D. (1962). Political and Economic Development in Nigeria. Western Boundary. Oxford.

McCorquodale, (1932). The Hausa Kola Trade. The Structure of a commercial system in the Ghana and Borno... West Africa. 214, D. The Slave Trade and Western Africa.

Lovejoy, P. (1985). Islam, Trade and Religion. Capitalist agriculture, Royal Incomes and Ghana Regular Associations. In Modern Africa, by Watts M. (ed.), pp. 176-197 and 259-68. Berkeley: Institute of International Studies. Berkeley. California. Berkeley, pp. 261-290.

Mortimore, M.J. (1967). Land and population pressure in the Kano Close-settled Zone, Northern Nigeria. The Geographical Review 25, pp. 677-738.

Mortimore, M. (1972). Population pressure in the Hausa. K.D., and R.J.A. Kellner (eds.). Peoples and Environment of Africa. University of Edinburgh and Land Management...

Obadan, A. D. (1991). An Assessment of the Transport Recovery Programme in Nigeria.

Olusanya, A. (1995). Economic Liberalisation and the development of the Coping Strategies of Manufacturers in the Manufacturing sector. Research Institute for Social and Economic Research, Ibadan.

Shea, Philip (1975). The Development of an Export-Oriented Dyed Cloth Industry in the Kano Emirate in the 19th Century. Ph.D. thesis, University of Wisconsin, Madison.

Stamp, Sir L. and L.M. Stamp. (1949). Quality Standards for Water for Irrigation. The Kano River Project Board. KRP 67a. Board of Irrigation and Development. Sudan. 1967a. KRP., Vol. I, June 1964. MANR.

# Chapter Ten

## THE PRESENCE OF ARABS IN KANO

Abdallah Uba Adamu

### Introduction

Olzak (2006) argues that conventional treatments of ethnic mobilization find that inequality or the absence of democracy has systematically produced more ethnic conflict and protests. Yet this does not take into consideration the relative relationships between what is called 'moving populations'. For while parts of Nigeria suffer from long-rooted periodic ethnic conflicts, e.g. Jos in the Plateau State (Akanji 2011, Ambe-Uva 2011), the Nigerian 'Middle Belt' (Ioratim-Uba 2009) due to diversity of ethnicities and settler competition for resources, other states of the federation (e.g. Kano, Bauchi, Jigawa) had waves of racial movement and migration of Arabs with total absence of any conflict between the immigrants and their host African population.

That does not mean, however, an integrated immigration population was totally and successfully created. Arabs settlers in northern Nigeria, for the most part, refused to integrate with the African population-and mainly marry African populations with similar racial characteristics, e.g. Shuwa Arabs or the Toranke Fulani, who are the lightest skinned of the nine or so Fulani groupings. This does not necessarily translate as racism, however, because there were pockets of 'Fulani Arabs' who had split ancestry between African Fulani and Arab. Ironically, most of these Fulani Arabs seemed to have lost their languages – speaking neither Fulfulde nor Arabic; instead becoming linguistic Hausa. This raises the interesting issue of identities, and the precise point at which a person claims a particular identity; and indeed what defines a person's identity - racial characteristics, linguistic affinity, or residence?

This chapter traces the migrations of Arabs from North Africa and the Middle East to northern Nigeria, particularly Kano, and the various ways they influence, but are not influenced by, the culture and society of Kano. The arguments are framed with the context of Gordon

Chapter 10    Abdallah U. Adamu, in
A.I. Tanko and S.B. Momale (Eds.)
*Kano: Environment, Society and Development*
London & Abuja, Adonis & Abbey Publishers

Allport's (1954) Intergroup Contact Hypothesis that looks at the emergence of racial prejudice among immigrants and settlers, although it is preferably perceived as lack of desire to integrate to due to an innate desire to retain individual and group identities, rather than racism. In fact while the theory applies to the hostility shown to immigrants by settled groups, in northern Nigeria, the reverse is the case, in that the Arabs became a favoured settler group - over and above other indigenous African settlers in the same communities.

## From Across the Sahara

The Region of North Africa in its historical connection with old empires attracted different names. The Romans called the region *Barbary,* the land of Barbarians or the people who were pushed southwards to the fringe of the desert by the colonists. The Arabs, on the other hand, called the region the Maghreb, which means West; which was then the Western part of their world. Thus we had *Maghreb-al-Aksa* which meant Morocco (Hogben and Kirk-Green, 1966). This Region stretches from Bilad al Shinjil Mauritania in the West to the southern borders of Egypt in the East.

Despite the risks encountered in desert crossings, the people of North Africa and the inhabitants of Hausaland had established ethnic and cultural relationships for a long period of time, which survived centuries of cultural and social changes. The relationships were first established through migratory patterns, trade and scholarship. For instance, Bovill (1958) argues that;

> For centuries black slaves were carried across the desert to end their days as domestic servants, as concubines, as laborers, or as soldiers among the communities of the Maghreb: and with them came other products of the Sudan: ivory, ostrich feathers, hides, Kolanuts and above all gold...From the North there came, transported by the camel caravans organized by North African merchants, the good craved by the people of the Sudan, fine clothes, paper swords, and other merchandise that might be counted luxuries, together with that necessity of life-salt, mined in the depths of Sahara. It was not only material goods that the merchants brought with them, but also the knowledge and culture of a wider world, the world of Islam, new concepts of religion, of law and government, new forms of learning, new words to enrich local languages, new styles of architecture, new crops, new crafts and skills (Bovill 1958: p.xi).

Chapter 10   Abdallah U. Adamu, in
A.I. Tanko and S.B. Momale (Eds.)
*Kano: Environment, Society and Development*
London & Abuja, Adonis & Abbey Publishers

North Africa of today contains five modern states. They are Mauritania, Morocco, Algeria, Tunisia and Libya. Between North Africa and Bilad al Sudan, or West Africa south of the Sahara, to which Hausaland belongs, lies the great Sahara desert which cuts off the later region from the western world.

The people of Hausaland and the inhabitants of North Africa have been closely connected for many centuries through the caravan routes. The main tie has been commercial but the Arabs have also introduced a number of exotic elements in dress, food and religious practices. The link was strengthened in the eighteenth century when Katsina was the commercial centre for the trans-Saharan trade and an important centre of learning. However, long before this and right through antiquity, the migratory corridor linking Hausaland and North Africa had served to ferry thousands of traders, clerics and merchants to various areas.

The migratory influx to Hausaland continued beyond the various *Amirs* who ascended the Kano throne, particularly during the reigns of Yakubu dan Abdullahi Barja (1452-1463) to Babba Zaki (1768-1776). However, it was during Rumfa's reign (1463-1469) that the Maghreb, particularly Tripoli became identified with Kano with the coming of Al-Maghili. The settlement of Tripolitanians in Kano radically altered the character of the territory. A tradition had been established; that of making Kano a hospitable place for all migrants - particularly those willing to live in, and identify with, the cultural environment of their hosts. So far history has not recorded any influx of migrants with radically different ideological stands which may warrant an internal conflict between settlers and immigrants.

The pockets of wandering clerics, traders and scholars who moved in and out of the territory from all directions established a series of caravan routes between the Hausa territories and the Maghreb. Since late 16th century Katsina had established itself as the chief trans-Saharan caravan centre of the Hausa states and an important centre of learning and remained so until about 1815. The Jihad of 1804 further opened up Hausaland to more migrants, established the supremacy of Islam, and conveyed impressions of great wealth. These were enough to attract more Maghreb scholars, adventurers and merchants, especially Tripolitanians.

For most of its history, Tripolitania had served as a scene of violent conflicts between different peoples all in attempt to control the

| Chapter 10 | Abdallah U. Adamu, in |
|---|---|
| | A.I. Tanko and S.B. Momale (Eds.) |
| | *Kano: Environment, Society and Development* |
| | London & Abuja, Adonis & Abbey Publishers |

Mediterranean trade route this vital city controlled. For instance in 1510 Tripoli was captured by the forces of Ferdinand the Catholic of Spain, who turned it over to the Knights of St. John in 1530. The latter lost the region in 1551 to the Ottoman Turks, who ruled it either directly or through suzerains for the next 360 years. In 1711 the local governor, Ahmad Karamanli, won recognition from the Ottomans as hereditary pasha (governor), and his dynasty ruled Tripolitania for all but a few years until 1835. Under the Karamanli rulers, Tripoli levied tribute on and plundered shipping in the Mediterranean, a practice that led to the Tripolitan War with the United States in 1801-05. In 1835 Ottoman Turkey resumed direct rule of Tripolitania in an effort to forestall further French expansion in North Africa.

This created a vast pool of refugees who moved southwards and settled in northern Chad area from where many joined the lucrative caravan routes that radiated from Bornu to all other parts of Bilad al-Sudan (Boahen 1962). As a result of the Italo-Turkish War of 1911-12, the Italians occupied Tripoli in 1911 and acquired all of Tripolitania from Turkey in 1912 - establishing one of the most brutal colonial regimes in history. The ensuing struggles for independence created yet more refugees who fled the embattled land and sought for a more peaceful land to settle. Kano, in addition to being a great trading center, was also an important entrepôt from which trade routes radiated westwards through Gwandu and Fada Ngurma to Wagadugu, south-westwards through Bussa and Nikki to Salaga in Ghana (Boahen 1962). Further, the city was already host to Tripolitanians since Yakubu Dan Abdullahi Barja (1452-1463). It therefore became their second home. As Paul Staudinger reported in 1885 (during the reign of Muhammad Bello, 1882-1893):

> Kano is the capital of the richest and most flourishing province of present-day Hausaland. A tremendous quantity of treasures, that is according to the standards of the natives, lies stored within its walls...The reason for the prosperity of this metropolis is to be found...in the fact that Kano is the trade emporium for the whole of Hausaland and moreover the southern-most market of the Arabs. Perhaps sixty to eighty North Africans are permanent residents, but during the dry season several hundred of them live here. It is also then that huge caravans from different Tuareg tribes arrive with one of the most indispensable items of trade amongst all people-salt...So here is a confluence-all the articles of trade from the English and the French, from Niger and the Benue, together with all the European and local articles which the Arabs bring...A good many of the skilled Semitic

Chapter 10 | Abdallah U. Adamu, in
A.I. Tanko and S.B. Momale (Eds.)
*Kano: Environment, Society and Development*
London & Abuja, Adonis & Abbey Publishers

traders own permanent houses and live here married to natives (in Moody 1967: 42).

And although the tie with the Arabs had been commercial, the Arabs in Kano introduced a number of exotic elements in dress, food and religious practices that were to transform the city, as clearly Staudinger's further accounts show. It is not surprising that the most radical contribution to the changing social and cultural character of Kano was made by North Africans, particularly Libyans.[2] To this end; they used at least four documented caravan routes to getting to Hausaland. These are the:

1. Morocco-Toademi-Timbucku (with a branch consisting of Mabruk-Tuat),
2. Tripoli-Fezzan-Bornu,
3. Cyrenaica-Kufra-Wadai, and the
4. Ghadames-Air-Kano routes.

The Morocco route diminished in importance with the outbreak of hostilities in the Songhai Empire in 1590s and the subsequent territorial rivalries between competing forces of Tuareg, Fulani, Arab, Bambara and Moorish made the route insecure. Similarly internal wars in the Bornu Empire in 1830s reduced the security of the Bornu route and diverted its traffic to the Kano route. The remaining two routes, Ghadames and Wadai survived the ravages of Sudanic wars and became the main trade and migratory routes to Kano and Hausaland in general. They eclipsed only with the coming of colonialism from 1900.

The Wadai route was virtually religious as it was used mainly by the Sanusiyya brotherhood especially after 1843. *Zawiya*s (lodging, headquarters) of the brotherhood littered the route and served as the main pathway through which the brotherhood philosophy filtered to Hausaland. The Ghadames-Kano route was the most commercially important and was protected by Azger and Kel Owi Tuareg militia whose livelihood depend on the commercial success of the route; so they chose to defend it rather than, as was usually their practice, raid it.

Chapter 10 | Abdallah U. Adamu, in
A.I. Tanko and S.B. Momale (Eds.)
*Kano: Environment, Society and Development*
London & Abuja, Adonis & Abbey Publishers

Just as Kano was an important terminus and *entrepôt*, Ghadames was an important starting point where caravans from Tripoli, Tunis and Algeria assembled there before they departed to Kano. A report noted that:

> The pioneers of the caravan trade were the merchants of Ghadames, then as now a small unimportant town without local trade, near the Tunisian frontier, about 20 days from Tripoli, who by their superior intelligence, capabilities and honesty, and aided by the geographical position of their birth-place in reference to the caravan routes, established themselves many years ago in the town of Tripoli and enjoyed the monopoly of the trade. They sent periodically consignment of goods to their agents in Ghat, Kanem, Bornu, Kan and Timbuctu, receiving in exchange ivory, ostrich feathers and god dust for sale in Tripoli and subsequent export to European markets (Johnson 1976: 109).

Ghadames still retained in the 19th century the position it enjoyed in the days of Leo Africanus as the home of most of the bankers and wholesalers and the Headquarters of most of the trading firms operating in the interior (Boahen 1962: 354).

## The Ghadames- Aïr-Kano Route

The Ghadames to Kano route[3] was laboriously slow. The daily travel rate rarely exceeded 12 miles. It was six or seven weeks with costs and risks through places such as Zinder, Agades, Arlit, Ghat and Ghadames. In peaceful times, the caravan journey used to take about eighteen months, and the profits could be as high as 50%.

The goods carried southwards by the Saharan caravans in the 1890s were similar to those carried earlier in the centuries. The British consul in Tripoli estimated in 1891 that Manchester cottons, white long cloths formed 70% of the total. Others included Austrian wool and sugar, satin from Bohemia, tea from China (via Malta), Bulgarian perfume (via Constantinople), beads, jewellery and a small quantity of hardware, and some arms and ammunition (Johnson 1976). The northbound cargo from Kano to Tripoli was Kano cloth, ivory, ostrich feathers, hides and leather, and slaves (most of which came from Bornu, helped in great measure by Rabah's invasion). According to Johnson,

Chapter 10 | Abdallah U. Adamu, in
A.I. Tanko and S.B. Momale (Eds.)
*Kano: Environment, Society and Development*
London & Abuja, Adonis & Abbey Publishers

the most interesting of the business houses in Tripoli was that of El Haj Mohammed; the father was resident at Ghat, one of his sons, Mahomed (sic) el-Assouad ['the black'] of Ghadames was at Tripoli, and another son was at Ghadames; seven sons made purchases in the Sudan; 'they are all negroes'-evidently they have been marrying in Hausaland for some generations (Johnson 1976: 110).

Other famous trading houses with branches in Kano included the family business of Ganaba brothers (who later became central figures in Sanusiyya *tariqa*), El-Tseni family of Ghadames who intermarried with Tuareg families. When the caravans arrived in Kano,

Quarters are taken up by the Arabs and goods opened for sale and native produce bought. The length of stay, varying from six months to twelve months, depends upon the scarcity or otherwise of native products. A rude currency, consisting of strings of small shells of different values, is much used, also a few Maria Theresa dollars, but bartering is also frequent. From this point some few Arabs make their way to Sokoto and Timbuktu, but the trade there is not important (Johnson 1976: 112).

In order to meet the demand of Hausaland for North African goods and services, and at the same time expand their own trading activities therein, the Tripolitanians took with them a large number of Hausa apprentice workers to Tripoli and trained them in various trades. At the beginning of their training, the workers would be taught religious knowledge and Arabic language after which they would be divided into four groups.

The first group were taught tailoring - general cloth making and embroidery. The second group learnt leatherworks - such as shoe-making and horse riding accoutrements. The third group was given charge of shops to learn the art of buying and selling as well as keeping the records of the commodities and stores. They were taught simple arithmetic in order to keep accounts and record weight and measures. The women workers who made the fourth group were taught how to cook various North African dishes and sweets. They learnt how to prepare dishes such as *Alfatat, Alkubus, Gurasa, Kuskus, Kudun-Kurno, Sunnasir* and sweets like *Alkaki, Algaragis, Tammaset, Greba* and *Bakilawa* - which all soon enough became part of standard Kano cuisine.

Chapter 10 | Abdallah U. Adamu, in
A.I. Tanko and S.B. Momale (Eds.)
*Kano: Environment, Society and Development*
London & Abuja, Adonis & Abbey Publishers

Along with this training programme the Arabs established some trading posts in Tripoli, Ghat, Ghadames and Zinder as depots where commodities from Tripoli and Kano met and changed hands and destination. Trained workers were settled in these posts for various assignments. The trained leather workers who were brought to Kano were also settled at the following wards - where shoes and horse tackles were made - near their mentors: Dala, Chiromawa, Dukurawa, Mandawari, Marmara, Alfindiki and Zangon Kofar Mata. The tailors were settled at the following areas which supplied the markets with Arab ready-made clothes: Lungun-Bulala near Dala hill; Dandalin Turawa, and Zauran Mallam in Danbazzau wards amongst others.

The third group, the shop keepers, appeared to be the most important group among the Arab apprentice workers. This group represented their mentors in all their trading undertakings, travelling with the wares of their mentors from one place to another selling and buying. It was they who took Arab goods and commodities to places like Borno, Bida and Ilorin. They bought cattle from Chad and Adamawa and sold them in the south.

It should be pointed out that not all of the North African traders preferred to settle permanently in Hausaland for trading purposes. As a matter of fact, there were some who had very large trading interests in Kano but never came to see it. For example, a Trabulus businessman, Zumit, entrusted all his trading enterprise to his trained Hausa worker, one Abubakar who settled at Kofar Mata ward in the city. It was this Abubakar who took the trade caravan of his mentor from Kano to Tripoli and back. Abubakar also recruited his own workers and trained them to help him carry out successfully the business of his mentor in Kano.

According to Dumber (1971), the Tuareg of Agades, the Bugaje of Damargu (Tanut) and the Agalawa (Nigeriène Tuareg) donkey breeders had a big role in making the North African trade a success in Hausaland. Apart from their own trade in salt and potash from Agades and Bilma (Arklet) the Tuareg provided camels for transport. The Agalawa and the Bugaje were employed as camel and donkey drivers. The Agalawa soon became guides in caravan routes all over the Hausaland.

The Tripoli caravan trade established many camping areas (*Zango*) from Kano to Tripoli. Some of these *Zangos* such as Zinder

Chapter 10 | Abdallah U. Adamu, in
A.I. Tanko and S.B. Momale (Eds.)
*Kano: Environment, Society and Development*
London & Abuja, Adonis & Abbey Publishers

(Damagaran) and Damargu (Tarut) grew as important towns which tried to become commercial rivals to Kano.

## The Cyrenaica-Kufra-Wadai Route

The second caravan route was eastwards leading from Kano to Chad and peripheral regions. There were three groups of traders that used this route for trading activities from their countries to Kano. The first were Arabs and Tubu traders. The second were the Kanuri and the third were Udawa and Fulatamare. The first group, the Arabs among them the bakkara tribes of the Sudan brought large herds of cattle from the following towns in Sudan and Chad: Atiye, Bargazal (Bahrnal-Ghazal), Dagana, Abashe, Wadai.[4]

This was the route which led through Borno-Wadai-Darfur- Nile in Egypt (Johnston 1967). The travelling organization of Sudanese Arabs was similar to those of their counterparts who followed the first route: Tripoli-Kano. They too employed a number of apprentice workers who followed the cattle while the mentors remained at home. Some goods and other provisions were carried by Dan-Bahari breed of donkeys, by far larger and stronger than the normal Hausa donkeys, with tremendous body power and ability to carry heavy loads and endure long travels.

The Sudan-Chad cattle traders made many camping places along their routes. For example, when they entered Borno they always stopped at Gaidam and Nguru before they moved to the next camp at Mallam-Madori in Hadejia Emirate. From Mallam-Madori their next camping place was Danzomo town in Tumbi (now Gumel Emirate). It was from this town of Danzomo, that the traders used to split into two groups. Those who would like to sell their cattle quickly so that they could get their money and buy their needs in the city and go back home earlier would head for Wudil market. On the way they would pass through many towns like Kaugama, Ringim, Zugaci, Alitini, Gogel and lastly Wudil. On reaching the market at Wudil, the traders would meet their customers among whom were the cattle dealers from Ilorin and Bida. As the Wudil Market was held every Friday of the week, it was convenient for the Ilorin and Bida cattle buyers who came through Zazzau emirate. In that respect, the buyers would not have to come to Kurmi Market to make their purchases. Further, cattle

Chapter 10 | Abdallah U. Adamu, in
A.I. Tanko and S.B. Momale (Eds.)
*Kano: Environment, Society and Development*
London & Abuja, Adonis & Abbey Publishers

133

in Wudil market were cheaper especially towards the end of the day when the cattle owners were anxious to sell and go to the city.

The other group which intended to reach the Kurmi Market in Kano city would continue their journey and encamp at Gabari. It was from Gabari that the caravans would enter the city through Kofar Mata gate. Immediately after the city gate and still a little distance from the Kurmi Market was a shallow muddy stream, a tributary of 'Yar Zage River. In order to make their passage easier logs of trees were felled down and placed across the shallow stream so that people and animals could pass without getting stuck in the mud. The Arabs named this place *Al-Kantara* meaning a bridge in Arabic - thus unwittingly giving the area a name. The journey always terminated at 'Yan Shanu, east of the Kurmi Market.

The Sudan-Chad traders bought the following, amongst other things, in Kano: tea and sugar, horse tackle, swords and coral beads, earrings, bangles and anklets. They also bought the famous Kano woven cloths such as *Kore* and *Tukurdi* dyed cloth for women (*Marra-Wahada*), white and blue color gown (*Dawingashau*) black gown (*Chilin*), shoes and many other items.

The second group the Kanuri brought to Kano potash of different qualities such as *Ungurnu* and *Gwangwarasa*. They also came with mats for different uses; made grass-fiber containers such as *Sanho* and *Cukurfa* as well as twisted ropes. The Kanuri camping area in the city was (also) in the eastern part of the market. The place is now called *Zangon-Barebari* (the encampment of the Kanuri) after their Hausa name. Their trade site was always adjacent to 'Yan Shanu on the Northern part of the market, just across the Jakara River. The Kanuri trades in Kano were very much local and their articles were sold by Hausa traders in many old markets throughout the Emirate.

The last, but by far not the least, were the Uda tribes who came from Gegemi in Dabinanci, or Dabinuwa Island bordering Chad from the Republic of Niger. These tribes came to Kano with their flocks of sheep and goats. They also brought ostriches with their ornamental feathers. These ostrich feathers were among the articles that the North African Arab exported from Kano to other parts of the world.

It was not surprising to find that all these three groups of traders who followed the same routes lived near each other occupying a very large area east of the Kurmi Market. Thus places such as 'Yan Shanu,

Chapter 10 | Abdallah U. Adamu, in
A.I. Tanko and S.B. Momale (Eds.)
*Kano: Environment, Society and Development*
London & Abuja, Adonis & Abbey Publishers

'Yan Awaki and 'Yan Kanwa in the Kurmi Market are still known by such trade-linked names.

All these groups were under the protection of *Sarkin Zango*. The office of *Sarkin Zango* was usually held by a distinguished trader who travelled far and wide and can speak a variety of languages - a necessary qualification to understand the various linguistic groups under his domain. This type of *de facto* official was at certain times an interpreter in the Amir's palace as well as in the *Alkali* courts. Sarkin Zango was not an official of the Emirate like village or district head, but he was recognized by the *Amir* to host the traders and protect their business against unscrupulous native traders who might have been tempted to exploit the strangers. For this reason, the *Amir* appointed four of his own body guards (*Dogarai*) to help Sarkin Zango, so that the general public would know that the Sarkin Zango was *de facto* official of the palace. He hosted the Sudan-Chad traders, arranged for the sale of their cattle and other articles of trade and finally guided them to buy all their needs without being cheated by bad local traders. The Sarkin Zango fed his guest from the commissions he collected from the trade transactions.

## The Consolidation of the North African Community in Kano

The affairs of North African traders in Kano were under the control of a palace-appointed host, *Galadiman Kano*. This was because before the death of Sarkin Kano Dabo (1819-1846), the position of the Arabs was strengthened by a letter sent to Ibrahim Dabo by the Sultan of Sokoto to recognize a Ghadames merchant named Abande as the leader of the Arabs in Kano.

As far back as the reign of Sarkin Kano Abdullahi Barja (1438-52), Kano *Chronicle* records that the North African merchants were coming to Kano for trade. But the second Fulani *Amir* of Kano after the Jihad, Mallam Ibrahim Dabo (1819-1846) encouraged some of the Arabs to move to Kano from Katsina. This happened after the battle of Maradi in which Kano contingents under the leadership of the *Amir* participated. After the jihad the old Hausa dynasty of Katsina was driven away and finally settled in Maradi from where they continually raided the northern and western parts of the territory (see Barth 1890, Landeroin and Tilho1911, and Smith 1967).

Chapter 10    Abdallah U. Adamu, in
A.I. Tanko and S.B. Momale (Eds.)
*Kano: Environment, Society and Development*
London & Abuja, Adonis & Abbey Publishers

It was the inability of Katsina rulers to protect the Sahara traders that made the entire community, both Arabs and their Katsina middlemen and agents migrate to Kano[5] under their leader Abdullahi Kutkut. The newcomers settled at Kulkul on the western side of the *Kasuwan-Kurmi* [market by the jungle] by the main city market. The area became *Kulkul* due to the inability of the *Kanawa* to pronounce Abdullahi Kutkut's name properly.[6]

The arrival of Katsina and Wadai Arabs in Kano swelled the number of the North African traders already resident in Kano. *Amir Ibrahim Dabo*, realizing the importance of the old Kano tradition of respecting guests, entrusted the affairs of the Arabs in the hand of *Galadiman Kano*. Under the Galadima, there was an officer called *Gado-da-masu*, who as the protocol officer in the palace became the host of the Arabs. He was the one who would usher in all the foreign visitors to the palace for audience with the Amir. He looked after the accommodation of the Arabs in the wards around the Kurmi market such as:

- Dandalin Turawa,
- Durmin Kulkul (Yalwa),
- Shatsari,
- Dala,
- Dukurawa,
- Jingau,
- Alfindiki,
- Zaitawa,
- Kofar Wambai, and
- Yan Awaki.

A token number of fighting men under the command of *Gado-da-Masu* were always prepared to protect the Arab traders to and from the borders of the Emirate.

### Social Organization

The North African Arabs in Kano were divided into two racially separated groups. The first group were the citizens of Morocco, Tunisia, Libya and some parts of the Sudan. These controlled the trade

Chapter 10 | Abdallah U. Adamu, in
A.I. Tanko and S.B. Momale (Eds.)
*Kano: Environment, Society and Development*
London & Abuja, Adonis & Abbey Publishers

process in Kano. The second group was composed of African trade agents who worked for the Arabs. The members of the first group were mostly Arabs, and that of the second group were Hausa and Kanuri. The two groups were not known to have inter-married, and from all records it seemed that they maintained superior-subordinate relationship. However, there were many instances of intermarriages between the North Africans and their Hausa hosts, especially drawn from the Hausa elite class.

The Arabs made the decisions, employing their African agents to implement them. Both Arab financiers and African agents met regularly to work out various commercial strategies. Gradually the African agents adopted the Arab culture - wearing Arab clothes and bearing Arab names; in effect, becoming Black Arabs. Thus names such as Gashash, Bin Howaid, Zumit and Talib are common among contemporary families in Kano.

In their relationships with the Emirate administration, the Arabs enjoyed respect and confidence in the Amir's palace especially at the time of the *Amir* Abdullahi who was their host when he was the *Galadiman Kano*. The Palace gates were opened to them, and they used to pay their respects every Friday after offering the Friday prayers. It was during such occasion that new arrivals from North Africa were introduced to the Amir.

The Arabs settlers in Kano greatly admired and respected the entire leadership of the jihad of Shehu Usman Danfodiyo, and were especially comfortable with the Islamic leadership of the Kano Emirate. They respected all the famous Ulama of Hausaland and regarded them as their own Ulama. As for the *Amir* of Kano they addressed him the same way they used to address the Turkish sultans. Thus they addressed the *Amir* in such Arabic words as *Maulana Sultan Kano*, meaning Lord the *Amir* of Kano. An example of the high regards which the North African Arabs had for the Amirs of Kano was seen in the will of a Moroccan merchant who fell sick in Kano. The merchant, realizing that he was dying in Kano and had no relation around to hand over to him his properties, wrote a letter to the *Amir* of Kano Abdullahi Bin Dabo requesting the *Amir* to take over the property and put it into *Baital Mal* for the benefit of all the Muslims in the Emirate if none of his blood relation came to claim the property.

| Chapter 10 | Abdallah U. Adamu, in |
| | A.I. Tanko and S.B. Momale (Eds.) |
| | *Kano: Environment, Society and Development* |
| | London & Abuja, Adonis & Abbey Publishers |

Further, in their relation with Government of Kano, the Arabs proved themselves loyal and reliable friends, refraining from undue political interference in the Emirate affairs, since by and large, not only were they welcome in the community, but had all the privileges of high status foreigners. For instance, when the Arabs were asked to choose their representative in the palace, the Arabs in most cases choose one of their African agents to be their representative in anything affecting both the palace and the entire Kano community. This representative at the Amir's palace was *Mai Unguwar Larabawa,* who used to liaise between them and the palace.

Thus the Arabs always refrained from direct interference in internal affairs of the kingdom; preferring to allow their African agents to deal with all the matters concerning the community. These African agents, representing the Arabs, were trusted with the office of the Emirate treasury, *Ma'ajin Kano,* throughout the period of Jihad until 1963. Thus these Arab representatives in the palace were very successful in bringing harmonious relationship between the Arabs and the Kano community. One of the famous among them was Mas'ud Al-Faqih Bin Bubakar. Mas'ud was given the name of Al-Faqih because of his rich knowledge of Islamic jurisprudence.

### Commercial Activities

The establishment of the Jihad Government in Hausaland increased the demand for Arab products and merchandise. The Ulama and their disciples needed papers to write their dissertations; members of aristocratic class needed popular North African textile materials for their robes and turbans. The embroidered North African *Jubba* and its Tunisian trousers as well as their *Kalabus* hat were also in great demand. The Arab trading activities soon covered a very wide area across Hausaland from Chad in the east to Ilorin and Bida in the West. Some of the articles the Arabs brought across the desert could be put into following categories:

- *Horse Tackle:* With decorated robes and embroidered saddle covers ready-made embroidered cloth such as *jubba, Fulmuran, Zubuni, Jauha* and *Alkyabba.*

Chapter 10 | Abdallah U. Adamu, in
A.I. Tanko and S.B. Momale (Eds.)
*Kano: Environment, Society and Development*
London & Abuja, Adonis & Abbey Publishers

- *Textile Materials:* Such as white and brown calico, Silken materials, pink and sky blue (*Hatsaya* and *Muwambal*), Turbans of different colors including white harsa.
- *Thread and Natural:* Such as *Warwar* which was used for weaving *barage* cloth in Sakkwato, *Al-harini Mahudon*, used for embroidered native gowns, perfume and increase, paper, tea, sugar, and other materials.

The North African Arabs on the other hand, dealt in many articles of trade from Hausaland, not only for the North African markets, but also for both internal and external trades, in and outside their homeland. For example they dealt in:

- Hides and Skins,
- Ostrich feathers,
- Elephant tusk and rhinoceros' horn,
- Dyed shinning blouse gowns and turbans (*Kore* and *Turkudi),* and
- White and blue woven blankets.

Others were

- Millet and guinea corn,
- Calabash of different uses,
- Mortars and pestle,
- Wooden soup bowls,
- Straw-made food covers (*faifai).*
- Cattle,
- Sheep and Goats, and
- Borno Horses

Thus by this time a well-established community comprising of Arab elements from North Africa, the Sudan and Yemen had fully established itself in Kano. Subsequently there was the second influx of Arabs from Katsina and Zinder. One group settled at *Dandalin Turawa* [recreation place for white people] which became an extension of the *Kulkul* ward. Another settled at *Jingau* - an area to the

| Chapter 10 | Abdallah U. Adamu, in |
| | A.I. Tanko and S.B. Momale (Eds.) |
| | *Kano: Environment, Society and Development* |
| | London & Abuja, Adonis & Abbey Publishers |

north west of the Amir's palace where they kept their camels. Yet another group of Wadai origin and shoemakers by profession also came from Zinder and Katsina to settle at the foot of Dala hill where they established shoe factories principally to supply the needs of other Arabs. These latter arrivals were not the only shoemakers in the now bustling community since there were many local shoe merchants earlier trained as apprentices in North Africa by their Arab mentors. The earlier Arabs of Ghadames also established factories at Jingau where they made *Lantami* [Hausa: meaning "tongue" i.e. slippers with a large tongue] shoes for the Amirs of the western Sudan, some of which were even exported to Tripoli.

Like every newly emergent community in a strange land, the new settlers felt the need for a place where they could obtain their own sort of food so an inn called *Al-findiki* (from the Arabic *al-Funduq* an inn) was built and there such wheat-based foods as *al-kaki* [a small cake or biscuit made from sugar, wheat flour etc. and then fried], *al-kubus* [wheaten pudding eaten with soup], *al-garagis* [similar to *al-kaki* but baked not fried], *Gurasa* [flat wheaten loaves], *Kuskus* [cous-cous] and many other dishes were first introduced to Hausaland. These new foods attracted the attention of the *Amir* and ruling classes who sent their female slaves to be taught the new techniques. Thus from Kano, *al-Kama* or wheat foods spread to the rest of Hausaland.

The Arab enrichment of Hausa culture of Kano did not end there. When the Hausa leather workers saw the newly established shoe factories of Dala and Jingau-Alfindiki they were not slow in learning the new methods and styles. Indeed, so well and so quickly did they learn that they came to dominate the trade. It was they who introduced the silk embroidered slippers which were exported to Sokoto, Gwandu, Nupe and Adamawa for use by the upper classes.

Commercially, the industrial patronage by the Arabs stimulated the growth of industries in Kano. They financed local craftsmen by giving them advanced payments which enabled them to produce the desired commodities for the Arabs. One area that enjoyed this form of advanced-fee stimulus is the dyeing industry. For long time in the history of Kano the only dyeing industry known by the outsiders was the famous Kura-Bunkure dyeing industry which produced *Turkudi* or *Dan Kura* and other colored materials. But with strong Arab patronage and capital, other dyeing industries sprang-up in Kano city near the

Chapter 10 | Abdallah U. Adamu, in
A.I. Tanko and S.B. Momale (Eds.)
*Kano: Environment, Society and Development*
London & Abuja, Adonis & Abbey Publishers

Arabs wards, in addition to Karofin Kura and Karofin Bunkure in Rano district. The places in the city included:

- Karofin Kwalwa,
- Karofin Sheshe,
- Karofin Kofar Mata,
- Karofin Zage,
- Karofin Wanka da Shuni,
- Karofin Sudawa,
- Karofin Dagauda and
- Karofin Dala.

Another industry that received special attention of the Arabs was the leather industry. To stimulate the production of hides and skin in large quantities, the Arabs helped establish tanning industries in:

- Majemar Adakawa,
- Majemar Arzai,
- Majemar Kirfi and
- Majemar Kofar Wambai or Dukaui.

Other craftsmen that benefited from the development of trade in Kano were the woodworkers, black smiths and calabash decorators.

## Political Leadership

Before the *Amir* of Kano Ibrahim Dabo died in 1846, he received a letter from his overlord, the *Sarkin Musulmi* of Sokoto ordering him to recognize one al-Hajj Abande as the permanent agent of the Ghadames government in Kano. As the majority of the Arabs in Kano were originally from Ghadames or Ghat, the Ghadames authorities felt that there was a need for a consulate to look after the commercial and personal interests of their people. The appointment of Al-Hajj Abande gave the Arabs greater confidence and a feeling of security with the result that their markets in Dandali and Al-Findiki expanded greatly. Trade goods from Middle East and Europe became commoner than ever before to their extensive North African contacts. Local traders were employed as agents and they were given goods and money with

Chapter 10 | Abdallah U. Adamu, in
A.I. Tanko and S.B. Momale (Eds.)
*Kano: Environment, Society and Development*
London & Abuja, Adonis & Abbey Publishers

which to trade. Long distance traders (*fatake*) traveling to Borno and Chad in the East were financed as were others who traveled to Bida, Borgu, Gwanja and Dagombe. These activities resulted in the city of Kano becoming one of the busiest and wealthiest markets in West Africa.[7] By 1855 there were a number of *masu kudi* or men of sufficient wealth to be distinguished from their fellows in both the Arab and Hausa communities.

It should be recalled that the predominantly Arab mercantile community in Kano had hitherto remained neutral from the political intrigues of the Kano Emirate; preferring to concentrate their attention purely on commercial activities. However, the appointment of al-Hajj Abande as some sort of Consul dragged them into the political matrix of the Emirate.

As an Ambassador or Consul of a foreign government, Al-Hajj Abande became a great friend of the Kano Court; the rulers of Kano, especially Abdullahi, the fourth Amir (1855-1882), made him their confidant. This favour brought the Arabs to the palace frequently, either to pray for the success of a war-like expedition or to give gifts of swords and other military hardware to the Amir's war machinery. As the friendship between the Arabs and the Abdullahi became so close, the former enjoyed a considerable amount of security and protection for their activities. Perhaps not unexpectedly, this close association with foreign powerful influence and the local political forces brought the Arabs deep into a series of Kano palace political controversies.

### Arabs and Sufism in Kano

The Arabs contribution to its religious life was as important. The Arabs had their own Ulama who used to perform various religious ceremonies for the Arab community such as marriages, funeral and naming ceremonies as well as *Eid* and Friday prayers. Some of their Ulama were Hudana of Jingau who was an authority in Jewish History; Talib at-Tuwat, the Imam of their mosque; and Sheikh Abdul-kareem Muradal-Marakishi who lived in 'Yan Awaki wards.

Long before the arrival of the Arabs as a forceful community, the Qadiriyya *tariqa* [the path, a Sufi practice] had many followers in Kano. Yet it was the Arabs who regularized the process through the

Chapter 10 | Abdallah U. Adamu, in
A.I. Tanko and S.B. Momale (Eds.)
*Kano: Environment, Society and Development*
London & Abuja, Adonis & Abbey Publishers

establishment of regular weekly prayer meetings for new members of the movement. The Arabs also emphasized the use of *bandiri,* a sort of tambourine without the jingles - drums, which were played every Thursday evening following afternoon meeting.

Muhammadu Bello, first *Sarkin* Musulmi (1817 to 1837) in his two books on the Qadiriyya, *Miftah al-Sadad fi aqsam hadhihi 'l-bilad* and *al-Durar al-zahiriya al-salasil al-qadiriya* outlined all the procedures of the *hadra* [the weekly meeting of the brethren and the procedures of the meeting, in Hausa often as a synonym of tariqa]. Although there were no attempts to hold the weekly meetings by him or anyone else it should be noted that while Bello, like his father Shaykh Uthman, received the *wird* of the Qadiriyya from al-Mukhtar al-Kunti (1729 to 1811) the main source of most Qadiriyya spiritual genealogies in the Western Sudan, it was not until three Arabs from different parts of North Africa settled in Kano and began to hold weekly meetings of their individual tariqa, sometimes after 1883, that the practice of *bandiri* was adopted and spread.

The first of these men was Al-Hajj Muhammad Sagaiya al-Ghadamsi, who founded his *Zawiya* [a lodge, meeting place of members of the tariqa] in his house in the Alfindiki ward. The second was Shaykh Talib at-Tuwati[8] who introduced the Sanusiyya *tariqa* after settling in *Dandalin Turawa.* The third was Aliyu Musa, the first leader of the Shadhiliyya[9] in Kano.

Of these three *turuq* only the *Sanusiyya* ultimately failed to attract the people of Kano and this was because its leaders were not settlers but traders who only remained for short periods before returning to their homes.[10] However, its members were active. When Shaykh Talib returned to his home he was succeeded by Al-Hajj Ali Bishir. The new leader raised funds and constructed the first proper *Zawiya* to be built. According to the practice of the Sanusiyya, the *ikhwan* or brothers had to build and maintain their own mosque and meeting place but, as their number was small, Ali Bishir appealed to the other Arabs to take some responsibility towards its upkeep. The Arabs maintained the mosque and used it for their *id* celebrations and Friday prayers, until *Amir* Abbas (1903-1919) asked them to use the main city Mosque and to integrate with the other Muslims. This was not without some international reasons.

| Chapter 10 | Abdallah U. Adamu, in |
| --- | --- |
| | A.I. Tanko and S.B. Momale (Eds.) |
| | *Kano: Environment, Society and Development* |
| | London & Abuja, Adonis & Abbey Publishers |

For example, in 1909 about six years after the British conquest of Kano, the French army in Niger Republic intercepted a group of important wealthy Kano traders of Tripoli origin on their way to Kano for their usual trading purposes. Fika (1968) gave the names of these merchants as Muhammad Nassauf, El-Ghazla, Hadi Bushaghour, and Sa'id Ganaba. These merchants were arrested by the French on the suspicion of being Sanusiyya adherents. Although they were later released, an intelligence report was sent to the British Resident in Kano alerting him to the possible dangers of these new Tripolitanian arrivals waging a jihad against British and French colonial interests. A careful discussion between the then British Resident, Mr. Temple and the then *Amir* Muhammad Abbas confirmed the baseless nature of these allegations as the Tripolitanian Arabs had been living in Kano for decades without incident.

Thus, to allay the fears of the British, who may now start feeling uneasy with the activities of highly mobile and resourceful members of a society without much control, *Amir* Abbas then requested the Arabs to integrate their religious activities in the main Central mosque, to further confirm to the British and their allies that there was no hidden agenda in the Arab presence in Kano.

When Ali Bishir finally left Kano for his own country, he left the mosque in charge of the Shadiliyya leader Ali Musa. The Shadiliyya *ikhwan* undertook responsibility for its maintenance and held their weekly meetings there up to the present time.

## The British Occupation and the Migrant Lebanese in Kano

The British occupation of Kano in 1903 dealt more on creating effective colonial machinery that allowed maximum exploitation of colonized peoples, whereas other people who have arrived and settled in the Kano territory more or less integrated with the society, thus contributing to its rich diversity, the British came strictly as overlords, with a specific mission and agenda: that of control and economic exploitation.

Right on their heels was another group of Arab settlers whose presence had a lot of impact on Kano. These were the Lebanese. Working in close cohort with the British (albeit the British with considerable disdain and reluctance), they significantly altered

Chapter 10    Abdallah U. Adamu, in
A.I. Tanko and S.B. Momale (Eds.)
*Kano: Environment, Society and Development*
London & Abuja, Adonis & Abbey Publishers

the economic structure of the territory.Unlike the Tripolitanian Arabs a century before them, the Lebanese refused to integrate in the mainstream Kano social fabric. Indeed the only thing that made them different from the British was the fact that instead of coming to rule and exploit, as the British did, the Lebanese came to exploit. Like the British, they were indifferent to the mainstream life of *Kanawa*, although unlike the British they were ready enough to go and live into every nook and corner of the territory in the pursuit of their commercial interests. As Albasu (1989: 28) noted,

> The Lebanese in Kano are secretive about their motives for migration. The bulk of the Lebanese came to Kano in the 1930s and they were Muslims. It was a period when Lebanon fell under French rule and was also a period of the Great Depression. So it was not clear whether they came in protest (or anticipation) of a repressive French rule or in response to the Depression and its attendant economic difficulties.

While the other Arabs, especially the North Africans came to Kano through the Sahara, the Lebanese came through the Niger Delta - down south. By then the British had already established full control and thus their movements were carefully recorded. But since they were not in sufficient quantity to constitute a threat to British interests, they were largely ignored by the British, who treated them with the same contemptuous disdain they reserved for any other race.

The railroad link between Lagos and Kano, completed in 1911, opened up the territory to penetration via the coast in full force. The Lebanese have been steadily migrating from Lebanon to various parts of the world in droves since the 19th century. The age of exploration and stories of fabulous wealth to be made in uncharted lands by those few who settled in these lands served to attract yet more others, who established a large settlement in Lagos colony. Their penetration into the interior was hampered by the British who controlled access to the area and were not willing to allow any interest other than their own into the areas.

The first Lebanese whose migration was recorded by the colonial officers were two brothers who came to Kano from Lagos in 1903, although they did not settle in the territory until 1907 (Albasu 1989). However, the first migrant to settle permanently in Kano city was

Chapter 10 | Abdallah U. Adamu, in
A.I. Tanko and S.B. Momale (Eds.)
*Kano: Environment, Society and Development*
London & Abuja, Adonis & Abbey Publishers

recorded as Seman Naoum in 1912. Like all the other Lebanese that were to follow, he was basically a trader in European goods.

The cultural aloofness of the Lebanese in early Kano were noted in the fact that when the British decided to implement the policy of racial separation and create their own reservation areas, the few Lebanese settlers applied for permission to leave the city and settle in the European areas. The British refused to allow the Lebanese to be their neighbours. Instead, in "1913 an area consisting of twelve plots was marked out west of the railway for "colored traders" (Albasu 1989: 206) meaning the Lebanese.

This area (the entire stretch of present-day Ibrahim Taiwo Road in Kano, starting from [today's] Radio Kano and ending at El-Duniya/Kwanar Singa junction) eventually became the Syrian Quarters, and from 1915 a home to any non-European who wished to pitch his business in the area; although it was dominated by the Lebanese. Seman Naoum the first Lebanese to settle in Kano city, almost immediately moved to the new settlement - ending perhaps the shortest duration of migrant stay in the territory. Eventually more Lebanese arrived in Kano, but they were never fully integrated into the Kano ethnic identity in the same way the other Arabs were. There were three reasons for this.

First, most of the early Lebanese to Kano were Christians and had little empathy with the Muslim Hausa. Again, they refused to stay in the city where they stand out, unlike other Christian African migrants (e.g. the Yoruba) who blended. Secondly, the subsequent Lebanese arrivals were Shiite Muslims creating a wider gap between the predominantly Hausa Sunni Muslims and their own brand of Islam. Third, they simply did not consider the African population as part of their anthropological universe. The few that did married Hausa women often ended up divorcing them when they got wealthy enough to get a wife imported for them from Lebanon (Albasu 1989). The Lebanese adopted this same strategy in other parts of West Africa where they settled. Fouad Khuri (1968: 90) recounts such practices - and their consequences as follows:

> The divorce of African wives by their Lebanese husbands, resulting from the latter's acquisition of wealth and the subsequent enlargement of their community, has created a mulatto group which recognizes itself to be neither African nor Lebanese but a separate, enclosed community. This is

Chapter 10 | Abdallah U. Adamu, in
A.I. Tanko and S.B. Momale (Eds.)
*Kano: Environment, Society and Development*
London & Abuja, Adonis & Abbey Publishers

true of Sierra Leone, Guinea, Senegal and in other West African countries where children belong to the father's kin and where the conflict in cultural practices between the Lebanese and the Africans has alienated the mulattoes from both groups.

The conflict in cultural practices between the Kano Lebanese and the Kano Hausa was, as said earlier, due to the Shiite/Sunni divide which is simply irreconcilable even if both the sides are ready to accommodate each other's views.

From Albasu's accounts, the first main business the Lebanese got involved in was cattle run from Kano to Lagos via Ibadan. They were, however, forced to pull out due to hostilities from long-established Hausa cattle dealers. Further, the success of the cattle-trade relied heavily on the credit system, which the Lebanese were unfamiliar with. Their next focus was kolanut trade running smack into the same ethnic monopoly they encountered in cattle-trading. The kolanut trade had been dominated by the Hausa caravans. It was made clear to the few Lebanese adventurous enough to join the caravans that they were not welcome. They then attempted to create alternative sources for the kolanut by bringing different species from what was (and possibly still is) their main home base in Africa Sierra Leone, especially through the coastal routes. This failed when the Sierra Leone variety of kolanut started to be grown in large quantities in western Nigeria. They had to pull out of that also. They struck lucky, however, with the boom in groundnut demand.

The demand for, of all things, soap, led to demands for groundnut oil which was found by European industrialists to be a better ingredient than animal fat. Demand for groundnut shot up with the use of groundnut oil in margarine manufacture. Large export of groundnuts however began after the railroad was opened in 1911.

Right from the beginning the trade was dominated by European firms. The Lebanese got involved only as dealers for the firms. Local Hausa traders were used as middlemen to procure the commodity. These middlemen such as Alhasan Dantata, Umaru Sharubutu, Maikano Agogo and Adamu Jakada and others were to form the nucleus of an oligarch class in the economic history of Kano, neatly supplanting the Europeans when they left.

However, in 1925 the European firms resolved (for an undocumented and therefore unknown reason) to stop dealing with

Chapter 10    Abdallah U. Adamu, in
A.I. Tanko and S.B. Momale (Eds.)
*Kano: Environment, Society and Development*
London & Abuja, Adonis & Abbey Publishers

Hausa middlemen which created a gap quickly filled by the Lebanese. With accumulated capital from their previous commercial forays, they now become groundnut buyers. With the Europeans buying only from the Lebanese, the latter formed a cartel which dictated the prices of purchase from the farmers (usually low) and sale to the firms (usually high). In addition, the Lebanese had by then made significant inroads into the road haulage. Thus a combination of European preferential patronage, Lebanese monopoly on the most lucrative trade deal of the decade, coupled with ownership of the haulage mechanism created a pull-factor that attracted more Lebanese to Kano as settlers from 1925.

While clearly maintaining a racial aloofness from the local populace, [11] the Lebanese were nevertheless ready to settle in areas no European would; adapt a life-style similar to that of the environment. More significantly, they were also ready to learn the local language if only to gain the confidence of the "natives", in the process of driving a hard bargain for the products they wanted to purchase. Throughout the colonial interregnum, the Lebanese adaptability remained a constant source of irritation to the British who encountered them in whatever economic activity they engage.

The indigenous merchants with the capital to compete with the Lebanese, seeing that they have been effectively marginalized, protested to Emir Abdullahi Bayero (1926-1953) who in turn lodged a complaint with the colonial authorities which led to the relaxation of the laws.

In compliance, and to break the Lebanese monopoly in the groundnut trade, the European firms opened canteens in various rural locations such as Daura, Mai Aduwa, Dambatta, Malam Madori, Kazaure, Gagarawa and others. Surprisingly enough, this was to enable the European firms to buy groundnut directly from the source in the hands of the same people (Hausa) that they resolved not to buy a few years earlier. This was perhaps due to the policy change instituted as a result of the protests of indigenous merchants to the Emir. Sensing a change in action (and possible fortunes), the Lebanese moved quickly in 1929 to acquire plots in the same canteen locations as the European firms. Since they had already penetrated deep into the hinterland, living there was quite an easy task.

The world-wide recession of the 1930s, followed by the onset of World War II reduced the value of Nigeria's agricultural products.

Chapter 10 | Abdallah U. Adamu, in
A.I. Tanko and S.B. Momale (Eds.)
*Kano: Environment, Society and Development*
London & Abuja, Adonis & Abbey Publishers

When the groundnut boom ended, the Lebanese next attempted to go into beans and maize production facing the same stonewall of ethnic dominance and monopoly from the Hausa, so they abandoned that. Ironically, during the war years, the European firms formed a cartel which refused to patronize non-European traders, particularly the Lebanese. Saul Raccah (not really a Lebanese, though associating with them), was the first to be allowed to join the cartel in 1941 and only after a legal protest. Constitutional changes and politics ensured the complete pull-out of the Lebanese from the agricultural commodities to textiles and industrial concerns.

Although unsettled by the British conquest of Kano in 1903, the Tripolitanian Arabs did not feel threatened since they had been so entrenched in the city culture to be easily removed. However, two factors motivated a movement of quite a few of them from the city to a new-layout at the outskirts of the city created by the British. First, with the arrival of railroad to Kano in 1911 it was clear that the trans-Saharan trade route of camels, donkeys and mules is now a dead-end. The Tripolitanian Kano Arabs, already aware of world-wide trends in trade through their Mediterranean links, clearly perceived the new rail as heralding an era of improved movement of goods; more volume more variety all brought faster, cheaper and more efficiently. As noted by Johnson (1976: 99), in 1909,

> The Arab traders at Kano already appreciate the advantages of comparatively rapid transport, and the more valuable imported articles of trade are now forwarded from England, Morocco and Tripoli by means of the parcel post. These traders will not be slow to recognize the benefits that the railway will confer by reducing the risks to loss and facilitating the realisation of their more bulky exports, and it seem more than probable that the large trans-Saharan trade to Tripoli will be diverted to the Niger.

Thus quite a few of the Kano Arabs seized the opportunity of enhanced commercial participation and moved out of the city. Although large scale movement did not probably happen until after 1949 when the lay-out was fully completed, nevertheless many did move to the Syrian Quarters initially in 1919. To the British, the Lebanese and the Tripolitanian Kano Arabs are variations of the same theme, and as such are combinable.[12] The commercial focus of those

Chapter 10 | Abdallah U. Adamu, in
A.I. Tanko and S.B. Momale (Eds.)
*Kano: Environment, Society and Development*
London & Abuja, Adonis & Abbey Publishers

whose choice was to remain in the city changed to Bornu and the Chad Basin (Paden 1973: 31).

Secondly, the movement of some of the Kano Arabs out of the city would have been encouraged by the British to clearly stem any "mahdist" inclinations as these more aware citizens may incite among ordinary "natives". This was made all the more evident by the fact that when the British opened the first western type school in 1909, among the first set of "commoners" to attend the school were some Kano Arabs[13] at a time when the school was being experimented on Kano Mallams or the children of the ruling houses (Williams 1960, Graham 1966).

The British apprehension was strengthened by the concern that traditional links (though never really military) between the Kano Arabs and North Africa might facilitate the transfer of some of the tensions in the Maghreb to northern Nigeria at the eve of World War I (Paden 1973: 256).

To appease local merchants (essentially the oligarch cartel, but with an eye also on the Kano Arabs), the British created Fagge-Ta-Kudu, intended as a trading and residential area for indigenous traders so as to enhance their participation in the modern trade. The rather stringent building conditions specified for residency in Fagge-ta-Kudu made it difficult for many of the first allottees - all *Kanawa* - to actually utilize the land. Further, the location of the site at a valley (thus *kwari*, depression) made it unattractive to the indigenous oligarchs.

The Lebanese, already entrenched in the also newly created Syrian Quarters and thus looking for areas to expand, seized up the opportunity and entered into agreements with the allottees where they built the houses according to the colonial specifications, and could stay for as long as 20 years rent-free, after which they were to relinquish the house to the allottee. Changes in laws in 1953 however gave the Lebanese occupants the right of perpetual occupancy in these plots - giving them both Syrian Quarters and Fage-ta-Kudu, and in the process automatically dispossess the original Hausa allottees. Thus with the few Tripolitanian Kano Arabs already settled, both Fage Ta Kudu and the Syrian Quarters became more or less Arab quarters. Incidentally, Fage-Ta-Arewa, north to Fage-Ta-Kudu, was to also have its own "Arab Quarters" in the form of Yemenites.

Chapter 10 | Abdallah U. Adamu, in
A.I. Tanko and S.B. Momale (Eds.)
*Kano: Environment, Society and Development*
London & Abuja, Adonis & Abbey Publishers

## Contemporary Yemenite Arrivals in Kano

In addition to the Tripolitanian Arabs, now fully *Kanawas*, another set of Arabs (beside the Lebanese who remained culturally monolithic and as such, as much outsiders to Kano's cultural makeup as the inhabitants of Sabon Gari) that enriched the urban ecology of Kano were the Yemenite Arabs.[14]

The contemporary Yemenite settlement in Kano, like that of the Lebanese, was a colonial phenomenon. Agricultural practices and crops seemed to indicate some elements of early Yemenite arrival in the territory of Kano perhaps as a result of the collapse of the Ma'arib dam in Yemen in 5th century B.C.; and that they were most likely to have introduced dry-season farming, certainly introducing new Middle-eastern crops such as *albasa* (onion) and *alkama* (wheat) to the Kano agricultural system. The hypothesis of Yemenite migration in antiquity traces the settlers from Aden Region near the Ma'arib Dam, thus their familiarity with advanced agricultural practices.

The Yemenite arrival in Kano was a direct result of demand for skins and hides in European markets, particularly the United States. Towards late 19th century, Max Klein, an American industrialist established buying stations for leather and hides at Aden, Mogadishu, Mombasa and Dar es Salaam. Local merchants under a European manager made the trade effective, prosperous and lucrative by penetrating into the hinterland and buying the product. By 1905 when he re-located, he had established an effective network for the purchase of hides and leather. The popularity of "morocco leather" and the realization that it was actually Sokoto leather made Klein shift his operations from East Africa to North Africa. However, unable to repeat his success of using local agents to secure skins and hides in North Africa, he appointed his East African Agent, Luigi Ambrosini, to set up a buying station in the British occupied territories of Northern Nigeria (Shenton 1974).

On arrival in Kano, for that was effectively Northern Nigeria in the early stages of the occupation (Kaduna became ready as a newly built capital only in 1917) Ambrosini decided to repeat his East African formula by using local agents to purchase skins and hides. By now, however, he was working for the UAC. Realizing the Islamic nature of

| Chapter 10 | Abdallah U. Adamu, in |
| --- | --- |
| | A.I. Tanko and S.B. Momale (Eds.) |
| | *Kano: Environment, Society and Development* |
| | London & Abuja, Adonis & Abbey Publishers |

Kano and the surrounding territories, Ambrosini decided to import Yemenites nationals, where he had a strong base and use them as the local buying agents.

Thus perhaps not surprisingly, virtually all the Yemenites imported by the British in Kano were from South Yemen with capital city of Aden which itself was a part of the British Empire from 1839 to 1967.[15] The Yemenite choice, beside existing bureaucratic network already in place by Ambrosini, was based on the Yemenite experience with raising goats, sheep and cattle on a far more massive scale than *Kanawa*. They therefore effectively knew the leather trade.

Also being Arabs and Muslim (unlike the Lebanese who, although with a lot of Christian members, were avoided in all transactions by the British as much as possible) means that they would be more acceptable in the hinterland than the British. Again the British avoided the Lebanese in this partnership because the Yemenites were hired and therefore worked for the UAC or other subsidiaries of UAC. This was to lay the foundation for the subsequent engagement in the civil service. The Lebanese, on the other hand, were independent free-agents, also trying to cut in whereever the British trade direction went. Despite the Nigerian passports which made it easy to use Nigeria as a base (never really having accepted themselves as Nigerians), the Lebanese showed little inclination to be employed in the civil service like the Yemenites.

The first Yemenite arrival was Hassan Ali from Aden who settled first at Abuja Road (House No J6 in former France Road) Sabon Gari in 1919, followed by Abdulmalik who later became a P.Z. Agent (Bako 1990: 142).

Al Halaf, another Yemenite came from Aden through the Lagos to Kano rail in 1928, [16] and later encouraged others to follow him. Even though the British were willing to experiment with importing people from other parts of the world to help them exploit colonized territories, they were not ready to do it on massive scale, as they did with the establishment of Sabon Gari. This was possibly because the Yemenite would come to Kano with an enhanced awareness of what they wanted and with their militant background of historical conflicts, could easily constitute a security risk if imported on large scale. The earlier arrivals were therefore quite few, and carefully selected by L. Ambrosini.

Chapter 10 | Abdallah U. Adamu, in
A.I. Tanko and S.B. Momale (Eds.)
*Kano: Environment, Society and Development*
London & Abuja, Adonis & Abbey Publishers

The Yemenite agents were given monthly stipends and food rations, which are doubled if the agent gets married, especially to a local woman. Marriage bonded the agents to the community, and made them more acceptable - which in turn made them more productive to the colonial machination. What made it particularly easier was the fact that the Yemenite, unlike the Lebanese in Kano, married out of desire to be part of the community. The Lebanese, on the other hand married local women principally to negotiate access into hinterland markets. Once they became well established and rich, they divorced the local wives and 'imported' Lebanese wives from Lebanon. It was the Yemenite adaptability to life in Kano, as distinct from a preserved Aden[17] that made the Yemenite indelible streaks in the cultural configuration of Kano.[18] What made it even more variegated was the trans-Arab marriage relationships between the Yemenite Arabs and the Tripolitanian Arabs many of whom were literally neighbours, leading to the emergence of a distinct Kano Arab.

While it was principally the UAC that took the bulk of the responsibility for the importation and welfare of the Yemenite in Kano, other subsidiaries such as GBO, PZ and John Holt also got involved in the skins and hides and employed the Yemenites. Eventually, however, they became the sole licensed agents of PZ only.

Further, their responsibilities were widened to include other articles of trade. Thus they became outlets through which manufactured and imported goods brought into the country by PZ were sold at the village level. In spreading them to the rural areas, the European firms settled them into the already created canteens (which came to be referred to as *kanti*). Commodities sold in the *kanti* stores included textile, salt, sugar, detergents and spices. Upon sale of these commodities, the Yemenite agents were then required to purchase hides and leather for the parent company and send them via either road transport or railroad link to Kano. This was facilitated by the network of rail terminals in most of the major villages.

After World War II the demand for groundnut seemed to suddenly explode, and Kano, being a major agricultural basin, was poised to provide a hungry Europe with the base material needed to re-build bodies battered by the years of war. The colonial administration, using the existing company structure, now aided by a series of locally

Chapter 10 | Abdallah U. Adamu, in
A.I. Tanko and S.B. Momale (Eds.)
*Kano: Environment, Society and Development*
London & Abuja, Adonis & Abbey Publishers

**153**

absorbed oligarch agents readily got involved (see for instance Bashir 1983, 1985).

In the 1950s and with the prospects of Nigerian gaining independence by the end of the decade, it was clear that some alterations to British-Yemenite arrangement would have to be made. As a process of disengagement, the status of the Yemenite agents was changed to *Factor* in 1956. Under this arrangement, the Yemenite were no longer in the employee of the companies they represented. Initially, there were protests against being called Factor. But an elaborate explanation from the authorities seemed to palliate their fears. The Factor status gave them independence to sell their hides, leather and groundnut to any company or anyone they wished, but they must first seek clearance from the main company. This gave them some freedom to transact with whoever they liked. Those who accepted this arrangement had the name FACTOR stenciled on their frontage of their shops in the various locations.

In the 1960s when Nigeria gained independence, the status of the Yemenites was not clear. First the Yemeni Government sent a delegation to Nigeria specifically to the Yemenite communities asking them to repatriate to Yemen. Many choose to stay in Nigeria. This was as a result of an earlier meeting held between the community members and the Premier of the Northern Region, Sir Ahmadu Bello where their future plans were discussed. At the meeting the Premier assured that by the virtue of religion, and the inter-marriage patterns, the Yemenite are *de facto* Nigerians (at least Northern Nigerians). The Sardauna drew parallels to the earlier arrivals of the Tripolitanian Arabs, and in antiquity, the Yemenite migratory cluster to indicate that for all the Yemenites, Kano was home, and had been home for centuries. They were therefore asked to consider Kano (or other territories) their home. However, those who wanted to go back to Yemen were quite free to do so; but they were all urged to stay. To make it even easier for them, the Indigenization Decree promulgated excluded them; thus treating them as full Nigerians.

| Chapter 10 | Abdallah U. Adamu, in |
|---|---|
| | A.I. Tanko and S.B. Momale (Eds.) |
| | *Kano: Environment, Society and Development* |
| | London & Abuja, Adonis & Abbey Publishers |

## Intergroup Contact, Migrations and Community Formation

According to Castles (2002), two main models of migration and incorporation dominated academic and policy approaches in the late twentieth century. First, the settler model, according to which immigrants gradually integrate into economic and social relations, re-united or formed families and eventually became assimilated into the host society (sometimes over two or three generations). Second, the temporary migration model, according to which migrant workers stayed in the host country for a limited period, and maintained their affiliation with their country of origin.

Sociological explanations of migration focus on the importance of cultural and social capital. Cultural capital refers to knowledge of other societies and the opportunities they offer, as well as information about how to actually go about moving and seeking work elsewhere. Arab migrations to northern Nigeria fit very well with this explanation in the sense that there is a considerable similarity - bounded in religious norms - between the immigrants and natives. This, perhaps not surprising and despite the clear racial divide, did not raise many issues of racism and prejudice - precisely because the Arab immigrants are those in minority, and occupy privileged positions of economic power.

Elsewhere, considering that the World War II and its aftermath owe a lot of its mechanism to racial prejudices in Europe, it is not surprising that intergroup contact theories emerged after the war. In 1954 Gordon Allport assessed why prejudice among groups existed. He determined issues which if controlled would lead to improved group relations and reduced conflict and prejudice among groups. He proposed his Contact Theory, also known as the Intergroup Contact Theory. Many research studies have been performed using his contact theory to assess intergroup contact, attitude change and the reduction of prejudice (judgments formed without sufficient warrant) in various groups such as racial groups and disabled children with positive outcomes (Pettigrew and Tropp 2006). This theory, elegant as it is in explanation of intergroup perception, becomes useful in understanding Arab presence among the Hausa of Nigeria in the absence of any reported overt racism between the Arabs and their African hosts.

| Chapter 10 | Abdallah U. Adamu, in |
| --- | --- |
| | A.I. Tanko and S.B. Momale (Eds.) |
| | *Kano: Environment, Society and Development* |
| | London & Abuja, Adonis & Abbey Publishers |

Intergroup threat and conflict theorists (Blalock 1967; Blumer 1958; Riek, Mania, and Gaertner 2006; Stephan and Renfro 2003) demonstrate that perceived threat at the individual level underlies hostile attitudes towards immigrants. In many countries, immigrants evoke both material and symbolic threat perceptions (e.g., risk of losing economic resources, cultural and value differences of immigrants; Falomir et al. 2004). Intergroup contact theorists (Pettigrew and Tropp 2006), in contrast, show that opportunities for and frequency of contact with immigrants (e.g., friendships) lead to more tolerant attitudes through a reduction of perceived threat.

If politicized and confounded with other societal problems such as crime, the presence of immigrants in one region of a country may foster threat perceptions in other parts with little or no immigrant population. Intergroup contact theory, on the other hand, contends that culturally diverse societal contexts increase opportunities for and frequency of contacts with immigrants, giving rise to more positive attitudes towards them (Wagner et al. 2006; Schluter and Wagner 2008). It is suggested that intergroup contact effects leading to a reduction in prejudice occur when individuals are exposed to immigrants at a proximal level (e.g., municipality) where immigrants and members of the national majority can truly interact in their daily activities (Wagner et al. 2006; Schmid et al. 2008). "Culturally distinct" immigrant groups, whose members may wear visible signs of cultural or religious affiliation such as headscarves or other attire (and are sometimes also "visible" in terms of skin colour or ethnic features differing from national majority), are usually ranked low on the ethnic hierarchy.

The proportion of immigrants in a country or region is frequently used as a measure of cultural diversity without differentiating between different groups. But some immigrant groups are viewed more positively than others and enjoy a better reputation. In other words, in everyday thinking ethnic and immigrant groups are ranked as more or less attractive social partners and within society there is substantial consensus on this "ethnic hierarchy" (Hagendoorn 1995).

While the Arab presence in Kano for hundreds of years has altered the social anthropology of the territory, yet the Arab presence was not felt in many other spheres of public discourse. Beside the influence on Hausa on some items of food and clothing, even areas predominantly

Chapter 10    Abdallah U. Adamu, in
A.I. Tanko and S.B. Momale (Eds.)
*Kano: Environment, Society and Development*
London & Abuja, Adonis & Abbey Publishers

settled by Arabs are barely distinguished from the ethnic Hausa indigenes. This is because the Arab community are 'living apart together' with the Hausa community due to their inability to fully integrate, even though many have lost their original mother tongue. Interestingly enough, this lack of integration is not just between the Arabs and their African hosts, but also amongst the Arabs themselves. Thus there is little cultural interactivity between the Maghreb, Yemeni and Middle Eastern Arabs resident in Kano - with each occupying its self-designated 'quarters' and not venturing into others. Further, for the most part, the Arabs in Kano seemed impervious. The main group of Arabs in Kano that seemed focused or interested in international events were the Lebanese, who once in a while hold demonstrations through peaceful marches in the city on international issues that affected only Lebanon, but not other parts of the Arab world.

Ethnographic interactions I had with a sample of the Yemeni Arabs in Kano reveal a strong desire on their part to project themselves as 'Kanawa' or 'Hausa' when dealing with non-Arab hosts; but retaining a strong Arab identity with their kin. This is similar to Frode Jacobsen's (2009) study of the Hadrami Arabs from the Hadramawt provide in southern Yemen who migrated and settled in Indonesia. Integration with Indonesian society, however, is much easier for these Yemeni Arabs on the basis of racial similarities, than with African populations of northern Nigeria. Jacobsen (2009: 2) opens the door to further research by stating that:

> A few but very interesting recent anthropological studies of Hadrami communities around the Indian Ocean reveal that the fate of these migrant communities differ significantly from country to country, and even between different towns within the same country (as is the case for India), suggesting the need for in-depth ethnographic studies of each of the ways that Hadrami migrant cultures and societies have developed.

This would form a basis for a deeper ethnographic study of Hausa Arabs in a subsequent study on Race, Culture and Identity. This should provide insights into how intergroup contact theory applies to what I call 'reversed racial configurations' -which studies how a White minority becomes integrated into a Black majority.

Chapter 10 | Abdallah U. Adamu, in
A.I. Tanko and S.B. Momale (Eds.)
*Kano: Environment, Society and Development*
London & Abuja, Adonis & Abbey Publishers

# References

Adamu, Mahdi. 1974. *The Hausa Factor in West African* History. Ph.D. thesis, University of Birmingham.

Adamu, Muhammad Uba. 1968. 'Some Notes on the Influence of North African Traders in Kano', *Kano Studies*, 1 (4): 43-49.

Adamu, Muhammad Uba. 1998. Further notes on the influence of North African traders in Kano, being a paper presented at the International Conference on Cultural Interaction and Integration between North and Sub-Saharan Africa, Bayero University Kano, 4th -6th March, 1998.

Adamu, Muhammad Uba. 2000. Confluences and Influences - the Emergence of Kano as a City-State. Kano: Munawwar Books Foundation.

Akanji, Olajide O. 2011. 'The problem of belonging': the identity question and the dilemma of nation-building in Nigeria. *African Identities*, 9 (2): 117-132.

Albasu, Sabo U. 1989. *The Lebanese in Kano: An immigrant community in a Hausa-Muslim society in the colonial and post-colonial periods.* Department of History, Bayero University, Kano

Allport, Gordon W. 1954. *The Nature of Prejudice.* Reading, MA: Addison-Wesley.

Ambe-Uva, Terhemba Nom. 2011. 'Identity Politics and the Jos Crisis: Evidence, Lessons, and Challenges of Good Governance.' *World Futures: The Journal of General Evolution*, 67 (1): 58-78.

Bako, Ahmad. 1990. A Socio-Economic History of Sabon Gari, Kano, 1913-1989. Unpublished Ph.D. thesis, Department of History, Bayero University, Kano.

Barth, Heinrich. 1857. *Travels and Discoveries in North and Central Africa: Being a Journal of an Expedition Undertaken Under the Auspices of H.B.M.'s Government*, in the Years 1849-1855. New York: Harper & Bros.

Bashir, Ibrahim L. 1983. The Politics of Industrialization in Kano: Industries, Incentives and Indigenous Entrepreneurs, 1950-1980. Unpublished Ph.D. thesis, Boston University.

Bashir, Ibrahim L. 1985. 'Classicism, Conflict and Socio-Economic Transition in a changing society: The Case of Kano Oligarchy.' *Kano Studies* (New Series) 2 (3): 120-137.

Chapter 10 | Abdallah U. Adamu, in
A.I. Tanko and S.B. Momale (Eds.)
*Kano: Environment, Society and Development*
London & Abuja, Adonis & Abbey Publishers

Blalock, Hubert M. 1967. *Toward a Theory of Minority-Group Relations*. New York: Wiley.

Blumer, Herbert. 1958. *Race Prejudice as a Sense of Group Position*. Pacific Sociological Review 1:3-7.

Boahen, Adu A. 1962. 'The Caravan Trade in the Nineteenth Century.' *Journal of African History*, Vol. III (2): 349-359.

Castles, Stephen. 2002. 'Migration and Community Formation under Conditions of Globalization.' *International Migration Review*, 36 (4), 1143-1168.

Clapperton, Hugh et al. 1826. *Narrative of travels and discoveries in Northern and Central Africa: in the years 1822, 1823, and 1824*. London: John Murray, 1826.

Falomir-Pichastor, Juan Manuel, Daniel Munoz-Rojas, Federica Invernizzi, and Gabriel Mugny. 2004. 'Perceived In-Group Threat as a Factor Moderating the Influence of In-Group Norms on Discrimination Against Foreigners.' European Journal of Social Psychology 34 (2):135-53.

Fika, Adamu M. 1978. *Kano Civil War and British Over-rule, 1882-1940*. Oxford: University Press.

Graham, Sonia F. 1966. *Government and Mission Education in Northern Nigeria, 1900-1919 - with special reference to the work of Hanns Vischer*. Ibadan: University Press.

Hagendoorn, Louk. 1995. 'Intergroup Biases in Multiple Group Systems: The Perception of Ethnic Hierarchies.' In European Review of Social Psychology, ed. Wolfgang Stroebe and Miles Hewstone, 199-228. London: Wiley.

Ioratim-Uba, Godwin Aondona. 2009. 'Language endangerment and the violent ethnic conflict link in Middle Belt Nigeria.' *Journal of Multilingual & Multicultural Development*, 30 (5): 437-452,

Jacobsen, Frode F. 2009. *Hadrami Arabs in Present-day Indonesia-An Indonesia-oriented group with an Arab signature*. New York: Routledge.

Johnson, Marion. 1976. 'Calico-Caravans: The Tripoli-Kano Trade after 1880.' *Journal of African History*, Vol XVII (1): 95-117.

Johnston, Hugh Anthony Stephen. 1967. *The Fulani Empire of Sokoto* London: Oxford University Press.

Marty, Paul. 1931. *L'islam et les tribus dans la colonie du Niger*. Paris: Geuthner, 1931.

Chapter 10 | Abdallah U. Adamu, in
A.I. Tanko and S.B. Momale (Eds.)
*Kano: Environment, Society and Development*
London & Abuja, Adonis & Abbey Publishers

Moody, Joanna E. 1967. 'Paul Staudinger: An Early European Traveller to Kano.' *Kano Studies* 1 (3): 38-53.

Olzak, Susan. 2006. *The Global Dynamics of Racial and Ethnic Mobilization.* Stanford: The University Press.

Paden, John. 1973. *Religion and Political Culture in Kano.* Berkeley: California University Press.

Pettigrew Thomas F. 1971. *Racially Separate or Together?* New York: McGraw-Hill.

Pettigrew, Thomas F. and Linda R. Tropp. 2006. 'A Meta-Analytic Test of Intergroup Contact Theory.' Journal of Personality and Social Psychology 90 (5): 751-83.

Riek, Blake M., Eric W. Mania, and Samuel L. Gaertner. 2006. 'Intergroup Threat and Outgroup Attitudes: A Meta-Analytic Review.' *Personality and Social Psychology Review* 10 (4): 336-53.

Schluter, Elmar, and Ulrich Wagner. 2008. 'Regional Differences Matter: Examining the Dual Influence of the Regional Size of the Immigrant Population on Derogation of Immigrants in Europe.' International Journal of Comparative Sociology 49 (2/3): 153-73.

Shenton, Robert. 1977. 'A Note on the Origins of European Commerce in Northern Nigeria.' *Kano Studies,* New Series, 1 (2): 63-67.

Smith, Michael Garfield. 1967. "A Hausa Kingdom: Maradi under Dan Baskore" in *West African Kingdoms in the Nineteenth Century,* ed. Daryll Forde and P.M. Kabery, 93-122. London: Oxford University Press.

Stephan, Walter G., and C. Lausanne Renfro. 2003. 'The Role of Threat in Intergroup Relations.' In *From Prejudice to Intergroup Emotions: Differentiated Reactions to Social Groups,* ed. Diane M. Mackie and Eliot R. Smith, 191-207. New York: Psychology Press.

Tilho, Jean-Auguste-Marie. 1911. *Documents scientifiques de la Mission Tilho* (1906-09), Vol. 2, Paris: Imprimerie Nationale.

Trimingham, Joseph S. 1958. *Islam in West Africa.* London: Oxford University Press.

Wagner, Ulrich, Oliver Christ, Thomas F. Pettigrew, Jost Stellmacher, and Carina Wolf. 2006. 'Prejudice and Minority Proportion:

| Chapter 10 | Abdallah U. Adamu, in |
| | A.I. Tanko and S.B. Momale (Eds.) |
| | *Kano: Environment, Society and Development* |
| | London & Abuja, Adonis & Abbey Publishers |

Contact Instead of Threat Effects.' Social Psychology Quarterly 69 (4): 380-90.

Watson, Godwin. 1947. *Action for Unity.* New York: Harper.

Williams, D. H.. *A short survey of education in Northern Nigeria.* Kaduna: Government Printer, 1960

Williams, Robin M. Jr. 1947. *The Reduction of Intergroup Tensions.* New York: Soc. Sci. Res.Counc.

**Notes**

1. This Chapter is substantially updated from a series of other papers previously published by Dr. Muhammad Uba Adamu, and noted in the references. However, this update is also going to be the basis of an entirely new publication titled *Race, Culture and Identity: The Emergence of Hausa Arabs in Northern Nigeria* by the present author.

2. Although reference is constantly made to Tripolitanian Arabs, who later became *Kano Arabs*, it should be pointed out early enough that Arabs of Yemenite origin also contributed to the gene pool of Kano. Geographical reference points of the Arabs in this book is therefore for the purpose of distinguishing the contributions of the clusters of Kano Arabs.

3. As told to Muhammad Uba Adamu and related to me by Mahadi Ganaba, a Kano Arab who recalled the routing from his tradition, in an interview, Kano, 1966. See also Johnston (1967).

4. Interview with Alhaji Bature in his house at Kofar Wambai, 1965, where the Chad-Kano traders used to encamp.

5. Clapperton, who visited Kano and Katsina early in 1824, reported that "the principal commerce of the country (is) being carried on at Kano since Felatah conquest; nevertheless there (is) still a considerable trade," (p.391). There was still a sizeable community of Ghadames merchants there as well as another at Kano. Barth makes it clear that there was still a Ghadames community in Katsina when he visited the town in 1850 largely due to the fact that the route to Nupe (from Katsina) was practicable for camels while that from Kano was only suitable for horses and asses. However, "all the principal foreign merchants migrated to Kano, where they were beyond the reach of this constant struggle," Barth, 1857, Vol. I:.280.

6. This tradition is sustained in some cases up to the 20th Century. For instance, one of the most busiest junctions in Kano city is the *Tal'udu Junction*. From the name, one could mistakenly assume it had Arabic origins. Actually it was a corruption of Taylor Woodrow, the international construction company that constructed the busy highway.

7. While the focus of this study is on the impact of migrants on the cultural development of Kano, it must be stressed that Hausa in general and Kanawa in particular have also impacted the lives of other kingdoms, as demonstrated by Mahdi Adamu (1974).

Chapter 10 | Abdallah U. Adamu, in
A.I. Tanko and S.B. Momale (Eds.)
*Kano: Environment, Society and Development*
London & Abuja, Adonis & Abbey Publishers

8. Shaykh Talib is probably to be equated with Shaykh Muhammad Talib b. Mubaraq, originally from Ain Salah, who was initiated into the Sanusiyya by Sidi Muhammad al-Sanni, one of the leading missionaries of the Sanusiyya who was sent to Zinder, Bornu, and Bagirmi in 1897-8. He visited Kano in the course of his mission (Trimingham 1959). Marty (1931: 188) suggests that as-Sunni came to the area as early as 1892. He adds that Shaykh Talib was living in Zinder in 1931.

9. The Shadiliyya represents a doctrine rather than an organized tariqa. It is common in the far west of the Sudan, most groups are closed communities (Trimingham, 1959: .96-97).

10. Most of the adherents of the Sanusiyya were Arabs from the Fezzan, and Cyrenaica. With the decay of the Saharan trade they were among the first to abandon Kano concentrate on the Sanusi controlled Benghazi-Wadai route. Also the political decline of the Sanusiyya in face of European aggression must have played a part in its declining appeal to the inhabitants of the Sudan.

11. There were, for instance, very few incidences of inter-racial marriage involving the Lebanese; and according to Albasu, such marriages usually occur when the Lebanese is newly arrived, lonely and has no money to send for a bride from Lebanon. However, the moment he makes it and becomes wealthy, he usually divorces the African wife and marry a Lebanese one. Marriage by a Lebanese woman to an African is considered "an unforgivable betrayal" (see Albasu, particularly pages 405-409).

12. The Hausa generally perceive people as either *turawa* (white, or light skinned) or *baki* (Negroid or dark-skinned). The British in Kano preferred to be called *Turawa* (whites), rather than *Nasara* (Christians) - which was what the Kano people were calling them on their arrival; thus the place where the British stayed was called *Nassarawa* (where the *Nasara* live) - much to the chagrin of the British who detest the *Nasara* appellation. The preference of British for the term *Turawa* to refer to themselves, thus reinforced the apparent racial superiority of the Tripolitanian Kano Arabs who already lived in *Dandalin Turawa* (playground of the whites) in the city. However, there was no recorded evidence even from the folkloric oral tradition of any form of racism on the part of the Tripolitanian Kano Arabs or their ancestors. Their aggregation and clustering in clannish modes was no more racial than the same clannish cluster adopted by the Fulani and the Hausa in Kano. The clannish brotherhood merely serves as a forum for exchanging commonly shared preferences - a natural enough activity of any ethnic cluster. However, this does not seem to extend to the new generation of Lebanese in Kano. According to Albasu,

> The foundation settlers were poor, had little capital and had to work hard and save. Many of their children, however, now have adopted a flamboyant and vulgar lifestyle which irritates many and is the object of much criticism and resentment. Their contact with Africans is often limited to business associates, employees and domestic servants. They have often come to consider themselves increasingly as superior to the Hausa, and they flaunt their wealth, fancy sport cars, and high life style. (Albasu 1989: 414.)

Chapter 10 | Abdallah U. Adamu, in
A.I. Tanko and S.B. Momale (Eds.)
*Kano: Environment, Society and Development*
London & Abuja, Adonis & Abbey Publishers

13. Two notables were Ahmed Matident, who attended the Hanns Vischer (*Dan Hausa*) School and Katsina High College; and Muhammad Munir, Katsina High College. For more details, see Muhammad Uba Adamu, *Further notes on the influence of North African traders in Kano*, being a paper presented at the International Conference on Cultural Interaction and Integration between North and Sub-Saharan Africa, Bayero University Kano, 4th-6th March, 1998.

14. I am not as yet aware of records, besides those of antiquity, of arrival of contemporary arrival of Yemenites in the Kano territory. This is an area that seems to attract less attention, considering that the Yemenites were more entrenched in the Northern Nigerian economy than the Lebanese.

15. Yemen seemed to suffer from fractious history [from violent natural disasters (Ma'arib dam breakage in late 6th century) to being trampled by Egyptian, Ottoman and British armies in various stages of its history. Yemen as a republic was formed on May 22, 1990, when the People's Democratic Republic of Yemen (also called Yemen [Aden], or South Yemen) officially merged with the Yemen Arab Republic (also called Yemen [San'a`], or North Yemen).

16. Based on a series of interviews held by Muhammad Uba Adamu and related to me, with a number older Yemenite generations in Kano who were among the first wave of arrivals. Dr. Adamu said the interviews were held in various places in Kano in the 1970s. The main informants were the then notable Yemenite leaders such as Sa'if Nayer (80 years at the time of the discussions), Abdulla Nayer (78), Galeb Ahmed (90), Ali Ahmed (78), Ahmed Furhan (90), Fauz Hashim (age not indicated).

17. There is no San'a, Saba, Aden or even Ma'arib Roads in Kano to entrench the Yemenite homeland identity; but there is a Beirut Road, populated by, of course, predominantly the Lebanese. Appendix 1, however, gives a list of some of the inner city wards that have substantial Arab population. The point is that only the Lebanese seem to resist a high degree of integration, by enclaving themselves in the old 'Syrian Quarters' of the metropolitan Kano, which included Beirut Road. Other Arabs simply settled among the Hausa in the city.

18. Many of the earlier Yemenites came with their womenfolk. However, the latter Yemenites were, by and large, quite willing to marry (permanently) outside their dominant ethnic communities -- leading to the growth of many notable hybrid Yemenite-Fulani, and Yemenite-Hausa families not only in Kano, but throughout the northern territories. Further, the latter Yemenites seemed to have lost their Arabic language, using the Hausa as their only primary language of communication - further confirming their integration.

Chapter 10 | Abdallah U. Adamu, in
A.I. Tanko and S.B. Momale (Eds.)
*Kano: Environment, Society and Development*
London & Abuja, Adonis & Abbey Publishers

## Appendix 1: Ward Settlement of Arabs in Kano City

Of the 124 wards in the old Kano city, at least 25 were settled mainly by Tripolitanian Arabs and their variants. The settlement pattern of the 25 I given below

| S/N | Ward | Main Settlers |
|---|---|---|
| 1 | Adakawa | Adarawa (Nigeriène) |
| 2 | Agadasawa | Agadès Tuareg (Nigeriène) |
| 3 | Alfindiki | Tripolitanians |
| 4 | Alkantara | Tripolitanians |
| 5 | Arzai | Tripolitanians |
| 6 | Bakin Zuwo | Tripolitanians |
| 7 | Cediyar 'Yan-gurasa | Tripolitanians |
| 8 | Dandalin Turawa | Tripolitanians |
| 9 | Dogon Nama | Agalawa (Nigeriène Tuareg) |
| 10 | Dukurawa | Tripolitanians |
| 11 | Durumin Arbabi | Agadès Tuareg (Nigeriène) |
| 12 | Jingau | Tripolitanians |
| 13 | Madigawa | Agalawa (Nigeriène Tuareg) |
| 14 | Mai-Aduwa | Tripolitanians |
| 15 | Mararraba | Agalawa (Nigeriène Tuareg) |
| 16 | Rijiya Biyu | Tripolitanians |
| 17 | Sabon Sara | Agalawa (Nigeriène Tuareg) |
| 18 | Sanka | Tripolitanians |
| 19 | Sharfa]i | Tripolitanians |
| 20 | Sharifai | Tripolitanians |
| 21 | Shatsari | Tripolitanians |
| 22 | Sudawa | Sudanese |
| 23 | Tudun Makera | Tripolitanians |
| 24 | Yalwa | Agalawa (Nigeriène Tuareg) |
| 25 | Zango | Azben (Aïr Tuareg) |

Chapter 10 | Abdallah U. Adamu, in
A.I. Tanko and S.B. Momale (Eds.)
*Kano: Environment, Society and Development*
London & Abuja, Adonis & Abbey Publishers

# Chapter Eleven

## KANO CULTURAL MOSAICS

Ibrahim Badamasi Lambu

### Introduction

The concept of a "cultural mosaic" helps us conceptualize the diversity of regional and global culture. To some degree, it is possible to classify and differentiate one culture from another. This assertion ignores the problem of determining boundaries (Lambu, 2011a). While the natural landscapes sometime provide relatively influential cultural boundaries, there is often a great deal of interchange and mixing where cultures meet. This Chapter illustrates that ethnicity and cultural identity are not rigid. It also illustrates the cultural complexity that exist in very small areas of Kano like Badawa and Giginyu where cultural diversity is very pronounced. Religion is one of the major differences addressed in this paper because all crises in Kano has religious undertone.

From the geographer's perspective, the cultural transformation in contemporary Kano has reduced the distinctions between people of different cultural and ethnic background where the Hausa culture 'swallows' others. While this is occurring, other processes of fragmentation are occurring within the state especially in the religious culture of Kano. For example, polarization of brotherhood with Izala sect is becoming more pronounced than ever in the religious sphere of the Region (Lambu, 2011b) and this development accelerated sharp rivalry by introducing new religious teachings and practices. The old Ulama who acquired Islamic education through traditional way are most inclined to either Tijjaniya or Kadiriya Islamic sects while the elites and the modern Ulama (who read Islam under formal setting) constitutes the majority in Izala sect (Wakili, 2009). Even Christianity displays similar fashion where sects' affiliations are linked to ethnicity, origin and location (Lambu, 2011b). For instance the Christian Society of Nigeria (CSN) in Kano is Igbo inclined, while Christian Pentecostal Fellowship of Nigeria has Yoruba taste and ECWA/TEKAN is dominated by the Hausa Christains and other

| Chapter 11 | Ibrahim B. Lambu, in |
| | A.I. Tanko and S.B. Momale (Eds.) |
| | *Kano: Environment, Society and Development* |
| | London & Abuja, Adonis & Abbey Publishers |

165

Northern migrants. Note that the situation may appear different elsewhere but this reflects the situation in Kano.

## The Geography of Religion in Kano City

Islam is one of the dominant social institutions within Kano with over 99% (Adamu 1999, Ashafa 1982). While there are different varieties of Islamic faith most notably the *Sufi* orders of Kadiriyyah and Tijjaniyyah as well as the revolutionary Izala sect and the disguised buds of Shiites there are also Christian sects as presented on the Fig.11.1.

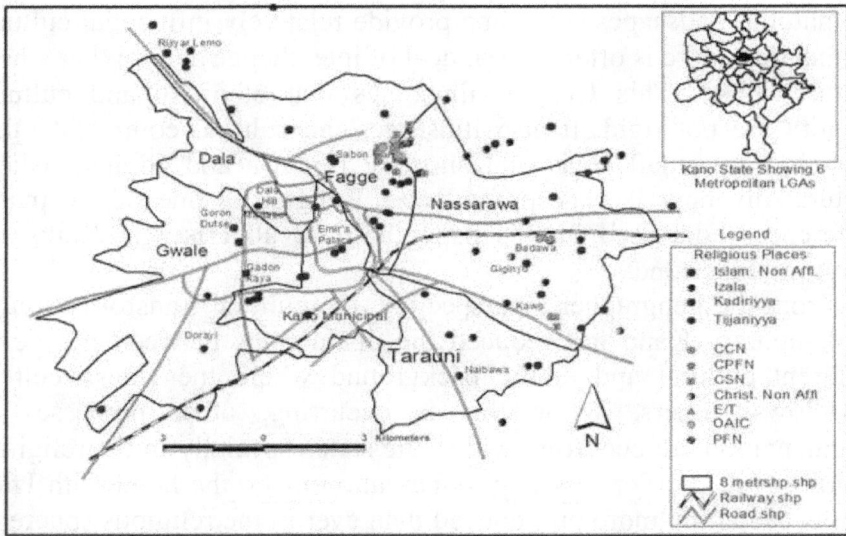

Source: Field Work (2011)

**Figure 11.1: Kano Metropolis Showing Areas of Religious Culture**

It is important to place Kano within the larger African community of Islam (Lambu, 2011b). While most people think about the Middle East as the Islamic world, Africa has become an important Islamic region in its own right. Contemporary estimates indicate that approximately one in three Africans is a Muslim. Islam is the predominant religion in Kano and even non Muslims are partially Islamized either in dress, in swearing oaths or in the forms of greetings

Chapter 11    Ibrahim B. Lambu, in
A.I. Tanko and S.B. Momale (Eds.)
*Kano: Environment, Society and Development*
London & Abuja, Adonis & Abbey Publishers

(uttering "Salam") especially in markets and other business arenas. In the city it is possible to establish the geographic pattern of religious clusters. Clearly, it is easy to say that the Muslims are the majority in the ancient city as well as the surrounding areas. However, it is possible to make exception in the Sabon Gari and other parts of Kano where there are mixtures of the Muslims and the Christians.

Islamic religion expanded from the center (in the old Kano city) radially to the peri-urban Kano dating back to 999AD (Adamu, 1999). Christianity, on the other hand, came to Kano with colonialism. For this the oldest Church in Kano was in 1926 (though older ones might have existed unnoticed). Trend Surface interpolation shows clearly the sphere of influence of the different religious land-marks (mosques, cemetaries, churches and schools) in the metropolitan Kano (Figure 11.2). It can be seen that while for most part of the metropolis, Islamic land-marks dominate, toward the northeastern part of Kano a sign of 'confluence' exists around Kawo, Giginyu and Badawa. These areas form the 'cultural melting pot' in Kano where people of different cultures and beliefs live together.

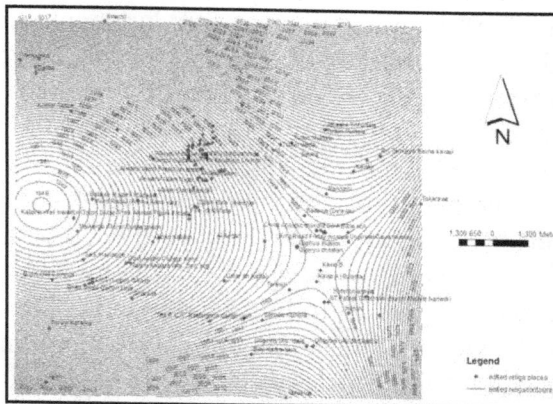

**Fig. 11.2 Trend Surface Mapping of Religious Distribution**

In order to explain the existence of border areas between the influences of the two religions, it is possible to trace it back to the colonial period. In other words, Kano (from colonial times) may be seen to continue to exist as a dual city with its one side having a large Muslim population spreading all over the metropolis but with a 'confined' area of non-Muslim populations.

Chapter 11 | Ibrahim B. Lambu, in
A.I. Tanko and S.B. Momale (Eds.)
*Kano: Environment, Society and Development*
London & Abuja, Adonis & Abbey Publishers

Generally, the analysis proves that in the case of Kano, as may be true for other cities in Nigeria, religious division is particularly acute because Nigeria's religious geography is strongly regionalized and in Kano, Christians are primarily localised around the Sabon Gari (including Kawo, Badawa and Giginyu) while the Muslims are heavily concentrated in the old city and the surrounding suburbs.

Christianity has its initial history in Kano from 1905 with the advent of colonialization in Kano (Paden 1973). The contingent of the Christian Missionary Society (CMS) that arrived Kano were not immediately accepted by the then Emir of Kano Aliyu in 1900, for which reason they settled at Zaria and later established their Mission in 1905 in the town (Crampton 1979 and Wakili 2009). That initial resistance to Christianity in Kano made the mission to focus attention to rural areas especially in the Maguzawa (Pagans) communities (Ubah: 1988, in Wakili 2009). It was much later that the Protestant Mission Churches like the Sudan Interior Mission (SIM), the Sudan United Mission (SUM) and Church Missionary Society (CMS) devised the use of western medical services and clinics including missionary schools as well as the use of the local language (Hausa) in sermons (Wakili, 2009), paving the way for Christianity in Kano.

Indigenization of the SIM was made by renaming it to Evangelical Churches of Western Africa (ECWA). The ECWA was dominated by Hausa Christians and other northern minorities. Kano as the economic capital of the north received the highest influx of other tribes who came to work in the newly established industrial factories. By 1966, there were over fifty six churches around the colonial established Township (the Sabon Gari). It was not long before it was clear that each of the dominions had an ethnic dominance. For instance, the Roman Catholics were dominated by the Igbo migrants while the orthodox Protestants were populated mostly by Yoruba group, while the northern Christians identified with the ECWA. Despite this pattern, the Pentecostals distinguished itself as a trans-ethnic dominion as its membership cut across all people from the different ethnic groups. Over time, the intense local resistance strengthened the Christian movements, uniting the believers irrespective of their differences. This gave birth to the Christian Association of Nigeria (CAN) which is more than a religious association as it also protects the political interests of its members.

Chapter 11 | Ibrahim B. Lambu, in
A.I. Tanko and S.B. Momale (Eds.)
*Kano: Environment, Society and Development*
London & Abuja, Adonis & Abbey Publishers

## The Kano Cultural Landscapes

One important dimension of Islam is that it sometimes serves as a trans-national and a trans-ethnic source of identity for its followers. This aspect of the faith is highly relevant to the situation of Kano. Muslims in the city have connection with other Muslims around the world. This connection is often expressed in the cultural landscape. Mosques, for example, often have architectural similarities with mosques in the Middle East. Minarets over mosque are the most visible element of this commonality; and a sign of architectural influence by the Muslim world - the Middle East. Sometimes the link between Nigerian Muslims and those in other countries is extremely direct. Saudi Arabia is one country with direct cultural ties with Kano. Apart from the mosques, houses in Kano share similar architectural designs as in many Islamic countries. Mode of dressing and ways of life are also similar.

Beyond trans-national identity, Islam has influenced and shaped the geographies of "sense of place" in conveying the meanings, emotional associations and unique characteristics that are associated with particular places. In this sense Kano is associated with many Islamic places and practices like the mosques, *Jumaat* (i.e. Friday) prayers and *Eid* celebrations among others. Another way through which Islam presents a "sense of place in Kano" is through the call to prayers, five times daily. This is important in the establishment of the daily rhythms of life in the city. The crier's loud voice, usually broadcast over a public address system, is an ever-present reminder to Muslims and non-Muslims alike that Islam is a dominant social institution in Kano.

Another socio-cultural practice that is variably influenced in Kano by Islam is polygamy. While the practice might have existed in the Region before the coming of Islam as practiced by the then *Maguzawa*, the Islamic religion is closely related to the contemporary practice of polygamy where maximum of four wives are allowed and this has contributed in the maintenance of social decency in Kano. The practice is particularly popular in the rural areas where the household is the fundamental unit of economic production. By having up to four

Chapter 11 | Ibrahim B. Lambu, in
A.I. Tanko and S.B. Momale (Eds.)
*Kano: Environment, Society and Development*
London & Abuja, Adonis & Abbey Publishers

wives, the head of the household gain access to the labour of many of the children from the different wives.

Age is another important social criterion within the society of Kano especially with rural communities. Every person is born into an "age set." These age-based groups facilitate social, educational and developmental activities of their members. They also emphasize the rites of passage that individuals go through during their lives. The oldest age sets are generally the most respected and powerful within local social life where hand shake is age-determined. Persons usually achieve the highest age level of full adulthood between the ages of 40 and 50. There are many examples of the way that status based on age manifests itself in Kano and in sub-Saharan Africa more broadly. Another important aspect of "generational geographies" is that retired persons often return to their homes to act as leader in the family or even the community. This is particularly important for those who lived in the city for much of their life. Many of these returnees maintain a house in their home area while they are semi-permanently away from their home area.

One important aspect of culture is language. Language is considered critical because it contains the collective histories and stories of its speakers. Whenever small minority languages become "extinct," much history and cultural richness is lost. Even with processes of cultural homogenization at work, Kano remains a linguistically unique area in Nigeria. Hausa is the official language in the Kano Palace despite the claim that the Emirate belongs to the Fulani clan.

## *Cultural Changes in the 20ᵗʰ Century*

Important changes in the twentieth century have diminished the importance and the nature of some of these cultural, religious and social norms. The coming of both Islam and Christianity has been the most important development impacting these socio-cultural institutions in and around Kano. Urbanization and modernization have also played important roles in these processes of change. The dynamism of the colonial and post-colonial periods, however, is not unique to the history and the geography of Kano, Nigeria or even Africa at large. African societies, like those throughout the world,

Chapter 11 | Ibrahim B. Lambu, in
A.I. Tanko and S.B. Momale (Eds.)
*Kano: Environment, Society and Development*
London & Abuja, Adonis & Abbey Publishers

have continually undergone social and cultural change of one kind or another. Youths through films and media adopt western cultures (viewed as immoral) from dresses, food and music and that is why many in Kano in the 21$^{st}$ century are yet to accept western education especially for the females.

Of course gender roles vary by geographical locations across Nigeria. In many parts of southern and central Nigeria, trading is principally carried out by women. For example, Yoruba women have a strong tradition as prominent and successful traders. In northern Nigeria and particularly Kano, however, trading is almost exclusively a male occupation. Mainly due to the practice of female seclusion (i.e. purdah), women of childbearing age are rarely seen in the public, and therefore, rarely serve as traders. With globalization, women are now out more than ever in the history Kano. Western education, media and communication industries expose the women to the present levels enabling them to unfold the shell of purdah. However with the high level of unemployment, even the educated women are left with limited options where matrimonial homes under polygamy continues to give shelter to the educated (sometimes graduate ladies) who are ready to join as second, third or even fourth wife especially if the groom is economically august.

## Conclusion

In most societies especially in Africa, both Islam and Christianity struggle to display presence and prestige; hence the proliferation of landmarks in different parts of our societies forming cultural mosaics. In Kano the continued proliferations of many cultures may be seen as fulfilments of the desire to be seen and heard. The concept of a transitional region illustrates the fact that ethnic and cultural characteristics are constantly changing, in some places much faster than others. Cultural dynamism may apply to Kano, Nigeria, Africa or even the international cultures as well. The cultural complexes and systems of present-day Kano are combination of those of many years ago. While it is impossible to take a static view of culture for illustration, it is also important to keep in mind that the culture is subject to change. It is the nature of the change that varies across spaces and cultures. As opposed to the views expressed especially in

Chapter 11    Ibrahim B. Lambu, in
A.I. Tanko and S.B. Momale (Eds.)
*Kano: Environment, Society and Development*
London & Abuja, Adonis & Abbey Publishers

the western world that African societies are static, the truth is that no culture can remain static for any long period especially as it continues to interact.

Kano people have been and will continue to interact with one another and with others from outside the Region. Existing stratification of wards in the ancient city of Kano like Dandalin Turawa, Karofin Sudawa, Nassarawa, Ayagi, and Tudun Nufawa all attest to the above fact. The concept of "fictive kinship" illustrates this idea very well as the level of inter marital relationship confuses the issue of identifying Kano man on facial, skin colour or any stereoscopic description. Many in Kano may have the *genes* of the Egyptians, the Sudanese, the Lebanese, the Malian, etc. which come from either of the parent. Kano's polity explains its old aged adage '... *ko da me kazo an fika'* [meaning '... there's someone ... better'] to infer that it is ready to accept and assimilate.

## References

Adamu, M.U (1999). Confluences and Influences: The emergence of Kano as a City State, Munawwara book foundation, Kano Ashafa, A.M. (1982). The Islamization of Kano before the Jihad: Kano study vol.1 No 3, 1982/85

Keegan, S (2009) Qualitative research: good decision making through understanding people, cultures and markets Typeset by Saxon Graphics Ltd, Derby Replika Press Pvt Ltd.

Lambu, I.B. (2011a); Culture and Nature: The co-actors in Climate Change, 52nd ANG, UDUS; Sokoto 2011

Lambu, I.B. (2011b): Culture and Development; In the Politics and Economy of Wudil, ABU Press Limited

Lambu I.B. (2011c): Culture and Nature: The co actors in climate change, a paper presented at 52nd Association of Nigerian Geographers (ANG) Usumanu Danfodio University Sokoto 2011.

Lambu, I.B. (2012a): Culture: Its Mystery and Paradox in Nigerian Leadership and Development, in Governance, Leadership and Nigerian Economy. A publication of Faculty of Social and Management Sciences, Bayero University Kano-Nigeria

Chapter 11 | Ibrahim B. Lambu, in
A.I. Tanko and S.B. Momale (Eds.)
*Kano: Environment, Society and Development*
London & Abuja, Adonis & Abbey Publishers

172

Lambu, I.B. (2012b): Cultural values and Environmental Sustainability in Nigeria; A publication of Faculty of Social and Management Sciences, Bayero University Kano-Nigeria

Lambu, I.B. (2012c): The role of culture on the sustainable use of energy for national development, a paper at International Conference on the future of Energy use in the Nigeria's Dry lands: Challenges and Opportunities from $12^{th}$ - $15^{th}$ November 2012 by DFID and DELPHI, Mumbaiyah BUK

Lambu, I. B. (2013): A Geographical Analysis of Religious Landscapes of Kano Metropolis, Unpublished PhD Thesis, Department of Geography, Bayero University, Kano

Liman, M.A. and Adamu, Y.M (2005): Urbanization and Spatial Development of Urban centers, in Northern Nigeria A century of Transformation 1903-2003, Arewa House; ABU.

Mahmud, A. (2007): An assessment of Tourism potential of Rurum, Kano state Nigeria. An unpublished M.Sc thesis, Geography Department B.U.K

Muhammad, I. T. (1999): Daular Usmaniyya; Rayuwar Shehu Usman Danfodiyo da Gwagwamarmayarsa. Hudahuda publishing company Ltd, Samaru Road Zaria.

Muhammad, A. (2010): The Paradox of Boko Haram, Moving image publishing ltd

Morril, R.L. and Kelley, M.B. (1970): 'The simulation of hospital use and the estimation of location efficiency', Geographical Analysis; John Wiley &Sons New York.

Nathan, G. (2000): Disaggregating Culture in Culture Matters; Basics Books ltd New York.

Neuman, W.L. (2003): Social Research Methods, U.S.A; Pearson Education Inc

Olofin, E.O (1985): Some aspect of the physical Geography of Kano region and some related responses.

Olofin, E.O (1989): Human responses to the Natural environment in Kanoregion Paden, J.N (1973): Religion and Political Culture in Kano; University of California press, Berkeley Los Angeles.

Sada, M. (2009): Space Technology for National Development. NASRDA quarterly magazines, vol.3 issue 5 2009.

Sambo, A.A. (2005): Research Methods in Education; Stirling-Horden Publishers (Nig.) Ltd.

| Chapter 11 | Ibrahim B. Lambu, in |
| | A.I. Tanko and S.B. Momale (Eds.) |
| | *Kano: Environment, Society and Development* |
| | London & Abuja, Adonis & Abbey Publishers |

173

Stace, L (2000): Culture, Mental model and National prosperity in Culture Matters; Basics Books ltd New York.

Wakili, H. (2009): Religious pluralism and Conflict in Northern Nigeria; Research report No 2 CRD, Kano

Yakubu, A.M. Jumare, I.M. Saed, A.G. (2005): Northern Nigeria: Century of Transformations, 1903-2003, Arewa House 2005.

Yusuf, L. (2009): Crises in cultural relevance and the role of culture in national development,     MAJASS; vol.1 No.1

Zaharadeen, M.S. (2011): Mosques as Learning Centers in Islam; The case of Sokoto Caliphate: A paper delivered at International Conference on the contribution of the Islamic world to Education 16th and 17th March, 2011 Bayero University Kano.

| Chapter 11 | Ibrahim B. Lambu, in |
| --- | --- |
|  | A.I. Tanko and S.B. Momale (Eds.) |
|  | *Kano: Environment, Society and Development* |
|  | London & Abuja, Adonis & Abbey Publishers |

**174**

# Chapter Twelve

## RURAL MARKETS

Ishaq Aliyu Abdulkarim

### Introduction

Rural Markets are defined as those segments of overall market of any economy, which are distinct from the other types of markets like stock market, commodity markets or Labor economics. Rural Markets constitute an important segment of the overall economy. For example, in the USA, out of about 3,000 counties, around 2,000 counties are rural, that is, non-urbanized, with population of 55 million. Typically, a rural market will represent a community in a rural area with a population of 2,500 to 30,000. In rural markets, trade like in urban market is characterized by direct sales but of small quantities of produce by producers to village traders and by retail sales to rural consumers. The rural markets normally form part of a local network and are usually arranged on a periodic basis, or specific week days. They are commonly organized at a central place in a village or district centre or beside a village's access road.

In many developing countries, rural markets are as important for the national economy as exports and international trade (Bromley, 1971). The role played by rural marketing systems in the economic development and the transformation of the economy of peasant farming societies has been widely recognized as being crucial for integrating these communities into the national economy and culture (see, Skinner, 1964; Hodder, 1965; Good, 1970; Bromley, 1971). Dixon (1974 cited in Lado 1988),for example, described the rural marketing systems as the most important 'multiplier' of economic development and a network through which information, new ideas and modern techniques can flow into the rural areas.

Rural markets in Nigeria constitute significant features of the rural economic landscapes of most of the communities (Gana, in Oguntoyinbo *et al* eds, 1983). The major characteristic of rural markets in Nigeria is when they occur and this attribute arises from the fact that the amount of effective demand encompassed by the market

Chapter 12 | Ishaq A. Abdulkarim, in
A.I. Tanko and S.B. Momale (Eds.)
*Kano: Environment, Society and Development*
London & Abuja, Adonis & Abbey Publishers

175

is often insufficient to provide an adequate profit level for traders. Because of the inadequacies in the rural economic structure, rural areas are gingered to set up structures that will enable them to benefit from the organization of production. Individually, settlements are so small that there are no viable markets, but collectively they are viable, and hence the organization in to periodic rural markets.

The rural markets of Nigeria perform three economic functions simultaneously: local exchange, internal trade, and central place functions (Eighmy 1972). The local exchange function represents a small scale division of labour, and mediates family level surpluses and deficits. For a single item of food, such as a yam, there is little spatial separation of production, market, and consumption sites. Similarly, depending on the storage qualities of the food item, there may be little temporal separation of production and consumption, and the services performed at the market site are correspondingly simple. This local exchange function is present at all levels of development, but requires no more than a subsistence economy. The internal trade and central place functions are correlates of a larger scale division of labor, increases in local wealth, and the spatial extension of a monetized exchange economy. Internal trade implies specific complementarities between spatially separated food surplus and deficit areas and requires a transport net capable of carrying commodities at a reasonable cost. Where a commodity is produced in excess of local demand, rural markets serve as bulking points in the internal trade sequence.

Holdder (1961) in his classification of markets gave the following for rural markets: (i) the rural daily market, which is often only for fresh meat; (ii) the rural periodic night market; and (iii) the rural periodic day market. Of these, the rural periodic day market is easily the most widespread and important type of local market that is clearly significant in the Kano Region.

The concepts of range and threshold explain the periodicity of rural markets. Stine (1962) employed the concept of range and threshold or maximum and minimum range respectively in the explanation of market periodicity. McKim (1972) has suggested that the location of markets relates to the distribution of population and settlements and Hill and Smith (1972) add the degree of mobility of traders and consumers. In Yorubaland (Nigeria), Hodder (1961) believed that the size and distribution of population was not important and that rural markets tended to space out at 10-kilometre intervals,

Chapter 12 | Ishaq A. Abdulkarim, in
A.I. Tanko and S.B. Momale (Eds.)
*Kano: Environment, Society and Development*
London & Abuja, Adonis & Abbey Publishers

even if there was no settlement at that location; this represented the maximum walking distance for those wishing to attend. Jackson (1971), in Southern Ethiopia, however, believed that population and market densities were closely allied.

Kura (2008) after realising that markets in rural Kano show low threshold and purchasing power, notes that prices of good in the markets depend on seasonality. Majority of the marketers are ruralites selling mostly agricultural produce and livestock. Also, it is not only the market that determine the prices of good but also the middle-men (*Dillalai*). The influence of the middle-men in the rural markets can never be overemphasized such that those who are not complying with their prices might end up going home with their products.

The social role of rural markets in the developing world can be as important to those taking part as the economic one. In northern Nigeria, Scott (1972) observed that women, in particular, visited the markets for social reasons. Market day is a time for relatives and friends to meet, and markets have a large number of catering establishments associated with them which are used for these various social gatherings. In this chapter, the evolution, characteristics, types, and the contribution of rural markets to the economy of the Kano Region are discussed.

## Evolution of Rural Markets in the Kano Region

For some of the poorer people in Nigeria most of who are in the rural areas, markets provide essential opportunities for the exchange and barter of locally produced goods and for the sale of livestock and the purchase of manufactured consumer goods. Academic literatures have shown the evolution of markets in Nigeria. Hodder (1965) suggested that the bartering system was a possible origin of rural markets, but nowadays barter is being replaced by cash transactions. Shopping points for long distance trading in Yorubaland were known to have emerged as important market centres (Hodder, 1969). At Abadi in Egba country, a caravan of 4000 people were sometimes gathering as far back as the mid- nineteenth century (Ibid, 1969). In the study of markets in the Zaria Division, Gana (1973) found that journeys made for religious purpose on Friday were not significantly different from shopping visits. Hill, (1972, quoted in Kura, 2008) in her work on

Chapter 12 | Ishaq A. Abdulkarim, in
A.I. Tanko and S.B. Momale (Eds.)
*Kano: Environment, Society and Development*
London & Abuja, Adonis & Abbey Publishers

Katsina Province found that there was a strong correlation between the occurrence of rural markets centers and Fulani cattle routes.

Similarly, Kura (2008) in his study on Kura Local Government (LGA) found that the old route passing from Kano through Kumbotso to Kura District led to the emergence of important markets in the district. Similarly, the building of central mosque in the settlements also led to the emergence of rural markets as many people congregate there for the Friday Jum'at Prayers.

It is a well known fact that there are nucleated settlements in Islamic Hausa society, and as such a strong desire by the people to have Friday mosques. These mosques are usually established with a traditional market, so that people can come to the village or town with a dual purpose of performing both religious and economic functions. However, there are some markets that are recent creation and those that evolved as a result of relocation because of the need for expansion. For example, the Janguza market is a recent creation (20 years old) and was relocated from Tashan Kadiri in Tofa LGA.

From the foregoing, and the discussion with some stakeholders [Leaders of the markets (*Sarakunan Kasuwa*) and traders] of some rural markets, it is evident that transportation routes and the Friday mosques were the major factors that contributed to the evolution of rural markets in the Kano Region. For instance, the markets in Kura, Rano, Bichi, Wudil, Tofa, Kwankwaso, Gora, Madobi, Rikadawa, Kubarachi and Kiru among others have their market days on Fridays. Thus, marketing calendars are social and cultural in origin. They not only regulate the frequency of a market and define the length of the "market week" for a given area, but often have a pervasive and subtle impact on other aspects of economic and social life which are only remotely associated with markets. Where markets are a relatively recent innovation, as in some ex-colonial areas, market calendars are commonly based on some variation or multiplier of an imported, western seven-day week. By contrast, in areas such as northern Nigeria (Islam is dominant) where market networks predate Western contact, periodic cycles in use today are based on traditional indigenous calendars (natural or Islamic) and show little evidence of yielding to the European manner of reckoning time. The features of most of these markets reflect the traditional and Islamic influence in the Region.

Chapter 12 | Ishaq A. Abdulkarim, in
A.I. Tanko and S.B. Momale (Eds.)
*Kano: Environment, Society and Development*
London & Abuja, Adonis & Abbey Publishers

## Characteristics of Rural Markets

Ultimately, the performance of marketplaces as development nodes is related to their degree of articulation with their local hinterlands and with the urban centres, transportation networks, and organizational frameworks that compose the spatial system of which they are part. Rural market (most of which are periodic) systems are vital features of the space economy of most developing countries in Africa. The markets comprised by these systems are greatly diversified in terms of locational pattern and timing, size, nature and scale of economic functions Good (1975). Lado (1988) opined that a majority of rural markets are characterized by periodicity, by mobility of sellers (among locations and productive activities), and by agglomerations of sellers. Although it is well known that periodicity occurs in both complex and less-developed economies, its significance in "peasant economies" (such as rural Kano) is not the fact of its occurrence but rather the degree to which it accounts for the relative location of markets and sets the rhythm regulating the circulation and convergence of people and goods. Most of the rural markets in the Region are periodic. However, there are pockets of daily rural markets most of which are specialized in either livestock or vegetables.

In the area of shelter, most of the rural markets in the Region do not have well-defined stalls but are held in the shade of convenient trees, usually by the roadside. They have few shelters mostly of thatched roofs supported by wooden poles and these are normally erected by sellers to protect themselves from sun rays and rainfall. However, some of these markets have noticeable permanent shelters as a result of the intervention by the local authorities. These are usually covered with corrugated iron roofs supported with brick walls.

In terms of locational pattern and timing, they are mostly located along road side, and center of the village. Fridays are mostly market days as earlier explained, Sundays are market days for Dambatta and Kachako while Badume Market operates twice in a week (Sundays and Wednesdays). The Gezewa, Tudun Wada Dankadai and Bunkure Markets operate on alternate days. Rahama and Darki Markets operate on Saturdays and Thursdays respectively. Most of them are day markets while some are evening and night (Janguza) Markets. Rural markets are an integral part of not only the rural economy, but also of

Chapter 12 | Ishaq A. Abdulkarim, in
A.I. Tanko and S.B. Momale (Eds.)
*Kano: Environment, Society and Development*
London & Abuja, Adonis & Abbey Publishers

**179**

the urban economy, its importance can never be over emphasized as it affects both rural and urban dwellers.

The male gender dominates in the markets unlike what is obtainable in the southern part of Nigeria. This is associated with the religious belief (Islam) which moderates the movement of women outside their homes. This is because the Kano Region is an Islamic region and as such women are confined to domestic affairs rather than selling in the market. However, women are still found in the market, most of them old Hausa women, young girls and Fulani women. The old women are mostly engaged in the sales of such items as locust bean spice (*Daddawa*), '*Fura da Nono*' (mostly Fulani women), and local traditional vegetable spices (*Zogale, Yadiya, Rama, Lamsir* etc.). Some women are usually engaged in selling food to the marketers while others usually sell groundnut oil and the spices produced from groundnut (*Kuli kuli*).

The products of these markets are mostly the agricultural produce and local farm implements. It include all types of grains grown in northern Nigeria, cassava, chickens, livestock, milk (*nono*), butter from cattle (*man shanu*), honey and and blacksmith wares among others. There are also manufactured goods in the markets such as textile materials, beverages, confectionaries, plastic products and drugs. The range of products in the markets varies from market to market. While some markets specialize in foodstuff, others are in vegetables while in others it is livestock.

## Types of Rural Markets in the Kano Region

In the Kano Region, peasant farming is not exclusively 'subsistence-oriented', in the sense that all production is entirely for consumption, and a certain proportion may be offered for sale in the rural markets. Based on the number of market days per week, there are four major types of rural markets exist in the Kano Region. They are (i) rural daily markets; (ii) rural two day markets; (iii) twice a week rural markets; and rural weekly markets.

### Daily Rural Markets

Daily rural markets in the Region are mostly specialized markets, for fresh vegetables and livestock. They usually hold in the day time and

Chapter 12 | Ishaq A. Abdulkarim, in
A.I. Tanko and S.B. Momale (Eds.)
*Kano: Environment, Society and Development*
London & Abuja, Adonis & Abbey Publishers

some in the evening and night. They do not only serve the immediate rural areas, but also serve as a bulking point for some urban requirement for these produce. Good examples of these are the specialized livestock market in Tamburawa and Badume (day and night markets respectively) and Kwanar Gafa (Vegetables) night market.

**Table 12.1: Some Notable Daily Rural Markets in the Kano Region**

| LGA | Name of Market | Market Days | Main Products |
|---|---|---|---|
| Dawakin Kudu | Kwanar Dawakin Kudu | Daily | Livestock (cattle, sheep and goats) |
| | Tamburawa | Daily | Livestock |
| Kura | Karfi | Daily | Rice, Tomatoes, Pepper |
| | Gundutse | Daily | Sugarcane |
| Tsanyawa | Tsanyawa | Daily | Foodstuffs |

*Source: Kano State Commercial and Industrial Guide, (2003), Updated with Field Survey, 2010*

### Every other Day Markets

These types of markets operate every two days. When the market is held on a certain day, the following day will be a rest day. This is as a result of the fact that the sellers who are mostly the producers need the free day to gather their produce and prepare for the next market day such as the Tanburawa, Bunkure and Kofa markets (Table 12.2).

### Twice Weekly Rural Markets

The markets here operate twice in a week with the days being rotational but fixed. There are two types, the day and the night markets. For example, the Janguza Market in Tofa local (a twice weekly market) holds on Thursdays and Sundays from around 4.00pm to 10.00 pm in the night. Other examples include the Ajingi Day Market (Tuesday & Sunday), Garo Market (Saturdays & Tuesdays), and Tofa Market (Fridays & Mondays) (Table 12.3).

| Chapter 12 | Ishaq A. Abdulkarim, in |
| | A.I. Tanko and S.B. Momale (Eds.) |
| | *Kano: Environment, Society and Development* |
| | London & Abuja, Adonis & Abbey Publishers |

## Seventh Day Rural Markets

These types of markets are held once in a week. Usually a day of the week is chosen by a rural community as its market day. In choosing a market day, the rural communities take into cognizance market days of the adjoining rural communities to avoid clash. The concept of threshold is in play here. Because of the low population, the subsistence nature of the rural communities, and the fact that individual settlements are so small and markets are not viable, collectively they became viable and hence organize themselves into what is called market rings. The market ring includes all the settlements participating in marketing on periodic basis. Example of Seven day markets in the region are the Karaye (Wednesday), Kiru (Thursday), Gwiwa (Wednesday), Furji (Thursday), Ajingi (Tuesday), Maraganta (Saturday), Maigatari (Thursday), Balare (Sunday), and Larabar Zango (Wednesday) just to mention a few (Table 12.4).

**Table 12.2: Some Every Other Day Rural Markets in the Kano Region**

| LGA | Name of Market | Market Days | Main Products |
|---|---|---|---|
| Bunkure | Bunkure | Every other day | Rice, Vegetables, Foodstuff, & Chickens |
| Bebeji | Kofa | Every other day | Rice, Vegetables, Foodstuff, & Chickens |
| Gezawa | Gezawa | Every other day | Foodstuff, Vegetables |
| Tudun Wada | Tudun Wada | Every other day | Foodstuff & General Goods |

*Source: Kano State Commercial and Industrial Guide, (2003), Updated with Field Survey, 2010*

**TABLE 12.3: Some Twice Every Week Rural Markets in the Kano Region**

| Local Government | Markets | Market Days | Main Products |
|---|---|---|---|
| Ajingi | Ajingi | Tuesday & Friday | Livestock, cloths Blacksmith Ware |
| Bagwai | Bagwai | Sunday & Wednesday | Maize, Corn, Millet |
| Bichi | Badume | Wednesday & Sunday | Maize, Millet, Livestock, Honey |
| Dawakin Tofa | Dawakin Tofa | Friday & Tuesday | Livestock, Grains |
| | Gwarmai | Sunday & Wednesday | Livestock, Grains |
| Kabo | Garo | Saturday & Tuesday | Food Items |
| Sumaila | Sumaila | Friday & Tuesday | Foodstuff |
| | Janguza | Thursday & Sunday | Vegetables, Livestock |
| Rimin Gado | Yelwa Danziyel | Monday & Friday | Food Items |

*Source: Kano State Commercial and Industrial Guide, (2003), Updated with Field Survey, 2010*

| Chapter 12 | Ishaq A. Abdulkarim, in
A.I. Tanko and S.B. Momale (Eds.)
*Kano: Environment, Society and Development*
London & Abuja, Adonis & Abbey Publishers |

## Table 12.4 (a - c): Some Notable Seven Day Rural Markets in the Kano Region

### a. Northern Part

| Local Government | Markets | Market Days | Main Products |
|---|---|---|---|
| Gwiwa | Gwiwa | Wednesday | Millet, Chickens, Beans, Milk |
| | Furji | Thursday | Livestock |
| | Maraganta | Saturdy | |
| Kafin Hausa | Kafin Hausa | Tuesday | Foodstuff, Livestock |
| | Bulangu | Wednesday | Livestock, Foodstuff, Blacksmith Ware |
| Maigatari | Maigatari | Thursday | Livestock |
| | Jabo | Thursday | Foodstuff, Livestock, Blacksmith Ware |
| Hadejia | Matachi | Friday | Foodstuff, Livestock |
| | Marma | Saturday | Foodstuff, Livestock |
| | Malamadori | Tuesday | Foodstuff, Livestock |
| | Gujungu | Sunday | Foodstuff, Livestock |
| | Kore | Thursday | Foodstuff |
| Gabasawa | Zakirai | Friday | Grains, Livestock |
| Kunchi | Sodawa | Sunday | Foodstuff, Groundnut |
| | Matan Fada | Wednesday | Livestock, Millet |
| | Shuwaki | Thursday | Edible Leaves, Food items |
| Minjibir | Ladin Dankade | Sunday | Food Items |
| Tsanyawa | Dumbulum | Tuesday | Foodstuff, Livestock |

*Source:* Kano State Commercial and Industrial Guide, (2003), Updated with Field Survey, 2010

Chapter 12 | Ishaq A. Abdulkarim, in
A.I. Tanko and S.B. Momale (Eds.)
*Kano: Environment, Society and Development*
London & Abuja, Adonis & Abbey Publishers

## b. Central Part

| Local Government | Markets | Market Days | Main Products |
|---|---|---|---|
| Bagwai | Gogori | Friday | Livestock, Food items |
| | Romo | Monday | Livestock, Food items |
| | Kiyawa | Thursday | Livestock, Food items |
| | Gandaya | Sunday | Livestock, Food items |
| Makoda | Kunya | Fridays | Foodstuff, Livestock |
| Kabo | Kabo | Friday | Foodstuff, Sheep |
| Rimin Gado | Rimingado | Wednesday | Foodstuff |
| | Yalwa | Wednesday | Foodstuff |
| Shanono | Shanono | Monday | Foodstuff, Livestock |
| Tofa | Tofa | Friday | General Goods |
| Madobi | Kwankwaso | Friday | Maize, Millet, Groundnut, Rice |
| | Madobi | Friday | Maize, Millet, Groundnut, Rice, Livestock |
| | Kafin Agur | Friday | Maize, Millet, Groundnut, Rice |
| | Kubarachi | Friday | Maize, Millet, Groundnut, Rice, Livestock |
| | Rikadawa | Friday | Maize, Millet, Groundnut, Rice |
| Kura | Kura | Friday | Rice, Wheat, Maize |
| | Danhassan | Monday | Rice, Wheat, Maize |
| Dawakin Kudu | Tsakuwa | Sunday | Foodstuff, Livestock |
| | Ladinmakole | Sunday | Chickens, Milk, Butter |
| Gaya | Gaya | Friday | Foodstuff, Livestock |
| Wudil | Wudil | Friday | Cattle, Foodstuff |
| | Darki | Thursday | Foodstuff, Livestock |
| Dutse | Shuwarin | Monday | Foodstuff, Livestock |
| Kiyawa | Kiyawa | Friday | Foodstuff, Livestock |
| | Larabar Tambarin Gwani | Wednesday | Foodstuff, Livestock |
| Warawa | Larabar G/Sarim | Wednesday | Foodstuff |
| Agingi | Larabar Zango | Wednesday | Livestock, Foodstuff |
| | Balare | Sunday | Milk, Foodstuff & Vegetables |

**Source:** *Kano State Commercial and Industrial Guide, (2003), Updated with Field Survey, 2010*

Chapter 12 | Ishaq A. Abdulkarim, in
A.I. Tanko and S.B. Momale (Eds.)
*Kano: Environment, Society and Development*
London & Abuja, Adonis & Abbey Publishers

## c. Southern Part

| Local Government | Markets | Market Days | Main Products |
|---|---|---|---|
| Bebeji | Bebeji | Friday | Foodstuff |
| | Konar Dangora | Friday | Rice, Vegetables, Foodstuff, & Chickens |
| Karaye | Karaye | Wednesday | Foodstuff |
| Rogo | Sundu | Sunday | Sugarcane, Foodstuff |
| | Jajaye | Friday | Sugarcane, Foodstuff |
| Kiru | Kwanar Dangora | Friday | Foodstuff |
| | Kiru | Thursday | Foodstuff |
| Garun Mallam | Garun Mallam | Friday | Wheat, Vegetables, Millet |
| Rano | Rano | Friday | Foodstuff, Vegetables, Milk, Butter |
| Doguwa | Doguwa | Tuesday | Foodstuff, Livestock |
| | Sabuwar Kaura | Saturday | Foodstuff, Livestock |
| | Maganda | Wednesday | Foodstuff, Livestock |
| | Falgore | Friday | Cattle, Maize, Milk, Butter |
| Garko | Garko | Sunday | Rice, Milk, Chickens |
| | Dala | Monday | Foodstuff, Groundnut |
| Kibiya | Kibiya | Tuesday | Foodstuff, Vegetables |
| Takai | Takai | Tuesday | Foodstuffs |
| | Kachako | Sunday | Foodstuffs |
| Gwaram | Gwaram | Friday | Livestock, Milk, butter, Grains |

**Source:** *Kano State Commercial and Industrial Guide, (2003), Updated with Field Survey, 2010*

## Contribution of Rural Markets to the Economy of the Region

The role played by rural markets in the economic development and the transformation of the economy of peasant farming societies has been widely recognized as being crucial for integrating these communities into the national economy and culture (Lado 1988, citing examples from, Bohannan and Dalton, 1962; Skinner, 1964; Hodder, 1965; Belshaw, 1965; Good, 1970; Bromley, 1971).

The rural markets in Kano contribute greatly to the economy of the Region. They are a source of income (not only to the people, but also the government) and employment to many rural dwellers; source of food for the urban dwellers (grains, milk, butter, chickens, vegetables, fruits such as water melon, livestock); source of raw materials for the

Chapter 12 | Ishaq A. Abdulkarim, in
A.I. Tanko and S.B. Momale (Eds.)
*Kano: Environment, Society and Development*
London & Abuja, Adonis & Abbey Publishers

industries in urban Kano (groundnut for groundnut oil, hide-and-skin for leather work, maize for improved maize flour, Table 12.5); market for urban goods (manufactured goods such as cloth, provisions drugs); and an avenue for the diffusion of information, innovation and new ideas and modern techniques can flow into the rural areas.

**Table 12.5: Some Produce of Rural Markets utilised by Urban Industries**

| Type of Goods | Industrial Uses | User Industries |
|---|---|---|
| Maize | Cornflakes, Maize grits, maize bran, germ oil, flour, malted maize starch, glucose, dextrose | Feed millers, flour mills, beverage industries |
| Cassava | Cassava chips, flour starch, gari and tapioca | Feed millers, flour mills, soft drink industries. |
| Sugarcane | Molasses, burgesses, sugar | Bakery, confectionaries, soft drinks |
| Millet | Flour, millet grit, malted millet | Feed millers, flour mills, beverage industries |
| Wheat | Flour, bran | Flour mills |
| Groundnut | Groundnut oil, cake | Oil mills, confectionaries |
| Livestock | Meat, yoghurt, ice cream, powered milk, butter, cheese, milk | Meat, dairy, bakery, beverage industries |

*Source: Kano State economic Empowerment and Development Strategy-Policy Framework and Project Summary (2005)*

## Conclusion

Rural markets in the Kano Region like most markets in northern Nigeria evolved as a result of two major factors; transportation routes and the presence of Friday Mosques. The characteristics of the markets show a clear rural one with little urban influence. Most of the markets are periodic with few daily markets. Four major types of markets exist, and are usually situated by the roadside with few well-defined stalls. The types of product are mostly agricultural, and few manufactured goods usually from the urban centre which are required to satisfy the needs of the rural people.

Rural markets, as part of the economy of the Region, have untapped potential (being a major part of the economy). There are several difficulties confronting the effort to fully explore these rural markets. The concept of rural markets in Nigeria, as in several other countries, is still in evolving shape, and the sector poses a variety of challenges, including understanding the dynamics of the rural markets and strategies to supply and satisfy the rural consumers. Development

Chapter 12 — Ishaq A. Abdulkarim, in
A.I. Tanko and S.B. Momale (Eds.)
*Kano: Environment, Society and Development*
London & Abuja, Adonis & Abbey Publishers

of infrastructures such as roads, and market stalls, as well as proper policy measures like those that will check the excesses of the middlemen who mostly control prices, and integration of all the markets into the Region's economy will enhance the viability and sustenance of the markets. This will go a long way in improving the markets, and help the rural marketer grow their businesses which will in turn lead to growth in their farm produce.

## References

Bromley, R. J. (1971) Markets in the Developing Countries: *A Review Geography*, Volume 56: 124-132.

Bromley, R. J., Symanski, R. and Good C. M. (1975) The Rationale of Periodic Markets, *Annals of the Association of American Geographers*, Vol. 65, No. 4, pp. 530-537

Eighmy T. H. (1972) Rural Periodic Markets and the Extension of an Urban System: A Western Nigeria: *Economic Geography*, Vol. 48, No. 3, Spatial Structure and Process in Tropical West Africa pp. 299-315

Good, C. M. (1971), *Rural markets and trade in East Africa*, University of Chicago Press, Chicago)

Good, C. M. (1975), Periodic Markets and Traveling Traders in Uganda, *Geographical Review*, Vol. 65, No. 1 pp. 49-72

Hill, P., and R. H. T. Smith (1972), The Spatial and Temporal Synchronization of Periodic Markets: Evidence from Four Emjrates in Northern Nigeria. *Economic Geography*, 48: 345-355.

Hodder, B. W. (1961) Rural Periodic Day Markets in Part of Yorubaland. *Trans. IBG.* (Old Series), 36: 149-159.

Hodder, B. W. (1965) Some Comments on the Origins of Traditional Markets in Africa South of the Sahara. *Transactions of the Institute of British Geographers*, No. 36, pp. 97-105

Hodder, B. W. (1965) Some Comments on the Origins of Traditional Markets in Africa South of the Sahara. *Trans. IBG.* (Old Series), 36: 99-1 05.

Jackson, R. T. (1971) Periodic Markets in Southern Ethiopia, *Trans. IBG* (Old Series) 53: 31-41.

Kano State Commercial and Industrial Guide (2003) First Edition.

Chapter 12 | Ishaq A. Abdulkarim, in
A.I. Tanko and S.B. Momale (Eds.)
*Kano: Environment, Society and Development*
London & Abuja, Adonis & Abbey Publishers

187

Kano State economic Empowerment and Development Strategy-Policy framework and Project Summary (2005).

Kura, L. S. (2008) Spatio-Temporal Pattern of Periodic Markets in Kura Local Government, Kano. (Unpublished)

Lado, C. (1988) Some Aspects of Rural Marketing Systems and Peasant Farming in Maridi District, *Transactions of the Institute of British Geographers*, New Series, Vol. 13, No. 3), pp. 361-374

McKim, W. (1972) The Periodic Market System in North-eastern Ghana. *Economic Geography*, 48: 333-344.

Oguntoyinbo, J. S., Areola, O. O. and Filani, M. (eds. 1983), *A General Geography of Nigeria* (Second Edition); Heinemann Educational Books Nigeria Limited.

Scott, E. P. (1972), The Spatial Structure of Rural Northern Nigeria: Farmers, Periodic Markets and Villages. *Economic Geography*, 48: 316-332.

Skinner, G. W. (1964) Marketing and Social Structure in Rural China. *Journal of African Development Studies*, 24: 3-43.

Chapter 12 | Ishaq A. Abdulkarim, in
A.I. Tanko and S.B. Momale (Eds.)
*Kano: Environment, Society and Development*
London & Abuja, Adonis & Abbey Publishers

**188**

# Chapter Thirteen

## POVERTY

### Julius Afolabi Falola

### The Meaning of Poverty

In writing about poverty, the first question to ask and which will be addressed is what is it? Poverty is a condition where one is unable to meet the basic needs for food, clothing and shelter. Distinction is often made between absolute poverty and relative poverty. The centrality of the food component to poverty is captured in absolute poverty which is synonymous with destitution, a condition which occurs when people cannot obtain adequate resources (measured in terms of calories or nutrition) to support a minimum level of physical health (Cp. Business Dictionary.com). Relative poverty on the other hand is inability to enjoy what is considered a minimum level of living standards acceptable and possibly enjoyed by the bulk of the population. This condition described as relative poverty varies considerably between and within nations and over time. The relativity of poverty is revealed in a discussion with a colleague who drew attention to poverty having to do with 'contentment' because a sense of poverty might derive from seeing other's affluence. As illustration consider this popular tale among Hausa people.

> Once upon a time, there was a man who felt that he was the poorest of all the poor people of his time, simply because he owned nothing except the skin (*warki*) he used to wrap his wrist. One day, he went to the king of his town and pleaded that the king should command his servants to kill him. The king asked him: "what offense have you committed deserving death?" The man replied: "I am the most wretched man in this town and for that I see no reason why I should continue living".

> The king ordered his servant, the *hauni* (head cutter) to lead the man to the stake, where the king used to behead criminals. Killing at the stake in the town attracted crowd. When he was about to be killed, he overheard someone in the crowd requesting the servant to offer him the skin the man was wearing. Suddenly the man requested the servants to lead him back to the king and told him that "today I saw someone who is more wretched than

Chapter 13 | J. Afolabi Falola, in
A.I. Tanko and S.B. Momale (Eds.)
*Kano: Environment, Society and Development*
London & Abuja, Adonis & Abbey Publishers

**189**

I am. Kindly release me and from now on I will be contended with what I have" [3]

Clearly poverty is to do with the level of living. Thus, it is multi-dimensional. Income alone, however defined can neither fully describe nor explain it. This is because it involves variables such as nutrition (food intake) and health, clothing (use of clothes and footwear), shelter (occupancy and quality of dwellings), education and individual development through learning, leisure (protection from overwork), security (safety and administration of justice) social environment (social contacts and recreation) and physical environment (housing condition, exposure to harmful and other pollutants), command over goods and services, employment and quality of working life, social opportunity and participation (Smith 1977).

These conditions are not same for all persons both in the urban and in the rural areas of the Kano Region. However inequalities are more obvious in the cities than in the rural. For in the cities one can see affluence side by side with destitution; high quality residential forms juxtaposed the slums; very clean and environmentally sanitised alongside those with heaps of solid wastes etc. We shall consider some of these using documentary data from publications of the Federal Bureau of Statistics, the National Population Commission and reports.

## The Nature of Poverty in the Region

### *Four Measures of Poverty*

In its survey the NBS (2012) adopted four measures of poverty as absolute, the relative, Dollar per day and what was termed the subjective. Absolute (objective) is measured as food energy intake using 3000 calories as expected minimum calorific intake for the average Nigerian. Relative measure of poverty was derived from summing the expenditure of the households where households with expenditure greater than two-thirds of the total household per capita expenditure are non-poor while those below it are poor. Further,

---

[3] *See Magana Jari ce for the detail of the story*

| Chapter 13 | J. Afolabi Falola, in |
| | A.I. Tanko and S.B. Momale (Eds.) |
| | *Kano: Environment, Society and Development* |
| | London & Abuja, Adonis & Abbey Publishers |

households with less than one-third of total household per capita expenditure are core-poor (extreme poor) and those greater than one-third of total expenditure are moderate poor. The dollar per day is taken as the amount of money that will afford the individual the barest livelihood support. The subjective poverty measure is a self-assess poverty measure based on the opinion of households.

Using the food, absolute, relative and dollar per day definitions (Table 13.1) Jigawa is found to be poorer than Kano. All measures classed 71% to 79% of Jigawa as poor and 48% to 72% in Kano. Poverty appears to be highest when the relative measure is used. If poverty is measured as those that live on less than $2 per day (this translates to about N300) many government employees, most of who have an average household size of seven people and who earn N18,000 are in the category of the poor since the household lives on 85 naira or $0.57 per day. One can understand why ranges from 66% in Kano to 74% in Jigawa State.

**Table 13.1: 2010 Poverty Numbers for Absolute, Relative and Dollar/day**

| State | Food Poverty | | Absolute Poverty | | Relative Poverty | | Dollar per day based on adjusted PPP | |
|---|---|---|---|---|---|---|---|---|
| | Food poor | Non poor | Poor | Non poor | Poor poor | Non | Poor | Non poor |
| Jigawa | 71.1 | 28.9 | 74.1 | 25.9 | 79.0 | 21.0 | 74.2 | 25.8 |
| Kano | 48.3 | 51.7 | 65.6 | 34.4 | 72.3 | 27.7 | 66.0 | 34.0 |
| National | 41.0 | 59.0 | 60.9 | 39.1 | 69.0 | 31.0 | 61.2 | 38.8 |

*Source: NBS (2012) Nigeria Poverty Profile 2012, www.tuerivers.org/ 28/12/2012*

Based on the opinion of members of household (self assessment/ subjective measure) Kano is ahead of Jigawa in poverty level (Table 13.2). Same trend is revealed from household assessment of their livelihoods (Table 13.3).

**Table 13.2: Subjective Poverty Measure 2012: Core Poor, Moderate, Poor, and Non-poor**

| State | Core Poor | Moderate Poor | Non-Poor | Total |
|---|---|---|---|---|
| Jigawa | 35.6 | 56.0 | 8.4 | 100.0 |
| Kano | 53.4 | 40.8 | 5.8 | 100.0 |

*Source: NBS (2012) Nigeria Poverty Profile 2012, www.tuerivers.org/ 28/12/2012*

| Chapter 13 | J. Afolabi Falola, in
A.I. Tanko and S.B. Momale (Eds.)
*Kano: Environment, Society and Development*
London & Abuja, Adonis & Abbey Publishers |

**Table 13.3: Household Assessment of Livelihood: Subjective Poverty Measurement**

| State | Very Poor | Poor | Moderate | Fairly rich | Rich |
|---|---|---|---|---|---|
| Jigawa | 4.9 | 30.7 | 56.0 | 7.3 | 1.0 |
| Kano | 11.5 | 41.9 | 40.8 | 5.2 | 0.6 |

*Source: NBS (2012) Nigeria Poverty Profile 2012, www.tuerivers.org/ 28/12/2012*

## Employment Status

A large percentage of men are employed compared to women where we define employment as being engaged in income generating activities. In the Jigawa portion of the Region close to half of the women were unemployed in the 12 months preceding the survey compared to about a third in Kano (Table 13.4), which is a reflection of the huge urban population. However, if this high proportion of men were employed, the questions are: Are they employed all year round? If employed on what type of job? Table 13.5 shows that most were in agriculture (largely small holders) and sales and services.

**Table 13.4: Employment Status: Women and Men (2008)**

| State | | Employed in the 12 months preceding survey | | Not employed in the 12 months preceding the survey |
|---|---|---|---|---|
| | | Currently Employed | Not currently Employed | |
| Jigawa | Women | 45.4 | 4.7 | 49.9 |
| | Men | 98.3 | 0.6 | 0.6 |
| Kano | Women | 47.3 | 13.8 | 38.6 |
| | Men | 85.3 | 3.2 | 11.5 |

*Source: National Population Commission, Nigeria Demographic and Health Survey 2008*

**Table 13.5: Occupation: Women and Men Age 15-49 in the Kano Region**

| TYPE | JIGAWA | | KANO | |
|---|---|---|---|---|
| | Women | Men | Women | Men |
| Professonal/Technical/Managerial | 0.7 | 5.5 | 1.2 | 8.1 |
| Clerical | 0.2 | 1.5 | 0.1 | 2.6 |
| Sales & Services | 57.7 | 30.4 | 59.3 | 38.9 |
| Skilled Manual | 38.7 | 10.6 | 38.3 | 20.1 |
| Unskilled Manual | 0.0 | 3.4 | 0.3 | 6.6 |
| Agriculture | 2.4 | 48.6 | 0.5 | 22.2 |
| Missing | 0.3 | 0.0 | 0.3 | 1.5 |

*Source: National Population Commission, Nigeria Demographic and Health Survey 2008*

Chapter 13 | J. Afolabi Falola, in
A.I. Tanko and S.B. Momale (Eds.)
*Kano: Environment, Society and Development*
London & Abuja, Adonis & Abbey Publishers

## *Education*

As regards education, which is often taken to be positively related to income and occupation and therefore level of living, close to 50% and slightly more than 50% of Kano and Jigawa respectively have no Western education. About 25% are nursery-primary in Kano and 21% in Jigawa. The proportion in the secondary level education was 22% and 18% respectively. Post-secondary and tertiary educations were still abysmally low (Table 13.6). Even this education is skewed in favour of the male segment of the population in the Region as 76% and 59% of women aged 15-49 have no Western education in Jigawa and Kano respectively (Table 13.7). This contrasts with the 56% and 39% for men in the respective States. There were more with some primary education than there were those who completed it both for male and female in the Region.

**Table 13.6: Distribution of Population by Educational Attainment in 2006**

|              | KANO      | %     | JIGAWA    | %     |
|--------------|-----------|-------|-----------|-------|
| Total        | 7,213,948 | 100   | 3,306,315 | 100   |
| None         | 3,320,983 | 46.04 | 795,589   | 54.31 |
| Nursery      | 984,912   | 13.65 | 389,235   | 11.77 |
| Primary      | 811,380   | 11.25 | 321,476   | 9.72  |
| JSS          | 520,101   | 07.21 | 178,102   | 5.39  |
| SSS/SEC/TTC  | 1,083,752 | 15.02 | 407,084   | 12.31 |
| OND/NCE      | 210,160   | 02.91 | 75,951    | 2.30  |
| Univ.Grad/HND| 114,227   | 1.58  | 35,060    | 1.06  |
| Postgraduate | 35,593    | 0.49  | 9,431     | 0.30  |
| Others       | 132,840   | 01.84 | 94,387    | 2.85  |

**Table 13.7: Educational Attainment by Women and Men; Age 15-49 (2008)**

| Educational Attainment | WOMEN  |       | MEN    |       |
|------------------------|--------|-------|--------|-------|
|                        | Jigawa | Kano  | Jigawa | Kano  |
| No Education           | 76.0   | 59.5  | 56.4   | 39.9  |
| Some Primary           | 12.3   | 14.4  | 19.7   | 19.4  |
| Completed Primary      | 7.3    | 10.4  | 10.7   | 11.6  |
| Some Secondary         | 1.0    | 5.1   | 5.6    | 11.0  |
| Completed Secondary    | 0.8    | 4.7   | 3.0    | 8.6   |
| More than Secondary    | 0.6    | 1.8   | 3.6    | 7.2   |
| Missing                | 2.0    | 4.1   | 0.9    | 2.2   |
| Total                  | 100.0  | 100.0 | 100.0  | 100.0 |

*Source: National Population Commission, Nigeria Demographic and Health Survey 2008*

Chapter 13 | J. Afolabi Falola, in
A.I. Tanko and S.B. Momale (Eds.)
*Kano: Environment, Society and Development*
London & Abuja, Adonis & Abbey Publishers

## *Housing*

After food and clothing another reflection of poverty is housing. In this we use the constructional materials for the walls and roofing as well as the kitchen and toilet facilities (Tables 13.8-13.11). As regards materials for the wall, mud was used for most of the houses where in Jigawa nearly three quarters (72.7%) and more than half in Kano (57.4%). While mud walls are ubiquitous, it is more so in the rural than in the urban areas. This indeed why most settlements have borrow pits from which have been mined the constructional materials. While this reflects the traditional forms, the problem is that the walls are unable to stand against rain wash and it is not uncommon to find walls collapsing under intensive rains. Others are wood, stone, cement blocks/bricks. As regards the latter, it is more in Kano (24.4%) than in Jigawa (9.3%) which is more dominated by rurality.

**Table 13.8: Material for Wall**

| State | Mud/ Reed | Wood | Stone | Cement Blocks/Bricks | Metal/Zinc Sheet | Other | Total |
|---|---|---|---|---|---|---|---|
| Jigawa | 554,869 (72.7%) | 111,559 | 31,512 | 75,289 (9.3%) | 20,292 | 16,789 | 810,310 |
| Kano | 920,458 | 177,342 | 39,691 | 390,442 (24.4%) | 57,545 | 17,857 | 1,603, 335 |
| Total | 1,475,327 | 288,901 | 71,203 | 465,731 | 77,837 | 34,646 | |

**Source:** *National Population Commission, Nigeria Demographic and Health Survey 2008*

Again for roofing thatch and earth/mud/bricks are very prevalent as the two together accounts for 44% as against 28% corrugated roofing sheets. Slates/asbestos, cement/concrete and roofing tiles are more of the features of the urban housing than the rural. Thus they are more to be seen in Kano than in Jigawa States (Table 13.9).

Chapter 13 | J. Afolabi Falola, in
A.I. Tanko and S.B. Momale (Eds.)
*Kano: Environment, Society and Development*
London & Abuja, Adonis & Abbey Publishers

**Table 13.9: Regular Households by Type of Main Material Used for Roofing of Dwelling Unit**

| Material | Jigawa | Kano | Total | % |
|---|---|---|---|---|
| Thatch | 189,049 | 275,973 | 465,022 | 19.27 |
| Wood | 141,949 | 274,816 | 416,765 | 17.27 |
| Earth/Mud/Mud Bricks | 274,113 | 332,906 | 607,019 | 25.15 |
| Corrugated Metal/Zinc Sheet | 154,176 | 522,475 | 676,651 | 28.03 |
| Slate/Asbestos | 19,926 | 89,321 | 109,247 | 4.53 |
| Cement/Concrete | 16,681 | 76,120 | 92,801 | 3.84 |
| Roofing tiles | 7,742 | 21,581 | 29,323 | 1.21 |
| Other | 6,674 | 10,143 | 16,817 | 0.70 |
| Total | 810,310 | 1,603,335 | 2,413,645 | 100 |

*Source: National Population Commission, Nigeria Demographic and Health Survey 2008*

## Facilities in Houses

Pit latrine is the dominant toilet facility while water closet is an exception. Use of nearby bush is more prevalent in Jigawa than in Kano. Largely an urban phenomenon occurrence of public toilet is about equal in the Region (Table 13.10).

**Table 13.10: Types of Toilet Facilities within Households**

| Type of Toilet | Jigawa | Kano | Total | % |
|---|---|---|---|---|
| Water Closet (WC) | 36,303 (4.5%) | 145,360 (9.1%) | 181,663 | 7.53 |
| Pit Latrine | 473,766 (58.5%) | 1,173,309 (73.2%) | 1,647,075 | 68.24 |
| Bucket/Pan | 99,277 | 103,463 | 202,740 | 8.40 |
| Toilet Facility in another (different dwelling) | 41,529 | 67,221 | 108,750 | 4.51 |
| Public Toilet | 38,244 (4.7%) | 68,395 (4.3%) | 106,639 | 4.42 |
| Nearby (bush/field) | 116,819 | 38,532 | 155,531 | 6.44 |
| Other | 4,372 | 7,055 | 11,427 | 0.47 |
| Total | 810,310 | 1,603,335 | 2,413,645 | 100 |

*Source: National Population Commission, Nigeria Demographic and Health Survey 2008*

Electricity supplies is still very rare where in Jigawa about 80% have no supply while in Kano it is about 50% (Table 13.11). The regular source of water for domestic uses is not any better as wells are the chief source where for all; it is as high as 42%. Borehole and rainwater are about equal in their importance just like water vendors and river/stream/spring. Piped-borne supply inside dwelling and

| Chapter 13 | J. Afolabi Falola, in
A.I. Tanko and S.B. Momale (Eds.)
*Kano: Environment, Society and Development*
London & Abuja, Adonis & Abbey Publishers |

195

outside dwelling are low being just about one-tenth put together (Table
13.12). The conclusion from this data is that water supply is poor with
their deleterious effect on human health in the Region. Here the urban
areas are hardly better than the rural with the prevalence of water
vendors in the urban areas.

**Table 13.11: Access to Electricity (2008)**

| STATE | YES | NO | MISSING | NUMBER |
|-------|-----|----|---------|--------|
| Jigawa | 18.6 | 81.0 | 0.4 | 862 |
| Kano | 49.6 | 50.1 | 0.3 | 1,882 |
| Jigawa | 20.5 | 79.2 | 0.3 | 4,660 |
| Kano | 51.5 | 48.2 | 0.2 | 10,209 |

*Source: National Population Commission, Nigeria Demographic and Health Survey
2008*

## Solid Waste Disposal

Solid waste disposal methods adopted in the Region are collection
largely by public authorities and dumping in both approved and
unapproved dump site. A high proportion burn the waste while others
buried the waste (Table 13.13). This is a reflection of poverty in the
provision of facilities for proper waste management. In the Region
waste disposal problem is more of an urban phenomenon as the rural
know the value of household solid waste for their soil improvement.

**Table 13.12: Main Sources of Domestic Water for Households (2006)**

| Source | Jigawa | Kano | Total | % |
|--------|--------|------|-------|---|
| Piped-borne inside dwelling | 48,416 | 89,249 | 137,665 | 5.70 |
| Piped-borne outside dwelling | 43,417 | 58,766 | 102,183 | 4.23 |
| Tanker Supply/Water Vendor | 27,404 | 114,276 | 141,680 | 5.87 |
| Well | 239.483 | 771,420 | 1,010,903 | 41.88 |
| Bore-hole | 234,888 | 162,506 | 397,394 | 16.46 |
| Rain Water | 130,264 | 301,460 | 431,724 | 17,89 |
| River/Stream/Spring | 80,047 | 80,374 | 160,421 | 6.65 |
| Pond/Lake/Dam/Pool | 3,952 | 14,332 | 18,284 | 0.76 |
| Other | 2,709 | 10,952 | 13,661 | 0.57 |
| Total | 810,310 | 1,603,335 | 2,413,645 | 100 |

*Source: National Population Commission, Nigeria Demographic and Health Survey 2008*

Chapter 13 | J. Afolabi Falola, in
A.I. Tanko and S.B. Momale (Eds.)
*Kano: Environment, Society and Development*
London & Abuja, Adonis & Abbey Publishers

**Table 13.13: Distribution of Regular Household by Method of Solid Waste Disposal**

| Method | Jigawa | Kano | Total | % |
|---|---|---|---|---|
| Collected | 208,347 | 433,151 | 641498 | 26.58 |
| Burned by household | 106,899 | 193,333 | 300,232 | 12.44 |
| Public Approved Dump Site | 162,136 | 346,022 | 508,158 | 21.05 |
| Unapproved Dump Site | 119,888 | 222,133 | 342,021 | 14.17 |
| Burnt by household | 181,493 | 359,746 | 541,239 | 22.42 |
| Other | 31,547 | 48,950 | 80,497 | 32.34 |
| Total | 810,310 | 1,603,335 | 2,413,645 | 100.00 |

**Source:** *National Population Commission, Nigeria Demographic and Health Survey 2008*

## Special Categories of the Poor

The special categories of the poor are the women, children and the disabled (more appropriately referred to as physically challenged). The women and the children are the most vulnerable of the society. They are largely powerless in social and economic decisions and this adversely affects their fortunes. It has been accurately judged that:

> All basic indicators of their survival, development, and participation and protection in the society are unfavourable. The infant and maternal mortality rates have remained high, while school enrolment for children (especially girls), life expectancy, immunisation coverage, literacy level and access to basic social services have remained low (Jigawa SEEDS, 75).

Discussing the constraints to the development of women and children, it is noted that the natural tendency to always perceive women and children as vulnerable is the foremost constraint to their development, a situation that ought not to be so as women are custodian of the societal *amanat* while the children are the future of the society. Another constraint is the cultural barrier that limits their social inclusion - the phenomenon that impedes on their educational attainment and participation on one hand and for the discrimination that women face in access to both social and economic opportunities (Jigawa SEEDS, 75).

There are the disabled made poor because of the inability of the social system to translate disability to ability - leaving the physically

Chapter 13 | J. Afolabi Falola, in
A.I. Tanko and S.B. Momale (Eds.)
*Kano: Environment, Society and Development*
London & Abuja, Adonis & Abbey Publishers

challenged at the mercy of the society. The total disabled from the disability status 6 years ago (2006) measured in relation to seeing, hearing, speaking, mobility, mental challenge etc. for Jigawa was 120,904 persons spread through age zero to more than 85 while that for Kano was 239,377 persons. For every disabled adult, there will be one or two escorts of able bodied persons that will be doubling or tripling the number of beggars' category (NPC, 2010).

As regards the children among them, as would be expected, the disabled are less likely than the non-disabled children to go to school and they often do not receive specialized medical care and assistance for rehabilitation that they need to lead normal lives (NPC 2010). Consequently, they resort to street begging for their survival or end up with unscrupulous guardians. Most of the disabled children face a difficult future and adulthood with few prospects of achieving self reliance.

## Reasons for Poverty in the Region

There are several reasons for the prevalence of poverty in the region. The following are notable:

### *Decline of Agriculture*

There has been great decline of agriculture in the Region especially in the once major source of foreign earnings - groundnut production. The Kano region took the lead and experienced phenomenal increase in commercial production of groundnut dating back to 1912 when the railway from Lagos was extended to Kano (Udo 1970). The pyramids which were part of the landscape until 1981 have become history. While there has been great effort at promoting large-scale irrigation (although managed by small holders) and thus extending dry season farming beyond the farmers, such practices are more of an enclave development as they are not ubiquitous as ramified. Even the widespread small-scale irrigation was once bedevilled by the challenges of maintaining the petrol pumps and high operational costs owing to scarcity of petrol (Falola and Sangari 1994).

### *Low Paying Job*

Chapter 13 | J. Afolabi Falola, in
A.I. Tanko and S.B. Momale (Eds.)
*Kano: Environment, Society and Development*
London & Abuja, Adonis & Abbey Publishers

There is also the problem of low paying jobs engaged in by those living in poor residential quarters in the city. The occupational status in selected urban quarters in Kano Metropolis portrayed in Table 13.14 reveal preponderance of trading/business which is basically petty trading. It is common to have kiosks or shops with everyone selling similar wares. There are the artisans many of whom are not more than labourers on daily rates. There are small holders whose farms are located in the urban periphery where agriculture is competing for space with residential developments that are leap-frogging. There are also the drivers and motorcyclists. The latter's fortunes have been dashed by a recent ban on their operations in Kano metropolis.

**Table 13.14: Occupational Status in Selected Slum Areas within Kano Metropolis**

| Occupational Status | Kurna | Gwale | Brigade | Total | % |
|---|---|---|---|---|---|
| Unemployed | 10 | 8 | 4 | 22 | 3.64 |
| Artisan | 36 | 26 | 104 | 166 | 27.48 |
| Trading/Business | 92 | 98 | 36 | 226 | 37.42 |
| Farming | 16 | 54 | 4 | 74 | 12.25 |
| Driving/Cyclist | 18 | 12 | 40 | 70 | 11.59 |
| Public Service | 28 | 6 | 12 | 46 | 7.62 |
| Total | 200 | 204 | 200 | 604 | 100.00 |

**Source:** *Adapted from Aliyu (2007:17)*

The economy of Jigawa State is largely characterized by informal sector activities with agriculture as the major economic activity. Specifically, over 80% of the population is engaged in small holder agriculture and animal husbandry; trade in agricultural goods, livestock and other consumer goods are largely on small and medium scale; other informal sector activities include blacksmithing, leather-works, tailoring services, auto repairs, metal works, carpentry, tanning, dyeing, food processing, masonry etc. Modern industrial sector is skewed in favour of Kano metropolis and is yet to gain any footing in Jigawa State apart from small-scale industries particularly in areas of food processing and other agro-allied activities

Chapter 13 | J. Afolabi Falola, in
A.I. Tanko and S.B. Momale (Eds.)
*Kano: Environment, Society and Development*
London & Abuja, Adonis & Abbey Publishers

**199**

## Seasonality of Employment

As regards seasonality of employment, about two-thirds of the women and men in Jigawa and Kano are engaged all year round while four-fifth of women are engaged all year round in Kano. That occupation is continuous all year for a large percentage of women is understandable being largely domestic (and not jobs outside the house) and, for men both opportunity for dry season farming in the region and sales and services make them engaged year round. In broad terms nearly one-third experience seasonality in their occupation (Table 13.15).

**Table 13.15: Continuity of Employment: Women and Men (2008)**

| Continuity of Employment | Jigawa | | Kano | |
|---|---|---|---|---|
| | Women | Men | Women | Men |
| All Year | 67.2 | 69.1 | 82.4 | 67.5 |
| Seasonal | 30.1 | 30.1 | 10.1 | 29.0 |
| Occasional | 1.3 | 0.6 | 6.6 | 3.0 |
| Missing | 1.4 | 0.3 | 0.9 | 0.4 |

*Source: National Population Commission, Nigeria Demographic and Health Survey 2008*

The picture in relation to type of earnings is clear from the type of employer. The women and men are largely family and self employed (Table 13.16). To be family employed within the region is the same as not being paid in cash for work done!

**Table 13.16: Type of Employer: Women and Men Age 15-49**

| Type Of Employer | Jigawa | | Kano | |
|---|---|---|---|---|
| | Women | Men | Women | Men |
| Employed by Family | 34.8 | 74.6 | 22.9 | 14.2 |
| Employed by Non-Family | 1.1 | 9.9 | 0.5 | 18.8 |
| Self-Employed | 63.9 | 15.5 | 76.1 | 67.0 |
| Missing | 0.2 | 0.0 | 0.5 | 0.0 |

*Source: National Population Commission, Nigeria Demographic and Health Survey 2008*

## Discordance between Population and Livelihood Support

Population size is a good correlate of poverty. In the Region, attention appears not to be given to measures of the scourge of poverty - the size of population in relation to the resources to support it. The survey conducted by the NPC (2009) reveals that the mean age at first

Chapter 13    J. Afolabi Falola, in
A.I. Tanko and S.B. Momale (Eds.)
*Kano: Environment, Society and Development*
London & Abuja, Adonis & Abbey Publishers

marriage for Kano is 15 and a median of 14 just as with many northern states, while the nation's mean is 18 with a median of 17. Indeed by age 19, 42% are mothers in the northwest geopolitical zone in which Kano groups. It was found that 87.7% are married by age 19. This is in spite of the fact that two-thirds of the population are aware of methods of contraception.

In Jigawa State the social characteristics of the population reveal why poverty may be prevalent. For instance the State has a total fertility rate of about 6.2 children per woman of childbearing age (a little above the national average), while the average household size was about 6.7 almost all of which were headed by males. Furthermore the State's population is predominantly rural (90%); the distribution in terms of sex is almost equal between male (50.8%) and female (49.2%). About 60% of household heads were self-employed with agriculture as their main occupation. In terms of age distribution, the 2002 CWIQ Survey indicates that 45.2% of the population was made up of young people below the age of 15; 49.0% between the ages of 15 and 59 while 5.8% were people aged 60 and above. With very high dependency ratio of almost 1.0; meaning that there is almost one dependent to every economically active person in the population. By implication about half of the population is not economically active. If as we know the economically active is already poor by the definition of poverty, it is not surprising that there is a ravaging poverty in the population.

## *Low Level of Literacy*

The literacy level/rate, as factor is both a cause and effect of poverty. There is generally a low level of literacy in the Region as the DHS EdData Survey of year 2012 reveals that only 31.9% of male children age 5-16 are literate. This implies that 67.8% cannot read or write. A very large proportion of this will be female. Even among the 31.9% only about half (16.4%) can read whole sentence. The picture is much grimy for the female children among which about three-quarters cannot read at all. Children in urban area are found to be twice as likely as children in the rural areas to be literate. Also, the higher the economic status of the child's household, the higher the literacy rate. The economically disadvantaged are low in everything. Without such

Chapter 13 | J. Afolabi Falola, in
A.I. Tanko and S.B. Momale (Eds.)
*Kano: Environment, Society and Development*
London & Abuja, Adonis & Abbey Publishers

**201**

education for many and possibly the required skill, even for those who have gone to school, most are not prepared for any employment even if there is any.

The clear evidence of the foregoing is in the army of male child beggars exported from the rural areas into the urban areas while myriads of female children are found hawking in the rural but particularly in urban areas. The latter phenomenon is said to enable the mothers have access to cash from the accumulated savings from the trade to prepare them (female children hawkers) for marriage which cash cannot be available if the child were to go to school. How else can poverty be explained?

But it is important to ask why school attendance is low and dropout rates high. Again the northwest geopolitical DHS EdData provides three major reasons among others as cost-related, the child factors and the school factors. As regards costs parents indicated inability to bear the monetary cost on one hand and the need for the labour of the children for family works. The child factors ranged from being too young to the child not having interest, being sick or disabled. The school factor however ranks highest (70.6%). Such factors as distance to school being too far, to travel to school being unsafe, school being of poor quality, schooling considered as being unimportant and the fact that those who went to school are not having jobs after all!

Other causes of poverty were identified by those who suffer it at an interactive forum with the poor tagged Talakawa Summit chaired by the Jigawa State Governor in 2009 to include:

- Poor state of rural infrastructures such as rural roads which not only limits economic activities but significantly contributes to high maternal and infant mortality in the State.
- Poor and unreliable power supply which profoundly constrains the development of micro, small and medium scale enterprises and the level of socioeconomic living conditions of the people;
- Security or lack of water particularly in Fadama lands which negatively affects agricultural production during the dry season;

Chapter 13 | J. Afolabi Falola, in
A.I. Tanko and S.B. Momale (Eds.)
*Kano: Environment, Society and Development*
London & Abuja, Adonis & Abbey Publishers

- Generally low level of economic activities in the State occasioned by poor patronage and the effects of globalization that threatens the survival of local businesses; and
- Lack of, or poor access to, capital or other means of production and economic empowerment particularly credit facilities and or production equipment.

## The Way Forward

If poverty will be eradicated, then the first point to address is to ensure access of youths to qualitative and functional education which is a very potent tool of socioeconomic transformation. This means giving due attention first to the primary and secondary school levels. It must be said apart from the various efforts of previous administration specified in the SEEDS, the administrations in Jigawa and Kano States appear to pay special attention to education and empowerment schemes. In the Kano section of the Region, Institutes and tertiary education institutions have been established in the last two years. However it is not sufficient for schools to be built and equipped, people must be made to attend them.

There must be a deliberate attempt to eliminate the constraints to agricultural development which have been aptly identified in the SEEDS document to include: addressing the accelerating land degradation; inherently low productivity small holder system, heavy reliance on traditional simple farm implements and production methods; poor state of basic infrastructures; heavy dependence on rain-fed agriculture in an ecologically unstable region prone to drought and flooding, high post-harvest losses due to poorly organised storage; and poor funding of production activities; and poor access to the markets (Jigawa SEEDS n.d.; Kano State Economic Empowerment and Development Strategies - K-SEEDS 2004; Falola, 1992). There must be a pragmatic decision on population policy which should begin with age at marriage and the adoption of appropriate family health practices.

The poor state of rural social and economic infrastructures including rural feeder roads, electrification and water supply among others must be addressed. The States, Local Governments and other

---

Chapter 13    J. Afolabi Falola, in
A.I. Tanko and S.B. Momale (Eds.)
*Kano: Environment, Society and Development*
London & Abuja, Adonis & Abbey Publishers

development partners need to agree on a sustainable approach to tackling this ever lingering challenge to development.

It is quite evident that "urbanisation is proceeding somewhat ahead of the Regions" capacity to control or manage the process without some alarming consequences (Cp. Smith 1977:23). This is reflection of failure of the planning process which includes implementation of plans and associated monitoring to ensure compliance. Surely, slums can be cleared and waste management challenge can be solved by public action.

## References

Aliyu, M.K. (2007), Evaluation of Urban renewal Programme to Slum Improvement in Urban Kano, *Unpublished MSc Land Resources (Administration) Thesis*, Bayero University, Kano.

Falola, J. Afolabi. 1992. An Alternative Strategy for the Organisation of Grain Storage and marketing in Nigeria, *Unpublished Research paper for Postgraduate Diploma in Rural policy and Project Planning*, Institute of Social Studies, The Hague, the Netherlands.

*Falola, J. Afolabi and D.U. Sangari (1994)* The management *of* small-scale irrigation in the Kano region' pp. 77-81 in Kolawole, A, Scoones, I., Awogbade, M.O. and Voh, J.P. (eds.) *Strategies for the Sustainable Use of Fadama Lands in Northern Nigeria*, CSER/ABU and IIED (London)

Jigawa State Government. n.d. Jigawa State Economic Empowerment and Development Strategy (JIGAWASEEDS)

Jigawa State Government of Nigeria. 2008. Communiqué of the Talakawa Summit, Dutse, October 18, 2008. Summit,www.citad.org/jigawa.talakawa-summit.htm, October 23, 2012

Kano State Government. 2004. Kano State Economic Empowerment and Development Strategy (K-SEEDS)

Kano State Government. Giant strides of Gov. Rabi'u Musa Kwankwaso, kano.gov.ng 20/02/2013

National Bureau of Statistics (2012) Nigeria Poverty Profile 2012, www.tuerivers.org/ 28/12/2012

National Population Commission (NPC) [Nigeria] and ICF Macro .2009. Nigeria Demographic and Health Survey 2008. Abuja, Nigeria: National Population Commission and ICF Macro

Chapter 13 | J. Afolabi Falola, in
A.I. Tanko and S.B. Momale (Eds.)
*Kano: Environment, Society and Development*
London & Abuja, Adonis & Abbey Publishers

**204**

National Population Commission. *2010. 2006 Population and Housing Census Priority Table XI - population Distribution by Age, Sex and Disability Status*. NPC, Abuja, Nigeria.

National Population Commission (NPC) [Nigeria] and RTI International, 2011. *Nigeria Demographic and Health Survey (DHS) EdData Profile 1990, 2003, and 2008: Education Data for Decision making, 2011*. Washington, DC, USA: National Population Commission and RTI International

Smith, D.M. 1977. *Human Geography: A welfare approach*, Edward Arnold, London

Udo, R.K. 1970. *Geographical Regions of Nigeria*, Heinemann, Ibadan

| Chapter 13 | J. Afolabi Falola, in |
| | A.I. Tanko and S.B. Momale (Eds.) |
| | *Kano: Environment, Society and Development* |
| | London & Abuja, Adonis & Abbey Publishers |

**205**

# Part III
# Resource Utilisation and Management

# Chapter Fourteen

## SOIL FERTILITY MANAGEMENT

Maharazu Alhaji Yusuf

### Introduction

The farming system in the Kano Region is dominated by smallholder farming, mostly at subsistence level. A smallholder farmer is the one who posses small farm plot, using mostly crude implements with very little investment, using mainly self and family labour. For centuries, the indigenous smallholder farmers in the Region have been devising numerous methods to cultivate land under the prevailing conditions of soils and climate. The soil resources being dynamic and a bowl, in which nutrients are cycled in the agricultural systems, need to be efficiently managed in order to maintain and protect the food production system. This makes the farmer to adopt diverse soil and fertility management technologies (Yusuf, 2001). These soil management strategies are manifested in the form of fallow, fertilization/manuring, cultivation systems and agronomy which vary from place to place depending upon the soils, landforms, rainfall availability, technology and other socio-economic variables.

The issue of soil fertility management by the smallholder comes as a consequence of the ever increasing need to increase food production for the family, especially in areas where the ratio of land to population is very high as in the case of the intensively cultivated Kano Close-Settled Zone (higher cultivation density areas), or where land is highly susceptible to the vagaries of weather as in the case of the more arid areas of the Kano Region.

The soil fertility management technologies are all the techniques employed by the farmer to conserve and improve the fertility of his farmland. They are mostly soil property improvement techniques aiming at conserving soil nutrients and improvement of soil conditions for crop production. The smallholder farmer in northern Nigeria and the Kano Region in particular have been devising some of these techniques before the knowledge of modern laboratory and some have proved excellent in conserving and improving soil fertility (Yusuf,

Chapter 14 | Maharazu A. Yusuf, in
A.I. Tanko and S.B. Momale (Eds.)
*Kano: Environment, Society and Development*
London & Abuja, Adonis & Abbey Publishers

2001). The improving techniques could be in terms of fertilization/manuring, employment of some cropping systems and patterns (e.g. crop rotation, mixed cropping, alley cropping, fallowing, weed controls, residue uses) and agroforestry. The adoption of these varies with environment (soils and landforms) and other resources (Jones and Wild, 1975; Mortimore, 1995).

However the fertility management technologies employed by the indigenous smallholder farmers of the Kano Region is not much exposed to scientific scrutiny. Much is yet to be known especially how the farmer has been adopting and adapting under climatic uncertainty and economic restrictions.

**The Farming System in the Kano Region**

The Kano Region as described also includes an open countryside characterised by high concentration of rural population with intensive arable farming. The area physiographically includes the upper and middle drainage basins of Rivers Kano, Hadejia, Katagum and Jama'are up to the confluence; forming the Yobe (Rachkam and Rose Innes, 1978; Olofin, 1987). This Region exhibits differences in terms of relief, soils, population density and economic activities. These differences help to characterise the farming system and so the soil fertility management. Therefore the Kano Region can be divided into three, based on physiography and farming system (Figure 14.1). The farming system is defined as a unit consisting of human group (usually household) and the resources it manages in the production of crops and or animals (livestock) under the prevailing factors such as climate, soils, land quality and tenure, and other socio-economic variables (Beets, 1990).

Chapter 14 | Maharazu A. Yusuf, in
A.I. Tanko and S.B. Momale (Eds.)
*Kano: Environment, Society and Development*
London & Abuja, Adonis & Abbey Publishers

**208**

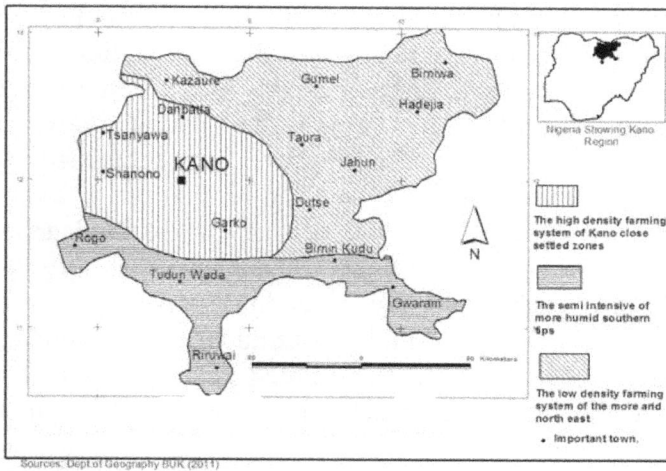

**Fig 14.1: The Distribution of the Farming Systems of the Kano Region**

In the Region, there are three farming systems with regards to differences in the soil fertility management strategies. The three divisions include:

i) The high density farming system of the Kano Close-Settled Zone;
ii) The low density farming system of the more arid North East; and
iii) The semi intensive farming system of more humid southern tips.

## The High Density Farming System of Kano Close-Settled Zone

This enclosed the area known as Kano Close-Settled Zone which is described as the vast rural settlements around the Kano city as node (Figure 14.1). There is great concentration of rural population with intensive subsistence farming by smallholder farmers. This is located at the centre of the Region, with irregular shape and ellipse, extending some 100km from Kano city to the south east and only 50km in other directions (Hill, 1977). The whole zone lies on the Basement Complex with dominance of sandy ferruginous soils, though very low in

Chapter 14 | Maharazu A. Yusuf, in
A.I. Tanko and S.B. Momale (Eds.)
*Kano: Environment, Society and Development*
London & Abuja, Adonis & Abbey Publishers

209

inherent soil nutrients but is light, freely draining, sandy loams which proved highly amiable to intensive cultivation. It lies within gently undulating plains and it is drained mostly by seasonal rivers. To the west and southern parts of the Region, the soils have developed from the Basement Complex with wind-blown sands. Whereas to the east is the unconsolidated sediments of the Chad Formation.

In this zone almost 80 - 90% of the surface land area is under rainfed arable cultivation of subsistence crops such as sorghum, millet, maize and some cash crops like groundnut, cowpea and pepper. For decades these farmlands are under continuous cultivation with plenty application of organic manure, sourced mainly from the farmers owned domestic animals, household sweepings and ashes (Harris, 1996; Yusuf, 2010).

The total annual rainfalls ranging from 750mm to 900mm a year is adequate for crops cultivation and the prevalence of drought is less. Due to high population density and suitably fertile soils the indigenous smallholder farmer has developed diverse and appropriate soil fertility management techniques that help to sustain the farming system for centuries (Hill, 1977; Mortimore and Adams, 1999). There are higher diversity of soil fertility management in this zone than anywhere in northern Nigeria wider range in use of different agronomic techniques, tillage and fertilization.

## The Low Density Farming System of the More Arid North East

This occupies the more arid north eastern part of the region and exclusively lies within the Chad formation (Figure 14.1). The soils are derived from the unconsolidated sediments which are predominantly sandy or sandy loam (Olofin, 1987) especially on the well drained interfluves. There are ancient stabilised dunes where brown and dark brown soils occur especially around Jahun and Birniwa.

There exist an extensive farming system, the farmlands are big and fallow lands are common and a part of the soil fertility management technique. The smallholder farmer uses long handled hoes like *ashasha* and *sungumi* which are adaptive to extensive farming operation. There are an extensive cultivation of mainly millet, sorghum and cowpeas. Other crops include *Citrulus lanatus (guna)* and benniseed as cash crops in especially the far northern part of the

Chapter 14 | Maharazu A. Yusuf, in
A.I. Tanko and S.B. Momale (Eds.)
*Kano: Environment, Society and Development*
London & Abuja, Adonis & Abbey Publishers

zone. Organic manure is available but used mostly in the infields (farms near the village) because of distance (Yusuf, 1998), while fallowing is frequently used for fertility regeneration (Mohammed, 1996). The rural population density is low at 100 to 250 persons per square kilometre. Only about 40 - 60% of the land area is under cultivation during the short rainy season with less than 750mm rainfall.

## *The Semi Intensive Farming System of More Humid Southern Tips*

This comprise of the southern tips of the region including the more wetter areas of Tudun Wada - Ririwai; the much more water shade of Challawa river around Rogo and the Birnin Kudu and Gwaram axis. The landforms are mainly the Basement Complex and the relief is undulating only in the southern tips of Riruwai where exist rock complexes and hills which occupy up to 45% of the surface area (Olofin, 1987).

The soils are derived from the highly weathered Basement complex and with wind drift material which covers the regolith of the ancient rocks. Due to the relative high annual rainfall of 800 - 1000mm, the soils are highly leached and acidic. They are silty loam to loam.

The farming system is fairly intensive only that the farms are relatively larger than in the Kano close-settled zone, possibly due to lower population density. There is the appearance of the Guinea Savanna particularly in areas south of Tudun Wada. Thus, vegetation is denser especially under reserve conditions. Some level of mechanisation mainly in the use of tractors for ridging is employed. The cultivation is oriented a little to commercialise farming with intensive cultivation of cash crops such as pepper, onions, rice, maize and cassava on commercial basis.

Traditional soil fertility management is still dominant; thus there is more use of inorganic fertilizer especially for cash crops. Fallow fields are common and mainly for the purpose of soil fertility regeneration.

Chapter 14 | Maharazu A. Yusuf, in
A.I. Tanko and S.B. Momale (Eds.)
*Kano: Environment, Society and Development*
London & Abuja, Adonis & Abbey Publishers

## Nature of Soil Fertility Management in the Region

Across the Region, the nature of Soil fertility management depends on land availability, agronomy, climate, soil types and other resources at the smallholder's disposal. In this vast area where farming system is dominated by smallholder peasant farming, the farmer cultivating his plots using simple implements to feed his family and derive small cash income from sale of a portion of the produce. The soil fertility management technologies adopted in every zone is summarised in Table 14.1. Over the years however, the farmers have developed and adapted different soil fertility management technologies to improve or maintain the soil fertility of their farmlands. These agricultural techniques can be divided into five: fallow, fertilization, agronomic practices, cultivation technologies and residue managements. In each of the three zones there are differences in terms of adaptability, usage and improvement of soil nutrients.

These managements are land or soil treatments adapted by the smallholder farmer which are mostly aimed at improving soil fertility. However some of these management technologies can also be weed control or moisture management, though they do in a way have serious positive or negative impact on soil properties. The management strategies and technologies are described below.

### *Fallow*

Fallowing is a deliberate abandonment of farmland without cropping for variable period of time, ideally to allow the land to rest and regenerate its fertility naturally. There are various systems and types of fallow, depending on the area and the purpose of fallow - such as bush fallow, intermittent fallow, and fallow under shifting cultivation or land rotation. In any situation the weeds and the perennial bushes and scrubs are allowed to invade the fallow fields and in most tropical conditions, are subjected to grazing (Beets, 1990).

The conventional fallow system in the Kano Region is only significant in the low cultivation density areas of north east and the more humid of the southern tips. And these were purposely for fertility improvements. This is the practice of many indigenous farming communities in low density areas of West African Savanna as reported

Chapter 14 | Maharazu A. Yusuf, in
A.I. Tanko and S.B. Momale (Eds.)
*Kano: Environment, Society and Development*
London & Abuja, Adonis & Abbey Publishers

by Areola (1979); Mark and Evedenberge (1991); Mortimore (1991); and Abubakar (1995). The period of fallow differs with land availability and other fertility management resources such as manure, draft power and improved tillage. In the high cultivation density zone, because of high pressure on land there could only be intermittent fallow in which land that has been cultivated for two to three years is left fallow for a year or two before it is cultivated again (Table 14.1). This type of fallow was found to be unsustainable and lowers the fertility status of the farmlands (Yusuf, 1994; 1996).

Fallow, as a soil fertility improvement technique, is absent in the high intensive farming system of the Kano Close-Settled Zone, but extensively adopted in the Low density farming system and in the more humid semi-intensive farming system (Table 14.1). The reasons for none improvement of nutrients in the high intensive farming system of the Kano Close-Settled Zone is that fallow fields are badly managed in these areas because they rarely occur, and where they occur, are under persistent grazing by the tethered-domestic animals and grass cut over by the neighbouring farmers which takes away soil nutrients. Moreover the fallow plots becomes bare even during the high peak rainfall period (July and August) when the arable crops are high enough (in the cultivated fields) to protect the soil from erosion and leaching of soil nutrients. Thus fallow is a bad management in the high cultivation density areas.

## *Manuring/Fertilization*

Fertilization is an application of organic or inorganic materials to the soils to supply certain elements for the growth of crops. The indigenous smallholder farmer in Kano Region appreciates the value of organic manure which he applies in form of pen manure, domestic household wastes (ashes, sweepings etc), kraal dung and composted farm waste and residues.

Livestock manure provides a low-cost supply of nutrients and organic matter with which farmers can improve soil fertility and so is an important component of their soil fertility management strategy (Harris and Yusuf, 2001). The addition of manure improves soil water holding capacity, cation exchange capacity, and soil structure. These in turns reduce erosivity of the soil. Manure is also a source of

| Chapter 14 | Maharazu A. Yusuf, in |
| | A.I. Tanko and S.B. Momale (Eds.) |
| | *Kano: Environment, Society and Development* |
| | London & Abuja, Adonis & Abbey Publishers |

nitrogen, phosphorus, potassium and range of micronutrients (Yusuf, 1995, Yusuf 2010). Farm yard manure is known to reduce the acidification of soil that comes from continued cropping, particularly where ammonium fertilizer are often used (Ofori and Potaley, 1965; Duponit de Direchin 1967 and Pien, 1971; Djokoto and Stephens, 1996).

Table 14.1 outlines the major types of organic manure used in different parts of the Kano Region. These include livestock manure, rotational manuring, compound refuse/waste, poultry and night soil. It can be seen that these types of organic manures are highly and intensively used in the high density Kano Close-Settled Zone. However for some manure types like poultry manure are preferred and used mainly for vegetables such as onions and pepper whereas night soil is mainly used for grain crops (Yusuf, 2010).

In the low density farming system, manure is generally used extensively in the nearby farms as its use is constrained by parking (transport) (Yusuf, 2010). Nonetheless poultry and night soils are not much recognised in this farming system. In the more humid semi-intensive farming system, the use of organic manure is adapted. However, rotational manuring, compound sweepings and night soil are not much in used.

Due to inadequacy of inorganic fertilizer, owing to its high costs in recent years, smallholder farmers resort to the use of organic manure with high efficiency, especially in the high population and cultivation density farming areas of the Kano Region. It was reported that, it is deemed necessary for every household in the Kano Close-Settled Zone to keep small ruminants (goats, sheep) for the purpose of generating manure (Harris, 1996; Yusuf, 1995). Besides this, there are few able farmers who still apply inorganic fertilizer such as compound fertilizers (NPK), calcium-ammonium-nitrate (CAN) and urea, mostly to cereal grain crops (sorghum and millet) and superphosphate (SUPA) to legume crops (groundnuts and cowpea).

## Agronomic Methods

The agronomic practice refers to the cropping systems, composition, density and pattern adopted in a particular area. The smallholder farmer in the Kano Region adopts several cropping patterns and

| Chapter 14 | Maharazu A. Yusuf, in |
| | A.I. Tanko and S.B. Momale (Eds.) |
| | *Kano: Environment, Society and Development* |
| | London & Abuja, Adonis & Abbey Publishers |

intensity so as to maximize yield and conserve fertility. These include crop rotation, mixed cropping or intercropping and monocropping of certain crops, such as legumes solo or grain solo (Table 14.1). Cropping system and pattern is a function of environment (soil and climate) and soil fertility. In more humid areas of the southern tips and the Kano Close-Settled Zone with the use of manuring, intensive cropping and mixed cropping with high density cropping are possible; whereas in low rainfall areas (Low density farming system) only few crops with sparse cropping pattern are possible. In all these situations, the fertility of the farmlands is affected negatively or positively by any of these cropping systems.

Mixed cropping is the art of growing two or more crops intermingled in the same field. In this pattern, certain crop combinations are mutually beneficial. There is the economic advantage of increasing return per hectare and some positive effects on soil fertility and quality. In this, different layers of crops have better protection of soil against the impact of rain drops and consequently surface compaction and erosion are reduced. This lowers bulk density and porosity is maintained (Jones and Wild, 1975; Powel, 1986). It was also found that this system enables the exploitation of the soil nutrients at different depths, which is more efficient, and extended over longer periods of time.

It was reported that cereal (sorghum and millet) may benefit from association with legumes (groundnut and cowpea). Though there are few studies on the impact of legumes on soil fertility unless in experimental farms, it is hardly possible to have continuous annual legumes under smallholder farming. Moreover, studies on productivity and fertility of soil under legumes-grain mixtures (groundnut and cowpeas) which are believed to be nitrogen fixers, provide no information about the amount of nitrogen fixed (by these crops) and how much is left in the soils at the end of the season (Jones and Wild, 1975; Smalling, 1993).

The diversification of cropping system and pattern are only and mostly evident in the high intensive farming system of Kano Close-Settled Zone of the Kano Region. Table 14.1 gives three basic cropping or agronomic methods across the three zones in the Kano Region i.e. crop rotation, mixed cropping and legumes mono culture. In the high density farming system of the Kano Close-Settled Zone,

| Chapter 14 | Maharazu A. Yusuf, in |
|---|---|
| | A.I. Tanko and S.B. Momale (Eds.) |
| | *Kano: Environment, Society and Development* |
| | London & Abuja, Adonis & Abbey Publishers |

crop rotation and mixed cropping are adopted and used to improve or manage the fertility of the soils whereas legume or grain mono cropping are only aimed to maximize productivity. However, in both low density farming system and the more humid semi intensive farming system, mono and mixed cropping are meant to maximised productivity of the crops. A smallholder farmer in the area may grow groundnut, beniseed or millet as major crop only to see that he gets much of the crop rather than for fertility improvement.

## Cultivation Methods (Tillage System)

Soil tillage under the Savanna environment is primarily aimed to control weeds and modify or improve the physical condition of soils within the rooting depth of crops, to incorporate organic residues and for better soil water use efficiency. It was reported that cultivation affects rooting systems i.e. the root extension which is liable to affect moisture and nutrients uptake and so determine crop growth and yield (Jones and Wild, 1975).

There are basically three methods of land tillage (cultivation) under the indigenous smallholder condition in the Region: Hand cultivation which involves the use of hand-hoe long or short in planting and weeding, ox-ploughing which makes use of animal power to cultivate the land, especially in weeding and ridging and the use of tractor. The use of hand-hoes throughout the crop cultivation periods ensures minimum soil disturbances; the depth hardly exceeds 10cm. On the other hand, ox-plough which is more popular in the high intensive farming system of Kano Close-Settled Zone and the more humid semi intensive farming system of the southern tip of the Kano Region. This system mixes the soil more vigorously and could reach a depth of up to 20 to 30cm. And this may affect the physical and chemical soil properties and have impacts on soil conditions generally (Yusuf, 2001). These technologies are said to have drastic effect on soil properties and management due to the vigorous churning of the soils in this practice (Ox-plough and tractor) and it can result to loss of some nutrients (Kowal and Kassam, 1978; Yusuf, 2001).

The basic tillage system in the high intensive farming system and the low density farming system are hand cultivation and use of ox-plough. The primary objective is weed control i.e. to suppress and

Chapter 14 | Maharazu A. Yusuf, in
A.I. Tanko and S.B. Momale (Eds.)
*Kano: Environment, Society and Development*
London & Abuja, Adonis & Abbey Publishers

clear the unwanted weeds in the farms to allow the cultivated crop to have the sole advantage of the soil nutrients and sunlight. However, ox-plough in the high intensive farming system is additionally for moisture management, thus farm plots which are ox-ploughed retain more moisture than those under hand plough (Yusuf, 1994). The use of tractor is only evident in the more humid semi intensive farming system. This is because the farms are relatively larger in size allowing adequate movement of the tractor, and the farming practice is more commercialised with relatively higher investment. On the other hand, use of tractor in the high intensive farming system of Kano Close-Settled Zone is impracticable as the farm plots are highly fragmented, with many fields less than 0.5 hectare. Moreover the extensive nature coupled with low investment in the low density farming system did not make use of tractor feasible.

## *Residue Management and Soil Fertility*

Residues in the broadest sense include all non-grain parts of cultivated crop plants and grass weeds grown on the farm (Beets, 1990). The use and disposal of these residues have important role in the productivity of the farming system and fertility of farm plots of the smallholder in the Region.

Crop residues is used in several ways to improve soil fertility as it decomposes readily to yield the available forms of mineral nitrogen, sulphur and phosphorus (Brady, 1975), it also helps to improve the soil conditions thereby improving its water relationships and diffusibility of carbon dioxide and oxygen through the soil. Moreover residues incorporation provides food for the soil micro organisms, especially, the nitrogen fixers (White, 1997).

The impact of cropping and crop residues on soil fertility manifest in many ways. Crop residues such as millet and sorghum stalk and legumes (cowpeas and groundnut) straws are used as mulching material in which they are left on the farms. This helps to protect soils against rain drops and wind shear; conserves soil moisture and modifies the microclimate of the near ground atmosphere (Briggs and Courtney, 1989). When the residues decay in situ, the carbon, oxygen and other nutrient elements assimilated during the crop growth are released to the soil. The incorporation of residues into the soil helps to

Chapter 14 | Maharazu A. Yusuf, in
A.I. Tanko and S.B. Momale (Eds.)
*Kano: Environment, Society and Development*
London & Abuja, Adonis & Abbey Publishers

improve soil organic matter content and thereby improve soil structure (Beets, 1990).

Burning of residues like grain stalk increase potassium and calcium, returning to the soil in form of ash. There are significant losses of nitrogen, phosphorus and sulphur in smoke and a high percentage of other soil nutrients are easily lost through leaching (Briggs and Courtney, 1989).

Residue burning or bush burning are only very much relevant in the more humid semi intensive system of the southern tip, and mostly aimed to clear farms from unwanted bushes and residues from the previous cultivation.

The farming system of the more humid southern tip of the Region requires that these residues are left *in situ* to decompose and be incorporated into the soils. These help to improve soil condition and fertility. Though the incorporation of residues (to improve fertility) is limited by ability to easily decompose (decay) into the soils, mainly due to the rainfall, temperature and relative humidity of the farming area zone. For example longer dry season in the low density farming system does not allow this incorporation of residues with soils to work properly. Whereas residues, mulching and burning are absent in the high intensive farming system, simply because residues are essentially used for other purposes like animal feeds and construction. However, in the intensive farming system of Kano Close-Settled Zone, the use of residues as soil fertility improvement is absent as all types of residues are effectively used by the farmer: cereal stalks used for construction and fencing while legume hay/straw form excellent livestock feeds.

## Conclusion

Three agro ecological zones were identified in the Kano Region, i.e. the high intensive farming system of Kano Close-Settled Zone, low density farming system of the far north east and the more humid semi intensive farming system of the southern tip of the region. Each of these areas has significant variability in terms of farming system and soil fertility management. The high intensive farming system is very intensive in population and farming intensities where over 90% of the area is under intensive smallholder cultivation. Moreover the climate in terms of rainfall and soil factors couple with the use of organic

Chapter 14 | Maharazu A. Yusuf, in
A.I. Tanko and S.B. Momale (Eds.)
*Kano: Environment, Society and Development*
London & Abuja, Adonis & Abbey Publishers

manure, allow this intensive system to be sustainable for over a century (Mortimore, 2007). All kinds of manures are used for improving soil fertility, while crop rotation and mixed cropping are other measures of improving soil fertility. But fallow is not recognised as soil fertility improvement method as this is restricted by the non-availability of land and overgrazing by the tethered livestock that overexploit the few fallow fields rendering it infertile.

The low density farming system occupies most zone of the Chad formation. The area has low population density, low rainfall and therefore extensive farming operations prevails. Fallow system is widely used and accepted as soil improvement method. Manures are only used in nearby farms. While mixed cropping and mono cultures are only meant for maximising crop productivity rather then for soil fertility improvement. Due to the extensive nature of this area, inorganic fertiliser is economically impossible and the use of ox-plough is mainly for weed control.

In the more humid farming system of the southern tip of the Kano Region, the rainfall is relatively higher and soil is heavier, but with low population and farming densities. These allow partially commercial rainfed farming, thus most of fertility management techniques are positively feasible. The use of fallow, organic and inorganic manures, use of agronomic methods and tillage are meant to improve soil fertility. It is observed that the residue use is not consciously meant for improving fertility but a means of clearing farms. Therefore it is relatable to assume that any agroecology with same type of physical and socioeconomic characteristics in the Savanna region of West Africa would exhibit same soil fertility management techniques.

Chapter 14    Maharazu A. Yusuf, in
             A.I. Tanko and S.B. Momale (Eds.)
             *Kano: Environment, Society and Development*
             London & Abuja, Adonis & Abbey Publishers

## Table 14.1: Types and Uses of Different Soil Fertility Management Technologies among the Three Zones in the Kano Region

| | SOIL FERTILITY MANAGEMENT | High Intensive Farming System of Kano Close-Settled Zone | Low Density Farming System of far North East | More Humid, Semi Intensive of the Southern Tips |
|---|---|---|---|---|
| A | *Fallow* | | | |
| | 1. Short Fallow 2-4 years | Incidental and intermittent, not improve fertility | Extensively adopted, and improve fertility | Adopted and improve fertility |
| | 2. Long Fallow 5-10 years | Absent | Extensively adopted, and improve fertility | Adopted and improve fertility |
| B | *Fertilization/Manuring* | | | |
| | 1. Organic Manure | | | |
| | i) Livestock Manure | Intensively used & improve fertility | Used only on nearby farms & is constrained by transport | Adopted and used |
| | ii) Rotational manuring | Used & improve fertility | Extensively used mainly by pastoralists. | Not much in use |
| | iii) Compound Waste/refuse | Used & improve fertility | No much use | Not much in use |
| | vi) Poultry manure | Used & mainly on vegetables and high value crops | No any significant use | Some uses to vegetables (pepper & onion) |
| | v) Night soil | Use on grain crops | Not in use | Not in use |
| | vi) Inorganic Fertilizer | Use by few rich farmers | No much in use | Much use especially for cash crops |
| C | *Agronomic Methods* | | | |
| | i) Crop rotation | Adapted and improve fertility | Not much in use | Manage soil fertility |
| | ii) Mixed cropping | Manage fertility | Maximising productivity | Maximising productivity |
| | iii) Legumes mono culture | Maximising productivity | Maximising productivity | Maximising productivity |
| D | *Cultivation Methods* | | | |
| | i) Hand Cultivation | Weed control | Weed control | Weed control |
| | ii) Ox-ploughing | Weed control and moisture management | Much use for weed control | Much use for weed control |
| | iii) Tractor | Not in use | Not in use | Very much in use as rigger |
| E | *Residue Management* | | | |
| | i) Residue mulching | Absent | Some use | Some use |
| | ii) Residue/Bush burning | Absent | Some use as farm clearance | Very much in use to clear farm |

| Chapter 14 | Maharazu A. Yusuf, in
A.I. Tanko and S.B. Momale (Eds.)
*Kano: Environment, Society and Development*
London & Abuja, Adonis & Abbey Publishers |

# References

Abubakar S. M. (1995) 'Role of Fallowing on Soil Renewal under a dry savanna climate: An example from the Kabomo Area of Katsina State': Paper presented at the National workshop on Land Administration and Management in Northern Nigeria. Bayero University Kano 12th - 16th March 1995.

Areola, O. (1979) `In search of an approach to the management of savanna fallow soils', *Savanna* Vol.8 (1) 39-44

Beets, W.C. (1990) *Raising and sustaining productivity of smallholder farming systems in the ropics,* AgBe Alkmaar, Holland

Bennet, G.J.; A. A. Hutcheon; W. B. Kerr; J. R. Mansfield and L. J. Rackham (1978) *Land Resources of Central Nigeria. Environmental Aspects of the Kano plains. vol.1 Land forms and soils.* Land Resource Report 20, Land Resource Center, UK Ministry of Overseas Development, Tolworth.

Brady, N. C. (1974). *The Nature and Properties of Soils*, Macmillan Publishing co., New York.

Briggs, D. and Courtney, F. (1989) *Agriculture and Environment. The physical Geography of Temperate Agricultural Systems.* Longman scientific and Technical. Essex. England.

Djokoto, R. K. and D. Stephens (1961) 'Thirty long-term experiments under Continuous cropping in Ghana. Crop yields and responses to fertilizers and manures.' *Emp. expl. Agric.*, 29, 181-195.

Dupont de Dinechin, B. (1967) 'Resultats conceenant les effets compares des fumures minerale et organique.' *Colloque sur la fertilite des sols tropicaux, Tana narive,* 2,1411-1428.

Harris F. (1996) *Intensification of Agriculture in Semi-arid Areas: Lessons from the Kano Close Settled Zone, Nigeria.* Gatekeeper series No. 59. International Institute for Environmental Development. London.

Harris, F. and Yusuf, M. A. (2001) 'Manure Management by Smallholder Farmer in the Kano Close-settled Zone, Nigeria.' *Journal of Experimental Agriculture* 37:319-332. Cambridge University Press.

Hill, P. (1977) *Population,, Prosperity and Poverty: rural Kano 1900 and 1970.* Cambridge: Cambridge University Press.

Chapter 14 | Maharazu A. Yusuf, in
A.I. Tanko and S.B. Momale (Eds.)
*Kano: Environment, Society and Development*
London & Abuja, Adonis & Abbey Publishers

Jones, M.J. and Wild, A. (1975) *Soils of the West African Savanna. The maintenance and improvement of their fertility. Technical Communication, No.55, Commonwealth Bureau of soils,* Harpenden.

Kowal, M. J. and Kassam, A. H. (1978) *Agricultural Ecology of the Savanna: A Study of West Africa.* Clarendon Press, Oxford.

Mark, S.F. and Freudenberger, K.S. (1993) *Fields, Fallow, and Flexibility" Natural Resource Management in Ndam mor Fademba, Senegal.* RRA. Dryland programme. No. 5 International Institute for Environment and Development. IIED. London.

Mohammed, S. (1996). *The Farming System of Dagaceri in Jigawa state, Nigeria.* Working Paper 2. Soils, Cultivars and Livelihoods in North Eastern Nigeria. Department of Geography University of Cambridge/Department of Geography, Bayero University, Kano.

Mortimore, M. And Willard, K. (1991) *Profile of Technology change; Environmental Change and Dryland management in Machakos District, kenya 1930-1990.* ODI working paper No.57 Overseas Development Institute, London.

Mortimore, M. J. (1995) `Caring for the soil, Agricultural expansion, population growth and natural resource degradation in the Sahel' Workshop, Senderborg, Denmark.

Mortimore, M. and Adams, W.M. (1999) *Working the Sahel: Environment and Society in northern Nigeria.* Routledge, London.

Mortimore, M; J. Adams and F. Harris (2000) *Poverty and Systems Research in the Drylands.* Gatekeeper series no.94 International Institute for Environment and Development. (IIED). London.

Ofori, C. S. and Potakey, V. A. (1965) 'Effect of fertilizers on yield of grop under mechanical cultivation in the coastal savanna area in Ghana.' *Proceeding, OAU/ATRC symposium on maintenance and improvement of soil fertility,* Khartoum.

Olofin, E.A. (1987) *Some Aspect of physical Geography of the Kano Region and Related human responses.* Departmental lecture note series No.1, Department of Geography, Bayero University, Kano.

Pieri, C. (1971) 'Survey of the fertilization trails on rainfed areas in Mali from 1954 to 1970.' *IRAT publication.* Translated STRC/OAU-J.P.26, Dakar.

Powell, J.M. (1986) Manure for cropping: a case study from central Nigeria. *Experimental Agriculture* 22, 15-24.

Chapter 14 | Maharazu A. Yusuf, in
A.I. Tanko and S.B. Momale (Eds.)
*Kano: Environment, Society and Development*
London & Abuja, Adonis & Abbey Publishers

Rachkam, L.J. and Ross Innes, R. (1978) *Land Resources of Central Nigeria. Environmental aspects of the Kano plains*. Vol. 2 climate and vegetation. Land Resource Division, Rep. 20. ODA, London

Smalling, E. (1993) *An agro-ecological Framework For Integrated Nutrient Management: - with special reference to Kenya*. Doctoral thesis, Agricultural University, Wageningen, The Netherlands.

Russel, E. W. (1973) Soil *Conditions and Plant Growth*, Longman, London.

Yusuf, M.A. (1994) 'The Influence of Agricultural Management on Present and Potential Soil Quality under Smallholder Conditions: A case study of Tumbau (Kano Close Settled-Zone).' M.Sc. Thesis (Land Resources), Department of Geography, Bayero University, Kano.

Yusuf, M. A. (1996). *The Farming System of Tumbau in Kano state, Nigeria*. Soils, Cultivars and Livelihoods in North Eastern Nigeria. Department of Geography University of Cambridge/Department of Geography, Bayero University, Kano.

Yusuf, M. A. (1998) 'Adaptive Soil Management in the Semi - Arid Northern Nigeria.' Proceedings of Department for International Development (DfiD) *Soils, Cultivars, Livelihoods and Nutrient Dynamics in Semi-arid northern Nigeria*. NRI, Department of Geography, University of Cambridge/Department of Geography, Bayero University Kano.

Yusuf, M. A. (2001). 'Soil Assessment and Indigenous Soil Management in the Semi-Arid North Eastern Nigeria' Unpublished PhD Thesis to the Department of Geography, Bayero University Kano.

Chapter 14    Maharazu A. Yusuf, in
         A.I. Tanko and S.B. Momale (Eds.)
         *Kano: Environment, Society and Development*
         London & Abuja, Adonis & Abbey Publishers

# Chapter Fifteen

## WATER RESOURCE DEVELOPMENT AND MANAGEMENT

Adamu Idris Tanko

## Introduction

Although the Kano Region as defined by this book is referring to the political States of Kano and Jigawa (see Chapter one), this Chapter widens the scope by discussing water resource within the hydrological boundaries traversing the states of Kano, Jigawa, Bauchi, Yobe, Borno and to some extent Plateau in central Nigeria. The area, located approximately between Latitude $10^{0}00$'N and $13^{0}20$'N and Longitudes $7^{0}25$'E and $11^{0}00$'E covers parts of the north west and north-east Nigeria covering over 84,000 $km^{2}$ and supporting the livelihood of over 15 million people through agriculture, fishing, livestock keeping and municipal water supply. The area cuts across two major geological formations of the Basement Complex at the upstream (characterized by hard impermeable strata) and the Chad formation in the middle and lower parts which is overlain by the relatively flat soft sand gravels and clays (see Chapters one and three). Bawden et al. (1973) describes the area as belonging to the Region of the northern plains characterized largely of extensive flat or very gently undulating plains sloping gradually from over 1000m above sea level in the south and west of Kano to less than 300m near the Lake Chad. Olofin (1987) describes the feature of the central area as having extensive longitudinal dunes and extensive alluvial flats existing in the inter-dune area. Generally, the river system within the area has extensive floodplains which provide means for various socio-economic activities through the utilization of a variety of ecological processes. A study (Aminu et al., 2006) reveals that in the area, the river is the most important resource upon which more than 90% of the population depend for their livelihoods. Hence, there is rapid rise in population (doubling in most of the riparian states in less than 30 years).

Chapter 15 | Adamu I. Tanko, in
A.I. Tanko and S.B. Momale (Eds.)
*Kano: Environment, Society and Development*
London & Abuja, Adonis & Abbey Publishers

Demographically, the ethic composition of the people living in these communities is mostly the Hausa-Fulani at the upstream of Hadejia valley, Fulani-Warji-Hausa-Karekare in the upstream of River Jama'are-Katagum-Komadugu-Gana; while Kanuri/Bedde-Hausa dominate the mid-stream in Yobe, and Kanuri dominate in Borno up to the Lake Chad. The average population size for the riparian communities was reported to be between 2,000 and 6,000 households except for very few communities where the average could be as high as 10,000 (Afromedev, 2006). The mid-basin especially around the Hadejia-Nguru Wetlands is characterized by excessively flooded and *typha*-infested areas and which forms one of the low density areas in the country (Bird and Tanko, 2004).

The level of urbanization and its antecedents characterize the upstream of the river systems, while there is a significant dependency on river resources both in terms of fishing and dry season irrigation (organized and unorganized) along the river channels, and this has attracted many people from different part of the country. Away from the river channels is mainly the practice of wet season upland farming which is greatly hindered by the limitation in climate. Pastoralism among the Fulanis and livestock rearing among the settled population is highly engaging as a means of income generation and survival (see Chapter sixteen). Main occupation in the area includes: upland crop production, fishing, irrigated crop production and livestock production. Main agricultural outputs produced include onion, sugar cane, tomato, carrot and pepper, garden egg, wheat and rice in the dry season; while in the wet season sorghum, millet cowpea, groundnuts and cassava are the main products. Other major economic activities include livestock rearing, fishing, trading (local and cross-border) and hunting. However, most of these economic activities are greatly affected by poor land and water resources management practices.

## Water Resources Development

### *Surface Water Resources*

The Region is primarily drained by four major river systems: the Hadejia, the Jama'are, the Komadugu-Gana and the Yobe (Fig 15.1). The Hadejia River is formed by the confluence of the Challawa and

Chapter 15 | Adamu I. Tanko, in
A.I. Tanko and S.B. Momale (Eds.)
*Kano: Environment, Society and Development*
London & Abuja, Adonis & Abbey Publishers

Kano Rivers near Kano City from where it flows in an eastward direction and joined about 400km downstream by the Jama'are River near the town of Gashua (see Chapter three). About 300km below this confluence, the Hadejia River is joined by the Gana River west of Damasak from the Komadugu-Yobe River. This area covers a total land area of 84,138km$^2$ and is part of a larger basin draining to the Lake Chad.

The river system is clearly differentiated by the gross change in surface geology where the river passes from the Basement Complex rocks to the Chad Formation sediments. In the upland area, the rivers have tributaries and are gaining streams. In the lowland area, the rivers are losing their water due to three principal mechanisms namely: losses to ground water, losses to evaporation or evapotranspiration and losses to non-returning river channels.

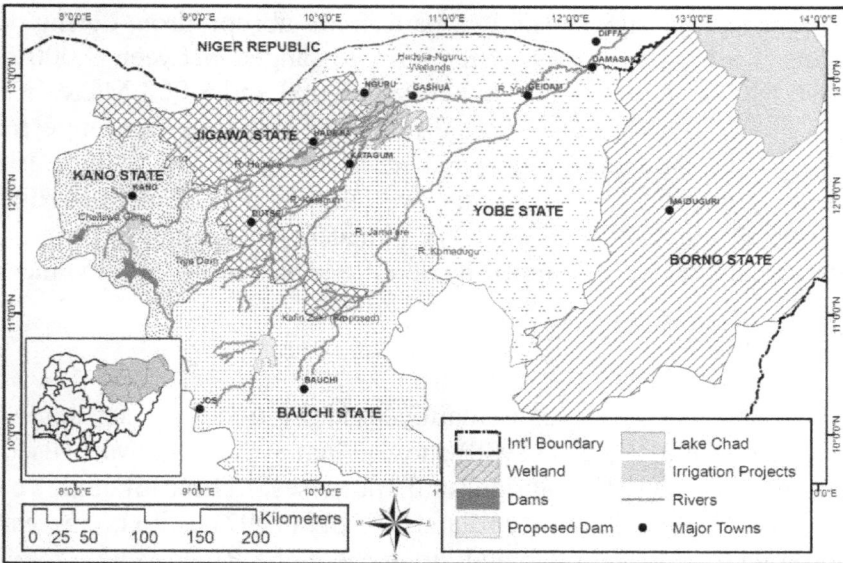

**Figure 15.1: The Hadejia-Jama'are-Komadugu-Yobe Basin (H-JKYB)**

Chapter 15 | Adamu I. Tanko, in
A.I. Tanko and S.B. Momale (Eds.)
*Kano: Environment, Society and Development*
London & Abuja, Adonis & Abbey Publishers

## Groundwater Resources

The groundwater is recharged mainly from the runoff water contributed by the major rivers. There is, however, very little information on the extent of groundwater recharge and the area covered. Carter and Alkali (1996) explained that at the downstream of Gashua, seepage into the alluvial aquifer is limited by the extensive clay cover overlying the aquifer and channel seepage is the main groundwater recharge mechanism with vertical infiltration severely restricted.

Thompson and Hollis (1995) modelled the water balance in the Hadeji-Nguru Wetland and show that the mean groundwater recharge amounted to 33% of the total river flow input with local rainfall contributing only 13% of the water balance. Based on this model, they show that groundwater storage beneath the flood plains of the wetland was largely stable between 1964 to 1971 and 1975 to 1982. The groundwater storage showed a pattern of abrupt drop during two periods. From 1964 to 1971, the storage ranged between 9,000 and 10,000 MCM; then dropped to between 7,000 and 8,000 MCM in the period 1972 to 1975. The storage remained stable at this range from 1975 to 1982 and finally dropped to about 5,000 MCM after 1986. This drop in groundwater storage was largely as a result of reduced flooding in the 1980s. From 1964 to 1987, the groundwater storage was estimated to have dropped by about one half of its initial values.

## Water uses

In the Kano Region water is mainly used for two purpose; domestic and agricultural. IWACO (1988) showed that 80% of the water used in the area is used for agricultural purposes. These include crop production, livestock and woodlands. IUCN (1997) estimate the water requirements to sustain demand along the Yobe River to be a total of 3637.52 MCM per annum (made up of 12.1, 13.2, and 1.7 MCM for irrigation, livestock and woodlands respectively). From 1975, the government of Kano State (initially of Kano and Jigawa States) constructed more than 20 earth-filled dams in the basins of Rivers Kano and Challawa primarily to serve remote villages where groundwater was insufficient to meet consumptive demands. Most of

Chapter 15 | Adamu I. Tanko, in
A.I. Tanko and S.B. Momale (Eds.)
*Kano: Environment, Society and Development*
London & Abuja, Adonis & Abbey Publishers

these dams were small impoundments of less than 100 hectares. There were of course a few of the dams in the categories of the medium-and large-scale dams (Tanko, 2010). There are also large, public irrigation schemes especially at the upstream of the Hadejia River system. There are medium irrigation schemes along the Yobe River system managed by the Borno State Ministry of Agriculture. There are also small-scale and farmer-managed irrigation schemes all over the Region being promoted by the Agricultural Development Projects (ADPs) and these are mainly along the valleys of the River system.

Water Resource Development practices in the Kano Region began in the late1960s and was basically to address natural water deficiency due to climatic shortfall and also the hydrological conditions. Early attempts and strategies especially in harnessing the surface water resources included the creation of artificial ponds, use of Shaduf pits, improved spring and stream intake and the construction of dams, reservoir and irrigation canals (Olofin, 1987). Birnin Kudu dam, completed in 1969, primarily for domestic purpose, was traced as the first earth-filled dam in the Kano Region. The second was the Bagauda Dam which was completed in 1971 for the purpose of water provision for the pilot scheme of the Kano River Irrigation Project Phase 1 (KIRP 1) at Kadawa. Initially, the Dam not only succeeded in providing the water for the irrigation at the pilot level, it also improved the water in-take for municipal water supply (Tanko 1994).

The largest dam in the Region is the Tiga with a maximum storage capacity of about 1,900 MCM and a surface area at that capacity of 178 $Km^2$, completed in 1974. It was primarily a multi-purpose dam for irrigation, municipal water supply, fishing and hydro-power generation. The Challawa Gorge Dam completed in 1992, has a storage capacity of 900 MCM with a designed maximum valve release capacity of $86m^3/s$ (Afromedev, 2006). The statistics of the storage and yields of the two dams are summarized in Table 15.1. Both Tiga and Challawa Gorge Dams contribute raw water to Kano City Water Supply and feed two large, partly finished, formal irrigation schemes, namely the Kano River Irrigation Project (KRIP) and the Hadejia Valley Irrigation Project (HVIP) (Table 15.2). The KRIP was designed in two phases. Phase I (KRIP-I) has a total irrigable area of 22,000 ha and the Phase II (KRIP-II) was designed to irrigate an additional 40,000 ha.

Chapter 15 | Adamu I. Tanko, in
A.I. Tanko and S.B. Momale (Eds.)
*Kano: Environment, Society and Development*
London & Abuja, Adonis & Abbey Publishers

**Table 15.1: Tiga and Challawa Gorge Reservoirs - Storage and Yields**

| Reservoir | Total Storage Volume Mm³ | Annual Average Inflow Mm³ | Ratio Volume/ Inflow | Average Annual Yield Mm³ |
|---|---|---|---|---|
| Challawa Gorge | 930 | 380 | 2.5 | 267 |
| Tiga | 1,345 | 900 | 1.5 | 768 |
| Combined | 2,275 | 1,280 | 2.0 | 1,065-1,090 |

NB: Losses from seepage and evaporation are put at 141 Mm³ for Tiga and Challawa Gorge, respectively: Parkman 2000

The outlet works at Tiga dam are deficient at present because the valve release capacity is limited to a maximum of $47m^3/s$ at full retention level. In response to seepage at the Dam it has also been necessary to draw the spillway level down by 2.5m to avoid excessive surcharging during floods. This change was made in 1992 and it effectively reduced the live storage capacity to 1,283 MCM (IUCN/NIWRMC, 2011). In an emergency situation, the limited capacity of the outlet works prevents the reservoir level being reduced rapidly hence the need to keep the level down. Since its storage volume far exceeds the average annual inflow (Table 15.1), the reduction in storage capacity does not significantly affect its average annual yield (Tahal, 1992).

**Table 15.2: Annual Water Demand in the Kano Region**

| Use | Annual Demand (Mm³) |
|---|---|
| Kano City Supply (for domestic and indusrial use) | 215.36 |
| Kano River Irrigation Project (KRIP) | 123.50 |
| Hadejia Valley Irrigation Project (HVIP) | 24.16 |

Withdrawals of the water requirement for KRIP and HVIP follow rigid design prescriptions:

i. fixed irrigation is done six days or four days in a week with one day off irrigation.;

ii. Releases from dams and diversions to cultivated areas are planned weekly.

iii. Local reservoirs control irrigation of fields.

iv. The estimated irrigation water demand per hectare for HVIP is much higher than that of KRIP phase I.

Chapter 15 | Adamu I. Tanko, in
A.I. Tanko and S.B. Momale (Eds.)
*Kano: Environment, Society and Development*
London & Abuja, Adonis & Abbey Publishers

v. Gravity of surface irrigation method (a great water waster) is practiced both in the KRIP and HVIP. No sprinkler system is yet adopted. High cost of sprinkler equipment and their maintenance is accorded greater priority consideration in the choice of irrigation method than the low availability and high value of water in the basin.

There is no system in place for the application of release rules from the dams that would match the integrated needs of the downstream users, either in terms of time or flows, nor is there currently adequate flow measurement at critical points in the basin including the dam outlet points. A large amount of improvement would need to be made to the present defective and inadequate infrastructure in order to permit a reasonable degree of knowledge of laws, let alone their control in various parts of the Region.

In addition to the situation on the Hadejia system, a dam is proposed on Jama'are system a Kafin Zaki. The purpose of the dam is to provide water for irrigation of an area totalling 84,000ha. Works on Kafin Zaki dam were started and then stopped a number of times. It is not certain up to now whether technical and/or political considerations will allow for the development of the dam. Bauchi State Government has, for the past five years continued the effort to get the proposal for the dam accepted by all major stakeholders in the Basin.

## Water Management Challenges in the Region

Water management challenges in the Kano Region, according to Tanko (2006) and IUCN-KYBP-Afromedev (2006) include the following:

1. Increasing population in the basin;
2. Non-availability and the non-usability of basic meteorological data as well as the presence of information of stream gauging in non-useable forms;
3. Limited knowledge about available water and about the nature and magnitude of water demands;
4. Cases of conflicts between and among cultivators and herders over shared resources, which are eminent, most of which erupt

Chapter 15 | Adamu I. Tanko, in
A.I. Tanko and S.B. Momale (Eds.)
*Kano: Environment, Society and Development*
London & Abuja, Adonis & Abbey Publishers

**231**

due to inadequate information and incomprehensible land legislation;

5. Scarcity of water due to climatic variations;
6. An invasive spread of *typha* grass causing macrophyte and silt blockages in the Hadejia-Nguru Wetland preventing the Hadejia River from contributing adequately to the Yobe River and primarily causing drop in the potentials of agricultural land in the Region;
7. Competitive unilateral development and operation of the two River Basin Development Authorities (RBDAs) in the Region, and
8. Lack of sufficient robust instrument to foster effective cooperation among the riparian parts of the Basin.

Rapid population growth in the Region is conventionally viewed as a major problem. By the year 2025 the population of the Region is projected to rise to over 25 million from the 15 million in 1991 (IUCN-KYBTF-Afromedev, 2006). This and migration in pursuit of livelihood by the pastoralists, fishermen and environmental refugees as a result of increased desertification, have intensified the competition for scarce land and qualitative water resources around the floodplains of the region resulting in frequent conflicts. Similarly the growing human and animal populations are in part responsible for the cultivation of marginal land, increased deforestation, depletion of grazing land and reduction of fallow period, which have seriously degraded the land in the riparian part of the Region. The majority of this population is comprised of women and children under the age of 15, who are vulnerable and deprived of their means of livelihood through degraded environment and inadequate water resource development. With declining per capita income, poverty has reached critical levels in most part of the Region (see Chapter 13). Immediate actions that will facilitate proper targeting of the poor and design of effective measure for poverty reduction are necessary to make progress towards improved living conditions.

Field research conducted between 2006 and 2008 in the riparian parts of the Region indicated the frequency of bridal marriages, population growth and migration situation in most of the communities (Tanko, et al. 2008). All the communities reported that bridal

Chapter 15 | Adamu I. Tanko, in
A.I. Tanko and S.B. Momale (Eds.)
*Kano: Environment, Society and Development*
London & Abuja, Adonis & Abbey Publishers

marriages were very high and more frequent during the harvest and dry season (*Kaka and Bazara* - read Chapter Two), estimates of 12 marriages in the communities were recorded per month per community. The marriages take place immediately after harvest period (*Kaka*). The report further indicated that presently on the average more people were migrating into the Region especially from the drier northern part.

Studies by a team of experts commissioned by the H-JKYBTF (2006) to among others, ascertain the status of the existing meteorological stations in the Basin discovered that there had not been a coordinated hydro-meteorological data management system since the late 1970s and early 1980s when all meteorological data were being sent to the National Meteorological Office at Oshodi, Lagos for analyses, archiving and dissemination. In the case of the hydrological data, the data were centrally collected, collated and analyzes by the National Water Resource Institute, Kaduna that was producing the Annual Hydrological Year Book. The last Year Book was produced in 1986 when the function was taken over by the Department of Hydrology and Hydrogeology of the then Federal Ministry of Water Resources. The team also found out that although currently, various agencies were collecting and keeping the hydro-meteorological data from their stations, the data collecting efforts were not continuous and consistent to the extent that one could hardly come across a consistent 10 year data from any of the existing stations in the Basin.

Water Audit Exercise carried out in 2006 with the aim of assessing the current status of water resources in the Region concluded that there was declining trend in rainfall in the Region since the 1980s(IUCN-KYBTF-Afromedev, 2006). This was related to some climatic variables including thepotential evapotranspiration which was discovered to vary from between 3.7mm/day and 8.2mm/day with a mean annual value of 2,200mm. The implication of the rate of evaporation is higher than rainfall in the region. This phenomenon also accounts for high losses from all water bodies in the Region.

The available surface water according to the report indicated a range between 2,609 MCM and 5,845 MCM depending on the climatic patterns. This highlights the importance of appropriate water management plan for the Region. The analysis showed that Hadejia sub-basin contributes 60% (30% from Tiga area, 20% from Challawa

| Chapter 15 | Adamu I. Tanko, in |
|---|---|
| | A.I. Tanko and S.B. Momale (Eds.) |
| | *Kano: Environment, Society and Development* |
| | London & Abuja, Adonis & Abbey Publishers |

Gorge area and 10% from unregulated area) of the surface water resources, while Jama'are sub-basin contributes 40% to the KYB at Gashua. While these proportions remain essentially constant the amount of water contributed by each sub-basin varies with climatic scenario.

**Table 15.3: Summary of Annual Surface Water Resources in the Kano Region**

| Catchment Unit | Climatic Pattern (Annual Ration) | | | | |
|---|---|---|---|---|---|
| | Normal | Wet | Extra wet | Dry | Extra dry |
| Tiga unit | 1,343,280.31 | 1,711,370.29 | 1,753.81 0.30 | 1,307.31 0.36 | 1,040,100.40 |
| Challawa unit | 651,520.15 | 907,320.16 | 851,26 0.15 | 429.60 0.12 | 150,860.06 |
| Unregulated unit | 558,740.13 | 773,370.13 | 726,48 0.13 | 378.52 0.10 | 130,110.05 |
| Jama'are sub-basin | 1,738,230.41 | 2,453,250.42 | 2,453,250.42 | 1,544,320.42 | 1,287,000.84 |
| **Total** | **4,291,771.00** | **5,845,311.00** | **5,784,801.00** | **3,659,751.00** | **2,608,911.00** |

*Source: IUCN-NIWRMC, 2009*

The ground water recharge to the shallow aquifer underlying the floodplains in the Region are clearly by river channel seepage, floodwater infiltration or direct rainwater infiltration, or combination of all three. Floodplain recharge is the major mechanism of recharge to the shallow floodplain aquifer. According to the IUCN-KYBTF-Afromedev (2006), in the Hadejia River and Hadejia-Nguru Wetlands (about $1,250km^2$) recharge ranges between 73mm and 197mm, with an average of 132mm, while in the Yobe sub-basin ($1,150km^2$) the estimated recharge is 50mm. The $500km^2$ Jama'are sub-basin has an estimated recharge rate of 100mm. These figures give the estimated total recharge to the shallow aquifers in the flood plains of all the sub-basins as 250mm.

The potential sources of surface water pollution in the region are mainly from the industrial estates in the densely populated Kano and also the largest irrigation projects. Effluents from especially the Sharada and Challawa Industrial Estates are openly drained into the open river channels without any form of treatment. Moreover, the effluents from the Bompai are similarly discharged into the Jakara River/Dam. In addition to these, waste water from large and small-irrigation projects may contain insecticides and nutrients from fertilizers. All these are obvious sources of water pollution in the Region. Field visit on many occasion by final year students offering water Resources Evaluation in the Department of Geography at

Chapter 15 | Adamu I. Tanko, in
A.I. Tanko and S.B. Momale (Eds.)
*Kano: Environment, Society and Development*
London & Abuja, Adonis & Abbey Publishers

Bayero University always report that most of the water resources infrastructures in the Region suffer from massive backlog of neglected maintenance. For example, the distribution system in Metropolitan Kano is in extremely poor condition. Unaccounted water is estimated to be in excess of 60% of total production. Water mains are blocked and other problems include lack of flow proportioning structures at critical positions in the river system, inadequate maintenance of irrigation canals and structures resulting in high losses.

Cases of conflicts between, especially the pastoral and farming groups were reported by Hadejia (1993), Milligan (2002) and Tanko (2006) among others. For several years the herding community and the farmers' groups engage one another in serious battle over the communality of both the available water and land resources, annually. Milligan (2002) reported a death toll of at least 210 people during two decades. The understanding of most analysts is that the Land Use Act (1979) does not adequately cater for the needs of the herding groups while giving so much to rhetoric emanating from policy-making and donor organisation which offer little hope to nomadism and pastoralism.

The invasive spread of typha grass (known locally as "*Kachalla or Roba*"- Hausa) over the last two decades along water channels and subsequently the floodable land including the Fadamas has a great threat to the local economy. Many of the local farmers only began to notice typha in the late 1980s, but by 2000 more that 60 percent of low lying floodable agricultural lands had been taken over by typha grass. According to a Department for International Development, Joint Wetlands Livelihood (DFID-JWL) document, in 1985 only 12ha of farmlands in Madachi village had been invaded by the weed, but by 2000 this figure had expanded to 216ha: roughly 80 percent of the field hitherto under cultivation in the village. On the average therefore, production dropped to around 20 percent of the land's potential.

Downstream of Madachi, along the Marma channel and around the Nguru Lake, typha invaded over 200km$^2$ of formerly arable land (Figure 15.1). Along some stretches of the Marma Channel, e.g. at Kirigidi and Matafari in Kirikasamma LGA, typha grass has taken over local farming and grazing land to such an extent that it now fills the horizon (i.e. as far as the eyes can see in every direction). Of course, for most of the Region downstream of the Hadejia Barrage,

Chapter 15    Adamu I. Tanko, in
A.I. Tanko and S.B. Momale (Eds.)
*Kano: Environment, Society and Development*
London & Abuja, Adonis & Abbey Publishers

tracts of productive land once utilized for wheat and rice cultivation are now totally swamped by typha.

Some other problems of the typha include the provision of vast breeding ground for fresh water snails, mosquitoes and other insects, leading to increased incidence of diseases like Bilhazia and malaria in humans and liver fluke in livestock. Moreover, typha provides a roosting place for flying crop-pests, like quelea birds, resulting in bird infestation and extensive crop damage, particularly rice, wheat and sorghum. In another development, the presence and invasion of typha is associated with the rise in the level of peach-groundwater table causing potash intrusion on surrounding land, salinizing the soils and rendering it useless to farmers and graziers (Tanko, 1999).

Two River Basin Development Authorities (HJRBDA and CBDA) are responsible for water management in the entire catchment (up to the Chad). The activities show little, if any coordination. The limited knowledge about available water and about the nature and magnitude of the water demands remain a major constraint to improved water management in the basin. Hence, this leads to competitive unilateral development and operations between them revealing insufficient robust instruments to foster effective cooperation among the riparian States in the Region. It is evident that lack of such instruments will likely result in weak mechanisms for clearly assigning benefits to each riparian country and state. Over the last decades, this unilateral development has limited RBDA's and indeed the Lake Chad Basin Commission's (LCBC's) ability to assert themselves as strong champion using appropriate coordination mechanism to effectively promote regional development. To optimize the basin's opportunities, it is imperative for the basin's riparian countries to empower the LCBC and ensure that it is fully committed to the preparation of key legal instrument and institutional mechanisms for joint investments and development within its catchment region and the Kano Region too.

Scarcity of water with substantial portion of available water source that can possibly be economically exploited having already been developed. The potential surface water requirements in the Hadejia sub-basin by estimation of the late nineties are 2.6 and 1.8 times larger than the mean available surface water resources, for the Hadejia and Jama'are Rivers, respectively. Analysis suggests that in a wet year, the

Chapter 15    Adamu I. Tanko, in
A.I. Tanko and S.B. Momale (Eds.)
*Kano: Environment, Society and Development*
London & Abuja, Adonis & Abbey Publishers

peak flow at Wudil is twice that of normal year, while that of dry year is half of the normal year. However, the peak flow obtained in a very wet year is lower than the minimum peak flow (500Mm$^3$/week) obtained in a pre-dam era.

## Poor Land and Water Management Practices

This coupled with water variability basin wide, contributes to severe ecosystem degradation in an already poverty-stricken environment. The increased needs for energy and limited access to electricity, compels the basin population to use wood fuel including charcoal for domestic purposes, resulting in deforestation and biodiversity loss from over-exploitation. Cumulatively, these factors are perpetuating a vicious cycle of environmental degradation which is in turn directly threatening rural communities whose livelihood is dependent upon the very ecosystem. Over the years, the combination of recurrent drought and flood periods, high population growth rate and inadequate water resources development for meeting the needs of a growing population, have further increased poverty and put severe pressure on the land and water resources. Reversing the Region's environmental degradation would call for concrete actions that will offset the poor land and water resources practices, which negatively affect natural resources use and promotion of these practices that facilitate natural resources management.

## Unutilized Development Potential

The Region is endowed with considerable natural water resources. However, their inadequate development and management have resulted in sub-optimal benefits. Given this situation, improvements in both agriculture and livestock production-the primary sector of the basin-can be achieved by optimizing benefits from existing water infrastructure. Furthermore, adequate water resources development and management can facilitates incremental benefits associated with increased productivity and incomes. Current development opportunities in the basin include: (i) over 1 million ha of irrigable land of which less than 40 percent are developed and less than fifty percent of which is actually irrigated, (ii) substantial hydropower

Chapter 15 | Adamu I. Tanko, in
A.I. Tanko and S.B. Momale (Eds.)
*Kano: Environment, Society and Development*
London & Abuja, Adonis & Abbey Publishers

potential but none is developed, (iii) navigable waterways but little is currently exploited. Additional opportunities include the development of fisheries, watershed management and ecotourism, all of which could provide incremental benefits associated with existing large infrastructure. Immediate actions are required to assist the River Basin Authority and the riparian state governments to develop a clear framework that will, in an integrated manner, tap these opportunities.

## Inadequate Operation and Maintenance of Existing Water Infrastructure:

Inadequate operation and maintenance are heavily impeding the effective management of existing hydraulic assets. Such situation overtaxes infrastructure and defers maintenance that could generate multiple benefits to the basin's population. While it is apparent that additional infrastructure is required to effectively mitigate the seasonal and annual variability of the water resources, improved operation and maintenance of the existing ones will ensure greater efficiency and long-term sustainability. Adequate operation and maintenance of existing large water infrastructure such as Challawa Gorge, Tiga and Bagauda are constrained by varied issues ranging from inappropriate maintenance and conflicting planning to poor funding. The situation is similar for small water infrastructure. Investments are required to rehabilitate and upgrade existing infrastructure and to establish a clear framework of interventions that will promote sustainable management of valuable assets, as well as optimization and development of the existing water resources potential.

Flood occurrences were particularly recorded in 1992, 1993, 1993, 1998, 2001, 2007, 2010 and 2012. The extremely large floods combined with uncoordinated reservoir operations resulted in the displacement of tens of thousands of people in 1998. The flood in 2001 took the lives of over 200 people and displaced over 35,000. Furthermore, contrary to what was expected after the completion of the dams, the timing of the floods in the Hadejia Nguru Wetlands (HNW) became less predictable and even resulted in dry-season floods. Along the Marma Channel in the HNW, the flooding has become more or less permanent since 2001. Some villages like Dabar Magini had to be moved to the west of Nguru Lake while the Hadejia-

Chapter 15 | Adamu I. Tanko, in
A.I. Tanko and S.B. Momale (Eds.)
*Kano: Environment, Society and Development*
London & Abuja, Adonis & Abbey Publishers

Nguru road was for over a year, from 2001, almost completely rendered inaccessible during the west season.

## *Changes in River Ecologies and Socioeconomics due to Dams*

Studies into the morphology of the River Kano, Northern Nigeria in the late 1970s indicated several morphological changes after the completion of the Tiga Dam in 1973. Some of these changes included river incision at the dam's downstream environment as well as the drying out of the floodable areas, known locally as the fadama land (Agboola, 1979; Olofin, 1987). At the upstream locations high levels of sedimentations and severe floods were noted, mainly as the natural vegetation around the dam location was removed (Tanko, 1994; 1999).

Another dimension of the challenges is the ecological changes in the forms of changing flood patterns (Tanko, 2010). This presents a significant concern amongst people in the downstream environment of both Tiga and Challawa Dams (Bird and Tanko, 2004). Whilst overall there has been a reduction in rainfall runoff and river flows in the area over the last 30 years (partly due to climate change but also the impact of dam and irrigation project construction in the area) a significantly increased proportion of this water has been diverted into the northern river sub-system and finds its way via the Marma channel to Nguru Lake (IUCN/HNWCP, 1998; JEWEL, 2003). Since the construction of upstream dams and barrages, the river regime has also changed, with the peak flows sometimes being attenuated and constant discharge being sent down the river throughout the dry season. The studies also showed that there has been a significant change in sediment patterns in the river system resulting in the partial closing of some channels (including the link channels to the lower Hadejia and also the Burum Gana river system as well as the exit to Nguru Lake). This sedimentation has been exacerbated by the sudden invasion of *Typha* weed which thrives on the perennial wet conditions in the river system (Bird and Tanko, 2004). The same report also indicated that the end result is that water levels in Hadejia Lake are now higher than in living memory and remain so all year, even in the height of the dry season, to the point of threatening important public facilities in the town. The lack of variation in water level in the lake is resulting in reduced ecological bio-diversity and threatening the sustainability of the

Chapter 15 | Adamu I. Tanko, in
A.I. Tanko and S.B. Momale (Eds.)
*Kano: Environment, Society and Development*
London & Abuja, Adonis & Abbey Publishers

Ramsar registered wetland (i.e. the Hadejia-Nguru Wetlands) and also the economic livelihood of the people in the area.

## Drive towards Integrated Water Resource Management

From the above, it is obvious that there is the absence of an integrated approach to water resources management in the Kano Region and beyond. This coupled with high water demands and competitions for water by a wide range of users have degenerated into various degrees of physical and human induced conflicts. Efforts are now being made at reversing the trend.

At the moment there are about six government organisations and a few non-government organizations concerned with the integrated management of the water resources of the entire Hadejia-Jama'are-Komadugu-Yobe Basin (H-JKYB). The Federal Ministry of Water Resources, which is the apex organ of government in the Nigerian water sector, empowered by Decree 101 of 1993 to be responsible for policy formulation and coordination for water resources development in the country. It has been managing the water resources of the H-JKYB through the two River Basin Development Authorities (H-JRBDA) and the Chad Basin Development Authority (CBDA). There is also a Coordinating Committee suported by a Technical Advisory Committee (TAC) on the H-JKYB in the Federal Ministry of Water Resources. This committee was setup by the National Council on Water Resource to coordinate the management and use of water in the Basin.

From 2006 efforts at developing an Integrated Water Resource Management (IWRM) led to the identification of stakeholders to include all major and minor resource users. This led to the evolvement of consensus over a number of issues relating the water resources and other Common Pool Resources (CPRs) management. The consensus was achieved through meeting and separate training and capacity building workshops on Institutional Rights and Responsibilities, access rights and conflict management, poverty and livelihoods issues in the H-JKYB. In January 2003 it was identified and agreed by the stakeholders that:

Chapter 15 | Adamu I. Tanko, in
A.I. Tanko and S.B. Momale (Eds.)
*Kano: Environment, Society and Development*
London & Abuja, Adonis & Abbey Publishers

a. There was poor coordination between institutions that have the statutory responsibilities for managing water resources in the H-JKYB;

b. There were identified gaps and overlaps in the responsibilities of these institutions, and

c. There was need for capacity strengthening of stakeholders in order to improve coordination among them.

In February 2003 the Stakeholders agreed and reached a common understanding on types and frequency of conflicts that existed between the various resources users of CPRs. In May 2003, consensus was reached on the fact that water was the most important resource in the Basin upon which all other CPRs were dependent and the need to concentrate efforts towards solving the water problem was paramount.

In line of these, stakeholders were engaged in capacity building training in IWRM, hydrological baseline data collection, river profiling and satellite image interpretations. A result of the IWRM capacity building has been the formation of IWRM Committees at different parts of the Basin. This was undertaken with the objective of instituting advocacy/awareness campaigns in the different parts of the Basin with the aim of putting in place an Integrated Water Resource Management (IWRM) plan. It was considered that the successful achievement of the goal of IWRM for the basin, should ultimately lead to the resolution of all the identified physical problems. In turn this would result in enhanced livelihoods for the population, particularly the poor who rely on the common pool resources especially water and land.

The major successes to date include getting the government conviction and commitment towards the provisions of funds in mitigating identified problems and for carrying out researches for better understanding of the problems. This has led to the formation of Hadejia-Jama'are Komadugu-Yobe Basin Trust Fund (H-JKYBTF). Secondly, the ability to draw community leaders who mobilized communal labour and excavators from responsible government agencies, to clear typha grass and other aquatic vegetation that had blocked flows at the bifurcation of the two channels and further along the Burum Gana was also a positive development. As a result of this later development, about 1,000 hectares of land that had been lying

Chapter 15   Adamu I. Tanko, in
A.I. Tanko and S.B. Momale (Eds.)
*Kano: Environment, Society and Development*
London & Abuja, Adonis & Abbey Publishers

**241**

dormant for many years were, from 2008, put under dry season cropping. Fishermen and farmers who had migrated from the area are now returning. It is a pity the security challenges faced in the Region (from 2011) is posing even more serious challenges. However, there is more commitment to take on bigger water management challenges by more communities and other stakeholders.

## Conclusions

The Chapter reviews water management issues in the Kano Region that they were found to be essentially arising from absence of sustainable development strategy and population pressure. As they were products of unsustainable resource-use practices, they have led to decline in access to water for different user groups. The Kano Region in collaboration with all other riparian States in the Hadejia-Jama'are Komadugu-Yobe Basin partnered in the formation of a Trust fund (H-JKYBTF) towards the collective need for Integrated Water Resource Management (IWRM). This is the newer outlook and adjustment of the existing River Basin Systems that was collectively agreed upon by all stakeholders towards harmonization of activities towards meeting effective water demand and supply within the Basin.

Efforts are being made that target land use planning that integrates water resources development. Activities of different user groups within the Region should be coordinated in relation to other resources and user groups. What may appear to be very difficult to combat are the ecological changes, e.g, the occurrences and infestations of aquatic weeds owing to the perennial water-looks within the Region. While efforts at dredging the original channels and opening of new open drains are currently being made, more technical efforts are needed.

Researches and focused planning must be geared towards meeting the demands of the various stakeholders within any particular basin will certainly bring harmony and development that the goals of the IWRM may be attained.

Chapter 15 | Adamu I. Tanko, in
A.I. Tanko and S.B. Momale (Eds.)
*Kano: Environment, Society and Development*
London & Abuja, Adonis & Abbey Publishers

# Reference

Afromedev (2006) Catchment Management Plan for Integrated Natural Resources mangemnet of Komadugu Yobe Basin, FMWR-IUCN-NCF Komadugu Yobe Basin project. Afromedev Consultancy Services Limited, Abuja.

Agboola, S.A (1979), Agricultural Atlas of Nigeria, Oxford University Press, London

Aminu A.; J.M. Jibrin, A. Suleiman, A. Mustapha (2006). Improving Land and water Resources Management Study, FMWR-IUCN-NCF Komadugu Yobe Basin Project, Kano.

Bawden, M.,G. jones and A judith (1973). The physiography of Northern plains.Interim Report, Overseas Development Administration, Land Resources Division. Surrey, UK.

Bird, A. and Tanko, A.I. (2004), Remote Sensing Report," Technical Report submitted to DFID/JEWEL project, Nigeria, july.

Carter, R.C.and A.G. Alkali (1996).Shallow ground water study in the North-east arid zone of Nigeria. Quarterly j.Eng,.Geol 29:341-355.

Hadejia, I.A (1993), 'Land - use Conflict in Guri District of Jigawa State' Paper Presented to the National Policy Workshop on Utilization and Sustainability of Fadama in Northern Nigeria

IUCN (1997), Water management options for the Hadejia-Jama'are-Yobe River Basin, Northern Nigeria. Hadejia-Nguru Wetlands Conservation Project Report. The World Conservation Union.

IUCN/HNWCP (1998), Water Management Options for the Hadejia-Jama'are-Yobe River Basin, Northern Nigeria, Report for Hadejia-Nguru Wetlands Conservation project

IUCN-KYBP-Afremedev (2006), Water Audit for Komadugu Yobe Basin, A Technical Report Submitted to IUCN,Kano Office, Nigeria.

IWACO (1988), Study of the water resources of in the Komadougou-Yobe Basin. Nigeria - Niger joint Commission for Cooperation, Niamey, Niger republic.

JEWEL, (2003) poverty, Environment & Livelihoods Issues Relating to Corps in the Hadejia-Nguru Wetlands, A report to the joint Wetlands Livelihood Project (JEWEL), funded by the DFID, UK

Chapter 15    Adamu I. Tanko, in
A.I. Tanko and S.B. Momale (Eds.)
*Kano: Environment, Society and Development*
London & Abuja, Adonis & Abbey Publishers

Milligan, R.S. (2002), Searching for Symbaosis: Pastorslist-Farmer Relations in North-East Nigeria, A Thesis for the Degree of D.Phil in Geography, University of Sussex, Brighton, UK

H-JKYBTF (2006), Trust Fund Hydrological Network Enhancement Report, A Technical Report prepared by Experts Drawn from the National Water Resource Insitute, Mando, Kaduna, IUCN-KYB Project, Kano Office, and KYBTF, Damaturu.

Olofin, E.A. (1987), Some Aspects of the Physical Geography, Bayero University, Kano, Nigeria

Tahal Consultants Ltd (1992) Environmental Impact Assessment Analysis of Kano River Irrigation Project Phase 1., Federal Ministry of Water Resources/World Bank, November 1992.

Tanko, A.I. (2010), Mega Dams for Irrigation in Nigeria: Nature, Dimension and Geographies of Impact in Brunn, S. (ed.) Mega Engineering Projects in the World. Springer Publishers, pp. 1617-1631.

Tanko, A.I (1999), Changes in Soil and Water Quality, and Implication for Sustainable Irrigation in the Kano River Project, Kano State, Nigeria. Unpublished Ph.D. Thesis. Geog. Dept., BUK December 1999.

Tanko, A.I. (2006), Improving Land and Water Resources Management in the Komadugu-Yobe River Basin-North Eastern Nigeria and South-Eastern Niger. A Mid-term project Evaluation Report submitted to the FMWR-IUCN-NCF Komadugu Yobe Basin Project.

Chapter 15   Adamu I. Tanko, in
A.I. Tanko and S.B. Momale (Eds.)
*Kano: Environment, Society and Development*
London & Abuja, Adonis & Abbey Publishers

# Chapter Sixteen

## BIODIVERSITY AND WILD FOODS

Salisu Mohammed

### Introduction

Biodiversity is the totality of living diversity; variety; multiplicity; range; or mixture of species from the molecular to the ecosystems level which includes the distinct species of all living things on this planet Earth. The entire ecosystems are part of this definition of biodiversity because flora and fauna are dependent on one another for their survival and to focus on just an individual species, would be thoughtless, unthinking, imprudent, ill-judge, unwise, hasty, rash, short-ranged, limited or restricted, since no species could exist outside its ecosystem or outside the community of other living things in which it has evolved.

Biodiversity is also the degree of variation of life forms within given species, ecosystem, biome, or an entire planet. Biodiversity can equally be a measure of the health of ecosystems and it is in part a function of the climate. The existence of a *global carrying capacity* limiting the amount of life that can live at once is also the question of whether such a limit would cap the number of species and influence general biodiversity. Charrier (in SPORE, 1994) believed that the word 'biodiversity' is a contraction of 'biological diversity' and it includes all living organisms (both individuals and groups) and their relationship with one another. That it is not just a collection of individuals but an interaction system where the characteristics of the individuals are no less important than their functions.

In the Kano Region, biodiversity has included many aspects from flora, fauna and even agro biodiversity (Mohammed, 2006) and from food production to medical research that all over the world people use at least 40,000 species of plants and animals everyday. The genetic resources here refer to the biological materials such as genes, individuals or species taken from biodiversity and used by man for agricultural, industrial and medicinal purposes. According to Bunting and Barbara (1995), most of the collections of plant genetic resources

Chapter 16    Salisu Mohammed, in
              A.I. Tanko and S.B. Momale (Eds.)
              *Kano: Environment, Society and Development*
              London & Abuja, Adonis & Abbey Publishers

in the world consist of, or are derived from individual accessories assembled by explorers or collectors, and these accessories are the unit of genetic resources. Thus to be useful, the accessories have to be documented, their origins have to be recorded and their characteristics described. They identified that in real life, the genetic resources are not homogenous botanical entities but variable and flexibly adaptable artifacts of man.

On the one hand, many people are said to depend on wild species for some or all of their food, shelter, and clothing as clearly demonstrated by the study conducted by Mohammed and Harris (2003) on wild foods in Northern Nigeria. As functions of biodiversity in many rural areas of Africa, wild foods are eminent, renowned, important, distinguished, famous, prominent, outstanding, as they provide diversity, vitamins and minerals in the diet of many rural poor. They are also important at times of food shortage. In most parts of Northern Nigeria, biodiversity is characterized by floral and faunal species of the particular ecozone.

This Chapter attempts to identify biodiversity situation and functions within the Kano Region with specific reference to floral biodiversity. Two areas were chosen for comparison; Dagaceri at the extreme north of the Region with Sahelian Savanna ecotype of northern Nigeria and Tumbau within the Kano Close-Settled Zone (KCSZ) with Sudan Savanna vegetation.

This latitudinal transect has identified floral and faunal disperities within the Region as influenced by the climate as evident in the studies of Kowal and Knabe (1972) on the climate of northern Nigeria which emphasise the relevance and significance of latitudinal transect studies in understanding the pattern of rainfall which goes with vegetation and natural biodiversity. The two areas of the case study cover the Sudan and Sahel savanna ecozones.

## Case Study Sites and Characteristics

### *Tumbau*

The first study area is Tumbau and it is the close to Kano Metropolis and it falls within latitudes 12°00' N to 12°08'N and longitudes 8°50'E to 8°58'E (Figure 16.1). Tumbau is part of Kano Close Settled Zone

Chapter 16 | Salisu Mohammed, in
A.I. Tanko and S.B. Momale (Eds.)
*Kano: Environment, Society and Development*
London & Abuja, Adonis & Abbey Publishers

(Mortimore, 1987). It is located some thirty kilometers south of Gezawa, the Headquarters of Gezawa Local Government in Kano State. The predominant ethnic group is Hausa and their major occupation is subsistence agricultural production while the major crops grown include principally millet, sorghum, cowpea and groundnut.

## Dagaceri

The second study area to the Northeast is Dagaceri, which is some thirteen kilometers to the north of Birniwa town in Birniwa Local Government Headquarters of Jigawa State and a distance of about 200km from Kano. It is a typical Manga settlement. However, it is presently composed of three ethnic groups living together - the Manga, Kanuri and Hausa. The Manga speaking Kanuri are found dominating the eastern half of the settlement while the western half is dominated by the Hausa settlers (Figure 15.2). Most of the Hausa settlers came to the village in the 1960s and 1970s from Damagaram, Niger Republic after drought periods, which stroke their area. They came and settled to form groups of Islamic scholars. The total population of the village in 1975 was estimated to be 738 people (Mortimore, 1989:83).

The two areas are under intensified aridity on an ecological and demographic gradient. Annual rainfall totals decreases from Tumbau to Dagaceri (Tables 16.1 and 16.2). So also is the population density and access to markets. All these areas fall within the semi-arid part of Sudano Sahelian Zone (SSZ) of North East Nigeria which according to Maduakor (1991) comprises of the former Kano State (now Kano and Jigawa States), and the former Borno State (now Borno and Yobe States).

**Table 16.1: Annual rainfall in Tumbau and Dagaceri (1992-1995)**

| Study Area | Annual totals | | | |
|---|---|---|---|---|
| | 1992 | 1993 | 1994 | 1995 |
| Tumbau | 664.0mm | 553.14mm | * | 379.7mm |
| Dagaceri | 331.5mm | 359.33mm | 403.5mm | 326.0mm |

*Souce: Rainfall data, Bayero University/Cambridge Universty project on Soil, Cultivar and Livelihoods in North East Nigeria.*
* Rainfall data not available for the year

Chapter 16 | Salisu Mohammed, in
A.I. Tanko and S.B. Momale (Eds.)
*Kano: Environment, Society and Development*
London & Abuja, Adonis & Abbey Publishers

Table 16.2 defines the relationship between rainfall and evaporation in 10 days period as reflected by the mean onset and cessation of rainfall in the two case study sites (Tumbau and Dagaceri).

**Table 16.2: Mean annual rainfall, mean onset and mean cessation of the rainy season at Tumbau and Dagaceri**

| Village | Mean Annual | Mean Onset Period | Mean Cessation Period |
|---|---|---|---|
| Tumbau | 534.60 | 10 days period in June | $2^{nd}$ 10 days period in September |
| Dagaceri | 355.20 | Dagaceri $2^{nd}$ 10 days period in July | $2^{nd}$ 10 days period in September |

*Source*: *Rainfall data, Bayero University/Cambridge Universty project on Soil, Cultivar and Livelihoods in North East Nigeria.*

The general ecosystem is concerned not only with the mean annual rainfall but also in its distribution through the season and the reliability between years which sustains biodiversity. The coefficient of variability (CV) of annual rainfall has been identified as another way of experiencing rainfall reliability. Mortimore (1989) agreed with the idea of Glober et al (1954), Manning (1951 and 1956) Sivakumar et al (1984) Sivakumar (1990) that rainfall variability is very important to the live of the people of rural drylands and biodiversity.

However mean rainfall fails to show the significance of long time change in the Sahel region between the 1960s and 1990s. Annual rainfalls decline by 25-30% or more at the majority of rainfall stations including those in Northern Nigeria and southern Niger which significantly affects the ecosystems and biodiversity. Such a treat also means an increasing frequency and intensity of the drought even with obvious implication for the production of crops and fodder. Indications are that the decline has ended and the average rainfall has increase since the early 1990s, but not to the levels enjoyed before the 1960s. Such long term treat reflects oscillations that have characterized the Sahel on geological time scale and adds to the riskness of the farming and livestock keeping and biodiversity

| Chapter 16 | Salisu Mohammed, in |
| | A.I. Tanko and S.B. Momale (Eds.) |
| | *Kano: Environment, Society and Development* |
| | London & Abuja, Adonis & Abbey Publishers |

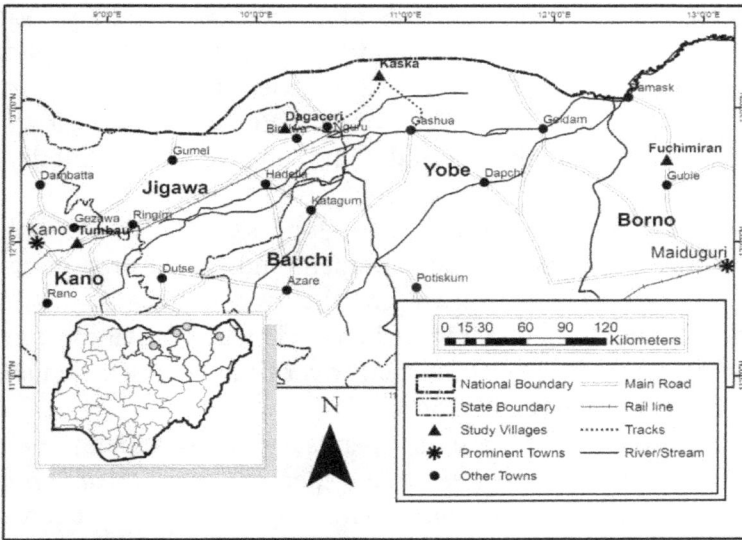

**Figure 16.1: Case Study Sites**

Essentials of Regional Biodiversity and Wild Foods Studies in Tumbau and Dagaceri within Kano Region:

i. The temperature and rainfall distributions follow a sharply seasonal pattern with the months October - April, May or June being very dry (with relative humidity of <20%), and July-September being wet (with relative humilities often >80%). The dry season is associated with prevailing easterly winds often bearing dust plumes from the desert (popularly and locally called harmattan) while the rainy season is associated with the invasion of a maritime air mass with storm development along the convergence zone.

ii. The mean annual rainfall ranges from about 400mm around Dagaceri to 600-800mm around Tumbau with high coefficients of variation (around 30%). Rain events are few intense and sometimes damaging and from the 1960s until 1990s averaging rainfall decline throughout the Sahel region by up to 33%. The frequency of agricultural droughts increased and depth to water tables increased in many areas, For example rainfall at Tumbau fell from 830mm to 650mm between 1931 and 1960 and the early 1990s and further north the changes were worse.

| Chapter 16 | Salisu Mohammed, in |
| --- | --- |
| | A.I. Tanko and S.B. Momale (Eds.) |
| | *Kano: Environment, Society and Development* |
| | London & Abuja, Adonis & Abbey Publishers |

iii. Perennial rivers are scarce as most rivers flow only seasonally. Also wetlands are scarce and confined to the flood plains of rivers or inter-dune depressions. The water table is normally 20-40m below the ground and fluctuates from year to year depending on the rainfall and this controls biodiversity functions.

iv. Soils are derived from former dune sands with low inherent fertility, weak profile development and scarce organic carbon. They are easily blown in the wind, creating areas of degradation or deposition (dunes). Under cultivation the soils are prone to lose their nutrients over time unless replenished by long fallows or fertilization.

v. The natural vegetation is open savanna woodland including many thorny *Acacia* tree species (*A. seyal, nilotica, sieberiana,*) *Ziziphus (mucronata, spina-christi*), regenerating shrubs (*Guiera Spp, Boscia Spp and A. ataxacantha*) and perennial or annual grasses (*Andropogon gayanus*) (in wetter and drier locations respectively) and forbs (*Leptadania pyrotechnica*). In natural depressions river valleys and around seasonal ponds larger trees benefit from more abundant and shallow ground water forming small areas of dense woodland adapted to the site and soil conditions. The number of woodland and grassland species identified in the region is reported to be more than 400.

vi. Under intensive agriculture woodland has been cleared over very wide areas and the land converted to fields and fallows however on these fields trees are protected (Mohammed, 1994) and in some cases exotic species from further south are often found.

vi. Risk is endemic in production systems owing to the variability of the rainfall and its associated threats which significantly affect biodiversity.

Tables 16.3`a-i' presents the floral and faunal biodiversity situations and functions in Tumbau. Similarly, Tables 16.4`a - i' present that of Dagaceri.

Chapter 16 | Salisu Mohammed, in
A.I. Tanko and S.B. Momale (Eds.)
*Kano: Environment, Society and Development*
London & Abuja, Adonis & Abbey Publishers

## Table 16.3a: Trees at Tumbau

| Botanical Name | Status | Indigenous name | Ecological/biodiversity Functions |
|---|---|---|---|
| *Balanites aegyptiaca* | Wild/Domesticated | Adua | Econs resource, medicinal |
| *Cordial Africana* | Wild | Alullubarimi | Fodder |
| *Simerubacae danzieliis* | Wild | Ararrabi | Fodder |
| *Acacia senegalensis* | Wild/Domesticated | Bagaruwa | Medicinal, econs resource |
| *Conbretacae dalzielii* | Wild | Bakar tsamiya | Fodder |
| *Ficus anomani* | Wild | Baure | Fodder, medicinal |
| *Ficus trichopoda* | Wild | Bauren kiyashi | Fodder |
| *Commiphora kerstingii* | Wild | Bazana | Fodder |
| *Ficus thonningii* | Wild | Cediya | Fodder, medicinal |
| *Azadirachta indica* | Domesticated | Dalbejiya | Medicinal, econs resource |
| *Phoenix dactylifera* | Wild | Dabino | Medicinal, edible and econ resource |
| *Commiphora Africana* | Wild | Dashi | Fodder |
| *Isoberlinia doka* | Wild | Doka | Construction |
| *Berlinia auriculata* | Wild | Doka rafi | Hedges |
| *Parkia biglobosa* | Wild | Dorowa | Medicinal, econs resource |
| *Vitex doniana* | Wild | Dinya | Edible, medicinal |
| *Tamarindus spp* | Wild | Farar tsamiya | Fodder |
| *Ficus platyphylla* | Wild | Gamji | Fodder, medicinal |
| *Gardenia aqualla* | Wild | Gaude | Hedges |
| *Faidherbia albida* | Wild/Domesticated | Gawo | Fodder |
| *Barassus aethiopium* | Wild | Giginya | Medicinal, edible |
| *Vigna subterranean* | Wild | Gurjiya | Fodder |
| *Annona senegalensis* | Wild | Gwandar dawa | Medicinal, edible |
| *Butyrospermum paradoxa* | Wild | Kadanya | Fodder, edible medicinal |
| *Bauhinia thonningii* | Wild | Kargo | Medicinal |
| *Diospyros mespiliformis* | Wild | Kanya | Edible, medicinal |
| *Prosopis Africana* | Wild | Kirya | Medicinal |
| *Ficus glumos* | Wild | Kawari | Edible, fodder |
| *Manilktara obovata* | Wild | Kirya dutse | Medicinal |
| *Strychnos spinosa* | Wild | Kokiya | Edible |
| *Adansonia digitata* | Domesticated | Kuka | Edible, medical, econs resource |
| *Sterculia setigera* | Wild | Kukkuki | Medicinal |
| *Aframomum melegueta* | Wild | Kunfar gada | None |
| *Ziziphus spina Christi* | Wild | Kurna | Edible, medicinal |
| *Khaya senegalensis* | Wild | Madaci | Medicinal |
| *Pterocarpus erinaceus* | Wild | Madobiya | Medicinal |
| *Ziziphus jujube* | Wild | Magarya | Edible, medicinal |
| *Cassia arereh* | Wild | Malgi | Medicinal |

Chapter 16 | Salisu Mohammed, in
A.I. Tanko and S.B. Momale (Eds.)
*Kano: Environment, Society and Development*
London & Abuja, Adonis & Abbey Publishers

| Botanical Name | Status | Indigenous name | Ecological/biodiversity Functions |
|---|---|---|---|
| *Ziziphus mucronata* | Wild | Magaryar kura | Medicinal |
| *Daniellia oliveri* | Wild | Maje | Medicinal |
| *Cassia arereh* | Wild | Malga | Medicinal |
| *Cissus populnea* | Wild | Malleduwa | Fodder |
| *Syzygium guineensis* | Wild | Malmo | Medicinal |
| *Anogeissus leocarpus* | Wild/Domesticated | Marke | Fodder |
| *Grewia bicolour* | Wild | Marken dutse | Medicinal |
| *Erythrina senegalensis* | Wild | Minjirya | Medicinal |
| *Ceiba pentadra* | Wild | Rimi | Econs resources |
| *Securidaca longipenculata* | Wild | Sanya | Medicinal |
| *Ficus iteophylla* | Wild | Shirinya | Edible |
| *Cussonta orboea* | Wild | Takandra giwa | Fodder |
| *Detarium senegalensis* | Wild | Taura | Edible medicinal |
| *Entada sudanica* | Wild | Tawatsa | Fodder, medicinal |
| *Tamarindus indica* | Domesticated | Tsamiya | Edible, medicine |
| *Combretaceae sokodense* | Wild | Wuyan damo | Fodder, medicinal |
| *Ficus abutilifolia* | Wild | Yandi | Fodder |
| *Celtis integrifolia* | Wild | Zuwo | Fodder |
| *Not identified* | Wild | Karki | Medicinal |

*Source: field studies 2007*

### Table 16.3b: Herbaceous Plants at Tumbau

| Botanical Name | Status | Indigenous name | Ecological/biodiversity Functions |
|---|---|---|---|
| *Not identified* | Wild | Abanacha | Consumption |
| *Ipomoea akuatica* | Wild | Awarwaro | Pasture |
| *Cyperus rotindus* | Wild | Aya aya | Pasture |
| *Lidigofera girecta* | Wild | Baabah | Dying and econs resources |
| *Nymphaea lotus* | Wild | Bado | Medicinal and consupmtion. |
| *Jaetropa Curcas* | Domesticated | Binidazugu | Fencing, exudates treats ringworm |
| *Crotalaria spp* | Wild | Biya rana | Medicinal |
| *Not identified* | Wild | Bunsurun Fadama | Medicinal |
| *Eragrostis cilianensis* | Wild | Bunsurun Fage | Medicinal |
| *Potulaca olaracea* | Wild | Daburin Shanu | Pasture |

Chapter 16 | Salisu Mohammed, in
A.I. Tanko and S.B. Momale (Eds.)
*Kano: Environment, Society and Development*
London & Abuja, Adonis & Abbey Publishers

252

| Botanical Name | Status | Indigenous name | Ecological/biodiversity Functions |
|---|---|---|---|
| *Vossia cuspidate* | Wild | Damba | Pasture |
| *Thelepogon elegans* | Wild | Datarniya | Pasture |
| *Centuarea perrottetii* | Wild | Dayi | Pasture |
| *Impomoea asrifolia* | Wild | Duman rafi | Medicinal |
| *Schwenckia Americana* | Wild | Ferfetsi | Medicinal and pasture |
| *Andropogon Gayanus* | Wild | Gamba | Fencing, local pen, fodder |
| *Solanum incanun* | Wild | Gautan Kaji | Pasture |
| *Mitracarpum verticillatum* | Wild | Goga masu | Medicinal (Skin treatment) |
| *Dactyloctenium aegyptium* | Wild | Gude-Gude | Pasture |
| *Curcurbitaceae vulgaris* | Wild | Gunar Shanu | Pasture |
| *Waltheria indica* | Wild | Hankuha | Medicinal |
| *Digitoria debilis* | Wild | Harkiya | Pasture and mulching |
| *Urelytrum thyrsiodes* | Wild | Jema | Withch medicine |
| *Ceratotheca sesamoides* | Wild | Kalkashin doki | Medicinal |
| *Pennisetum hordeoides* | Wild | Kansuwa | Roofing, fencing |
| *Ceralluma dalzielii* | Domesticated | Karan masallaci | Medicinal |
| *Mucuna pruriens* | Wild | Karar | Fencing |
| *Smilacaceae kraussiana* | Wild | Kayar bera/kusu | Pasture |
| *Cynodon dactylon* | Wild | Kiri-Kiri | Rope, weaving, pasture |
| *Amocphophallus* | Wild | Kunen jaki | Medicine against snake, scorpoin |
| *Commelina forskalaei* | Wild | Kununguru | Pasture |
| *Randia nilotica* | Wild | Kwanarya | Treatment of urino-genital disease |
| *Gisekia pharnaciodes* | Wild | Lallen Shamuwa | Pasture |
| *Citrus orantifolia* | Wild | Lemun Tsuntsu | Pasture |
| *Syzygium guineense* | Wild | Malmo | Pasture |

Chapter 16 | Salisu Mohammed, in
A.I. Tanko and S.B. Momale (Eds.)
*Kano: Environment, Society and Development*
London & Abuja, Adonis & Abbey Publishers

| Botanical Name | Status | Indigenous name | Ecological/biodiversity Functions |
|---|---|---|---|
| *Euphorbia virta* | Wild | Nonon Kurciya | Medicinal |
| *Cassia occidentalis* | Wild | Rai-rai/rai dore | Ornamental purpose, medicinal |
| *Kigelia Africana* | Wild | Rawaya | Pasture, medicinal |
| *Acacia ataxacantha* | Wild | Rukuki | Consumption |
| *Tephrosia bracteolate* | Wild | Sabani | Medicinal |
| *Compositea alexandrina* | Wild | Suradu | Medicinal |
| *Cleome gynandra* | Wild | Taba da mashi | Pasture |
| *Coctus spectabilis* | Wild | Tabarmar zomo | Medicinal (fly gel) |
| *Cassia tora* | Wild | Tafasa | Consumption, medicinal, econs resource |
| *Imperata cylindrical* | Wild | Tofa | Pasture |
| *Acanthaceae campestris* | Wild | Tsamiyar maharba | Dying |
| *Loudetia togoensis* | Wild | Tsintsiya | Sweeping, boarderline Control of erosion |
| *Loudetia phragmitoides* | Wild | Tsintsiyar dutse | Sweeping, hedges, farm demarcation |
| *Eleusine indica* | Wild | Tuji | Pasture |
| *Calotropis procera* | Wild | Tumfafiya | Mix with white cola for farin jinni (med} |
| *Graminae serobicualatum* | Wild | Tumbin Jaki | Pasture |
| *Striga senegalensis* | Wild | Wuta-wuta | Pasture |
| *Vigna reticulate* | Wild | Yadiya | Consumption, medicinal |
| *Hibiscus asper* | Wild | Yakuwar jeji | Animals fodder |
| *Impomea hispida* | Wild | Yaryadi | Pasture |
| *Datura Metal* | Wild | Zakami | Stimulant, medicinal |
| *Amaranthaceae viridis* | Wild | Zaki banza | Pasture |

**Source:** *field studies 2007*

Chapter 16 | Salisu Mohammed, in
A.I. Tanko and S.B. Momale (Eds.)
*Kano: Environment, Society and Development*
London & Abuja, Adonis & Abbey Publishers

## Table 16.3c: Shrubs and biological functions

| Botanical Name | Indigenous name | Ecological/biodiversity Functions |
|---|---|---|
| *Acacia nilotica* | Bagaruwa | Dyeing |
| *Euphorbiaceae curcas* | Bini da zugu | Fencing, boarder line |
| *Not identified* | Cihun | Consumption |
| *Commiphora Africana* | Dashi | Fencing, tooth treatment |
| *Dichrostachys cinerea* | Dundu | Fueling shed, against desertification |
| *Iridaceae discoren* | Farin ganye | Medicinal |
| *Mormodica balsamina* | Garafuni | Medicine for Abdominal pain |
| *Lagenari vulgaris* | Gora | Roofing, weapon |
| *Anona senegalensis* | Gwandar dawa | Consumption, |
| *Hyphaene thebaica* | Kaba | Roofing, rope, mat, desertification |
| *Bauhinia thonningii* | Kargo | Starch, roof making |
| *Lawsonia inermis* | Lalle | Dyeing, decoration |
| *Acacia ataxacantha* | Rikuki | Consumption |
| *Cassia goratensis* | Runhu | Used by women after birth in hot water |
| *Portulaca oleraceae* | Ruba tari | Roofing, desertification |
| *Guiera senegalensis* | Sabara | Skin treatment: rashes |
| *Dichrostachys cinerea* | Sarkakiya | Fencing, medicinal |
| *Vernonia amygdalina* | Shuwaka | Soup, medical and econ resource |
| *Luffa cylindrical* | Soso | Used with soap in bath |
| *Euporbia poisonii* | Tinya | Medicinal, poison |
| *Ximenia Americana* | Tsada | Edible |
| *Moringa oleifera* | Zogala | Consumption, medicinal |

**Source:** *Adapted from Salisu et al 2006*

## Table 16.3d: Plant Species used in house construction and craft at Tumbau

| Hausa Name | Scientific name | Location/distribution within the village area | Biodiversity Function |
|---|---|---|---|
| Tabila | *Boscia senegalensis* | Southern and northern part of the village | Construction |
| Sabara | *Guiera senegalensis* | Southern part | |
| Maina | *Azadirachta indica* | Within the village and on farms | Fuel wood substitute |
| Tumfafiya | *Calotropis procera* | Northwest Part | Fence and roofing |
| Giyyaya | *Mitrigyna inermis* | Northern part of the village | Craft |
| Kirya | *Prosopis Africana* | Forest reseve near wudil | Fence |

**Source:** *Fieldwork 2006*

| Chapter 16 | Salisu Mohammed, in A.I. Tanko and S.B. Momale (Eds.) *Kano: Environment, Society and Development* London & Abuja, Adonis & Abbey Publishers |
|---|---|

## Table 16.3e: Species of wild trees with edible fruits at Tumbau

| Hausa Name | Scientific name | Location/distribution within the village area | Biodiversity Function |
|---|---|---|---|
| Dorowa | *Parkia biglobossa* | Many stands scattered over the village area | Edible fruit Seed use as soup ingredient |
| Dinya | *Vitex doniana (sweet)* | Western part | Edible fruit |
| Kurna | *Ziziphus spina Christi* | Northern part | Edible fruit |
| Tsamiya | *Termarindus indica* | Northern and southern part | Edible fruit |
| Kanya | *Peutadesma btyracea* | Southern part | Edible fruit |

*Source: Fieldwork 2006*

## Table 16.3f: Plant Species used for Medicinal Purposes in Tumbau

| Hausa Name | Scientific name | Location/distribution within the village area | Biodiversity Function |
|---|---|---|---|
| Marke | *Anogeissus schimperii* | South east of the village | Roots used |
| Maina | *Azadirachta indica* | Within the village and on farms | Leaves |
| Kattakara | *Combetum glutinosum* | Southern part | Bark |
| Tabila | *Boscia senegalensis* | Southern and northern parts | Roots |
| Tsada | *Zimenia Americana* | North and northwestern part | Leaves |
| Sanya | *Securedaca longipedunduculata* | By the fadama to the southern part | Roots, Bark and leaves |

*Source: Fieldwork 2006*

## Table 16.3f: Plants Used as Food

| Hausa Name | Scientific name | Biodiversity Function |
|---|---|---|
| Tafasa | *Cassi tora* | Wild food |
| Yadiya | *Leptadadia pyrotechnica* | Wild Food |
| Zogala* | *Moringa oleifera* | Domesticated food |

*Source: Fieldwork 2006*

*Zogala is also planted within compounds for fencing or just for its edible leaves. In such cases it connot be regarded wild

## Table 16.3g: Grass Species used for Roofing and Fencing in Tumbau

| Hausa Name | Scientific name | Location/distribution within the village area |
|---|---|---|
| Jema | *Veriveria nigrita* | Within farm boundaries, fallow land and strong ground |
| Roba | *Echinochloa pyramidalis* | Close to the river |
| Kansuwa | *Pennisetum pedicellatum* | Within farm boundaries |

*Source: Fieldwork 2006*

| Chapter 16 | Salisu Mohammed, in A.I. Tanko and S.B. Momale (Eds.) *Kano: Environment, Society and Development* London & Abuja, Adonis & Abbey Publishers |
|---|---|

## Table 16.3h: Wild Animal Species used for bush meat (Kamukamu) and medicinal purpose

| Hausa Name | English name | Biodiversity Function |
|---|---|---|
| Kurega | Squirrel | Kamukamu |
| Damo | Iguana Lizard | Kamukamu |
| Kadangare | Ordinary lizard | Kamukamu |
| Guza | Large Iguana lizard | Kamukamu |
| Kwankiya | Snake | Medicine |
| Jemage | Bat | Medicine |
| Bodari | Skunk | Medicine |
| Bushiya | Hedgehog | Kamukamu and medicine |
| Beguwa | Porcupine | Kamukamu and medicine |

*Source: Fieldwork 2006*

The iguana lizard and porcupine are mostly found around the Fadama area to the south of Tumbau. The other animals have no specific location. The people said, that 'one can run into them any where at any time within the village area.

**Table 16.3i: Fish Species caught in Tumbau area**

| Hausa Name | English Name | Scientific Name |
|---|---|---|
| Tarwada | Mud Fish | *Clarlas Spp* |
| Minjirya | Electric fish | *Malapterrurus* |
| Lulu | Butterfly fish | *Schilbemystus* |
| Tsage | Tiger Fish | *Hydroynus Spp* |
| Kuku | Catfish | *S.schale* |
| Gaiwa | African Long fish | *Protopterus annectens* |
| Jari* | Not known | Not Known |
| Musku* | Not known | Not Known |
| Barya* | Not known | Not Known |

*Source: Fieldwork 2006*
*English names and Botanical names not known

| Chapter 16 | Salisu Mohammed, in |
|---|---|
| | A.I. Tanko and S.B. Momale (Eds.) |
| | *Kano: Environment, Society and Development* |
| | London & Abuja, Adonis & Abbey Publishers |

# Biodiversity of Dagaceri (Biodiversity functions and wild food use in Dagaceri)

### Table 16.4a: Trees of Dagaceri

| Botanical Name | Indigenous name | Ecological/biodiversity Function |
|---|---|---|
| *Acacia nilotica (sub tomentosa)* | Adua | Econs resource, medicinal |
| *Acacia tortilis* | Kandili | Medicinal, econs resource |
| *Acacia seyal* | Farar Kaya | Fodder |
| *Acacia sieberiana* | | Fodder, medicinal |
| *Adansonia digitata* | Kuka | Medicinal, econs resource |
| *Albizia chevalieri (harrns)* | | Medicinal, edible and econ resour |
| *Anogeissus schimperi* | | Fodder |
| *Anona senegalensis* | Gwandar daji | Medicinal, econs resource |
| *Azadirachta indica* | Maina | Edible, medicinal |
| *Balanites aegyptiaca* | | Fodder |
| *Bauhinia ruffescens* | | Fodder, medicinal |
| *Bauhinia thonningii (Schum)* | | Hedges |
| *Cassia sieberiana (Linn.)* | | Fodder |
| *Combretun glutinosum* | Katakara | Medicinal, edible |
| *Commiphora Africana* | | Fodder |
| *Faiderbia albida* | Gawo | Medicinal, edible |
| *Ficus ingens (miq-miq var ingens)* | | Fodder, edible medicinal |
| *Ficus platyphylla (Del.)* | Gamji | Medicinal |
| *Hyphaene thebaica (Linn.)* | Goruba | Edible, medicinal |
| *Maerua angolensis* | | Medicinal |
| *Maerua crassifolia* | | Edible, fodder |
| *Moringa oleifera* | Zogale | Medicinal |
| *Prosopis Africana* | Kirya | Edible |
| *Sclerocarya birrea (Hoesch)* | | Edible, medical, econs resource |
| *Stereospermum kunthiamum (Lam.)* | | Medicinal |
| *Sterculia bsetigera* | | Edible, medicinal |
| *Stylosanthes errecta* | | Medicinal |
| *Tamarindus indica* | Tsamiya | Edible, medicinal |
| *Terminalia aviccenioides* | | Medicinal |
| *Vitex doniana (sweet)* | | Medicinal |
| *Ximeniua Americana (Linn.)* | | Medicinal |
| *Ziziphus mauritiana (Lam.)* | | Medicinal |
| *Ziziphus mucronata* | | Fodder |
| *Zizphus spina Christi* | Kurna | Medicinal |

*Source:* Field Studies 2007

Chapter 16 | Salisu Mohammed, in
A.I. Tanko and S.B. Momale (Eds.)
*Kano: Environment, Society and Development*
London & Abuja, Adonis & Abbey Publishers

## Table 16.4b: The shrubs of Dagaceri

| S/N | Botanical Name | Indigenous name | Ecological/biodiversity Functions |
|---|---|---|---|
| 1 | *Acacia ataxacantha* | Adua | Econs resource, medicinal |
| 2 | *Boscia senegalensis* | Tabila | Medicinal, econs resource |
| 3 | *Calotropis procera* | Tumfafiya | Fodder |
| 4 | *Cassia tora (Linn.)* | Tafasa | Fodder, medicinal |
| 5 | *Ceasalpinia goratensis* | | Medicinal, econs resource |
| 6 | *Euphorbia balsamifera (Ait.)* | Makira | Medicinal, edible and econ resource |
| 7 | *Guiera senegalensis* | Sabara | Fodder |
| 8 | *Lawsonia inermis* | Lalle/Nalle | Medicinal, econs resource |
| 9 | *Leptadania pyrotechnica (Decne.)* | | Edible, medicinal |
| 10 | *Euphorbia poisonii* | Tinya | Fodder |
| 11 | *Hyphaene thebaica (Frond)* | Kaba | Fodder, medicinal |

**Source:** *Field Studies 2007*

## Table 16.4c: Herb of Dagaceri

| Botanical Name | Ecological/ biodiversity Functions | Botanical Name | Ecological/ biodiversity Functions |
|---|---|---|---|
| *Abutilon mauritianum* | Fodder | *Hibiscus asper (Hook). (Dalz.)* | Food |
| *Acantospermum hispidum* | Fodder | *Hibiscus sabdariffa (var. imtermedius)* | Food |
| *Achyranthes aspera* | Fodder | *Hibiscus sabdariffa (var. ruber)* | Food |
| *Alysicarpus vaginalis (del)* | Fodder | *Indigofera astragulina (D.C)* | Medicine |
| *Andropogon gayanus* | Fence/roofing | *Kohontia grandiflora* | Medicine |
| *Andropogon pseudopricus* | Fodder | *Kylinga eracta (Schumind.) (Thenn.)* | Medicine |
| *Amaranthus viridis* | Fodder | *Lageraria vulgaris (Seringe)* | Fodder |
| *Boerhavia erecta (Linn.)* | Medicinal | *Laggeria aurita (Linn.)* | |
| *Brachiana distichophylla* | Medicinal | *Leucas spp.* | |
| *Cenchrus biflorus (Roxb)* | Medicinal/Fodder | *Leucas martinicensis (Jacq) Ait* | |
| *Cenchrus biflorus (Dalz)* | Fodder | *Leptadania lancifolia (Decne)* | Wild food |
| *Celosia leptostachya* | Madicinal | *Mitracarpum verticillatum (vatke)* | |
| *Ceralluma dalzielli* | Medicinal | *Momordica balsamina* | Medicinal |
| *Ceratotheca sesamoides* | Medicinal | *Pennisetum pedicellatum* | Medicinal |
| *Centuarea alexandrina* | Medicinal | *Pergularia tomentosa (Linn.)* | Medicinal |
| *Chameochrista mimosoides* | Medicinal | *Peristrophe bicalyculata (Retz)* | Medicinal |

Chapter 16 | Salisu Mohammed, in
A.I. Tanko and S.B. Momale (Eds.)
*Kano: Environment, Society and Development*
London & Abuja, Adonis & Abbey Publishers

| | | | |
|---|---|---|---|
| | | Mers. | |
| Chrozophora brachiana | Medicinal | Polycarpaaea linearifolia (DC) | Medicinal |
| Chrozophora senegalensis | Fodder | Portulaca oleracea (Linn.) | Medicinal |
| Corchorus olitorius | Medicinal | Ricinus communis | Medicinal |
| Conyza attenuate | Medicinal | Rageria adenophylla | Medicinal |
| Crinum yuccaeflorum | Medicinal | Sesamum spp. | Medicinal |
| Crotolaria aranaria | Medicinal | Schizachyrium exile (Stapf) | Medicinal |
| Crotolaria aschrek (Forsk.) | Medicinal | Schaenefeldia gracilis | Medicinal |
| Crotolaria aschrek (Linn.) | Medicinal | Scoparia dulcis (Linn.) | Medicinal |
| Cucumis melo (Lin) | Medicinal | Securidaca longepedunculata (Fres) | Medicinal |
| Cucumis prophetarum | Medicinal | Senna italica (mill) | Medicinal |
| Cyperrus platycaulis (Bak) | Medicinal | Senna occidentalis | Medicinal |
| Datura inoxia | Medicinal | Sesbania aegyptiaca (poir) | Medicinal |
| Desmodium lastocarpum | Medicinal | Solanum incanum (Linn) | Medicinal |
| Dicoma tomentosa (cass) Dalz. | Medicinal | Sonchus oleraceus | Medicinal |
| Eragrostis ciliaris (Lingulata) W. D Clayton. | Fodder | Spermacoce stachydea (DC) | Medicinal |
| Euphorbia convolvuloides (Hosch) | Medicinal | Striga spp. | Medicinal |
| Euphorbia polycmoides (Hosch) ex bois. | Medicinal | Tephrosia humilis (Gull & Perr) | Medicinal |
| Evolvulus alsinoides (Linn.) | Medicinal | Tephrosia purpurea | Medicinal |
| Feretia cantheioides (Hiern) | Medicinal | Trianthema pentadra | Medicinal |
| Fimbristylis hispidula (valv.) kuntt. | Medicinal | Trianthema portulacastron | Medicinal |
| | | Vernonia ambigua | Medicinal |
| | | Vernonia perroffetii (Sch. Bip) | Medicinal |
| | | Watheria Americana | Medicinal |

*Source:* Field studies 2007

## Table 16.4d: Trees Species used for house construction and craft in Dagaceri

| Hausa Name | Scientific Name | Location |
|---|---|---|
| Kirya | Prosopis Africana | Gume and gana village areas 30km north of Dagaceri |
| Kalgo/Kargo | Bauhania thonningii | Village farmland and kalimbo forest reserve |
| Maina | Azadarichta indica | Within the village and on farmlad |
| Katakara | Combretum glutinosum | Southern part |
| Kalimbo | Leptadenia pyrotechnica | Fallow land mostly in the forest reserve |
| Gawo | Faidherbia albida | Eastern and northern part of the area |

*Source:* Fieldwork 2006

Chapter 16 | Salisu Mohammed, in
A.I. Tanko and S.B. Momale (Eds.)
*Kano: Environment, Society and Development*
London & Abuja, Adonis & Abbey Publishers

## Table 16.4e: Species of Wild trees with edible fruits in dagaceri

| Hausa Name | Scientific Name | Location |
|---|---|---|
| Adua | *Balanite aegyptiaca* | On farmland to the east |
| Dinya | *Vitex doniana* | On farms and fallow land to the south |
| Kurna | *Ziziphus Spins Christi* | Within the village and on farmlands |
| Magarya | *Ziziphus maurutiana* | On farms and fallow lands to the north |
| Gwandar daji | *Anonna senegalensis* | In the kalimbo forest reserve |

*Source: Fieldwork 2006*

## Table 16.4f: Plant Species use for medicinal purposes in Dagaceri

| Hausa Name | Scientific Name | Location |
|---|---|---|
| Sansani | *Stereospernum kinthianum* | East and west along Dagaceri kukawa |
| Maina | *Azadirachta indica* | Within the village and southwest alog the pathway to wargale village |
| Katakara | *Combretum glutinosum* | Is the southern part along the pathway to Katikimiram |
| Sharagamda | Unknown | Southern and Northern part |
| Marke | *Anogeissus schimperii* | Western part |

*Source: Fieldwork 2006*

## Table 16.4g: Species of Wild plants and edible leaves in Dagaceri

| Hausa Name | Scientific Name | Location |
|---|---|---|
| Raidore | *Cena occendetale* | |
| Tafasa | *Cassia tora* | |
| Yadiya | *Leptadenia lancifolia* | |
| Zogale* | *Moringa oleifera* | |

*Source: Fieldwork 2006*

They are found in the village and on farmlands
*Zogale is also planted and found within compound for fencing or just for edible use in such case it cannot be regarded as wild.

## Table 16.4h: Grass Species Used for Roofing and Fencing in Dagaceri

| Hausa Name | Scientific Name | Location |
|---|---|---|
| Gamba | *Andropogon Gayanus* | Farm boundaries |
| Janramno/Janrauno | *Hyporhaenia* | Fallow lands |

*Source: Fieldwork 2006*

## Table 16.4i: Animal Species used for Medicinal Purpose

| Hausa Name | English Name | Location |
|---|---|---|
| Kurege | Squirrel | |
| Damo | Iguana Lizard | |
| Zomo | Rabbit/Hare | |
| Bushiya | Hedgehog | |

*Source: Fieldwork 2006*

These animals are said to be found mostly in the Kalimbo Forest Reserve, some 20km north of Dagaceri. A few rabbits, hedgehogs, big rats and skuncks are however encountered once in a while in the bushes within the village area.

Chapter 16 | Salisu Mohammed, in
A.I. Tanko and S.B. Momale (Eds.)
*Kano: Environment, Society and Development*
London & Abuja, Adonis & Abbey Publishers

Attempt has been made to present the status of all identified (in the local languages) floral biodiversity in the two case study areas (Table 16.5) and in grouping them into trees, shrubs and herbs (Table 16.6). Whereas the trees are recognisable as large perennial woody plants which grow to a height of several feets and typically has single erect main stem with side branches, the shrubs and herbs are differently smaller.

**Table 16.5: Floral Biodiversity of Dagaceri with Local Names in Hausa, Fulbe and Kanuri**

| PLANTS | HAUSA NAMES | KANURI (MANGA) | FULBE NAMES | Status |
|---|---|---|---|---|
| *Abuliton mauritiana* | Kyablu | Kyaulu | Nebbawa | Wild |
| *Acacia ataxacantha* | Sarkakiya | Duzu | Korawul | Wild |
| *Acacia nilotica subs. Tomentosa* | Bagaruwa | Kanga' ar | Gawari | |
| *Acacia tortilis (Hvm)* | Kandili | Kandil | Shilluki | Wild |
| *Acacia seyal* | Dakwara | Kolwal | Dibbehi | Wild |
| *Acacia sieberiana (Hvm)* | Farar kaya | Karamga | Bulbi | Wild |
| *Acanthos permum hispidum* | Kashin yawo | Biri yawure | Kashin yawo | Wild |
| *Achyranthes aspera (Linn)* | Kaimin kadangare | Sheri-kadiye | Ni'embu'udi | Wild |
| *Adansonia digitata* | Kuka | Kuwwa | Bokki | Wild |
| *Albizia chevalieri (Harrins)* | Katsari | Kayari | Fadawonduhi | Wild |
| *Alycarpus vaginalis, (Del) A. violescens (Schindl)* | Gadagi | Ngadagi | Kadagire | Wild |
| *Amaranthus viridis (Linn)* | Zaki banza | Kari nasaraye | Kakkaba kuri | Wild |
| *Andropogon gayanus (Kunth)* | Gamba | Suwu lame | Gambaho | Domesticated |
| *Andropogon pseudopricus (Stapf)* | Shuci | Suwu buro | Bulude | Wild |
| *Anogeissus schimperii (Hvm)* | Marke | Marye | Kojohi | Dom and wild |
| *Anona senegalensis (Hvm)* | Gwandar daji | Ndussa | Dukkuhi | Wild |
| *Azadachta indica (Hvm)* | Maina | Ganye | Sharbihi | Domesticated |
| *Balanites aegyptiaca L . (Del)* | Aduwa | Bizoo | Adduwahi | Dom and wild |
| *Bauhinia rufescens (Lam)* | Matsattsagi | Sizi | Nammari | Wild |
| *Bauhinia thonnigss (Schum)* | Kargo | Ka'al | Barkihi | Dom and wild |
| *Boerhaavia erecta (Linn)* | Zankon gada | Not known | Not known | Wild |
| *Boscia senegalensis* | Tabila | Tabula | Bultuhi | Wild |
| *Brachiaia distichophylla (Stapf)* | Garaji | Kirkanar | Hardiyaho | Wild |
| *Calotropis procera (Ait)* | Tumfafiya | Kayau | Babambi | Wild |
| *Cassia tora (Linn)* | Tafasa | Tawaza | Tafasa'a | Wild |
| *Cassia steberiana (Linn)* | Marga | Kiska tizirai | Dawohi | Wild |
| *Ceasalpinia goratensis (Fressen)* | Runhu | Rumbu | Rumfuhi | Wild |
| *Celosia leptostachya (Benth)* | Tozalin mage | Fenziran gambazue | - | Wild |
| *Cenchrus biflorus (Roxb)* | Karangiya | Ngibi | Kebbe | Wild |
| *Cenchrus biflorus (Daiz)* | Karangiyar bera | Ngibin garimaye | Nyabkabre | Wild |
| *Ceralluma dalziellii NE BC* | Wutsiyar damo | Korofuron | Girle | Wild |
| *Ceratotheca sesamoides* | Yodo | Kaskazi | Yaudo | Wild |
| *Centuarea alexandrina (Del) C. praecox. (Oliv) C. Rhizocephala (Dalz)* | Dayi | Kamga | Dayije | Wild |
| *Chamaecrista mimosodes* | Bagaruwar kas | Kiska tamzuwu | Fadawonduhi | Wild |
| *Chrozophora bracchiana (Vis)* | Gyada-gyada | Kwalji-kwalji | Biridihi | Wild |
| *Chrozophora senegalensis (A. juss)* | Damagi | Klangadi | Dusur | Wild |
| *Corchorus olitorius (Linn)* | Lalo | Gamsaina | Liolalo | Wild |
| *Cembretum glutinosum (Perrott. Ex. Dc)* | Kattakara | Kazaga'ar | Doki | Wild |
| *Commiphora africana (Hvm)* | Dashi | Kabi | Dasihi | Wild |
| *Conyza attenuata (Dc)* | Goron mayu | Bunchale | - | Wild |
| *Crinum yuccaeflorum (Salisb)* | Albasar kwadi | Ngariyo goggo | Albasar kutiji | Wild |
| *Crotalaria arenaria (Linn)* | Manta uwa | Simozo | Manta uwahi | Wild |

Chapter 16 | Salisu Mohammed, in
A.I. Tanko and S.B. Momale (Eds.)
*Kano: Environment, Society and Development*
London & Abuja, Adonis & Abbey Publishers

| PLANTS | HAUSA NAMES | KANURI (MANGA) | FULBE NAMES | Status |
|---|---|---|---|---|
| *Crotalaria schrek (Forssk)* | Jar birana | Kingal gakki kime | Biyaranahi budehi | Wild |
| *Crotalaria aschrek (Linn)* | Farar birana | Kungalgakki bull | Biyaranahi budehi | Wild |
| *Cucumis melo (Linn)* | Gurji | Nguryi | Gurji | Wild |
| *Cucumis prophertarum (Linn)* | Ciccidu | Cicidu | Shubbel wainabeh | Wild |
| *Cyperus platycaulis (Bak)* | Jiji | Jiji | Goyai | Wild |
| *Datura inoxia* | Zakami | Gorgo mukkabe | Zakami | Wild |
| *Desmodium lasiacarpum (Dc)* | Dankadafi | Sazimo | Dangere | Wild |
| *Dicoma tomentosa (Cass) (Dalz)* | Garkuwar bera | Kamgabi | Lailaiduwa | Wild |
| *Eragrostis ciliaris, and E. lingulata (W.D) Clayton* | Komayya | Burasa | Saraho | Wild |
| *Euphorbia balsamifera (Alt)* | Aguwa/makira | Dumara | Fuddasardihi | Wild |
| *Euphorbia convolvuloides (Hosch)* | Nonon kurciya | Kiska kyamma | Nonon kurciya | Wild |
| *Euphorbia poisonii (Linn)* | Tinya | Kiska dal | Burohi | Wild |
| *Euphorbia polycmoides (Hoschst) ex. Boiss)* | Kwallin kuda rimin kiyashi | Kiska arumma | Kojeluyil | Wild |
| *Evolvulus alsinoides (Linn)(Daiz)* | Kafi mallam | Malam bakoina | Kafi malam | Wild |
| *Faidherbia albida* | Gawo | Karau | Gawari | Wild |
| *Feretia canthioides (Hiern)* | Kuru kuru | Kuru-kuru | Bakin lalle | Wild |
| *Ficus inges (Miq-miq var ingens)* | Shirinya | Kazu | Shediyahi | Wild |
| *Ficus platyphylla (Del)* | Gamji | Ngabura | Dundehi | Wild |
| *Fimbristylis hispidula (Kunth.Sub.Sp)* | Gude-gude | Millam filazaye | - | Wild |
| *Guiera senegalensis (Lam)* | Sabara | Chabara | Giloki | Wild |
| *Hibiscus asper(Hook) (Daiz)* | Yakuwar kwadi | Karasu karaye | Seruje | Wild |
| *Hibiscus sabdariffa (var intermedius)* | Jar yakuwa | Karasu kime | Falle bodaje | Wild |
| *Hibiscus sabdaruffa (var ruber)* | Farar yakuwa | Karasu bull | Falle danije | Wild |
| *Hyphaene thebica (Linn) (Big) Hyphaene thebaica (Small)* | Goruba | Kargim | Gellowul | Wild |
| *Hyphaene thebica (Small)* | Kaba | Ngilai | Bali | Wild |
| *Indigofera astragulina (Dc)* | Kaikayi komakan mashekiya | Kiska mazafurum | Kaikayi komakan mashekiya | Wild |
| *Kohontia grandiflora (Dc)* | Rimin samari | - | - | Wild |
| *Kyinga erecta (Schumid)(Thenn)* | Gemum kwado | Jawo kattiya | Jiji | Wild |
| *Lageraria vulgaris (Seringe)(Daiz)* | Duma | Kabezo | Laifahi | Wild |
| *Laggeria aurita (Linn-f) Bentt ex C. B. CL* | Namijim goro | Kiska kuwumbal | - | Wild |
| *Lawsonia inermis (Linn)* | Lalle | Nalle | Poldi | Wild |
| *Leptadania lancifolia Decne* | Yadiya | Njera | Yadiya | Wild |
| *Leptadenia pyrotechnica (Decne)* | Kalimbo | Karimbo | Suwalewul | Wild |
| *Leucas spp* | Hanaratse | Doyinnagaduwe | Kayan tsohuwa | Wild |
| *Leucas martinicensis (Jacq) Ait f.* | Kanbarawo | Klabarwuye | Kuagujjo | Wild |
| *Maerua angolensis* | Cicciwa | Kiska Ta'anda | Bisidoyil | Wild |
| *Maerua crassifolia (Forssk)* | Jiga | Ngijiga | Jariyahi | Wild |
| *Mitracarpum verticillatum (vatke)* | Gogamasu | Cuwokiri | Gududel | Wild |
| *Momordica balsamina* | Garafuni | Daddayi | Habiru | Wild |
| *Moringa oleifera lam.* | Zogale | Alinga | Zogalihi | Wild |
| *Ocimum spp.* | Kafi amarya kanshi | Kiska kariwa | Kafi amarya kanshi | Wild |
| *Pennisetum pedicellatum (Trin)* | Kansuwa | Fuuraa | Bulude | Wild |
| *Pergularia tomentosa (Linn)* | Fataka | Taulaha | Taulagawa | Wild |
| *Peristrophe bicalyculata (Retz) Nees.* | Tumanim Dawaki | Diyesikel | Korlandahu | Wild |
| *Polycarpaea linearifolia (Dc) and p. coymbosa (Lam)* | Bakin suda | Ngiladiyya | Bakin suda | Wild |
| *Portulaca oleracea (Linn)* | Fasa kaba | Kiska lelenobe | Killiningil | Wild |
| *Prosopis africana (Linn)* | Kirya | Sinzim | Kohi | Wild |
| *Ricinus communis* | Zurman | Kula-kula | Zurman | Wild |
| *Rogeria adenophylla* | Shekara tsayel Baba rado | Muzum muzum | Shekara tsaye | Wild |
| *Sesamum spp.* | Ridin kadangare | Nomengiri | Ridi barewa | Wild |

| Chapter 16 | Salisu Mohammed, in A.I. Tanko and S.B. Momale (Eds.) *Kano: Environment, Society and Development* London & Abuja, Adonis & Abbey Publishers |
|---|---|

| PLANTS | HAUSA NAMES | KANURI (MANGA) | FULBE NAMES | Status |
|---|---|---|---|---|
| *Schizachyrium exile (Stapf)* | Janruno | Nawuro | Janrauno | Wild |
| *Sclerocarya birrea (A. rich)* | Daniya | Kuma | Edi | Wild |
| *Schoenefeldia gracilis* | Kalawo | Kalawu | Joenekeral | Wild |
| *Scoparia dulcis (Linn)* | Romafada | Romafada | Shashatau | Wild |
| *Securidaca longependunculata (Fres)* | Uwar magunguna | | Alali | Wild |
| *Senna italica (mill)* | Bauren kiyashi | Shayagurum | Hirarannahi | Wild |
| *Senna occidentalis (Linn. Link.)* | Raidore | Raidore | Balbaleriwarde | Wild |
| *Sesbania aegyptiaca. (Poir) or S. polycarpa* | Zamarke | Caccawo | Ga'andi | Wild |
| *Solamum incanum (Linn)* | Idon saniya | Simfeye | Gittonoye | Wild |
| *Sonchus oleraceus* | Farar bafulatana | | Bafulatanahi | Wild |
| *Spermacoce stachydea (Dc)* | Alkamar tururuwa | Febe | - | Wild |
| *Striga spp* | Wuta-wuta/kudiji | Kujiji | Kuduji | Wild |
| *Sterculia setigera (Del)* | Kukkuki | Chawo | Bobbari | Wild |
| *Stereospermum kunthianum (Cham)* | Sansami | Kawau | Golombi | Wild |
| *Stylosanthes errecta (P.Benax)* | Kumba shahu | Kiska klamiya | Jirehi | Wild |
| *Tamarindus indica (Linn)* | Tsamiya | Tamzuwu | Jahmi | Wild |
| *Teptrosia humilis (Gulland pers)* | Tsintsiyar maharba | Yoyal | Buwurdi | Wild |
| *Tephrosia purpurea (pers)* | Maragowa | Maranguwa | Nebbambi | Wild |
| *Terminalia avicennioides* | Baushe | Kmada | Baushi | Wild |
| *Trianthema pentadra (also Boehaavia and Merremia angustifolia)(Dalz)* | Gadonmaciji | Bazari kandirai | Filowel | Wild |
| *Trianthema portulacastrum* | Babbajuji | Brima | Jini mutuhi | Wild |
| *Vernonia ambigua* | Mekiya | Brembremi | Jigawal | Wild |
| *Vernonia perroffettii (Sch.Bip)* | B'urzu | | | Wild |
| *Vitex doniana (Sweet)* | Dinya | Ngarbi | Bummehi | Wild |
| *Watheria americana (Linn)* | Hankunfa | Klaklabelu | Kafaffi | Wild |
| *Zimenia amricana (Linn)* | Tsada | Dandul | Chabbullli | Wild |
| *Ziziphus mauritiana (Lam)* | Magarya | Kaluso | Jabi | Wild |
| *Ziziphus mucronata* | Magaryarkura | Kiska bulluwe | Gulum | Wild |
| *Ziziphus spina-christi (L)Desf.* | Kurna | Kurna | Kurnahe | Wild |

**Source:** *Adapted from Mohammed, 1995 and updated*

**Table 16.6: Grouping of plants into Trees, Shrubs and Herbs**

| HERBS | TREES | SHRUBS |
|---|---|---|
| *Abutilon mauritianum* | *Acacia nilitica (Sub tomentosa)* | *Acacia ataxacantha* |
| *Acanthospermum hispidum* | *Acaccia tortilis* | *Boscia senegalensis* |
| *Achyranthes aspera (Linn)* | *Acacia seyal* | *Cassia tora (Linn)* |
| *Alysicarpus vaginalis De. And A. violescence (Schindl)* | *Acacia sieberiana* | *Cassia tora (Linn)* |
| *Andropogon gayanus (Kuntt)* | *Adansonia digitata* | *Ceasalpinia goratensis* |
| *Andropogon pseudopricus (Stapt)* | *Albizia chevaliert (Harrins)* | *Euphorbia balsamifera* |
| *Amaranthus viridis (Linn)* | *Anogeissus schimperi* | *Guiera senegalensis* |
| *Boerhavia erecta (Linn)* | *Anona senegalensis* | *Lawsonia inermis* |
| *Brachiari distichophylla (J. M. Dalz)* | *Azadirachta indica* | *Leptadenia pyrotechnica (Dene)* |
| *Cenchrus biflorus (Roxb)* | *Balanites aegyptiaca* | *Euphorbia poisonii* |
| *Chenchrus biflorus (Dalz)* | *Banhinia ruffescens* | *Hyphaene thebaica (Small)* |
| *Chenchrus biflorus (Daiz)* | *Bauhinia jhonningii (Schum)* | |
| *Celosia leptostachya (Benth)* | *Cassia sieberiana (Linn)* | |
| *Ceralluma dalzielli N. E. Br.* | *Combretun glutinosum* | |
| *Ceratotheca sesamoides Eudl.* | *Commiphora Africana* | |
| *Centuarea alexandrina, C. Praecox and C. Rhizophora* | *Faidherbia albida* | |

Chapter 16   Salisu Mohammed, in
A.I. Tanko and S.B. Momale (Eds.)
*Kano: Environment, Society and Development*
London & Abuja, Adonis & Abbey Publishers

| HERBS | TREES | SHRUBS |
|-------|-------|--------|
| *Chameochrista mimosoides* | | |
| *Chrozophora brocchiana* | | |
| *Chrozophora senegalensis (A. juss)* | *Ficus ingens – (Mig-Mig var ingens)* | |
| *Corchorus olitornis (Linn)* | *Ficus platyphylla (Del)* | |
| *Conyza attenuata D. C.* | *Hyphaene jhebaica (BIS) (Linn)* | |
| *Crinum yuccaeflorum (Salis b).* | *Maerua angolensis* | |
| *Crotalaria aranaria (Linn)* | *Maerua crassifolia* | |
| *Crotalaria aschrek (Forsk)* | *Moringa oleifera (Lam)* | |
| *Crotalaria aschrek (Linn)* | *Prosopis Africana* | |
| *Cucumis melo (Linn)* | *Sclercarya birae (N. rich) Hoschst* | |
| *Cucumis prophetarum* | *Stereospermum kunthianum (Lam)* | |
| *Cyperrus platycaulis (Bak)* | *Sterculia sefigera* | |
| *Datura inoxia* | *Stylosanthes errecta P. Beawx* | |
| *Desmodium lasiorcarpum (Dc.)* | *Tamarindus indica* | |
| *Dicoma tomentosa (cass.) (Daiz)* | *Terminalia aviccenioides* | |
| *Eragrostis cilaris and E. lingulata (W. D. Clayton)* | *Vitex doniana (sweet)* | |
| *Euphorbia convolvuloides (Hosch)* | *Ximenia amricana (Linn)* | |
| | *Ziziphus mauritiana (Lam)* | |
| *Euphorbia polycmoides (Hoschst) ex. Boiss* | *Ziziphus mucronata* | |
| *Evolvulus alsinoides (Linn)* | *Ziziphus spina christi (Desf.)* | |
| *Feretia cantheioides (Hiern)* | | |
| *Fimbristylis hispidula (Valv.) kuntt* | | |
| *Hibiscus asper (Hook) (Daiz)* | | |
| *Hibiscus sabda riffa (var. intermedius)* | | |
| *Hibiscus sabda riffa (var ruber)* | | |
| *Indigofera astragulina (Dc)* | | |
| *Kohontia grandiflora (D.C)* | | |
| *Kylinga ercta (Schumid) (thenn)* | | |
| *Lageraria vulgaris (Seringe)* | | |
| *Laggeria aurita (Linn)* | | |
| *Leucas spp.* | | |
| *Leucas martinicensis (Jacq) Ait* | | |
| *Leptadania lancifolia (Decne)* | | |
| *Mitra carpum vertiallatum (Vatke)* | | |
| *Momordica balsamina* | | |
| *Pennisetum pedicellatum* | | |
| *Pergularia tomentosa (Linn)* | | |
| *Peristrophe bicalyculata (Retz) Mers.* | | |
| *Polycarpaea linearifolia (DC) and P. caymbosa (Larm)* | | |
| *Portulaca oleracea (Linn)* | | |
| *Ricinus communis* | | |
| *Rageria adenophylla* | | |
| *Sesamum spp.* | | |
| *Schizachyrium exile (Stapf)* | | |
| *Schaenefeldia gracilis* | | |
| *Scoparia dulcis (Linn)* | | |
| *Securidaca lengepedunculata (Fres)* | | |
| *Senna italica (Mill)* | | |
| *Senna occidentalis (Linn)* | | |
| *Sesbania aegyptiaca (poir) or S. Polycarpa* | | |
| *Solanum incanum. (Linn)* | | |
| *Sonchus oleraceus* | | |
| *Spermacoce stachydea (DC)* | | |
| *Striga spp.* | | |
| *Tephrosia humilis (Guill & perr)* | | |
| *Tephrosia purpurea* | | |

Chapter 16 | Salisu Mohammed, in
A.I. Tanko and S.B. Momale (Eds.)
*Kano: Environment, Society and Development*
London & Abuja, Adonis & Abbey Publishers

| Trianthema | pentadra | |
|---|---|---|
| Trianthema | portulacastrum | |
| Vernonia | ambigua | |
| Vernonia | perroffetii | (Sch. Bip) |
| Watheria | americana | (Linn) |

**Source:** *Adopted from Mohammed (1996)*

## Discussion

The first attempt made in order to conserve biodiversity or the curtailing of threat to genetic erosion was the establishment ex-situ, Gene Banks. Gene Banks are amongst the several important strategies that address the conservation of plant genetic diversity. Therefore, establishment of gene banks is a giant effort to conserve genetic resource as the basis of biodiversity and agro biodiversity. In effect, many gene banks were established in the 1960s and this is because plant breeders discovered that the biodiversity on which they depended was beginning to disappear. As a result, presently there are some 50 large gene banks in the world to which the principle of free access applies, and in theory any breeder may receive in response to a simple request a sample of any variety

The main responsibility of these gene banks is to conserve and preserve genetic resources as well as to make them available on request. Many problems were identified with gene banks or the ex-situ mode of genetic conservation. These include:

a. Gene banks or the international plant breeding system has not been very effective where agro-ecological environments are more variable and the need and are more diverse. As Ceccarelli (1999:36) explains, this is because peoples' needs are not well understood and there are few genetically uniform products for on farm testing and selection. Thus, the testing and selections are made on stations where conditions are quite different from the farm in the target environment.

b. Most of the gene banks (or formal sectors) are mainly interested in commercial agro-bio diversity. Thus, the varieties developed are often unsuitable for the diverse agro-ecological conditions and needs of small farmers.

c. Although some of the larger gene banks contain impressive number of accessions local farmers usually do not have easy

| Chapter 16 | Salisu Mohammed, in |
|---|---|
| | A.I. Tanko and S.B. Momale (Eds.) |
| | *Kano: Environment, Society and Development* |
| | London & Abuja, Adonis & Abbey Publishers |

access to the materials they have donated in especially agro biodiversitry.

It could be stated here that though gene banks play the role of conventional solution to the conservation of plant germplasm and biodiversity, which are based on collection of genetic materials from centers of origin and elsewhere, that are stored in controlled and periodically regenerated, they are seen as important sources of material for plant breeding programmes and other research activities. Despite their problems as identified above, gene banks will still continue to be a basic element in conservation programmes and promoter of biodiversity.

Identifying some lapses with gene banks or the ex-situ conservation of biodiversity, inter alia has created the possibility of a little shift in paradigm on sustainable biodiversity and germplasm conservation in order to curtail the process of genetic loss.

An option that is attracting attention is the possibility of carrying out genetic resource maintenance and management in the field. This is also referred to as the in-situ conservation in addition to the ex-situ alternative of gene banks.

The *in-situ* conservation has included the importance of recognizing the roles of both the environmental factors and farmer intervention in land race development. In-situ conservation has been emphasized for the following reasons:

a. In areas of high genetic diversity,
b. land races are often evolved through crossing with wild or weedy relatives and farmers play a crucial role in selecting adapting new materials.

The development of land races from wild species illustrates that local gene development is an effective system of crop development. According to ODI (1996), farmers land development in agrobiodiversity involves a careful selection of plant material adapted to varied (and often changing) growing conditions and preferences whose result has been of complex and continually evolving collection of local crop varieties. It also reflects interaction with wild species adaptation to changing farming conditions and responses to the economic and cultural factors that shapes farmers priorities. It is

Chapter 16 | Salisu Mohammed, in
A.I. Tanko and S.B. Momale (Eds.)
*Kano: Environment, Society and Development*
London & Abuja, Adonis & Abbey Publishers

understood that the *in situ* location for genetic resource is the farm and the wild, and for this reason, this method can play a very vital role in its conservation.

Farmers' varieties in agro biodiversity are uniquely adapted to genetically diverse cultivars. They are repositories of traits that have evolved in local environments over long periods of time as a result of cultivation and selection. As sources of adapted genes, the varieties have been the raw materials from which the modern and often higher yielding crop varieties have been developed. The conservation of local land races is therefore of critical importance both for scientific crop improvements and subsistence agriculture and biodiversity (ILEIA, 1999: 30).

Numerous land races provide food security to many people especially at subsistence level and also act as a primary source of breeding material for modern varieties (MVs). The use of land races also contributes to stable food production and income especially in agro biodiversity and marginal environments where the impact of modern varieties is limited.

The convention on Biological Diversity or biodiversity (CBD) has recognized the continued maintenance of traditional varieties in-situ, as an essential component of sustainable agricultural development.

The primary objective of *in situ* is to conserve biodiversity of traditional crop varieties on the farms and wild. This practice is self supporting as well as favouring evolutionary process. However, in-situ conservation may not be fully adequate for the maintenance of material or gene for the fact that farmers may not wish to continue planting particular varieties or crops if better varieties become available. Also the genetic make up of materials can change when farmers change production practices. Evidently the significance of local involvement in genetic resources conservation is increasingly recognised.

Important questions to be asked here are:

a. How do local people see genetic resource or biodiversity conservation?
b. How do the local people conserve genetic resources or biodiversity?

Chapter 16 | Salisu Mohammed, in
A.I. Tanko and S.B. Momale (Eds.)
*Kano: Environment, Society and Development*
London & Abuja, Adonis & Abbey Publishers

In order to answer the first question, it can be said that local people view genetic resource conservation in terms of its importance to their livelihood. In this case genetic resource conservation can hardly be dissociated from usage. This decision to conserve a variety depends largely on its usefulness and ILEIA (1999:33) re-emphasized that people have managed germplasm for thousands of years under complex and changing conditions and thus contemporary usage of *'conservation'* has failed to capture the dynamics of adoption and selection, and as such it is safe to make the remarks that the development of land races from wild species by the farmers' selection strategy has illustrated that local development process is an effective system of crop improvement. However, many people in various areas do not feel that they are the custodians of something geneticists want to preserve for future use. Their perception of biodiversity and crop diversity is pragmatic and more related to managing their immediate individual life styles and economic needs. Thus in the case of agrobiodiversity, the aspects that seem particularly important to farmers include the search crop diversity and earliness to increase their ability to cope with adverse weather conditions.

On the second question, local people in the high risk environments in places such as the drylands do conserve genetic resources or biodiversity in the process of varietal and species selection in order to deal with the environmental problems, and as such, the process of conservation has been seen in many cases as a specialized activity in which few individuals in a community are considered local conservers. Such individuals in the community have considerable knowledge of genetic resources conservation that has a more conscious and systematic approach to crop conservation. Furthermore, the value of conserving the genetic diversity still cultivated in traditional system is undisputed. It is becoming increasingly clear that the farmers in both high and low potential areas will always need genetic diversity to buffer them against environmental hazards, changing market conditions and as insurance for the future. Thus, such challenges show combined development with the maintenance of farmers' genetic diversity. However, as earlier identified, there are various studies which are *'enhancing'* and not *'extractive'* in approach that identify the importance of incorporating local knowledge of farmers especially in developing countries (e.g Howes and Haugurud, 1990).

Chapter 16 | Salisu Mohammed, in
A.I. Tanko and S.B. Momale (Eds.)
*Kano: Environment, Society and Development*
London & Abuja, Adonis & Abbey Publishers

Also Boncodin and Vega (1999) added in summary that local people conserve preferred cultivars by continuously planting them on their farms, home gardens and plots. Furthermore, from the problems identified above, it is important that local knowledge of farmers and stakeholders has to be incorporated in biodiversity and crop genetic diversity conservations. This is particularly necessary as one of the most important sectors of Nigerian economy is the agricultural sector, therefore progress in understanding the genetic diversity and management of indigenous cultivars should strengthen the subsistence agricultural sector as extension services should benefit from a better understanding of the needs for and impact of new technologies.

The need to conserve biodiversity in the words of TAC in SPORE (1994):

'Many plants and animals species are disappearing thereby deflating the world's genetic resource. Our heritage of biodiversity is under serious threat and one of the themes of international discussion about the environment is to devise what measure should be taken to reduce the threat'.

Many factors have been identified to be responsible for genetic loss, for instance, forests are cut down, land is cleared, bush fires rage, land is over grazed, there is resource misuse, there is misuse of fertilizer and pesticides; irrigation is mismanaged and there is pollution; plant and animal habitats are destroyed, industrial activities and urban proliferation compound the problem. Specifically, it has been identified that the richness and range of the diversity of farmers' land races which develop as result of careful selection of plant materials adapted to varied and often changing growing conditions and preferences which is tantamount to the production of a complex and continually evolving collection of local crop varieties that reflect interaction with wild species. Adaptation to changing farming conditions and response to the economic and cultural factors has shaped farmers' priority which is now under threat because of changing nature of agricultural production which includes widespread adoption of crop modern varieties (MVs), which are the products of formal plant breeding. The MVs often provide yield increases and other advantages that result in their being sown over large areas.

A question may be asked here that if the adoption and use of MVs and other agricu ltural technology in agro biodiversity brings

Chapter 16 | Salisu Mohammed, in
A.I. Tanko and S.B. Momale (Eds.)
*Kano: Environment, Society and Development*
London & Abuja, Adonis & Abbey Publishers

significant benefit to farmers, why then should we be concerned with their land races and the preservation of crop genetic diversity as a whole? ODI (1996) has provided an answer to the above question that many advances of modern plant breeding have been possible because of the wide range of genetic material provided by land. In other words, farmers' land races have provided a backbone to the production of modern varieties. Thus the very success of modern plant breeding now threatens the source of genetic diversity on which further progress depends as farmers find it less demanding to maintain the diverse mixture of land races develop by their ancestors.

It is also noted that the widespread use of MVs raises questions about the stability of crop production and the threat of disease or pest attack. MVs are more uniform than land races that may increase their susceptibility to pest or pathogens, but many MVs owe their acceptance to the fact that they are more resistant than the varieties they replace. The principal threat to yield stability from MVs use is the increasing uniformity and continuos cropping that their use endangers. Large areas planted to a single variety are potentially a cause of concern, no matter what the source of the variety.

Additionally, the preservation and utilization of biodiversity and agro biodiversity is of particular importance to the more marginal, diverse agricultural environment where modern plant breeding has had much less success. Farmers in these areas tend to be poorly served by public research and extension systems. These areas are often centres of diversity for many crop species. However, increasing poverty is forcing many of these farmers to be more dependent on non farm source of income with consequent reduction in their capacity to grow and maintain the range of local varieties that they have been accustomed to manage. It could also be stated that the maintenance of a wide and evolving range of local varieties of local crop land races is threatened by the advent of intellectual property protection for crop varieties (see UNRISO, 1994:54), accelerated by the formation of the World Trade Organization. The increasing application of plant breeders' right has several implications for plant genetic diversity. For a new variety to be legally protected, it must be subject to very precise description including the requirement that it be distinct, uniform and stable (DUS), which could be a disincentive to the promotion of intrinsically diverse land races or of variety mixtures.

Chapter 16    Salisu Mohammed, in
             A.I. Tanko and S.B. Momale (Eds.)
             *Kano: Environment, Society and Development*
             London & Abuja, Adonis & Abbey Publishers

## Biodiversity Problems in Tumbau and Dagaceri

I.   Slow growth rates of indigenous trees, especially under conditions of drought. This constraint discourages would-be tree planters from using them rather than the fast-growing and very drought-resistant neem (*Azadirachta indica*) which is planted on farms and within the villages. Nurseries are few, far away and the selection of species available restricted; all are managed by the forestry department and there are no private nurseries.

II.  Premature and indiscriminate cutting of trees. Transhumant herds pass through both areas and their keepers cut branches of browse trees for feeding their animals, without permission though on private land whether they are ready for cutting or not.

III. Lost of fodder, fruit and *kaba* (the fibrous shoots of *hyphaene thebaica*.). Field boundary plants which provide fodder are prone to theft and farmers hoist bundles of millet stalks onto the trees to secure them from people (Tumbau).

IV.  The fruit trees raised on farms are prone to harvest by unknown persons (both villages). This fear is a constraint to growing exotic fruit trees in the open fields. The dum palm that is systematically harvested for *kaba* for the making mats and rope has a strong market value and may be taken by people (not necessarily the owners). This tendency runs counter to increasing privatization of ecosystem resources and a decline of *social policing* and local courts or district heads may not always uphold private rights. Livestock theft is also on the increase in less densely populated areas further east. Dagaceri area is characterized by drylands conditions (Plates 15.2 and 15.3) and the biodiversity is resilient and adapted to the conditions of aridity (Plate 15.4).

The study in Dagaceri shows that there are less number of biodiversity due to less rainfall also there is large number of wild plants which contribute to the local diet. They were predominantly used to supplement staples in meals (e.g as spinach leaves).

Chapter 16 | Salisu Mohammed, in
A.I. Tanko and S.B. Momale (Eds.)
*Kano: Environment, Society and Development*
London & Abuja, Adonis & Abbey Publishers

Biodiversity management in Tumbau has been supported by various efforts to control indiscriminate cutting of trees. Fuel wood is sourced mostly from lower plants such as shrubs and other woody plants and not grown trees (Plate 15.5). Preserving biodiversity also takes place at the molecular level in the conservation of genetic diversity (Mohammed 2006).

In the year 2006 while establishing community of neem plantation in Dagaceri, a team of researchers (including the author) traveled over 60km from the village to be able to source for *Kirya* (*Prosopis africana*) post to be used in fencing the plantation because it could resist termite destruction. *Kirya* is indeed an endangered species in the area.

## Conclusion

This Chapter has shown that wild resources in the Kano Region are linked to biodiversity and poverty considering their role in livelihoods. Moreover, it has been shown that wild foods and biodiversity are important strategy for rural communities and it is apparent that many species are of value to household's needs. The wild foods play a role in livelihoods in providing an improved diet in terms of nutritional value and diversity, and in supplementing the food needs of rural households particularly at times of famine. They also provide opportunities for income generation.

Agro biodiversity continues to characterize farming practices (Mohammed, 2006), though there is a risk of loss as new improved varieries replaces *traditional* ones as main food providers. Tumbau has a greater degree of agro diversity than dagaceri and Ririwai has the greatest.

In addition to the threats posed by rainfall uncertainty and population growth, Tumbau and Dagaceri face a number of constraints in managing the ecosystem and biodiversity, especially to increasing its capacity to produce more food, goods and services in the long term. Biodiversity is directly involved in water purification, recycling nutrients and providing fertile soils. Finally, biodiversity of semi arid environment is under threat, and plants and animals species seem to be more insecure to this threat.

Chapter 16 | Salisu Mohammed, in
A.I. Tanko and S.B. Momale (Eds.)
*Kano: Environment, Society and Development*
London & Abuja, Adonis & Abbey Publishers

# References

Boncodin, R. and Vega, B., (1999) Local Views on Genetic Resource Conservation: *in* ILEIA News letter, vol. 15 3/4

Bunting A.H and Barbara. T, (1995) 'Plant genetic resources: Preservation of genetic' resources 423-27 *in: complexes d' especes, flux de genes et resources des plantes.* Collogues international, Paris 8-10 Janvier

Ceccarelli, S. 1999. *A methodological study on partispatory barley breeding 1.* Selection phase. Euphytical. Aleppo: ICARDA

Glover, J., Robinson, P. and Henderson (1954) Provisional maps of the reliability of annual rainfall in East Africa. *Quart, J. R. Met. Soc.* 80 78-80

Grove, A. T. (1973) 'Desertification in the African environment. In: Dalby and church (eds.), op. cit.

Howes and Haugerud 1990 Plant resources. Improving the relevance of breeding in *Africa'experimental Agriculture* 26: 341-62

ILEIA (Information on Low External input and sustainable agriculture)(1999) *Seeds for Agrobiodiversity*: ILEIA foundation Leusden, the Netherlands. Vol.15 nos. 3/4

Kowal, J. M. and Knabe, D. T., (1972) *An Agroclimatological Atlas of the Northern states of Nigeria,* Zaria, ABU press Nigeria.

LEISA (Low External Input and Sustainable Agriculture) (1999), *Seeds for agrobiodiversity Vol. 15* no. 3/4: A quarterly newsletter, ILEIA foundation, Leusdan, the Netherlands.

Maduakor, R.O., (1991) physical and hydraulic properties of soils of the sudano-sahelian regions of Nigeria. IN Sivakumar, M. U. K., Wallace, J. S., Renard, C. and Ciroux, C. (eds.). *Soil and water balance in the sudano sahelian zone.* Proceedings of the Niamey workshop, International Association of hyrological sciences (IAHS) publication no. 199 pp. 229-240

Manning, H. L., (1951) Confidence limits of expected monthly rainfall *J. Agric. Sci. Camb.* 40 169-76

Manning, H. L., (1956) The statiscal assessment of rainfall probability and its application in Ugandan Agriculture. *Proc. Roy. Soc. London (B)* 144 460- 80

Chapter 16 | Salisu Mohammed, in
A.I. Tanko and S.B. Momale (Eds.)
*Kano: Environment, Society and Development*
London & Abuja, Adonis & Abbey Publishers

Mohammed S. (1994) Evaluation of multipurpose uses of trees, shrubs and grasses. Condition of access and smallholder management in a village in semi arid North Eastern Nigeria. Unpublished M.Sc. Land Resources Thesis, Bayero University, Kano, Nigeria.

Mohammed S. 1996 'The farming system of Dagaceri Jigawa State Nigeria.' *Soils Cultivars and Livelihood in Northeast Nigeria,* Working paper 2. Kano: Department of Geography Bayero University

Mohammed S. (2006) `Adaptive Management of of Cultivar Diversity in semi arid Northern Eastern Nigeria`.Unpublished Ph.D Thesis, Bayero University, kano, Nigeria

Mohammed Salisu, and Frances Harris (2003), *Relying on nature wild field in Northern*

*Nigeria: AMBIO Vol XXXII no 1 Feb. 2003.* The Royal Swedish Academy Sciences: 24 - 29

Mortimore, M. J. (1987) The lands of Northern Nigeria: some urgent issues IN Mortimore, m., et al (eds.) op. Cit. Pp.13-23

Mortimore, M. J. (1989) *Adapting to drought farmer, famines and desertification in West Africa.* Cambridge: Cambridge University Press.

ODI, (1996) The Erosion of crop genetic diversity: challenges, strategies and uncertainties, ODI, London.

Sivakumar, M. V. K., Huda, A. K. S. and Virmani, S. M., (1984) hysical environment of sorghum and Millet growing areas in South Asia. Pg. 63-83 in agrometreology of sorghum and millet in the semi arid tropics; proceedings of the International sym posium, 15-20, Nov. 1982, ICRISAT center, India. Patancheru A.P. 502 324 India: International Crop Research Institute for the semi arid Tropics.

Sivakumar, M. V. K., (1990), Exploiting rainy season potential from the onset of rains in the sahelian zone of west Africa. *Agriculture and Forest Metreology.* 51 321-32

SPORE (1994) 'Biodiversity: Our common heritage'.Technical center for agricultural and Rural cooperation (CTA) No. 54 1-3 CTA, wageningen, the Netherlands

Chapter 16 | Salisu Mohammed, in
A.I. Tanko and S.B. Momale (Eds.)
*Kano: Environment, Society and Development*
London & Abuja, Adonis & Abbey Publishers

**275**

# Chapter Seventeen

## PASTROLISM

Saleh Bashayi Momale

### Introduction

Pastoralism has traditionally been defined as a farming system where livestock (such as cattle, sheep, goats, and camels) are taken to different locations in search of fresh pastures, or simply the extensive grazing of livestock dependent on natural pastures (FAO, 2002). This narrow definition has been challenged by contemporary scholars. Pastoralism is presently viewed as a complex, diverse, and extremely dynamic system of traditional livestock breeding and securing of livelihoods by the breeders, who continuously adapt to evolving social, political and economic conditions at local, national and regional levels (Hesse and MacGregor, 2006). Thus, pastoralism is not only viewed from the perspective of livestock production, but also from human perspectives looking at the livelihoods of the breeders. Pastoralism is thus a livelihood system that integrates livestock husbandry with other activities, as a rational economic activity with strong social, environmental and cultural objectives. It is a system regulated by ecology and complex modes of social, political and economic organizations (Hesse and MacGregor, 2006).

Studies of pastoralism address the dynamics of dryland ecosystems and the livelihood objectives pursued by pastoral communities in response to key environmental and market drivers. It deal with issues of maintaining an optimal balance between pastures, livestock and people in a highly uncertain and variable environment, to meet both immediate and future livelihood needs of the pastoral families.

### Livestock Breeding Practices in the Kano Region

There are three categories of livestock breeders in the Kano Region. The first are nomadic pastoralists made up of full-time livestock breeding families whose major preoccupation is the herding of livestock, mainly cattle and sheep. The percentage of this group is increasingly reducing because of the continuous spontaneous

Chapter 17 | Saleh B. Momale, in
A.I. Tanko and S.B. Momale (Eds.)
*Kano: Environment, Society and Development*
London & Abuja, Adonis & Abbey Publishers

sedantarisation of pastoralists on the one hand, and the increasing migration of this group into the sub-humid zone of Nigeria. This group does not have areas of permanent settlement, but continue to oscillate from the northern parts of the Region to the most southernmost parts. They often cross regional and national boundaries into the middle belt and southern parts of Nigeria to the south and into North-eastern parts of Nigeria and Niger Republic to the North.

The second are agro-pastoralists who combine traditional livestock breeding with crop cultivation. They establish semi-permanent to permanent settlements but practicing split migration in response to seasonal variability in climatic conditions. They are currently the most dominant group of livestock breeders in the Kano Region and widely spread across all parts of the Region. Livestock holdings per household greatly vary among families ranging from as low as 20 cattle per household to as high as over 500 cattle per household.

The third are crop producers who maintain and breed some livestock. This practice is increasingly gaining prominence due to the increased use of ox-plough and ox-drawn carts on one hand and the fattening of livestock as a means of generating wealth. Again, a number of wealthy crop producers, traders and peri-urban civil servants invest in livestock breeding where the animals are kept at the custody and care of poorer pastoral families. The practice of fattening has also gained prominence within major urban centres of the Region, particularly in Metropolitan Kano.

The types of movements associated with pastoralism in the Kano Region can be summarized as follows:

i. Daily movement of livestock in search of grazing and water returning to the same camp at the end of the day.

ii. Seasonal movement of herds in response to availability of natural pasture, water and availability of grazing fields. Generally speaking, the pattern of movement is for pastoralists and their livestock to move from the north to the south during the dry season and from the south to the north during the wet season. In the Kano Region however, the patterns of movements reflects mobility from densely cultivated to less densely cultivated areas during the cropping (rainy) season and vice versa during the dry season. In addition, the irrigation sites

Chapter 17    Saleh B. Momale, in
A.I. Tanko and S.B. Momale (Eds.)
*Kano: Environment, Society and Development*
London & Abuja, Adonis & Abbey Publishers

and floodplains of major rivers witness large influx of pastoralists during the dry season.

iii. Long range movement of pastoralists from parts of Niger Republic and the northern parts of the Region to the most southernmost parts to the central parts of Nigeria.

iv. Total outmigration from the Kano Region to other parts of Nigeria, particularly the central and south-eastern parts of Nigeria. There has also been migration of many pastoral families to northeastern parts, particularly into Bauchi, Gombe, Adamawa and Taraba States and Republic of Cameroon.

The nature of livestock breeding and the type of mobility associated with each type of breeding technique is simplified in Table 17.1.

**Table 17.1: Classification of Pastoralism based on type of Mobility**

| Breeding Technique | Type of Mobility often adopted by the Breeders | | |
|---|---|---|---|
| | Continuous movement of livestock | Split/Seasonal Movement of livestock | Short distance oscillations or confinement of livestock |
| Full time livestock breeding | Nomadic Pastoralists | Transhumant pastoralists | Sedentary pastoralists |
| Livestock breeding with little cropping | - | Transhumant agro-pastoralists | Sedentary agro-pastoralists |
| Livestock breeding with farming | | Semi-sedentary pastoralists | Sedentary agro-pastoralists/ commercial livestock farmers |

## *Distribution of Pastoralists in the Kano Region*

Within the Kano Region, there are areas of high pastoralists and livestock concentration during the wet and dry seasons. In the wet season, the areas of highest concentration are found in Tudun Wada, Doguwa, Rano, Sumaila, Albasu and Gaya LGAs, with the highest density within the Falgore Game Reserve and its adjoining areas. Areas of medium concentration include the remote rural areas of Kiru, Gwarzo and Karaye Local Governments. However, pastoralists are found scattered throughout the State including the peri-urban areas of Metropolitan Kano. In Jigawa State, the areas of high concentration are found in Kaugama, Gumel, Birniwa, Garki and Birnin Kudu Local Governments. Areas of medium concentration are found in Kazaure, Kirikasama and Babura Local Governments.

Chapter 17 | Saleh B. Momale, in
A.I. Tanko and S.B. Momale (Eds.)
*Kano: Environment, Society and Development*
London & Abuja, Adonis & Abbey Publishers

During dry season period, the pastoralists are widely distributed where livestock feed on crop residue particularly during the early parts of the dry season. However, the highest concentrations are found within the floodplains of the Hadejia River. This extends along the extensive floodplains from Wudil in Kano State into Auyo, Hadejia, Guri and Kirikasama in Jigawa State. During the late part of the dry season, very high concentrations are found within the Kano River Irrigation Project (KRIP) and other irrigations schemes including the Watari, Magaga, Bagwai, Tomas and Hadejia Valley Irrigation Projects (HVIP).

The Kano Region is one of the rural areas with high population density in sub-Saharan Africa. As such, there is stiff competition over access to land and this has tended to erode pastoralists access to grazing lands during the wet season. Thus, Kano and Jigawa States are among the few States in Nigeria without extensive gazette grazing reserves. This has negatively affected livestock production under traditional breeding systems. The *hurmis*, which were traditional grazing areas carved out around villages, have been significantly encroached upon by farming activities.

In addition, to the erosion of grazing areas (*hurmis*), stock routes utilized for daily grazing and migration has witnessed significant encroachment. Thus, mobility of pastoralists and livestock has been constraint, leading to periodic conflicts between pastoralists and farmers, particularly in Jigawa State.

Unlike in other States of Northern Nigeria, the Kano Region has the lowest sizes of grazing reserves that have been established by Government. For example, data from the Kano State Ministry of Agriculture shows that there are only three grazing reserves/pasture plots in Kano State covering a land area of about 253 hectares. In Jigawa State, the Ministry of Agriculture has records of 323 grazing reserves/areas and pasture plots spread across 21 Local Governments with a total land area of 106,474.5 hectares (Table 16.6). High level of farmer encroachments has been reported within these demarcated grazing reserves, grazing areas and pasture plots. This was the result of the failure of State Governments to gazette and protect the areas from enchroachment. In addition, infrastructure and services are poorly developed within these areas. Thus, the vast majority of pastoralists in the Kano Region depend on fallow lands, uncultivated

Chapter 17 | Saleh B. Momale, in
A.I. Tanko and S.B. Momale (Eds.)
*Kano: Environment, Society and Development*
London & Abuja, Adonis & Abbey Publishers

marginal fields and forest reserves as grazing fields and sources of pasture.

Despite the encroachment on grazing areas and stock routes, there is close association of livestock breeders with settled farmers for generations in the Kano Region with a positive correlation between population density and livestock concentration (Hendy, 1977). Bourn and Wint (1994) using aerial surveys of livestock distribution in countries like Chad, Mali, Niger, Nigeria and Sudan, have established positive correlation between livestock concentration and farming activities. Though most cattle are owned by pastoralists, many of these pastoralists also cultivate crops, and over the centuries and decades, a growing proportion of them have adopted settled, mixed farming practices. The pastoralists also prefer to live and co-exist closely with agricultural communities than inhabit isolated hinterlands. Thus, there is high level of livestock breeding and crop cultivation in the Kano Region. This symbiotic relationship is based on rural exchanges of cereals, crop residues, farm yard manure and other social and cultural exchanges.

## Contributions of Livestock Breeding

Globally, about 40 million persons, almost half of them African pastoralists, depend on livestock for their livelihoods. Livestock contribute about 40% of the global value of agricultural output and support the livelihood and food security of about a billion people (FAO, 2009). Traditional livestock breeding produces about 23% of the world's beef supply with a high proportion of this originating from Africa. Sub-saharan Africa represents 40% of the world's rangeland areas in the arid and semi-arid zones. At household level, livestock contributes directly to nutritional food security and income required for variety of purposes like clothing, health care and cultural functions. It provides farm yard manure, drought power and some raw materials required for variety of purposes at household and community levels.

The African Union Pastoralists Policy Framework (2007) quoted the United Nations' Food and Agriculture Organization 2005 figures, which indicate that the continent has 235 million cattle, 472 million goats, 21 million pigs and 1.3 billion poultry, all valued at about $65 billion. Based on the same statistics, there are 314 million poor people who live on less than $1 a day in Africa, half were highly dependent

Chapter 17 | Saleh B. Momale, in
A.I. Tanko and S.B. Momale (Eds.)
*Kano: Environment, Society and Development*
London & Abuja, Adonis & Abbey Publishers

upon livestock for their livelihoods and 80 percent of whom were in pastoral areas.

Nigeria has the largest population of livestock in West and Central Africa with about 16.6 million cattle, 35.5 million sheep and 56.5 million sheep (FAO, 2009), contributing 20% of the nation's Gross Domestic Product(GDP). Over 90% of the ruminant livestock population are owned and managed by traditional livestock breeders (Maina, 1999). Table 16.2 presents statistics of ruminant livestock and poultry in Nigeria.

**Table 17.2: Population of Cattle, Sheep, Goats and Poultry in Nigeria**

| Livestock type | 2000 | 2005 | 2010 (projected) |
|---|---|---|---|
| Cattle | 15 202 357 | 15 875 267 | 16 577 962 |
| Sheep | 28 202 149 | 31 547 883 | 35 519 759 |
| Goats | 44 156 517 | 49 959 046 | 56 524 075 |
| Poultry | 118 063 699 | 150 682 522 | 192 313 325 |

**Source:** *Federal Ministry of Agriculture: Department of Livestock, FAO Statistics, 2008*

Within the Kano Region, livestock production is among the major socio-economic activities of the people, predominantly practiced by Fulani Pastoralists. Largely managed under pastoral systems, the dominant livestock species involved are cattle, sheep and goats which are kept in open ranges feeding on natural pastures within the rural landscapes of the Kano region. Within the urban areas, smaller numbers of sheep and goats are reared within households, but often allowed to roam the streets particularly within the low density residential areas and slums of the metropolis.

Data on the population of livestock within the region are scanty since census of livestock is seldom undertaken in Nigeria. Figures from the Livestock Resources Survey of 1990 - 1992 showed that there were over a million cattle in Kano State alone. From livestock, the most important products derived are beef, dairy products and hides and skins. In addition, manure, farm power (work bulls) and other products like bones and blood possess enormous economic value.

There has also been a significant increase in demand for livestock products (meat and milk). This is a common worldwide phenomenon that Delgado et al. (1999) call the 'livestock revolution'. The increased demand makes labour-intensive feeding methods, such as fattening economical. Thus, hundreds of people are now engaged in livestock

Chapter 17 | Saleh B. Momale, in
A.I. Tanko and S.B. Momale (Eds.)
*Kano: Environment, Society and Development*
London & Abuja, Adonis & Abbey Publishers

fattening particularly in the Metropolitan and peri-urban Kano. However, what has remained poorly developed is dairy production. This could be attributed to the ready availability of imported powdered milk that satisfies the need for milk at comparatively cheaper prices.

To derive beef, millions of livestock are slaughtered annually in Nigeria and the Kano Region. In Kano State for example, transhumant livestock rearing provides 65% of beef, 40% of sheep and goat's meat and 70% of milk available on the market (Moutari and Tan, 2008). Table 17.3 provide data on the estimated number of ruminant livestock slaughtered in Nigeria and the Kano Region to provide beef and other livestock products. It should be noted that this number could be higher because some of the livestock slaughtered in villages and outside the slaughter houses have not been included in the statistics in the Table.

**Table 17.3: Livestock Slaughtered in the Kano Region for Selected Years**

| Livestock Type | 2000 | | 2005 | | 2008 | |
|---|---|---|---|---|---|---|
| | Nigeria | Kano Region | Nigeria | Kano Region | Nigeria | Kano Region |
| Cow | 1,882,529 | 210,815* | 2,350,845 | 62,844* | 2,522,956 | 105,126 |
| Sheep | 3,432,551 | 333,663* | 2,902,405 | 162,179* | 1,464,094 | 219,837 |
| Goats | 5,390,302 | 638,332* | 4,576,544 | 638,332* | 2,462,315 | 226,767 |
| Camels | 16,281 | No data | 54,055 | 20,932* | 58,412 | 16,224 |

* Data not available for Jigawa State
**Source:** *Federal Ministry of Agriculture: Department of Livestock, FAO Statistics, 2009*

The livelihood of not only the livestock breeders but also a wide ranging segment of the Nigerian population involve in the purchase, marketing, transportation and selling of livestock products and by-products. Thus, the breeding of livestock, the marketing life- animals and the processing and marketing of beef and other products are important sources of employment and revenue to governments in all States of the country. Table 17.4 presents the average prices of beef and life ruminant livestock for some selected years.

Chapter 17 | Saleh B. Momale, in
A.I. Tanko and S.B. Momale (Eds.)
*Kano: Environment, Society and Development*
London & Abuja, Adonis & Abbey Publishers

**Table 17.4: Prices of Some Livestock Products and Life Animals in Nigeria (in Naira)**

| Product/Livestock type | 2001 | 2005 | 2008 |
|---|---|---|---|
| Beef (per metric ton) | 226 890.00 | 375 830.00 | 586 026.21 |
| Mutton (per metric ton) | 171 970.00 | 279 080.00 | 543 979.23 |
| Goat meat (per metric ton) | 208 410.00 | 338 920.00 | 543 221.50 |
| Cock (per metric ton) | 221 030.00 | 362 880.00 | 569 036.30 |
| Cattle (per head) | .. | .. | 71 475.84 |
| Sheep (per metric ton) | .. | .. | 15 202.92 |
| Goats (per metric ton) | .. | .. | 8 385.58 |
| Camel (per metric ton) | .. | .. | 64 944.44 |

*Source:* National Bureau of Statistics, Annual Abstract of Statistics, FAO Statistics, 2009

The supply and processing of dairy products is an important economic activity associated with livestock breeding. In Nigeria and the Kano Region, cattle and sheep are the suppliers of dairy products, with milk from cows being the most dominant source. The milk is collected daily by the breeders and processed into different forms for consumption. Milk is directly consumed, and it can also be processed to provide other nutritional foods like yoghurt, butter, and cheese. Table 17.5 contains data on the value of dairy products for some selected years in Nigeria. It is important to note that accurate and reliable statistics relating to the production, consumption and value of dairy products in Nigeria are grossly inadequate.

The largest quantity of milk produced by pastoralists are marketed locally without undergoing industrial processing while the remaining is normally consumed by pastoral households. Marketing of milk is one of the most dominant means of income generation for women in pastoral societies. Thus it is common to find pastoralists women hawking milk and yoghurt in all the cities, towns and villages of the Kano Region. Important areas providing milk and other dairy products in the Region are Falgore, Rano, Bunkure, Birnin Kudu and Babura in the rainy season. Kura, Garun Mallam, Bagwai, Hadejia and Auyo are important areas providing milk in the dry season.

Within Metropolitan Kano, the Kofar Wambai market is serving as the Headquarters of milk marketing, with products including fresh milk, yoghurt and butter brought from all parts of the rural hinterland. In addition, thousands of pastoral women from the adjoining settlements also market their products within the Metropolis. Thus, *fura da nono* is among the commonest drinks consumed by traders,

Chapter 17 | Saleh B. Momale, in
A.I. Tanko and S.B. Momale (Eds.)
*Kano: Environment, Society and Development*
London & Abuja, Adonis & Abbey Publishers

artisans and civil servants during the day time particularly in the urban and peri-urban areas of the Region.

**Table 17.5: Value of Milk Products by Commodity (2004-2008)**

| Product | 2004 | 2007 | 2008 |
|---|---|---|---|
| Milk and cream of =<1% fat, not concentrated or sweetened | 40,829,395 | 347,600* | 3,348,259* |
| Milk and cream in solid forms of =<1.5% fat | 829,969* | 178,758,576 | 348,000,000 |
| Milk and cream in solid forms of >1.5% fat, unsweetened | 7,195,749* | 226,875,496 | 494,877,427 |
| Milk and cream, concentrated or containing added sugar | .. | 14,557,649 | 165,553,570 |
| Milk and cream, concentrated or containing added sugar or other sweet | .. | .. | 2,931,301 |
| Milk and cream in solid forms of >1.5% fat, sweetened | 13,344,016 | .. | .. |
| Concentrated milk and cream, unsweetened (excluding in solid form) | 4,559,400 | .. | .. |
| Buttermilk, curdled milk and cream, etc (excluding yogurt) | 55,896,000* | 155,253,875 | .. |
| Products consisting of natural milk constituents | 5,003,896 | 12,144,188 | .. |
| Butter | .. | 3,196,879 | .. |
| Fats and oils derived from milk (excluding butter/dairy spreads) | .. | 12,875,567 | 153,486* |

* Years with inadequate data
*Source: National Bureau of Statistics, Abstract of Statistics, 2009 (FAO Statistics)*

Milk and milk products are grossly inadequate in meeting both the rural and urban demand of the products. Thus, Nigeria is a net importer of dairy products from the Western countries of Europe such as Netherlands, Denmark and Spain. Therefore, imported powdered milk in various forms is dominating the supply of milk products utilized by households and petty traders in tea, coffee and other drinks. In a like manner, powdered milk is mixed to produce liquid yoghurt by small scale factories in many urban centres and is sold in local shops and super markets.

Chapter 17 | Saleh B. Momale, in
A.I. Tanko and S.B. Momale (Eds.)
*Kano: Environment, Society and Development*
London & Abuja, Adonis & Abbey Publishers

## Land use intensification and Inadequacy of Grazing Areas

Rapid population expansion has been recorded within the Kano Region. In 1952, the Kano Province had a population of 3,396,350 with only 14% of the population residing in urban areas of 5,000 people and above. By 1991, the population has grown to over eight million people with 30% residing in urban areas of over 20,000 people. This growth and structural change in the population has several impacts on livestock breeding.

One of the impacts of population growth is the significant decrease in the amount of uncultivated fields and land under fallow (due to larger numbers of farmers). This led to decrease in availability of grazing areas during the wet season. On the other hand, increased cultivation of cereals to meet both urban and rural demand for foodcrops led to increase in the supply of crop residues that could be used as animal feeds during the dry season. In Kano, Jigawa and Katsina, the grain needed for urban consumption increased more than nine times from 62,000 tonnes in 1952 to 585,000 tonnes in 1991 (Tiffen, 2004). However, the increased production of crop residues provides for a change in animal feeding strategies adopted by pastoralists with increased reliance on crop residue than undertaking long range dry season migration into central Nigeria.

One of the response mechanisms to the increasing alienation of pastoralists' access to grazing areas was the enactment of the 1965 Grazing Reserve Law that empowers Government at the State level to carve out land and designate it as a grazing reserve for the exclusive use by Pastoralists (Momale, 2007). While hundreds of thousands of hectares of land have been acquired and demarcated as grazing reserves in various parts of Northern Nigeria, the Kano Region has the lowest sizes of grazing reserves in all States of Northern Nigeria as earlier stated. Table 16.6 shows the distribution and sizes of the *hurmis* and grazing reserves in the Region.

One of the effects of inadequacy of grazing areas in the Kano Region is the out-migration of pastoralists to central and other parts of Nigeria. Thus, hundreds of pastoralists indigenous to the Kano Region are now found in the States of Kaduna, Kogi, Nasarawa, Enugu, Abia and FCT Abuja among others. They have adapted to nomadic lifestyles or have established semi-permanent settlements in various villages and communities in those States.

| Chapter 17 | Saleh B. Momale, in |
| | A.I. Tanko and S.B. Momale (Eds.) |
| | *Kano: Environment, Society and Development* |
| | London & Abuja, Adonis & Abbey Publishers |

To guarantee the sustainability of pastoralism in the Kano Region, there is need to provide grazing areas. Support need to be provided to encourage the adoption of improved breeding techniques through breeds improvement, pasture production and formulation of supplementary feeds to address inadequacy of feed resources.

## Problems facing Pastoralism in the Kano Region

There are several constraints facing traditional livestock breeding in the Kano Region. The problems are quite similar to those confronting pastoralists in other parts of Nigeria and other countries of sub-Saharan Africa. In a survey conducted by the Pastoral Resolve (2004), (and personal communication), the following problems were identified as the major problems facing pastoralists in the Region.

i.   Inadequate of grazing land in all parts of the Region, leading to high levels of concentrations in the few Grazing Reserves and Forest Reserves. The high level of concentration has resulted to excessive overgrazing in the Region's uncultivated fields. The gross inadequacy of grazing lands and pasture has led to decreasing productivity, decline in milk yield and degradation in the genetic quality of the livestock breeds.

ii.  High level of blockage and encroachment of cattle routes to grazing and watering points which constrict livestock mobility and forces the breeders to utilize motorways as migratory routes with all its attendant problems such as vehicular accidents and extortion by security agencies.

iii. High level of competition over grazing areas and pastures as well as over crop residues due to the Influx of pastoralists from other States. This competition results to high cost of crop residues and available supplementary feeds like groundnut cakes, cotton seed cakes and bio-organics.

Chapter 17 | Saleh B. Momale, in
A.I. Tanko and S.B. Momale (Eds.)
*Kano: Environment, Society and Development*
London & Abuja, Adonis & Abbey Publishers

### Table 17.6: Grazing Reserves and Areas in the Kano Region

| S/N | LGA | No. of Grazing Reserves/Areas | Total Sizes of the Area in Hectares |
|---|---|---|---|
| | **Kano State** | | |
| 1 | Bichi | 1 | 804 |
| 2 | Gaya | 1 | 200 |
| 3 | Tudun Wada | 1 | 1,249 |
| | **Total** | **3** | **2,253** |
| | **Jigawa State** | | |
| 1 | Jahun | 39 | 1,649 |
| 2 | Maigatari | 8 | 850 |
| 3 | Sule Tankarkar | 13 | 750 |
| 4 | Kiyawa | 9 | 3,571 |
| 5 | Kirikasama | 14 | 9,800 |
| 6 | Kafin Hausa | 21 | 16,000 |
| 7 | Birnin Kudu | 20 | 4,912.5 |
| 8 | Dutse | 16 | 6,024 |
| 9 | Garki | 10 | 17,213 |
| 10 | Ringim | 18 | 20,226 |
| 11 | Taura | 15 | 8,844 |
| 12 | Gumel | 15 | 1,500 |
| 14 | Gwaram | 24 | 2,973 |
| 15 | Gwiwa | 9 | 1,076 |
| 16 | Hadejia | 25 | 1,074 |
| 17 | Kaugama | 23 | 2,511 |
| 19 | Roni | 11 | 1,796 |
| 20 | Birniwa | 10 | 920 |
| 21 | Kazaure | 23 | 4,785 |
| | **Total** | **323** | **106,474.5** |

*Source: PTF Pastoral Development Programme, 1997*

iv. Gross inadequacy of supplementary feeds that can be purchased by pastoralists to supplement the feeding of their animals particularly during the dry season.

v. Inadequacy of watering facilities forcing livestock and their breeders to concentrate along the major river systems and irrigation sites during the dry season.

vi. Low milk yield associated with poor feeding, diseases and decline in the genetic quality of the animals particularly cattle. This is negatively affecting family livelihoods and the level of income available to women resulting in poor nutrition, clothing, child care and provision of household essential needs.

vii. Poor quality of water for livestock consumption due to contamination of watering channels by fishermen, farmers and excessive use of ponds by livestock.

Chapter 17 | Saleh B. Momale, in
A.I. Tanko and S.B. Momale (Eds.)
*Kano: Environment, Society and Development*
London & Abuja, Adonis & Abbey Publishers

viii. Recurring conflicts between pastoralists and farmers with weak institutional mechanisms for the management of the disputes and prevention of violence. Higher levels of conflicts are recorded within the Hadejia River Valley than in the other parts of the Region.

ix. The practice of bush burning which destroys dry matter and crop residue that is beneficial in feeding livestock.

x. Inadequacy of veterinary services including diagnostics, quality drugs and treatment of diseases. This has led to the preponderance of many animal diseases (Fascioliasis, Helminth, Tryps, FMD, CBPP, PPR, NCD and Coccidiosis) with fatalistic effects on livestock productivity.

xi. High level of infestation of wet season grazing areas with biting flies (Mosquitoes, Black flies, Glossina, Midges, Horse flies, Tabanids) particularly in areas closer to the major river systems forcing pastoralists to migrate during the wet season.

xii. Weak extension services associated with gross inadequacy of extension workers, absence of well packaged extension messages and weak reach out to pastoral groups.

xiii. Inadequate availability of farm inputs (such as fertilizers, pesticides, herbicides, improved seeds and implements) required by the pastoralists for the cultivation of subsistence crops.

xiv. High level of illiteracy among the pastoral communities and inadequate enrolment of children into schools. There is also ineffective teaching and learning in the existing nomadic schools and other rural schools attended by the pastoralists' children.

xv. Insufficient representation of the pastoralists' communities in the various organs of government resulting in weak articulation of their needs and inadequate government interventions in promoting improved livestock breeding.

xvi. Excessive fines charged for crop damage, which is often associated with extortion by traditional leaders, vigilante and law enforcement agencies. There is also undue harassment and molestation from crop farmers and constituted authorities on the slightest opportunity.

xvii. Inadequate and weak provision of social services to the Pastoralists communities such as human health services,

Chapter 17 | Saleh B. Momale, in
A.I. Tanko and S.B. Momale (Eds.)
*Kano: Environment, Society and Development*
London & Abuja, Adonis & Abbey Publishers

xviii. portable water supply, educational services and accessible roads infrastructure.

Inadequate availability and access to credit facilities and other sources of finance to invest in improved management of livestock.

## Pastoralists - Farmer's Conflicts in the Kano Region

A major problem facing pastoralism in Nigeria are conflicts involving pastoralists and farmers. These conflicts revolve around the issues of access to, and use of natural resources that are increasingly becoming scarce in all parts of the country. The causes of these conflicts have been attributed to inadequate grazing and cropping areas, degradation of land due to desertification and other improper land management practices, crop destruction by livestock, encroachment on livestock migratory routes and grazing areas by farmers and other land users, competition over *fadama* resources and lack effective mechanism for the peaceful resolution of disputes between the pastoralists and farmers. Table 17.7 summarises some of the causes of conflicts that are triggered by pastoralists and farmers.

**Table 17.7: Two sides of the Pastoralists – Farmers' Conflicts**

| Conflicts are caused by farmers when they … | Conflicts are caused by Pastoralists when they … |
|---|---|
| • deliberately encroach into grazing fields, stock routes and watering areas; <br> • block access routes to grazing fields and watering points; <br> • leave harvested crops within the farms beyond the appropriate time of harvest; <br> • leave crop residue unprotected; <br> • Intentionally provoke herd boys/migrating pastoralists while on transit | • allows animals to damage crops at any stage of the crop growing season; <br> • migrate/move with large herds that are difficult to control; <br> • allow immature youths to herd cattle that results in crop damage; <br> • allow animals to trespass protected areas like forest/wild life reserves; community plantations and other reserved areas; and <br> • refuse to pay farmers compensation for crop damage |

Within the Kano Region, the levels of conflicts are low. The most frequent violence is recorded along the Hadejia Valley (especially around Kirikasama, Guri and Hadejia) extending into the Hadejia – Nguru Wetlands in Jigawa and Yobe States. Other areas where violent conflicts have been recorded include Gwarzo, Gaya, Wudil, Rano and

Saleh B. Momale, in
A.I. Tanko and S.B. Momale (Eds.)
*Kano: Environment, Society and Development*
London & Abuja, Adonis & Abbey Publishers

Birnin Kudu Local Governments. Efforts put in place to minimize the conflicts include the establishment of conflict resolution committees at State and Local Governments level, the opening of migratory stock routes and the massive enlightenment of both pastoralists and farmers on the need for peaceful and harmonious coexistence.

## Conclusion

Traditional livestock breeding is highly important to the inhabitants and economy of the Kano Region. The system of traditional livestock breeding has not been static, but has been dynamic adapting to emerging economic, social and political challenges. It has responded to ecological and land use changes and has expanded over the years. There is increasing demand in livestock products and the prices of all types of livestock had increased. This potential need to be adequately harnessed to ensure the Region will continue to produce substantial parts of its livestock products needs.

Pastoralism is also contributing to food security and poverty reduction. It can do more with appropriate interventions by governments at all levels. Provision of support services like extension, veterinary care and training on one hand and the promotion of private sector investments in the livestock industry will further support food security and poverty reduction. Policy makers need to further recognize the role of livestock as safety nets against vulnerability to poverty and initiate appropriate policies and implement programmes that will reinforce this important function.

Livestock breeding is negatively affected by land degradation, desertification and the impact of climate change. On the other, with appropriate policies, the livestock sector can positively contribute to the mitigation of these environment effects. Livestock convert dry matter into organic manure that will contribute to land reclamation. It can contribute to reduced greenhouse emissions thereby mitigating the level of climate change. Thus, policies and programmes should be pursued to achieve these dual benefits of managing the environment and contributing to improved peoples livelihoods.

There is also the need to manage the diverse problems facing the pastoralists. This requires strategies that will guarantee pastoralists access to land and other critical resources as well as their sustainable management. The management of risks associated livestock diseases is

Chapter 17 | Saleh B. Momale, in
A.I. Tanko and S.B. Momale (Eds.)
*Kano: Environment, Society and Development*
London & Abuja, Adonis & Abbey Publishers

291

essential by developing an effective framework for the provision of an effective herd health management system. Again, addressing the recurring conflicts between pastoralists and farmers is essential for peaceful and harmonious relations.

Efforts by all stakeholders should be strengthened to improve its level of productivity by making investments in improved technologies and practices for breeding and feeding of livestock. Training and capacity building for pastoralists need to be strengthened, supported by an effective educational and extension service delivery. The enlightenment and mobilization of the pastoral communities on one hand their involvement in policy formulation and implementation is required to ensure acceptability of interventions and sustainable achievement of impacts.

**References**

African Union Pastoralist Policy Framework, 2007: Pastoralism in Africa and Pastoralist Leaders Meeting, Inception Workshop, Shaba, Isiolo, Kenya, 9 - 11 July 2007

Awogbade, M. O. 1983, *Fulani Pastoralism: Jos Case Study*, Centre for Social and Economic Research, ABU Zaria

Baba, J. M. 1986, Reconciling Agricultural and pastoral Land Use Systems in Nigeria, in *Perspectives on Land Administration and Development in Northern Nigeria*, ed. Michael Mortimore et al, Department of Geography, Bayero University, Kano

Blench, R. 2004, *Natural Resource Conflicts in North-Central Nigeria: A Handbook and Case Studies*, Mallam Dendo Limited, Cambridge, UK

Bourn D. and Wint W. 1994, *Livestock, land use and agricultural intensification in sub-Saharan Africa*, Pastoral Development Network Working Paper 37a, Overseas Development Institute, London, UK

Delgado, C., Rosegrant, M, Steinfeld H., Ehui, S., and Courbois, C., 1999, *Livestock to 2020: The Next Food Revolution, 2020 Vision Initiative Food, Agriculture and Environment*, Discussion Paper 28, International Food Policy Research Institute, Washington D.C.

Ezeomah, C. 1987, *The Settlement Patterns of Nomadic Fulbe in Nigeria: Implications for Educational Development*, Cheshire: Deanhouse Limited,

Chapter 17 | Saleh B. Momale, in
A.I. Tanko and S.B. Momale (Eds.)
*Kano: Environment, Society and Development*
London & Abuja, Adonis & Abbey Publishers

Federal Republic of Nigeria (FRN), *Official Gazette No. 2, Vol. 96, February 2009, Legal Notice on Publication of 2006 Census Final Results*

Food and Agricultural Organisation, 2002, *FAO Animal Production and Health Paper - 150*, FAO, Rome

Food and Agricultural Organisation, 2009, *The State of Food and Agriculture: Livestock in the Balance*, FAO, Rome

Food and Agricultural Organisation, 2011, *World Livestock 2011: Livestock in food security*, FAO, Rome

Hadejia, I. A 1993: Land Use Conflicts in the Guri District of Jigawa State; Paper presented at the National Policy Workshop on Utilisation and Sustainability of Fadama in Northern Nigeria, Maiduguri

Hendy C.R.J. 1977, *Animal production in Kano State and the requirements for further study in the Kano Close-Settled Zone*, Land Resources Report 21, Land Resources Division of the Overseas Development Administration, Tolworth, Surrey, UK

Hesse C. and Macgregor, J. 2006, *Pastoralism: Drylands' Invisible Asset*? IIED Paper No. 142

Ingawa, S.A. Ingawa, G. Tarawali and R. von Kaufmann, 1989, *Grazing Reserves in Subhumid Nigeria: Problems, Prospects and Policy Implications*, African Livestock Policy Analysis Network (ALPAN), Network Paper No. 22, December 1989, Addis Ababa

Kano State Agricultural and Rural Development Authority, 1986, *Report on the 1984 Large Scale Reconnaissance Survey*, Kano State Agricultural and Rural Development Authority, Kano, Nigeria

Maina, J. A. 1999: Management of Common Property Resources for Sustainable Livestock Production in Nigeria; Paper presented at the DFID Workshop on Land Tenure, Poverty and Sustainable Development in Sub-Saharan Africa, February 1999, UK

Momale, S. B. 2003: Resource Use Conflicts in Agricultural and Pastoral Areas of Nigeria: in *Land Tenure Systems in Nigeria, Evolving Effective Land Use Policy for Poverty Alleviation*; LandNet, Nigeria

Mortimore, M. 1993, The Intensification of Peri-Urban Agriculture: The Kano Closed Settled Zone, 1964 - 1986, In *Population Growth and Agricultural Change in Africa*, Gainesville University Press, Florida ed. Turner II, B. L., G. Hyden and R. W. Kates

| Chapter 17 | Saleh B. Momale, in |
| --- | --- |
| | A.I. Tanko and S.B. Momale (Eds.) |
| | *Kano: Environment, Society and Development* |
| | London & Abuja, Adonis & Abbey Publishers |

Mortimore, M. 2001, Hard Questions for 'Pastoral Development': A Northern Nigerian Perspectives, *Elevage et gestion de parcours au Sahel, Implications pour le development, ed. E. Tielkes*, Schlecht et P. Hierrnaux, Ulrich

Moutari, M. and Su Fei Tan, 2008, Securing Pastoralism in East and West Africa: Protecting and Promoting Livestock Mobility, Niger/Nigeria Desk Review

Petroleum (Special) Trust Fund, 1997, The Pastoralists Development Programme, Working Paper I: Grazing Reserves and Stock Routes in Nigeria, Abuja, Nigeria

Shettima, A. G. and Usman A. Tar, 2008, Farmer - Pastoralists Conflicts in West Africa: Exploring the Causes and Consequences, *Information, Society and Justice, Volume 1.2, June 2008, pp 163 - 184,* London Metropolitan University, UK

The Pastoral Resolve (2004), Community Needs Assessment for Pastoral Communities in Kura, Bunkure and Garun Malam LGAs, Kano State, Internal Working Document, Kaduna

Tiffen, M., 2004, *Population pressure, migration and urbanisation: Impacts on crop-livestock systems development in West Africa,* Drylands Research, UK.

Chapter 17 | Saleh B. Momale, in
A.I. Tanko and S.B. Momale (Eds.)
*Kano: Environment, Society and Development*
London & Abuja, Adonis & Abbey Publishers

294

# Chapter Eighteen

## EDUCATION

### Nuratu Mohammed

## Introduction

Infrastructure is the platform and the bedrock upon which development occurs. The United States' National Infrastructural Improvement Act of 2006 identified these amenities to include water supply and distribution system, communications, electricity, waste collection and treatment facilities, surface transportation facilities, road and mass transit facilities, airports and airways facilities, resource recovery facilities, waterways, levees and related flood control facilities, docks or ports, school buildings and hospitals/medical facilities. Satisfactory provision and access to those basic structures and facilities that support positive economic performance requires massive financial commitments, ability to work around the difficulty in benefit-split that is private/public as well as handle the attendant high externalities (Usman, 2010). In many parts of the developing countries including Nigeria, infrastructural facilities are largely characterized by government ownership and management as a result of the capital expenditure involved in the provision of such services. The educational facilities and services in the Kano Region are examined in this Chapter.

## The Education Facilities

In all countries of the world, education is recognized as the cornerstone for sustainable development. It is the fulcrum around which the quick development of economic, political, sociological and human resources of any country revolve. Education is one of the indices used in measuring the development of a nation and the standard of living or poverty level of a society in comparison with the Human Development Index (HDI) which focuses on human development/knowledge measured in terms literacy or formal education (Adesemowo, et al, 2008). According to the Federal

Chapter 18 | Nuratu Mohammed, in
A.I. Tanko and S.B. Momale (Eds.)
*Kano: Environment, Society and Development*
London & Abuja, Adonis & Abbey Publishers

Government of Nigeria (2004), the National Policy on Education is meant for education to serve as the greatest investment that the nation can make for quick development of its economic, political, sociological and human resources. Education has been adopted as the instrument par excellence for effecting national development. It is unanimously agreed that education is the key factor to economic, political and socio-cultural development in essence education is a powerful tool for societal progress and development.

## *Forms of Education in the Kano Region*

Two main forms of education can be identified in the Region and these are the religious and western both of which are taken under formal, semi-formal and informal arrangements. The religious/Islamic education pre-dated the coming of western education in Northern Nigeria. The spread of Islam was accompanied by the teaching and learning of the Arabic language and the Islamic education to enable the adherents of the religion recite and understand the Qur'an and Islamic system. In this way, two forms of Islamic schools are found in the Region: *Makarantar allo/ Tsangaya* and the *Makarantar Islamiyya.*

In both schools, education is based on the basic philosophy of the life of the Muslim; submission and obedience to the will of Allah. The objective of Islamic education is to promote the Islamic cultural practices and way of life. To Muslims, the education is crucial to the moral, social and spiritual development of an individual. According to Ajibade (1991) the Islamic system of education is divided into three stages: The first stage which is equivalent to elementary education is *ibtidiyyah*, the second stage is the *i'dadiyya* which corresponds to secondary school and the third stage *Thanawiyyah* which is the highest stage and equivalent of the university stage (Abiri el al, 2005).

The advent of colonization saw the introduction of western education which came to the Kano Region after its first introduction in southern Nigeria. This found stiff opposition by parents. Over time, the opposition began to wane, that the Islamic schools began to be modified to incorporate western education forms and features; giving birth to Islamiyya schools. The schools came to design curriculum with a blend of the Islamic and western education thus incorporating

Chapter 18 | Nuratu Mohammed, in
A.I. Tanko and S.B. Momale (Eds.)
*Kano: Environment, Society and Development*
London & Abuja, Adonis & Abbey Publishers

Islamic disciplines of Qur'anic recitation, Islamic history and the traditional primary school subjects of English, reading and writing, arithmetic, health education and domestic science (Field observation, 2010). The government as part of its efforts to develop and promote the education in the Region introduced financial grants to the established Islamiyya schools and towards the establishment of new ones. Today there exists in the Region as many Islamiyya and Qur'anic schools as there are western type of schools (Table 18.1).

## The Western Education

The western schools came to the Region as formal English oriented schools characterized by specially built institutions (schools, colleges, universities) with formalized and highly structured curricula (programmes). Another mark of western schools is the award of prescribed certificates after completing specified curriculum designed for different levels and courses taught by the use of approved methods, facilities and examinations. The western oriented schools are divided into the following levels; pre-primary/nursery, primary, secondary and tertiary education (Abiri et al, 2005).

**Table 18.1: Registered Islamiyya and Qur'anic /Tsangaya and Ilmi Schools in Kano Region**

| Types of Schools | Jigawa | | Kano | |
|---|---|---|---|---|
| | N/S | N/ST | N/S | N/ST |
| Islamiyya | 42 | 88,018 | 4,623 | 1,517,843 |
| Qur'anic/Tsangaya | 259 | 14,731 | 13,635 | 1,272,844 |
| Ilmi | 140 | 16,214 | 4,150 | 214,294 |
| **Total** | **441** | **118,963** | **22,408** | **3,004,981** |

*Source: Computed from data at the Research and documentation Unit, office of the special adviser on education and information technology, Kano State*
*Key: N/S=Number of schools; N/St=Number of students*

## Pre-primary and Primary Education

These forms of education are treated in separate sections (i.e. Sections 2 and 3 respectively) in the National Policy on Education (NPE) of the Republic of Nigeria 1977 and 1981. In the document the pre-primary education is described as education given in an educational institution to children aged 3-5years and it is conceived of as nursery or preparatory education. Prior to the launching of the Universal Primary

---

| Chapter 18 | Nuratu Mohammed, in |
|---|---|
| | A.I. Tanko and S.B. Momale (Eds.) |
| | Kano: Environment, Society and Development |
| | London & Abuja, Adonis & Abbey Publishers |

Education (UPE) private nursery schools had been in existence in the Region however over the years a number of private nursery schools had more than double in number. In a recent survey of the number of primary schools in Kano State it was found out that there were over 20,000 private nursery/primary schools. The number of pre-primary and primary schools and enrolment in Jigawa State is shown in Table 18.2.

**Table 18.2: Number of Pre-primary and Primary Public Schools, Teachers and Enrolment in Jigawa State**

| | Number of schools | Number of teachers | | | Number of pupils | | |
|---|---|---|---|---|---|---|---|
| | | Male | Female | Total | Male | Female | Total |
| Pre-primary only | - | - | - | - | 11,585 | 10,392 | 1,977 |
| Pre-primary and primary | 1,817 | 12,128 | 1,642 | 13,770 | 286,831 | 195,499 | 482,330 |
| Primary only | 1,817 | 12,128 | 1,642 | 13,770 | 275,246 | 185,107 | 460,353 |

*Source: Ministry of Education, Jigawa State*

## *Primary Education*

Primary education in Nigeria refers to education given in an institution for the children aged 6-11 years according to the National Policy on Education. At this level emphasis is placed on the acquisition of the basic skills of reading, writing and arithmetic. Prior to the launching of the Universal Primary Education in 1976, the total number of enrolments were insignificant as a result the costs of education and the apprehension expressed by parents earlier mentioned in this write-up. However, the number of schools and enrolment continue to be on the increase since the launching of free Primary education in 1976 under the Universal Primary Education (UPE) programme and the Universal Basic Education (UBE) in 1999 which have been the response of Government in expanding educational opportunities to the teeming population of the country. Similar to the case in Jigawa State (Table 18.2) enrolment in Kano continued to be on the increase. Tables 18.3 and 18.4 show the number of primary schools, total enrolment (male and female), number of teachers and number of classrooms in the Region.

| Chapter 18 | Nuratu Mohammed, in |
| | A.I. Tanko and S.B. Momale (Eds.) |
| | *Kano: Environment, Society and Development* |
| | London & Abuja, Adonis & Abbey Publishers |

**Table 18.3: Primary schools in Kano State: 1999-2009**

| Year | Number of schools | Male Enrolment | Female Enrolment | Number of teachers | Number of Classes |
|---|---|---|---|---|---|
| 1999 | 2270 | 1,288,997 | 519,774 | 19,015 | 2,645 |
| 2000 | 2424 | 1,517,433 | 607,970 | 19,022 | 2,645 |
| 2001 | 2752 | 1,681,285 | 672,514 | 21,954 | 3,050 |
| 2002 | 2985 | 1,681,756 | 725,569 | 26,535 | 3,050 |
| 2003 | 3068 | 1,264,636 | 541,569 | 26,535 | 2,902 |
| 2004 | 3450 | 1,509,336 | 658,532 | 25,999 | 3033 |
| 2005 | 3454 | 1,609,303 | 658,320 | 25,999 | 9,600 |
| 2006 | 3626 | 1,704,848 | 780,549 | 34,611 | 9,609 |
| 2007 | 4146 | 1,958,645 | 985,795 | 35,855 | 9,702 |
| 2008 | NA | NA | NA | 42183 | NA |
| 2009 | 663 | 2,030,369 | 965,276 | 45,232 | 9,809 |

*Source: SUBEB Kano, 2010*

Going by Table 18.3, it can be inferred that there is gender gap in enrolment into the primary schools. To address the situation various administrations since the 1976 universal education programme have attempted to bridge the gender gap. Some ways by which governments in the Region try to bridge this gap is by encouraging parents to send their daughters to school and providing education free up to the secondary level (in Kano State) and up to the university level (in Jigawa State). Despite these attempts the rate of girls' enrolment is still much lower than that of the boys. Recently, the Kano State Government, in recognition of the role of primary schools in the development of education, has built over 800 one storey additional blocks of classes with 400 offices all over the 44 Local Government Areas of the State.

As earlier pointed out the number of schools and enrolments is on the increase, however one of the challenges facing western education in contemporary times is the issue of adequate qualified teaching staff to handle the number of students. Table 18.4 shows the staff strength by qualification in Kano State.

Chapter 18 | Nuratu Mohammed, in
A.I. Tanko and S.B. Momale (Eds.)
Kano: Environment, Society and Development
London & Abuja, Adonis & Abbey Publishers

**299**

Table 18.4: Number of Teachers by Qualification

| Qualification | Number of Teachers | | Total |
|---|---|---|---|
| | Male | Female | |
| Graduate with teaching qualification | 470 | 157 | 627 |
| Graduate without teaching qualification | 181 | 48 | 229 |
| NCE | 5,825 | 1,559 | 7,384 |
| Pivotal Teachers Training Prog. (PTTP) | 7,420 | 1,605 | 9,025 |
| Grade II Teachers (GRII) Pass | 570 | 63 | 633 |
| Grade II Teachers (GR II) Referred | 2,330 | 353 | 2,863 |
| SIS | 3,996 | 596 | 4,592 |
| SSCE | 3,381 | 587 | 3,968 |
| Others | 8,187 | 841 | 9,028 |
| **Total** | **36,443** | **6,938** | **43,381** |

*Source: SUBEB Newsletter, 2008*

## Secondary Education

The National Policy on Education (2004) states that secondary school education is the education children receives after primary education and before the tertiary stage. Secondary education level went through several changes. Before the most recent change, the 6-3-3-4 system - comprising six years of primary, three years each in the junior secondary (JSS) of and the senior secondary school (SSS), and four years at the tertiary level. In recent times, there are agitations for another system; to operate the Basic Education of nine years of primary and junior secondary, three years of senior secondary and four years of tertiary education (9-3-4). What this system entails is that the first three years of primary school education is to be known as local basic and the whole classes four (4) to six (6) of the primary school education is to be called middle basic and the whole of junior secondary school level is to be called upper basic and senior secondary school is to remain as it has been. As in the case of the primary schools the number of secondary schools (both Junior and Senior) increased over the years as a result of government involvement in making education universal.

Chapter 18 | Nuratu Mohammed, in
A.I. Tanko and S.B. Momale (Eds.)
*Kano: Environment, Society and Development*
London & Abuja, Adonis & Abbey Publishers

**Table 18.5: Number of Junior and Senior Secondary Schools and enrolments in Kano State**

| Year | Number of schools | Total enrolmt | Female enrolmt | Number of teachers | Classes |
|---|---|---|---|---|---|
| 1999 | 313 | 199,660 | 69,881 | 311 | 11,796 |
| 2000 | 334 | 210,660 | 70,581 | 4,420 | 120,996 |
| 2001 | 351 | 401,957 | 140,688.1 | 3,511 | 241,174.2 |
| 2002 | 351 | 401,966 | 140,688.1 | 4,020 | 241,179.6 |
| 2003 | 433 | 428,652 | 150,018.75 | 5,021 | 258,175 |
| 2004 | 452 | 472,574 | 165,400.9 | 5,365 | 283,544.4 |
| 2005 | 452 | 492,950 | 172,533.15 | 6,179 | 295,770 |
| 2006 | 516 | 623,730 | 218,305.5 | 8,097 | 374,238 |
| 2007 | 595 | 517,598 | 181,159.3 | 8,097 | 310,558.8 |
| 2008 | 757 | 531,531 | 186,035.85 | 12,822 | 318,918.6 |

*Source: Planning, Research and Statistics, Ministry of Education, Kano State 2010*

The number of schools continued to increase as the demand for education also increases. The data collected from the Kano State Senior Secondary Schools (KSSSMB, 2013) shows a total of 9,749 schools and student population of 481,808. Information obtained from the Kano State Senior Secondary Schools Management Board revealed that there was approximately 9,039 qualified teaching staff in the Senior Secondary Schools in Kano State (Data Unit, KSSSSMB, 2013).

**Table 18.6: Number of public secondary schools, teachers and enrolment in Jigawa State**

| | Number of schools | Number of teachers | | | Number of pupils | | |
|---|---|---|---|---|---|---|---|
| | | Male | Female | *Total* | Male | Female | *Total* |
| Junior secondary | 334 | 2,904 | 207 | *3,111* | 47,926 | 25,684 | *73,610* |
| Senior secondary | 114 | 1,887 | 128 | *2,015* | 36,897 | 10,689 | *47,586* |

*Source: Jigawa State Ministry of Education*

The secondary schools in the Region usually offer the following field of study:

- Science;
- Arts;
- Vocational; and
- Commercial

Some of the Science and Technical based Secondary Schools in the Region are the Dawakin Kudu and Dawakin Tofa Science Schools,

Chapter 18 | Nuratu Mohammed, in
A.I. Tanko and S.B. Momale (Eds.)
Kano: Environment, Society and Development
London & Abuja, Adonis & Abbey Publishers

301

Gaya Technical School and Kano Technical College. Despite the establishments of science secondary schools from 1977 to cater for the manpower needs including the teaching of Science subjects, much more efforts are required in that direction. As such one of the problems of secondary education in Kano region is inadequate teachers in the field of sciences.

## *Tertiary Education*

Tertiary education is that education received after secondary education also known as post-secondary education. For admissions into tertiary institution, candidates need to have required credits/qualification. It is in pursuance of this objective, that the Region has established a number of quasi or intermediate tertiary institutions to cater for students with deficiencies in some subjects required for them to gain entrance into universities, and this type are tagged remedial schools for remedial studies.

Some of these are the college of arts, science and remedial studies, established in 1972 where diploma program which are affiliated to various institutions are offered, in addition to remedial studies. In addition to the colleges of remedial students, vocational and technical institutions at tertiary level are also forms of English style/western education found in the Region. Some of these are listed in Table 18.7.

## *University Education*

In recognition of the important contribution of education towards the development of the human resources vis-a-vis the development of manpower capacities and capabilities, Kano State has established two State funded universities. The first is the University of Science and Technology (KUST) in 1999 and the second is the Northwest University in 2012, which commenced academic activities in April 2013. In addition to these, there are two Universities funded by the Federal Government. The first is the Bayero University established in 1977 and the second is the Federal University, Dutse in Jigawa State established in 2011.

Chapter 18 | Nuratu Mohammed, in
A.I. Tanko and S.B. Momale (Eds.)
*Kano: Environment, Society and Development*
London & Abuja, Adonis & Abbey Publishers

**Table 18.7: List of Tertiary Vocational Institutions in the Kano Region**

| List of Vocational institutions | Kano | Jigawa | Total |
|---|---|---|---|
| Polytechnic | Kano | Hussaini Adamu | 2 |
| Management studies | Kano | Dutse | 2 |
| School of Social and Rural Development | Rano | - | 1 |
| School of Environmental Studies | Gwarzo | - | 1 |
| College of Agriculture | Danbatta | Hadejia | 2 |
| School of Legal Studies | Aminu Kano | Ringim | 2 |
| School of Information Technology | Kano | Kazaure | 2 |
| School of Nursing | Kano | Birnin Kudu | 2 |
| School of Health technology | Kano and Bebeji | Jahun | 3 |
| School of Clinical assistant/Hygiene | Danbatta | Hadejia | 2 |
| School of Midwifery | Danbatta | - | 1 |
| Colleges of Education | Kano and Bichi | Gumel | 4 |

*Source: Ministry of Higher Education, Kano State and Jigawa State Ministry of Education*

## Private Sector Participation in Educational Development of the Region

As a result of the high demand for education, private participation in education in the Region is assuming significance. To this end a number of private proprietary schools are found in every part of the Region. Some of these schools have met acceptable standard but many are below the standards. As a result of observable inadequacies in some of these private proprietary schools the Ministry of Education in Kano State established a Department charged with the responsibility of inspecting, monitoring and coordinating the schools. The Department has so far registered many of the schools as presented in Table 18.8, and similar information for Jigawa State is presented in Table 18.9.

**Table 18.8: Registered Private Schools in the Kano state**

| Number | Number |
|---|---|
| Schools | 6,905 |
| Student Enrolment | 205,519 |
| Teacher | 11,845 |

*Source: Private Institution Department, Ministry of Education Kano State*

| Chapter 18 | Nuratu Mohammed, in |
| | A.I. Tanko and S.B. Momale (Eds.) |
| | Kano: Environment, Society and Development |
| | London & Abuja, Adonis & Abbey Publishers |

**Table 18.9: Number of Private Schools by level in Jigawa State**

| | Numbers of Schools | | Numbers of Schools |
|---|---|---|---|
| Schools with primary classes | 81 | Of which: Primary only | 24 |
| Schools with junior secondary classes | 4 | Of which: Junior secondary only | 4 |
| Schools with senior secondary classes | 2 | Of which: Senior secondary only | 2 |

*Source: Jigawa State Ministry of Education*

Going by the above tables showing the number of the private institutions in the region it could be seen that there are more private institution in Kano state than in Jigawa state. The reason for this is not far-fetched, Jigawa use to be part of greater Kano State not until 1991 when it was created out of the old Kano State.

## References

Abiri, J.O., O.E. Abdullahi, Amaela, S., Daramola, C.O. (2005) *Perspectives on History of Education in Nigeria.* Ibadan: Emolay-Jay.

Adesemowo, P.O. Solorade, O.A.T & Okubanjo, O. (1999), *The Psychology and Meaning of Learning.* Lagos: Merrified publishers

Ajibade, E. (1991) *Nigerian Educational Policy Issues, Problems and Strategies in Eighties and Beyond.* Ibadan: Emia Publishers

Federal Government of Nigeria (2004): *National Policy of Education.* Lagos: NERDC Press.

Usman, N. Esther (2010) *Funding issues and infrastructural development in Nigeria* being A paper presented at the 51st annual conference of the Association of Nigerian Geographers (ANG), Anyigba,                                                                 2010.

Chapter 18 | Nuratu Mohammed, in
A.I. Tanko and S.B. Momale (Eds.)
*Kano: Environment, Society and Development*
London & Abuja, Adonis & Abbey Publishers

**304**

# Chapter Nineteen

## PASSENGER TRANSPORT SERVICE

Isah Umar Farouk and Muhammad Abubakar Liman

### Introduction

Throughout the inhabited world, transport in one form or another is a basic and essential part of the daily rhythm of life. It is generally regarded as one of the most important factors involved in the process of economic development. In fact, material development of any kind is virtually impossible without appropriate transport (Brain and William, 1998; Liman 2008). Thus, the need for a transport system with which to move people and goods from one location to the other, or from one section of the settlement to the other, changes with the society's mode of production. At its best form, the agrarian economy only led to the use of animal-drawn transport. The industrial settlement is by far a bigger settlement than its predecessor and both mechanical and motorized transports are products of the industrial economy (Adeneji, 1984; Liman, 2008; Aminu, 2010). Also, the form and pattern of movement are more heightened in an industrial or industrializing settlement than that which obtains in agrarian settlements. Thus nowadays, the urban dweller resides and works in different settlements or different areas of the urban landscape.

The intimate relationship between transport and the economy is widely recognized but only represents half of the picture. The other half of the picture is provided by transport's intimate relationship with social arrangements and therefore its role in social organizations and transformations (Atubi and Onokala, 2005; Liman, 2008; Akinlayo, 2010). Together, and in a complementary manner, economic arrangements and different social arrangements organize space and society differently. In the end, it is transportation - different transport modes and how they are organized - that determines the social as well as the spatial linkages between the economic and social fabric of society and ultimately the overall growth of the settlement. Indeed, it can be said that a settlement is only as big as its transportation system.

The complex travel demands of settlements vary from one settlement to the other and so does the resulting maze of daily

Chapter 19 | Isah U. Farouk & Muhammad A. Liman, in
A.I. Tanko and S.B. Momale (Eds.)
*Kano: Environment, Society and Development*
London & Abuja, Adonis & Abbey Publishers

movements which, though complex, is not without order or pattern. It is this regularity, among other things, that has given birth to transport service in the industrial settlement (Davies and Warnes, 1980). Indeed, the urban settlement can be judged and ranked on the availability, regularity and effectiveness of the transport service catering for its inter-urban as well as intra-urban movements (Liman, 2008; Remi, 2009; Ibrahim, 2010). This Chapter traces the development of road transport service in the Kano Region and highlights its availability, regularity and effectiveness with the attendant issues that policy should address.

A transport route is the normal path between two termini, one being the starting terminus and the other being the destination terminus where vehicles turn round to make a round trip. At the national scale every State capital can be seen as a node and a terminus while at a lower scale of a State, every Local Government headquarters can be seen as a node and a terminus. Kano and Dutse are both State capitals and can be seen as nodes in the country. Furthermore, as State capitals each is connected to the Local Government headquarters within its State. The spatial receptacle where road transport routes start from and/or terminate is here more commonly referred to as a motor park. The city scale represents a further lower scale with different parts of the city serving as nodes and possible termini. Within the city a node, or more, will develop from where many road transport routes start and/or terminate. Such a terminus is known as a transfer terminal.

Thus, there are many motor parks in Kano metropolis; some recognized by the authorities and therefore legal, while others are not recognized by the authorities and therefore illegal. The latter are usually without building infrastructure and therefore further distinguishable by their road side operations while the former have built infrastructure and, in comparison, operate with more orderliness (see Table 19. 1).

| Chapter 19 | Isah U. Farouk & Muhammad A. Liman, in |
| | A.I. Tanko and S.B. Momale (Eds.) |
| | *Kano: Environment, Society and Development* |
| | London & Abuja, Adonis & Abbey Publishers |

**Table 19.1: Some Motor Parks in Kano Metropolis**

| Sno | Motor Park | Abbreviations Used | LGA |
|-----|------------|--------------------|-----|
| 1. | City Motor Park | CTMP | Municipal |
| 2. | Ibo Road Motor Park | IRMP | Fagge |
| 3. | Kofar Wambai Motor Park | KWMP | Fagge |
| 4. | Shahuchi Bus Stop | SCBS | Municipal |
| 5. | Tashar Kuka Motor Park | TKMP | Dala |
| 6. | Unguwa Uku Motor Park | UUMP | Tarauni |
| 7. | 'Yan kaba Motor Park | YKMP | Nassarawa |
| 8. | 'Yan Kura Motor Park | YKura | Fagge |

In addition, the passenger vehicles are mostly buses and taxi cabs that should normally carry 10 and 4 passengers respectively. One of the characteristics of passenger transport service is that of squeezing more people than officially allowed in the vehicle. Thus, on average, the vehicles take 12 and 6 passengers for buses and taxi cabs respectively. In other words, a taxi cab takes half a bus and so the average for taxi cabs was first converted to Passenger Bus Unit (PBU) and added to the average for buses - making it seem as if all the vehicles were buses. These were then plotted against the destination settlements to show the strength of, and connections arising from, the travel pattern(s).

The picture here only represents part of the whole but enough to reveal the pattern of connections and their strength as well as the transport corridors in the Kano Region. Even though one should expect a higher number of travel data than is being presented here this may not necessarily affect the pattern as we believe settlements are equally affected by the dearth of available data. This notwithstanding, sufficient data have been captured to make the points central to the Chapter. The data available therefore informs the reader of the development and management of road transport service as well as the issues arising from such an important livewire of the Kano Region.

## Inter-Urban Transport Service in the Kano Region

Modern transport (i.e. motorized transport) owes its origins to the industrial revolution, but for settlements in Nigeria modern transport is the baby of colonial rule (Liman, 2008). Thus, the establishment of Kano as a railway terminus of the Baro-Kano line in 1911, and its subsequent extension to Nguru in 1930, not only established modern commercial rail transport in the Kano Region but established the

Chapter 19   Isah U. Farouk & Muhammad A. Liman, in
A.I. Tanko and S.B. Momale (Eds.)
*Kano: Environment, Society and Development*
London & Abuja, Adonis & Abbey Publishers

region firmly within the ambit of industrial economy. Settlements like Madobi, Ringim, Gagarawa, Taura, Kaugama, Birniwa, and Mallam Madori, (each of which is an LGA headquarters in the Kano Region today), Dan Gora, Jogana, Mabiya, Garun Gabas, Dabi, and Buramusa not only became aligned on the new rail network but became additionally important as nodes on the new economic system (see fig. 19.1). Being linear the new economic system could be joined at any of the nodes on the new rail transport system and thus, all nodes on the system had equal potential of being important. For Kano, being both a rail terminus and a point from where the rail line extends further a field established her, more and more, as a centre of a region.

While it is understandable that the new rail system could not have connected all the existing important settlements in the region one wonders why the rail line avoided Bebeji and Hadejia. Nonetheless, road development projects were started in 1946 to complement the railway network in the country and to replace the need for porters in the inland provinces (see Liman and Adamu, 2005). Existing important towns in the Kano Region, such as Bebeji, Gumel and Hadejia that were by-passed by the railway network bounced back to a new lease of life. The new road system links up with Kano which, again, further confirms it as a central point in the Kano Region. Road transport is more flexible than rail transport system and as a testimony of the importance of the new transport system some settlements even relocated to the roadside or in close proximity to the newly-born road and vehicular transport network system. This attraction between the new transport system and the settlements led, among other things, to the development of contemporary inter-urban road transport service in the country as far back as the 1950s.

Chapter 19 | Isah U. Farouk & Muhammad A. Liman, in
A.I. Tanko and S.B. Momale (Eds.)
*Kano: Environment, Society and Development*
London & Abuja, Adonis & Abbey Publishers

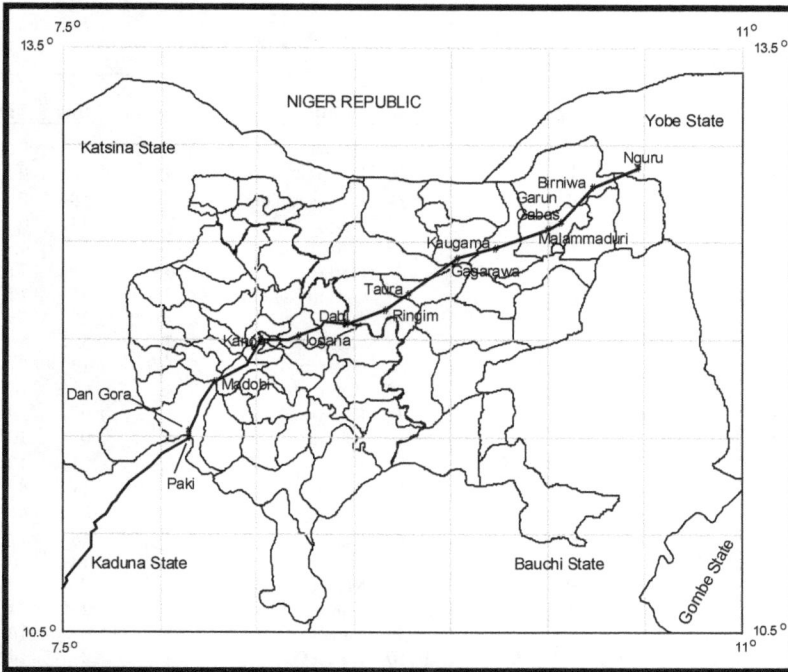

**Fig. 19.1:  Rail Transport Service across the Kano Region**

The strength of the linkages, in terms of road transport service, between Kano metropolis and other settlements in the Kano Region is shown in Table 19.2. The six LGAs that make up Kano metropolis together constitute the origin and are therefore represented as the motor parks. The LGA Headquarters in both Jigawa and Kano States remain the destinations for road transport service in the region. With the exception of Miga, for which there was no data, the PBU represents the road transport service data for LGA headquarters in the region the lowest being 4 and 85 being the highest. The linkages can be looked at in 4 categories of weak (1 - 10), fairly strong (11 - 30), strong (31 - 50), and very strong (51 and above). Thus, the one case of no data representing 1.6% and the 14 cases of weak linkages which constitute 21.5% together make up about 23% of weak or no linkages. The remaining 77% of the linkages is made up of fairly strong (27 cases making up 41.5%), strong (20 cases making up 30.8%) or very strong (3 cases making up 4.6%).

Chapter 19 | Isah U. Farouk & Muhammad A. Liman, in
A.I. Tanko and S.B. Momale (Eds.)
*Kano: Environment, Society and Development*
London & Abuja, Adonis & Abbey Publishers

**309**

Table 19.2:   Road Transport Service Linkages in the Kano Region
*Source: Fieldwork, 2011*

| S/no | Destinations | From | Bus | Taxi | PBU | Sno | Destinations | From | Bus | Taxi | PBU |
|------|--------------|------|-----|------|-----|-----|--------------|------|-----|------|-----|
| 1 | Auyo | 7 | 8 | 12 | 13 | 35 | Dambatta | 8 | 49 | 0 | 49 |
| 2 | Babura | 5 | 7 | 0 | 7 | 36 | Dawakin Kudu | 4 | 20 | 0 | 20 |
| 3 | Biriniwa | 7 | 20 | 12 | 26 | 37 | Dawakin Tofa | 4 | 18 | 0 | 18 |
| 4 | Birnin Kudu | 6 | 30 | 35 | 48 | 38 | Doguwa | 2,3 | 34 | 0 | 34 |
| 5 | Buji | 6 | 30 | 29 | 45 | 40 | Gabasawa | 7 | 4 | 45 | 27 |
| 6 | Dutse | 6 | 55 | 60 | 85 | 41 | Garko | 4 | 0 | 7 | 4 |
| 7 | Gagarawa | 7 | 4 | 2 | 5 | 42 | Garum Mallam | 2,3,6 | 40 | 13 | 47 |
| 8 | Garki | 7 | 13 | 14 | 20 | 43 | Gaya | 4,6 | 20 | 33 | 37 |
| 9 | Gumel | 7 | 28 | 25 | 40 | 44 | Gezawa | 7 | 5 | 55 | 33 |
| 10 | Guri | 3,7 | 26 | 8 | 29 | 46 | Gwarzo | 4,5 | 13 | 74 | 50 |
| 11 | Gwaram | 3,7 | 22 | 13 | 28 | 47 | Kabo | 4 | 0 | 14 | 7 |
| 12 | Gwiwa | 7 | 10 | 8 | 14 | 49 | Karaye | 4 | 0 | 39 | 19 |
| 13 | Hadejia | 7 | 23 | 18 | 31 | 50 | Kibiya | 4 | 0 | 10 | 5 |
| 14 | Jahun | 6 | 24 | 28 | 38 | 51 | Kiru | 3,6 | 25 | 17 | 34 |
| 15 | Kafin Hausa | 3,6 | 24 | 7 | 28 | 52 | Kumbotso | 6 | 11 | 8 | 15 |
| 16 | Kaugama | 7 | 5 | 9 | 9 | 53 | Kunchi | 3 | 6 | 5 | 8 |
| 17 | Kazaure | 5 | 28 | 8 | 31 | 54 | Kura | 6 | 16 | 17 | 24 |
| 18 | Kirikasamma | 7 | 18 | 13 | 24 | 55 | Madobi | 1,6 | 14 | 30 | 29 |
| 19 | Kiyawa | 6 | 20 | 30 | 35 | 56 | Makoda | 3 | 8 | 6 | 11 |
| 20 | Maigatari | 7 | 20 | 7 | 23 | 57 | Minjibir | 3,7 | 35 | 13 | 42 |
| 21 | Malam Maduri | 7 | 7 | 6 | 9 | 59 | Rano | 4 | 0 | 10 | 5 |
| 22 | Miga | | 0 | 0 | 0 | 60 | Rimin Gado | 4 | 0 | 14 | 7 |
| 23 | Ringim | 7 | 18 | 8 | 21 | 61 | Rogo | 4 | 0 | 17 | 9 |
| 24 | Roni Sule | 3,6 | 22 | 8 | 26 | 62 | Shanono | 1 | 0 | 18 | 9 |
| 25 | Tankarkar | 7 | 28 | 8 | 32 | 63 | Sumaila | 4,6 | 33 | 25 | 46 |
| 26 | Taura | 7 | 18 | 8 | 21 | 64 | Takai | 4,6 | 34 | 24 | 46 |
| 27 | Yankwashi | 6 | 8 | 6 | 11 | 66 | Tofa | 4 | 0 | 40 | 20 |
| 28 | Ajingi | 4 | 0 | 8 | 4 | 67 | Tsanyawa | 5 | 15 | 0 | 15 |
| 29 | Albasu | 6 | 12 | 7 | 15 | 68 | Tudun Wada | 2 | 20 | 7 | 23 |
| 30 | Bagwai | 1,3 | 22 | 4 | 25 | 69 | Ungogo | 2,4 | 50 | 40 | 70 |
| 31 | Bebeji | 2,3,6 | 44 | 18 | 53 | 70 | Warawa | 7 | 18 | 13 | 24 |
| 32 | Bichi | 4,5 | 31 | 10 | 36 | 71 | Wudil | 4,6 | 20 | 38 | 40 |
| 33 | Bunkure | 4 | 0 | 10 | 5 | | | | | | |

The Kano Region is satisfactorily connected by road transport service from Kano metropolis to the various destinations in the region (see Table 19.3). This is reflected in the total of 1,662 PBU leaving Kano metropolis on a daily basis out of which 699 PBU (42%) head for settlements in Jigawa State and 963 PBU (58%) head for other settlements in Kano State. The near fifty-fifty split of passengers between the two States attests to the high attraction of Kano metropolis in the region in terms of road transport service. It is however important to note that 60% of the commercial traffic (in terms of the PBUs) leaving Kano metropolis do so from Unguwa Uku and 'Yan Kaba Motor Parks. The skewness is indicative of the characteristics of road transport service, its infrastructure, its

Chapter 19 | Isah U. Farouk & Muhammad A. Liman, in
A.I. Tanko and S.B. Momale (Eds.)
*Kano: Environment, Society and Development*
London & Abuja, Adonis & Abbey Publishers

organization, and the participation of stakeholders (an examination of each of which is beyond the scope of this paper).

**Table 19.3: Motor parks servicing different destinations in Jigawa State**

| To Destinations in | From Motor Park | | | | | | | | Total PBUs |
|---|---|---|---|---|---|---|---|---|---|
| | 1 | 2 | 3 | 4 | 5 | 6 | 7 | 8 | |
| Jigawa State | 0 | 0 | 52 | 0 | 38 | 290 | 319 | 0 | 699 |
| Kano State | 23 | 115 | 121 | 193 | 75 | 278 | 109 | 49 | 963 |
| Total PBUs | 23 | 115 | 173 | 193 | 113 | 568 | 428 | 49 | 1,662 |

*Source: Fieldwork, 2011*

## Intra-urban Transport Service in Kano metropolis

Intra-urban transport service is a necessary complement of inter-urban transport service (Oyesiku, 2003; Liman, 2008). Indeed Liman (2008) maintains that intra-urban transport service in Kano metropolis came up as complementary to the rail system (like it did in Britain) and to the air link between Kano and the outside world. These (the railway station and the airport) remained the transfer terminals for intra-urban transport service until the first passenger bus service started in the 1950s. However, with the suspension of rail transport service in the country, the railway station has become inactive as a transfer terminal. The development of bus service in Kano metropolis and the active stakeholders is shown in Table 19.4. The latter includes the service providers (popular sector, private sector, public sector, and the managers), the consumers, and the government. The popular sector is made up of a pool of individually owned buses offering transport service for profit. According to Liman (2008, op. cit.) there are about 2,300 buses servicing Kano metropolis on a daily basis managed by agents, known as *"Yan Kamasho"* - an association that has evolved into the National Union of Road Transport Workers (NURTW). The NURTW manages the passengers, the drivers, and the bus owners as well as the operations of transport service in the Kano Region. It is "largely responsible for whatever semblance of order there is in the general conduct of affairs relating to commercial transport service" (Liman, 2008). The popular sector remains the longest serving and active participant, for over fifty years in Kano metropolis, in transport service delivery and organization.

The private and public sectors have a history of epileptic participation in transport service delivery and organization generally.

Chapter 19 | Isah U. Farouk & Muhammad A. Liman, in
A.I. Tanko and S.B. Momale (Eds.)
*Kano: Environment, Society and Development*
London & Abuja, Adonis & Abbey Publishers

While the former is made up of a pool of buses owned by individual companies or group of companies offering transport service for profit, the public sector is made up of a pool of buses owned by government offering transport service either as a welfare package or for profit. "Yakamata Motors is the only private company popularly known to have participated in the commercial transport service sector in Kano. Government participates once in a while, and currently in the name of Kano line" (Liman, 2008, p. 34). Private sector or public sector transport service operation is more organized, formal and rigid than obtains in the popular sector. This notwithstanding the popular sector has shown more resilience and had survived competition against the private and public sectors. At the moment, both private and public sectors do not run intra-urban transport service in Kano metropolis any more.

The bus service in Kano has developed slowly, each time after the leap-frog growth of the settlement over the years. Initially, three transfer terminals (Bata, Jakara, and 'Yan Kura) developed to service the settlement. With varying success (due mainly to the different governments' big stick) Shahuci had served as a transit point over the years but now re-confirms its position as a transfer terminal. Thus, there are four bus transfer terminals in Kano metropolis with definite routes. The degree of connectivity still leaves much to be desired. On the one hand, although in physical space Bata to 'Yan Kura is less than 2km apart the two transfer terminals are not connected by bus. However, Bata-Jakara, Jakara-Shahuci, Jakara-'Yan Kura, and Shahuci-'Yan Kura connections also exist. On the other hand, with the exception of Kano city as a node (served by 14 routes), other nodes on the different routes are weakly connected (see Table 19.5). Only Kabuga (*Tasha*), Kurna, Panshekara, and Tarauni are connected by three routes each. Brigade, Hotoro, Kwanar Madobi, Mariri, Na'ibawa, Rijiyar Zaki (*Tasha*), Sharada, Sheka, Yan Kaba, and Zoo Road are each connected by two routes. All other nodes served by bus service are connected by only one route.

Taxi cabs have no definite route and have taken a long time developing their terminals. Thus, in addition to the airport taxi cab terminal similar taxi service is being offered at each of the legal motor parks and other favoured locations such as Gidan Murtala, Zoo road, BUK (old site) and Kabuga. In other words, there are more taxi cab terminals in Kano metropolis than there are bus terminals. Without

| Chapter 19 | Isah U. Farouk & Muhammad A. Liman, in
A.I. Tanko and S.B. Momale (Eds.)
*Kano: Environment, Society and Development*
London & Abuja, Adonis & Abbey Publishers |

definite route their connectivity is even lower than that obtainable from the bus routes. In general however, there are more taxi cabs servicing Kano metropolis on a daily basis and these are coordinated by NURTW which manages the passengers, the drivers, and the taxi cab owners.

Chapter 19 | Isah U. Farouk & Muhammad A. Liman, in
A.I. Tanko and S.B. Momale (Eds.)
*Kano: Environment, Society and Development*
London & Abuja, Adonis & Abbey Publishers

**Table 19.4: Development of Bus Service Routes within Kano metropolis**

| Sector | From Bata to | From Jakara to | From Yan kura to | From Shahuci to |
|---|---|---|---|---|
| Popular<br><br>1951-1960 | Panshekara<br>Tudun Wada | Asibiti<br>Gwauron Dutse<br>Gwammaja | Mandawari | |
| 1961-1970 | | Asibiti - Yan Kura | Gwammaja | |
| 1971-1980 | Kabarin Raka<br>Kwana Hudu<br>Kawaji | Gwammaja - Kurna | Mandawari - Gwale<br>Gwammaja - Kurna<br>Rijiyar Lemo | |
| 1981-1990 | Airport area<br>Badawa<br>Brigade2<br>Dakata<br>Hotoro<br>Kano city4<br>Kawo-Giginyu<br>Mariri<br>Na'ibawa<br>Panshekara<br>Sharada<br>Yan Kaba<br>Zoo road-Sheka | Asibiti - Gwale<br>Asibiti - Hotoro<br>Asibiti - Mariri<br>Asibiti - Na'ibawa<br>Asibiti - Panshekara<br>Asibiti - Sharada<br>Asibiti - Zoo Road<br><br>Rijiyar zaki (tasha) | Bachirawa<br>Dawanau<br>Kano city2<br>Mandawari - S/titi<br>Kabuga<br>Kurna<br>Rijiyar lemo | |
| 2000-2010* | | | | Unguwa uku -<br>Tarauni<br>Court Rd -<br>Karkasara<br>Sheka - Gidan Zc<br>Yankura -Kabuga<br>Tasha<br>Agadasawa –<br>Makwarari -<br>K/Gabari<br>Jakara -Kwanar<br>Dala - Gwammaj |
| Private (Yakamata Motors)<br><br>1990s | Badawa<br>Kawo<br>Tarauni<br>Yan Kaba<br>Zoo Road | | | |
| Public<br>(Kano Line)<br><br>1990s | Kwana Hudu<br>Kabarin Raka<br>Mandawari<br>Na'ibawa<br>Panshekara<br>Tudun Wada<br>Yan Kaba | Asibiti<br>Asibiti - Zoo road<br>Asibiti - Tarauni | BUK<br>Dawanau<br>Rijiyar Lemo | |

*Sources: Liman, (2008) & Fieldwork, 2011*

Chapter 19 | Isah U. Farouk & Muhammad A. Liman, in
A.I. Tanko and S.B. Momale (Eds.)
*Kano: Environment, Society and Development*
London & Abuja, Adonis & Abbey Publishers

**Table 19.5: Bus route nodes and connectivity within Kano metropolis**

| To (Nodes) | From (Transfer Terminals) | | | | |
| --- | --- | --- | --- | --- | --- |
| | Bata | Jakara | Yan kura | Shahuci* | Totals |
| Airport Area | x | | | | 1 |
| Bachirawa | | | X | | 1 |
| Badawa | x | | | | 1 |
| Bela | x | | | | 1 |
| Brigade | xx | | | | 2 |
| BUK New site | | | X | | 1 |
| Court Road | | | | X | 1 |
| Dakata | x | | | | 1 |
| Dawanau | | | X | | 1 |
| Gwauron Dutse | | X | | | 1 |
| Gidan Zoo | | | | X | 1 |
| Giginyu | x | | | | 1 |
| Hotoro | x | | | X | 2 |
| Janguza | | | X | | 1 |
| Kabuga (Tasha) | | | Xx | X | 3 |
| Kwanar Madobi | x | X | | | 2 |
| Kano City | xxxxx | Xxxxx | Xxx | X | 14 |
| Karkasara | | | | X | 1 |
| Kawaji | x | | | | 1 |
| Kawo | x | | | | 1 |
| Kurna | x | X | X | | 3 |
| Mariri | x | | | X | 2 |
| Na'ibawa | x | | | X | 2 |
| Panshekara | x | X | | X | 3 |
| Rijiyar Lemo | | | X | | 1 |
| Rijiyar Zaki (Tasha) | | X | X | | 2 |
| Sharada | x | | | X | 2 |
| Sheka | x | | | X | 2 |
| Tudun Wada | x | | | | 1 |
| Tarauni | x | X | | X | 3 |
| Unguwa Uku | | | | X | 1 |
| Yan Kaba | xx | | | | 2 |
| Yan Kura | | X | | X | 2 |
| Zoo Road | x | X | | | 2 |
| Totals | 27 | 13 | 12 | 14 | 66 |

Source: Compiled from Liman, (2008); and *Fieldwork, 2011

| Chapter 19 | Isah U. Farouk & Muhammad A. Liman, in |
| --- | --- |
| | A.I. Tanko and S.B. Momale (Eds.) |
| | *Kano: Environment, Society and Development* |
| | London & Abuja, Adonis & Abbey Publishers |

315

While in general bus services are never designed to provide door-to-door service a number of factors have combined to ensure that not even taxi cabs could offer such a service. In addition to the slow development of bus service in Kano metropolis, lack of effective urban planning and traffic control as well as the bad state of township roads have combined to make the *"Achaba"* (motorcycle service) and tri-cycle (*Adaidaita Sahu*) more appealing and effective than they normally should have been. Thus, started as far back as 1983 the *"Achaba"* continued to wax stronger until it was banned in 2013 following security challenges. Now *"Achaba"* service is only available away from Kano Metropolis. While it helped to solve some of the transport problems of the inhabitants there was a general feeling that it was more of a menace especially in the metropolis.

## Conclusions

Kano metropolis owes a large measure of its vibrancy to its trans-saharan, colonial and post-colonial transport connections; today it is served by at least six major road networks - Zaria-Jos, Gwarzo, Bichi, Dambatta-Kazaure, Ringim-Hadejia-Nguru, and Wudil (Azare-Jama'are axis, Damaturu-Maiduguri axis, and Bauchi axis). Such consistent and elaborate transport connections underscore the importance of transportation - different transport modes and how they are organized - in economic development. Making the roads better would go a long way in increasing safety. Leaving such an important livewire of the Kano Region to informal and semi-formal institutions for 50 years is far from the ideal situation. Although they deserve commendations but asking people equipped only with agrarian society ideals to handle equipment of the industrial society is hardly fair. As a result, in the present arrangements consumers are relegated to the bottom of the stakeholders' ladder and hardly have a fair deal; consumers are simply not protected. Formal institutions need to be created to organize and manage transportation in the Kano Region. For instance, a fundamental characteristic of commercial vehicles (buses, taxi-cabs, or *"Achabas"*) in the Kano Region is that they operate wait-and-load system at terminals and pick–and-drop-anywhere system in between the terminals. The resultant unsightly long queues of vehicles only confirm that there are more vehicles than are being demanded for.

| Chapter 19 | Isah U. Farouk & Muhammad A. Liman, in |
| | A.I. Tanko and S.B. Momale (Eds.) |
| | *Kano: Environment, Society and Development* |
| | London & Abuja, Adonis & Abbey Publishers |

In addition, the attendant chaos created, apart from the environmental impact, give a bad reputation to motor parks and transfer terminals.

On a final note, it is highly regrettable that even as we venture into the information era we are plagued by the "normal" refusal to make data available! That the informal and semi-formal institutions even keep some records is commendable - this study would not have been possible without such data. Admittedly there is no guarantee the situation would be different if transportation is managed by formal institutions but at least it would be known who is failing in his duties and can be taken to task. Considering the much done on the transport modes, the little done on the organization and management of transport, as well as the current and potential economic role of passenger transport service in the Kano Region nothing short of re-structuring will do justice to all the stakeholders.

## References

Abimbola, O. O. (2009) "Efficacy of bus transit in metropolitan Lagos", *Journal of Logistics and Transport*, Nigerian Institute of Transport Technology (NITT), Zaria, Vol.1 No.2, pp.17-27

Adeneji K. (1984), "Urban Development and Public Transport in Nigeria" *Third World Planning/Review*, vol.5 No.4, Nov. 1984, pp. 383-394

Ahmad Y. A. (2007), "Okada (motorcycle) transport as a veritable means of urban transportation in Ilorin, Nigeria" Geo-studies Forum: *An International Journal of Environmental and Policy Issues*, pp. 443-452

Akinlayo, S. B. (2010) "Integrated Transport system as a panacea for sustainable public transport development in Nigeria", *Journal of Logistics and Transport*, Nigerian Institute of Transport Technology (NITT), Zaria, Vol.2 No.1, pp.73-86

Aminu, Y. (2010) "Capacity building in road transportation management - options for Africa", *Journal of Logistics and Transport,* Nigerian Institute of Transport Technology (NITT), Zaria, Vol.2 No.1, pp.1-7

Atubi, A. O and Onakala, P. C (2005), "Effective Road Transportation and Communication Network, A Basis for Rural Development and

Chapter 19 | Isah U. Farouk & Muhammad A. Liman, in
A.I. Tanko and S.B. Momale (Eds.)
*Kano: Environment, Society and Development*
London & Abuja, Adonis & Abbey Publishers

**317**

Transformation in Benin City, Nigeria" *International Journal of Economic and Development* Issues, Vol. 5 Nos. 1 & 2, pp. 149-153

Brain, T. and William, R. B. (1998), "Inter-urban Transport", in Hoyle, B. and R. Knowles (Ed) *Modern Transport Geography*, 2nd revised edition, John Wiley & Son Ltd, pp.159-161

Dambazau, A. M. M. (1998) "The Spatial Distribution of Motor Parks and Bus Stops in Urban Kano", Unpublished B.Sc. Dissertation, Department of Geography, Bayero University, Kano

Davies, P. W. & A. M. Warnes (1980), *Movement in Cities: Spatial perspective on urban transport and travels*, Methuen, London

Ibrahim, J. M. (2010) "Understanding intra-urban commuting characteristics in Kano metropolitan area", *Journal of Logistics and Transport*, Nigerian Institute of Transport Technology (NITT), Zaria, Vol.2 No.1, pp.108-117

Liman, M. A. and Y. M. Adamu (2005), "Urbanization and the spatial development of Urban Centres", in Yakubu, A. M.; I. M. Jumare; and A. G. Saeed (eds.) *Northern Nigeria: a century of transformation, 1903-2003*, Arewa House

Liman, M. A. (2008) "Policy Dialogue and Public Transport System in Kano: Problems, Challenges and the Way Forward" Key note Address, Policy Dialogue on Traffic Management and Public Transport System in Kano, Centre for Democratic Research and Training, BUK, Mambayya House, pp. 31-39

Obimah, L. (1995) "Characteristics of Commercial Bus Transport along Brigade-Sabon Gari-Bata Route", Unpublished B.Sc. Dissertation, Department of Geography, Bayero University, Kano

Oyesiku O. K. (2003) "Policy Directions in Urban Transportation" in, I. Vandu-Chikolo (ed.), *Perspective on Urban Transportation in Nigeria*", pp. 171-174

Remi, J. (2009), "Transport infrastructure management and human capital development", *Journal of Logistics and Transport*, Nigerian Institute of Transport Technology (NITT), Zaria, Vol.1 No.2, pp.102-107

Umar, S. (1991) "Commercial Transport Routes in Metropolitan Kano", Unpublished B.Sc. Dissertation, Department of Geography, Bayero University, Kano

Chapter 19 | Isah U. Farouk & Muhammad A. Liman, in
A.I. Tanko and S.B. Momale (Eds.)
*Kano: Environment, Society and Development*
London & Abuja, Adonis & Abbey Publishers

**318**

# Chapter Twenty

## TRANSITION INTO THE INFORMATION ERA

Muhammad Abubakar Liman

### Introduction

The world is witness to at least three major technological "revolutions" each of which has changed life and living for the better. The first is known as the Agricultural revolution (or the Neolithic revolution) which led to the transition from a wandering to a sedentary Man in an agrarian society. It involved the domestication of plants and animals as well as cultivating and raising them for sustenance. This achievement marked the beginning of agricultural production and food grain was in abundance. It also marked the beginning of true civilization in which Man consciously determined what he wanted rather than wait for the bounties of nature.

The second was the Industrial Revolution which revolutionized all aspects of life by introducing new processes and techniques of doing things based, predominantly, on non-agricultural production. Whereas the Agrarian society relied on food and natural power the industrial society relied on harnessing and creating energy from the elements as its primary and transforming resource. Thus, the advent of industrial manufacture to replace craft manufacture, the introduction of motorized transportation means, as well as many other things we today take for granted were products of this era. Also, telecommunications (any process of communication over a considerable distance), the necessary equipment for transferring sound (radio, telephone), video (television) and digital text (telefax), as well as the computer (an umbrella term for all machines that take commands or inputs to work on them according to specified instructions, and give results or outputs) are not only products of the Industrial era but featured prominently in the industrial society. It was the machine age.

Back in 1970s Alvin Toffler warned of an impending change and the speed with which it was catching up with us (Toffler, 1971), and this materialized with the intimate union of the computer and

Chapter 20 | Muhammad A. Liman, in
A.I. Tanko and S.B. Momale (Eds.)
*Kano: Environment, Society and Development*
London & Abuja, Adonis & Abbey Publishers

telecommunications which marks the on-set of the Information era, marking the beginning of the third "revolution". Computer inputs and outputs (whether sound, video, or text) are transformed to, described, measured, and stored in bits (from Binary Digit) or its multiples. Thus, Information and Communications Technology (ICT) refers to the processing and distribution of data (whether sound, video, or text) using the computer and telecommunications in digital electronics (the process by which data is converted into digital format or binary digit signals). But the most important creativity in the use of information is in the agreement to share it - sharing of both the most flimsy of ideas to the most significant of ideas - in archive form or real time basis. The web of connectivity, as a result or because of sharing, gave birth to the internet as the centre of the information technology mediated world and creates flows of electronic signals which are transported on what is now described as the information superhighways.

The ICTs form the backbone of the structural transformations leading us into the information era and the effects that characterize the incipient informational society are pervasive - not limited to any part of the world or any sector of endeavour. How is the Kano Region located in the new world of the information era? What are the telltale signs as well as implications and challenges of such a positioning for the Region?

Probably the preponderance, as well as ownership, of functional mobile phone sets is the real evidence of the arrival of the information era to Nigerian space. From 1999, when the race to join the information bandwagon was flagged off in Nigeria, there was a scramble by different telecom providers to conquer the somewhat virgin space. The Global System for Mobile communications (GSM) and the Code Division Multiple Access (CDMA) are the two telecommunication technologies that featured in the race. The technology behind sending communication signals require somewhat free space and involve harmful microwave radiation. As a result, there is a general requirement of height to ensure safety and so, in the absence of very tall buildings, the communications antenna is housed in the massive and somewhat grotesque structure -telecommunications masts (TCM) - which is anchored to the ground. Thus, one of the most glaring evidence of the arrival of the information era is the presence of GSM TCMs littering the country. Like the story of the curving out of

Chapter 20 | Muhammad A. Liman, in
A.I. Tanko and S.B. Momale (Eds.)
*Kano: Environment, Society and Development*
London & Abuja, Adonis & Abbey Publishers

Nigeria by the British which dragged the people into the industrial era the incursion of the TCMs into the Nigerian space herald a new era as they (the TCMs) are the visible connections of the Nigerian space (geographic space) to the cyberspace.

The aim of this Chapter therefore is to examine the distribution of the TCMs being the spatial materiality supporting the space of flows in the Kano Region. Thus, the telecom providers were approached for the coordinates of their TCMs located in Kano and Jigawa States. Of the major telecom providers only Zain and Glo (Globacom) responded favourably within the time frame of this write-up. When plotted against the Local Government Area (LGA) map of the Kano Region a count was made of the TCMs in the various LGAs in both Kano and Jigawa states.

The data was collected in 2010 from two major telecom providers' installations (Globacom and Airtel). Every telecom provider is gunning for population concentrations (settlements) while the logistics, for a variety of reasons, dictates that most of the installations are done either in settlements and/or along transport corridors. Thus, although one should expect a higher number of TCMs than is being presented here this may not necessarily affect the pattern of distribution more so as some of the telecom providers (especially Etisalat, being a late comer to the scene) have resorted to sharing the TCMs. Moreover, the CDMA antennas do not necessarily depend on the TCM as the GSM antennas do and so may not be included in both the captured data and the ones not available to this study.

Nevertheless, sufficient TCMs that are fixed to the ground have been captured in this data to make the point central to the Chapter. The data available therefore does not inform the reader of the use as well as the extent of use of the information network, or the information products available to the Kano Region. Rather, it is a documentation of the spatial distribution of an important feature of the information era in the Kano Region.

## Conceptual Framework

The idea of a globalizing world is not new. Four previous attempts at globalizing the world by the various religions, slavery, colonialism, and modernization failed (Adamu, 2005: 515) or did not succeed as

| Chapter 20 | Muhammad A. Liman, in |
| | A.I. Tanko and S.B. Momale (Eds.) |
| | *Kano: Environment, Society and Development* |
| | London & Abuja, Adonis & Abbey Publishers |

**321**

desired. However, there is no denying that the ICT has created a global village (Global Electronic Village) as well as the formation of a global economy (Castells, 2000; Sassen, 2000; Ya'u, 2004). Getting in touch with any part of the world - a few kilometers away or thousands of kilometers away - is instant. As a result, capital flows, labour markets, commodity markets, information, raw materials, management, and organizations of the global economy are internationalized, fully interdependent and the economy works as a unit in real time on a planetary scale requiring societies (capitalist or socialist) to adjust appropriately in the new informational world (Castells, 2000: 560). From the point of view of information and/or communications the world is now truly global - with no frontiers and no barriers. It is a borderless space.

Additionally, Man as a rational being has had to contend with the need for information in, especially, decision-making. With the advent of the information era, information progressively and increasingly becomes the basis for decision-making, production, and consumption making it the critical raw material for all social processes and social organizations and therefore a crucial factor in competitiveness and productivity. Thus, there is the growth in quantitative size and qualitative importance of information processing activities in both goods production and services delivery (Castells, 2000). As a complement to the volume of information available, the new technology has massive storage capacity. Indeed a staggering 2,000 classics have been published on one CD-ROM (Cochrane, 1995: 27). Today, a lot more can be squeezed into a DVD. Thus, in this new era investment in telematics surpasses investment in other industrial machinery (Graham & Marvin, 2000:569).

The readiness to share the vast amount of available data/information coupled with the instantaneous and interactive nature of the new technology has stimulated international trade in services such as education, finance, health and telecommunications (Ya'u, 2004). The new technology is working wonders in classroom learning as well as remote or distant education. Even disciplines that are necessarily cautious of innovations (and therefore necessarily conservative), like medicine, have no option but to join the bandwagon of the information age and to advantage.

| Chapter 20 | Muhammad A. Liman, in |
| | A.I. Tanko and S.B. Momale (Eds.) |
| | *Kano: Environment, Society and Development* |
| | London & Abuja, Adonis & Abbey Publishers |

With every development in space-adjusting technologies the idea of an imploding world, like that of a globalizing world, became stronger. Thus, the settlements formed as a result of the Agricultural revolution became transformed with the advent of the industrial revolution as industrial cities. Rural populations were attracted to the city and together with the improved health and standard of living cities exploded. By the year 2000 London, Tokyo, New York, Cairo, Seoul, Calcutta, Bombay, Shanghai, Peking, Mexico city, Sao Paulo, and Rio de Janeiro were all mega cities. Increasingly the inhabitants of the world are living in cities while the supporting rural population became smaller but more efficient - thanks to the industrialization of agriculture. Now

> ...cities are being restructured from internally integrated wholes to collections of units which operate as nodes on international, and, increasingly, global economic networks. It is increasingly impossible to understand the forces that are shaping the restructuring of cities from a purely local perspective (Graham & Marvin, 2000: 570).

This heightens the borderlessness of space that it reawakens the fear that geography has come to its end (see Adamu, 2005: 520).

It is true that the telecommunicated space is a space of flows (often referred to as cyberspace) rather than the space of places (geospace or geographic space). The former, is characterized by "spacelessness" as well as "timelessness" and therefore virtual space (having the essence or effect but the not the appearance or form) while geographic space is marked by physical location separated by physical distance and therefore real space (Castells, 2000: 565; Ogunsanya, 2007: 74). But the webs of connectivity in cyberspace create flows of electronic signals akin to spatial interaction flows and have definite spatial materiality. As a result, we now have two realities; one that is physical (and can be touched) and the other which, though virtual, is no less real. This is much so as "the location of ICT equipment, the associated infrastructure, and the users of ICT all exist in real geographic space. …[and] it is more rational to think that ICT has bound geospace and cyberspace together" (Ogunsanya, 2007: 77). After all, the space of flows does have spatial materiality (Castells, 2000).

However, productive forces of the economy are now intimately linked to cultural capacity of society "because knowledge generation

Chapter 20 | Muhammad A. Liman, in
A.I. Tanko and S.B. Momale (Eds.)
*Kano: Environment, Society and Development*
London & Abuja, Adonis & Abbey Publishers

**323**

and information processing are at the roots of the new productivity" (Castells, 2000: 560). In other words, the extent to which the Kano Region, for instance, benefits from, and participates in, the new information era depends on its knowledge base and how much ICT infrastructure and equipment it can afford. Thus, the global village is made up of asymmetrical space of communication flows arising from the uneven appropriation of a global communication system (Castells, 2000). This only means an inevitable global spatial differentiation of the global space based on the acquisition and use of ICTs. To drive the point home, the spatial differentiation does not stop at the global or regional levels; it is also to be found at the national and lower levels of society. But this time the intensity of the new type of differentiation is higher than has been experienced and borders on polarization.

**The Kano Region**

The Kano Region, situated in Nigeria, is largely made up of the former Kano state from which the present Kano and Jigawa states were curved out. The two states are contained within latitudes 10.54° N and 13.04° N and longitudes 7.69° E and 12.70° E.

The area is a large and predominantly agricultural region that is dominated by Kano as the largest settlement and most prominent commercial centre. Although the industries in Kano were crumbling by the time the country was joining the information bandwagon it is still the most industrialized settlement in the Region. Each state is divided into LGAs with Jigawa having 27 LGAs (numbered 1–27 in Fig. 20.1) and Kano having 44 LGAs (numbered 28–71 in Fig. 20.1). In addition to Kano all other LGA Headquarters are prominent settlements from which nearly all the LGAs take their names.

Chapter 20 | Muhammad A. Liman, in
A.I. Tanko and S.B. Momale (Eds.)
*Kano: Environment, Society and Development*
London & Abuja, Adonis & Abbey Publishers

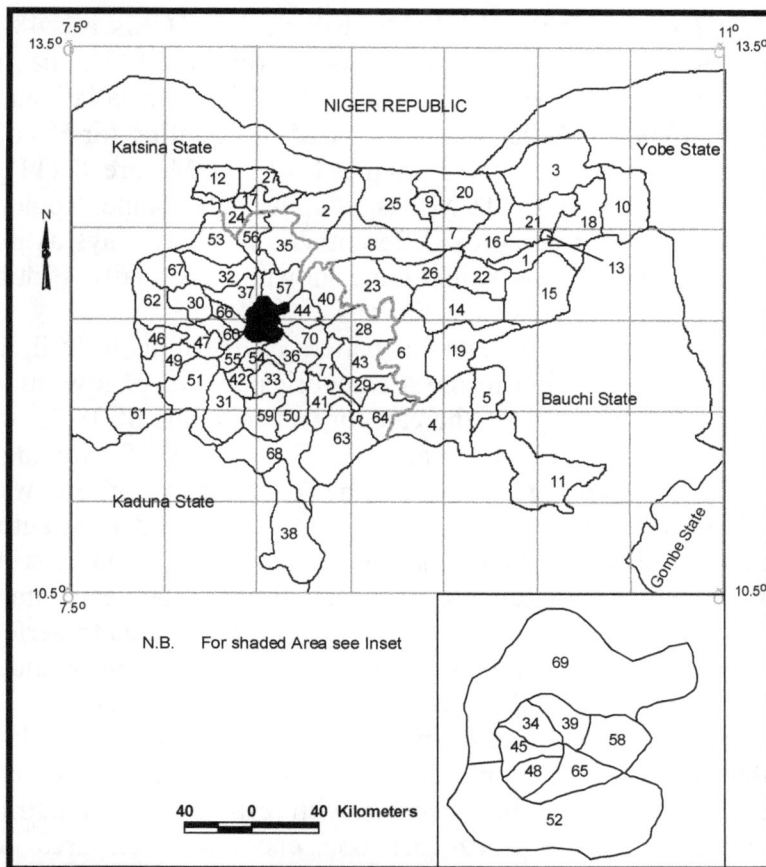

**Fig. 20.1: Map of Jigawa and Kano states showing the LGAs**
Note that Numbers in LGAs are the same as the "Sno" in Table 20.1

## The Distribution of the TCMs in the Kano Region

Table 20.2 shows the distribution of TCMs in the Kano Region which adds up to 310 with 70 in Jigawa state and 240 in Kano state. Thus, with 23% of the TCMs located in Jigawa state and 77% located in Kano state the coverage of the region seems fairly distributed as no LGA is without TCM installations. The LGAs have between 1 and 27 TCMs, though beginning to depart from the usual pyramidal structure of most distributions; many have few while the few have many. The significance of this is better appreciated looking at the TCM distribution in 4 categories of 1-3 (low), 4-6 (moderate), 7-10 (high),

Chapter 20 | Muhammad A. Liman, in
A.I. Tanko and S.B. Momale (Eds.)
*Kano: Environment, Society and Development*
London & Abuja, Adonis & Abbey Publishers

and 11-27 (very high). The LGAs having 1-3 TCMs are 48 (68%) accounting for 31% of TCM installations while the LGAs having 4-6 TCMs are 13 (18%) accounting for 19% of TCM installations. There are only 2 (3%) LGAs having 7-10 TCMs accounting for 5% of TCM installations while the LGAs having 11-27 TCMs are 8 (11%) and accounting for 45% of TCM installations. The Kano Region as a geographic space is certainly differentiated in many ways as many of the chapters in this book would have shown; it is equally, if not more, differentiated by its TCM installations.

Table 20.1 further reveals this pattern of distribution. Still, looking at the TCM distribution in the 4 categories above (of low, moderate, high, and very high) gives the category value totals of 38,32, 0, 0 for Jigawa, 59, 28, 14, 139 for Kano, and 97, 60, 14, 139 for the entire Kano Region. This means that the distribution of Jigawa state somewhat conforms to the traditional pyramidal structure of distributions. But the Kano state and the Kano Region distributions depart from this structure. It may well be speculative to attach too much importance to it, as it is not highly accentuated as to perfectly fit the polarization characteristic of the information era, but it should not be ignored as it is very likely a beginning in that direction.

Mapped out according to the four categories mentioned above the distribution is equally impressive and reveals more. As expected the Kano Region is highly differentiated with respect to TCM distribution. Going south-west to north-east one encounters an area of low telecommunicated space then followed by the high telecommunicated space of Kano metropolis and then back to a low telecommunicated space. From the Kano-Jigawa boundary one enters a moderately telecommunicated space followed by a low telecommunicated space which is only punctuated by the moderately telecommunicated space of Hadejia LGA.

The first noticeable pattern is the dominance of Kano metropolis which, for all practical purposes, covers six LGAs (Dala, Fagge, Gwale, Municipal, Nassarawa, and Tarauni) - and parts of Kumbotso and Ungogo (Fig. 20.2). With 106 TCMs it has more TCMs than Jigawa State and accounts for one-third (34%) of all the TCMs in the Kano Region! Then again, housing only about one-third of the population of Kano State it accounts for about 44% of all TCMs in the

Chapter 20 | Muhammad A. Liman, in
A.I. Tanko and S.B. Momale (Eds.)
*Kano: Environment, Society and Development*
London & Abuja, Adonis & Abbey Publishers

State! As it is, Kano remains an unrivalled telecom city in the Kano Region and no doubt one of the telecom cities of Nigeria.

**Table 20.1: Distribution of TCMs in the Kano Region by LGAs**

| Sno | State | LGA | TCM | Sno | State | LGA | TCM |
|---|---|---|---|---|---|---|---|
| 1 | Jigawa | Auyo | 2 | 37 | Kano | Dawakin Tofa | 7 |
| 2 | Jigawa | Babura | 4 | 38 | Kano | Doguwa | 1 |
| 3 | Jigawa | Biriniwa | 3 | 39 | Kano | Fagge | 27 |
| 4 | Jigawa | Birnin Kudu | 4 | 40 | Kano | Gabasawa | 3 |
| 5 | Jigawa | Buji | 1 | 41 | Kano | Garko | 2 |
| 6 | Jigawa | Dutse | 5 | 42 | Kano | Garum Mallam | 1 |
| 7 | Jigawa | Gagarawa | 1 | 43 | Kano | Gaya | 2 |
| 8 | Jigawa | Garki | 3 | 44 | Kano | Gezawa | 6 |
| 9 | Jigawa | Gumel | 2 | 45 | Kano | Gwale | 12 |
| 10 | Jigawa | Guri | 1 | 46 | Kano | Gwarzo | 2 |
| 11 | Jigawa | Gwaram | 6 | 47 | Kano | Kabo | 2 |
| 12 | Jigawa | Gwiwa | 1 | 48 | Kano | Kano Municipal | 11 |
| 13 | Jigawa | Hadejia | 3 | 49 | Kano | Karaye | 2 |
| 14 | Jigawa | Jahun | 3 | 50 | Kano | Kibiya | 1 |
| 15 | Jigawa | Kafin Hausa | 5 | 51 | Kano | Kiru | 3 |
| 16 | Jigawa | Kaugama | 1 | 52 | Kano | Kumbotso | 11 |
| 17 | Jigawa | Kazaure | 2 | 53 | Kano | Kunchi | 0 |
| 18 | Jigawa | Kiri Kasama | 1 | 54 | Kano | Kura | 2 |
| 19 | Jigawa | Kiyawa | 3 | 55 | Kano | Madobi | 2 |
| 20 | Jigawa | Maigatari | 3 | 56 | Kano | Makoda | 1 |
| 21 | Jigawa | Malam Maduri | 4 | 57 | Kano | Minjibir | 1 |
| 22 | Jigawa | Miga | 1 | 58 | Kano | Nassarawa | 26 |
| 23 | Jigawa | Ringim | 3 | 59 | Kano | Rano | 2 |
| 24 | Jigawa | Roni | 1 | 60 | Kano | Rimin Gado | 2 |
| 25 | Jigawa | Sule Tankarkar | 2 | 61 | Kano | Rogo | 2 |
| 26 | Jigawa | Taura | 4 | 62 | Kano | Shanono | 2 |
| 27 | Jigawa | Yankwashi | 1 | 63 | Kano | Sumaila | 3 |
| 28 | Kano | Ajingi | 2 | 64 | Kano | Takai | 3 |
| 29 | Kano | Albasu | 2 | 65 | Kano | Tarauni | 16 |
| 30 | Kano | Bagwai | 2 | 66 | Kano | Tofa | 3 |
| 31 | Kano | Bebeji | 7 | 67 | Kano | Tsanyawa | 2 |
| 32 | Kano | Bichi | 4 | 68 | Kano | Tudun Wada | 3 |
| 33 | Kano | Bunkure | 2 | 69 | Kano | Ungogo | 22 |
| 34 | Kano | Dala | 14 | 70 | Kano | Warawa | 5 |
| 35 | Kano | Dambatta | 2 | 71 | Kano | Wudil | 5 |
| 36 | Kano | Dawakin Kudu | 4 | | | | |

**Source:** *Fieldwork, 2010*

Chapter 20 | Muhammad A. Liman, in
A.I. Tanko and S.B. Momale (Eds.)
*Kano: Environment, Society and Development*
London & Abuja, Adonis & Abbey Publishers

Table 20.2: TCMs Distribution pattern in the Kano Region

| TCM | JG | KN | Total (KR) | Sum (JG) | Sum (KN) | Sum (KR) |
|---|---|---|---|---|---|---|
| *1* | 9 | 4 | 13 | 9 | 4 | 13 |
| *2* | 4 | 17 | 21 | 8 | 34 | 42 |
| *3* | 7 | 7 | 14 | 21 | 21 | 42 |
| *4* | 4 | 3 | 7 | 16 | 12 | 28 |
| *5* | 2 | 2 | 4 | 10 | 10 | 20 |
| *6* | 1 | 1 | 2 | 6 | 6 | 12 |
| *7* | 0 | 2 | 2 | 0 | 14 | 14 |
| *11* | 0 | 2 | 2 | 0 | 22 | 22 |
| *12* | 0 | 1 | 1 | 0 | 12 | 12 |
| *14* | 0 | 1 | 1 | 0 | 14 | 14 |
| *16* | 0 | 1 | 1 | 0 | 16 | 16 |
| *22* | 0 | 1 | 1 | 0 | 22 | 22 |
| *26* | 0 | 1 | 1 | 0 | 26 | 26 |
| *27* | 0 | 1 | 1 | 0 | 27 | 27 |
| | *27* | *44* | *71* | *70* | *240* | *310* |

**JG** = Jigawa state    **KN** = Kano state    **KR** = Kano Region

The second noticeable pattern is the general distance-decay from Kano metropolis accentuated along the motor transport corridors that traverse Dawakin Tofa and Bichi LGAs, Dawakin Kudu and Bebeji LGAs, Gabasawa and Gezawa LGAs, and Wudil LGA. Within Jigawa State this pattern is tempered by Babura LGA in the north-west, Malam Madori and Kafin Hausa LGAs in the north-east, Dutse and Taura LGAs in the east, and Birnin Kudu and Gwaram LGAs in the south-east.

## Discussion and Conclusion

Bell (1976) notes that the fact that while the industrial society is based on machine technology and structured on labour and capital the post-industrial (informational) society will be based on intellectual technology and structured on information and knowledge suggests that we need conscious planning and monitoring of structures that mediate our position in the information era. Underlying the eleven elements of the informational society he mentions is the fact that the informational society will not displace the industrial society just as the latter, in its turn, did not displace the agrarian society before it. "The new

Chapter 20 | Muhammad A. Liman, in
A.I. Tanko and S.B. Momale (Eds.)
*Kano: Environment, Society and Development*
London & Abuja, Adonis & Abbey Publishers

developments overlie the previous layers, erasing some features and thickening the texture of society as a whole", (Bell, 1976: 6). This position becomes more significant amid reports that Africa is presently at the bottom of the ICT ladder as well as a consumer of ICTs (Castells, 2000: 561; Ya'u, 2004: 15-16). There is a need for conscious effort towards providing more ICT infrastructure as well as creating more awareness to its relevance as well as creating more information products.

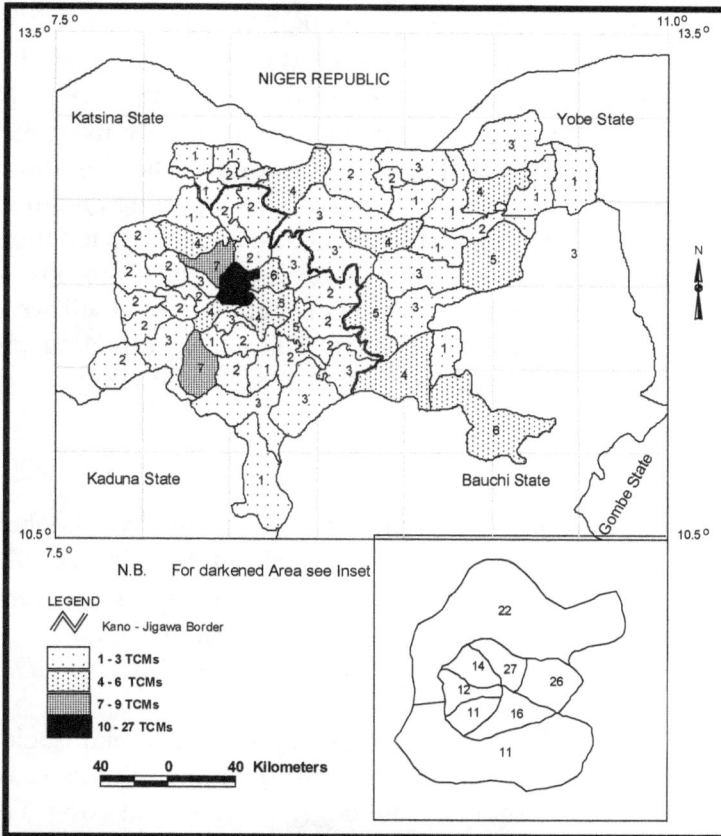

**Fig. 20.2 Distribution pattern of TCMs in the Kano Region**

The incursion of the TCMs into the Kano Region has no doubt further differentiated its space. At the moment it would appear that population remains a key factor in the distribution of TCMs in the Kano Region. However, as purchasing power of the population means

Chapter 20 | Muhammad A. Liman, in
A.I. Tanko and S.B. Momale (Eds.)
*Kano: Environment, Society and Development*
London & Abuja, Adonis & Abbey Publishers

**329**

higher demand and consumption the significance of population as a factor can be used to great advantage or otherwise. But the speed with which the TCMs sprang up as well as the apparent competition between the telecom providers resulted in the clustering of the TCMs in a locality that one wonders what principles decide their location. Is this unsightly clustering a necessary price to pay? As the antennas are of varying strengths - they have different ranges and probably thresholds - why can't we have some order? At any rate if sharing information and the information superhighways is a necessary feature of the information era why not sharing the TCMs?

Indeed, the distribution of the TCMs in Nigeria and the Kano Region, in particular, raises more questions. What this points to is the need for immediate research. Probably a similar study like this one all over the country is the starting point. Secondly, there is the need to know how the actors (telecom providers) are capturing and/or creating space as well as the nature of the telecommunicated space they create and how it is mediated. Then there is the need to know what information products consumers are consuming. Above all we need to know how the telecommunicated space is affecting markets (particularly transfer of goods to market as well as pricing).

## References

Adamu, F. L. (2005), "'Think Globally, Act Locally': Globalisation and Glocalisation in Northern Nigeria", in Yakubu, A. M.; I. M. Jumare; and A. G. Saeed (eds.) *Northern Nigeria: a century of transformation, 1903-2003*, Arewa House pp. 515-526

Bell, D. (1976), "The Coming of Post-Industrial Society", *Dialogue*, vol. 11, No. 2, pp. 3-11

Castells, M. (2000); "European Cities, the Informational Society, and the Global Economy" in LeGates, R. T. and F. Stouts (eds.), *The City Reader*; 2nd Edition, Routledge, London and New York, pp. 557-567.

Cochrane, P. (1995), "The Information Wave" in Emmott, S. J. (ed.), *Information Superhighways: multimedia users and futures*, Academic Press, London, pp. 17 - 33

Graham, S. and S. Marvin (2000); "The Transformation of Cities: Towards Planetary Urban networks" and "Telecommunications

Chapter 20 | Muhammad A. Liman, in
A.I. Tanko and S.B. Momale (Eds.)
*Kano: Environment, Society and Development*
London & Abuja, Adonis & Abbey Publishers

**330**

and Urban Futures"; in LeGates, R. T. and F. Stouts (eds.), *The City Reader*; 2nd Edition, Routledge, London and New York, pp. 568-578.

Ogunsanya, A. A. (2007), "Geography in the Information and Communication Technology Age", *Nigerian Geographical Journal*, Vol. 5, No. 1, The Nigerian Geographical Association

Sassen, S. (2000); "A New Geography of Centres and Margins: Summary and Implications"; in LeGates, R. T. and F. Stouts (eds.), *The City Reader*; 2nd Edition, Routledge, London and New York,pp. 208-212.

Short, J. R. (1996), *The Urban Order: An introduction to Cities, Culture, and Power*; Backwell Publishers Ltd., Oxford

Toffler, A. (1971), *Future Shock*, The Brodley head, London,

Ya'u, Y. Z. (2004), "The New Imperialism & Africa in the Global Electronic Village", *Review of African Political Economy*, Vol. 31, No. 99, ICTs 'Virtual Colonisation' & Political Economy (Mar., 2004), pp. 11-29

Chapter 20 | Muhammad A. Liman, in
A.I. Tanko and S.B. Momale (Eds.)
*Kano: Environment, Society and Development*
London & Abuja, Adonis & Abbey Publishers

# Chapter Twenty One

## GENDER AND GENDER MAINSTREAMING

Mairo Haruna

### Introduction

Gender in the cultural sense refers to the socially created - not biologically based - distinctions between feminity and masculinity. People are born either as biological female or male or have to acquire a gender identity (Boserup, 1970; Falola, 2001). Thus gender itself refers to the distinction between men and women based on social, cultural and ideological processes including for example, socialism, whereby the dresses a woman should wear are distinct from that which men should wear, educational processes which men discriminates against sex not merely in opportunities or exposure but even in terms of education. For example, domestic science and nursing for girls or women and Engineering for boys or men (Falola, 2001). Gender or the social relations between men and women is responsible for the gendered division of labour which required the allocation of and the exclusion along gender lines (Falola, 2001) and how these allocations are socially and economically valued. In a household or family, men and women are likely to play different roles regarding decisions or responsibilities for activities such as child care. The essential biological sexual division of labour applies to a small subset of reproductive labour namely pregnancy, child birth and perhaps breast feeding. Some schools of thought regard sexual division of labour as natural; these are essentialist and largely conservative (Moser, 1993:3-4; Bhatta, 2001).

In the Kano Region, gender division of labour is greatly influenced by social, cultural and religious practices and norms passed down from generation to generation. These practices shape the nature of women's activities/work and their access to resources in the Region. Some of the gender issues relating to women in the Kano Region discussed in this Chapter include: women reproductive and productive roles, education, politics/governance and access to important resources.

Chapter 21 | Mairo Haruna, in
A.I. Tanko and S.B. Momale (Eds.)
*Kano: Environment, Society and Development*
London & Abuja, Adonis & Abbey Publishers

# Gender Issues

## *Women Productive and Reproductive Roles*

African women like their counterparts in other parts of the world make immense contributions to society through their triple role of production, reproduction and community service. The production role of women includes the production of goods in areas such as farming, industry and wage employment that cover diverse fields. Women play major roles in the reproduction of the family mainly child bearing and rearing and household chores such as fuel wood collection, fetching water, cooking, laundry and cleaning.

The reproductive activities of women in the Kano Region are considered more important than any other activity that women do as the reproduction of children generates the provision of abundant labour required for production of agricultural commodities especially in the rural agrarian societies (Mohammed 2004). Because of the importance attached to the reproduction of human labour force and women's reproductive roles, girls are married at an early age particularly in the rural areas. Research in some rural areas of the region showed that by age thirteen many of the girls are married (Mohammed, 2012).

**Table 21.1 Marriage Age for Females in Rural Kano Region**

| Age (years) | Female Cooperatives members N= 200 | % | Female non Cooperative Members N -= 110 | % |
|---|---|---|---|---|
| 8 -13 | 160 | 80 | 70 | 64 |
| 14 -19 | 40 | 20 | 40 | 36 |
| **Total** | **200** | **100** | **110** | **100** |

*Adapted from Mohammed (2004)*

The productive activities of women are in agricultural and non agricultural activities such as small and large scale trading, civil service (at different parastatals and levels depending on one's qualification) and craftsmanship. The women are also involved in food preparing/cooking and selling. For example, a substantial number of women in Chediyar *'Yan Gurasa* Ward in Dala Local Government of

Chapter 21 | Mairo Haruna, in
A.I. Tanko and S.B. Momale (Eds.)
*Kano: Environment, Society and Development*
London & Abuja, Adonis & Abbey Publishers

Kano are involved in *Gurasa* production (a local bread/snack of Arabian origin) and selling which is a very vibrant economic activity in that part of the metropolis. Women in the civil service are mainly the urban based women. Table 21.2 shows that about a substantial number of the women interviewed in a study in Kano metropolis are civil servants, while the remaining constituted women doing other home based activities such as tailoring and knitting.

The agricultural activities of women include crop production (farming), food processing and livestock rearing. Table 21.3 shows the major farming activities of women in Kura, a rural agricultural settlement in Kano State. However, most of the women who work on the farm are the old women, the widowed and young unmarried girls. The young married women and women of child producing age usually practice farming by proxy delegating their husbands or brothers to manage their farms. Most of the women engage in food processing in their homes. This can be explained by the fact that Kura is a predominantly Muslim and Hausa society where women are not allowed to work outside their homes. Most of the women however process agricultural products in their compounds.

**Table 21.2 Income and Occupation of some Women in Kano metropolis**

| Occupation | Annual Income (in thousands of naira) | | | | % |
|---|---|---|---|---|---|
| | <200 | 200-299 | 300-399 | >400 | |
| Civil service | | 41 | 53 | 48 | 70.8 |
| Trading | 21 | | | | 09.1 |
| Others | | 11 | 10 | - | 20.1 |
| | - | | | | |
| | | 46 | - | - | |
| | - | | | | |
| Total | | 98 | 63 | 48 | 100 |
| | 21 | | | | |

*Source:* Ma'moun (2006)

Chapter 21 | Mairo Haruna, in
A.I. Tanko and S.B. Momale (Eds.)
*Kano: Environment, Society and Development*
London & Abuja, Adonis & Abbey Publishers

**335**

**Table 21.3: Proportion of Women Performing Specific Farm Operations in Kura**

| Farm Operation | Kura Ward n = 25 | | Dan-Hassan Ward n = 25 | | Karfi Ward n= 25 | | Dukawa Ward n=25 | | All Wards N = 100 |
|---|---|---|---|---|---|---|---|---|---|
| | No: | % | No: | % | No: | % | No: | % | % |
| Land preparation | - | 0 | - | 0 | - | 0 | - | 0 | 0 |
| Ridging Planting | - | 0 | - | 0 | - | 0 | - | 0 | 0 |
| | 8 | 32 | 9 | 36 | 8 | 32 | 6 | 24 | 31 |
| Transplanting (rice seedlings) | 8 | 32 | 10 | 40 | 8 | 32 | 4 | 16 | 32 |
| Fertilizer application | 7 | 28 | 10 | 40 | 8 | 32 | 4 | 16 | 29 |
| Weeding | 2 | 08 | - | 0 | 3 | 12 | 4 | 16 | 09 |
| Harvesting | 2 | 08 | - | 0 | 3 | 12 | 4 | 16 | 09 |
| Processing farm produce | 10 | 40 | 15 | 60 | 15 | 60 | 14 | 56 | 54 |

*Source: Haruna (2004)*

## Women and Education

Globally, education is conceived as a process that helps to develop the whole human being physically, mentally, morally, politically, socially and technologically to enable one function in any given environment. Education performs a major role in reshaping and equipping the mind with skill and knowledge. There is a general consensus that education in human beings involves desirable change in behaviour through the process of learning.

In the Kano Region, two general types / forms of educational systems are recognized.

    a.   The Islamic education system and
    b.   The Western education system

### a. Women and Islamic Education

The major ethnic groups in the Kano Region are the Hausa and Fulani who are predominantly Muslims. Islam was introduced to Hausa land

Chapter 21 | Mairo Haruna, in
A.I. Tanko and S.B. Momale (Eds.)
*Kano: Environment, Society and Development*
London & Abuja, Adonis & Abbey Publishers

as early as the 10<sup></sup> Century AD by traders from North Africa and spread widely in the mid-fifteenth century during the immigration of nomadic Fulani into Hausa land. However, it was not until the 19<sup></sup> Century that Islam became more firmly established as a result of the efforts of Islamic preachers during the Fulani jihad. With the introduction of Islam came the spread of Arabic and Islamic literature, Mosques and Quranic schools were established where learning took place. Islamic education is based on the basic philosophy of life of the Muslim, which are submission, understanding and adoption of the Islamic way of life. To Muslim parents therefore, Islamic education is very important, for it is through such an education that their children can grow to be religiously minded and to become adults of good character. Therefore nearly every girl child in the Region starts her first years of education in Islamic schools which are characterized by informal syllabus and time. Thus, it is rare to meet a woman or grown up girl in the Region who is not literate in the Arabic text or cannot recite the Quran. Even if a girl is not privileged to have attended western schools, she would have gone through the Islamic school(s). This is particularly true with the exception of some rural areas where girls do not attend even the Islamic schools. A study in six villages in Jigawa and Kano States showed that about 49% of the women sampled in the villages are not literate in western terms, more than half of the sample had some form of Quranic education and about 35% have not had any form of education (Mohammed, 2004).

The parents of those who do not attend schools claim they do not have enough money to fund their children's education and prefer sending them to hawk mainly cheap items. It is the proceeds obtained from hawking of items/goods that is saved to purchase marriage items and cooking utensils for the girl when she is married off. Most of the girls in the rural areas who attend the western schools hardly complete the primary education or proceed to secondary or tertiary institutions as they are assumed to be old enough to be married out. In the urban areas such as the Kano metropolis, western schools are attended by girls in addition to Islamic schools. Today, there are many women who are Islamic scholars teaching, preaching and giving sermons on Islamic issues in gatherings and the media.

Chapter 21 | Mairo Haruna, in
A.I. Tanko and S.B. Momale (Eds.)
*Kano: Environment, Society and Development*
London & Abuja, Adonis & Abbey Publishers

**Table 21.4 Educational level of some Rural Women in the Kano Region**

| Educational Level | Female Cooperatives members N = 200 | % | Female Non-Cooperative Members N = 110 | % |
|---|---|---|---|---|
| Not literate | 53 | 26.5 | 54 | 49.1 |
| Quranic Educ. | 115 | 57.5 | 40 | 36.4 |
| Primary Educ. | 25 | 12.5 | 15 | 13.6 |
| Secondary | 7 | 3.5 | 0.9 | |
| Total | 200 | 100 | 110 | 100 |

*Source: Mohammed (2004)*

## b. Women and Western Education

Western education was introduced into Northern Nigeria at a much later date than in the southern parts of the country. For many years, strong resistance was shown for western education in the North. One of the main reasons for this resistance was that it was associated with Christianity and the Northerners, majority of whom are Muslims and who had a well established system of education saw it as a threat to their own faith (Fafunwa, 1974). This attitude towards western education held by Muslim parents was more pronounced with regard to female education as parents were reluctant to expose their daughters. As a result, the total number of enrolment into primary schools in the region was low, but rose significantly with the Universal Primary Education Policy in 1976. During the past three decades, women's educational attainment levels in the Region have risen significantly due to modernization, investment by the States in education and some political reforms. With enlightenment and modernization, parents now see it even necessary to send their children to school to obtain the western education in addition to Islamic education. Today there are a lot of both private and public primary and secondary schools in the region. Though the rate of enrolment in schools has risen over the years, the percentage of girls' enrolment is still much lower than for the boys (Table 21.4). There are also adult education classes attended by women in the evenings.

With increased enrolment of the girl child into schools many girls and women have graduated from secondary schools and enrolled in institutions of higher learning and graduated with various certificates ranging from Diplomas, HND, B.Sc, BA, MBBS, B. Sc, B. Tech, and B. Arch among several others. Today, the Kano Region has a few

| Chapter 21 | Mairo Haruna, in |
|---|---|
| | A.I. Tanko and S.B. Momale (Eds.) |
| | *Kano: Environment, Society and Development* |
| | London & Abuja, Adonis & Abbey Publishers |

338

female Professors, a number of consultant gynecologists, female lawyers, engineers, teachers, lecturers, doctors and many nurses.

**Table 21.4 Primary Schools within the Kano Region**

| Year | Number of schools | Total enrolment | Female enrolment | Number of teachers | No. Classrooms |
|------|-------------------|-----------------|------------------|--------------------|----------------|
| 1996 | 329 | 1,307,956 | 498,192 | 24,907 | 26,937 |
| 1997 | 3669 | 1,585,562 | 592,612 | 27,242 | 26,937 |
| 1998 | 3613 | 1,229,675 | 548,038 | 99,624 | 28,296 |
| 1999 | 3860 | 1,472,964 | 651,978 | 28,540 | 33,003 |
| 2000 | 3860 | 1,771,130 | 678,007 | 29,717 | 33,498 |
| 2001 | 4186 | 1,650,222 | 623,824 | 32,998 | 33,688 |
| 2002 | 4245 | 1,662,940 | 575,492 | 34,726 | 34,452 |
| 2003 | 4612 | 1662,940 | 903,749 | 49,236 | 35,285 |
| 2004 | 5133 | 1,889,339 | 772,389 | 41,606 | 35,452 |
| 2005 | 5167 | 1,975,564 | 750,080 | 41,356 | 35,467 |

*Source: National Bureau of Statistics (2006)*

## *Women and Governance*

The Nigerian women, in spite of their numerical strength, resourcefulness and capability, are grossly underrepresented in political positions especially at the decision making level. Some of them who ventured into politics have not fared better in a scenario that is dominated by men. However, this situation is gradually changing as women now contest for positions in election. The women in the northern part of the country are not very active participants in politics. This is partly due to the Islamic and the Hausa culture of keeping women away from political activities which are seen as basically men's areas. Since mid twentieth century however, women involvement in politics in the Region gradually improved though at a slow rate. It started in the 1950s when women like late Hajia Gambo Sawaba, late Hajia Asabe Reza, and late Hajia Rabin Mato joined in the struggle for independence and continued participating in politics after independence. Though these women were active in the then political activities, they did not contest for any office in elections. Their contributions to politics in the Kano Region however are greatly acknowledged by many writers.

Women in the Region rarely contest in elections and even where they do, they end up losing because the stake is very high. Political participation today requires a lot of human and material resources. For this reason women do not go beyond the primary levels in their

Chapter 21 | Mairo Haruna, in
A.I. Tanko and S.B. Momale (Eds.)
*Kano: Environment, Society and Development*
London & Abuja, Adonis & Abbey Publishers

political parties. Women also lack support from their husbands, families and the society. The most active participants in politics are usually not educated and do not belong to the elite class in the society. However, they are active in the electioneering process. They participate in mobilizing and sensitizing their fellow women on parties' manifestos and also partake in campaigning activities. It is reported by the media that a substantial percentage of the votes cast in the region are women's votes who want their voices heard and their needs met. Though the women rarely contest for posts in elections, they are given political appointments to serve as Commissioners and Special Advisers to the Governor. This enables them contribute their own quota in the development of the Region. These are usually educated women who may be employed in the civil service. However, this is also limited as only a few of them are presently in the States cabinets in Kano and Jigawa states.

## *Women's Access to Resources*

Gender structuring refers to the socio-economic relations between males and females that are characterized by differential assignments of labour roles. Economic relations of resources are affected by the existing labour relations. This in turn influences women's access to the resources. Because women's role is seen as basically domestic or home based, they would normally not be deemed as deserving of certain resources such as land, credit and other technologies. Whitehead (1981) in her analysis of gender differences in the control of resources acknowledges that while production is segregated sexually at the household level, the picture is rather blurred at the level of the state or nation. For development to be sustainable, women who formed half of the world's population (Pratt, 2004) and who contribute between 60-80% of the time put to agriculture need to have access and control over the means of production and training. Important resources women need to have access and control over are land, capital and credit, technology and information. Others include health services, training and education. Thus empowerment of women would mean increased access to and control over resources (Bangesser, 1995: 17; Bhatta, 2001:3; Mohammed, 2004: 52).

Chapter 21 | Mairo Haruna, in
A.I. Tanko and S.B. Momale (Eds.)
*Kano: Environment, Society and Development*
London & Abuja, Adonis & Abbey Publishers

Studies in the Kano Region have shown that access to resources by women is governed by factors such as available capital, raw materials, educational level/training, male predisposition and market. Many of the women in a study by Mohammed (2004) got their start up capital for economic activities for example from their spouses, where the consent to start a business has been given, but the capital in most cases is low particularly in the rural areas. Women's lack of access to credit from commercial banks has been attributed to lack of collateral, educational level and non participation in particular political parties (Haruna, 2004).

Women also have access to land for agricultural purposes and landed properties mostly through inheritance (Haruna, 2004) by virtue of the Islamic practice which allocates a daughter half of what the son gets and a wife one-eighth of her deceased husband's property. Educated and urban women also receive land for residential purposes through government allocation (Table 21.6) but the disparity in allocation between men and women is evident. The pattern is more clearly illustrated in Figure 21.1.

**Table 21.5 Percentage of Women having Access to Specific Agricultural Resources in Kura**

| Agricultural Resources | Kura Ward n = 25 | | Dan- Hassan Ward n = 25 | | Karfi Ward n = 25 | | Dukawa Ward n = 25 | | All Wards N = 100 |
|---|---|---|---|---|---|---|---|---|---|
| | No | % | No | % | No | % | No | % | % |
| Land | 22 | 88 | 23 | 92 | 22 | 88 | 19 | 76 | 86 |
| Local farming tools | 19 | 76 | 22 | 88 | 21 | 84 | 24 | 96 | 86 |
| Capital/loan | 8 | 32 | 5 | 20 | 5 | 20 | 6 | 24 | 24 |
| Tractors | 2 | 08 | Nil | 0 | 1 | 04 | Nil | 0 | 3 |
| Processing machine | 10 | 40 | 2 | 08 | Nil | 0 | Nil | 0 | 12 |
| Fertilizer | 17 | 68 | 10 | 40 | 12 | 48 | 14 | 56 | 53 |
| Drought animals | 5 | 20 | 5 | 20 | 1 | 04 | 2 | 08 | 13 |
| Extension services | 5 | 20 | 10 | 40 | 10 | 40 | 6 | 24 | 31 |

*Source: Haruna, 2004*

Chapter 21  Mairo Haruna, in
A.I. Tanko and S.B. Momale (Eds.)
*Kano: Environment, Society and Development*
London & Abuja, Adonis & Abbey Publishers

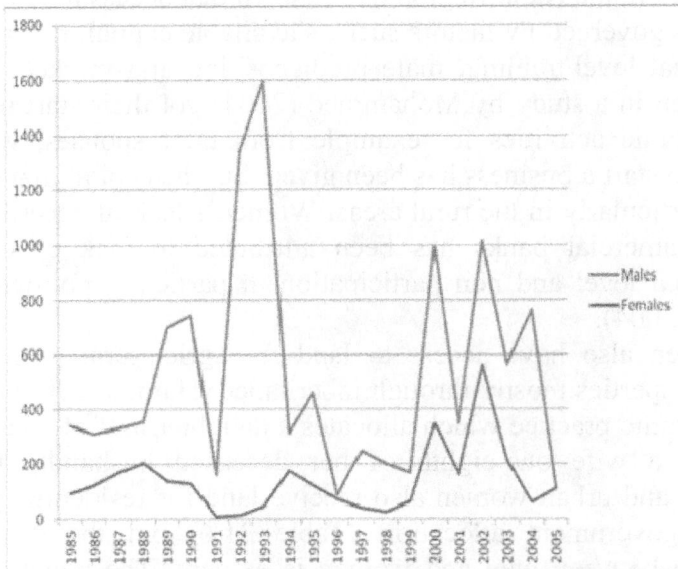

**Figure 21.1: Pattern of Government Residential Land Allocation in Kano Metropolis (1985-2005)**

**Table 21.6 Pattern of Government Residential Land Allocation in Kano Metropolis (1985)**

| Year | No. of sampled Applications | Treated Applications | Untreated Applications | Allocation | | | |
|------|------|------|------|------|------|------|------|
| | | | | Male | % | Female | % |
| 1985 | 550 | 433 | 117 | 340 | 78.5 | 93 | 21.5 |
| 1986 | 450 | 434 | 16 | 311 | 58.2 | 123 | 23 |
| 1987 | 500 | 500 | 50 | 332 | 66.4 | 168 | 33.6 |
| 1988 | 600 | 52 | 38 | 357 | 63.5 | 205 | 36.5 |
| 1989 | 850 | 836 | 14 | 700 | 83.7 | 136 | 16.3 |
| 1990 | 900 | 874 | 26 | 745 | 85.2 | 129 | 14.8 |
| 1991 | 200 | 170 | 30 | 161 | 94.7 | 9 | 5.3 |
| 1992 | 1400 | 1357 | 43 | 1342 | 98.9 | 15 | 1.1 |
| 1993 | 1700 | 1646 | 53 | 1600 | 97.1 | 47 | 2.9 |
| 1994 | 500 | 490 | 10 | 314 | 64.1 | 176 | 35.9 |
| 1995 | 600 | 583 | 17 | 462 | 85.9 | 121 | 20.8 |
| 1996 | 200 | 160 | 40 | 87 | 54.4 | 73 | 45.6 |
| 1997 | 300 | 289 | 11 | 248 | 85.8 | 41 | 14.2 |
| 1998 | 250 | 229 | 21 | 202 | 88.2 | 27 | 11.8 |
| 1999 | 250 | 231 | 19 | 168 | 72.7 | 63 | 27.3 |
| 2000 | 1400 | 139 | 61 | 993 | 74.2 | 346 | 25.8 |
| 2001 | 550 | 514 | 36 | 350 | 68.1 | 164 | 31.9 |
| 2002 | 1600 | 1576 | 24 | 1014 | 64.3 | 562 | 35.7 |
| 2003 | 800 | 781 | 19 | 567 | 72.6 | 214 | 27.4 |
| 2004 | 850 | 825 | 25 | 764 | 92.6 | 61 | 7.4 |
| 2005 | 350 | 225 | 125 | 114 | 50.7 | 111 | 49.3 |

*Source: Ma'moun (2007)*

Chapter 21 | Mairo Haruna, in
A.I. Tanko and S.B. Momale (Eds.)
*Kano: Environment, Society and Development*
London & Abuja, Adonis & Abbey Publishers

# Conclusion

This Chapter reveals a number of critical issues related to women in the Kano Region. First, is the fact that more importance is attached to the reproductive role of women particularly in the rural areas. As a result, girls in the rural areas are married off at an early age. In the urban centres, the practice is not the same as most girls are enrolled in primary and Quranic (Islamiyya) schools and even proceed to secondary and tertiary Institutions. Women's educational attainment levels in the region have risen significantly due to modernization, investment by the state in education and some political reforms. However, female and male literacy in the region indicate that basic literacy is still a struggle for both men and women and gender gaps are still evident.

Secondly, women in the Region are also involved in other productive activities such as agricultural and non-agricultural activities such as small and large scale trading, wage employment and craftsmanship. However, they are constrained by inadequate or total lack of resources, cultural practices and the male predisposition.

Thirdly, the women are grossly underrepresented in political positions especially at the decision making level. Some of them who have ventured into politics have not fared better in a scenario that is dominated by men. Political appointments are usually given to women who are educated and in the civil service.

Lastly, there has not been any deliberate policy to help women who mostly find it difficult to acquire adequate resources for example, from the point of acquiring farming or residential plots, capital and training, through the process of procuring technical support to actual construction or production.

In conclusion, the prospect for enhancing the role of women in national development is a function of significant social values. These have to do mostly with the class, gender and power structures. However, there is no doubt that the emerging situation with regards women's role in development and access to resources is part of the resurgence of national consciousness of governments in the developing countries of the world to remove whatever impediments on the way of access of women to production resources. It is significant to restate that there are no working legal enactments that are working

Chapter 21 | Mairo Haruna, in
A.I. Tanko and S.B. Momale (Eds.)
*Kano: Environment, Society and Development*
London & Abuja, Adonis & Abbey Publishers

against access and use of women to certain resources and privileges. We have cultural and behavioural tendencies arising from long existing practice both in the traditional and modern setting. The extent and magnitude of the practices and the effect which they have on the pace of urbanization and economic development generally can only be precisely determined following further research.

## References

Bangassar, L.C. (1995), *Advancement of Women* Notes for Speakers. United Nations.

Bhatta, G (2001), "Of Geese and Ganders" Mainstream Gender in the context of Sustainable Human Development, *Journal of Gender Studies* Vol. 10, No .1 Oxfordshire, Great Britain

Boserup, E (1970), *Women's Role in Economic Development*, St. Martins Press, New York.

Fafunwa, A. B (1974), *History of Education in Nigeria,* George Allen and Unwin, London.

Falola, J.A. (2001) "Towards the sustainability of the Sustainer: Women and Technological Interventions in rural Production systems" in Baba, K.M., Mohammed, I. Kyiogwom, U.B. and Bello, H. M. (eds.) *Rural resources Development and sustainability; proceedings of the Ninth Annual conference of the Nigeria Rural Sociological Association.* NRSA/UDU, pp 9 - 18.

Haruna, Mairo (2004) Access to resources and the participation of women in agriculture in Kura, Kano State. Unpublished M.Sc. thesis Bayero University, Kano

Ma'moun, U. B. (2007) Access to residential land by Women in Kano metropolis. Unpublished M.Sc thesis. Bayero University, Kano

Mohammed, N. (2004), Influence of Cooperatives on Female Participation in Income Generating Activities in Parts of Kano and Jigawa States, Nigeria. Unpublished PhD thesis, Bayero University Kano.

Mohammed, N (2012) Gender participation in Environmental Management in Tofa Local Government Area of Kano State: Implications for sustainable development. British journal of Arts and Social science Vol. 9 No 12 http//www.bjournal.co.uk/NJASS. aspr

Chapter 21    Mairo Haruna, in
A.I. Tanko and S.B. Momale (Eds.)
*Kano: Environment, Society and Development*
London & Abuja, Adonis & Abbey Publishers

Moser, CON (1993) *Gender Planning and Development: Theory, Practice and Training.* Routledge, London

National Bureau of Statistics (2006) *Abstract of statistics*, Federal Government of Nigeria, Abuja

Pratt, G (2004) *Working Feminism.* Edinburgh: Edinburgh University Press and Philadelphia: Temple University Press

Chapter 21 | Mairo Haruna, in
A.I. Tanko and S.B. Momale (Eds.)
*Kano: Environment, Society and Development*
London & Abuja, Adonis & Abbey Publishers

**345**

# Chapter Twenty Two

## MATERNAL HEALTH IN RURAL KANO

Yusuf Muhammad Adamu

### Introduction

Medical Geography or Geography of Healthcare as it is sometimes called "Uses the concepts and techniques of the discipline of Geography to investigate health-related topics. Subjects are viewed in holistic terms within a variety of cultural systems and diverse biosphere. Drawing freely from the facts, concepts and techniques of other social, physical and biological sciences, medical geography is an integrative, multistranded subdiscipline that has some room within its broad scope for a wide range of specialist contributions ... Geographic variations in health has long been studied under such disciplinary rubrics as geographic pathology, medical ecology, medical topography, geographical epidemiology, geomedicine and so forth" (Meade & Earickson, 2000:1)

The fact that studies in women's health is coming to the forefront of health priorities in many countries, makes it important for Medical Geographers to participate, not only that, it is only geographers that can best assist the achievement of one of the major objectives set by the Safe Mother Initiative in 1987 of getting "country and locale-specific information on maternal mortality". Efforts to reduce maternal mortality appeared to centre on the causes of maternal death viewed from clinical angle with no clear focus on women themselves nor their circumstances (PMM Network, 1995). This, necessitate the involvement of Social Scientists in many programmes aimed at preventing maternal mortality. For instance, it was the research efforts of medical geographers, medical sociologists and anthropologists put together that pointed out that delay in seeking and receiving care was the major cause of maternal death (Thaddeus and Maine 1990). This outcome has helped to draw the attention of certain funding agencies notably Carnegie Corporation of New York to support intervention projects in the Third World Countries. In the Sokoto State (now Sokoto, Kebbi States) Carnegie Corporation supported a project on the Prevention of Maternal Mortality and Morbidity between 1990 and

Chapter 22 | Yusuf M. Adamu, in
A.I. Tanko and S.B. Momale (Eds.)
*Kano: Environment, Society and Development*
London & Abuja, Adonis & Abbey Publishers

1995. The project was able to identify various socio-cultural, geographical and economic factors that serve as predisposing factors greatly influencing maternal morbidity and mortality. This led to intervention efforts among which is the re-training of Traditional Birth Attendants so that they can administer certain complications and be able to refer cases they seem not to understand or fail to control. Other interventions provision of emergency obstetric first aid boxes in health institutions and in conjunction with National Union of Road Transport Workers provided transport for emergency obstetric cases. This effort has greatly improved women's lives of the area, for example, the report further states that obstructed labour dropped from about 50/1000 in 1995 to 10/1000 in 1995 so also the fatality rates of post partum haemorrhage, ruptured uterus has remarkably dropped.

The concerns of Medical Geography, according to McGlashan (1972), lie in the local variations of those environmental conditions which are causatively related to human health or as explained by Howe (1972), it is a comparative study of the incidence of diseases and the distribution of physiological traits in people belonging to different communities throughout the world and the correlation of these data with features of the environment. It is, as described by Barrette (1986), centred on mortality and morbidity, on the distribution of disease patterns, health-care facilities, patient and physical spatial behaviour. It is about different medical systems in different areas of the world. Its concern is diffusion of disease and medical ideas. It studies spatial problems at different scales, but seldom studies health per se. It therefore is an important tool of analysing this problem of maternal mortality. This study is a contribution by geographers to the understanding of mortality studies in Africa and specifically in the Kano Region considering the increasing rapid population growth, increasing poverty, inequality, and the deteriorating condition of health-care system in the Region .

Obstetric complications have been recognized as the major cause of mortality and morbidity among women in reproductive age particularly in the developing countries (WHO, 1987; Mahler 1987; Smyke 1991). Globally, there are 430 maternal deaths for every 100,000 live birth, with Eastern and Western Africa accounting for the highest rates and ratios (World Health Day, 1998). Up to 99% of all maternal deaths and morbidity take place in developing countries

Chapter 22 | Yusuf M. Adamu, in
A.I. Tanko and S.B. Momale (Eds.)
*Kano: Environment, Society and Development*
London & Abuja, Adonis & Abbey Publishers

where also there are high birth rates (about 86% of the world's total). Sadly, the African continent registers the highest number of maternal deaths in the world, with more than 253,000 women dying during pregnancy or following childbirth annually (WHO, 2000).

The risk of a woman dying because of pregnancy or childbirth varies around the world. While the chances of a woman dying in developing countries is 1:48 (WHO, 1996) in developed countries it is one in several hundreds. The mortality ratios vary, but they are higher in developing countries than the developed countries (Table 22.1). The unfortunate thing is that the ratios in the Kano region are the highest. This makes it imperative to look at the relevant issues that do influence maternal heath in the area. Table 22.2 shows the life time risks of dying from pregnancy-related complications and a comparison of maternal mortality ratios from regions of Africa and geo-political zones of Nigeria.

**Table 22.1: Comparison of Maternal Mortality Ratios from Regions of Africa and Geo-political zones of Nigeria**

| Study | Year | MMR per 100 000 | Region |
|---|---|---|---|
| WHO | 1996 | 1200 | Eastern and Southern African |
| WHO | 1996 | 360 | Middle East and North Africa |
| WHO | 1996 | 1000 | Western and Central Africa |
| WHO | 1996 | 1100 | Sub-Saharan Africa |
| Harrison, KA | 1997 | 100 | Nigeria |
| WHO | 1996 | 1546 | North-East Nigeria |
| Aboyeji AP | 1998 | 532 | Ilorin (North Central Nigeria) |
| Ujah et al. | 1999 | 739 | Jos (north Central Nigeria) |
| Etuk et al. | 2000 | 600 | Calabar (South-South Nigeria) |
| Olatunji, AO & Sule-Odu, AO | 2001 | 1700 | Sagamu (South-West Nigeria) |
| Okaro et al. | 2001 | 1406 | Enugu (South-East Nigeria) |
| Adamu, YM | 2003 | 2420 | Kano (North West, Nigeria) |

*Sources: Various*

**Table: 22.2 Women's Lifetime Risk of Dying from Pregnancy-Related Complications.**

| Region | Risk of dying |
|---|---|
| Africa | 1 in 16 |
| Asia | 1 in 65 |
| Latin America & the Caribbean | 1 in 30 |
| Europe | 1 in 1400 |
| North America | 1 in 3700 |
| All developing countries | 1 in 48 |
| All developed countries | 1 in 1800 |

*Source: World Health Organization, 1996*

| Chapter 22 | Yusuf M. Adamu, in A.I. Tanko and S.B. Momale (Eds.) Kano: Environment, Society and Development London & Abuja, Adonis & Abbey Publishers |

The socio-economic and psychological costs of these deaths to the family and community levels are indeed considerable. This is so, perhaps, because of the class of families involved are poor and powerless, those who set national and international health priorities have for long neglected this tragic and agonizing situation faced by millions of people in the Third World countries (Royston and Armstrong 1989). The most regrettable thing is that most of these deaths are preventable.

## Obstetric Causes of Maternal Deaths in Rural Kano

Kano State has the highest maternal mortality ratios in Africa and the world. The maternal mortality ratio of Kano State is 2420/100,000 while the rate is 802/100,000, (Adamu, 2003). These ratio and rate are not only disturbing but also unacceptable. Within the decade of 1990-1999, sixty-seven women died in one ward: Kausani in Wudil Local Government in rural Kano State. While Eclampsia is the major cause of death among women (accounting for 31%) in urban Kano, community based data from Kausani ward shows that Anaemia is the major cause of mortality (Adamu, 2003). Community based data from Kausani shows that Anaemia was responsible for 38.8% maternal deaths, followed by prolonged obstructed labour accounting for (13.4%) maternal deaths. Postpartum haemorrhage has accounted for 7.5% followed in order by malaria and Caesarean section accounting for 6.0% maternal deaths each. Retained placenta, Kakanda and ante-partum haemorrhage accounted for 3.0% each. Chest problem, cerebro-spinal Meningitis and Gastric Enteritis accounted for 1.5% each. The 14.9% of the causes could not be ascertained so are considered not known. Although hospital based data from Wudil General Hospital for the period of study (1990-1999), 3 year data (1997-1999) which was available shown on figure 22.1 suggests that Anaemia is really an important cause of maternal deaths in rural Kano.

Chapter 22 | Yusuf M. Adamu, in
A.I. Tanko and S.B. Momale (Eds.)
*Kano: Environment, Society and Development*
London & Abuja, Adonis & Abbey Publishers

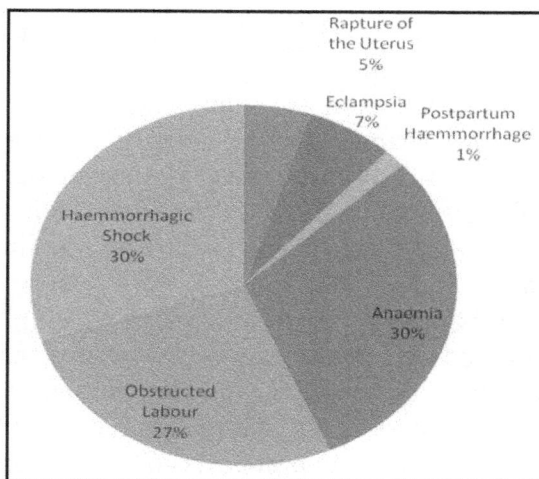

**Fig. 22.1: Causes of Maternal Death in Rural Kano**

## Socio-Cultural Determinants of Maternal Health in Rural Kano

The age at which girls are given out in marriage is an important determinant of their future lives and health. Women are physically and psychologically ready to start child bearing at certain age. In rural Kano, early marriage is a rule rather than an exception. Girls are married from the age of 9-17. A study conducted by Adamu (2003) shows that 57.9% of 107 women interviewed were married up between the ages of 10-14. While only two girls were married at the age of nine and ten (accounting for 0.9%), four (3.7%) were married up at the age of 12. Twenty-five were married at the age of 13 (23.4%), 33 at the age of 14 (30.8%) and 37 married at the age of 15 (34.6%) Finally at the age of 16 and 17 only 6 girls (three each) were married at the ages of 16 and 17. It is clear that ages 13-15 are the prime age of marriage in the study area as they accounted for almost 89% of the total 107 women interviewed. This implies that under normal circumstances, all girls could be married, between the ages of 3-15.

The study also shows that girls in rural areas generally experience their first pregnancies at a tender age of 13. However, the prime age of first pregnancy in the area is between the ages of 15 and 17. This implies that since these girls start child bearing at such tender age, they stand the risk of a number of complications and, in the long run,

Chapter 22 │ Yusuf M. Adamu, in
A.I. Tanko and S.B. Momale (Eds.)
Kano: Environment, Society and Development
London & Abuja, Adonis & Abbey Publishers

very high parity. It also means that their chances of dying are many folds that of their counterparts living in urban Kano where majority of the girls are enrolled in primary schools and thereby delaying their early marriage. This factor is sufficient to explain why women in the rural Kano are in a very high risk of dying coupled with other unfavourable factors against them, as we shall see in due course. The reasons for such early marriages in rural Kano include the ones described below.

The majority population of rural Kano is Muslim. Islam prohibits pre-marital sex and the preservation of virginity has strong social relevance. Parents ensure that their female children's social security is protected, by marrying them out at a tender age when they are in their early adolescence. This is in an attempt to prevent them from sexual promiscuity and premarital pregnancies that can damage the image of their entire family.

Early marriage, in rural Kano is also influenced by the statue of the girl. If the statue of a girl is big even at an early age, she stands the "chance" of getting someone to marry her. Chronologically, it is also socially unacceptable for a person to allow his daughter to grow up to 16-17 years in his house. She is considered as leftover (*kwantai*) and the person will lose his public respect; it is also a sign of failure not to get one's daughter married as soon as she is 12 or 13 years old. People who are poor however, delay the marriage of their daughters because of the costs involved.

Although girls are allowed, as their male counter-parts, to attend Qur'anic schools and to gain Islamic education, it is not the same with *"Makarantar Boko"* or Western education school. This is because of the cultural practices in the area of marrying girls early. When girl-child is not in a primary school, the excuses of delaying her marriage under the guise of schooling are not there.

## Antenatal and Obstetric Care Services in Rural Kano: Women Access to the Services

Majority of the women (88%) do not attend antenatal care. Only 19% indicated that they attend antenatal care for what they call *"a duba lafiyarsu"* (meaning, "To be examined"). The women gave a wide range of reasons as to why they do not attend antenatal care services

Chapter 22 | Yusuf M. Adamu, in
A.I. Tanko and S.B. Momale (Eds.)
*Kano: Environment, Society and Development*
London & Abuja, Adonis & Abbey Publishers

available at the General Hospital, Wudil. Majority (44.8%) attribute their inability to go for antenatal services to financial constraints. The major occupation for the people in the study area is subsistence farming, although some of the people cultivate crops like cassava, groundnuts and vegetables for community purposes. The women are solely dependent and most are not involved in any income generation activity. The women as well as the male eat mainly carbohydrates foods from sorghum, maize and millet (although they also contain some percentage of proteins).As such, many do not eat foods that are rich in protein like beans, fish, and beef because they could not afford it. Although some of them produce beans, it is produced to generate income not for consumption at home. The money realised from the sales are used for ceremonies and other day-to-day activities. Going to the hospital involves money (for travel and drugs) there is also the fear that new things might be diagnosed which will involve spending money (which they do not have). All these, make them to stay away from hospital unless it is necessary.

## Factors Affecting Access to Maternal Health

(a) Husband's denial: this accounted for 17.2%; this is an important barrier to antenatal care service use. But why is it important? There are five fundamental reasons as follow:

(b) Cost: Since these women are dependent on their husbands, even when they earn some income, all the financial commitment of going to antenatal rest with the husband. The fear of costs makes most husbands reluctant to allow their wives to go rather than practice of seclusion (purdah). Instead of spending money on antenatal care, they will use it for the naming ceremony, which is socially very relevant until all alternatives have been exhausted.

(c) Purdah; there are people who actually practice seclusion, as a practice, their wives are not allowed to go out for anything, not even visiting their parents until when it is absolutely necessary. People who practice seclusion (*Tsari*) do not allow their wives to go out.

(d) Fear of 'unfaithfulness': The fear that some women might be unfaithful discourages some men from allowing their wives to go to hospital routinely.

Chapter 22 | Yusuf M. Adamu, in
A.I. Tanko and S.B. Momale (Eds.)
Kano: Environment, Society and Development
London & Abuja, Adonis & Abbey Publishers

(e) Health workers attitude: During a Focus Group Discussion, many people complained about the attitude of health workers, which they claim discourage them from allowing their wives to attend antenatal care services. Some of the allegations against health workers are extortion, maltreatment and partiality. They argued that they are made to pay monies that are not actually being charged by the government. Secondly, when they bring their spouse (mostly late to the hospital) they are maltreated by the hospital staff, that infringes on their ego and keep them off. They also complain of partiality, hospital sub-staff (labourers) use their positions to break protocol particularly when you give them a tip. This attitude also discourages many husbands from allowing their wives to go for antenatal care.

(f) God's will: Hausa community has a strong belief in God as the Alpha and Omega. The conviction that God is the Chief determinant of everyone's fate and destiny make Hausa people very fatalistic in nature. On things that one finds oneself helpless, the common consolation is "it is the will of God that this should happen to me".

(g) Fatalism: is another crucial attitude of all reasons why women do not attend antenatal services as it accounted for 17.2%. Most women feel that they do not go for ANC because God has destined that they would not. This explanation is an attempt to be faithful and not to put anyone at fault.

(h) Women's Perception of their Condition: First pregnancy is always a serious business among Hausa women. An old-aged practice of modesty or *kunya* is still relevant, a woman is encouraged to always show some modesty about her first pregnancy (this practice is still common among the rural communities in Kano). As observed by Trevitt (1973) a woman is scolded for the slightest signs of immodesty. It then implied that all problems associated with the pregnancy should be hidden, and may not be made public when it is necessary and mainly through an intermediary. When a woman delivers her first child, she is discouraged from calling him by his real name or showing love and affection to the child openly. On the other hand, another cultural practice of *"Juriya"* (i.e. Endurance) encouraged women to endure all the pains during labour and childbirth.

| Chapter 22 | Yusuf M. Adamu, in |
|---|---|
| | A.I. Tanko and S.B. Momale (Eds.) |
| | *Kano: Environment, Society and Development* |
| | London & Abuja, Adonis & Abbey Publishers |

This belief has affected Hausa women's view or perception of what is normal and what to expect. So minor complications or their symptoms are considered normal for pregnancy and in cases like bleeding or severe pains or obstructed labour, they believe no cause to go for antenatal. Experience has taught their elders how to treat minor symptoms or ailment. Only 2.3% of the women felt that they are on course and so have no reason to bother themselves with the trouble of going to antenatal care. While 3.4% of these women realized that they need assistance from the health centre, but are only careless in not going for it.

This negligence may actually be rooted in the cultural perception of what is normal and when is it necessary for them to go for ANC. Some women (9.2%) however said they have no reason for not going. In fact, they did not feel like going.

(i) Some women (2.3%) gave *"zaman kauye"* (village life) as their reason of not going for ANC. But what does *"zaman kauye"* imply? From our own understanding, it implied the inadequacies of village life all hinged on ignorance and poverty. They do not know why they need to trouble themselves in going to the hospital while they have alternatives. This necessitates the need for health education.

(j) Distance: Finally, distance also acts as a barrier for some number of women (2.3%). Many of the husbands complained that the distance to Wudil General Hospital is much, both physical distance and costs matter here. In the absence of vehicular transport most women have to travel an average of 2km or more on foot to the main road (Gaya-Wudil) before getting one, except for some cases where women are taken on motorcycle or on some market days. A number of the men felt that if they have the resources, distance might not be a serious obstacle. In a nutshell, all these factors like negligence, no reason and *"zaman kauye"* bother on ignorance.

(k) Place of delivery: Of the 107 women interviewed 103 (96.3%) have previously delivered at home without a skilled attendant, despite the fact that they had in the past experienced some complications. Only 4 (3.7%) have previously delivered at the hospital, and that was out of necessity, mainly due to prolonged labour and that, their husbands could afford to finance them.

Chapter 22 | Yusuf M. Adamu, in
A.I. Tanko and S.B. Momale (Eds.)
Kano: Environment, Society and Development
London & Abuja, Adonis & Abbey Publishers

In order to encourage women to attend antenatal services, to improve their hygiene and nutrition, health workers compose songs, which the women are taught. The songs are for mobilization and enlightenment. The women are made to sing the songs, so that they can always remember the messages contained therein. They are also encouraged to have some exercises, which may help improve their health particularly at late stage of pregnancy. Part of the one of the songs runs thus:

| | |
|---|---|
| *dawo da mai dadi* | **Translated thus:** |
| *Na je asibiti saboda dana* | Child! Having a child is sweet |
| *Na sha manja saboda dana* | I went to the hospital for my child |
| *Na ci ayaba na sha lemo* | I ate palm oil for my child |
| *Na sha miyar alayaho saboda dana* | I ate banana and oranges for my child |
| | I ate vegetable soup for my child |

Women at the antenatal ward at the Wudil General Hospital sing this song with enthusiasm. This action is however frown at by some men who pointed out that going to the hospital for ante-natal is "nothing more than giving the nurses an opportunity to teach their wives songs and dances". This factor has prevented and is preventing women from enjoying this life saving services. Women have no grudges against that. However, those who have the power to permit the woman to go out are not comfortable.

Hausa women generally consider pregnancy as a very serious and life threatening situation. In fact, pregnant women are said to have one leg in this world and another in the hereafter, implying that until a woman delivers safely, she should expect the worst. This fatalistic belief had some effect on the way women see and perceive pregnancy. That is why when a woman delivers safely relations and friends come to rejoice with her for having made it; that practice is called "Barka" and is practiced in all Hausa communities.

Women who deliver at home have reasons for doing so. Table 22.3 summarises the reasons.

Chapter 22 | Yusuf M. Adamu, in
A.I. Tanko and S.B. Momale (Eds.)
*Kano: Environment, Society and Development*
London & Abuja, Adonis & Abbey Publishers

**Table 22.3: Why Women Deliver at Home**

| Reason | Respondent | | |
|---|---|---|---|
| | Number | % | 95% CI(%) |
| It is easier at home | 27 | 26.2 | 17.7-34.7 |
| God's will | 18 | 17.5 | 10.2-24.8 |
| Precipitate labour | 17 | 16.5 | 9.3-23.7 |
| Financial constraints | 14 | 13.6 | 7.0-20.2 |
| No reason | 8 | 7.8 | 2.6-13.0 |
| Husband's preference | 7 | 6.8 | 1.9-11.7 |
| Distance | 5 | 4.9 | 0.7-9.1 |
| Others | 7 | 6.8 | 1.9-11.7 |
| Total | 103 | 100 | ----- |

*Source: Adamu, 2003*

Although the respondents gave a multiple reason for home delivery, four are adjudged as important. They are financial constraint (13.6%), God's will (17.5%) and perceived simplicity (it is easy at home) 26.2%, and precipitate labour (16.5%). Financial constraint and God' will are already explained above.

## *Factors Affecting Place of Delivery*

A number of factors are found to affect the choice of place of delivery and are explained below:

### *(a) "It is easier at home"*

Twenty-Seven women (27.2%) said home delivery is easier. However, they said this not because majority of them have had a nasty experience in hospital delivery, but because they want to avoid the many perceived "inconveniences" of hospital delivery which include exposing their nakedness to male health workers, compulsory shaving of pubic hair, and harassment by the midwives and so on. This similar view was found by Kisekka et al (1992) in their study in Zaria area. Women prefer to deliver at home with people they are familiar with and who understand them and their problems.

### *(b) Precipitate Labour*

Normal labour, according to Encarta Encyclopedia (1999) "begins with irregular contractions of the uterus that occur every 20 to 30 minutes. As labour progresses, the contractions increase in frequency

Chapter 22 | Yusuf M. Adamu, in
A.I. Tanko and S.B. Momale (Eds.)
Kano: Environment, Society and Development
London & Abuja, Adonis & Abbey Publishers

357

and severity. The usual length of labour for a mother expecting her first child is about 13 to 14 hours, and about 8 or 9 hours in a woman who has given birth previously."

Under normal circumstance, therefore a primigravidae would deliver within 14 hours from the onset of labour while multigravida should do so within 10 hours. If a woman in any of the category does not deliver within that limit, she is considered to have a prolonged labour that needs assistance. In rural Kano, women have their perception of what is considered a normal labour. Table 22.4 shows that 88.8% of the women interviewed view normal labour to last for not more than 24 hours, 8.0% consider 48 hours normal while 1.9% considered 8 hours normal and 1.9% not sure.

**Table 22.4: Duration of Normal Labour**

| Normal labour | Frequency | % |
|---|---|---|
| 24 hours | 95 | 88.8 |
| 48 hours | 8 | 7.5 |
| 8 hours | 2 | 1.9 |
| Don't know | 2 | 1.9 |
| Total | 107 | 100 |

*Source: Adamu, 2003*

This implies that when a woman in the study area does not deliver after 14 or 10 hours as the case may be she still feels that her labour is normal. She would only start to seek for assistance after 24 hours. Since they have their limit, they consider labour that is completed before 24 hours as normal.

One woman gave the presence of elders (who can assist at delivery) as her reason for home delivery; two others (1.9%) gave father-in-law's permission as a barrier to their access to ANC. This will suggest that they live in an extended family compound where the head of the household is in full control and his decisions affecting the family are final. Therefore, even if their husbands are willing to allow them to go and deliver at the hospital, their father's decision can prevent that. For these two women in particular, their in laws are Qur'anic teachers who have apathy to modern medicine. One said she does not know where she would deliver it therefore depends on the circumstance. Yet another woman interestingly point to the fear of *"Gori"* as reason to why most women detest hospital delivery. *"Gori"*

| Chapter 22 | Yusuf M. Adamu, in |
| | A.I. Tanko and S.B. Momale (Eds.) |
| | *Kano: Environment, Society and Development* |
| | London & Abuja, Adonis & Abbey Publishers |

is a word that usually refers to ones bad or shameful behaviour, some one's weakness or cowardice. Women who deliver at the hospital might be tagged as cowards or something like that. A woman may be scolded with these words *(Ba ta yi haihuwar dadi ba)* (she had a bitter delivery). It is also ego killing.

### (c) *Attendants at the Last and Next Delivery*

Of the 107 women, only four have been, and are expecting to be attended by a midwife during delivery. The rest have been and would be by a family member or a TBA. As so because 42% of these women (most of whom are multigravidas) had experienced complications in the past most of which were treated at home.

### (d) *Previous Complications Experienced*

Over half of the women interviewed (58%) argued that they had not experienced any serious complication in their previous birth. The 42% of who point to eight complications. Majority (40.0%) had had prolonged labour in their last delivery, 15.6% were Anaemic, 13.3 had Postpartum Haemorrhage, and 8.9% had PPH due to "Kakanda" cut (is an important complication that almost all women interviewed said they have experienced at least once in their live times). Miscarriage account for 4.4% while APH, pre-eclampsia and retained placenta occurred in 2.2% each.

### The Role of Traditional Birth Attendants and Surgeons

Although there are divergent views on the relevance of TBA and their incorporation into modern health services (Royston and Armstrong, 1989) there is no doubt that they play an important role in assisting women to some complications usually after delivery and by providing post natal advice to them in developing countries. In the study area, there are six practicing TBAs, two in Kausani, one each in Gurbo, Gaci, Manga and Rege.

The interview with Isumuha, a 70-year-old TBA at Gurbo is very revealing. She has over 30 years working experience and has cut the umbilical cord of more than 500 babies from her estimate. The role of the TBA according to Isumuha is as follows:

| Chapter 22 | Yusuf M. Adamu, in |
|---|---|
| | A.I. Tanko and S.B. Momale (Eds.) |
| | Kano: Environment, Society and Development |
| | London & Abuja, Adonis & Abbey Publishers |

i)   To cut the umbilical cord of the baby;
ii)  To bath the baby;
iii) To remove the placenta;
iv)  Where there is retained placenta to attempt manual removal;
v)   To give the mother some medicines;
vi)  And to bath dead women before burial.

TBAs do not actually deliver women; they come only after the woman has delivered i.e. they give post natal care services like removing retained placenta, stopping PPH etc. Women at home, mainly relatives and co wives do the job of delivering women. They are not formally trained, but are experienced. Isumuha explained that they refer some cases (e.g. retained placenta and PPH) to hospital when they have tried and cannot succeed. As for prolonged labour, it is the Qur' anic Malams that gives rubutu (a kind of sacred water or philtre made by washing the verses of the Quran) to the women, although they (the TBAs) also give some herbs (usually during labour) to ease delivery.

There are two types of traditional surgeons in the study area, Kakanda incisor and the barbers. Barbers are male and do minor surgeries like removing clitoris (for girls) and circumcision (for boys). The only woman surgeon in the study area is Ramai who makes incision for women who suffer from Kakanda. By the time of the interview, Ramai began her work about five years, having inherited it from her mother. Whenever she is invited she would first examine the woman and affirm if the problem is Kakanda or not. If it is not she would leave. If it is, she would give the woman an option of pastry or incision. Most women prefer pastry. Those who are anaemic are usually excluded from the exercise. Over these five years, Ramai gave pastry to over 200 women and had performed incision on over 50 women. Some women lose small quantity of blood, some more all in her area of coverage: Kausani, Masama, Gaci, Turari and Rege.

The term *"Kakanda"* has become difficult to understand in modern medical sense. Attempts have been made to find the English equivalent of the term, but have proved difficult. The medical doctor and midwives at the General Hospital Wudil and my female research assistant could not say exactly what Kakanda is. Dr. Tijjani the

Chapter 22 | Yusuf M. Adamu, in
A.I. Tanko and S.B. Momale (Eds.)
*Kano: Environment, Society and Development*
London & Abuja, Adonis & Abbey Publishers

Medical Director of Wudil General Hospital does not believe there is anything called Kakanda, as far as he is concerned the incision is done to draw the attention of the woman from the pains of labour. However, Mrs. Amadi a midwife argued that Kakanda is Cancroids that is resulting from infection (septicaemia) due to poor hygiene.

A Traditional Birth Attendant describes Kakando as follows: Kakanda is something like membranes that flow and cover the birth canal of a woman in labour. When that happens a woman cannot deliver. The Kakanda can be treated either by *"nani"* (pasting of alum) or by incision. If it is not serious, alum can be pasted on the birth canal. After some hours, it will break and some watery fluid will be released and the woman can deliver. On the other hand, if it is complicated, the surgeon will use a razor blade and make incision. After the incision the woman will lose some blood after which the woman can deliver. Whatever is the case, the condition needs further investigation, but most importantly there is the need to discourage women from it through health education and increased access to emergency obstetric care in the area.

## Conclusion

This Chapter examines some maternal health issues in rural Kano with particular reference to Kausani ward of Wudil local government area. The Chapter reveals that the Kano Region has the highest maternal mortality rate and identifies the factors responsible for such trend. It is very important to understand that the high maternal mortality ratios are not simply resulting because there are no enough health facilities and manpower but also greatly influenced by social and cultural practices. Any effort that would target the reduction of maternal deaths and morbidity in rural Kano must have a clear understanding of the social and cultural practices. It is only by changing and modifying certain practices and changing certain perceptions that rural women would have the right access to services provided by government and non governmental agencies. Changing mind sets is therefore crucial.

Chapter 22 | Yusuf M. Adamu, in
A.I. Tanko and S.B. Momale (Eds.)
Kano: Environment, Society and Development
London & Abuja, Adonis & Abbey Publishers

# References

Adamu, Y.M. (2003) A Geographical Analysis of Maternal Mortality in Kano State, Being a PhD thesis submitted to the Department of Geography, Bayero University, Kano, Nigeria.

Greenwood, A. et al. (1987) A prospective study of pregnancy in a rural area of the Gambia, West Africa. *Bulletin of the World Health Organisation*, 65 (5): 635-644.

Harrison, K.A. (1997) Maternal Mortality in Nigeria, the real issues. A commentary. *African Journal of Reproductive Health.* 1, 7-13.

Kisekka, M.N; Ekwempu, C.C, Essien, E.S, Olarukoba, B.M. (1992) Determinants of Maternal Mortality in Zaria Area, in Kisekka, M.N (Ed) (1992) *Women's Health Issues in Nigeria,* Tamaza Publishing Company Limited, Zaria.

Okoro, J.M, Umezulike,AC; Onah, H.E;. Chukwuali, L.I; Nweke, P.C., (2001) Maternal Mortality at the University of Nigeria Teaching Hospital, Enugu, Before and After Kenya. *African Journal of Reproductive Health.* 5, 90-97

Olatunji, A.O and Sule-Udu, AO. (2001) Maternal Mortality at Sagamu, Nigeria-A ten year Review (1988-1997). *Nigerian Postgraduate Medical Journal*: 8, 12-15

Onwuhafua, P.I, Onwuhafua, A.; Adze,J. (2000) The challenge of reducing maternal mortality in Nigeria. *International Journal of Gynecology and Obstetrics.* 71, 211-213

Royston, E. and Armstrong, S. (eds.) (1989) Preventing of maternal mortality. *World Health Organisation*, Geneva.

Safe Motherhood Newsletter, 1991, *World Health Organization*, Geneva.

Smyke P. (ed.) (1991) Women and Health. Zed Books Ltd., Zed Press, London.

Ujah, I A.; Uguru, I.A; Aisien, O.A; Segay AS; Otubu, J.A. (1999) How safe is motherhood in Nigeria? the trend of maternal mortality in a tertiary health institution. *East African Medical Journal* 76, 436-439

World Health Organisation (1996). *Coverage of maternity care; a listing of available information.* WHO, Geneva.

Chapter 22 | Yusuf M. Adamu, in
A.I. Tanko and S.B. Momale (Eds.)
*Kano: Environment, Society and Development*
London & Abuja, Adonis & Abbey Publishers

World Health Organisation (1999) *Reduction of maternal mortality: a WHO/UNFPA/UNICEF/World Bank statement*. Geneva, World Health Organization.

World Health Organization Reducing maternal mortality: A challenge for the 21st century. *WHO/AFRO Press Releases*. 28 August-2nd Septembser 2000

World Health Organization (1986), *Measuring Reproductive Morbidity*, Report of a technical working group, Geneva.

World Health Organization and UNICEF (1996) *Revised 1990 Estimates of maternal mortality, a new approach by WHO and UNICEF*. WHO and UNICEF Geneva.

World Health Organization (1977) *International classification of diseases. Manual of the international statistical classification of diseases, injuries and causes of death*. Ninth Revision. Geneva.

World Health Organization (1997) *Maternal Health Around the World* (poster) WHO and The World Bank. Geneva

Chapter 22 | Yusuf M. Adamu, in
A.I. Tanko and S.B. Momale (Eds.)
Kano: Environment, Society and Development
London & Abuja, Adonis & Abbey Publishers

# Part IV
# Issues in Development: Case Studies

# Chapter Twenty Three

## URBAN PLANNING IN THE CONTEXT OF RAPID GROWTH

Aliyu Danshehu Maiwada

### Introduction

In recent decades, Nigeria has experience the phenomenon of urbanization on a scale more rapid than many other countries in Africa south of the Sahara. This has led to rapid expansion of existing cities and creation of new urban centres. Rapid urban growth reflects migration of people to cities as well as natural increase among urban residents.

Kano metropolis as one of the leading commercial and industrial centre is therefore experiencing this rapid growth rate. Although estimates of its population growth vary widely, analysis of the different estimates indicates the rapid growth rate. In 1932 the population was estimated to be only 83,000; but by 1952 it has reach 131,361. In the 1963 census, 330,000 people were recorded; hence an implied growth of 7.7% between 1952 and 1963. The official estimate for 1983 was 900,000. According to the 1991 population census, Kano metropolis has a population of about 1.6 million. Finally according to 2006 census the population of Kano metropolis is estimated to be between 2.5 to 3 million people.

This rapid growth is accompanied by aerial expansion as more and more surrounding rural areas are absorbed into the urban sphere; and also in-filling of every available open space within the existing built up areas. In a study, Sekandi (1994) estimated the total area of Kano metropolis increased from 122.7km$^2$ in 1966 to 154.6 km$^2$ in 1981, an increase of about 25% on the average, the expansion rate of about 2km$^2$ per annum. The same study also shows the decline of agricultural land use from 57.2% in 1962 to 38.8% in 1981, but residential land use increased from 22% to 44%, thus more than doubling. The estimated built area in 1991 stood at 659km$^2$, a further evidence of horizontal expansion of residential land. Today this rate of expansion has been maintained as a result of construction of the

Chapter 23 | Aliyu D. Maiwada, in
A.I. Tanko and S.B. Momale (Eds.)
*Kano: Environment, Society and Development*
London & Abuja, Adonis & Abbey Publishers

365

western and the eastern by-pass roads as well as institutional developments in the peri-urban area. During all times from 1962 to 2010 the pattern and direction of this growth is linear haphazard (see Chapter 6). It mainly follows the axis formed by major transport line coming into the city.

This Chapter examines how the institutional and administrative framework is coping with rapid growth, assessing the achievement and impediments and to make recommendations for sustainable urban development.

## Institutional and Admnistrative Frame Work for Planning

### *The Colonial Period*

The British colonial administration was established in 1903. This brought about substantial change in commerce, economy, administration and technology which resulted in the transformation of Kano into a modern industrial and commercial centre. These changes resulted in a substantial increase in the population which was mainly accommodated outside the old walled city. Thus by 1937 the new township was well developed according to colonial policy and guidelines. In particular, the cantonment proclamation of 1904 and the township ordinance of 1917 were strictly enforced in Kano. The cantonment later called government reservation (GRA) area was built in accordance with Garden city concept. It was a low density development separated from the old wall city and other areas by a building-free zone. In 1913 Sabon Gari was laid out to provide accommodation for the southern Nigerians mainly Christian, Tudun Wada to accommodate other northern Nigerians, and after the Second World War, Gwagwarwa was developed. All the layouts in Sabon Gari, Tudun Wada and Gwagwarwa were of the grid-iron pattern and the density much higher than the GRA. Also a commercial area was developed between Fagge and the railway station; and an industrial area was developed at Bompai in 1959.

One of the weaknesses of the colonial urban planning in Kano was the lack of establishment of strong municipal administration. The system of indirect rule effectively prevents the whole city from being administered by single authority. The old city remained under the

Chapter 23 | Aliyu D. Maiwada, in
A.I. Tanko and S.B. Momale (Eds.)
*Kano: Environment, Society and Development*
London & Abuja, Adonis & Abbey Publishers

control of native administration, while the township was administered separately by the colonial government in accordance with the township ordinance of 1917, where Kano was declared as a second class township.

Finally it is important to note that no overall plan was prepared for the whole of the area, but layout plans for commercial, residential and industrial areas in the township were prepared by the department of works.

## Post Colonial Period

As a result of rapid growth of Kano; the Northern Nigerian government established the Greater Kano Planning Authority (GKPA) in 1962; in accordance with the Nigerian Town and Country Planning Laws (1946). The authority was to function as planning authority, with powers to prepare planning schemes and to control the development of city; but by 1966 it was functioning on a very restricted basis. The major achievement of the authority was the preparation of Greater Kano Development Plan and some investment in housing and roads. The authority could not function effectively because of financial and jurisdictional problems.

The creation of Kano State in 1967, with Kano metropolis as the capital led to more rapid growth of Kano; hence another planning authority was established, known as Metropolitan Kano planning and Development Board. The functions of the board was planning and control of development within the entire planning areas of metropolitan Kano and adjoining districts of Ungogo and Kumbotso. The board was abolished in 1976 and was replaced by the Kano State Urban Development Board (KSUDB) as the sole planning authority for all urban areas of Kano State including metropolitan Kano. In 1990 KSUDB was renamed Kano State Environmental Planning and Protection Agency (KASEPPA) by virtue of Edict No. 15 of 1990. Its activities were enlarged in scope and areal extent to include environmental protection. However with the creation of ministry of environment in 1999 and the Refuse Management Agency in 2005, KASEPPA was renamed Kano Urban Planning and Development Agency (KNUPDA) and all aspect of environmental sanitation and protection were transferred to the Ministry Environment.

Chapter 23 | Aliyu D. Maiwada, in
A.I. Tanko and S.B. Momale (Eds.)
*Kano: Environment, Society and Development*
London & Abuja, Adonis & Abbey Publishers

## Organizational Framework for Planning In Metropolitan Kano

There are many organizations involved in Urban Administration and Development. These range from the main line bodies such as the Ministry of Land and Physical Planning, and KNUPDA with more broad power for control of land use, to more limited organizations established to provide facilities and services, such as Housing Cooperation, Water Board, and the Power Holding Company of Nigeria (PHCN).

### *Kano State Urban Planning and Development Authority (KNUPDA)*

This planning authority has undergone metamorphosis since its establishment in 1962, as the Greater Kano Planning Authority as mentioned earlier. But the agency remains the same except for minor adjustments. The Kano Sate Environmental Planning and Protection Edict No. 15 of 1990 under Sections 17 and18, empowers the Authority to perform the following functions:

i. Prepare or cause to be prepared and keep under continuous review land development plans for the urban areas of the state.
ii. Control the development and the use of land in all urban areas of the state.
iii. Preserve buildings and other objects of architectural, historic and artistic interest and places of national interest and beauty.
iv. Administer any laws controlling and regulating the construction of any building or other structures.
v. Collect and publish demographic, economic, environmental, social and other relevant information about urban areas and the land development plans that are being or have been prepared by such urban areas.
vi. Design and provide industrial, commercial, and residential layouts.

Despite all these powers conferred on the Agency by the Edict and other relevant laws, the urban environment in Kano Metropolis still manifests a physical pattern of development that has little or no bearing with these laws and regulation.

Chapter 23 | Aliyu D. Maiwada, in
A.I. Tanko and S.B. Momale (Eds.)
*Kano: Environment, Society and Development*
London & Abuja, Adonis & Abbey Publishers

## Ministry of Land and Physical Planning

The process of land acquisition and allocation in Kano State is controlled by this Ministry. The Land Tenure Laws of Northern Nigeria (1962) and the Land Use Act (1978) are the main legislations governing the process of land acquisition and allocation. In effect both legislations nationalized land by vesting control of all lands in the Governor of the state. The duties of the ministry include; land assembly and the payment of compensation; the processing of applications for matters related to land including allocation, permission for alienation, valuation of property, transfer of land grant, land subdivision, lease, and change of use; the collection of land rents; and the keeping of a register land ownership.

## Other Agencies

There are many other agencies that are directly involved in urban development, among them is the State Housing Cooperation; established in 1980 to implement housing programs in the State, also agencies that provide services such as Water Board; Sustainable Kano Projects and many others.

## Urban Planning and Development in Practice

## Master Plans

The only Master Plan statutory approved is the 1963 Trevallion Plan; prepared for the Greater Kano Planning Authority. The overall aim of the plan reflects the factors which created the perceived need for planning in Kano in the first place, the need to cater for the problem arising from the rapid growth of Kano. The proposed physical plan was designed to permit the evolution of a compact urban environment in keeping with the traditional pattern of physical development in Kano, for maximum economy of operation. To achieve this objective, the neighbourhood concept was used, and the whole urban area was divided into six sectors of group III, each with population of about 140,000 people, the sector group III was to be subdivided in sectors

Chapter 23 | Aliyu D. Maiwada, in
A.I. Tanko and S.B. Momale (Eds.)
*Kano: Environment, Society and Development*
London & Abuja, Adonis & Abbey Publishers

group II and I each with its own centre and populations of 36,000 and 6000 respectively: The whole arrangement was designed in order to ensure the provision of services at the level at which they could be used effectively and economically.

In the rural areas within metropolitan boundary, there was a proposal for a gradual increase in the size of the settlement and the proper provision of public and social facilities, and seven new villages were proposed. The main policy was to ensure that the villages are large enough to support facilities.

Specific proposals were made for housing, industrial and commercial development. Also the plan proposed standards for the provision of public and social services, transport and communication. Finally, a program was prepared for the implementation of these proposals during the 20 year period (1963-1983). This plan was revised in 1980 (Metropolitan Kano Master Plan (1980-2000). This review superimposed a form of proposed development based on hexagonal shaped neighbourhoods, with green belts.

## *Implementation of the Master Plan*

The overall objectives of the plan for maintaining compact urban development have not been achieved. Also the proposed structure of the town, based on the neighbourhood concept remains only on paper. Many areas have been developed without provision of essential facilities and services and development control has not been fully enforced in most part of the metropolis. However, the location of industries in Sharada and Challawa industrial estates are based on the proposal of the plan. Also some roads in the metropolis are based on the recommendation of the master plan.

## *Preparation of Layouts*

A major activity of KNUPDA and the Ministry of Lands and Physical Planning, is the preparation of layouts for residential, industrial, or commercial developments. According to Kano State Handbook (1991) the Agency designed 34 residential layouts, 13 commercial layouts and four industrial layouts between 1977 and 1990; also the Ministry of Lands and Physical Planning developed 12 layouts during the same

Chapter 23 | Aliyu D. Maiwada, in
A.I. Tanko and S.B. Momale (Eds.)
*Kano: Environment, Society and Development*
London & Abuja, Adonis & Abbey Publishers

period. However, a number of criticisms can be made of the KNUPDA Layouts (Home, 1986).

a. Insufficient attention to infrastructure costs and Layout efficiency: The main infrastructure cost is roads, and yet official layouts show as much as 55% of the total land area reserved for roads.
b. Plot sizes are unnecessarily large especially for the low and medium density layouts.
c. Development charges are unrealistically low. Such generous plot sizes make it impossible to levy an affordable development charge, to provide sufficient capital for roads and infrastructure as planned. Since plots are offered at economically low price, there allocation becomes a form of political patronage.
d. Layouts are often not developed as planned. Land reserved for public open space and other public facilities; may be illegally subdivided, especially if the provision of facilities is delayed. Unrealistically large plots get subdivided. A lease requirement that development be undertaken within a fixed period of 2 years is not enforced, and there is black market in the unauthorized and speculative sale of undeveloped plots.

## Illegal Development

A major problem in Nigerian towns, as in many developing countries, is subdivision and development of land without the knowledge or approval of planning authorities. Most new development takes place on land with only customary title and effectively outside KNUPDA control. This so called illegal development arises in various ways, sometimes local government layouts are prepared by Local Government without professional planning and without informing the planning authority. Sometimes a farmer may make his own subdivision and sell the plots through ward head and illegal land dealers. This is because compensation for compulsory purchase is paid on only disturbance basis which would be a fraction of the open market value (price). It is therefore not surprising farmers on the urban edge prefer to sell their plots illegally to private buyers, rather than

Chapter 23 | Aliyu D. Maiwada, in
A.I. Tanko and S.B. Momale (Eds.)
*Kano: Environment, Society and Development*
London & Abuja, Adonis & Abbey Publishers

wait for the government to acquire. In such a situation sub-division often take place faster than demand, contributing to high vacancy rates in some unauthorized subdivision. The so called illegal areas on the urban periphery can hardly be considered squatter settlements and not all of them are overcrowded slums with bad living conditions. The plot holders have usually paid money to the customary land holders, so that their occupancy is legal according to the customary tenure but illegal according to the State Government.

The illegal areas may have electricity and pipe water, and may offer tolerable living conditions. They are, however an unplanned form of development, usually poorly related physically to the road network. Public facilities such as road access, drainage and building setbacks may be lacking.

### Some Impediments to Effective Planning in Kano Metropolis

i. Absence of up to date flexible master plan to guide the growth and development of the town;

ii. Institutional framework is marred by overlapping jurisdiction and powers of various agencies; hence there is lack of coordination;

iii. Inadequate financial and human resources for smooth and timely acquisition of land for public sector development projects;

iv. Lack of community participation in the planning process;

v. Land allocation policy does not favour the low-income group, but only the most strategically positioned members of the managerial bourgeoisie, the political class, top businessmen have been granted a disproportionate share of statutory land rights.

vi. The high level of subsidy in land allocation coupled with the inefficiency in the bureaucracy has encouraged corruption in the allocation process, reducing it to a form of patronage. The corruption in the allocation process encourages the use of land for speculative practices, and reinforces the trend toward higher prices and resultant inaccessibility of land.

Chapter 23 | Aliyu D. Maiwada, in
A.I. Tanko and S.B. Momale (Eds.)
*Kano: Environment, Society and Development*
London & Abuja, Adonis & Abbey Publishers

## Recommendations

There is a need for the preparation of a structure plan; which consist of a written statement accompanied by diagrammatic illustration setting out and justifying broad land use policies (but not detailed land allocation) for the city, policies for the management of traffic and measures for the improvement of the physical environment.

Structure plans 'indicate' action areas where major change, by development, redevelopment or improvement, may be expected; and then local plans which are conceived as detailed elaborations of the broad policies incorporated in the structure plan can be prepared to provide a detailed basis for development control; and to coordinate the development and other use of land.

Finally a subject plan which deals with specific aspects of planning, such as housing, conservation, recreation can be prepared when there is a need. Community participation is essential for planning to succeed. Urban planning should provide for extensive consultation at all stages of the process. Such participatory approaches will lead to clear objectives for planning interventions. It encourages a feeling of ownership and utilizes people's extensive knowledge about their local environments. Also it proposes public awareness through media campaign working groups; strengthen urban management instrument; encourage community involvement in environmental protection; and the construction and provision of facilities and services. Finally community participation will promote transparency and accountability in the planning process.

Population pressure in Kano Metropolis is mainly a result of lack of another growth centre that will relieve pressure on Kano. There must be a deliberate attempt to develop such centres through deliberate government and private sector investments in such other smaller towns around the Kano Region.

## Conclusion

The fact remains that, in spite of the level of economic, social and cultural development, there is no overlooking the inevitable and indispensable need to regulate and enforce control of our urban environment. Just as land use decisions made years back affect the

Chapter 23 | Aliyu D. Maiwada, in
A.I. Tanko and S.B. Momale (Eds.)
*Kano: Environment, Society and Development*
London & Abuja, Adonis & Abbey Publishers

quality of today's urban environment, so decisions made today and tomorrow will shape the quality of urban life for future generation.

Reluctance or inability to provide affirmative guidance for land development in the cities will not of course prevent development from occurring. Rather, inaction or ineffective action now will allow undirected and haphazard development as is happening in Kano. Therefore, inaction or ineffective action represents a decision about the future urban environment; just as careful, positive action does.

There is a crying need to ensure a rational measure of orderly organization, exploitation and management of urban environment for the present and future good of the environment. This requires a strong political, legislative and financial support of all the planning and implementing agencies and strengthening of all support institutions throughout the state.

## References

Garba, S.B.(1993) Urban Land Management Problems and Low income Housing: case study of the Kano metropolitan Area paper presented at DEMO 93 International Conference in Nigerians indigenous Building Materials, Kongo Zaria

Hameed, R. and Nadeem, O. (2006) Challenges of Implementing Urban Master Plans: The Lahore Experience. *World Academy of Science, Engineering and Technology*, 24 2006.

Home, R.K. (1986) Urban development boards in Nigeria: The Case of Kano. *CITIES*

Kano State Urban Development Board (1980) *Metropolitan Kano 2000 Master Plan*, Kano.

Koehn, P. (1984) 'Development' Administration and Land Allocation in Nigeria - *Rural Africana* No 18 winter Michigan State University.

Maiwada, A.D. (1995) Towards a more effective and acceptable planning system in Kano. Unpublished paper presented at Dinner organized by NITP in honor of its members

ISoCaRP 2000 Millennium Report - IsoCaRP. Wyporel, B. (2000)

Travellion, B.A.W. (1966) *Metropolitan Kano: Report of a Twenty Year Development Plan 1963-1983*, Greater Kano Planning Authority, Kano State Government.

Chapter 23    Aliyu D. Maiwada, in
A.I. Tanko and S.B. Momale (Eds.)
*Kano: Environment, Society and Development*
London & Abuja, Adonis & Abbey Publishers

# Chapter Twenty Four

## SPATIAL DISTRIBUTION OF PRIMARY HEALTH CARE FACILITIES IN THE METROPOLIS

Mohammed Ahmed

### Introduction

Health care services are activities geared towards the provision of a comprehensive package of integrated care to beneficiaries through the primary, secondary and tertiary levels. This includes increasing both demand and supply of services with the goal of expanding coverage for improving the health status of the citizenry. It is recognized that health care services in Nigeria are provided by a multiplicity of health care providers - public, private including for profit and not for profit, patent medicine vendors and the traditional health care providers (Israel and Sunday, 2009 ).

Nigeria operates a pluralistic health care delivery system with the orthodox and traditional health care delivery systems operating alongside each other, albeit with hardly any collaboration. Both the private and public sectors provide orthodox health care services in the country. In 2005, the Federal Ministry of Health (FMOH) estimated a total of 23,640 health facilities in Nigeria of which 85.8% are primary healthcare facilities, 14% secondary and 0.2% tertiary. 38% of these facilities are owned by the private sector, which provides 60% of health care in the country (Federal Ministry of Health, 2005). While 60% of the public primary health care facilities are located in the northern zones of the country, they are mainly health posts and dispensaries that provide only basic curative services (NCH, 2009).

It is in recognition of the importance of healthcare facilities to sustainable development that various levels of health care facilities are established by al the three levels of government in Nigeria. Government always budget huge amount of money for the health sector. Since the goal of any development effort by the government is to improve the well-being of the generality of the people it governs, making adequate planning for healthcare delivery will be a right step

Chapter 24 | Mohammed Ahmed, in
A.I. Tanko and S.B. Momale (Eds.)
*Kano: Environment, Society and Development*
London & Abuja, Adonis & Abbey Publishers

in the right direction. But adequate planning could only be based on adequate information on the existing health facilities in the area for planning purposes. The Chapter sets out to provide the information on the existing and type of healthcare facilities in the Kano Metropolis.

Metropolitan Kano comprises of eight Local Governments: Dala, Fagge, Gwale, Municipal, Nassarawa, Tarauni, Kumbotso and Ungogo. The Metroplois lies within Latitudes 11°52'22''N to 12°07'19''N and Longitudes 8°34`56''E to 8°47'11''E and is about 472 meters above sea level. Kano Metropolis is bounded by Minjibir LGA to the North East and Gezawa to the East, Dawakin Kudu to the South East, Madobi and Tofa to the South West and Dawakin Tofa to the North West (Yusuf, 2011).

Kano Metropolis is today one of the fastest growing cities in Nigeria and the largest in the whole of the Northern part of the country. In 1931, the population of Kano Metropolis was 96,805 persons. This figure rose to 130,170 persons in 1952 and by 1963, it was 295,432 (Maiwada, 2000). According to the 1991 population census, Kano State had a figure of 5,810,340 people, out of which Kano metropolis accounted for 1,432,255 representing 24.3% of total population of the State. By 2006 census, the population rose to 9,383,683 people with that of Kano Metropolis rising to 2,165,223 (Census, 2006).

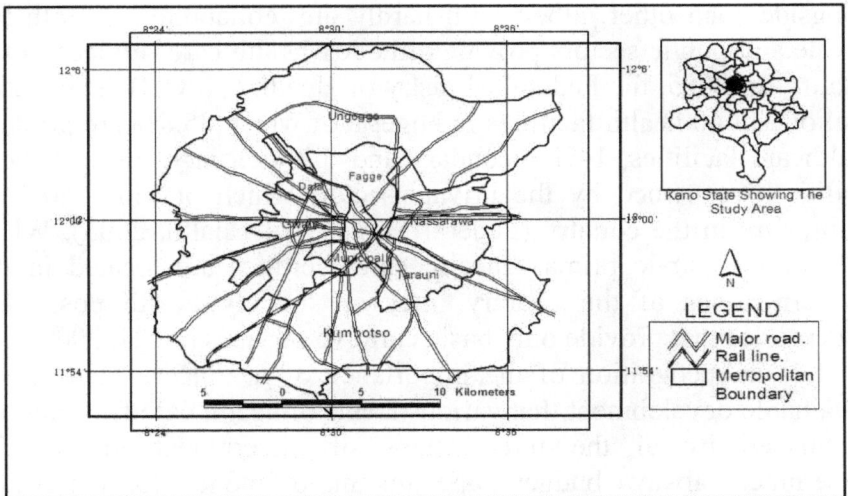

**Figure 23.1: Kano Metropolis**

Chapter 24 | Mohammed Ahmed, in
A.I. Tanko and S.B. Momale (Eds.)
*Kano: Environment, Society and Development*
London & Abuja, Adonis & Abbey Publishers

## Concept of Primary Healthcare

The ideal model of primary health care was adopted in the declaration of the International Conference on Primary Health Care held in Alma Ata in 1978 (known as the "Alma Ata Declaration "), and became a core concept of the World Health Organisation's goal of Health for all (WHO, 2011). The Alma-Ata Conference mobilized a "Primary Health Care movement" (PHC) of professionals and institutions, governments and civil society organizations, researchers and grassroots organizations that undertook to tackle the "politically, socially and economically unacceptable "health inequalities" in all countries.

In other words, PHC is an approach to health beyond the traditional health care system that focuses on health equity-producing social policy (Barbara, 2011). According to Public Health Agency of Canada (2011), PHC includes all areas that play a role in health, such as access to health services, environment and lifestyle.

Primary Health Care (PHC) is a conceptual model which refers to both processes and beliefs about the ways in which health care is structured. PHC encompasses primary care, disease prevention, health promotion, population health, and community development within a holistic framework, with the aim of providing essential community-focused health care (WHO, 1978; Shoultz & Hatcher, 1997).

A transdisciplinary understanding of Primary Health Care (PHC) acknowledges the role of health care providers from diverse disciplines, within a philosophy and framework of PHC that is guided by the principles of access, equity, essentiality, appropriate technology, multisectoral collaboration, and community participation and empowerment (WHO, 1978). A PHC philosophy recognizes that health and health services occur within particular physical environments and their historical, socio-political, economic, and cultural contexts that shape the social determinants of health for individuals, families, groups, communities, regions, or countries. Each discipline contributes to health and health services delivery within a PHC model, both in a unique sense, and through collaborative interdisciplinary practice. Indeed, as constructed to address numerous principles and contexts, the components of PHC can vary tremendously. As Calman and Rodger (2002) noted, primary health

Chapter 24 | Mohammed Ahmed, in
A.I. Tanko and S.B. Momale (Eds.)
*Kano: Environment, Society and Development*
London & Abuja, Adonis & Abbey Publishers

377

care cannot exist as a "cookie-cutter response" to health issues. Moreover, a consensus process engaged in by Haggerty et al. (2007) resulted in 25 operational definitions of primary care attributes, thereby suggesting that the task of conceptualizing PHC is not an easy one.

PHC forms an integral part of the country's health system. While the main focus of PHC is the health of individuals, families and communities, PHC is equally concerned with addressing the overall social and economic development of communities, thereby targeting the social determinants of health. PHC embodies a spirit of self-reliance and self-determination; it is driven by and implies community empowerment and building community capacity and resilience: "The fundamental premise of (community development) is that when people are given the opportunity to work out their own problems, they will find solutions that will have a more lasting effect than when they are not involved in such problem-solving" (Lindsey, *et al* 1999).

**Development of Health Care Facilities in the Kano Region**

Chapter Seven gives the population growth of the Kano Metropolis from the colonial periods. Health care provision in Kano has always been anchored by the Kano State Ministry of Health that aims at the attainment of a level of health that enable the citizens to achieve socially and economically productive lives through primary health care system. According to Mousa-Booth (1987), it was in reckoning with this aim that the Kano State Ministry of Health first established and thereafter continues to embark on the expansion of what is now known as the Murtala Mohammed Hospital. For instance, after its establishment, by 1970 it was realised that the then existing maternity block was inadequate to cope with intake for child deliveries in the Metropolitan Kano. A new block was started in late 1970 and completed early 1972 with 60 bed wards and a nursery operating theatre. It was at the same time Nassarawa Hospital (now known as Abdullahi Wase Hospital) was improved and upgraded to provide more quality services as a secondary health facility.

Around 1972 Kano State had seven Hospitals located in the city and other important towns such as Hadejia, Birnin Kudu, Gumel, Kazaure and Danbatta. Other health facilities were the Eye Hospital

Chapter 24 | Mohammed Ahmed, in
A.I. Tanko and S.B. Momale (Eds.)
*Kano: Environment, Society and Development*
London & Abuja, Adonis & Abbey Publishers

ran by the Sudan Interior Mission and the Orthopaedic Hospital which was by that time under the Ahmadu Bello University. In addition to these, there were 28 dispensaries spread all over the Kano Region. Of this, 18 belonged to Local Government Authorities while the remaining 10 were owned by voluntary missions. During this period there was only one Dental Centre situated in Kano Metropolis manned by two dental surgeons, technical and other auxiliary staff.

Between 1977 and 1980 the government, through the Health Ministry, in its effort to improve its services especially with the increase in demand associated with increased population, almost all the existing hospitals were upgraded. More clinics were established to put more emphasis in improving rural health care delivery. By 1982, additional fifteen health care facilities were established in some selected areas within the Region.

By the second half of 1984, the Ministry began to upgrade some health centres alongside constructing new ones as basic health clinics and primary health centres. This Chapter describes the geography of the healthcare facilities within the Region with particular focus on Metropolitan Kano which is the centre of the social and economic activities of the Kano Region.

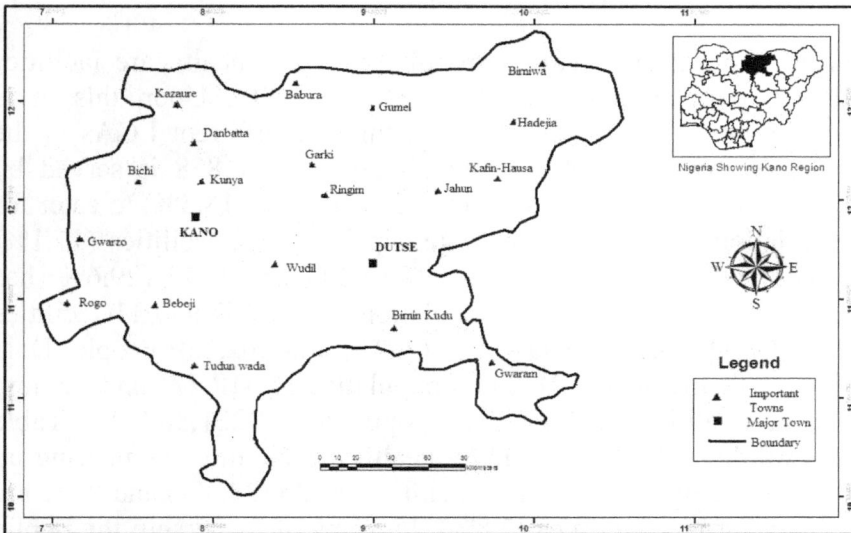

**Figure 24.2: important towns in the Kano Region**

| Chapter 24 | Mohammed Ahmed, in<br>A.I. Tanko and S.B. Momale (Eds.)<br>*Kano: Environment, Society and Development*<br>London & Abuja, Adonis & Abbey Publishers |

## Distribution of Healthcare Facilities in Kano Metropolis

From data obtained at the Kano State Ministry of health, there are different types of health facilities in the Metropolis. These include Primary, Secondary and Tertiary health facilities owned and managed by both the Public and Private sectors.

**Table 24.1: The Distribution of Healthcare facilities in Kano Metropolis**

| LGA | Type | | | Ownership | | | HCF (%) | Population (2006) |
|---|---|---|---|---|---|---|---|---|
| | Primary | Secondary | Tertiary | Public | Private | Total | | |
| Fagge | 4 | 3 | 0 | 7 | 0 | 7 | 6.5 | 198,828 |
| Kumbotso | 20 | 0 | 0 | 20 | 0 | 20 | 18.5 | 295,979 |
| Municipal | 9 | 3 | 0 | 11 | 1 | 12 | 11.1 | 365,525 |
| Nassarawa | 16 | 15 | 1 | 19 | 13 | 32 | 29.6 | 596,669 |
| Ungogo | 10 | 1 | 0 | 11 | 0 | 11 | 10.2 | 369,657 |
| Gwale | 8 | 0 | 0 | 7 | 1 | 8 | 7.4 | 362,059 |
| Dala | 8 | 2 | 1 | 11 | 0 | 11 | 10.2 | 418,777 |
| Tarauni | 5 | 1 | 1 | 6 | 1 | 7 | 6.5 | 221,367 |
| Total | 80 | 25 | 3 | 92 | 16 | 108 | 100 | 2,828,861 |

**Source:** *Kano State Ministry of Health (2012) and NPC (2006)*

From Table 24.1, Kano Metropolis with 108 healthcare facilities serves the population of 2,828,861 (NPC, 2006). Upon this, it is possible to show the spatial spread within the different LGAs in the municipality. Fagge LGA with population of 198,828 is served by seven facilities (6.5%). Kumbotso has 20 facilities (18.5%) to cater for the population of 295,979. The Municipal with 12 facilities (11.1%) has a population of 365,525. Nassarawa LGA with 32 (29.6%) has 596,669 people. Ungogo has a population of 369,657 and 11 facilities (10.2%). Gwale has eight facilities (7.4%) and 362,059 people. Dala also has 11 facilities (10.2%) but a population of 418,777 and Tarauni with seven facilities (6.5%) and the population of 221,367. The Table also shows there are more Primary healthcare facilities numbering up to 80 (74.1%). Secondary health facilities are 25 (23.3%) and there are only three Tertiary facilities (2.8%). In terms of ownership the public (Government own facilities) has the highest number (92) of facilities

Chapter 24 | Mohammed Ahmed, in
A.I. Tanko and S.B. Momale (Eds.)
*Kano: Environment, Society and Development*
London & Abuja, Adonis & Abbey Publishers

representing 85.2% and the private health facilities are only 16 representing 14.8%.

This fact reveals that the distribution of Healthcare facilities is highest in Nassarawa LGA while Kumbotso LGA has the highest in the primary healthcare because of the vast land area covered. There is also a concentration of private healthcare facilities in Nassarawa LGA and this is because of the GRAs where many of the richer members of the society that can afford the cost of the services are residing in the area. Most of this people living in this area prefer to visit private facilities as against the public hospitals.

## *Explanation of the types of Health facilities in the Kano Metropolis*

According to Medical and Dental Council of Nigeria (MDCN) in Badru (2003), primary health centres are to undertake such functions as health education, diagnosis and treatment of common ailments through the use of appropriate technology, infrastructure and essential drug list. Bello (2007) described Dispensary and health posts are the type of health institution where minor treatments are giving to patients. Its establishment is to provide easy access to resident of a particular community or neighbourhood and they should therefore, be located within residential area. A population of 15,000 - 20,000 in any community should be served by dispensary health post, so that minor cases of illness which do not require the attention of a specialist medical personal could be immediately attended to. This type of health facility is to provide out-patient health services. Maternal and child health centre is another type of the primary health care which provides service in gynaecology, family planning and nutrition. A maternity clinic or maternity home is to serve an area of 20,000 - 30,000 people. Primary healthcare centres are to refer complicated cases to secondary health care facilities (popularly called the General Hospitals).

Secondary health centres are involved with prevention, treatments and management of minimal complex cases. Examples of secondary types of health facilities are the comprehensive health centres and general hospitals. The comprehensive health centres are often owned by private individuals(s) or a group of individuals. Bello (2007) explained that Health clinic and Comprehensive health centres are the type of health facilities that provide in-patient services, and are

Chapter 24 | Mohammed Ahmed, in
A.I. Tanko and S.B. Momale (Eds.)
*Kano: Environment, Society and Development*
London & Abuja, Adonis & Abbey Publishers

381

concern with the treatment of disease that are very common like fever, Malaria, Ulcer, and provides antenatal and postnatal care service. In this health facilities, patient are usually admitted. General hospitals have provisions for accident and emergency unit and diagnosis unit (including X-ray, scan machines and other pathological services) among other services (Badru, 2003). This occupies the status of being a second layer of health institutions and it is to be provided with certain acceptable standards and level of infrastructure. However, secondary health facilities are to refer the more complicated cases to the tertiary or specialist hospital.

Tertiary health institutions, also called specialist/teaching hospitals, handle complex health problems/cases either as referrals from general hospitals or on direct admission. It has such features as accident and emergency unit, diagnostic unit, wards units, treatment unit and out-patient consultation unit (Badru, 2003). All these units are to be equipped with the necessary facilities and staffed by highly skilled personnel. Teaching hospitals also conduct researches and provide outcomes to the government as a way of influencing health policies. This explains why this type of health institution is often university-based. Example is the Aminu Kano Teaching Hospital (AKTH).

Furthermore, teaching hospitals are supposed to be fully developed and accredited for teaching of various medical disciplines. They are to conform to international and acceptable standards. It should be stressed also that apart from the provision of infrastructure for health matters, there is also the need for availability of teaching materials and specialists in such fields as surgery, general medicine, paediatrics, obstetrics, dentistry, otolaryngology and psychiatry among other disciplines (Erinosho, 2005; Badru, 2003).

## *Mapping Healthcare Facilities*

Healthcare providers and hospitals can capture data, analyze and prepare quality visual presentations in forms of reports and maps for use in product planning. A geographic information system (GIS) is a computer based tool that organizes and displays data. In health organizations, GIS provides powerful tools for geographic and spatial

Chapter 24 | Mohammed Ahmed, in
A.I. Tanko and S.B. Momale (Eds.)
*Kano: Environment, Society and Development*
London & Abuja, Adonis & Abbey Publishers

analysis, and it allows visualization of data that may have gone unnoticed in spreadsheets, charts and other reports.

Physical access to primary health care remains a key issue in most low income countries in which a large proportion of the population often resides in rural areas at considerable distances from basic health services. Many studies show that physical access to health care is the most important determinant of the utilization of the heath care services. In addition, Tanser (2006) establishes strong correlation between physical access to primary health care and adverse health outcomes affecting adherence to demanding treatment regimes.

## Conclusion

The present distribution of healthcare facilities within the urban and rural areas in Nigeria is uneven with enormous implications on provision of effective health service. The concentration of secondary and private health institutions in urban wealthy neighbourhoods like Nassarawa GRA reflects the dominance of service delivery to the wealthy and more educated segment of the society and the inadequate and poorer service delivery to both the urban and rural poor. The importance of population concentration on the provision of health service delivery implies that areas with more concentrated populations like Metropolitan Kano are better served than those with dispersed and less densely populated rural areas such as the hinterland of the Kano Region.

The applications of appropriate data analysis techniques like GIS will greatly enhance understanding of the spatial distribution of population and health facilities, thereby providing planners with better understanding on how to effectively plan and organise health service delivery. This means that engaging in PHC research may constitute a form of social action in that social, economic and political determinants of health become part of interdisciplinary discourse. There is also need for increase multidisciplinary research on health so as to devise more effective strategies to improve health and health services delivery that will create positive social change, stimulate development and improve peoples' health condition and livelihoods in the Kano Region and beyond.

---

Chapter 24 | Mohammed Ahmed, in
A.I. Tanko and S.B. Momale (Eds.)
*Kano: Environment, Society and Development*
London & Abuja, Adonis & Abbey Publishers

# References

Ahmed, K. (1994), the impact of the regulated River Kano on wetlands in Drylands, The Hadejia Nguru Wetlands, and Paper presented at the first international conference on research for Development in the arid zone of Nigeria, Center for arid zone studies, University of Maiduguri June 19-25, 1994.

Badru, F.A. (2003). 'Sociology of Health and IlIness Relations' in Olurode, Lai and Soyombo Omololu (eds.) Sociology for Beginners, John West Ikeja: pp. 336-355. Central Bank of Nigeria (2005). Annuals Report and Statement of Account for the year ended 31st December, 2005, CBN, Abuja.

Barbara, S. (2011), "Politics, primary healthcare and health." *J Epidemiol Community Health* 65: 653-655 doi:10.1136/jech.2009. 102780

Bello, B.A. (2007) *Distribution of public primary health care facilities in Kano metropolis.* An unpublished B.Sc. Dissertation, Department of Geography Bayero University, Kano

Calnan, R. and Rodger, G.L. (2002) Primary Health Care: A new approach to health care reform Retrieved Oct 7, 2008 from Canadian Nurses Association Website: http://www.cnannurses.ca/ CNA/documents/pdf/publications/PHC_presentation_Kirby_6602 _e.pdf

Erinosho, O.A. (2005), Sociology for Medical, Nursing and allied Professions in Nigeria, Bulwark Consult, Abuja and Ijebu-Ode.

Federal Ministry of Health (2005) *Inventory of Health Facilities in Nigeria* Abuja: Federal Ministry of Health

Haggerty, J., Burge, F., Lévesque, J.F., Gass, D., Pineault, R., Beaulieu, MD., and Santor, D. (2007), Operational definitions of attributes of primary health care: Consensus among Canadian experts. *Annals of Family Medicine,* 5, 336-344

Hogg, W., Rowan, M., Russell, G., Geneau R., and Muldoon L. (2008), Framework for primary care organizations: The importance of a structural domain. *International Journal forQuality in Health Care,* 20, 308 - 313.

Institute of Medicine (1994). Defining primary care: An interim report, in: M. Donaldson, K. Yordy and N. Vanselow (Eds.) Washington, DC: National Academy Press.

Chapter 24 | Mohammed Ahmed, in
A.I. Tanko and S.B. Momale (Eds.)
*Kano: Environment, Society and Development*
London & Abuja, Adonis & Abbey Publishers

Israel, A. A. and Sunday O. A. (2009), Infrastructural distribution of healthcare services in Nigeria: An overview Journal of Geography and Regional Planning Vol. 2(5), pp. 104-110, May, 2009 Available online at http://www.academicjournals.org/JGRP ISSN 2070-1845

Lindsey, E., Sheilds, L. and Stajduhar, K. (1999) Creating effective nursing partnerships: relating community development to participatory action research Journal of Advanced Nursing, 29(5), 1238 - 1245.

Maiwada, A.D. (2000) *Disappearing open spaces in Kano metropolis.* Proceedings of the national Workshop on land administration and development in northern Nigeria, Department of Geography Bayero University Kano, Nigeria

NSHDP (2009) National Strategic Health Development Plan Framework (2009- 2015) TWG-NSHDP/ HEALTH SECTOR DEVELOPMENT TEAM

Public Health Agency of Canada (2011), *About Primary Health Care,* Accessed 12 July 2011.

Shoultz, J., and Hatcher, P. (1997) Looking beyond primary care to primary health care: An approach to community-based action. *Nursing Outlook,* 45(1), 23-26

Tanser, F. (2006) Geographical Information Systems (GIS) Innovations for Primary Health Care in Developing Countries innovations / spring 2006 *mitpress.mit.edu/innovations*

Tarlier, D.S., Johnson, J.L. and Whyte, N.B. (2003). Voices from the wilderness: an interpretive study describing the role and practice of outpost nurses. *Canadian Journal of Public Health,* 94(3), 180-184,

WHO (1978), Declaration of Alma-Ata, Adopted at the International Conference on Primary Health Care, Alma-Ata, USSR, 6-12 September 1978

WHO (2000), The World Health Report 2000 Health Systems: Improving performance (Geneva, Switzerland: World Health Organization, 2000).

WHO (2011). "International Conference on Primary Health Care, Alma-Ata: twenty-fifth anniversary". *Report by the Secretariat.* WHO. Retrieved 28 March 2011.

Chapter 24 | Mohammed Ahmed, in
A.I. Tanko and S.B. Momale (Eds.)
*Kano: Environment, Society and Development*
London & Abuja, Adonis & Abbey Publishers

**385**

Yusuf, I. (2010) Spatial Distribution of Police Stations in Kano Metropolis. An Unpublished B.Sc. Dissertation Submitted to the Department of Geography Bayero University, Kano

Chapter 24 | Mohammed Ahmed, in
A.I. Tanko and S.B. Momale (Eds.)
*Kano: Environment, Society and Development*
London & Abuja, Adonis & Abbey Publishers

**386**

## Appendix 24.1 Distribution of Healthcare Facilities in Kano Metropolis

| S/N | FAGGE  L.G.A. | Type | Ownership |
|---|---|---|---|
| 1 | I.D.HOSPITAL | Secondary | Public |
| 2 | SHEIK M. JIDDA GEN. HOSP. | Secondary | Public |
| 3 | SABO GARBA | Primary | Public |
| 4 | KRODA | Primary | Public |
| 5 | GALADIMAN FAGGE | Primary | Public |
| 6 | KWAJIRI | Primary | Public |
| 7 | ALHASSAN HOSPITAL | Secondary | Public |
|  | **KUMBOTSO   L.G.A.** |  |  |
| 1 | ABDULLAHI WASE | Primary | Public |
| 2 | SHEKAR BARDE | Primary | Public |
| 3 | PANSHEKARA | Primary | Public |
| 4 | MARIRI | Primary | Public |
| 5 | CHALAWA | Primary | Public |
| 6 | GURIN GAWA | Primary | Public |
| 7 | D/MALIKI | Primary | Public |
| 8 | ZAWACHIKI | Primary | Public |
| 9 | LIMAWA | Primary | Public |
| 10 | JA'OJI | Primary | Public |
| 11 | RINKUSAWA | Primary | Public |
| 12 | RIGA FADA | Primary | Public |
| 13 | SHEKAR MADAKI | Primary | Public |
| 14 | DANBARE | Primary | Public |
| 15 | U/RIMI | Primary | Public |
| 16 | ZARA | Primary | Public |
| 17 | MAI KALWA | Primary | Public |
| 18 | WAILARE | Primary | Public |
| 19 | NAIBAWA | Primary | Public |
| 20 | BAICI | Primary | Public |

Chapter 24 | Mohammed Ahmed, in
A.I. Tanko and S.B. Momale (Eds.)
*Kano: Environment, Society and Development*
London & Abuja, Adonis & Abbey Publishers

| S/N | FAGGE L.G.A. | Type | Ownership |
|---|---|---|---|
| | **MUNICIPAL L.G.A.** | | |
| 1 | M.M.S. HOSPITAL | Secondary | Public |
| 2 | HASIYA BAYERO PED. HOSP | Secondary | Public |
| 3 | NAGARTA SP. HOSPITAL | Secondary | Private |
| 4 | BAMALLI NUHU | Primary | Public |
| 5 | MARMARA | Primary | Public |
| 6 | YAN-AWAKI | Primary | Public |
| 7 | SHARADA | Primary | Public |
| 8 | F/GABAS | Primary | Public |
| 9 | EMIR PALACE | Primary | Public |
| 10 | F/KUDU | Primary | Public |
| 11 | MAYANKA | Primary | Public |
| 12 | KWALLI | Primary | Public |
| | **NASSARAWA L.G.A.** | | |
| 1 | M.A. WASE SPEC. HOSP. | Secondary | Public |
| 2 | SIR. M.S. GEN. HOSPITAL | Secondary | Public |
| 3 | IDEAL HOSPITAL | Secondary | Private |
| 4 | CATHERINE HOSPITAL | Secondary | Private |
| 5 | PARK HOUSE | Secondary | Private |
| 6 | ODUMMMA ESTATE HOSP. | Secondary | Private |
| 7 | MAIMUNA ALLAH RAYA HOS | Secondary | Private |
| 8 | GAMJI HOSPITAL | Secondary | Private |
| 9 | UNITY HOSPITAL | Secondary | Private |
| 10 | ANNURI HOSPITAL | Secondary | Private |
| 11 | WARSHU HOSPITAL | Secondary | Private |
| 12 | ECWCA EYE HOSPITAL | Secondary | Private |
| 13 | LAFIA SURGERY HOSPITAL | Secondary | Private |
| 14 | AHMADIYYA HOSPITAL | Secondary | Private |

Chapter 24 | Mohammed Ahmed, in
A.I. Tanko and S.B. Momale (Eds.)
*Kano: Environment, Society and Development*
London & Abuja, Adonis & Abbey Publishers

| S/N | FAGGE  L.G.A. | Type | Ownership |
|---|---|---|---|
| 15 | GWAGWARWA  FAMILY CLINIC | Primary | Public |
| 18 | T/WADA | Primary | Public |
| 19 | SCHOOL CLINIC | Primary | Public |
| 20 | GWAGWARWA MATERNITY | Primary | Public |
| 21 | KAWAJI | Primary | Public |
| 22 | BADAWA | Primary | Public |
| 23 | TORANKE | Primary | Public |
| 24 | GAMA | Primary | Public |
| 25 | T/MURTALA | Primary | Public |
| 26 | AMINU KANO TECH. HOSP. | Tertiary | Public |
| 27 | ALMU HOSPITAL | Secondary | Private |
| 28 | JAOJI | Primary | Public |
| 29 | UNGUWA UKU | Primary | Public |
| 30 | KUNDILA | Primary | Public |
| 31 | TARAUNI | Primary | Public |
| 32 | DARMANAWA | Primary | Public |
| | **UNGOGO      L.G.A.** | | |
| 1 | YADAKUNYA LEP. HOSP. | Secondary | Public |
| 2 | UNGOGO | Primary | Public |
| 3 | KADAWA | Primary | Public |
| 4 | RIJIYAR ZAKI | Primary | Public |
| 5 | BACHIRAWA | Primary | Public |
| 6 | RIMIN KEBE | Primary | Public |
| 7 | GAYAWA | Primary | Public |
| 8 | FANISAU | Primary | Public |
| 9 | Z/BAREBARI | Primary | Public |
| 10 | D/RIMI | Primary | Public |
| 11 | BACHIRAWA | Primary | Public |
| | **GWALE   L.G.A.** | | |

Chapter 24    Mohammed Ahmed, in
A.I. Tanko and S.B. Momale (Eds.)
*Kano: Environment, Society and Development*
London & Abuja, Adonis & Abbey Publishers

| S/N | FAGGE  L.G.A. | Type | Ownership |
|---|---|---|---|
| 1 | MARHABA SPEC. HOSP. | Primary | Private |
| 2 | F/YAMMA | Primary | Public |
| 3 | AISAMI | Primary | Public |
| 4 | K/NA'ISA | Primary | Public |
| 5 | FILIN MUSHE | Primary | Public |
| 6 | K/KABUGA | Primary | Public |
| 7 | K/DUKAWUYA | Primary | Public |
| 8 | DORAYI | Primary | Public |
|  | **DALA   L.G.A.** |  |  |
| 1 | ORTHOPEADIC HOSPITAL | Tertiary | Public |
| 2 | PSYCHAIATRIC HOSPITAL | Secondary | Public |
| 3 | S/BAKIN ZUWO MATERNITY | Secondary | Public |
| 4 | KURNA | Primary | Public |
| 5 | F/AREWA | Primary | Public |
| 6 | YALWA | Primary | Public |
| 7 | DALA | Primary | Public |
| 8 | SANI MAI NAGGE | Primary | Public |
| 9 | DORAYI | Primary | Public |
| 10 | UNGUWAR DABAI | Primary | Public |
| 11 | KABUGA | Primary | Public |
|  | **TARAUNI   L.G.A.** |  |  |
| 1 | AMINU KANO TECH. HOSP. | Tertiary | Public |
| 2 | ALMU HOSPITAL | Secondary | Private |
| 3 | JAOJI | Primary | Public |
| 4 | UNGUWA UKU | Primary | Public |
| 5 | KUNDILA | Primary | Public |
| 6 | TARAUNI | Primary | Public |
| 7 | DARMANAWA | Primary | Public |

Chapter 24 | Mohammed Ahmed, in
A.I. Tanko and S.B. Momale (Eds.)
*Kano: Environment, Society and Development*
London & Abuja, Adonis & Abbey Publishers

# Chapter Twenty Five

## HUMAN EXCRETA MANAGEMENT IN THE METROPOLIS

Oyelawo Abike Adekiya

### Introduction

Human excreta and the lack of adequate personal and domestic hygiene have been implicated in the transmission of many infectious diseases including cholera, typhoid, hepatitis, polio, cryptosporidiosis, ascariasis and schistosomiasis (Carr, 2001). Human waste is a highly efficient weapon of mass destruction. Faeces can carry 50 communicable diseases (see table 25.1). Where people have poor or no sanitation, human excrement gets tramped into living environment on feet and carried on fingers into food and drink (George 2012).

The World Health Organization (2000) estimates that 2.2 million people die annually from diarrheal diseases, and that high proportion of the population in the developing world are severely infected with intestinal worms related to improper waste and excreta management (WHO 2000). Human excreta transmitted diseases predominantly affects children under five than AIDS, tuberculosis or malaria. In graphic terms diarrhoea's death too is equivalent to two jumbo jets, full of children dying every four hours or one child every 15 seconds (George 2010).

The diarrheal prevalence rate in Nigeria is 18.8% and is one of the worst in Sub-Saharan Africa, above the average of 16%. An estimated 150,000 deaths mainly in children under five occur annually due to diarrhoea (UNICEF Nigeria 2009). Cholera infection has also continued to plague many Nigerian communities. From a low incidence rate in 2.02 in 1999 to 19.02 in 2002 (841.586 increase). Typhoid and paratyphoid cases have risen from a reported incidence rate of 22.38 in 1994 to 77.48 in 2002 (Federal Ministry of Water Resources, 2007).

The Nigerian government have drawn up numerous programmes and policies on sanitation, which encompasses a wide range of challenges including excreta disposal, hygiene, solid waste disposal

Chapter 25 | Oyelawo A. Adekiya, in
A.I. Tanko and S.B. Momale (Eds.)
*Kano: Environment, Society and Development*
London & Abuja, Adonis & Abbey Publishers

and drainage. Sanitation is a key input for poverty alleviation and is thus a priority within National Economic Empowerment Development Strategy 2 (NEEDS 2). Sanitation programmes in Nigeria is guided by the Federal Ministry of Agriculture and Water Resources and the Federal Ministry of Housing and Urban Development. The Federal Ministries with important agenda on sanitation include the ministries of Health and Education Programmes are implemented by the State Government Ministries and agencies, Local Government Areas, Communities and Civil Society Organization. The European Commission, United Nations Children's Fund, British Government Department for International Development, Water Aid and Unilever are supporting major sanitation programmes in the country (UNICEF Nigeria 2009).

Chapter 25 | Oyelawo A. Adekiya, in
A.I. Tanko and S.B. Momale (Eds.)
*Kano: Environment, Society and Development*
London & Abuja, Adonis & Abbey Publishers

**Table 25.1: Environmental Classification of Excreta related infections**

| Category | Infection | Pathogenic Agent | Dominant transmission mechanisms | Major control measures |
|---|---|---|---|---|
| I. Faecal-oral (non-bacterial) Non-latent. Low infectious dose | Poliomyelitis<br>Hepatitis A<br>Rotavirus diarrhea<br>Amoebic dysentery<br>Giardiasis<br>Balantidiasis<br>Enterobiasis<br>Hymenolepiasis | V<br>V<br>V<br>P<br>P<br>P<br>H<br>H | Person to person contact Domestic contamination | Domestic water supply improved housing Provision of toilets Health education |
| II. Faecal-oral (bacterial) Non-latent. Medium or high Infectious dose. Moderately persistent And able to multiply | Diarrheas and dysenteries<br>Campylobacter enteritis<br>Cholera<br>E.coli diarrhea<br>Salmonellosis<br>Shigellosis<br>Enteric fevers<br>Typhoid<br>Paratyphoid | <br><br>B<br>B<br>B<br>B<br>B<br>B<br>B | Person to person contact Domestic contamination Water contamination Crop contamination | Domestic water supply Improved housing Provision of toilets Excreta treatment prior to re-use or discharge Health Education |
| III. Soil Transmitted Helminthes Latent and persistent with no intermediate host. | Ascariasis (roundworm)<br>Trichuriasis (whipworm)<br>Hookworm<br>Strongyloidiasis | H<br>H<br>H<br>H | Yard contamination Ground contamination in Communal defecation area Crop contamination | Provision of toilets with clean floors Excreta treatment prior to land application |
| IV. Beef and pork tapeworms Latent and persistent with cow or pig intermediate host | Taeniasis | H | Yard contamination Field contamination Fodder contamination | Provision of toilets Excreta treatment prior to land application Cooking and meat inspection |
| V. Water-based helminiths Latent and persistent with aquatic intermediate host(s) | Schistosomiasis<br>Clonorchiasis<br>Diphyllobothriasis<br>Fasciolopsiasis<br>Paragonimiasis | H<br>H<br>H<br>H<br>H | Water contamination | Provision of toilets Excreta treatment prior to discharge Control of animals harbouring infection Cooking |
| VI. Excreta-related insect | Filariasis (transmitted by Culex pipiens mosquitoes) Infections in categories I-V, especially I and II which may be transmitted by files and cockroaches | H<br><br><br>M | Insects breed in various faecally contaminated sites | Identification and elimination of potential breeding sites Use of mosquito netting |

B = Bacterium     V = Virus
H = Helminth     M = Miscellaneous
P = Protozoon
*Source: Cairn Cross & Feachem (1993)*

Despite all these programmes, sanitation in Nigeria currently is not on the tract to meet the millennium Development Goal target of 70

Chapter 25 | Oyelawo A. Adekiya, in
A.I. Tanko and S.B. Momale (Eds.)
*Kano: Environment, Society and Development*
London & Abuja, Adonis & Abbey Publishers

percent access to safe sanitation, by the year 2015 (Federal Ministry of Agriculture and Water Resources, 2007).

This Chapter examines the practice of excreta disposal and personal hygiene among residents in two residential districts in Kano Metropolis. This is because for maximum health protection, it is important to treat and contain human excreta as close to the source as possible before it gets introduced into the environment. Numerous studies have shown that the incidence of many diseases is reduced when people have access to and make regular use of effective basic sanity installation (Carr, 2001). Sanitation was voted the best medical advance since 1840 over antibiotics and vaccines (George, 2010).

## Study Population

Kano Metropolis is the most industrial and commercial city in northern Nigeria. This study was carried out in two, high density residential districts within the Metropolis. The two districts are:

District I - Kano Municipal Council, this district is located within the old city. The major ethnic groups within this area are the Hausa/Fulani.

District II - Sabon Gari residential area is located outside the old city wall. The British Colonial Authority established the area in the 1930s to cater for migrants from southern Nigeria. The different ethnic groups found within this area include Igbos, Yorubas, Nupes, Tivs, and Edos among others.

In the Kano Municipal Council (KMC), ten wards namely Kofar Mata, Kurawa, Zango, Dambazau, Sheshe, Zango, Jujin 'Yan Labbo, Yakasai and Shahuchi were sampled. In Sabon Gari, ten streets namely Church Road, Niger Road, Aitken Road, Onisha Road, Abeokuta Road, Enugu Road, Court Road, Yoruba Road, New Road and Ilaro Road were studied. The survey sampled 20 households in each of the wards or streets within the residential districts. Sampling was done through random selection.

Questionnaire administration, in-depth interview and visual observation were used to obtain data. The questionnaire and in-depth interview were directed to women in each household. This is because culturally in Nigeria, women are saddle with the responsibility of caring for the family and cleaning of the house. The results of the

| Chapter 25 | Oyelawo A. Adekiya, in |
|---|---|
| | A.I. Tanko and S.B. Momale (Eds.) |
| | *Kano: Environment, Society and Development* |
| | London & Abuja, Adonis & Abbey Publishers |

investigations relating to the characteristics of the respondents, the personal hygiene and excreta disposal practices and the knowledge of respondents on the relationship between poor excreta disposal and diarrheal disease is presented in Tables 25.2; 25.3 and 25.4 respectively.

**Table 25.2: Socio-Economic Characteristics of Respondents**

| Educational Status | Kano Municipal Council | | Sabon Gari | |
|---|---|---|---|---|
| | Frequency | Percentage | Frequency | Percentage |
| Primary | 56 | 28 | 36 | 18 |
| Secondary | 49 | 24.5 | 119 | 59.5 |
| Tertiary | 24 | 12 | 45 | 22.5 |
| Arabic/Islamic | 71 | 35.5 | - | - |
| TOTAL | 200 | 100 | 200 | 100 |

**Table 25.3: Personal Hygiene and Excreta Disposal: Practice among Respondents**

| | Kano Municipal Council | | Sabon Gari | |
|---|---|---|---|---|
| | Frequency | Percentage | Frequency | Percentage |
| 1. Number of family per housing unit | | | | |
| 1 – 2 | | | | |
| 3 – 4 | 151 | 75.5 | - | - |
| 5 – 6 | 33 | 16.5 | 14 | 7 |
| 7 + | 16 | 8 | 50 | 25 |
| | - | | 136 | 68 |
| | 200 | 100 | 200 | 100 |
| 2. Source of water pipe-borne water | | | | |
| Borehole/hard pump vendor truck | 47 | 23.5 | - | - |
| | 45 | 22.5 | 80 | 40 |
| | 108 | 54.9 | 120 | 60 |
| | 200 | 100 | 200 | 100 |
| 3. Shared Toilet | | | | |
| Yes | 167 | 83.5 | 146 | 73 |
| No | 33 | 16.5 | 54 | 27 |
| | 200 | 100 | 200 | 100 |
| 4. Type of Toilet unfloored pit | | | | |
| Floored pit | 102 | 51 | 70 | 35 |
| Water system | 88 | 44 | 61 | 30.5 |
| Wrap and throw in drainage channels | 10 | 5 | 14 | 7 |
| | | | 55 | 27.5 |
| | 200 | 100 | 200 | 100 |
| 5. Toilet with Fly proof care | | | | |
| Yes | | | | |
| No | 48 | 24 | 39 | 19.5 |
| | 152 | 76 | 161 | 80.5 |
| | 200 | 100 | 200 | 100 |
| 6. Washing of hands after toilet usage | | | | |
| Yes | | | | |
| No | 200 | 100 | 200 | 100 |
| | - | - | - | - |
| | 200 | 100 | 200 | 100 |
| 7. Method of hand washing after toilet usage | | | | |
| Water only | | | | |
| Water and soap | | | | |
| Water and ash | 118 | 59 | 124 | 62 |
| | 20 | 10 | 76 | 38 |
| | 62 | 31 | - | |
| | 200 | 100 | 200 | 100 |

Chapter 25 | Oyelawo A. Adekiya, in
A.I. Tanko and S.B. Momale (Eds.)
*Kano: Environment, Society and Development*
London & Abuja, Adonis & Abbey Publishers

| | Kano Municipal Council | | Sabon Gari | |
|---|---|---|---|---|
| | Frequency | Percentage | Frequency | Percentage |
| 8. Frequency of cleaning daily | | | | |
| Twice a week | | | | |
| Once a week | 23 | 11.5 | 45 | 22.5 |
| Anytime/occasional | 69 | 34.5 | 56 | 28 |
| | 108 | 54 | 99 | 49.5 |
| | 200 | 100 | 200 | 100 |
| 9. Method of cleaning | | | | |
| Washing with water only | 30 | 15 | 54 | 27 |
| Washing with water and soap | 39 | 19.5 | 36 | 18 |
| Washing with water, soap and antiseptic | 27 | 13.5 | 18 | 09 |
| sweeping only | 104 | 52.0 | 92 | 46 |
| | 200 | 100 | 200 | 100 |
| 10. Condition of toilet | | | | |
| Poor | 132 | 66 | 114 | 57 |
| Fair | 42 | 21 | 28 | 14 |
| Good | 26 | 13 | 58 | 29 |
| | 200 | 100 | 200 | 100 |
| 11. Persons responsible for cleaning the toilet | | | | |
| Self (women) | 46 | 23 | 100 | 50 |
| Children | 24 | 12 | 54 | 27 |
| Paid labourers | 130 | 65 | 36 | 18 |
| Men | | - | 10 | 5 |
| | 200 | 100 | 200 | 100 |

**Table 25.4: Knowledge of Respondents on the Relationship between poor excreta disposal and diarrheal disease**

| | Kano Municipal Council | | Sabon Gari | |
|---|---|---|---|---|
| | Frequency | Percentage | Frequency | Percentage |
| Have you any number of your family had an upside of diarrhoea disease within the last Cement us | | | | |
| Yes | 200 | 100 | 200 | 100 |
| No | - | - | - | - |
| | 200 | 100 | 200 | 100 |
| Do you know that poor excreta disposal have a relationship with spread of diarrheal diseases | | | | |
| Yes | 190 | 95 | 200 | 100 |
| No | 10 | 5 | - | - |
| | 200 | 100 | 200 | 100 |
| Do you think improvement in excreta disposal will decrease the rate diarrhoea infection | | | | |
| Yes | 156 | 78 | 170 | 85 |
| No | 44 | 22 | 30 | 15 |
| | 200 | 100 | 200 | 100 |
| Do you know whether your children always washes their hands after using the toilet | | | | |
| Yes | 69 | 34.5 | 80 | 85 |
| No | 131 | 65.5 | 120 | 15 |
| | 200 | 100 | 200 | 100 |

Chapter 25 | Oyelawo A. Adekiya, in
A.I. Tanko and S.B. Momale (Eds.)
*Kano: Environment, Society and Development*
London & Abuja, Adonis & Abbey Publishers

# Results

From Table 25.2, over 60% of the respondents in Kano Municipal Council (KMC) have either Islamic education or only primary education. In Sabon Gari residential area 82% of the respondents finished from either the secondary or tertiary institution. Seventy three percent of the women in KMC are unemployed that means they are housewives and they stay home most of the times. However in Sabon Gari area, only 10% are housewives, 90% of the women are trading or employed in private and public sectors.

Information presented in Table 25.3, shows that the number of families residing in a housing unit is higher in Sabon Gari than in the KMC. In Sabon Gari 68% of housing units have more than seven families residing in them. In KMC however 76% of housing units have between 1 - 2 families residing in them. The sources of water in the two residential districts are mainly through vendor truck, 60% in Sabon Gari and 54% in KMC. In the two residential districts shared toilets among different families are very common, 84% in KMC and 73% in Sabon Gari. Un-floored pit toilet is the most common type of field in the two residential areas (51% in KMC and 35% in Sabon Gari). Twenty seven percent of respondents in Sabon Gari practice the wrap and throw method, here because of poor condition of toilets; residents defecate inside a nylon bag and then threw it inside the drainage channel behind the house or inside the pit latrine. Over 70% of the toilets in the two residential areas do not have a fly proof cover. The condition of toilets in the two areas are poor are very dirty (66% and 57% in KMC and Sabon Gari respectively). All the sampled women in the two residential areas agreed that they wash their hands after the use of the toilet. However over 58% of the women wash their hands with only water. Frequency of toilet cleaning in the two residential districts is poor, 54% and 49% in KMC and Sabon Gari districts clean their toilets occasionally. Method of cleaning of the toilet is mainly by sweeping, 52% and 46% in KMC and Sabon Gari respectively. In KMC, paid labourers (65%) are responsible for cleaning in toilet. However in Sabon Gari, 50% of the respondents (women) are responsible for cleaning the toilet.

From Table 25.4, all the women (100%) agreed that either they or member of their family have had an episode of diarrhoea disease in the

Chapter 25 | Oyelawo A. Adekiya, in
A.I. Tanko and S.B. Momale (Eds.)
*Kano: Environment, Society and Development*
London & Abuja, Adonis & Abbey Publishers

last 6 months. Over 90% of the respondents in the two areas also have the knowledge on the positive relationship between poor excreta disposal and spread of diarrheal disease. Over 70% of the women in the two residential areas are also of the view that improvement in excreta disposal will decrease the rate of diarrheal infection. Over sixty percent of residents (mothers) however agree that their children do not always wash their hands after the use of the toilet.

## *Water and Sanitation*

Despite the fact that access to an adequate water supply and sanitation is a fundamental and indeed arguably a right for all people (WHO 200), in Table 24.2 half of the people sampled do not have access to adequate water supply, rather they rely on water vendors. Increasing urbanization and concentration of poor in urban slums which is manifested in a number of families residing in a housing unit (see Table 24.3 especially in Sabon Gari) and a number of families sharing toilets is likely to be associated (in many cases) with higher risk of transmission of diarrhoea, thus posing much greater sanitation challenges (Carr, 2001).

Sanitation, as noted by George (2010) is a bargain. Every Naira invested in sanitation reaps an eight fold return because people will spend less on health costs and miss fewer days at work. In a 2008 Report, the World Bank calculated that poor sanitation cost Cambodia, Indonesia, the Philippines and Vietnam 1.3 - 7.2 percent of the gross domestic product (George 2010). As a disease - prevention mechanism sanitation is hard to beat, in either effectiveness or price. The treatment of lower acute respiratory illness in children under-fiver costs as much as US$ 264 per DALY (disability) - adjusted life year a standard health prevention unit of calculation). Sanitation cost $11 hygiene promotion cost $3 (George 2010).

Cairncross and Richard (1993) gave seven reasons why sanitation has to be marketed. These scholars noted that sanitation requires a different approach from conventional civil engineering. The seven reasons are as follows:

i)   Health improvement in general does not motivate many people to buy latrines, because the connection between latrine usage

Chapter 25 | Oyelawo A. Adekiya, in
A.I. Tanko and S.B. Momale (Eds.)
*Kano: Environment, Society and Development*
London & Abuja, Adonis & Abbey Publishers

and health is not clearly perceived. The desire for privacy, convenience or social status is usually more effective in generating demand.

ii) The cost is not a function of the design criteria. Rather the design criteria should depend on the price purchasers are willing to pay, while some programmes have offered latrines at heavily subsidized prices, most of these have reached only a tiny percentage of the target population.

iii) A modification to an existing practice or type of latrines is likely to be much easier to implement than a completely new package of technology. Before marketing a new product, it is essential to study what people already do and ask them what they think they need.

iv) The acceptability of the product (the sanitation technology) must be checked at every stage in its development by consulting likely purchasers and by offering prototypes to some of them. It is a good idea to offer a range of models.

v) The marketing operation requires constant monitoring of the consumer's response. Sanitation promotion, including the monitoring is best accomplished through a cadre of staff indirect content with the consumer in the field.

vi) The rate of installation depends on demand, and not on any preconceived project plan. Demand may take a long time to build up, as many people will wait until their neighbours have installed a latrine and found it to perform satisfactorily before they buy one for themselves. The most successful and sustainable programme have been led by consumers demand.

vii) There must be someone to provide "after-sale service" if the technology is not one to be discredited. Without good maintenance, any type of latrine soon become failed and offensive and may become a health hazard in itself.

## Policy Issues and Recommendation

Excreta disposal and personal hygiene practice in the two residential areas are poor, reflecting the condition that exists in Metropolitan Kano and other urban settlements of the Region. Over 70% of families in the two districts use shared toilets. Over 60% of the household use

Chapter 25 | Oyelawo A. Adekiya, in
A.I. Tanko and S.B. Momale (Eds.)
*Kano: Environment, Society and Development*
London & Abuja, Adonis & Abbey Publishers

**399**

latrines that are very poor and are not properly. The problem of excreta disposal is clearly as old as mankind itself and the need for careful disposal is highlighted in a number of religious books including Hindu, Islamic and Christian texts (Carr, 2001). A number of recommendations on effective human waste management in Kano Metropolis are suggested below:

**a.** Public awareness and enlightenment programmes on sanitary practices in dealing with human waste are to be carried out by the Federal and State Ministries of Health, Environment, Agriculture and Water Resources and Housing and Urban Development in print and electronic media. These programmes must be a continuous one. As Jack Sim, the founder of the World Toilet Organization noted the world can talk about eating (which he calls uploading) so it should be able to talk about downloading (George 2010);

**b.** Women that are saddled with the responsibilities of caring for the home need to be effectively involved in all sanitation programme (in design and selection of domestic facilities, environmental education programmes etc). Research conducted by Neto and Tropp (2000) in Southern Asia demonstrated that involving women in sanitation programmes has resulted in higher coverage, better maintenance of facilities, increased hygiene awareness and lower incidence of faecal-oral disease in the community.

**c.** The government is to compel landlords to provide adequate toilet facilities in houses meant for rentage. Shared toilets by different families are to be discouraged in the urban centre. A toilet per household with family size of at least 6 should be encouraged (i.e. 1 toilet per 6 persons, 2 toilets per 12 persons etc).

For the fact that Nigeria is yet to meet the MDG target of 70% access to safe sanitation by the year 2015, the following excreta disposal without water carriage or the ones that make use of little water are to be encouraged for the low income socio-economic classes.

Chapter 25 | Oyelawo A. Adekiya, in
A.I. Tanko and S.B. Momale (Eds.)
*Kano: Environment, Society and Development*
London & Abuja, Adonis & Abbey Publishers

## I.   *Ventilated Sand Plat Pit Latrine*

This is a slight modification to the conventional pit latrine. In the case of the ventilated san plat pit latrine, there is a provision of a vent (see fig 25.1) which makes it odour and fly free (if properly constructed). The latrine should also have a ceiling and screen window to keep out reptiles and rodents. The vent pipe should be at least 15cm in diameter and preferably higher than the latrine roof top. A screen should cover the top end of the vent pipe. This type of latrine is suitable for sites where the soil is self supporting (e.g. laterite soils).

## II.   *Ventilated Improved Pit Latrine (VIP Latrines)*

The VIP latrine is just like the ventilated san plat latrine but the pit is improved by lining it completely with concreted blocks, bricks or stone, to eliminate the risk of the pit side carving in.

## III.   *Offset Pit Latrine (Reid Odourless Earth Closet or ROEC Latrine)*

The offset pit latrine is different from the latrines discussed above, because the pit is not directly below the squatting slab, thus the users do not see the excreta. An added advantage is that the pit can also be emptied without disturbing the squatting slab.

## IV.   *Pour-Flush Latrine*

The pour-flash latrine is the conventional pit latrine, but the squatting slab carries a water seal bowl through which the excreta falls directly into the pit below, when as little as a litre of water is poured into the bowl to flash away the excreta. The water seal makes the latrine odour and fly free. The pit may be lined to preventing the wall caving in. A small quantity of water for flashing trust be provided. This latrine is very suitable if anal cleaning is done with water. The use of solid materials such as

---

Chapter 25 | Oyelawo A. Adekiya, in
A.I. Tanko and S.B. Momale (Eds.)
*Kano: Environment, Society and Development*
London & Abuja, Adonis & Abbey Publishers

**401**

corncobs, newspaper, leaves etc should be avoided to prevent blockage.

## V.  *Pour Flash Offset Latrines*

The pour flash offset latrine is like the conventional pour flash except that the pit is offset from the squatting slab which carries the water seal device. A sewer (pipe) is provided to connect the water seal bowl to the pit outside. Usually a vent is provided to enable the gases produced to escape. The pit can be duplicated so that when one is tiled, the other can be put in use. This makes the latrine permanent since the two pits can be used and destroyed alternatively.

## References

Adequate, Grace Olubukunmi (2001) Water Supply Environmental Hygiene and Health. A paper prepared for the 28th International Faith and Learning Seminar held at Babcock University Ilishan-Remo, Ogun State June 17 - 29 2001.

Carr, Richard (2001) Excreta - related infections and the role of Sanitation in the control of transmission in WHO (2001) *Water Quantity Guidelines, Standards and Health*, edited by Loma Fewtrell and Jamie Bertram, published by IWA Publishing London UK ISBN: 1900222280.

Federal Ministry of Agriculture and Water Resources (2007) *Strategy for Scaling up Rural Sanitation & Hygiene to meet M. Hennium Development Goal* Final Report, Federal Government of Nigeria, Abuja

George, Rose (2001) Nowhere to go: *The Rotation*, January 2010.

Neto, F. and Tropp, H. (2000) Water supply and Sanitation Services for all: global progress during the 1990s *Natural Resources Forum*, 24, 225-235.

UNICEF Nigeria (2009), Sanitation Fact Sheet Nigeria, UNICEF New York

WHO (2001) *Global Water Supply and Sanitation Assessment*, World Health Organization, Geneva.

Chapter 25 | Oyelawo A. Adekiya, in
A.I. Tanko and S.B. Momale (Eds.)
*Kano: Environment, Society and Development*
London & Abuja, Adonis & Abbey Publishers

Cairncross, S. and F. Richard, (1995) *Environmental Health Engineering in the Tropics: An Introductory Text*, Second Edition Wiley publishers.

Chapter 25 | Oyelawo A. Adekiya, in
A.I. Tanko and S.B. Momale (Eds.)
*Kano: Environment, Society and Development*
London & Abuja, Adonis & Abbey Publishers

**403**

# Chapter Twenty Six

## URBAN PRESSURE AND TREE COVER CHANGE

Roy Maconachie

## Introduction

Inextricably linked to the concept of land degradation, and the central focus of this Chapter, is the notion of vegetation loss. Although the protection of vegetation and the incorporation of useful trees into production systems has for centuries been an important part of livelihood strategies in the Kano Closed-Settled Zone (CSZ) (Mortimore and Adams, 1999), current discussions with a wide range of actors across the research transect, reveal that there is presently considerable concern for a perceived decrease in many tree species. If local perceptions of environmental change are, in fact, representative of what is actually being played out on the landscape, such a reduction in vegetation cover could have a significant impact on livelihoods in the CSZ, since a broad range of plants, grasses and tree products are reported as being vital resources in the household economy. Moreover, the vast majority of households interviewed in this study also demonstrated awareness that changes in vegetation cover had critical implications for the sustainability of other environmental resources, such as soil and water. Since there appears to be much interlinkage between the various types and manifestations of land degradation, local assessments of vegetative change may provide a useful indicator for assessments of other biotic resources as well. As Stocking and Murnaghan (2001: 7) point out, 'a reduction in vegetation cover through deforestation will almost always be accompanied by soil erosion, sedimentation of lower slopes and increased surface runoff'.

Although vegetation changes have always been apparent in the West African drylands, in recent decades growing numbers of researchers have noted that human activity is increasingly playing a major role in causing them (LeHouérou, 1997). The discussion in this Chapter contributes to the debate by exploring how local actors in the

Chapter 26 | Roy Maconachie, in
A.I. Tanko and S.B. Momale (Eds.)
*Kano: Environment, Society and Development*
London & Abuja, Adonis & Abbey Publishers

Kano CSZ currently *perceive* the relationship between people and woodland resources. More specifically, an attempt is made to elucidate the relationship between these perceptions and the issue of land degradation, taking into account some of the recent pressures that are associated with urban expansion. For the purpose of this Chapter, the analysis focuses on the 'degradation' of vegetation resources, rather than the more encompassing process of 'deforestation'. While 'deforestation' is broadly a term that is used to convey the total clearance of forest land for agriculture or other purposes, the concept of 'woodland degradation' is used to convey lesser anthropogenic changes in tree cover that do not imply a total clearance (Grainger, 1999: 179). The discussion is constructed around evidence obtained from the following three main sources:

    a.   Ninety household questionnaires administered at six study sites across a distance-decay research transect in urban and peri-urban Kano (see Figure 26.1);

    b.   Thirty focus group discussions, carried out with five different actor groups at each of the six sites;

    c.   One hundred questionnaire surveys designed to explore peri-urban energy consumption patterns, administered at Hotoro Arewa and Zangon Gabas, the two most peri-urban sites[4]

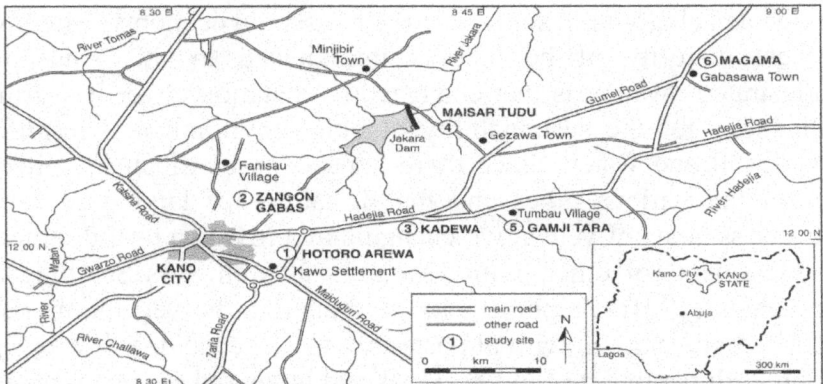

**Figure 26.1: Study Sites in the Kano Close-Settled Zone**

---

[4] The questionnaire survey initially administered in ninety households across the research transect, identified a number of issues concerning peri-urban fuelwood use which required further investigation. Accordingly, to shed light on some of these issues, an additional survey was designed and administered at one hundred households in Hotoro Arewa and Zangon Gabas, the two most peri-urban sites.

| Chapter 26 | Roy Maconachie, in |
| | A.I. Tanko and S.B. Momale (Eds.) |
| | *Kano: Environment, Society and Development* |
| | London & Abuja, Adonis & Abbey Publishers |

**406**

Local perceptions of land and society remain important considerations in any study of land degradation, since local actors base their land management decisions on how they *perceive* the environment, not necessarily on how it is in real terms. While this Chapter does not attempt to quantify changes in tree cover *per se*, or even to claim that overall tree cover is declining in real terms, it does offer an important insight into local perceptions of vegetation change. More specifically, the discussion reveals that perceptions vary considerably between actor groups, both temporally and spatially over the transect. This not only appears to affect the way that different social actors understand their environment, but it may also play a role in conditioning their differential behaviour within their surroundings. Thus, as new pressures on environment and society continue to 'ratchet up' stress in the Kano CSZ, livelihood patterns continue to adapt, and natural resources begin to take on new meanings for different individuals. As Warren (2002: 457) points out, new social arrangements, such as community-based management systems, also become more challenging, since they may be associated with radically different appraisals of the resource base and of its degradation. Ultimately, it would therefore seem that an appreciation of the dynamic and variable perceptions that local people hold of the vegetation base must be a central consideration in formulating meaningful environmental policies that include the livelihood needs of all social actors, and have a realistic chance of success.

In this study, it is worth noting that at some sites, the issue of woodland degradation was not perceived to be a serious problem, while at other localities, it was recognised as being much more of a threat to the environment and the sustainability of livelihoods. Similar observations concerning the changing localised contours of vegetation cover were revealed by Boerma (1999) in her long-term historical study into deforestation in the central highlands of Eritrea since 1890. Perhaps much like the pattern of vegetation change in Kano's CSZ, she concluded that change in tree cover is not a uniform or unilinear process, but rather 'a kaleidoscope of different processes both in time and space, with both loss and gain in tree cover being experienced at different points in…recent history' (1999: i). As such, it may well be the reality that in the Kano CSZ, there are 'pockets' of pressure where stress on the vegetation resource base is particularly great at any one point in time. If this is the case, it would be clearly unwise to

Chapter 26 | Roy Maconachie, in
A.I. Tanko and S.B. Momale (Eds.)
*Kano: Environment, Society and Development*
London & Abuja, Adonis & Abbey Publishers

**407**

extrapolate these localised incidents of change in woody cover to include the entire CSZ. Such a deduction would almost certainly paint an unrepresentative picture of the present situation concerning vegetation cover, and would undoubtedly contribute to reinforcing many of the 'deforestation myths' that have been so apparent in the past.

Related to this observation, and reflecting the importance of specific species of trees and grasses to livelihood portfolios in the Kano CSZ, local actors identified certain vegetation resources that were increasingly perceived to be under threat, but suggested that other species had not suffered a decline in prevalence. At this micro-level, it appeared that there were some very situation-specific trends in the observations that emerged, and understandably, local actors demonstrated a detailed knowledge in the vegetation species that had a direct bearing on their livelihoods. However, the translation of these observations from individual situations to wider perspectives should again be processed with an air of caution. Of vital importance, the issue of scale - both temporal and spatial - comes into play, particularly in research that explores the sustainability of resource management strategies in an unstable and fluctuating environment, such as that of the Kano CSZ. As Sullivan (1999) wisely comments:

> Clearly, information derived at the small-scale and in the short-term needs to be situated within an understanding of the range of dynamics that a system may display under different spatial and temporal conditions before degradation labels, and the attribution of blame associated with these, can be made with any degree of certainty (1999: 272).

As such, in the process of exploring local-level perceptions of vegetation cover in the Kano CSZ, the subsequent discussion in this chapter highlights some of the potential dangers in making degradation assumptions that concern resource use in a small 'sacrificial area' (Perkins and Thomas, 1993) and extrapolating these conclusions to vegetation landscapes over much greater spatial scales (Warren and Agnew, 1988; Dahlberg, 1994). The Chapter begins with a brief exploration of some variable perceptions of vegetation in the Kano CSZ by drawing on 'local knowledge', and highlighting the impressive insight that different actors have of indigenous plants, trees and shrubs. Such attention to local experience and knowledge demonstrates the complex and interacting factors that influence

Chapter 26 | Roy Maconachie, in
A.I. Tanko and S.B. Momale (Eds.)
*Kano: Environment, Society and Development*
London & Abuja, Adonis & Abbey Publishers

individual decisions to manage the vegetation base; it is argued that because people perceive the resource base in very different ways, the notion of land degradation is largely a social construct. The Chapter then goes on to explore more specifically the question of whether or not local actors actually consider woodland degradation to be occurring in the Kano CSZ. In some cases, it is shown that a reduction in the prevalence of certain species does not necessarily equate with a perception of degradation. In the latter half of the Chapter, some of the main forces that local people suggest are currently driving vegetation change are investigated, and the implications that these changes may have on livelihoods and sustainability are then considered.

## *Exploring Local Knowledge*

During the course of discussions with a wide range of actors, it immediately became apparent that local people hold an intricate knowledge of the plants, grasses and trees in their environment, and they are well aware of any vegetation changes that may be occurring. Other studies in West Africa confirm this observation, have demonstrated that local knowledge can be a rich source of information, and have shown that local people often possess a detailed and reliable understanding of vegetation changes (Wezel and Haigis, 2000; Amanor, 1994; Kinlund, 1996). This is perhaps not at all surprising, since for hundreds of years most farmers have recognised the value of many tree species for food, fibre, fodder, medicine, fuel and building materials[5]. Moreover, many edible fruits and leaves become especially important during the dry season, when local people rely on these products to supplement an otherwise poor diet, to feed to livestock, or to sell to generate much needed income. The value attached to such trees and shrubs in the environment has given rise to the typical Kano CSZ landscape, which is often referred to as 'farmed parkland' (Pullan, 1974), and is characterised by a sustainable agro-forestry strategy in which a wide range of tree species are protected and integrated into food production systems. As has also been confirmed in other studies, any degradation of the woody vegetation

---

[5] In an inventory of the major useful trees and plants conducted by Yusuf (1996) in Gamji Tara, local informants reported that there were over 43 useful tree species, more than 20 important domestic shrubs, and over 100 different species of useful annual grasses.

| Chapter 26 | Roy Maconachie, in |
| | A.I. Tanko and S.B. Momale (Eds.) |
| | *Kano: Environment, Society and Development* |
| | London & Abuja, Adonis & Abbey Publishers |

cover in a dryland environment can have a direct and profound impact on the lives of local people (Lykke, *et al.*, 1999).

Local informants spoke eloquently and at length about the many uses of tree products, and it quickly became evident that various tree species are valued differently, depending on their specific usefulness to diverse livelihood portfolios. For example, as one old farmer from Zangon Gabas explained, there are certain farm trees that are more beneficial to integrate into cropping systems than others:

> Some trees are better to have on your plot than others. The *Kuka* is excellent because it doesn't have too many leaves. But the *Tsamiya* has very broad leaves and it will make too much shade on the plot, so it is not as good for the crops. The *Gawo* tree produces fruits that animals love. So under the *Gawo*, you will see lots of animals, and they will drop their *taki* and make the soil rich. When you see the *Marke* tree, you know the land is not rich. The land around this tree becomes very hot and dry, even in the rainy season (Ibrahim, pers. com., 15 March, 2002).

Such an intricate knowledge of trees is, of course, not unique to land managers of the Kano CSZ, and in recent years there has been much interest in the value of indigenous knowledge in livelihood strategies and production systems elsewhere (see Richards, 1985; Chambers *et al.*, 1989; Scoones and Thompson, 1994). For example, in his study of farmers' responses to land degradation in Ghana, Amanor (1994) demonstrates that land managers often value and protect certain trees over others, as some species are believed to contribute more to site productivity. As the above quotation from Zangon Gabas illustrates, this would also appear to be the case in the Kano Region. However, in addition to having a preference for specific trees, discussions with local farmers in Kano also revealed that certain weeds and grasses were considered to be 'good' by land managers and encouraged to grow, while other species were recognised as harmful and were suppressed. According to one respondent from Maisar Tudu:

> If you want a rich plot, there is a kind of grass called *Rai-rai*, which means long life. At all times of the year that grass will remain green, and its presence is a good sign. There are many types of grasses that are good, like *Kiri-kiri*, *Yadiya*, *Dodandawa*, *Tofa*, *Tsidau*, and *Yawo*. If you see these grasses growing, the soil must be strong and fertile (Y. Abdulwahab, pers. com., 20 February, 2002).

Chapter 26 | Roy Maconachie, in
A.I. Tanko and S.B. Momale (Eds.)
*Kano: Environment, Society and Development*
London & Abuja, Adonis & Abbey Publishers

Alternatively, however, other respondents pointed out that there are also certain species of grasses that are considered to be harmful, and in fact serve as a visual indicator of land degradation. In the words of a young farmer from Kadewa:

> But some grasses are bad, like *Komaiya*[6], *Daburun Saniya*, or *Gasaya*. If you see them, it signifies that the place is not good and it is degraded. Also, where there is too much *Gogamasu* it indicates that the land is bad, and crops will not grow well. *Gogamasu* is a kind of grass that has an iritating effect on your skin. If you see *Burruku* and *Duman Rafi* growing, it means that the land is too sandy and not good for crops. Where ever you see those grasses, the land is infertile because those grasses like a cold, waterlogged environment. Under that grass, there is water only a few metres down (Nasiru, pers. com., 05 March 2002).

Thus, it became evident that in discussions concerning the relationship between vegetation and land degradation, it was not merely a loss of vegetation cover that was alarming to local land managers. Rather, many respondents associated a degraded landscape, with specific changes in vegetation species (particularly shrubs and grasses)[7], as well as a perceived decline in the prevalence of many valuable indigenous tree species such as *Dorawa* (*Parkia biglobosa*), *Rimi* (*Ceiba pentandra*) and *Kuka* (*Adansonia digitata*).

Interestingly, those respondents in the study who believed that tree cover was either stable or increasing in Kano's hinterlands, believed this was so because of the large number of exotic species, particularly *neem* trees (*Azadirachta indica*), that had been planted in recent years. The highly valued *neem* tree, a species originally indigenous to India, was first introduced to the Kano region during the Colonial era, and since then has been widely planted throughout the CSZ. Indeed, when international awareness of 'desertification' burgeoned following the 1972-4 Sahelian drought, governments in the northern Nigerian states

---

[6] Many farmers believed that *Komaiya* (*Eragrostis tremula*) was a particularly 'wicked' grass, as is suggested by the well known Hausa proverb, '*Komaiya koma wata*', which roughly translates to: "if there is *Komaiya* growing on your land, it is time to change to a new plot."
[7] In a related observation, Stocking (1996: 145) points out that although the majority of research supports the belief that vegetative cover is one of the most important factors in controlling soil erosion in tropical environments, it is not necessarily the case that vegetation always has a positive influence on the landscape in which it grows. He notes that in a series of laboratory experiments carried out by de Ploey (1981), two troughs of soil - one that was planted with bunch grass and one that was left bare - were exposed to conditions of simulated rainfall. After observing increased sediment loads under the trough planted with grass in comparison to the one that was bare, de Ploey concluded that vegetation was an 'ambivalent factor' in soil conservation strategies.

Chapter 26 | Roy Maconachie, in
A.I. Tanko and S.B. Momale (Eds.)
*Kano: Environment, Society and Development*
London & Abuja, Adonis & Abbey Publishers

became obsessed with shelterbelts and tree-planting schemes. Many of the young trees supplied by government afforestation programmes have been *neem* seedlings, due to their ability to grow quickly and withstand harsh environments.

Although most respondents demonstrated a common belief that trees were generally valuable for farm conservation, many individuals complained that they could not gain access to government seedlings due to their erratic availability, the difficulty of transporting them to their farms, or their high cost. Consequently, in the Kano CSZ, new trees are usually added to farm plots, simply by encouraging coppicing from lopped tree stumps, or by protecting seedlings which germinate naturally, in a process referred to locally as *sassabe*. In Gamji Tara, it was reported that some trees, such as *Dorawa (Parkia biglobosa)*, *Mangwaro (Mangifera indica)*, *Dabino (Phoenix dactylifera)* or *Rimi (Ceiba pentandra)*, needed to be fenced in the dry season in order to protect them from free-grazing livestock (Yusuf, 1996). Farmers also noted that many of the indigenous species of tree saplings, which they had protected around their plots and were encouraging to regenerate, grew very slowly, and it would take a long time before they would reach maturity.

This being the case, some respondents described alternative conservation techniques that they had adopted to compensate for a perceived reduction in trees on their land. Some of the practices mentioned included building low mud walls to slow down soil erosion, referred to as *ganuwa* in Hausa, or planting various indigenous species of grass, such as *Jemma (Urelytrum giganteum)*, *Gamba (Andropogon gayanus)*, *Tsintsiya (Eragrostis sp.)* or *Kiri-kiri (Cynodon dactylon)*, around the boundaries of farm plots. Once again, informants demonstrated a detailed knowledge of many different species of grasses that they believed were useful, and could be integrated into farming systems. It was also apparent that different grasses were used in different situations, depending on the severity of conditions, as is evident in the following statement by one young farmer from Gamji Tara:

> *Jemma* is one of the strongest of the grasses. It has the strongest roots and has the greatest perseverance for withstanding fast currents of water. *Gamba* seems to be one of the weaker grasses, and *Tsintsiya* is somewhere in the middle in terms of strength. *Jemma* can be submerged in water for a

| Chapter 26 | Roy Maconachie, in |
| | A.I. Tanko and S.B. Momale (Eds.) |
| | *Kano: Environment, Society and Development* |
| | London & Abuja, Adonis & Abbey Publishers |

solid month and it won't die. *Kiri-kiri*, or carpet grass, is an interwoven grass that is the strongest of all grasses. It is a flat grass that doesn't grow shoots (Alkasim, pers. com., 27 February, 2002).

Focus group discussions at all six sites along the transect revealed that many informants recognised that changes in the vegetation base had direct implications for the sustainability of other environmental resources. For example, a significant number of individuals realised that the leaf litter from most farm trees played a role in improving soil fertility, although they could not explain why this was so. Alternatively, other informants made a positive connection between tree cover and soil conservation. When one woman in Zangon Gabas was asked if the number of trees on her land had an effect on the quality of the soil, she responded:

> Yes, it has great effect, and we can see that the time when the quality of the land began decreasing coincides with the time when the trees really began disappearing. When there were no longer strong roots to hold the soil together, the wind began to blow the soil and there was much more sand. Also, there were no leaves to block the rain when it fell, or break the speed of the wind, so this was hard on the land (Shemawa, pers. Com., 15 May, 2002).

When further attention was given to exploring local knowledge of the relationship between trees and soil, it became evident that there was a complex matrix of factors that influenced management decisions. At each site, many people indicated that vegetation could play a key role in erosion control, maintaining soil structure, fertility enhancement, or the moderation of microclimates. As is indicated in Table 26.1, when specifically asked if changes in tree cover affected soil conditions, there was a high level of agreement among households that a correlation existed between the two.

Chapter 26 | Roy Maconachie, in
A.I. Tanko and S.B. Momale (Eds.)
*Kano: Environment, Society and Development*
London & Abuja, Adonis & Abbey Publishers

**Table 26.1: Do changes in tree-cover affect soil conditions? (N=15 at each site)**

| Site | Yes | | No | |
|---|---|---|---|---|
| | Number | % | Number | % |
| Hotoro Arewa | 12 | 80 | 3 | 20 |
| Zangon Gabas | 10 | 66.7 | 5 | 33.3 |
| Kadewa | 13 | 86.7 | 2 | 13.3 |
| Maisar Tudu | 11 | 73.3 | 4 | 26.6 |
| Gamji Tara | 14 | 93.3 | 1 | 6.7 |
| Magama | 11 | 73.3 | 4 | 26.7 |
| Total sample (N=90) | 71 | 78.9 | 19 | 21.1 |

*Source:* author's fieldwork

Further focus group discussions at each site elucidated many of the responses given in the household surveys. Farmers frequently spoke of how the colour of soil under trees changed to a 'richer shade of black', and if crops were planted in a location where a tree had been cut down, the land would be richer, and yields would be higher for three agricultural seasons. Interestingly, for unknown reasons, there was a strikingly high level of consensus that yields would return to normal levels after three years. The household questionnaire surveys also revealed that at all six sites, there were a number of other common perceptions concerning the relationship between trees and the soil. When asked about the effects that a reduction in the number of trees had on the soil, there were four overwhelmingly common responses, which are summarised in Table 26.2.

**Table 26.2: Effects of tree-cover change on soil conditions (N=90)**

| Stated effect of fewer trees on soil conditions | Mentioned by | |
|---|---|---|
| | Number | Total % of sample (N=90 |
| Makes soil more sandy | 19 | 21.1 |
| Reduces amount of shade which dries out soil | 17 | 18.9 |
| Reduces amount of leaf litter which makes soil less fertile | 16 | 17.8 |
| Exposes soil to wind and rain which increases erosion | 16 | 17.8 |
| Other effects mentioned | 3 | 3.3 |

*Source:* author's fieldwork

Local actors appeared to demonstrate a strong awareness that levels of vegetation were connected to site fertility, soil conservation, and the safe-guarding of other environmental resources. However, while farmers reported that they made conscious management decisions about trees and grasses based on this local knowledge, it was also evident that other structural factors often influenced their

| Chapter 26 | Roy Maconachie, in |
| | A.I. Tanko and S.B. Momale (Eds.) |
| | *Kano: Environment, Society and Development* |
| | London & Abuja, Adonis & Abbey Publishers |

decision-making abilities and shaped local practices. Thus, as is the case with the assessment of other environmental resources, the dynamics of vegetation change must also be situated in a broader livelihood context, where the factors that mediate people-environment relationships range from the micro-level to the macro-level. Later in this chapter, further attention will be given to tree management practices, with specific reference to how livelihood factors drive local decisions. But first, in the next section, the focus of the discussion will turn specifically to how perceptions of tree cover change are allied more broadly to the complex concept of land degradation.

## Perceptions of Vegetation Change: Is Woodland Degradation Occurring?

In the West African drylands, for over a century now, deeply held fears of deforestation have captured the imaginations of a wide range of observers, ranging from colonial administrators and government officials to development workers and environmentalists (Ribot, 1999). All too often, as an increasing number of studies have pointed out, much previous research concerning the relationship between society and environmental change in forest-savanna ecologies has been premised on neo-Malthusian assumptions (Fairhead and Leach, 1996). The prevailing orthodoxy has suggested that widespread deforestation has been driven by 'exploding' populations and their increasing poverty, which is causing irreversible environmental degradation (Myers, 1991). However, there is now a vast literature which recognises that many of these fears have been unfounded, and have unjustly supported highly inappropriate and draconian environmental policies that have often been damaging to local people (Cline-Cole, 2000; Fairhead and Leach, 1998; Tchamie, 1994).

One of the main problems with past studies that have endeavoured to assess the extent of vegetation change, is undoubtedly that they are frequently constructed around inaccurate baseline information and exaggerated forestry statistics (Fairhead and Leach, 1998). Since long-term environmental information is often difficult to obtain, many assessments of forest degradation are, in fact, based on observations of present situations, or comparisons between short time-series of data (Fairhead, 1998). Even attempts to assess the extent of tree cover change based on data which spans one or two decades, can be

Chapter 26 | Roy Maconachie, in
A.I. Tanko and S.B. Momale (Eds.)
*Kano: Environment, Society and Development*
London & Abuja, Adonis & Abbey Publishers

**415**

problematic since observed changes may be the result of several processes operating at various time scales (Rasmussen, 1999).

As has already been clarified, this chapter does not propose to make long-term comparisons of tree cover change, but rather concentrates on the perceptional aspects of environmental change in the short-term. By focusing on the normative nature of woodland degradation, a number of key questions can be explored which may help to shed light on why land managers behave in such different ways. For example, we might ask, how do perceptions of tree change vary with distance from Kano? What are the main factors that condition these perceptions? And although it is apparent that many people believe there are presently less trees than in the past, why is it that they do not always equate this with a perception of degradation? Questions such as these remain imperative, if we are to understand how local people understand their environment and formulate their land management decisions. Moreover, such an appreciation is crucial for policy makers if they are to prioritize the actions to be taken to improve environmental conditions in the future.

When asked about changes in tree cover, a high percentage of respondents in this study perceived that there were now fewer trees than in the past, even though they acknowledged that there were presently conservation laws in place to regulate the felling of trees on farmland. According to the questionnaire survey, over 82% of the households sampled reported that they now had fewer trees on their land than they did 20 years ago. Moreover, as is indicated in Table 26.3, although the perception that tree cover is currently diminishing was high at all six sites, households sampled at the three communities in closest proximity to Kano - Hotoro Arewa, Zangon Gabas, and Kadewa - demonstrated a very strong belief that tree numbers were presently on the decline.

| Chapter 26 | Roy Maconachie, in |
| | A.I. Tanko and S.B. Momale (Eds.) |
| | *Kano: Environment, Society and Development* |
| | London & Abuja, Adonis & Abbey Publishers |

**Table 26.3: Are there fewer trees on your land today than 20 years ago?**

| Site | Yes | | No | |
|------|-----|---|-----|---|
| | Number (N=15) | % | Number (N=15) | % |
| Hotoro Arewa | 13 | 86.7 | 2 | 13.3 |
| Zangon Gabas | 13 | 86.7 | 2 | 13.3 |
| Kadewa | 13 | 86.7 | 2 | 13.3 |
| Gamji Tara | 12 | 80 | 3 | 20 |
| Maisar Tudu | 11 | 73.3 | 4 | 26.7 |
| Magama | 12 | 80 | 3 | 20 |
| Total sample (N=90) | 74 | 82.2 | 16 | 17.8 |

*Source: author's fieldwork*

In the past, respondents explained, customary laws regulating the use of trees and other common resources were regarded not only as an important mechanism for securing equitable access to resources, but also played an important function in ensuring the most efficient use of the natural resource base between different actors, particularly in an environment with such a low and unpredictable rainfall. Although it should not be assumed that the absence of customary laws necessarily causes land managers to behave irrationally or opportunistically, over the years, as Boerma (1999: 48) points out, such regulations may have helped to clarify people's rights, to improve their ability to manage their resources effectively, and to help avoid disputes about entitlement to various resources. In this study, discussions revealed that to all intents and purposes, most of the customary laws concerning the felling of trees have now disappeared in many of the communities in Kano's hinterlands, and instead, many local governments have introduced new policies to regulate the exploitation of trees. For example, a large number of respondents spoke of a recently enacted law, whereby those who wished to lop a tree, or cut it down completely, were subject to pay a fine of 100 Naira or 200 Naira respectively. A number of respondents added, however, that these laws or penalties did not seem to stop people from cutting down trees, because they were not effectively monitored or enforced.

Although an overwhelming majority of respondents in the study articulated that there had been a diminution in vegetation cover in recent years, the reasons given for this perception varied greatly and fell into four main categories. First, the central reason mentioned related to an increased domestic demand for fuelwood. Secondly, it

Chapter 26 | Roy Maconachie, in
A.I. Tanko and S.B. Momale (Eds.)
*Kano: Environment, Society and Development*
London & Abuja, Adonis & Abbey Publishers

**417**

was suggested that difficult economic times and an increased demand for cash income had forced many people to rely on their natural capital stocks, such as trees, to make ends meet. Thirdly, it was believed that increased pressure on the land, and the accompanying changes in land use patterns that had developed, had led to many more trees being cut down. And fourthly, many land managers, especially elderly farmers, associated a perception of increasingly harsh climatic conditions with the natural death of trees, particularly many of the more cherished indigenous species. Broadly speaking, the majority of descriptions of vegetation change revealed by respondents in this study fits into one of these four main categories. In the next sections, each of these perceived reasons for change is dealt with individually, and greater attention is focused on the livelihood factors that drive local management decisions.

**Fuelwood Demand**

In the West African drylands, urban demand for fuelwood has long been assumed to be a major contributing force to the permanent deforestation of wooded savannas. According to Main (1995: 52), wood accounts for as much as three-quarters of total energy consumption in sub-Saharan Africa, while estimates of fuelwood dependency in the Sahelian countries suggest that consumption rates are even higher.[8] At the crux of this dependency, is the assumption that a rising urban demand for wood encourages traders to deplete rural tree stocks, and the cycle becomes circular and reinforcing as poor urban and peri-urban dwellers become vulnerable to rising woodfuel prices that they can no longer afford. As fuelwood becomes scarcer and urban prices continue to rise, it becomes more feasible for wood traders to travel even further a field to harvest supplies, driving prices even higher, and extending the ring of deforestation to greater distances.

During the 1980s, this narrative appears to have been a major theme in many studies relating to fuelwood supply and demand in West Africa, and came to be popularly referred to as the 'Woodfuel Gap' theory. The main premise of this theory was formulated on the

---

[8] Although the statistics may now be somewhat dated, a study by the Club du Sahel (1978) estimated that on average, in Sahelian countries firewood represents 82.12% of household energy consumption.

| Chapter 26 | Roy Maconachie, in |
| | A.I. Tanko and S.B. Momale (Eds.) |
| | *Kano: Environment, Society and Development* |
| | London & Abuja, Adonis & Abbey Publishers |

notion that increasing deforestation problems are interpreted as a problem of a growing gap between population-driven demand and diminishing resources, usually radiating out from centres of habitation in increasingly wider and wider circles. Today, of course, the idea of a 'Woodfuel Gap', and the assumptions that it is based on, have largely been discredited, but many studies continue to be influenced by its reasoning. For example, Kabré (1998) illustrates the idea of a supply-demand gap in his recent fuelwood study in the neighbouring country of Burkina Faso, by estimating the ever-increasing distances travelled by fuelwood lorries supplying Ouagadougou markets. He calculates: "Effectively, during the 1950's, the distance to travel was 25km compared to 85km in 1985; with 1.7km rate of increase a year this distance is 105km in 1997 and will reach 111km in 2000" (1998: 44). Ultimately, his study concludes, the overexploitation of timber stands will undoubtedly increase in years to come and become more catastrophic as Ouagadougou's ecological footprint expands, unless new sources of domestic fuels can be found.

Alternatively, Benjaminsen's (1998) two detailed case studies from Mali, in the Gourma region and the Diéli sub-region in the southern cotton zone, are critical of narratives framed around 'Woodfuel Gap' theory, arguing that such fuelwood orthodoxies unfairly blame local people for causing natural resource degradation. However, although Benjaminsen's research concludes that locally induced deforestation caused by fuelwood consumption does not appear to be an immediate environmental threat in the two case study areas, the investigation does suggest that the commercial exploitation of wood destined for urban markets is currently depleting fuelwood supplies. Specifically, it is pointed out that there is unusually high external pressure on the woody vegetation in the Diéli region due to the proximity of a major road linking two urban centres, and about half the quantity of wood being exploited from the area is being removed by fuelwood traders coming from outside to supply urban areas with wood (1998: 36).

The situation in the Kano CSZ appears to be radically different. Studies into fuelwood consumption and tree management in the inner and outer CSZ by Cline-Cole et al. (1990a; 1990b), provide a powerful counter-narrative to deforestation orthodoxies, and suggest that the maturity and density of trees actually increase in areas that are in closer proximity to urban centres, where there are greater

Chapter 26 | Roy Maconachie, in
A.I. Tanko and S.B. Momale (Eds.)
*Kano: Environment, Society and Development*
London & Abuja, Adonis & Abbey Publishers

population densities. Moreover, Mortimore's (1975) detailed research relating to fuelwood interaction between Kano and its hinterland, suggests that regions in the urban periphery have benefited from the close social and economic links that they share with the nearby city. Until the 1960s, it has been suggested that most of Kano's demand for fuelwood was satisfied by trees harvested within 26 kms of the city limits, within the so-called 'inner CSZ', an area that is now generally considered to be peri-urban in nature (Mortimore, 1998; Cline-Cole, 2000). However, by the early 1990s, Cline-Cole *et al.* (1990a) add that growing urban populations drove fuelwood traders to distances of more than 300km away in search of wood, and it became more cost effective for traders to purchase truckloads of wood from outside the CSZ.

While previous studies into Kano's fuelwood trade, such as those carried out by Cline-Cole and Mortimore, have provided important counter-narratives to fuelwood orthodoxies, the question remains as to why the majority of informants interviewed in this study had a radically different perception of their environment? It is, of course, worth noting that the studies carried out by Cline-Cole *et al.* (1990a; 1990b) were based on field research undertaken in the late 1980s. Moreover, Mortimore's seminal research on the fuelwood trade was conducted as far back as the late 1960s and early 1970s. Could it be the case that over the last decades, the introduction of powerful new external pressures has eroded the resilience of a once sustainable system? Indeed, since the earliest of these studies were carried out, urban ecological footprints have grown astronomically in size, and the far-reaching changes set in motion by the forces of globalisation have penetrated even the remotest of villages. We must therefore ask ourselves, have the abilities of local land managers to make sustainable tree management decisions been constrained in this period of radical change?

Although increased urban pressure has almost certainly put greater stress on tree stocks in urban hinterlands, Main (1995) notes that undoubtedly some reports of deforestation have been grossly over-exaggerated. In the Kano Region, one well-known study by Eckholm *et al.* (1984: 28) describes the presence of 'severe deforestation and collapse of a sustainable agricultural system' in Kano's urban hinterlands. Although the observations made during the present study failed to uncover any evidence of 'severe' deforestation caused by

Chapter 26 | Roy Maconachie, in
A.I. Tanko and S.B. Momale (Eds.)
*Kano: Environment, Society and Development*
London & Abuja, Adonis & Abbey Publishers

fuelwood exploitation, respondents in focus group discussions did raise a number of key concerns concerning the sustainability of local fuelwood supply in the near future. According to local voices, it would now seem that there is a pressing need to reconsider some of the issues concerning trees in the Kano CSZ.

Focus group discussions and the fuelwood questionnaire survey administered at Hotoro Arewa and Zangon Gabas suggested that in peri-urban localities, the perceived decline in the number of trees in recent years was thought to be the result of a number of factors. Specifically, in addition to an increase in the domestic use of trees for house building, it was commonly believed that there was a heightened demand in wood for cooking and heating water. This belief was not just based on the perception that a growing population was consuming more resources, but also that the rising cost and unreliable availability of kerosene had increased the demand for wood as the main source of fuel. For example, according to one individual at Hotoro Arewa:

> Your fuel choice will firstly be determined by economic factors. If you use firewood, it is the cheapest way. When women try cooking for a large family on a kerosene stove, the food will not be cooked well, and it will take too much time. The price of kerosene is very high today, and the cost is increasing with every day. When the kerosene is not available, it becomes very costly, and many cannot afford to buy it. With the hiking of petrol prices, it has made kerosene even more expensive, and many who used to use kerosene have stopped and switched to wood (Hamza, pers. com., 23 March, 2002).

Some respondents went on to suggest that the demand for wood was further being driven by a combination of high profit margins in the fuelwood economy, coupled with the effects of recent government energy policies which left people with a lack of viable energy alternatives. In agreement with the findings of this study, Odihi's (2003) recent research into deforestation in Yobe and Borno states notes that both the high cost and erratic availability of alternative energy sources have played a major role in strengthening fuelwood dependencies. Prior to the introduction of structural adjustment programmes (SAPs) in Nigeria in 1986, he points out that alternative forms of domestic energy, including kerosene and cooking gas (liquefied natural gas) were both affordable and available. At that time, Odihi suggests, a 12 kg cylinder of cooking gas cost less than

Chapter 26 | Roy Maconachie, in
A.I. Tanko and S.B. Momale (Eds.)
*Kano: Environment, Society and Development*
London & Abuja, Adonis & Abbey Publishers

421

three *naira*, would last an average family for one month, and was cheaper than kerosene and even fuelwood. By 1988, however, the situation was very different:

> The affordability index of fuelwood between 1988 and 1996 was between 7 and 9 for low-income households and 9 for both middle and high income ones. Kerosene availability declined from the favourable condition of index 6 in 1988 to 0 in 1994 and climbed back to 4 in 1996 for low-income households. The affordability index of gas was 0 in 1994 (i.e. it was not affordable) for over 70% of middle income households that were formerly using it (Odihi, 2003: 244).

In this study, cooking gas was not mentioned by any of the households surveyed as a current source of domestic fuel[9]. Table 26.4 summarises the main types of household fuel used being used in peri-urban areas, according to 100 households randomly surveyed in Hotoro Arewa and Zangon Gabas.

In addition to cost and availability factors, it was also suggested by many households that wood was preferred as the main source of fuel for a number of cultural reasons. For example, for families that have the financial means, it is a traditional Hausa custom for women to cook very large quantities of food every day, so that it can be shared with extended family or those in need, at a moments notice. Such substantial portions of *tuwo*, the staple food, can only be cooked in large pots on wood fires. Many respondents suggested that only those who had small families, or did not want to share their food with others, chose to cook on kerosene stoves.

---

[9] Odihi (2003: 242) notes that for both natural gas and kerosene, the supply and reliability of these energy sources has been greatly reduced by a variety of factors including, price fixing, tampering with metres and containers to reduce their capacity, adulteration, and a strong illegal trans-border trade.

Chapter 26 | Roy Maconachie, in
A.I. Tanko and S.B. Momale (Eds.)
*Kano: Environment, Society and Development*
London & Abuja, Adonis & Abbey Publishers

**Table 26.4: Primary fuel sources in Hotoro Arewa and Zangon Gabas**

| Main type of household fuel used | % of households (N=100) |
|---|---|
| Wood | 38 |
| Kerosene | 31 |
| Wood and Kerosene | 26 |
| Millet/sorghum stalks and wood | 2 |
| Millet/sorghum stalks | 1 |
| Ayafa (refuse from plastics factories) | 1 |
| Charcoal | 1 |

*Source: author's fieldwork*

Moreover, it was apparent that many individuals avoided kerosene because they believed that the stoves were too complicated, or they thought that it affected the taste of the food. As one respondent from Hotoro Arewa suggested:

The people here avoid buying kerosene if possible. They want firewood. Any food cooked on kerosene does not taste as good as if it is cooked on firewood. The *tuwo* tastes much better when it is cooked on wood, and in some villages, old men will not eat food cooked on kerosene (Usaini, pers. com., April 06, 2002).

Several respondents also made a direct connection between a perceived increase in the birth rate and an increase in fuelwood consumption. Such a perception can be attributed to the common Hausa cultural practice known as *wankan jego*, where newly delivered mothers bathe twice daily for 40 days in scalding hot water. This tradition obviously requires a large volume of fuelwood to heat water, and it is frequently possible to identify new mothers from the large piles of fuelwood outside their houses. In Table 26.5, the main factors determining choice of fuel selection are summarised, as revealed in the fuelwood questionnaire.

## Economic factors

Focus group discussions revealed that many informants associated difficult economic times and a rising demand for cash income with increased pressure on natural capital stocks, such as trees. According to the *West African Long Term Perspective* Study (WALTPS) carried by the Club du Sahel (1995), the non-farm share of rural household income in West Africa may presently be as high as 40% of total

Chapter 26 | Roy Maconachie, in
A.I. Tanko and S.B. Momale (Eds.)
*Kano: Environment, Society and Development*
London & Abuja, Adonis & Abbey Publishers

**423**

income. Such a growing dependency on non-agrarian income-generating activities, Bryceson (1997) adds, is largely being driven by a combination of three main forces: economic pressures undermining small scale agriculture, environmental degradation, and new economic and political opportunities which may have opened up in recent years. Smallholders in northern Nigeria do not appear to be exempt from these forces, and in the Kano CSZ, the process of de-agrarianisation is very apparent. In fact, in recent years, cash needs have become even greater for most people, and have been exacerbated by the rising costs of manufactured goods and food products, and a poor economic climate in Nigeria more broadly speaking. Meagher and Mustapha (1997) suggest that in Nigeria, as is the case in other sub-Saharan countries, the onset of structural adjustment programmes has been one of the most dramatic influences on the rising cost of food and agricultural inputs.

**Table 26.5: Reasons for household fuel choice**

| Fuel type | Reason for choice of household fuel | % of households (N=100) |
|-----------|-------------------------------------|------------------|
| Wood | Wood is the cheapest | 25 |
| Wood | Family is large, so wood is more economical | 18 |
| Wood | Food tastes better cooked on wood | 4 |
| Wood | Cannot cook some foods with kerosene, so wood must be used | 2 |
| Wood | Wood is more available | 3 |
| Wood | Cannot afford to buy kerosene stove | 1 |
| kerosene | Family is small, so kerosene is easier and cost effective | 19 |
| Kerosene | Kerosene is easier to use than wood | 9 |
| Kerosene | Kerosene is cheaper than wood | 8 |
| Kerosene | Do not like the smoke from wood | 6 |
| Kerosene | Kerosene is more easily available than wood | 4 |
| Kerosene | Kerosene is better for the environment | 1 |

*Source: author's fieldwork*

As non-agrarian income has become a 'lifeline' for many poor grassroots actors, off-farm activities have increasingly been pursued with greater vigour, and often at the expense of the natural resource base (Bryceson, 1997). For example, El Bashir (1997) describes how desperately poor rural people in Darfur, Sudan, have become dependent on fuelwood and grass sales to make ends meet, but in the process have accelerated environmental degradation. Likewise, Meagher and Mustapha (1997) argue that in the northern Nigerian

| Chapter 26 | Roy Maconachie, in |
|---|---|
| | A.I. Tanko and S.B. Momale (Eds.) |
| | *Kano: Environment, Society and Development* |
| | London & Abuja, Adonis & Abbey Publishers |

context, there is also a danger that off-farm activities could extract too much from the resource base and threaten the sustainability of production systems. It would appear that these concerns have great bearing on the discussion at hand concerning vegetation, since the sale of fuelwood, economic tree products, and even grasses and shrubs, is becoming an increasingly common method of generating income. As is noted by Cline-Cole (1995):

> Dependence on non-agricultural income increases with harvest failure, livestock mortality, population density, farming intensity, land scarcity, and proximity to large urban centres....The collection, processing and sale of sylvan products from both agricultural and non-agricultural land make important contributions to non-agricultural income, with fuelwood being, arguably, the most important of these (1995: 174).

In focus group discussions in this study, a number of individuals admitted that economic desperation had driven them to harvest the trees on their property and sell them for fuelwood. In fact, even in Gamji Tara, a community that Harris described in her 1995 study as being "away from the bias of the city...[where] farmers were not in frequent contact with Kano businesses and trade" (1995: 49), residents reported that fuelwood lorries from Kano now make regular visits to the village to buy trees from anyone who wishes to sell[10]. Likewise, at the furthest site at Magama, one resident commented:

> Here we don't have many ways of earning money, especially in the dry season, so some people cut down their trees to sell as firewood. We can sell our wood to the people from Kano city, who come here to buy it. There are lorries from Kano that drive out here and we can sell our wood for 15 or even 20 naira per bundle. In Magama, we use wood as our main fuel source, but even in the city people will now buy wood because kerosene is very costly, and many people are no longer using stoves (Dibi, pers. com., 19 February, 2002).

Most often, it was reported that financial strain occurred during the so-called 'hungry season' immediately preceding the harvesting of crops, or during cultural occasions that required gift-giving, such as weddings or naming ceremonies. With respect to the latter, Bryceson (1997) notes that economic stress has in many ways broken down

---

[10] During focus group sessions in Gamji Tara, informants reported that during the dry season, fuelwood lorries from Kano came to Gamji Tara as many as three times per week to collect wood.

Chapter 26 | Roy Maconachie, in
A.I. Tanko and S.B. Momale (Eds.)
*Kano: Environment, Society and Development*
London & Abuja, Adonis & Abbey Publishers

well- established channels of familial exchange, and although it may be the case that households still possess a sense of filial duty, economic crisis has left them with little disposable cash or time to spend on gift-giving to relations beyond their nuclear families. In this study, many respondents remarked that the cost of their economic responsibilities had risen dramatically in recent years, and a summary of the main household expenses requiring a cash income reported in the questionnaire survey are presented in Table 26.6. Overall, respondents indicated that their major financial commitments included hiring farm labour, purchasing food, buying clothes, and meeting the costs associated with household items consumed on a daily basis, such as soap, kerosene and soup ingredients. Although many of the households surveyed admitted that they sometimes bought fuelwood, this was not revealed as being a major household expense in the questionnaire survey. In fact, due to the rising costs of other household expenses, domestic energy expenditures were reported as being minimal, and many respondents admitted that in recent years, they had resorted to collecting fuelwood themselves or burning the sorghum or millet stalks from their farms.

According to the Sustainable Livelihoods Framework (see Scoones, 1998), it has been suggested that at any specific time, a household possesses up to five different types of 'capital assets' in its livelihood portfolio, with the five most common categories of capital being: natural, economic, human, physical, and social. According to this approach, households in effect 'juggle' combinations of these different types of capital, and if one category of capital is lacking at any given time, one form can be freely converted into another. As livelihood portfolios are dynamic and subject to change over time and space, it can thus be concluded that the responses and capabilities of various households are constantly in flux, as local circumstances change. As Warren *et. al* (2001) note, it would appear that some households may have a greater capacity to convert assets than others, depending on a variety of factors such as wealth, power, status, or household demography.

In desperate times, when individuals may not be able to readily rely on the 'social capital' or family networks that were once more accessible in the past, an over-reliance on the natural capital base may be the response of some households. Indeed, many of those interviewed in this study equated their perception of a diminution in

| Chapter 26 | Roy Maconachie, in |
| | A.I. Tanko and S.B. Momale (Eds.) |
| | *Kano: Environment, Society and Development* |
| | London & Abuja, Adonis & Abbey Publishers |

tree-cover with the economic stress that has been building over the past two decades. These sentiments are well summarised by an interviewee at Kadewa:

> The number of trees here has been drastically reduced. Numbers started to decline about 15 years ago, and as population has increased, tree numbers have continued to diminish. Today, we are in serious financial trouble, and it is common for people to cut down the trees, either on the farmland or in the compound, and sell them for firewood either in Jogana or Kano. As the number of people continues to increase, more wood is in demand for both *wankan jego*, and for fuelwood to cook. We have mainly cut down trees like *Dorawa*, *Rimi*, and *Kuka*, and now there are few. Cooking gas is too expensive for most people, so we buy wood from the city, but it is also expensive, so we try to burn our corn stalks. In the past, some of us used kerosene stoves, because kerosene was very cheap then. Only the rich can afford to use kerosene or gas cookers today (Zakari, pers. com., 2002).

Thus, for many respondents, current pressure on the number of trees was perceived to be related to a specific episode of economic stress, rather than merely population growth in general. The reasons given for a decline in tree cover frequently concerned conflicting land-use patterns that were being directed by increased urban pressures and greater economic stress. As such, it was revealed that not only do many people now rely much more heavily on the natural resource base to generate cash income, but as will be explored in the upcoming section, land hunger and the pressing need to increase yields on each plot may also have implications for the number of trees that farmers choose to integrate into the farming system.

Chapter 26 | Roy Maconachie, in
A.I. Tanko and S.B. Momale (Eds.)
*Kano: Environment, Society and Development*
London & Abuja, Adonis & Abbey Publishers

**Table 26.6: Household expenses by site**

| Expense | Hotoro Arewa number* | % | Zangon Gabas number | % | Kadewa number | % | Maisar Tudu number | % | Gamji Tara number | % | Magama number | % | Total (N=9 total number |
|---|---|---|---|---|---|---|---|---|---|---|---|---|---|---|
| labour hire | 14 | 93 | 12 | 80 | 8 | 53.3 | 15 | 100 | 11 | 73.3 | 6 | 40 | 66 |
| Food | 15 | 100 | 15 | 100 | 10 | 66.7 | - | - | 10 | 66.7 | 11 | 73.3 | 61 |
| Clothes | 10 | 67 | 10 | 66.7 | 7 | 46.7 | 6 | 40 | 2 | 13.3 | 15 | 100 | 50 |
| daily needs** | 2 | 13 | 1 | 6.7 | 4 | 26.7 | 8 | 53.3 | 11 | 73.3 | 12 | 80 | 38 |
| fodder (animal feed) | 3 | 20 | 2 | 13.3 | 6 | 40 | 3 | 20 | - | - | - | - | 14 |
| gifts(cultural)*** | 2 | 13 | 1 | 6.7 | 6 | 40 | - | - | 3 | 20 | 1 | 6.7 | 13 |
| motorcycle expenses | 2 | 13 | 3 | 20 | - | - | 1 | 6.7 | - | - | - | - | 6 |
| farm inputs**** | - | - | 1 | 6.7 | 1 | 6.7 | 1 | 6.7 | - | - | 2 | 13.3 | 5 |
| transportation to work | 1 | 6.7 | 1 | 6.7 | 1 | 6.7 | 1 | 6.7 | 1 | 6.7 | - | - | 5 |
| house repairs | - | - | - | - | 2 | 13.3 | - | - | 3 | 20 | - | - | 5 |
| vehicle expenses | - | - | 3 | 20 | - | - | - | - | - | - | - | - | 3 |
| petrol for irrigation pump | - | - | 2 | 13.3 | - | - | 1 | 6.7 | - | - | - | - | 3 |
| school fees | 1 | 6.7 | - | - | - | - | 2 | 13.3 | - | - | - | - | 3 |
| Taki | - | - | - | - | 2 | 13.3 | - | - | - | - | - | - | 2 |
| Medicine | - | - | - | - | - | - | - | - | 1 | 6.7 | - | - | 1 |
| Charcoal | - | - | - | - | - | - | - | - | 1 | 6.7 | - | - | 1 |

* number - refers to the total number at each site who mentioned the giver expense
** daily needs are defined as small items needed to maintain the household on a daily basis, and include such items as soap, kerosene soup ingredients
***gifts include all monies given for religious and cultural occasions, or for 'helping' those in need

****farm inputs are defined as chemical fertilisers or insecticides

*Source: author's fieldwork*

## Conflicting Land-Use Patterns

It has already been noted that for many years now, there has been an intense demand for agricultural land in the Kano CSZ. More recently however, beginning with the major changes in the Nigerian political economy that were set in motion during the oil boom years, increasing urban and peri-urban population densities, land fragmentation, and periods of climatic uncertainty have put much more strain on smallholder production systems. As such, Mortimore *et al.* (1999: 243) suggest that in the West African drylands, the major force presently driving the process of deforestation is the expansion of small-scale farming. Ribot's (1999: 293) extensive studies into local

Chapter 26 | Roy Maconachie, in
A.I. Tanko and S.B. Momale (Eds.)
*Kano: Environment, Society and Development*
London & Abuja, Adonis & Abbey Publishers

forest management in Burkina Faso appear to confirm this belief, and suggest that most of the current peri-urban vegetation clearing around Ouagadougou is not to meet urban fuelwood shortages, as is most frequently claimed (see, for example, Kabré (1998)), but rather to create more agricultural land. Other studies have also indicated that land clearance for agriculture has been identified as a principal cause of forest depletion (Leach and Mearns, 1988), and in the Kano CSZ, one contributing factor in a perceived diminution in tree cover may also be the high demand for agricultural land.

In the northern Nigerian dry belt, Odihi (2003) believes that recent government policies and a downturn in socioeconomic conditions have favoured agricultural expansion for many desperate people living on urban fringes. Based on research conducted in eight local government areas in Yobe and Borno states, he argues, "Unfavourable socioeconomic conditions such as mass retrenchment of workers, mass unemployment, increasing social burdens in circumstances of low wages, irregular or non-payment of salaries and soaring food prices have turned many people into farmers" (2003: 229). Although it would appear that the political and economic climate of Kano state is in a similar predicament to that of its northern neighbour states, and there is an equally strong desire for local farmers to increase output, the possibility for local actors to expand farming activities is somewhat more challenging. For at least three decades now, all available farmland has been under permanent cultivation, and the practice of fallowing rarely occurs, except under circumstances that are very out of the ordinary (Harris, 1996). Consequently, as the following statement illustrates, there is in fact very little possibility of creating further agricultural land, or rangeland for grazing animals:

> We use all the available places around here for grazing our animals, but the grazing land has disappeared because of the city. We have to spend a lot of money on animal feed now. We buy the feed simply because the *burtalis* and *makiyayas* we have now are few. There is no forest reserve. There is land hunger now, and people are desperately looking for farm plots. If you have enough food, you can do whatever you like (Baba, pers. com., March 10, 2002.)

Although it was apparent that many trees were considered to be beneficial for soil conservation and were a key economic asset in livelihood portfolios, it was almost unanimously mentioned that too

Chapter 26 | Roy Maconachie, in
A.I. Tanko and S.B. Momale (Eds.)
*Kano: Environment, Society and Development*
London & Abuja, Adonis & Abbey Publishers

**429**

much shade was considered to be bad for crops, and further reduced the amount of land that could be planted. Several informants mentioned that during the 1980s and early 1990s, there had been a short-stemmed variety of sorghum called *zauna inuwa*, that grew very well in the shade, but it was no longer possible to obtain these seeds. Accordingly, as it was not possible to plant in the shade, and it was extremely difficult to obtain additional farm plots to cultivate, informants reported that to increase the cultivable area and allow more sunlight to reach crops, many who were desperate for farmland had cleared all the trees from their plots. However, it was indicated that the incidence of land hunger does not only appear to be affecting farmers, but also pastoralists, who are desperate for rangeland to graze their animals. Indeed, several recent studies have highlighted the apparent emergence of pastoralist-farmer conflict, and the subsequent breakdown of a supposed state of symbiosis which once existed between the two groups (Williams *et al.* 1997; Milligan, 2002). Several respondents admitted that in recent years, trees had been the cause of land-use conflicts between Fulani pastoralists and local cultivators. Of specific concern to many individuals was the diminishing prevalence of the *Gawo* (or *Gao*) (*Faidherbia albida*) tree. The *Gawo*, a highly valued indigenous species, has been referred to as 'the dry season floral wonder of the Sahel' (Odihi, 2003), because it has the unique ability to remain green and produce fruit during the long dry season, at a time when most other trees are dry and leafless. Consequently, the *Gawo* is an important source of fodder for animal rearers at a time when feed is scarce. To discourage pastoralists from bringing cattle onto agricultural land, local farmers remarked that they frequently chopped down all *Gawo* trees, whose branches are traditionally used by the Fulani for cattle fodder[11]. The problem is illustrated by the following concerns of one young farmer:

> Some trees are good for the land, but some are bad. The *Gawo* tree causes problems for us because of the *Udawa* (Fulani who come to Nigeria from the Republic of Niger). They come and cut the branches, and often there are thorns which spread all around my plot and hurt me when I am working. Sometimes, the *Udawa* bring their animals onto my plot after the crops have already germinated, and they damage the plants. So for this reason, to

---

[11] Consequently, the decision by many farmers to cut down the *Gawo* trees on their plots may have also played a role in reducing the amount of *taki* available from Fulani cattle.

| Chapter 26 | Roy Maconachie, in |
| | A.I. Tanko and S.B. Momale (Eds.) |
| | *Kano: Environment, Society and Development* |
| | London & Abuja, Adonis & Abbey Publishers |

keep the *Udawa* off my land, I have cut down my *Gawo* trees. Afterwards,
I used the wood as fuel for cooking (Yakubu, pers. com., 2002).

Such reports of conflict between cultivators and pastoralists in the
Kano CSZ are undoubtedly increasing, and in recent years greater
contest for key resources has often led to violent clashes. Similar
findings are reported by Odihi (2003) in his extensive study of
deforestation-related activities and problems carried out in Yobe and
Borno States between 1991 and 2000. In fact, Odihi (2003: 239) goes
as far as to suggest that "[t]he increasing popularity of animal rearing
by urban residents, soaring price of fodder (*harawa*), mutual hostility
between herders and crop farmers which practically ended the long
existing symbiotic relationship between crop and animal production in
the zone seem to be at the expense of [the] Gao tree." In this study,
many of those interviewed also expressed great concern for the
manner in which the *Gawo* tree has 'ratcheted up' levels of tension
between local communities and the transitory *Udawa*, as is evident in
the following statement of one young farmer from Maisar Tudu:

> The *Udawa* do come here, and sometimes they stay for one or two months.
> The relationship we have with them is not cordial. Four years ago, one of
> the *Udawa* climbed one of our trees to lop the branches. We told him to get
> down, but he refused. Because of this a big fight started. Many people were
> wounded (Garba, pers. com. 25 February, 2002).

It appeared that most concern for farmer-herder relations was
evident at the transect sites in furthest proximity from Kano, where the
*Udawa* still regularly transit during the dry season. In comparison, at
Hotoro Arewa and Zangon Gabas, the two closest sites to Kano, focus
group informants suggested that as the number of *Gawo* trees had been
considerably reduced and the landscape had become progressively
more 'urban' in character, pastoralists now rarely used peri-urban areas
to graze their animals. At all transect sites, however, it was noted that
because local authorities were reluctant to enforce laws concerning
visiting Fulanis, most farmers in the region had stopped nursing young
*Gawo* saplings on their plots altogether. The relationship between
farmers and the *Udawa*, and the tension between them created by the
*Gawo* tree, illustrates the significant implications that land use conflict
can have on tree-growing decisions. Consequently, several farmers in
the study conceded that the absence of trees, such as the *Gawo,* could

Chapter 26 | Roy Maconachie, in
A.I. Tanko and S.B. Momale (Eds.)
*Kano: Environment, Society and Development*
London & Abuja, Adonis & Abbey Publishers

have played a role in the recent deterioration of peri-urban soil conditions.

## Climatic Factors

It must be finally noted that although most respondents in the study associated their perceptions of woodland degradation with anthropogenic factors, many individuals believed that certain vegetation species were diminishing as a consequence of declining amounts of rainfall. Low and variable amounts of rainfall are characteristic conditions of the Kano CSZ, it was very apparent that many respondents believed this to be having a significant impact on the regeneration of a large number of indigenous tree species. Moreover, it was suggested that because many African tree species are slow growers, and were not being replanted to the same extent as exotic species such as the *neem* tree, they were quickly declining in number. This perception is well-illustrated by one Fulani man at Gamji Tara:

> The indigenous trees such as *Dorawa* and *Gawo* are quickly disappearing. *Gawo* is becoming extinct because of the *Udawa*, and there are few seeds left to replant the *Dorawa*. When the *Dorawa* gets old, it stops producing seeds and dies. And we have not replanted *Dorawa* seeds previously because we have been using them for many things, like cooking *kunu*. So there are not many new Dorawa trees. We practice *sassabe* with the *Dorawa*, but it has a short period of seed production in its lifetime. *Dorawa* cannot withstand harsh environments like many other trees can. It is not as strong, and now there have been changes in the environment. The climate has become harsher and there is less rainfall. The roots of the *Dorawa* cannot travel deep into the soil to get enough water (Jibrin, pers. com., 26 February, 2002).

While it may be the case that low and variable amounts of rainfall are playing a role in retarding the growth of certain tree species, it is probably not the case that this factor alone is responsible for any significant reduction in their numbers. Indeed, most of the trees found in the Kano CSZ are extremely hardy, and for thousands of years have been withstanding extreme environmental conditions. Perceptions of an increasingly harsh environment have undoubtedly placed greater stress on local livelihoods, and may have accelerated the tendency for some individuals to exploit their natural capital base in times of

Chapter 26 | Roy Maconachie, in
A.I. Tanko and S.B. Momale (Eds.)
*Kano: Environment, Society and Development*
London & Abuja, Adonis & Abbey Publishers

intense pressure. For example, many respondents noted that in recent years there had been an increase in the activities of traditional herbalists who strip the bark from certain indigenous trees for medicine, in a practice known locally as *sassaka*. It was reported that in many localities, the bark was being removed at unsustainable rates and was causing a large number of trees to die.

Broader concerns for the climate may also be influencing perceptions of land degradation, and may have convinced some individuals that the widespread depletion of environmental resources is occurring (Dahlberg and Blaikie, 1999; Elias and Scoones, 1999). As is possibly the case with perceptions of soil fertility, it should not be ruled out that local perceptions of tree cover are also being framed by broader concerns, such as increased stress on livelihoods or negative changes in levels of well-being.

## Conclusion

Although in recent years, a number of influential studies examining woodland degradation in West Africa have been guided by more optimistic hypotheses concerning the relationship between people and physical resources (Fairhead and Leach, 1998; 1996), in this study, local perceptions suggest that in some locations within the CSZ, there may currently be some cause for concern. However, it was also revealed that livelihood circumstances and management strategies vary greatly both spatially and temporally, and extrapolating micro-level findings to wider scales thus remains problematic. Although it may be the case that 'pockets' of environmental pressure do exist, it would also be wrong to assume that the widespread degradation of all woodlands was occurring.

As Cline-Cole and Madge (2000: 5) suggest, in the Kano CSZ dryland forestry is essentially, "the product of the dynamic interplay between dominant and subordinate forces, between heterogeneous populations and varied interests".Tree management decisions are embedded in a complex political economy, involving the conflicting resource management interests of a wide range of actors, and this chapter has demonstrated that perceptions of tree-cover and the management decisions they drive vary greatly across the research transect. Although there are many practical and theoretical challenges to consider when integrating spatial scales and extrapolating from the

Chapter 26 | Roy Maconachie, in
A.I. Tanko and S.B. Momale (Eds.)
*Kano: Environment, Society and Development*
London & Abuja, Adonis & Abbey Publishers

micro-level to the macro-scale, in agreement with Marcussen and Reenberg (1999), micro-level studies still remain the best analytical point of departure for investigations of environmental change. Although it may be the case that different social actors hold radically different appraisals of their resource base and of its degradation, such an understanding of the dynamic and variable perceptions that local people hold of the natural resource base must be a central consideration in formulating meaningful environmental policies for the years to come.

## References

Amanor, K. S. (1994) *The New Frontier. Farmer Responses to Land Degradation: A West African Study*. Zed Books Ltd., London and New Jersey.

Benjaminsen, T.A. (1998) Fuelwood - Myths and Realities: Two Cases from Mali. In: Reenberg, A., H.S. Marcussen and I. Nielsen (eds.) The Sahel: Sahelian Perspectives - Myths and Realities. Proceedings of the 10th Danish Sahel Workshop, 5-8 January 1998. *SEREIN Occasional Paper No. 6*, University of Copenhagen, Copenhagen, pp.29-38.

Boerma, P. (1999) Seeing the Wood for the Trees: Deforestation in the central Highlands of Eritrea since 1890. Unpublished DPhil Thesis. School of Geography, University of Oxford.

Bryceson, D.F. (1997) De-agrarianisation: Blessing or Blight? In: Bryceson, D.F. and V. Jamal (eds.) *Farewell to Farms: De-agrarianisation and employment in Africa*. Ashgate, Aldershot, pp. 237-256.

Buba, L.F. (2000) Drought Occurrence and the Utilization of Rainfall for Agriculture in Northern Nigeria. In: *Issues in Land Administration and Development in Northern Nigeria,* Falola, A.J., K., Ahmed, M.A. Liman, A. Maiwada (eds.). Department of Geography, Bayero University, Kano.

Chambers, R., A. Pacey, and L. Thrupp (eds.) (1989), *Farmer First: Farmer innovation and agricultural research*. Intermediate Technology Publications, London.

Cline-Cole, R. (2000) Redefining forestry space and threatening livelihoods in colonial northern Nigeria. In: Cline-Cole, R. and C.

Chapter 26 | Roy Maconachie, in
A.I. Tanko and S.B. Momale (Eds.)
*Kano: Environment, Society and Development*
London & Abuja, Adonis & Abbey Publishers

Madge (eds.) *Contesting Forestry in West Africa*. Ashgate Publishing Limited, Aldershot, pp. 36-63.

Cline-Cole, R. (1995) Livelihood, sustainable development and indigenous forestry in dryland Nigeria. In: Binns, T. (ed.), *People and Environment in Africa*. John Wiley and Sons, Chichester, pp. 171-185.

Cline-Cole, R., J. Falola, H. Main, M. Mortimore, J. Nichol and F. O'Reilly (1990a), *Wood fuel in Kano*. United Nations Press, Tokyo.

Cline-Cole, R., H. Main, and J. Nichol (1990b) On fuelwood consumption, population dynamics and deforestation in Africa. *World Development, 18* (4), pp. 513-27.

Cline-Cole, R. and C. Madge (2000) Constructing, Contesting and Situating Forestry in West Africa: An Introduction. In: Cline-Cole, R. and C. Madge (eds.), *Contesting Forestry in West Africa*. Ashgate Publishing Limited, Aldershot, pp. 3-10.

Club du Sahel (1978) L'énergie dans la développement du Sahel. Situation perspectives, recommandations. *CILSS*, Ouagadougou.

Dahlberg, A.C. (1994) Contesting views and changing paradigms: the land degradation debate in Southern Africa. *Discussion Paper 6*, Nordiska Afrikainstitutet, Uppsala, Sweden.

Dahlberg, A.C. and P.M. Blaikie, (1999) Changes in landscape or in interpretation? Reflections based on the environmental and socio-economic history of a village in NE Botswana. *Environment and History 5*, pp. 127-174.

Eckholm, E., G. Foley, G. Barnard and L. Timberlake (1984) *Firewood: the energy crisis that won't go away*. Earthscan, London.

El Bashir, H. (1997) Coping with Famine and Poverty: The Dynamics of Non-Agricultural Rural Employment in Darfur, Sudan. In: Bryceson, D.F. and V. Jamal (eds.), *Farewell to Farms: De-agrarianisation and Employment in Africa*. African Studies Centre Research Series, Leiden. Ashgate, Aldershot, pp. 23-40.

Elias, E. and I. Scoones (1999) Perspectives on soil fertility change: a case study from southern Ethiopia. *Land Degradation and Development 10*, pp. 195-206.

Fairhead, J. (1998) Reframing deforestation: Escaping orthodoxies concerning deforestation in West Africa. In: Reenberg, A., I. Nielsen and H.S. Marcussen (eds.) The Sahel: Sahelian

Chapter 26 | Roy Maconachie, in
A.I. Tanko and S.B. Momale (Eds.)
*Kano: Environment, Society and Development*
London & Abuja, Adonis & Abbey Publishers

**435**

Perspectives-Myths and Realities. *SEREIN Occasional Papers 6*. Copenhagen, pp. 13-28.

Fairhead, J. and M. Leach (1998) *Reframing Deforestation: Global Analysis and Local Realities: Studies in West Africa*. Routledge, London.

Fairhead J. and M. Leach (1996), *Misreading the African Landscape: Society and Ecology in a Forest-Savanna Mosaic*. Cambridge University Press, Cambridge.

Grainger, A. (1999) Constraints on modelling the deforestation and degradation of tropical open woodlands. *Global Ecology and Biogeography, 8*, pp. 179-190.

Harris, F. (1996) Intensification of Agriculture in Semi-Arid Areas: Lessons from the Kano Close-Settled Zone, Nigeria. *Gatekeeper Series No. 59*. International Institute for Environment and Development, London.

Kabré, A. (1998) Degradation of natural resources - the need for sustainable management: plans for a better future. In: Reenberg, A., H.S. Marcussen and I. Nielsen (eds.) *The Sahel: Sahelian Perspectives-Myths and Realities*. Proceedings of the 10th Danish Sahel Workshop, 5-8 January 1998. SEREIN Occasional Paper No. 6, University of Copenhagen, Copenhagen, pp. 41-47.

Kinlund (1996) Does land degradation matter? Unpublished PhD Thesis, Stockholm University.

Leach, G. and R. Mearns (1988), *Beyond the Woodfuel Crisis: People, Land and Trees in Africa*. Earthscan Publications, London.

LeHouérou, H.N. (1997) Climate, flora and fauna changes in the Sahara over the past 500 million years. *Journal of Arid Environments* 37, pp. 619-647.

Lykke, A.M. B. Fog and E. Madsen (1999) Woody vegetation changes in the Sahel of Burkina Faso assessed by means of local knowledge, aerial photos, and botanical investigations. *Danish Journal of Geography-Special Issue*, Vol. 2, pp. 57-68.

Main, H. (1995) The effects of urbanization on rural environments in Africa. In: Binns, T. (ed.) *People and Environment in Africa*. John Wiley and Sons, Chichester, pp. 47-57.

Marcussen, H.S. and A. Reenberg (1999) On scale and disciplinarity in the study of natural resource use in the Sahel – lessons from the SEREIN research program. *Danish Journal of Geography – Special Issue*, 2, pp. 1-13.

| Chapter 26 | Roy Maconachie, in<br>A.I. Tanko and S.B. Momale (Eds.)<br>*Kano: Environment, Society and Development*<br>London & Abuja, Adonis & Abbey Publishers |

Meagher, K. and A. R. Mustapha (1997) Not by Farming Alone: The Role of Non-farm Incomes in Rural Hausaland. In: Bryceson, D.F. and V. Jamal (eds.) (1997) *Farewell to Farms: De-agrarianisation and Employment in Africa.* African Studies Centre Research Series, Leiden. Ashgate, Aldershot, pp. 63-84.

Milligan, R. S. (2002), Searching for Symbiosis: Pastoralist-Farmer Relations in North-East Nigeria. Unpublished DPhil Thesis, University of Sussex.

Mortimore, M. (1998) *Roots in the African Dust: Sustaining the Sub-Saharan Drylands.* Cambridge University Press, Cambridge.

Mortimore, M. (1975) Peri-urban pressures. In: Moss, R.P., and R.J.A.R. Rathbone (eds.) *The population factor in African Studies.* University of London Press Ltd., London, pp. 188-197.

Mortimore, M. and W. Adams (1999) *Working the Sahel: Environment and Society in Northern Nigeria.* Routledge Research Global Environmental Change Series, London.

Mortimore, M., F.M.A Harris, and B. Turner (1999) Implications of land use change for the production of plant biomass in densely populated Sahelo-Sudanian shrub-grasslands in north-east Nigeria. *Global Ecology and Biogeography,* 8, pp. 243-256.

Myers, N. (1991) *Population, Resources and the Environment: the Critical Challenges.* Bantam Books, New York.

Odihi, J. (2003) Deforestation in afforestation priority zone in Sudano-Sahelian Nigeria. *Applied Geography* 23, pp. 227-259.

Odihi, J. (2000) Making dams more beneficial in northern Nigeria. In: *Issues in Land Administration and Development in Northern Nigeria.* Department of Geography, Bayero University, Kano, pp. 261-270.

Perkins, J.J and D.S.G. Thomas (1993) Spreading deserts or spatially confined environmental impacts? Land degradation and cattle ranching in the Kalahari Desert of Botswana. *Land Degradation and Rehabilitation,* 4, pp. 179-194.

Pullan, R.A. (1974) Farmed Parkland in West Africa. *Savanna,* 3 (2), pp. 119-152.

Rasmussen, K. (1999) Land degradation in the Sahel-Sudan: the conceptual basis. *Danish Journal of Geography - Special Issue.* Vol. 2, pp. 151-159.

Chapter 26   Roy Maconachie, in
A.I. Tanko and S.B. Momale (Eds.)
*Kano: Environment, Society and Development*
London & Abuja, Adonis & Abbey Publishers

Ribot, J. (1999) A history of fear: imagining deforestation in the West African dryland forests. *Global Ecology and Biogeography* 8, pp. 291-300.

Richards, P. (1985) *Indigenous agricultural revolution: ecology and food production in West Africa.* Longman, London.

Scoones, I. (1998) Sustainable rural livelihoods: a framework for analysis. *IDS Working Paper 72*, Institute of Development Studies, Brighton.

Scoones, I.and J. Thompson (1994) Knowledge, power and agriculture -towards a theoretical understanding. In: Scoones, I. and J. Thompson (1994) (eds.) *Beyond Farmer First: Rural people's knowledge,agricultural research and extension practice.*
Intermediate Technology Publications, London, pp. 16-32.

Stocking, M.A. and N. Murnaghan (2001) *Handbook for the Field Assessment of Land Degradation.* Earthscan Publications, London.

Sullivan, S. (1999) The impacts of people and livestock on topographically diverse open wood and shrub-lands in arid north-west Namibia. *Global Ecology and Biogeography,* 8, pp. 257-277.

Tchamie, T.T.K. (1994) Learning from local hostility to protected areas in Togo. *Unasylva* 176 (45).

Warren, A. (2002) Can land degradation be simply defined? In: *Implementing the United Nations Convention to Combat Desertification (CCD): Past Experience and Future Challenges. Proceedings of the CCD Workshop, 26-27 February 2002, Denmark.* Marcussen, H.S., I. Nygaard and A. Reenberg (eds.). SEREIN Occasional Paper No. 14, Copenhagen, pp. 19-46.

Warren, A., Batterbury, S. P. J. and Osbahr H. (2001) Sustainability and Sahelian soils: evidence from Niger. *Geographical Journal,* 167 (4), pp. 324-341.

Warren, A. and C. Agnew (1988) An assessment of desertification and land degradation in arid and semi arid areas. *Drylands Paper,* 2, Drylands Programme, IIED, London.

Wezel, A. and J. Haigis (2000) Farmers perception of vegetation changes in semi-arid Niger. *Land Degradation and Development,* 11, pp. 523-534.

Williams, I., F. Mu'azu, U.M. Kaoje and R. Ekeh (1997) *A Brief Study of Conflicts Between Pastoralists and Agriculturalists in the North-east of Nigeria. A study for the Overseas Development Association* (ODA). Mimeo.

Chapter 26 | Roy Maconachie, in
A.I. Tanko and S.B. Momale (Eds.)
*Kano: Environment, Society and Development*
London & Abuja, Adonis & Abbey Publishers

Yusuf, M.A. (1996) The farming system of Tumbau, Kano State, Nigeria. *Soils, Cultivars and Livelihoods in North-east Nigeria. Working Paper No. 1.* Department of Geography, Bayero University, Kano.

## Personal communications

Abdulwahab, Y (2002) Maisar Tudu, farmer, personal communication, February 20, 2002.

Ahamed, A. (2002) Gamji Tara, farmer, personal communication, May 01, 2002.

Ali, S. (2000) Hotoro Arewa, farmer, personal communication, April 27, 2002.

Alkasin, U. (2002) Gamji Tara, farmer/vegetable seller, personal communication, Feb 27, 2002.

Amadu, U. (2002) Jakara irrigation site, vegetable farmer, personal communication.

Baba, Y. (2002) Zangon Gabas, bus driver/farmer, personal communication, March 10, 2002.

Basiru, M. (2002) Hotoro Arewa, civil servant/farmer, personal communication, April 21, 2002.

Dibi, G. (2002) Magama, civil servant/farmer, personal communication, February 19, 2002.

Garba, Y (2002) Maisar Tudu, tailor/farmer, personal communication, February 25, 2002

Hamza, A. (2002) Hotoro Arewa, farmer, personal communication, March 23, 2002.

Jibrin, U. (2002) Gamji Tara, Islamic teacher/farmer, personal communication, February 26, 2002.

Maikano, A. (2002) Hotoro Arewa, brick layer, personal communication, April 21, 2002.

Nasiru, M. (2002) Kadewa, farmer/sugar cane seller, personal communication, March 05, 2002.

Nuhu, J. (2002) Kwarin Dankukuru irrigation site, vegetable farmer, personal communication, April 16, 2002.

Sadanu, M. (2002) Kwarin-Dankukuru irrigation site, vegetable farmer, personal communication, April 16, 2002.

Sani, M. (2002) Kwarin Dankukuru irrigation site, vegetable farmer, personal communication, April 23, 2002.

| Chapter 26 | Roy Maconachie, in |
| | A.I. Tanko and S.B. Momale (Eds.) |
| | *Kano: Environment, Society and Development* |
| | London & Abuja, Adonis & Abbey Publishers |

Shemawa A. (2002) Zangon Gabas, housewife, personal communication, May 15, 2002.

Usaini, D. (2002) Hotoro Arewa, Bricklayer/farmer, personal communication., April 06, 2002.

Yakubu, H. (2002) Zangon Gabas, farmer, personal communication, April 27, 2002.

Zakari, A (2002) Kadewa, housewife, personal communication, March 05, 2002.

Chapter 26 | Roy Maconachie, in
A.I. Tanko and S.B. Momale (Eds.)
*Kano: Environment, Society and Development*
London & Abuja, Adonis & Abbey Publishers

# Chapter Twenty Seven

## HOUSEHOLD ENERGY

Ibrahim Baba Yakubu

### Introduction

This Chapter discusses household energy situation in the Kano Region. It examines the importance of energy at household level and its impact on the socioeconomic well-being of nations. Issues treated include: woodfuel as a major household energy source in Kano; urban energy demand and supply in Kano; sources of woodfuel and the household energy transition in Kano.

The importance of energy at household level and its impact on socioeconomic wellbeing is well known. The amount of energy consumed in the various sectors of the economy varies from country to country and according to level of development. While the industrialised countries use most of the world's energy, the less developed countries use the least. The pattern of use also differs. In this regard, Enger and Smith (2004) reported that the industrialized nations use energy equally within three sectors: residential, transportation and industrial, as against the predominant use of energy for residential purpose (cooking and heating) by the less-developed countries. They further reported that the amount of energy required for commercial and residential use varies also from country to country. This is because though a country with high GDP uses a large amount of energy, a lower percentage of its energy per capita is used for residential and commercial needs than does a less developed country. They gave example of 30 percent of the energy used in North America going to the residential and commercial sectors as against the 90 percent in India going to the residential sector. It is also worth noting that there is variation in residential energy use between countries and regions.

IEA (2008) reported that countries within the Organisation For Economic Co-operation and Development (OECD), comprising mainly developed economies has over 72 percent of its household energy requirements derived from electricity and natural gas and

Chapter 27 | Ibrahim B. Yakubu, in
A.I. Tanko and S.B. Momale (Eds.)
*Kano: Environment, Society and Development*
London & Abuja, Adonis & Abbey Publishers

proportionately used at 69 percent for space/water heating, 21 percent for appliances, while lighting and cooking consume 5 percent apiece. This contrasts remarkably with 53 percent of energy use at household derived from renewable sources, mainly biomass, and used predominantly for cooking in non OECD countries, including Nigeria. Educational background, cultural and traditional beliefs also affect energy consumption pattern. Studies in Northern Nigeria have shown that households whose heads' have little or no formal education (western education) consume more wood for domestic use than those with some formal education (Silviconsult 1991, Hassan 2008). In another instance Nierkik (1998) reported that electricity was initially rejected in West Rand of South Africa, because people believed that it would chase away their ancestral spirits. However, later awareness that electricity and the traditional fire can co-exist and the linkage of their ancestors maintained resulted in change of habit by the people, and clamour for electrification followed.

Generally Nigeria, as a country, is well endowed with energy resources. The main ones being crude oil, natural gas, coal tar, sand and biomass. Table 27.1 shows the energy reserve/potential for the country. The country has so far recorded more than 40 years of successful oil exploration and the country presently consumes considerable amount of liquefied petroleum gases, motor spirits, kerosene, diesel oil, fuel oil and gas oil.

**Table 27.1: Nigeria's Energy Reserves**

| Resource | Reserves | Reserves (Billion toe) | % Fossil |
|---|---|---|---|
| Crude oil | 33 billion bbl | 4.488 | 31.1 |
| Natural Gas | 4502.4 billion m³ (159 trillion scf) | 3.559 | 26.7 |
| Coal & Lignite | 2.7 billion tones | 1.882 | 13.0 |
| Tar Sands | 31 billion bbl oil equiv. | 4.216 | 29.2 |
| Sub-Total (Fossil Fuels) | | 14.445 | 100 |
| Hydro Electric Power (Large Scale) | 10,000 MW | | |
| Hydroelectric power (Small Scale) | 734 MW | Provisional | |
| Fuel wood | 13,071,464 has (forest land 1981 | Estimate | |
| Animal Waste | 61 million tones/yr | | |
| Crop Residue | 83 million tones/yr | | |
| Solar Radiation | 3.5-7.0 kWh/m²-day | | |
| Wind | 2-4m/s (Annual Average) | | |

*Source: Energy Commission of Nigeria*

Chapter 27   Ibrahim B. Yakubu, in
A.I. Tanko and S.B. Momale (Eds.)
*Kano: Environment, Society and Development*
London & Abuja, Adonis & Abbey Publishers

Proven crude oil reserves in the country stand at more than 20 billion barrels, while gas reserves are put at about 2.7 billion cubic meters. The abundance of oil and gas supplies in the country has played a significant role in accounting for Nigeria's heavy reliance on energy as a major foreign exchange earner. SOER (2008) reported that Nigeria possesses one of the least energy-efficient economies in the world with energy consumption per capita at 138kg of oil equivalent with an energy intensity of 0.476 in 1990.

Solar energy still remains a major potential source of energy in Nigeria, which is relatively untapped. In terms of annual total, the annual radiation level in Northern Nigeria has been reported by SOER (2008) to be about 190kcal while the level in the South is about 110kcal. Nigeria is also blessed with flowing rivers, both large and small, and hydroelectric power generation has been significant source of energy in the country.

Wood is however the main source of fuel especially to majority of the rural communities in Nigeria. Wood is also significant as a source of fuel to some urban dwellers and bundles of wood either dried or semi-dried, cut from forests, woodlands and swamps, are seen daily piled up along motorable roads awaiting transportation to major urban centres. Wood is also used for making charcoal for sale in large urban centres, and charcoal burning has become a major money making activity. Around cities such as Lagos, Ibadan, Kano, Enugu, Onitsha, Maiduguri and Sokoto, women and local farmers are engaged in the business. In the coastal region, trees such as *Rhizophora racemosa*, which has a high calorific value is widely used as firewood and especially for making charcoal.

SOER (2008) reported that 70 percent of the households in Nigeria use firewood as the main source of fuel for cooking, and that more than a quarter (26.6 percent) use kerosene, while only 1.1 percent use gas (Table 27.2).

Chapter 27    Ibrahim B. Yakubu, in
A.I. Tanko and S.B. Momale (Eds.)
*Kano: Environment, Society and Development*
London & Abuja, Adonis & Abbey Publishers

Table 27.2: Main Sources of Fuel for Cooking in Nigeria (%)

| Source of Fuel | Percent |
|---|---|
| Fuel Wood | 69.8 |
| Charcoal | 0.84 |
| Kerosene/Oil | 26.55 |
| Gas | 1.11 |
| Electricity | 0.52 |
| Crop Residue or Sawdust | 0.09 |
| Animal Waste | 0.07 |
| Others | 0.84 |
| Total | 100 |

*Source: National Bureau of Statistics (2005)*

## Woodfuel as Major Household Energy in Kano

Cline-Cole et al. (1990) have in a study in 1983, regarded as a watershed work on household energy situation in northern Nigeria, entitled "Woodfuel in Kano", investigated many aspects of woodfuel as the dominant household energy in Kano. Issues treated by this work ranged from supply and demand of, to policy issues in, woodfuel. It is important to revisit some of the issues raised by the work of Cline-Cole et al. (1990), with a view to recording some of the fundamental matters arising, 28 years after.

### *Urban Household Energy Demand and Supply in Kano*

The estimated consumption of woodfuel per person in an urban wood-using household in 1983 was 360kg of solid wood per year, according to the investigations of Cline-Cole et al. (1990). Today, the woodfuel consumption per person has been estimated at 372kg per year. Though, woodfuel is used in conjunction with a range of other fuels, persistent price shifts in kerosene and other fossil fuels, and logistic problems in the supply chain of other fuels may have increased the marginal demand in woodfuel at household level. On the basis of a model population of one million (1983), total consumption in Metropolitan Kano was estimated to be 383,000m$^3$. In the year 2010, total consumption of Metropolitan Kano was estimated at

Chapter 27 | Ibrahim B. Yakubu, in
A.I. Tanko and S.B. Momale (Eds.)
*Kano: Environment, Society and Development*
London & Abuja, Adonis & Abbey Publishers

2,298,000m³, with a population of 6 million, making allowances for non-wood-using households (32%) and non-household use.

## Sources of Woodfuel in Kano

Cline-Cole et al. (1990) reported that woodfuel (and now with the advent of charcoal) may be obtained from four main sources in 1983: plantations, natural forests, farmed parkland, and fallows or shrubland. In 2010, 22 years after, investigation indicates that Kano Metropolis imports about 72 percent of its woodfuel requirement from outside the Region. This finding corroborates the forecast of Cline-Cole et al (1990) when they noted that in the foreseeable future, Metropolitan Kano may be expected to import an increasing proportion of its woodfuel from outside its borders. There has also been massive importation of charcoal into Kano in recent years, where it has been estimated that for every 10 truck-load of petroleum products coming into the city from Southern Nigeria, at least four come along with about 20 bags of charcoal each. Furthermore, more and more households in the metropolis are today switching over to, or supplementing, woodfuel with charcoal at 13 percent and 18 percent respectively. The environmental burden of charcoal production and use has been reported to be high.

Woodfuel gathered from forested commons is an important source of domestic energy in rural areas of many poor countries (Cecelski et al., 1979; Heltberg et al., 2000). It has been estimated that more than 2.4 billion people rely directly on traditional biomass fuels for their cooking and heating, and in poor countries biomass use represents over half of residential energy consumption (IEA, 2005). Demands for fuelwood by subsistence agricultural households may be the leading cause of world deforestation (Amacher et al., 1993; Amacher et al., 1996). According to recent data, the global rate of deforestation continues to be alarmingly high - about 13 million hectares per year (Food and Agriculture Organization of the United Nations, 2005). In recent decades deforestation has come to be perceived as a global problem, because of the perception that the earth's resources are reaching the limits for supporting the world's population and economic systems (Schmink, 1994). Deforestation has created a situation of fuelwood scarcity to the point that an impending

Chapter 27 | Ibrahim B. Yakubu, in
A.I. Tanko and S.B. Momale (Eds.)
*Kano: Environment, Society and Development*
London & Abuja, Adonis & Abbey Publishers

"fuelwood crisis" looms in many settings (Dewees, 1989; Heltberg et al., 2000).

## Household Energy Transition in Kano

The "energy ladder" is a commonly used concept in models of domestic fuel choices in developing countries (Campbell et al., 2003; Alam et al., 1998; Davis, 1998; Leach, 1992; Hosier and Dowd, 1987). The principal notion underlying this concept is that households face a range of energy supply choices, which can be ordered from least to most technologically sophisticated. A transition from biomass fuels to more sophisticated alternatives occurs as part of the process of economic growth. Most empirical studies that have been done on the determinants of fuel transitions have linked factors such as income, access to electricity, and forest scarcity to fuel substitution (Alam et al., 1998; Campbell et al., 2003; Davis, 1998; Heltberg et al., 2000; Madubansi and Shackleton, 2007; Ouedraogo, 2006). Although there have been few studies of changing household fuel choices, evidence of the energy transition is mounting. Household energy surveys have found income to be a major determinant of the energy transition (Alam et al., 1998; Campbell et al., 2003; Davis, 1998; Ouedraogo, 2006). For example, Campbell et al. (2003) found that in the four largest cities in Zimbabwe higher income households were less likely to use wood as their primary cooking fuel, switching to kerosene and electricity. Ouedraogo (2006) found that households' firewood utilization rate decreased with increasing household income in the capital city of Burkina Faso. Access to electricity has been found to be another important determinant of the energy transition (Campbell et al., 2003; Davis, 1998; Ouedraogo, 2006). However, Madubansi and Shackleton (2007) found that the introduction of electricity into a rural region of South Africa had little impact on fuelwood consumption. Other factors associated with reduced consumption of fuelwood and instead uses of alternative fuels are forest scarcity and increased fuelwood collection time (Heltberg et al., 2000) and household size (Alam et al., 1998; Ouedraogo, 2006).

While it is widely assumed that consumer preference for woodfuel is an artifact of delayed modernisation, or of inefficiencies in the distribution of alternative energies, the work of Cline-Cole et al

Chapter 27 | Ibrahim B. Yakubu, in
A.I. Tanko and S.B. Momale (Eds.)
*Kano: Environment, Society and Development*
London & Abuja, Adonis & Abbey Publishers

showed that cooking requirements, capital costs, supply irregularities, and cultural attitudes are all relevant to the issue, and that at 1983-Kano prices, wood provided more energy per Naira than the alternatives for cooking and heating. Our present study shows that willingness to shift to other sources of energy for 2010 is as high 56 percent, but that the basic constrain to this transition is income. Respondents indicated that initial investments in the procurement of basic equipment for alternative sources of energy are beyond the reach of average households. The case in point usually cited was that of LPG (cooking gas) and kerosene stoves, whose initial costs may be between N7,000 and N38,000 and between N1,500 and N7,000 respectively. This is no doubt an area where policy makers may intervene by subsidising the initial costs of these cooking stoves for, in the early stages, the working households, thereby facilitating the much needed transition to cleaner energy sources.

## References

Alam, M. J. Sathaye, and D. Barnes (1998). "Urban household energy use in India: Efficiency and policy implications." *Energy Policy* 26 (11):885-891.

Amacher, G.S., W.F. Hyde, and B.R. Joshee (1993). "Joint Production and Consumption in Traditional Households: Fuelwood and Crop Residues in Two Districts in Nepal." *The Journal of Development Studies* 30 (1): 206-225.

Amacher, G.S., W.F. Hyde, and K.R. Kanel (1996). "Household Fuelwood Demand and Supply in Nepal's Tarai and Mid-Hills: Choice Between Cash Outlays and Labor Opportunity." *World Development* 24 (11):1725-1736.

Campbell, B.M., S.J. Vermeulen, J.J. Mangono, and R. Mabugu (2003). "The energy transition in action: Urban domestic fuel choices in a changing Zimbabwe." *Energy Policy* 31(6):553-562.

Cecelski, E., J. Dunkerley, and W. Ramsay (1979). "Household Energy and the Poor in the Third World."in *Resources for the Future*. Washington, D.C.

Cline-Cole, R. A., Falola, J. A., Main, H. A. C., Mortimore, M. J. and F. D. O'Reilly (1990). Wood Fuel in Kano. The United Nations University Press.

Chapter 27 | Ibrahim B. Yakubu, in
A.I. Tanko and S.B. Momale (Eds.)
*Kano: Environment, Society and Development*
London & Abuja, Adonis & Abbey Publishers

447

Davis, M. (1998). "Rural household energy consumption: The effects of access to electricity-Evidence from South Africa." *Energy Policy* 26 (3): 207-217.

Dewees, P.A. (1989). "TheWoodfuel Crisis Reconsidered: Observations on the Dynamics of Abundance and Scarcity." *World Development* 17(8):1159-1172.

Enger, E. A. and Smith, B. F. (2004). Environmental Science - A study of Interrelationships. McGraw Hill, New York.

Hassan, A. (2008). Analysis of Household Energy Utilisation in Katsina Metropolis. Unpublished Msc Thesis, Bayero University, Kano.

Heltberg, R., T.C. Arndt, and N.U. Sekhar. (2000). "Fuelwood Consumption and Forest Degradation: A Household Model for Domestic Energy Substitution in Rural India." *Land Economics* 76 (2): 213-232.

Hosier, R.H.and J. Dowd. (1987)."Household fuel choice in Zimbabwe: an empirical test of the energy ladder hypothesis." *Resources and Energy* 9:347-361.

IEA, (2008). World Trends in Energy Use and Efficiency. Energy Indicators, IEA/OECD, Paris http:/www.iea.org/Textbase/about/co pyright.asp

Leach, G. (1992). "The energy transition." *Energy Policy* 20 (2):116-123.

Madubansi, M. and C.M. Shackleton. (2007). "Changes in fuelwood use and selection following electrification in the Bushbuckridge lowveld, South Africa." *Journal of Environmental management* 83:416-426.

Ouedraogo, B. (2006). "Household energy preferences for cooking in urban Ouagadougou, Burkina Faso."*Energy Policy* 34(18):3787-3795.

Schmink, M. (1994). "The Socioeconomic Matrix of Deforestation." Pp. 253-275 in *Population and Environment: Rethinking the Debate*, edited by L. Arizpe, M.P. Stone, and D.C. Major. Boulder, CO: Westview Press.

Silviconsult (1991). Northern Nigeria Household Energy Study. Federal Forestry Management Evaluation and Coordinating Unit, Ibadan.

Chapter 27 | Ibrahim B. Yakubu, in
A.I. Tanko and S.B. Momale (Eds.)
*Kano: Environment, Society and Development*
London & Abuja, Adonis & Abbey Publishers

# Chapter Twenty Eight

## CLIMATE CHANGE

Luka Fitto Buba

### Introduction

Climate Change is a significant and lasting change in the statistical distribution of weather patterns over periods ranging from decades to millions of years. It may be a change in average weather conditions or the distribution of events around that average (e.g., more or fewer extreme weather events). Climate change may be limited to a specific region or may occur across the whole Earth.

Science has made enormous inroads in understanding climate change and its causes, and has helped to develop a strong understanding of current and potential impacts that affect people today and in coming decades. This understanding is crucial because it allows decision makers to place climate change in the context of other large challenges facing the nation and the world. There are still some uncertainties, and there always will be in understanding a complex system like the Earth's climate. Nevertheless, there is a strong, credible body of evidence, based on multiple lines of research, documenting that climate is changing and that these changes are in large part, caused by human activities. While much remains to be learned, the core phenomenon, scientific questions, and hypotheses have been examined thoroughly and have stood firm in the face of serious scientific debate and careful evaluation of alternative explanations.

### *The Climate Change Phenomenon*

Global warming has become familiar to many people as one of the important environmental issues of our day. Many opinions have been expressed concerning it, from the doom-laden to the dismissive. According to the National Academy of Sciences, the Earth's surface temperature has risen by about 0.5 degree Celsius in the past century, with accelerated warming during the past two decades. There is new

Chapter 28 | Luka F. Buba, in
A.I. Tanko and S.B. Momale (Eds.)
*Kano: Environment, Society and Development*
London & Abuja, Adonis & Abbey Publishers

and stronger evidence that most of the warming over the last 50 years is attributable to human activities. Human activities have altered the chemical composition of the atmosphere through the build-up of greenhouse gases - primarily carbon dioxide, methane, and nitrous oxide. The heat-trapping property of these gases is undisputed although uncertainties exist about how exactly the earth's climate responds to them.

Energy from the sun drives the earth's weather and climate, and heats the earth's surface; in turn, the earth radiates energy back into space. Atmospheric greenhouse gases (water vapour, carbon dioxide, and other gases) trap some of the outgoing energy, retaining heat somewhat like the glass panels of a greenhouse. Without this natural "greenhouse effect," temperatures would be much lower than they are now, and life as known today would not be possible. Instead, thanks to greenhouse gases, the earth's average temperature is a more hospitable 15.6°C. However, problems are certain to arise when the atmospheric concentration of greenhouse gases increases beyond the normal.

Since the beginning of the industrial revolution, atmospheric concentrations of carbon dioxide have increased nearly 30%, methane concentrations have more than doubled, and nitrous oxide concentrations have risen by about 15%. These increases have enhanced the heat-trapping capability of the earth's atmosphere. Sulfate aerosols, a common air pollutant, cool the atmosphere by reflecting light back into space; however, sulfates are short-lived in the atmosphere and vary regionally (IPCC, 2007).

Scientists generally believe that the combustion of fossil fuels and other human activities are the primary reasons for the increased concentration of carbon dioxide. Plant respiration and the decomposition of organic matter release more than 10 times the $CO_2$ released by human activities; but these releases have generally been in balance during the centuries before industrial revolution with carbon dioxide absorbed by terrestrial vegetation and the oceans.

What has changed in the last few hundred years is the additional release of carbon dioxide by human activities. Fossil fuels burned to run cars and trucks, heat homes and businesses, and power factories are responsible for about 98% of the U.S. emissions of carbon dioxide, 24% of methane, and 18% of nitrous oxide (IPCC, 2007). Increased

Chapter 28 | Luka F. Buba, in
A.I. Tanko and S.B. Momale (Eds.)
*Kano: Environment, Society and Development*
London & Abuja, Adonis & Abbey Publishers

agriculture, deforestation, landfills, industrial production, and mining also contribute a significant share of emissions. In 1997, the United States emitted about one-fifth of the total global greenhouse gases.

Estimating future emissions is difficult, because it depends on demographic, economic, technological, policy, and institutional developments. Several emissions scenarios have been developed based on differing projections of these underlying factors. For example, by 2100, in the absence of emissions control policies, carbon dioxide concentrations are projected to be 30-150% higher than today's levels (IPCC, 2007).

The last two decades of the 20th century have been remarkable for the frequency and intensity of extreme of weather and climate. For example, periods of unusually strong winds have been experienced in Western Europe. During the early hours of the morning of 16 October 1987, over fifteen million trees were blown down in south-east England and the London area. The storm also hit Northern France, Belgium and The Netherlands with ferocious intensity; it turned out to be the worst storm experienced in the area since 1703 (Houghton, 2004). Storm-forced winds of similar or even greater intensity but covering a greater area of Western Europe have struck since – on four occasions in 1990 and three occasions in December 1999 (McCarthy et al, 2001). In the Nigerian context, temperature characteristics have been found to exhibit similar trends to those of other regions of the world that indicate a rise in global temperatures. Buba (2009) clearly supports this position.

## Seasonal and Annual Distribution of Temperature

### Seasonal Temperature distribution

Figure 28.1 presents an overview of long-term monthly temperature distribution over Kano. This is believed to be truly representative of the situation over the Kano Region as a whole. It shows that temperature distribution over the Region closely follows the seasonal migratory pattern of the overhead sun. The main feature is that seasonal temperature values range between 21°C and 33°C. The annual temperature range is small. This goes to show that seasonal average

Chapter 28 | Luka F. Buba, in
A.I. Tanko and S.B. Momale (Eds.)
*Kano: Environment, Society and Development*
London & Abuja, Adonis & Abbey Publishers

**451**

temperatures in the Kano Region do not vary markedly; 22°C to 25°C for December, January and February; 23°C to 30°C for March, April and May; 26°C to 30°C for June, July and August; and 25°C to 27°C for September, October and November.

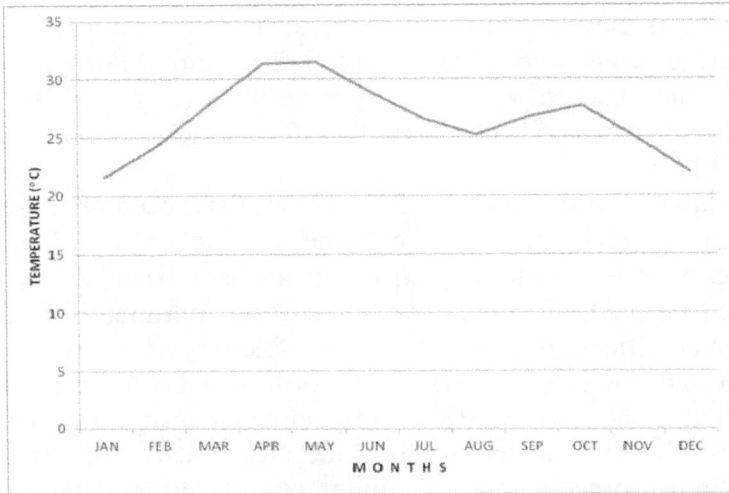

**Figure 28.1: Long-term Mean Monthly Temperature Distribution at Kano (1942-2010)**

The difference between minimum and maximum temperatures for the Region averages about 26°C. The lowest minimum monthly temperature, for January, of 13°C is compared to the lowest mean maximum temperature of 29°C, which is for January. For the same zone, the highest mean maximum which occurs in May and April, are respectively, 25°C and 40°C. All these go to confirm the well known fact that diurnal variations in temperature are more pronounced than inter-annual variations and the usual conceptualization of the night as the winter of the Tropics.

Inter-annual variation of temperatures is low over the Kano Region. The implication is that each year is very much like the other with respect to daytime temperatures. The monotony of high daytime temperatures from month to month and from year to year is a well known feature of tropical climates. This notwithstanding, one could identify temporal and spatial patterns in variability of mean monthly temperatures. In the more northern zones, coefficients of variability

Chapter 28 | Luka F. Buba, in
A.I. Tanko and S.B. Momale (Eds.)
*Kano: Environment, Society and Development*
London & Abuja, Adonis & Abbey Publishers

appear to be relatively higher in the months of December, January and February compared to other months of the year.

The coefficients of variability reveal a clear contrast between December to March on the one hand and the rest of the year on the other hand. In almost all the stations, the highest coefficients are for January followed by December. This pattern is much more pronounced in the northern areas. Generally, low variability of temperature highlighted explains the usual relegation of temperature parameters in the literature on climate variability in the Tropical areas, with more emphasis placed on rainfall which for all intent and purposes is characterized by wider variability.

## *Annual Temperature Anomaly Trends*

Temperature Anomaly time series were plotted for Kano and the Sudano-Sahelian Zone (see Figures 28.2 and 28.3), making it possible to assess the level of inter-annual fluctuation in each station's temperature. The general trends in temperature were assessed using the simple regression analysis technique. The dominance of negative signs is indicative of a general trend towards below normal temperature distribution, while positive signs points to above normal temperature conditions. The results are presented on the time series, in conjunction with the running means, line of least squares and their equation. The trend investigated with the simple regression analysis is a straight line, which gives the impression of continuous and regular increase in temperature. However in reality, the actual annual values fluctuate around the straight line to which the series have been fitted. The analysis gives a general direction of change, which in this case is increasing temperature. The yearly fluctuations may at first appear irregular or random. Further investigation of the series with the technique of five-year running mean indicate a tendency for periods of below normal to alternate with periods of above temperature whether in terms of the annual temperature or in terms of any of the components of seasonal temperature.

Chapter 28 | Luka F. Buba, in
A.I. Tanko and S.B. Momale (Eds.)
*Kano: Environment, Society and Development*
London & Abuja, Adonis & Abbey Publishers

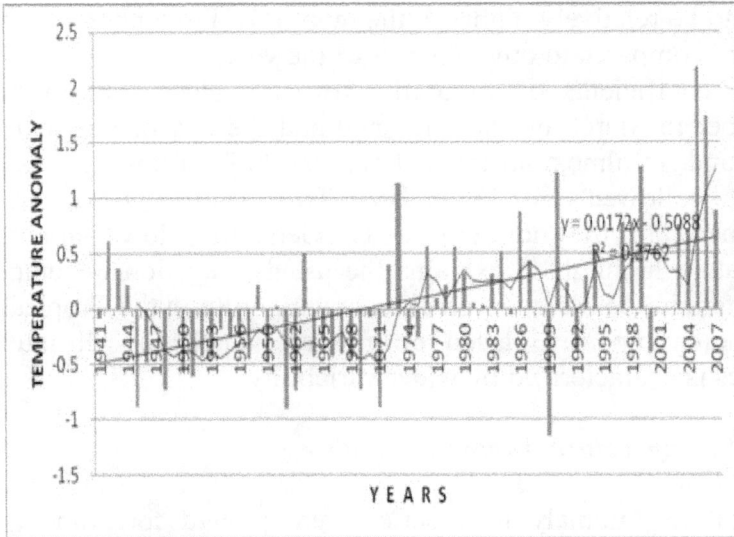

**Figure 28.2: Temperature Anomaly for Kano (1941 - 2007)**

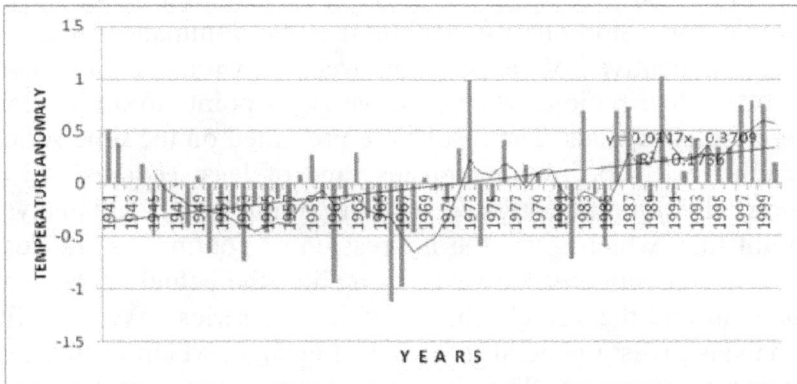

**Figure 28.3: Temperature Anomaly for the Sudano-Sahelian Zone (1941 - 2000)**

The evolution of average annual temperature anomalies shows two main periods over the Kano Region. The 1950s and 1960s are characterized by negative anomalies. The 1980s are marked by positive anomalies across the entire study area. The last decade (1990s) has shown more marked positive anomalies. This goes to show that temperature distribution over the area was normally

Chapter 28 | Luka F. Buba, in
A.I. Tanko and S.B. Momale (Eds.)
*Kano: Environment, Society and Development*
London & Abuja, Adonis & Abbey Publishers

454

distributed until fairly recent when it began to manifest an upward trend in response to the ongoing global warming phenomenon.

## Seasonal and Annual Rainfall Distribution

### *Monthly Rainfall distribution*

The main rainfall regime of the Kano Region is displayed as monthly precipitation for Kano. The region is characterized by unimodal seasonal rainfall distribution. The Region shows a peak in the month of August.

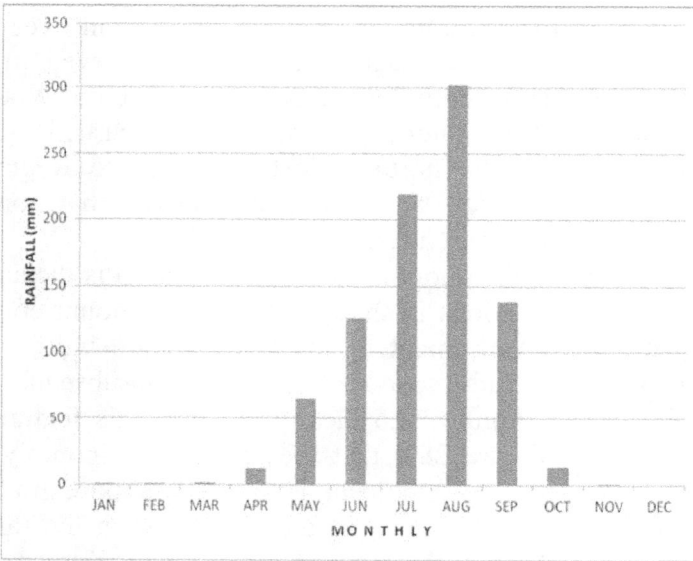

**Figure 28.4: Long-term Mean Monthly Rainfall distribution for Kano (1905-2007).**

The first season of the year includes the months of December, January and February (DJF): it is the major dry season in the Kano Region. The second season comprises the three months of March, April and May (MAM) and marks the beginning of the wet season. The third runs from June to August (JJA) and is the main wet season engulfing the entire region. The fourth season includes the months of

Chapter 28   Luka F. Buba, in
A.I. Tanko and S.B. Momale (Eds.)
*Kano: Environment, Society and Development*
London & Abuja, Adonis & Abbey Publishers

**455**

September, October and November (SON) and is transitory from wet to dry-marking the end of rains.

Rainfall usually starts in the month of May and ends in October over the Region. This feature of the onset of the rainy season is entrenched in the mechanism that determine the climates of West Africa in general and the area in particular. This indicates that the time for the onset of the rainy season as presented by the Nigerian Meteorological Agency (NIMET) and other climatologists has only changed slightly.

The cessation of rainfall in the Kano Region follows the same pattern with the onset, but in reverse order. Rainfall ceases in October over the region. The same explanation given with respect to onset above obtains.

In the light of the presentation above, rainy season over the area lasts five months on the average. Variation is observed in rainfall duration in relation to different locations over the Region. Whereas the rains start earlier and stop later in the southernmost parts, it starts later and ceases earlier in the northernmost parts of the Region. This situation is still controlled by the climatic factors that control the distribution of rainfall over Nigeria.

Closely related to the duration of the rainy season is the amount of rainfall received by stations in the area. Rainfall amount continue to increase with the advancement of the rainy season until a peak is reached in August. Rainfall amount then decreases subsequently until it eventually ceases. Figure 28.5 clearly captures this feature. It can also be seen from Figure 28.4 that the increase in monthly rainfall amount, from the onset until the peak is reached, is more gradual than the decrease from when the peak is attained to when the rains stop. This is in line with the findings of Kowal and Kassam (1978), Oguntoyinbo et al (1977), Buba (2000).

### *Long-term Annual Rainfall Distribution*

Rainfall in the Kano region is characterized by strong interannual variability. Figure 28.5 presents a descriptive statistics of annual rainfall for the stations in the Region. Mean rainfall is found was

Chapter 28 | Luka F. Buba, in
A.I. Tanko and S.B. Momale (Eds.)
*Kano: Environment, Society and Development*
London & Abuja, Adonis & Abbey Publishers

found to vary from over 1,174mm in the southern part of the Region to less than half that figure in the northern fringes.

Whereas mean annual rainfall varies significantly from one station to another (spatially), inter-annual (temporal) variation for individual stations is relatively small. The highest standard deviation (192) was recorded at Hadejia, while the lowest figure of 120 was found to hold in Gwaram. There is however no clear spatial trend in the spatial distribution of standard deviation values over the Kano Region. The only observation is that variation seems to increase with latitude (see Figure 28.6).

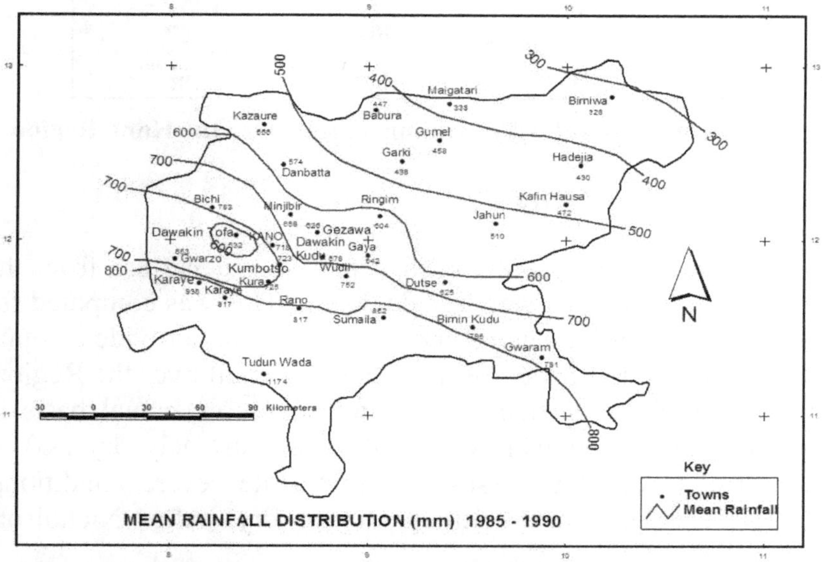

MEAN RAINFALL DISTRIBUTION (mm) 1985 - 1990

**Figure 28.5: Isohytes indicating Rainfall Distribution over the Kano Region**

Chapter 28 | Luka F. Buba, in
A.I. Tanko and S.B. Momale (Eds.)
*Kano: Environment, Society and Development*
London & Abuja, Adonis & Abbey Publishers

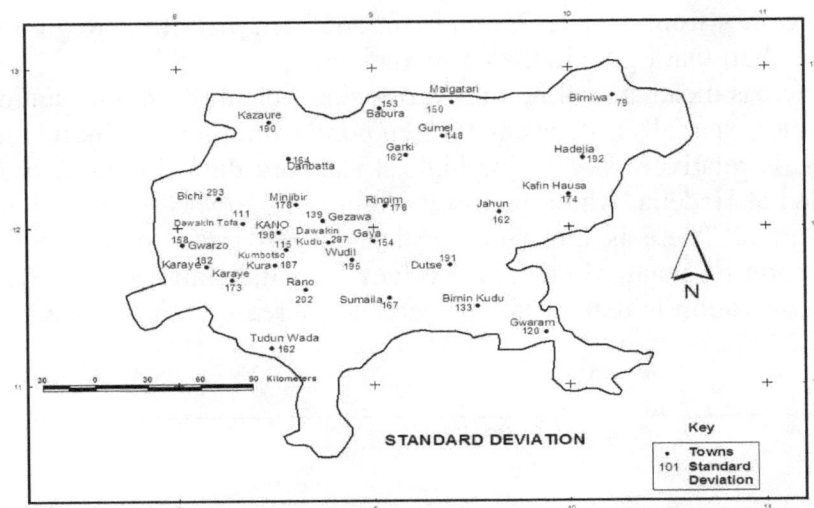

**Figure 28.6: Rainfall Standard Deviation Values over the Kano Region**

## *Annual Rainfall Time Series*

Rainfall is expressed as standardized departure - departure from the long-term mean divided by standard deviation. This was computed for Kano and the Sudano-Sahelian Zone. The departures provide a sound basis for examining the nature of interannual rainfall over the Region. It also gives information about the water status on annual basis in terms of whether a year can be described as extremely dry (-3) or extremely wet (+3). The classes of ±2 indicate severe conditions, while the ±1classes indicate mildly wet or dry (After Nicholson, 2000).

Figures 28.7 and 28.8 present clear pictures of rainfall fluctuations, particularly, in the Kano Metropolis, and generally, in the Kano Region. It can be seen that the temporal distribution of rainfall is quite variable. Actual rainfall, as indicated by the anomalies, fluctuates around the horizontal axis to which the series have been fitted. This demonstrates the relationship between the long-term mean and changes from one year to the other. The magnitude of the inteannual variation is also vividly captured (see Figures 28.7 and 28.8). This gives a clear picture of fluctuation in moisture status of individual years as being normal, moderately wet or dry, severely wet or dry and

Chapter 28 | Luka F. Buba, in
A.I. Tanko and S.B. Momale (Eds.)
*Kano: Environment, Society and Development*
London & Abuja, Adonis & Abbey Publishers

extremely wet or dry. By this it becomes possible to assess any year or couple of years as having normal, high or low moisture levels. All the stations considered commonly exhibit these fluctuations which are in conformity with the general nature of interannual rainfall in the tropical Region.

Figure 28.7 reveals that the early part of the 20th century (1915 - 1919) was characterized by normal moisture levels with more positive than negative anomalies/fluctuations. The 1920s, however, appear to have more negative fluctuations. The 1930s had normal moisture levels exhibiting positive departures. The period 1950 - 1967 can be described as wet, with significantly high moisture levels characterizing the period. The period 1967 - 1990 on the other hand recorded a sharp decrease in moisture levels, with 1970s and 1980s having severe droughts. The late 1990s seem to mark a recovery to normal moisture levels. These findings corroborate the similar opinions expressed by Hulme (2001), Nicholson (2001) and Buba (2000).

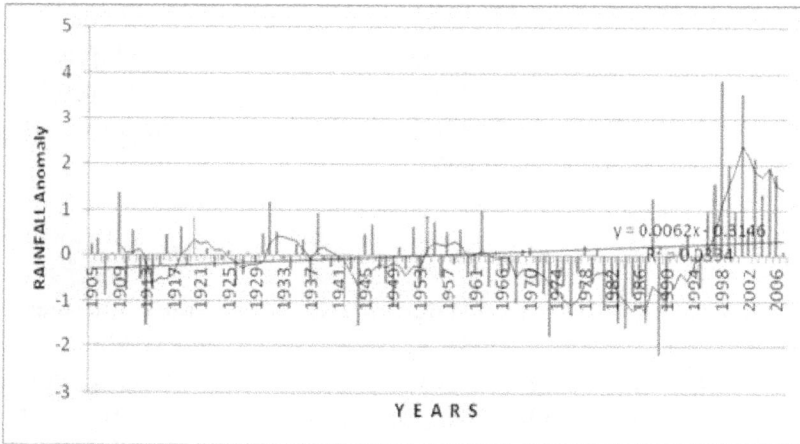

**Figure 28. 7 Long-term Rainfall Anomaly at Kano (1905 -2007)**

| Chapter 28 | Luka F. Buba, in |
| | A.I. Tanko and S.B. Momale (Eds.) |
| | *Kano: Environment, Society and Development* |
| | London & Abuja, Adonis & Abbey Publishers |

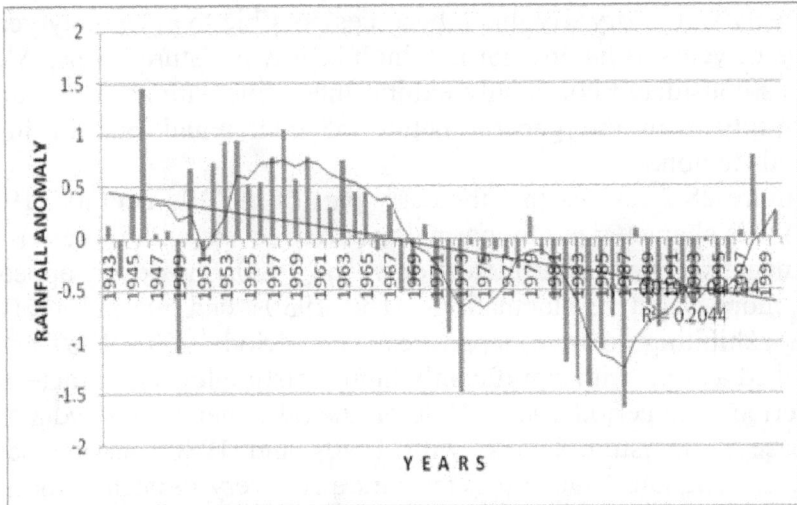

**Figure 28.8: Long-term Rainfall Anomaly for the Sudano-Sahelian Zone (1943 - 2000)**

A further investigation of the series, using the five-year running mean technique revealed a tendency for periods of above normal rainfall to alternate with periods of below average rainfall (see Figures 28.7 and 28.8). However, periods with sustained negative rainfall anomaly have persisted since 1968.

## Conclusion

This Chapter documents precipitation and temperature changes over larger part of the 20th century, over the Kano Region, where precipitation processes, climate variations and their spatial patterns are hitherto poorly documented. Rainfall results obtained agree with the main conclusions of other research works which focused on the sub-region (Nicholson, 1986, 2000; Hulme et al., 2001), and showed relatively wet conditions from the 1950s until the late 1960s, and drier conditions in the 1970s and 1980s. The precipitation evolution displays a shift between 1968 and 1971. The results of this will allow the appreciation of the effects of global warming at the local scale, because the impacts of climate change are more perceptible at this level.

Chapter 28 | Luka F. Buba, in
A.I. Tanko and S.B. Momale (Eds.)
*Kano: Environment, Society and Development*
London & Abuja, Adonis & Abbey Publishers

The temperature evolution of the Kano Region corresponds with that of the Inter-Tropical Convergence Zone (ITCZ) where years prior to 1980 were less warm and there was the very warm decade of the 1990s. Nevertheless, two periods clearly characterize the recent temperature evolution of Northern Nigeria pre- and post-1970. The first period reveals a temperature decrease or low temperatures and abundant precipitation. The second period is characterized by a general increase for all stations; all series show a relative precipitation decrease during the 1970s and 1990s compared to other decades. However, temperature and precipitation seem to increase from the 1990s.

It could thus be summarized that the temperature evolution over Northern Nigeria has been characterized by a warming during the last two decades after a long period of moderate temperatures. In this evolution of temperatures in the area, there are urban zones which have experienced marked warming, without any doubt linked to urbanization. However, even weak urbanization zones have experienced a general increase in temperatures, an indication of the sensitivity of the Kano Region to global climate change.

In summary, the temperature evolution of the Kano Region in Nigeria closely follows the Inter-Tropical Convergence Zone. It has been characterized by a warming during the last two decades after a long period of moderate temperatures which closely conform to IPCC's observations and prediction.

The Chapter also determined the degree of spatio-temporal variation of rainfall in the Kano Region. Monthly and annual rainfall data were analyzed to give information on coefficient of variability, rainfall anomaly indices and trends.

The results indicate that:

a. variability in annual rainfall totals is lower than those of monthly totals;
b. there is tendency for variability of annual totals to increase as totals decrease;
c. there has been a general trend towards aridity in most of the stations studied;

Chapter 28    Luka F. Buba, in
A.I. Tanko and S.B. Momale (Eds.)
*Kano: Environment, Society and Development*
London & Abuja, Adonis & Abbey Publishers

d. all the rainfall anomaly time series, when smoothed with five-year running means, reveal patterns characterized by oscillations;
e. the fluctuations are characterized by strong persistence and temporal dependencies; and
f. There appears to be regional variation in terms of rainfall fluctuations.

As regards temperature, the results also indicate the following:
i. there has been a general increase in temperatures for all stations since the 1950s;
ii. the annual temperature is characterized by a quasi-generalized increase for all stations; and
iii. However, temperature and precipitation seem to increase from the 1990s.

## References

AMCEN/UNEP, 2002: *Africa Environment Outlook: Past, Present and Future Perspectives. Earthprint*, Stevenage, 410 pp.

Adejuwon, J.O., Balogun, E.E. and Adejuwon, S.A. (1990): On the Annual and Seasonal Patterns of Rainfall Fluctuations in Sub-Saharan West Africa. *Int. J. Climatol.*, 10, 839 - 848

Adejuwon, J.O., Odekunle, T.O. and Adejuwon, S.A. (2006). Climate Variability in Nigeria. In Adejuwon, J.O. and Ogunkoya, O.O. (2006). (Ed.) *Climate Change and Food Security in Nigeria.* Obafemi Awolowo University Press.

Awosika, L.F., G.T. French, R.T. Nicholls, and C.E. Ibe, (1992). The Impacts of Sea Level Rise on the Coastline of Nigeria [O'Callahan, J. (ed.)]. In: *Global Climate Change and the Rising Challenge of the Sea.* Proceedings of the IPCC Workshop at Margarita Island, Venezuela, 9-13 March 1992. National Oceanic and Atmospheric Administration, Silver Spring, MD, USA, 690 pp

Ayoade, J. O. (1973): Annual Rainfall Trends and Periodicities in Nigeria. *Nigerian Geographical Journal* 16(2): 167-176

Chapter 28 | Luka F. Buba, in
A.I. Tanko and S.B. Momale (Eds.)
*Kano: Environment, Society and Development*
London & Abuja, Adonis & Abbey Publishers

Ayoade, J. O. and Akintola, F.O. (1982) A note on some characteristics of rainstorms in Ibadan, Nigeria. *Weather* 37 (2): 56-58

Boko, M., I. Niang, A. Nyong, C. Vogel, A. Githeko, M. Medany, B. Osman-Elasha,

R. Tabo and P. Yanda, 2007: Africa. *Climate Change 2007: Impacts, Adaptation and Vulnerability. Contribution of Working Group II to the Fourth AssessmentReport of the Intergovernmental Panel on Climate Change*, M.L. Parry, O.F. Canziani, J.P. Palutikof, P.J. van der Linden and C.E. Hanson, Eds., Cambridge University Press,Cambridge UK, 433-467.

Boxel, J. V. (2004). "Uncertainties in Modelling Climate Change" Climate Change: 33-42.

Brooks, N. L. G., M. (2000). Dust Variability over Northern Africa and Rainfall in the Sahel. *Linking Land Surface Change to Climate Change*. S. J. M. D. Kniverton. Dordrecht, Kluwer.

Brooks, N. (2004). Drought in the African Sahel: long-term perspectives and future prospects.Working Paper 61, Tyndall Centre for Climate Change Research, University of EastAnglia, Norwich, 31 pp.

Buba, LF, (2009) Evidence of Climate Change in Northern Nigeria: Temperature and Rainfall Variations. Unpublished. A Ph D Thesis submitted to Bayero University, Kano, Nigeria.

Chappell, A. and C.T. Agnew, 2004: (Modelling). Climate Change in West African Sahel rainfall (1931-90) as an artifact of changing station locations. *Int. J. Climatol.*, 24, 547-554.

Conway, D., C. Mould and W. Bewket, 2004: Over one century of rainfall and temperature observations in Addis Ababa, Ethiopia. *Int. J. Climatol.*, 24, 77-91.

Dennet, M.D., Elston, J., and Rodgers, J.A. (1985) An appraisal of rainfall trends in the Sahel. *Journal of Climatology* 5:353-347

Eklundh, L. and Olsson, L. (2003) Vegetation trends for the African Sahel 1982- 1999. *Geophys. Res. Lett.*, 30, 1430, doi: 10.1029/2002GL016772.

Fauchereau, N., S. Trzaska, Y. Richard, P. Roucou and P. Camberlin, 2003: Sea surface temperature co-variability in the southern Atlantic and Indian Oceans and its connections with the

Chapter 28 | Luka F. Buba, in
A.I. Tanko and S.B. Momale (Eds.)
*Kano: Environment, Society and Development*
London & Abuja, Adonis & Abbey Publishers

atmospheric circulation in the southern hemisphere. *Int. J. Climatol.*, 23, 663-677.

Folland CK, Palmer TN, Parker DE (1986) Sahel rainfall and worldwide sea temperature 1901-1985. *Nature* 320: 602-607

Folland, C. Owen, J. Ward, M.N. and Colman, A. (1991) Prediction of seasonal rainfall in the Sahel region using empirical and dynamical methods. *Journal of Forecasting* 10:21-56

Houghton, J. T., (2004). *Global Warming: The Complete Briefing.* 5 ed. Cambridge University Press.

Hulme, M. (2001). "Climatic Persepctives on Sahelian desiccation: 1973-1998." Global *Environmental Change* 11: 19-29.

Hulme, M., Doherty, R., Ngara, T., New, M., Lister, D. (2001). "African climate change: 1900-2100." *Climate Research* 17: 145-168.

Hulme, M., Doherty, R. Ngara T. and New, M (2005) Global warming and African climate change. *Climate Change and Africa*, P.S Low, Ed., Cambridge University Press, Cambridge, 29-40.

IPCC, (2007). Summary for Policymakers In: *Climate Change 2007: The Physical Science Basis. Contribution of Working Group I to the Fourth Assessment Report of the Intergovernmental Panel on Climate Change* [Solomon, S., D. Qin, M. Manning, Z. Chen, M. Marquis, K.B. Averyt, M.Tignor and H.L. Miller (eds.)]. Cambridge University Press, Cambridge, United Kingdom and New York, NY, USA

IPCC, (2007a). *Climate Change 2007: The Physical Science Basis. Contribution of Working Group I to the Fourth Assessment Report of the Intergovernmental Panel on Climate Change*, S. Solomon, D. Qin, M. Manning, Z. Chen, M. Marquis, K.B. Averyt, M. Tignor and H.L. Miller, Eds., Cambridge University Press, Cambridge, 996 pp.

Mortimore, M.J. and W.M. Adams, (2001). Farmer Adaptation, Change and Crisis in the Sahel'. *Global Environ. Chang.*, 11, 49-57.

Nicholson, S. E., (2001). Climatic and Environmental Change in Africa during the Last Two Centuries. *Climate Research* Vol 17: 123-144

Chapter 28 | Luka F. Buba, in
A.I. Tanko and S.B. Momale (Eds.)
*Kano: Environment, Society and Development*
London & Abuja, Adonis & Abbey Publishers

Nicholson, S. E., (2005). "On the Question of the "Recovery" of the Rains in the West African Sahel." *Journal of Arid Environments* 63: 615-641.

Nicholson, S.E. and Grist, J.P. (2003) The Seasonal Evolution of the Atmospheric Circulation over West Africa and Equatorial Africa. *J. Climate*, 16, 1013-1030

Obasi, G.O.P., (2005). The Impacts of ENSO in Africa. *Climate Change and Africa*, P.S Low, (ed.), Cambridge University Press, Cambridge, 218-230.

Tarhule, A. and Woo, M. (1998) Changes in rainfall characteristics in northern Nigeria. *Int. J. Climatol.* 18: 1261-1271

Tarhule, A. and Lamb, P.J., (2003). Climate research and seasonal forecasting for West Africans: perceptions, dissemination, and use? *B. Am. Meteorol. Soc.*, 84, 1741-1759.

Trenberth, K.E., Jones, P.D. Ambenje, P. Bojariu, R. Easterling, D. Klein Tank, A. Parker, D. Rahimzadeh, F. Renwick, J.A. Rusticucci, M. Soden B. and Zhai, P. (2007) Observations: Surface and atmospheric climate change. *Climate Change 2007: The Physical Science Basis. Contribution of Working Group I to the Fourth Assessment Report of the Intergovernmental Panel on Climate Change*, S. Solomon, D. Q. in, M. Manning, Z. Chen, M. Marquis, K.B. Averyt, M. Tignor and H.L. Miller, (eds.), Cambridge University Press, Cambridge, 235-336.

Chapter 28 | Luka F. Buba, in
A.I. Tanko and S.B. Momale (Eds.)
*Kano: Environment, Society and Development*
London & Abuja, Adonis & Abbey Publishers

# Chapter Twenty Nine

## DROUGHT AND DESERTIFICATION

Ahmed Maigari Ibrahim

## Introduction

Climate and weather systems are dynamic processes of the earth that constantly change. Naturally, extreme temperatures, rainfall variability, and intense air movement habitually occur. Therefore, periods of unusual dryness, i.e. droughts, are normal feature of climate and weather systems in all geographical regions, regardless of those areas considered as "wet" or "cold" as well as the semi-arid areas that are conventionally associated with drought. However, the preponderance and the dreadful repercussions of drought and its paraphernalia, in the semi-arid Tropics, in particular make drought and desertification a serious ecological disasters that not only require academic understanding but also proper planning and remediation measures. Kano Region as a sub-set of Semi-arid Tropic is bedevilled with the problems of drought and desertification of varying magnitude. This Chapter therefore focuses on the perception of drought and desertification in the Kano Region, the spatial distribution, attributed causative factors, repercussion and human response, among others.

## Drought

Conceptually, drought and desertification are very difficult to define due to the controversy involved among scholars and/or subject emphasis. For logical understanding and academic pedagogy, however, three main kinds of drought are considered. These are Meteorological, Hydrological, and Agricultural droughts. Meteorological drought is the delay in rainfall expectation or concentration of rainfall within a few months as against the long-term normal rainfall regime, or a deficiency of rainfall or moisture below normal during a particular period (Maigari, 2002). Conventional literature (Thambyahpillay, 1987; Mortimore, 1989a; Nicoholson and

Chapter 29 | Ahmed M. Ibrahim, in
A.I. Tanko and S.B. Momale (Eds.)
*Kano: Environment, Society and Development*
London & Abuja, Adonis & Abbey Publishers

Palao, 1993; and Agnew, 2000; etc) and rainfall records revealed that meteorological drought is evident in Kano Region in all of its ramifications; delay in rainfall expectation period, concentration of rainfall within few months, and inadequate rainfall amount.

Hydrological drought involves a reduction in water resources, such as stream-flows, lake levels, groundwater, under-ground aquifers, below a specified level for a given period of time. Therefore, it heavily relied on data for the availability and off-take rates in relation to the normal requirements of the system being supplied such as domestic, industrial and irrigated agriculture (UNDP, 1994). During the 1960s, 1970s and 1980s droughts, streams and rivers and to some extent dams and ground water levels had seriously reduced in many parts of the Kano Region. Notably among them include Kazaure, Danbatta, Wudil, Gumel, and Kafin-Hausa.

It is worth noting, however, that these two types can often be blurred as hydrological droughts may be caused by reductions in precipitation anywhere within the catchment area of a river or aquifer system. Thus, irrigated agricultural areas along river side may experience a hydrological drought as a result of a meteorological drought in the upland area (watershed) regardless of the levels of rainfall downstream.

On the other hand, Agricultural drought is the consistent high soil moisture deficit during growing season (Famer and Wigley, 1985). Thus it is the impact of meteorological and/or hydrological droughts on crop yields, as crops have particular temperature, moisture and nutrient requirements during their growth cycle in order to achieve optimum growth. It has been established, that inadequate moisture during growing cycle impairs on growth of crops and reduces yields. The common crops grown in the Kano Region, such as sorghum, millet, cowpea, groundnut, cotton, maize, and beniseed are highly vulnerable to drought. Improved crops varieties such as quick yielding and drought resistant seed varieties are now commonly used by small-holder farmers in the drought prone areas, particularly north of the 500mm isohyets line.

Chapter 29 | Ahmed M. Ibrahim, in
A.I. Tanko and S.B. Momale (Eds.)
*Kano: Environment, Society and Development*
London & Abuja, Adonis & Abbey Publishers

## Desertification

Desertification is the degradation of ecosystem in arid and semi-arid regions. According to UNEP (1977) 'it is the diminution or destruction of the biological potentials of land and can lead to desert like condition'. It is also viewed as a negative change from a productive to a less productive state or a transfer of the unproductive characteristics of one area, such as desert, to another (Mortimore, 1989a). Since the 1930s Dust Bowl in the Midwestern USA, desertification has been recognized as a problem, but the 1968 and 1973 great droughts in the Sahel made desertification an international issue. The desertified areas of the Kano Region are also of great concern both at local, state, national and international level.

### *Perception of Drought and Desertification*

Drought and desertification, like other natural calamities in the Kano Region are perceived in two main ways. The rural communities who are predominantly Muslims their religious believes and attitudes influenced their perception. Thus, most people believed that drought and desertification are an act of punishment or warning for wrong doings of contemporary societies. Some verses from the Glorious Qur'an such as the ones contained in Chapter Seven Verse 30 and Chapter Two Verse 27 attest to such believes: *'And indeed we punish the people of Fir'aun with seven years of drought and shortness of fruits (crops) that they might remember...'* (Q7:30). Other related verses include; Q2:22, Q2:164, Q6:99, Q7:30, Q16:10, and Q20:53 (See Maigari, 2006). In addition to this, still some proclaimed that human socioeconomic activities such as bush burning, deforestation and over-grazing, among others, induces the prevailing phenomenon of drought and desertification in the region and beyond. This agglomerative view is common among scientific and urban base communities.

| Chapter 29 | Ahmed M. Ibrahim, in |
|---|---|
| | A.I. Tanko and S.B. Momale (Eds.) |
| | *Kano: Environment, Society and Development* |
| | London & Abuja, Adonis & Abbey Publishers |

## Spatial Distribution

Historical evidence revealed that the incidences of drought were in the past been recorded throughout the Region. Thus there is no part of the Region that in the historical past had never experienced the incidence of drought. However, the severity of the experience varies from northern to southern parts of the Region and from one year to another. The areas north of the hydrological divide of the Region (Olofin, 1987) experiences more incidences of drought and evidence of desertification than the relatively wetter areas of the south such as Riruwai.

Precipitation Index (PI) based on seasonal rainfall records revealed that sixteen incidences of drought of varying magnitude were recorded in the Kano Region from 1931 to 2010. There were six incidences each of moderate drought with PI of < -0.84 and severe drought (PI = < - 1.28) and three extreme cases with PI of < - 1.65. Table 29.1 below provides the details.

Table 29.1: Incidences of Drought in the Kano Region: 1931 To 2010

| Magnitude | Years | | | | | | Frequency |
|-----------|-------|------|------|------|------|------|-----------|
| Moderate  | 1942  | 1972 | 1982 | 1985 | 1990 | 2004 | 6 |
| Severe    | 1949  | 1963 | 1975 | 1981 | 1983 | 1987 | 6 |
| Extreme   | 1944  | 1973 | 1984 |      |      |      | 3 |
| Total     |       |      |      |      |      |      | 15 |

*Source: After Mortimore, 2000*

With this background, there is no doubt that desertification is inevitable. Mortimore (1989b) has identified about seven indicators of desertification in the Kano Region and other sudano-Sahelian regions. These are: i) declining rainfall with persistent drought and associated dust storms and low humidity; ii) soil erosion by wind and water, loose or fragile soils and active sand dunes; iii) deforestation, scanty vegetation, tree mortality, the invasion of dryland species, and fodder scarcity; iv) diminishing groundwater and drying of surface ponds and streams; v) falling farm yield; vi) southward migration of livestock producers and/or farmers; and vii) food scarcity and increased human mobility.

Chapter 29 | Ahmed M. Ibrahim, in
A.I. Tanko and S.B. Momale (Eds.)
*Kano: Environment, Society and Development*
London & Abuja, Adonis & Abbey Publishers

## Causes of Drought and Desertification

Generally, drought and desertification are brought about by several interwoven physical and anthropogenic factors, notable among them include: high surface temperature, atmospheric disturbances, dust storm, and socioeconomic activities such as deforestation, bush burning, overgrazing, and excessive cultivation. Some studies such as Nicholsen (1981) and Ba et. al. (1995) reveal that drought in the Sahel is as a result of dynamic condition in weather system rather than the earlier connotation that the migration of the Inter-Tropical Convergence (ITC) is the mechanism that brings rain. Consequently in drought years, conventional rainfall fails to develop normally, and storms often produce dust rather than rain. This has been further evaluated by examining the relationship between the position of the ITC and rain (during the period 1983 - 1988). The results indicated that other than in one year (1988) there was no systematic difference between dry and wet years in the location of the ITC. Thus, the difference were readily apparent in the intensity and spatial extent of convection, which further confirms that '… the ITCZ appears to be displaced northward in some, but not all, wet years in the Sahel, but that no anomalous southward displacement is evident in dry years' (Ba et al. 1995:428). Drought in the Sahel therefore is more apparently linked with reduced convective activity.

Similarly, the occurrence of drought in the Kano Region cannot be far away from the above fact. Temperature inversion due to frequent incidences of dust storms during wet season (often May to June) makes the formation of cumulus clouds impossible thereby negates condensation and precipitation.

Desertification in the semi-arid Tropics generally, and the Kano Region in particular is the physical repercussion of persistent rainfall variability, soil desiccation and drought. However, the preponderance emergence of areas of loose or fragile soils and active sand dunes; scanty vegetation; and fodder scarcity suggest that deforestation and bush burning among others accentuates the magnitude of desertification in the far northern parts of the region. Danbatta, Maigatari, Suletankarkar, Gumel and Birniwa areas are some of the areas that desertification is more evident.

Chapter 29 | Ahmed M. Ibrahim, in
A.I. Tanko and S.B. Momale (Eds.)
*Kano: Environment, Society and Development*
London & Abuja, Adonis & Abbey Publishers

## Consequences

As death is always the fear of all mankind so also is drought and desertification to agriculture and ecosystem. Rainfall variability and frequent occurrences of drought (agricultural) have been persistently affecting crop production and invariably food security level of the Region. For example, the 1987 drought causes serious crop losses in the Region. Most of the crops affected are sorghum, millet, cowpea, and groundnut. According to CCDE (1988) Report, about 37 - 39% of the crops yield (sorghum, millet and maize) declined in the Kano region due to the 1987 drought. Table 29.2 shows the amount of crops lost in relation to 1986 annual rainfall deficit.

**Table 29.2: Estimated Crop Losses due to 1987 Drought in the Kano Region**

| KNARDA Zones | A. Rainfall (%) 1986 | Estimated Crop Losses (%) | | | |
|---|---|---|---|---|---|
| | | Sorghum | Millet | Cowpea | Groundnut |
| 1 | 83 | 15 | 15 | 10 | 10 |
| 2 | 63 | 70 | 50 | 60 | 40 |
| 3 | 86 | 25 | 15 | 25 | 20 |
| 4 | 66 | 65 | 75 | 80 | 75 |
| Overall | 76 | 38 | 39 | 44 | 25 |

*Source: After Mortimore, 1989b*

Apart from crop losses, drought in the Kano Region also favours ample breeding condition for the incursion of pest such as grasshoppers, locust, birds and rodents. During the 1987 drought, for example, an estimated insect population (grasshoppers) of 113,000 to 306,000/ha infested the northeastern part of the Region (KNARNA, 1987); thereby adding more stress on harvest. Places such as Maigatari, Birniwa and some parts of Gumel had no harvest. Equally, the decline in groundnut production in the entire northern parts of the Region was attributed to the rosette epidemic at the aftermath of the 1975 drought.

Frequent occurrence of drought also affects hydrological condition of the drought prone areas in the Region. Inadequate rainfall affects surface and underground water resources which in turn adversely affects the growth of crops and natural vegetation. A survey by

Chapter 29 | Ahmed M. Ibrahim, in
A.I. Tanko and S.B. Momale (Eds.)
*Kano: Environment, Society and Development*
London & Abuja, Adonis & Abbey Publishers

WRECA (1985) revealed a substantial fall in water table due chain incidences of 1982, 1983, 1984 and 1985 droughts in the Region. Moreover, increase in frequency of drought, especially from 1981 to 1985 and 1987 drought years has created an alarming evidence of soil desiccation; intensified aridity and desertification in Danbatta, Maigatari, Suletankarkar, Gumel and Birniwa areas.

Prolonged drought and desertification, quite often, results in severe shortages of life supporting resources, malnourishment, hunger, starvation, famine, rampant diseases and epidemics. The 1970s and 1980s drought in particular, have ravaged greater part of the rural population in the Kano Region and beyond. Several hundreds of people and thousands herds of livestock died due to hunger, starvation and epidemics. The prices of food stuff increased more than three-fold throughout the Region, while poverty and social vices were commonplace realities in both urban and rural areas.

## Human Response

The series of suffering and hardship during and the aftermath of drought and desertification in the semi-arid Tropics have made the inhabitants to devise adaptation measures since the phenomenon of drought and desertification cannot be easily and adequately overcome. In line with this Mortimore (1989b) indentifies three basic adaptation mechanisms by farmers, all of which are common to the Kano Region. These are: i) agro-pastoral management mechanism in order to use reduce rainfall more efficiently, which includes varying plant spacing, crop varieties, grazing circuits, and herd composition; ii) multi-sectoral economic strategies including short-term and long-term mobility and iii) mobilizing alternative foods from the ecosystem, substituting amongst market foods, or going without.

Moreover, with regard to farmer's response to soil degradation especially under permanent annual or bi-annual cultivation system, as obtained in the Kano Region, farmers have three options. These are: i) to abandon the farmland; ii) to continue using it as before, and iii) to invest in rehabilitating or improving it. However, Mortimore (1989b) stressed that, the choice of these options is determined by the farmer's economic resources.

| Chapter 29 | Ahmed M. Ibrahim, in |
| --- | --- |
| | A.I. Tanko and S.B. Momale (Eds.) |
| | *Kano: Environment, Society and Development* |
| | London & Abuja, Adonis & Abbey Publishers |

At the community and local levels, on the other, the practical response to drought and desertification are mainly constant prayers, repentance, and relief assistance. While at the state and national levels, the adjustment measure include: establishing of plant nurseries, shelter belt, and irrigation schemes in the drought prone areas of Kazaure, Danbatta, Maigatari, Gumel, and Birniwa among others. The former Kano State Government (now Kano and Jigawa States) had constructed about 38 earth dams in the Region in order to boast agricultural production, domestic water supply and employment. Disaster and Emergency Relief Agency is in operation in both Kano and Jigawa States and indeed in all States of the Federation to manage disaster and emergency situations.

## Conclusion

From the forgoing it can be well understood that drought and desertification are evil phenomena which if allowed can put humanity in a precarious situation. Therefore, the preponderance of drought and desertification in the Kano Region should not be seen as a regional affair, but rather a global crisis facing humanity. As such collective effort of all the stakeholders is required in managing and safeguarding the future of our common habitat. It is recommended that the resource management system in the Region should be improved to include working directly with resource managers and their communities; farmer's adaptation mechanisms should be improved and institutionalized; and environmental management system in should be coherently improved and pursued vigorously.

## References

Agnew, C. (2000), Using the SPI to Identify Drought. *Drought Network News*: 12, 6-12.
Ba M. B., Frouin, R., and Nicholson, S.E. (1995) Satellite-derived Inter-annual Variability of West African Rainfall during 1983-1988, *Journal of Applied Meteorology, 34*:428

Chapter 29  Ahmed M. Ibrahim, in
A.I. Tanko and S.B. Momale (Eds.)
*Kano: Environment, Society and Development*
London & Abuja, Adonis & Abbey Publishers

CCDE (1988) Report on Desertification and Desert Encroachment in Eleven Northern States of Nigeria. Kano: Consultative Committee on Desert Encroachment.

Famer G. and Wigley, T. M. L (1985) Climate Trends for Tropical Africa. A Research Report for the Overseas Development Administration, Norwich; Climate Research Unit North Anglia

KNARNA, (1987) Report on the Effect of Drought and Grasshopper Infestation on Field Crops in Kano State. Kano State Agriculral and Rural Development Authority.

Maigari A. Ibrahim (2004) *Introduction to Environmental Problems and Management.* Wa'adallah Environmental Consult, Kano Nigeria.

Maigari A. Ibrahim (2009) Environmental Degradation, Security and Peace in a Multi-religious Setting: Islamic Perspective. Paper presented at the 2009 3rd Quarter General Meeting of the Nigerian Inter-religious Council (NIREC) at Hotel Presidential, Port-Harcourt, 16th -18th August, 2009.

Mortimore, M. (1989a) *Adaptation to Drought: Farmers, Famines and Desertification in West Africa,* Cambridge University Press.

Mortimore, M. (1989b) The Causes, Nature and Rate of Soil Degradation in the Northernmost States of Nigeria and An Assessment of the Role of Fertilizer in Counteracting the Processes of Degradation. *World Bank, Environment Department Working Paper* No. 17

Mortimore, M. (2000) Profile of Rainfall Change and Variability in the Kano-Maradi Region, 1960-2000, *Dryland Research Working Paper* 25

Nicholson, S. E. (1981) Rainfall and Atmospheric Circulation during Drought Periods and Wetter Years in West Africa. *Monthly Weather Review.* 109

Thambyahpillay, G. G. R. (1987) Methodological and Climatological Perspective of Drought and Desertification in the Lake Chad Basin: Sahelo-Sudan Nigeria. International Conference, Water Resource of the Lake Chad Basin. Lake Chad Basin Commission, N'Djamena.

Olofin, E. A. (1987) *The Kano Region. Departmental Lecture Series,* Geography Department Bayero University Kano, Nigeria

| Chapter 29 | Ahmed M. Ibrahim, in |
| --- | --- |
| | A.I. Tanko and S.B. Momale (Eds.) |
| | *Kano: Environment, Society and Development* |
| | London & Abuja, Adonis & Abbey Publishers |

Nicoholson, S. E. and Palao, I. M. (1993) A Re-evaluation of Rainfall Variability in the Sahel, Part1: Characteristics of Rainfall Fluctuation. *International Journal of Climatology*, 13: 371-389.

UNDP, (1994) Drought and Famine - Department of Humanitarian Affairs/United Nations Disaster Relief Office, United Nations Development Programme, 1994, 53 p.

UNEP (1977) Report of the United Nation Conference on Desertification, Nirobi Kenya 29th August to 9th September, 1977.

WRECA (1985), Groundwater Monitoring in Kano State, Kano: Water Resources and Engineering Construction Agency

| Chapter 29 | Ahmed M. Ibrahim, in |
| | A.I. Tanko and S.B. Momale (Eds.) |
| | *Kano: Environment, Society and Development* |
| | London & Abuja, Adonis & Abbey Publishers |

# Chapter Thirty

## EROSION HAZARDS

### Kabiru Ahmed

## Introduction

There are reports of accelerated erosion in sub-Saharan Africa between 1960's and 2000, and this is explained by the ongoing land use intensification. Land use intensification is recorded in form of the expansion of the cultivated land and the disappearance of the fallow system in many places between 1960's and 2000 (Junge and Stahr, 2006) as well as the degradation of the traditional agroforestry farmed parkland system of the unified management of scattered farm trees and crops. The degradation of the unified management system is the decline in the density of farm trees between 1960's and 2000. This is due to the increased demand for tree products (Gijsbers and Knebel 1994 in Boffa, 2008, and Lericollais, 1989 in Boffa, 2008). A transect survey from the derived Savanna to the northern Guinea Savanna of Benin and Nigeria which was based on the interpretation of aerial photos and satellite images as well as interviews on the farming systems showed land use intensification and accelerated erosion between 1960's and 2000. In northern Nigeria, sheet erosion exposed iron-pan on lower slopes and destroyed farmland in some villages studied (Junge and Stahr, 2006).

In this Chapter erosion hazard is assessed in Kano State, and there is a relation between land use intensification and accelerated erosion in an area where the fallow system was reported to have disappeared and farm sizes to have declined (Ahmed, 1995). Erosion Hazard Assessment is an aspect of landform studies because erosion is a process of detachment and transport of land surface particles by, in this case, water as raindrop and as surface runoff. Erosion operates and leads to slope development as well as channel development. This means landform evolution depends on erosion, while certain landform characteristics are indicative of erosion hazard. In this Chapter, landform characteristics, both qualitative and quantitative, are used to indicate erosion hazard in Kano State.

Chapter 30 | Kabiru Ahmed, in
A.I. Tanko and S.B. Momale (Eds.)
*Kano: Environment, Society and Development*
London & Abuja, Adonis & Abbey Publishers

Erosion Hazard Assessment in the Kano Region, in this Chapter, does not include estimates of gully erosion hazard. It is nonetheless important because it indicates the magnitude of soil loss from agricultural land, and gives an idea of sedimentation rates in water reservoirs. Kano is an agricultural Region because more than two third of the land is cultivated and about 90% of the land is cultivable. There are over twenty dam reservoirs constructed by the government for multiple purposes (water supply, irrigation, and recreation). The situation in the Region makes erosion hazard assessment very relevant. Studies of soil nutrient losses showed considerable loss of nutrients in Samaru, Zaria (Kowal and Kassam, 1978 in Ahmed, 1989).

**Methods**

The only erosion data in the Region prior to the construction of dams was the sediment concentration measurements in the 1966-67 rainy seasons. The data for this presentation is from the mapping of three tier landscape pattern from aerial photographs (Ahmed, 1986), morphometric analysis from maps at 1:100,000 and 1:50,000 (Ahmed, 1986 and Ahmed, 1995), reservoir sedimentation measurements (Ahmed, 1989) and point erosion measurements (Ahmed, 1991). In addition, a parametric survey of erosion hazard was carried out from the interpretation of aerial photographs to map land utilisation types and surface discontinuities, transect survey was carried out of slope and erosion features mainly at intervals of 30-60m, while quadrats (100-100m) were used to sample the soil, vegetation, and land use. Laboratory analysis of soil pH, particle size, total nitrogen and organic carbon was made as described by Hesse (1971) and Ahmed (1999). Observations of land use changes and related accelerated erosion were made, while the depletion of farm trees was monitored between 2004 and 2008.

Chapter 30 | Kabiru Ahmed, in
A.I. Tanko and S.B. Momale (Eds.)
*Kano: Environment, Society and Development*
London & Abuja, Adonis & Abbey Publishers

# Landform Characteristics

## Three-tier Landscape Pattern

The pattern identified is the high land, upland, and lowland. The highland describes the landscape features that survived denudational processes such as the residual hills (ridges, mesa, and inselberg).This surface has the highest runoff coefficient because it is bare rock and has shallow soils. The landscape is called *Tsauni* in Hausa. The second tier is the upland or *Tudu*. It is an extensive plain with deep cultivated soils and woodland areas. The lowest tier is the lowland or *kwari* and it is essentially the floodplain, which is most intensively cultivated because of the fertile soil and the low water table.

The distribution of the three-tier landscape for catchments in the State shows that the upland is the most extensive (84.5%), the highland comes next at 11%, and the lowland at 4.5%. The highland has the highest erosion hazard because of the steep hillslopes and the skeletal soil. The lowland has the lowest hazard because of the gentle slopes and the floods, which deposit sediment. The upland has moderate hazard (Ahmed, 1986).

Table 30.1: Three-tier Landscape Patterns in Catchments

| River | Catchments Area km$^2$ | Highland % | Upland % | Lowland % |
|---|---|---|---|---|
| Gari | 1492 | 7.2 | 88.8 | 4.0 |
| Tomas | 715 | 0.9 | 94.6 | 4.5 |
| Jakara | 587 | 0.1 | 94.7 | 5.2 |
| Iggi | 1173 | 11.1 | 85.6 | 5.3 |
| Dogwalo | 844 | 35.9 | 60.8 | 3.3 |
| Average | | 11.0 | 84.5 | 4.5 |

## Landform Systems

Morphometric data on slope, drainage density, and hypsometric integral was used to identify units with similar characteristics and are called landform systems. The five units identified are more homogenous than the three-tier pattern identified earlier. A landform system has uniform erosion hazard. The granite hill-mesa-ridge landform system has the highest erosion hazard. This is essentially the upland with the highest altitude (820-600m), highest relief (270-50m),

Chapter 30 | Kabiru Ahmed, in
A.I. Tanko and S.B. Momale (Eds.)
*Kano: Environment, Society and Development*
London & Abuja, Adonis & Abbey Publishers

and highest drainage density (2 - 0.8km$^2$) and with a moderate slope exceeding 4°. The hypsometric integral indicates that less than half of the surface was exhumed (Table 29.2). The lowest hazard is in the floodplain or lowland. The upland is now sub-divided into three smaller landform systems (denudational plain, undulating plain, and interfluve plain). These are respective areas of moderately high, moderate, and moderately low hazard. The interfluve landform system has the highest hypsometric integral indicating that the least erosion took place there as less than half of the original surface was exhumed.

The lowest hazard on the interfluve plain landform system is attributed to the protective function of the woodland cover (Falgore Forest Reserve). The other two landform systems (denudational plain and undulating plain) have higher hazards. The denudational plain, of moderately high erosion hazard, is in the southern part of the State comprising of Rivers Kano, Challawa, Iggi, Dogwalo, and Gaya catchments. Rainfall is higher here and runoff (16-17%) is higher, so also is the erosion hazard. The undulating plain, of moderate hazard, in the north has lower rainfall, lower runoff (4-10%), the drift material has higher infiltration potential, and lower erosion hazard. The nature of erosion in the two areas is discussed below.

### *Rainfall, Slope, Soil, and Erosion*

Annual rainfall varies from about 800mm in the north to over 1000mm in the south. The rain starts in May/June and ends in September/October. There is a concentration of rain between July and September, when over 70% of the annual rainfall and runoff are recorded. Erosion rate in the denudational plain of moderately high hazard was estimated from reservoir sedimentation at 0.5mm/year and from reservoir survey at 0.22mm/yr (Ahmed, 1990). In the undulating plain, records of point erosion indicate that slope erosion started at the beginning of the rains when about 85mm cumulative rainfall was recorded. This was when enough runoff was recorded to detach and transport soil particles (Fig. 30.1). The erosion also varied with the slope gradient, and the steeper the slope the higher the erosion rate and the relationship was represented by the equation E=0.3 + 1.6S: where E is erosion in mm/year, and S is slope in degrees.

Chapter 30 | Kabiru Ahmed, in
A.I. Tanko and S.B. Momale (Eds.)
*Kano: Environment, Society and Development*
London & Abuja, Adonis & Abbey Publishers

**Table 30.2: Landform Systems and Erosion Hazard**

| Landform System | Landform | Average Slope (degrees) | Drainage density (Km/km$^2$) | Hypsometric Integral (%) | EROSION |
|---|---|---|---|---|---|
| **Hills-ridges** | Highland | Over 4 | 0.8-2 | 49 | High |
| **Denudational plain** | Upland | 1.5 | 0.8-1.2 | 45-55 | moderately high |
| **Undulating plain** | Upland | 1.0 | 0.5-0.8 | 53-57 | moderate |
| **Interfluve plain** | Upland | 0.5-1 | 0.7 | 62 | moderately low |
| **Floodplain** | Lowland | 0.5-1 | Variable | | Low |

The relevance of slope gradient and organic carbon content of soil in assessing erosion hazard for sustainable agriculture was emphasised and used to assess erosion (Ahmed, 1999) in the undulating plain landform system identified earlier to have moderate erosion hazard. Field data for parametric rating was collected at Rimaye and Lamba villages and was used to actualise a hypothetical parametric scheme based on slope and carbon content (Fig. 30.2). The scheme has three categories of parametric units and seven sub-categories (Table 30.3).

**Table 30.3: Hypothetical Parametric Classes Derived from Fig 30.2**

| Category | Sub-category(code) | Sub-category(rank) |
|---|---|---|
| **Sustainable** | AA | High |
| | AB | Moderately high |
| | AC | Moderate |
| | BA | Moderate |
| | BB | Moderately low |
| | CA | Moderately low |
| **Marginally Sustainable** | BC | Low |
| | CB | Low |
| | DA | Low |
| | CC | Very low |
| **Unsustainable** | DB | Very low |
| | DC | Extremely low |

The field and laboratory data was used to actualise the parametric classes by identifying three class limits for slope and four class limits for organic carbon (Table 30.4).

Chapter 30 | Kabiru Ahmed, in
A.I. Tanko and S.B. Momale (Eds.)
*Kano: Environment, Society and Development*
London & Abuja, Adonis & Abbey Publishers

**Table 30.4: Actual Class Limits Used For Ranking**

| Parameter | Class limit | Rank | Value (degrees) | Remarks |
|---|---|---|---|---|
| Organic carbon | A | Moderate | 0.9-1 | Requires no external input such as woodland and plantation |
| | B | Low | 0.7-0.8 | Manure is applied by farmers. Pastoralists reside in farms. |
| | C | Very low | 0.5-0.6 | Manure application is limited |
| | D | Extremely low | < 0.5 | Very limited manure is applied |
| Slope | A | Gentle | < 3 | Plains and interdune depressions, wash erosion is dominant |
| | B | Moderate | 3-6 | Gully erosion is dominant on valley slope |
| | C | Relatively steep | > 6 | Gully erosion and mass movement on hillslope and valley slope |

The actual class limits identified were used to rate land facets. Sample transects were rated in Rimaye and Lamba villages. The gentle cultivated slopes were rated as sustainable in terms of their erosion hazard while the relatively steep hillslopes were rated as unsustainable (Table 30.5).

**Table 30.5: Rating of Cultivated Slope Units along a Transect in Rimaye and Lamba Villages**

| Site | Land unit | Class limit | Value (carbon %) | Value (slope in degrees) | Remark |
|---|---|---|---|---|---|
| Lamba | Gentle slope | CA | 0.5 | 1-2 | Sustainable |
| | Moderately sloping | DB | 0.3 | 4-8 | Unsustainable |
| Rimaye | Cultivated lowland | CA | 0.5 | 0.5-2 | Sustainable |
| | Cultivated upland | DA | 0.4 | 1-2 | Marginally sustainable |

## *Vegetation and Erosion*

An estimated 75% of the Region is cultivated, while less than 10% is under woodland cover. The protective function of the woodland was investigated to establish a reason for protecting and planting more farm trees in order to reduce erosion on farmlands. Trees provide a protective cover because the tree canopy reduces the erosional impact of raindrops. The roots prevent erosion by holding the soil together

Chapter 30 | Kabiru Ahmed, in
A.I. Tanko and S.B. Momale (Eds.)
*Kano: Environment, Society and Development*
London & Abuja, Adonis & Abbey Publishers

and by enhancing infiltration and reducing surface runoff and sediment transport. On the other hand, tree removal increases nutrient loss, sediment transport and dissection of the landscape.

Morphometric data on stream order, basin gradient, drainage density, and percentage length of first order tributaries was used to assess the impact of vegetation on erosion and slope development. The study sampled small drainage basins with similar scale factors (area and basin order) and similar topographic characteristics (relief and gradient). The basins in the interfluve landform system turned up to have lower drainage densities indicating limited dissection of the landscape, and the higher percentage of the first order streams indicates less channel ramification and less slope development. This shows the protection of the landscape by the woodland and the landscape remains an extensive flat interfluve. The basins in the cultivated parkland have higher drainage densities and lower percentage of first order tributaries indicating more dissection and more channel development (Table 30.3). There is more slope development in the cultivated land. Erosion and slope development progresses with the decline of slope angle leading to the exhumation of hill slope and the interfluve plain, and the extension of the foot slope (Figure 30.3). There is need to protect farm trees in order to protect the surface against the high intensity rainfall and to enhance infiltration and reduce runoff.

The monitoring of farm trees from quadrats in two villages between 2004 and 2008 showed progressive decrease in the density of trees arising from cutting of trees exceeding the rate of planting new trees. The density of trees declined below the optimum recommended for agroforestry (Ahmed, 2010a).

Table 30.6: Morphometric Characteristics of Small Tributary Catchments in the River Kano

| Morphometric Characteristics | Basin 1 | Basin 2 | Basin 3 | Basin 4 |
|---|---|---|---|---|
| Basin Area (km$^2$) | 8.7 | 10.9 | 9.5 | 9.5 |
| Stream Order | 2.0 | 3.0 | 2.0 | 2.0 |
| Relief | 30.0 | 60.0 | 30.0 | 30.0 |
| Gradient | 8.1 | 7.7 | 8.5 | 8.5 |
| Drainage Density | 1.3 | 1.2 | 0.75 | 0.75 |
| First Order (%) | 50.0 | 39.0 | 75.0 | 75.0 |

Basins 1 and 2 are parkland basins, while Basins 3 and 4 are woodland basins.

Chapter 30 | Kabiru Ahmed, in
A.I. Tanko and S.B. Momale (Eds.)
*Kano: Environment, Society and Development*
London & Abuja, Adonis & Abbey Publishers

## Erosion Control

The studies have shown the protective function of trees in the control of the erosional impacts of rainfall, slope, and soils. The problem is that the protective cover is threatened by clearing more woodland for farmland and resettlement such as the dwindling Falgore Reserve. Farm trees are also depleted mainly to supply fuelwood. These developments arising from the construction of Tiga Dam and the increasing demand for fuelwood lead to accelerated erosion and the sedimentation of water reservoirs.

Field observations and measurements between 2004 and 2008 (Ahmed, 2010a, b) show the need to protect and plant more trees. In Rimaye village a hill, characterised earlier as an area of high erosion hazard and to be unsustainable for development, was observed to progressively lose its tree cover between 2004 and 2008. The hill is called '*dutsen kura*' (meaning hyena hill) because the dense woodland cover on the hill supported wildlife such as hyenas and monkeys. The hill is now almost bare except for few scattered shrubs exploited for fuelwood. The depletion of the tree cover is due to the increased demand for fuelwood by the members of the community. The removal of the cover resulted in accelerated erosion, flow concentration, and gully development. This threatens the farmland and settlement located below the hillslope and community members are battling to control the situation. The lesson here is that all hillslopes should be protected as a matter of policy and by law because they are areas of high erosion hazard and unsustainable to development.

On the cultivated upland, a survey of farm trees between 2004 and 2008 at Rimaye and Lamba villages showed depleting tree stocks (Ahmed, 2010 a, b) and densities were below the density recommended for effective agroforestry practices. There is the need for the farm trees to be better managed in order to achieve the recommendrd density needed to reduce erosion and maintain soil fertility.

Chapter 30 | Kabiru Ahmed, in
A.I. Tanko and S.B. Momale (Eds.)
*Kano: Environment, Society and Development*
London & Abuja, Adonis & Abbey Publishers

## Conclusion and Recommendations

Regional assessment of erosion hazard shows a three-tier landscape pattern and the highlands with steep slopes have the highest erosion hazard. The second most extensive tier (84.5%) is the cultivated upland and deserves some attention. Morphometric analysis showed this landscape unit to comprise of areas of moderately high erosion hazard, moderate erosion hazard, and moderately low hazard. The denudational plain landform system, in the southern part of the State has moderately high hazard estimated at 0.22-0.5mm per year in the cultivated parkland, this leads to soil degradation and sedimentation in the over 20 water reservoirs in the State thereby reducing their lifespan. The undulating plain landform system in the Sudan Savanna has lower rainfall, higher infiltration rates (6-15cm per hour according to Anon 1981 in Ahmed, 2000), and lower runoff less than 11%. Studies made show that erosion is a function of rainfall and slope gradient. A minimum of about 85mm of rainfall was required to satisfy the moisture deficiency at the beginning of the rain season and to generate runoff to detach and transport soil particles. There after the rate of erosion varied with slope gradient. Surveys conducted between 2004 and 2008 showed that the level of fertilizer application remained low while there was continued depletion of farm trees thereby reducing the level of litter input to the soil. The application of manure should increase and farm trees should be planted to replace cut trees.

Careful management of the cultivated land is recommended through manure application, mechanical protection such as by ridging to control runoff, and agroforestry practices. It is recommended to control the accelerated erosion, and reservoir sedimentation by protecting woodland reserves, enriching degraded reserves, establishing woodlots, protecting the vegetation on hillslopes, and protecting and planting farm trees to achieve the recommended density for effective agroforestry (Ahmed, 2010a).

Chapter 30    Kabiru Ahmed, in
A.I. Tanko and S.B. Momale (Eds.)
*Kano: Environment, Society and Development*
London & Abuja, Adonis & Abbey Publishers

# References

Ahmed, K. (1986), Landform Systems in the Rivers Kano and Gari Catchments, within the Hadejia-Jamaare River Basin, Kano Studies, New Series, Vol. 2, no 4

Ahmed, K. (1986), Erosion Hazard Assessment in the Savanna: The Hadejia-Jama'are River Basin, in Mortimore M., Olofin E. A., Cline-Cole R. A., and Abdulkadir A. (eds.), *Proceedings on the Workshop on Land Resources*, Department of Geography, Bayero University, Kano, Nigeria

Ahmed, K. and M. Musa (1989), The Bagauda Dam: Reservoir and the 1998 Failure, in Olofin E A and Patrick S (eds), *Land Administration and Development in Northern Nigeria: Case Studies.* Proceedings on the Second Workshop on Land Administration and Development in Northern Nigeria, Department of Geography, Bayero University, Kano, Nigeria

Ahmed, K. (1995), Some Constraints to Crop Production in Northwest Kano State, *Journal of Social and Management Studies*, Vol. 1 No 2

Ahmed, K. (1995), An Assessment of the Use of Vegetation in Soii Conservation in Kno Region, *Journal of Social and Management Sciences*, Vol. 2, No. 1, UNIMAID

Ahmed, K. (2000), The Kano Physical Environment, *www.kanoonline.com*

Ahmed, K. (2010a), A Survey of Farm trees in Kano State, Bayero Journal of Interdisciplinary Studies, BUK, accepted for publication.

Ahmed, K. (2010b), Towards a Sustainable Agricultural Development in Kano State, *Bayero Journal of Intredisciplinary Studies*, BUK, accepted for publication.

Boffa, J. M. (2008) West African Agroforestry Parklands'; Keys to Conservation Sustainable Management, FAO, *Corporate Document Repository,* http/www/fao/x3989/04.h

Junge, B. and Stahr K. (2006), Monitoring Land Use Intensification and Linkage to Erosion in Nigeria and Benin, Tropentag, Bonn, *www.tropendag.De/abstracts/links/junge_18q9dILK.pdf*

Chapter 30 | Kabiru Ahmed, in
A.I. Tanko and S.B. Momale (Eds.)
*Kano: Environment, Society and Development*
London & Abuja, Adonis & Abbey Publishers

# Chapter Thirty One

## DEMOCRATIZATION AND GOVERNANCE IN KANO STATE

Mahmoud Muhammad Lawal

### Introduction

There is a universal crave for good democratic government essentially because of its immense advantages and, by implication, because of the negative consequences of bad government (Oluwatosin, 2007: 180). Contemporarily, democracy is universally cherished and promoted by most nations, and as such Nigeria cannot be an exception. Since the return of democracy in 1999, the struggles have been on how to sustain and reinvent the democratic system to make it efficient and more acceptable to the generality of the people, who are the main beneficiaries of democracy. The return of democracy in Nigeria permeates all regions, states and local governments of the nation. Clearly Kano State, being part and a major player in Nigerian federation cannot be excluded from the benefits of democratic dividend.

This Chapter examines the overall democratization process in Nigeria, with specific focus on Kano State and its uniqueness, in the political firmament of the country. It reviews the process of democratization and governance in Kano, by highlighting the nature and character of the forces or actors that shape and determine politics in the State.

Similarly, the Chapter reviews the centrality of Kano as a commercial and industrial nerve center of Northern Nigeria, as well as its unique Islamic orientation and background of the people and its impact on the democratization and governance process in the State.

### *Conceptual Clarifications: The Interface*

In order to have conceptual clarity and also to appreciate the relevance of the concept of democratization, it is important to clarify and define the term democratization. Like several concepts in the social sciences,

Chapter 31 | Mahmoud M. Lawal, in
A.I. Tanko and S.B. Momale (Eds.)
*Kano: Environment, Society and Development*
London & Abuja, Adonis & Abbey Publishers

487

the concept of democratization is subject to various interpretations. It implies that the ultimate authority of governance rest with the people themselves.

Without doubt, democracy is about the rule of the majority; although the rights of the minority is equally protected and guaranteed. In this connection, therefore, democracy as a principle, system and a process of governance involves the satisfaction of certain basic rights and features that guarantees the workings of a democratic system. Diamond captures this succinctly: According to him:

> Democracy is a system of government that meets three essential conditions: Meaningful and extensive competition among individuals and groups especially political parties for all effective positions of governmental power; at regular intervals and excluding the use of force; a highly inclusive level of political participation in the selection of leaders and policies, at least through regular and fair election, such that no major (adult) social group is excluded, and a level of civil and political liberties; freedom of expression, freedom of the press, freedom to form and join organizations, sufficient to ensure the integrity of political competition and participation (Diamond, 1989: xvi)

Similarly, democracy is also defined as political competition through periodic elections, however democracy is not only built on elections, but elections serve as the core of the democratic process. Again, one of the fundamental goals of democracy is how to govern the society in such a way that power is seen to actually belong to the people (Ojo: 1999; 257). The expression of this power is through the elected representatives of the people, who are given mandates at certain periodic intervals to exercise them on behalf of the people. To this end, elections are central to the success and sustenance of democracy.

Consequently, democracy is built and sustained on the principles of government by the consent of the people that is public accountability, majority rule, recognition of the rights of the minority and the constitutional government, i.e. government by laws. On the other hand, democratization according to Adejumobi (1999: 4):

> … is a process through which the institutional infrastructures germane to the construction of a democratic polity are established (e.g. parliament, independent and impartial Judiciary, and Police, Press, etc.), civil liberties

Chapter 31 | Mahmoud M. Lawal, in
A.I. Tanko and S.B. Momale (Eds.)
*Kano: Environment, Society and Development*
London & Abuja, Adonis & Abbey Publishers

are codified and guaranteed, the rule of law suffices and a process of constitutionalism engineered.

In spite of the establishment of these institutions of democracy as pointed above, the democratization process is still a misnomer, and thus requires consistent struggles and prodding to make it work for the better. Omoweh, on the other hand, considers democratization as:

> ... a process of creating an enabling environment in both the policy and economy that allows people at all levels to exercise control and authority over their own affairs and improve their existential political, social and economic conditions without the intrusion of the state terror and counterproductive policies (Kieh, 1996 cited in Omoweh, 2000: 23)

Therefore, the ultimate goal of the political and economic democratization processes is to create a democratic society in which the fundamental and civil rights and their basic human needs like water, food, shelter, and health, are met and the access created for the people to meet and sustain these rights and needs (Omoweh, 2000: 23).

Having explained, the concepts of democracy and democratization, it is imperative to define governance and thereafter establish the linkage between these inter-related and useful concepts in political discourse. In the contemporary world of today, governance is used in different ways, to mean different things to different people. In some respects, the term governance is used to describe regime types, the nature and style of political system. Similarly, governance refers to the manner in which power is exercised in the management of a country's economic and social resources for development (Imam, 2004: 537). Governance broadly refers to the manner in which a government or state governs its territory and the people with juridical controls (Imam, 2004: 537). In other words, governance as a concept covers all aspects of the complex relations that exist between a government and the people. In this regard, since democracy is about the people and the way and manner through which their aspirations are met. Governance also involves the people and the government in the management and administration of their resources and affairs by a government duly elected and responsible to the people.

The relationship between democracy and governance is so strong that a good democratic government can promote and enhance good

Chapter 31 | Mahmoud M. Lawal, in
A.I. Tanko and S.B. Momale (Eds.)
*Kano: Environment, Society and Development*
London & Abuja, Adonis & Abbey Publishers

governance in a state. As such democratization provides a greater and better platform for good governance to flourish and succeed. In the first place, Huntington (1991) explains that democratization takes place in waves. According to him, there have been three major waves of democratization: the first was a long wave stretching from approximately 1820-1920 and affected largely countries in Europe and North America and the English dominions in the South (Australia and New Zealand); the second was rather short and took place in the two decades after the end of the Second World War and included, in addition to countries in Europe, many in Latin America, e.g. Brazil, Costa-Rica and Venezuela; the third wave began in the mid-1970s and still continues with countries also in Africa, Asia and Eastern Europe being pulled into the process (cited in Hyden: 1995; 50). He further contends that it is important to point out that each wave has been accompanied by a reversal; i.e. a return in many countries, though not all forms of authoritarian rule, (Hyden, 1995: 50). In the case of Nigeria, there has been this reversal particularly under the prolonged period of military rule from 1983 to 1999. And this reversal came with obstacles along the way in the entrenchment of democracy in the country. One of these obstacles is the military involvement in politics which has posed a serious roadblock to the process of democratization. For Sixteen years that the military had been in power, the institution desecrated all the noble institutions of democracy thus restraining every effort to institute a free and fair democratic process in Nigeria. It was only through sustained struggles by the civil society groups in the 1980s and 1990s that succeeded in ushering a civilian transition in 1999.

For Nwabueze, democratization must involve experimentation over time and thus has a wider meaning and encompasses more than multi-partyism. It must be seen in addition, to democratize the society, economy, politics, the constitution of the state, the electoral system and process, and the practice of government (1993: 2). He further contends that democratization must therefore involve concerted effort to instill the spirit of liberty, democracy and social justice in the people (1993: 3). Doing this requires respect for the underlying values and principles of democracy. In addition, Nwabueze listed twelve conditions which countries on the throes of democratization must

Chapter 31 | Mahmoud M. Lawal, in
A.I. Tanko and S.B. Momale (Eds.)
*Kano: Environment, Society and Development*
London & Abuja, Adonis & Abbey Publishers

imbibe and some of which include the rule of Law, multi-partyism, popular participation and efficient electoral system.

Thus, as an all-encompassing process, Olushola (1994:51) offers that democratization must be seen in essence and substance, as an autocentric process of social restructuring, in consonance with the prevailing societal values, ethics, norms and nuances of the generality of the society, in which this process of political and social changes are taking place (1994: 51). Consequently, all social forces must be involved in defending, promoting and entrenching democracy.

Osaghae (1994:45) is of the view that democratization may be defined as the process of moving from an authoritarian system to a democratic political system. This seems to be the popular perception of democratization among both scholars and politicians. But it is pertinent to understand that the movement from authoritarian system to a democratic system is but a necessary step in the democratization process. Having attained this stage, civil society and the generality of the people must strenuously organize to defend the tenets of democratization such as accountability of the rulers to the ruled.

According to Ake (1991) the trend towards democratization in the Third World Countries predate the cold war era. This started actually during the period of decolonization when a number of elites in many African countries embarked on nationalist agitations for self-determination and self-government. He asserts that it is true that Africa is democratizing but the democratization occurring in Africa does not appear to be in the least emancipatory. On the contrary, it is legitimizing the disempowerment of the ordinary people who seems to be worse off than they use to be because their political oppression is no longer perceived as a problem inviting solution, but a solution endowed with moral and political legitimacy (Ake:1991). Thus, the conduct of our "so called" democrats during this period of democratization leaves much to be desired and apparently this further perpetuates the political oppression of the ordinary people through excessive corruption by the political class.

Other scholars observed that the on-going trend towards democratization especially under the period of globalization is seen as a calculated attempt towards entrenching and legitimizing neo-liberal ideas in many places in the third world. It is therefore merely seen as a reflection of the expansion of capitalism as it will ultimately

Chapter 31 | Mahmoud M. Lawal, in
A.I. Tanko and S.B. Momale (Eds.)
*Kano: Environment, Society and Development*
London & Abuja, Adonis & Abbey Publishers

encourage openness to capital and the media. In essence, democracy and democratization has to reflect the culture, norms and behavior of the society in question, for as Richard Sklar sums up:

> Democracy... is a developing idea, its meaning is enriched by contributions from all cultures and nations. From that standpoint, democracy is not the property of one or another ideological camp; every country in the world is a veritable laboratory for the discovery of democratic principles and workshop for the construction of democratic machinery (cited in Olushola, 1994: 65).

Consequently, democratization from the above viewpoint varies from one country to another, especially as it reflects the uniqueness of the differing societies. Yet, democratization remains essentially a process of change towards the desired democratic order, which must be built and sustained by the people themselves.

According to Jega, democratization is essentially the process of bringing about "real" or "substantive", as opposed to "formal" democracy. The former, Martins argues, goes beyond the formal trappings of democratic political systems (such as multi-partyism and elections) to include such elements as accountability and genuine popular participation in the nation's political and economic decision-making process" (cited in Jega, 1995: 4). Thus, for Jega (1995: 4), democratization is a process which invests power with legitimacy, facilitates the creation of enduring political institutions, and nurtures responsible political pluralism. Also, it involves the promotion and defense of social justice and human rights

Accountability is an important element of both democracy and democratization, and in political and economic decision-making process. Therefore, efforts must be made to ensure an accountable and responsible process in governance, as it is the one of the hallmarks of good democratic governance.

## Kano in Socio-Economic Perspective

The history of Kano can be traced to 999 AD, when Bagauda, brought together all the several clans around the settlement of Dala under one political authority (Ibrahim, 2001). Since then Kano has transformed and expanded into a famous industrial and commercial center of note.

Chapter 31 | Mahmoud M. Lawal, in
A.I. Tanko and S.B. Momale (Eds.)
*Kano: Environment, Society and Development*
London & Abuja, Adonis & Abbey Publishers

Kano State was created in 1967 and currently has a population of 9,401,288 people according to the 2006 census. The State has various tribal groups, the dominant being Hausa, Fulani and several other ethnic groups from across the country. Kano city became a formidable political entity around the tenth and eleventh centuries as a result of the rapid physical, economic and social settlement in the Kano Region (Adamu, 1999 cited in Ibrahim, 2012: 86). In fact, Adamu further states that Kano has developed from a tribal society enriched by migratory trends, which led to an eventual mixture of the various migrants through integration and assimilation into an emergent and distinct political formation.... Before its conquest by the British forces, Kano was invariably the entrepot and chief distribution centre for different products which led to the flourishing of both international and domestic trades (1999:11 cited in Ibrahim, 2012:86). Presently, there are 44 Local Government Areas (LGAs) in Kano State; as such the State has the largest number of representation in the Federal House of Representatives because of its huge population.

In fact, Kano is considered as the second most important industrial centre in the country after Lagos, though, this position is gradually fading because of the absence of and collapse of socio-economic infrastructures such as electricity, water and good roads network. The predominant economic activities of the people of the Kano Region are commerce and agriculture. In fact, Kano is famous as a major region of cotton and groundnut production. Similarly, as a commercial centre, Kano boosts of several commercial and business activities such as textile, car business, estate development, general enterprises, banking, trade and finance. Some of the major markets for these business activities include Kurmi, Sabon Gari, Kwari and Singer Markets which are known for many international and local business links. Other important Markets in Kano are the Wapa Currency Market at Fagge, Akija automobile Market, Dawanau grain Market, Dawakin Kudu International cattle Market, and Yankaba Market which attracts traders and businessmen and women from far and wide into the City for commercial transactions. There are many other markets in rural and urban Kano State that operate mostly on weekly basis in several parts. Consequently, migrants from far and near were generally attracted by the booming commercial and trading activities in Kano,

Chapter 31 | Mahmoud M. Lawal, in
A.I. Tanko and S.B. Momale (Eds.)
*Kano: Environment, Society and Development*
London & Abuja, Adonis & Abbey Publishers

and have led to the settlement since pre-colonial times of Asians such as Lebanese, Syrians, and other Arabs in the City.

The climatic condition of Kano and its immediate environs is the tropical dry and wet climate (Olofin and Tanko, 2002: 14), with average warm and hot temperature throughout the year. The vegetation is generally Sudan Savanna with fertile land in most part of the State favouring agricultural production. The population of Kano is very high and it is endowed with great human and natural resources potentials. Kano has played a formidable role in the socio-economic development of the country since independence, with its own share of trials and tribulations. A key feature of the State is the predominance of Islam, since the time of Emir Muhammadu Rumfa, which was consolidated with the Jihad of Sheikh Othman Dan Fodio in 1804. As a result, Islam has continued to influence the democratic and governance machinery in the State, with several dynamics and paradoxes. In effect, Kano has played a tremendous role in the development of Islamic culture and scholarship in and around the Western Sudan. Today, Kano is considered as one of the great centers of Islamic intellectualism.

## Kano in the Democratization Process: The Dynamics and the Paradoxes

Muazzam (2009; 265-266) posits that:

> In terms of politics and political activity, Kano is known not only for its consistent stand as the home of oppositional politics in the north but also a beacon. Kano people are historically if not naturally contentious. It was a home to the Northern Elements Progressive Union (NEPU) in the first republic and the Peoples Redemption Party (PRP) in the second republic. This was all against the more "traditional" politics in the north of Nigeria....... Kano politics has always been riddled with intraparty rivalry, high level intrigues and even bitterness, factional cleavages and contest are deeply rooted in the politics of the state.

With this background of Kano politics, any person, group or political party that wants to remain relevant in the political calculations in Kano, then certainly one needs to enlist not only the support but the votes of several social groups with great influence in

Chapter 31    Mahmoud M. Lawal, in
A.I. Tanko and S.B. Momale (Eds.)
*Kano: Environment, Society and Development*
London & Abuja, Adonis & Abbey Publishers

the politics of the State. These groups include *Ma'aikata* (civil servants, teachers etc), *Yan kasuwa* (Businessmen, traders, merchants), *Malamai* (religious scholars), *Yan Boko* (Western educated), the politicians, youth and to some extent the traditional ruling groups (Muazzam, 2009, 267). These groups with high stakes in the political economy of the State have generally indulged in intrigues and political alliances in order to protect and promote their particularistic interests in the governance process in the State. In some situations, they have participated in influencing the outcome of many government policies and programmes with negative and/or positive consequences for the population of the State.

No region, state or locality is insulated from the national politics (Flint and Taylor, 2007: 257). In other words, whatever happens at the national or central level is felt or impacts on the local or state level. Consequently, the dynamics of democratization in Nigeria is usually played out in the politics of Kano.

Since the first States creation exercise of 1967 when Kano was created as part of the twelve States, the State has had its own share of political problems. The State was created under military regime; its first military governor was the late Police Commissioner Audu Bako, who ruled for the greater part of the civil war years 1967-1970. Audu Bako is believed to have laid the foundation of modern Kano with several developments in the areas of education, agriculture, rural development, infrastructures and health. His administration conceived and developed most of the existing infrastructures in the State such as Gidan Murtala which houses some of the key government ministries and establishments; Challawa Gorge dam; the Kano State College of Arts, Science and Remedial Studies; Tiga Dam Resort and a network of urban and rural roads. Two other Military governors ruled Kano to 1979, Col. Sani Bello and AVM Ishaya Aboi Shekari who handed over power to the first elected Governor, Late Muhammadu Abubakar Rimi on 1st October, 1979. The Second Republic was short-lived, as the military sacked the politicians on 31st December, 1983. However, within the four years period of Rimi, Dawakin Tofa and Bakin Zuwo administrations, Kano witnessed tremendous socio-economic transformations largely because of the populist ideology of the People's Redemption Party (PRP) that won elections and controlled government in Kano from October, 1979 to December, 1983. In line

Chapter 31 | Mahmoud M. Lawal, in
A.I. Tanko and S.B. Momale (Eds.)
*Kano: Environment, Society and Development*
London & Abuja, Adonis & Abbey Publishers

**495**

with the populist principles of the PRP government in Kano under Abubakar Rimi, the State witnessed massive development of social and economic infrastructures particularly in the area of education, rural water, electrification projects and roads development. The State invested heavily in the development of science education which led to the establishment of science schools for both boys and girls in places such as Dawakin Kudu, Dawakin Tofa, Garko, and Taura in the old Kano State.

From 1983 to 1999, the military held sway for sixteen (16) years with several stress and strains. Within the period, several forces and factors have influenced the changes that have taken place, for instance, the business community, the religious leaders and the emirate/traditional rulers have generally influenced the conception and implementation of public policies and programmes in the State, including the nominations and appointments of political office holders. Under military rule, the people struggled and made sacrifices during the period of the transition to democracy.

In fact, the period of the transition to democracy has been profoundly difficult, as it was dubbed "transition without end". Jega (2006: 11) captures this period more succinctly thus:

... the 16 years of military rule had been continuous and during which period militarism was deeply entrenched, with militarization taking a heavy toll on institutional processes and the psychology and behavior of the people, for example the years of military rule made the process of transition to democracy vexatious, democratic consolidation very slow and conflict-ridden, and the entire democratic experiment precarious and susceptible to authoritarian reversals

In 1999, the military finally handed over power to the civilians, and this saw, the People's Democratic Party (PDP) winning the elections in Kano. From 1999 and 2011, political power and leadership oscillated between the PDP and ANPP. First, Dr. Rabiu Musa Kwankwaso won elections on the platform of the PDP from 1999 to 2003, and then Malam Ibrahim Shekarau took over in 2003 to 2011. (See, Appendix 31.1: List of all (Civilian and Military) Governors of Kano State, since its creation in 1967). In April 2011 elections, the PDP again won the gubernatorial elections in Kano, partly due to the absence of internal party democracy in the ANPP, because the choice

Chapter 31 | Mahmoud M. Lawal, in
A.I. Tanko and S.B. Momale (Eds.)
*Kano: Environment, Society and Development*
London & Abuja, Adonis & Abbey Publishers

**496**

or rather the imposition of Salihu Sagir Takai as the anointed candidate of the outgoing Governor of the State Malam Ibrahim Shekarau really affected the political fortunes of the Party and hence the defeat of the ANPP at the April 2011 polls. An important feature of the democratic process in Kano is the unpredictability of the voting pattern of the electoral population in Kano.

The paradox of the democratisation and governance process in Kano has to do with the changing dynamics of governments in the State, for each new government means discontinuity in government policies with the attendant consequences in the cost implication for policy initiation, implementation and evaluation.

There is the crisis of leadership in the State, which is the root of the failure in the current democratisation process. In fact, the leadership is self-serving, corrupt, unfocussed and with poor vision especially under successive military regimes. Consequently, they have virtually wasted the resources and opportunities critical in handling state matters. As a result, the State has had its fair share of political and several religious crises, i.e. the July 10, 1980 political crises which led to the assassination of the Political Adviser to Late Governor Abubakar Rimi, and the attack on Radio Kano and the Triumph Publishing Company; the December, 1980 Maitastine uprising; the 1991 Reinhard Bonnke religious riots; the 1994 Gideon Akaluka incident; the 1995 Sabon Gari Market ethnic disturbances; the 2001 Anti- American protests against the attack on Afghanistan; the reprisal attacks of the 2004 Yalwan-Shendam crises; the 2002 Sagamu crisis and even the April 2011 post elections violence (Lawan, 2012: 52-54).

Kano is famous as a significant industrial, commercial trade route in the trans-Saharan period, and this has been sustained, because of the existence of many industries and business enterprises. There are several industries and companies situated in the Challawa, Sharada, Bompai and Dakata industrial areas involved in various manufacturing activities such as tanning, metal and steel, food and beverages, construction, motor assembly, wood products, textile products, chemical and pharmaceutical etc. However, the State has regrettably lost this enviable position, largely due to the economic recession that engulfed the country in the early 1980s as a result of the introduction of Structural Adjustment Programme (SAP); apparent neglect of the manufacturing sector of the economy by the State Government;

Chapter 31 | Mahmoud M. Lawal, in
A.I. Tanko and S.B. Momale (Eds.)
*Kano: Environment, Society and Development*
London & Abuja, Adonis & Abbey Publishers

**497**

epileptic supply of electricity; and poor infrastructural development of facilities required to sustain industrialization. The State Government during the period of democratization has poorly managed the economic resources of the State, as a result of which most of these industries collapsed. For instance, as at October 2010, 49 industries were operating below their industrial capacity while 126 industries have closed down in the Bompai industrial area (Radda et al, 2011, 33). In the Sharada/Challawa industrial area within the same period, 46 companies were operating below capacity and 106 have closed down completely (Radda *et al*, 2011, 44). As a consequence of the closure of these industries in Kano, many workers were retrenched or laid down which has compounded the crisis of unemployment and governance in the State.

Politics in Kano has lost its steam because of the absence of principles and ideology. In the First and Second Republics, the late Mallam Aminu Kano led a formidable party NEPU and PRP respectively to challenge conservative principles of the Northern People's Congress (NPC) and the traditional institutions in the State, which provided an alternative and a strong opposition platform for politics of principles and ideology to strive not only in the State but in the north in particular. In fact, democratic politics in Kano then was very exciting as politicians seriously engage in political confrontations, political rivalry and democratic debates on issues and programmes. Currently, politicians promote selfish and manipulative principles due to the ignorance and poverty that has ravaged the State, as such they dwell much on personalities rather than issues that will promote the greatest good for the greatest number. Consequently, politicians promote personality cults in the parties instead of entrenching internal democracy and strong democratic ethos for the consolidation of the democratic process in the Kano Region and Nigeria in general.

In effect, illiteracy and poverty are the twin threats to the survival of the democratization process in Nigeria. In fact, the 2011 post-election violence clearly illustrates the damaging effects of poverty and illiteracy in the democratic project in Nigeria.

Another major paradox of the democratisation process is the increasing and devastating impacts of the unemployed street beggars such as the *almajirai*, whose daily mobility in the urban centers has

Chapter 31 | Mahmoud M. Lawal, in
A.I. Tanko and S.B. Momale (Eds.)
*Kano: Environment, Society and Development*
London & Abuja, Adonis & Abbey Publishers

literally created a congested city, with unkempt environment as well as becoming nuisance in the traffic management of the State. This situation is further worsened by the adherence to conservative and age-old traditional practices that have no place in religious teaching.

A significant factor that is really affecting the pace of development and democracy in Kano in the last two years is the heightened and increased level of insecurity occasioned by the activities of militant groups particularly in the northern part of the country. The 20th January, 2012 violent bomb attacks in Kano which led to the killing of about 200 citizens of the State is a major challenge to the leadership in the State. Although, the spate of violence is not unique to Kano in the recent times but the country in general, however, the situation is inimical to sustaining the status of the State as a major trading and commercial hub of the north. In fact, this spate of violence has really affected the influx of traders and entrepreneurs in the State and the Region as well, and could thereby affect its political and economic fortunes.

In the final analysis, the trend and pattern of democratisation and governance in the Kano Region, clearly demonstrates that governance is for the rich-elite and the nobility, such that policies generally favours them, especially in the allocation and distribution of political, and socio-economic resources.

## Recommendations

It is imperative at this juncture to propose some recommendations towards promoting a better democratic culture and good governance in Kano State. The executive and the legislature must have the intellectual capacity to initiate and implement sound policies and projects that will meet the requirements and needs of the citizens of the State.

In the last fourteen years, the State has lost its enviable position as an industrial haven, because of harsh economic policies and the absence of basic infrastructures such as electricity supply, good roads etc. There is therefore the need to put in place functional infrastructures particularly electricity so as to revitalize the ailing and collapsed industries in the state. In fact, the State must as a matter of urgency embark on the construction of an Independent Power Project

Chapter 31 | Mahmoud M. Lawal, in
A.I. Tanko and S.B. Momale (Eds.)
*Kano: Environment, Society and Development*
London & Abuja, Adonis & Abbey Publishers

(IPP) so as to reduce the over-dependence on the national grid, thereby improving the investment climate. But it is imperative to note that, after 2011 elections the new administration in the State is beginning to address some of the infrastructural deficit by initiating sound and sustainable policies in various sectors of the economy in order to enhance its political status.

A serious defect in the governance process in Kano, is lack of proper planning and forecasting in an environment where there is ever-increasing population explosion coupled with the commercial pull factor which attracts in commercial traders and entrepreneurs into the State. Consequently, government must plan properly and forecast correctly to ensure a better future for the citizens.

The *almajiri* phenomenon is a major challenge to the political, economic and social development of the State hence serious and concerted efforts must be put in place to reduce the negative effects of the roaming *almajirai* in the urban centers of Kano. Poverty and ignorance have accentuated the culture of docility in Kano. Consequently, the citizens should not remain perpetually docile but should raise appropriate questions on all critical issues that affect them either directly or indirectly. The leadership in the State should appreciate such criticisms and questions in good faith and not misconstrue them as confrontational attacks on their manner of governance (Bello-Imam; 2004; 540).

Kano is famous as an industrial and commercial centre; as such the State government and the private sector should appreciate each other as complementary partners in the development process, so as to accelerate the overall transformation of the potentials of the state in national development. Similarly, government in the State should ensure that all economic, educational and social policies are aimed at eradicating poverty and expanding the choice that the citizens have in their lives and not worsen their conditions (Bello-Imam: 2004; 540-541).

A culture of disrespect for rule of law and order exists in Kano, both among the leaders and the led. For instance, road users hardly obey traffic rules and regulations which to a large extent compound the traffic congestion in the Metropolis. The attitude of especially the Okada (*'Yan Achaba*) riders is very depressing and uncultured. Thus, the recent ban on Okada business by the State Government is a step in

Chapter 31 | Mahmoud M. Lawal, in
A.I. Tanko and S.B. Momale (Eds.)
*Kano: Environment, Society and Development*
London & Abuja, Adonis & Abbey Publishers

the right direction. Similarly, people destroy the environment through the abuse of the landscape and destructive practice of unplanned business premises in all major roads particularly within Kano Metropolis.

Again, many political leaders have no democratic mindset as such, in many cases, they tend to impose their will on party membership without recourse to internal party democratic principles. Thus, there is the apparent need on the part of both the leaders and the citizens to subject themselves to the rule of law and due process, no matter how highly placed they are in the society.

The ultimate objective of any government anywhere in the world is to attend to the aspirations of the entire citizenry. Therefore, the State Government should priorities provision of basic infrastructures like roads, water, education, health and promote increased private sector participation. The civil society organisations (CSOs) should strengthen their activities in the State, particularly in the areas of civic education campaigns, greater political awareness for the citizens and effective mobilisation towards democratic deepening and good governance.

There is a high level of dependence on government in the State by the citizens for the provision of basic infrastructure and services, and this is associated with the notion of government as "father Christmas". Thus, the citizens must re-invent themselves through communal activities and programmes, and thereby consider governance as the responsibilities of both the governors and the governed, and therefore a collective responsibility of all. The citizens need to eschew negative traditional practices which hinder successful governance practice in the State. The Kano Region is blessed with fertile agricultural land; hence government should encourage agriculture through better agricultural programmes to make the State self-sufficient in food production, to produce even more for export.

With the vast land in the State, government needs to open up by constructing more roads and where necessary overhead bridges, as this will reduce the frustrating traffic congestion which is taking its toll on productivity, administration and overall development in the State.

Finally, the State along with the Federal Government and the community in general, must tackle the incessant security challenges confronting the State and people, if we must tap the benefits of democratization and good governance.

Chapter 31 | Mahmoud M. Lawal, in
A.I. Tanko and S.B. Momale (Eds.)
*Kano: Environment, Society and Development*
London & Abuja, Adonis & Abbey Publishers

# Conclusion

The task of enthroning democracy is a collective responsibility. Consequently, it requires courage, persistence, perseverance, and doggedness on the part of both the leaders and the led. It also requires democrats with democratic mindsets for it to survive. Similarly, democratisation and good governance cannot take place in an atmosphere of poverty, illiteracy, youth restiveness, violence, electoral fraud and insensitive leadership. Therefore, the greatest challenge that confronts the entire people of Nigeria, not only the *Kanawa* is to enthrone credible and selfless leadership that considers the people as the native force in the making of democracy.

# References

Olowu, D. Williams, A. and Soremekun, K. (1999): *Governance and Democratization in West Africa*, Dakar; CODESRIA

Nwabueze, B.O. (1993): *Democratization*, Ibadan: Spectrum Books Limited.

Omoruyi, O. et.al edited (1994): *Democratization in Africa; Nigerian Perspectives*, Volume one Benin City: Hima and Hima Limited.

Osaghae, M.O. (1994): *"Sustainable Democracy"*, in Omoruyi, O. et. al, Democratization in Africa: Nigerian Perspectives, Vol. one. Benin City: Hima and Hima Limited.

Ake, C. (1996): *"Is Africa Democratizing"?* Cass Monograph No. 5.

Adetula, V.A.O. (1997): Claude Ake and Democracy in Africa: A Tribute. *Afrigov Monographs No. 4*, Jos; Afrigov.

Hyden, G. (1995): "Conjunctures and Democratization", in Olowu, D., Soremekun, K. and Williams, A. (edited), *Governance and Democratization in Nigeria*, Ibadan: Spectrum Books Limited.

Muazzam, I. (2009) "The 2007 Elections and Popular Sovereignty in Kano State" in Jibrin Ibrahim and Okechukwu Ibeanu (Eds.) Direct Capture: The 2007 Nigerian Elections and Subversion of Popular Sovereignty, Abuja: Centre for Democracy and Development and Open Society initiative in West Africa (OSIWA)

Chapter 31 | Mahmoud M. Lawal, in
A.I. Tanko and S.B. Momale (Eds.)
*Kano: Environment, Society and Development*
London & Abuja, Adonis & Abbey Publishers

Onoge, O. (1997): *The Democratic Imperative in Africa*, Claude Ake Memorial Lecture Series No. 1, African Center for Democratic Governance, Jos, Plateau State.

Olofin, E.A. and Tanko, A.I. (2002): *Laboratory of Areal Differentiation: Metropolitan Kano in Geographical Perspective, Kano:* Adamu Joji Publishers.

Jega, A.M. (2006): *Democratization in Nigeria: Problems and Prospects,* 8th Claude Ake Memorial Lecture, Centre for Advanced Social Science, Port-Harcourt, Nigeria.

Ojo, E.O. (1999): *Towards Sustaining Democratic Values in Nigeria*, in Hassan Saliu (ed) Issues in Contemporary Political Economy of Nigeria, Ilorin; Haytee Books

Flinct, C. and Taylor, P. (2007), *Political Geography: World Economy, Nation-State and Locality*, England; Pearson Education Limited.

Omoweh, D.A. (2000): *"Democratization and the Development of the Nigerian Economy",* in the Central Bank of Nigeria, Financial and Economic Review, Vol. 24, No. 1. January/March, 2000.

Radda, S.I, Bello, I. and Aminu, S.D.(2011): The Nature of Police Patrol in Kano Metropolis, Kano; Benchmark Publishers.

Ibrahim, O.F. (2001): *Prince of the Times: Ado Bayero and the Transformation of Emiral Authority in Kano*, Asmara; Africa World Press Inc.

Ibrahim, F.O. (2012) "The 2004 Ethno-religious Conflicts in Kano State and the Identity Question" in Mohammed, H. (ed*) Nigeria's Convulsive Federalism: Perspectives on Flash-Points of Conflict in Northern Nigeria*, Ibadan: Cypress Concepts and Solutions Limited.

Lawan, M. M. (2012) "Periscoping the Causes of Ethno- Religious Conflicts in Nigeria's North West Zone" in Mohammed, H. (ed*) Nigeria's Convulsive Federalism: Perspectives on Flash-Points of Conflict in Northern Nigeria*, Ibadan: Cypress Concepts and Solutions Limited.

Chapter 31 | Mahmoud M. Lawal, in
A.I. Tanko and S.B. Momale (Eds.)
*Kano: Environment, Society and Development*
London & Abuja, Adonis & Abbey Publishers

**APPENDIX 31.1**: List of Governors and Military Administrators of Kano State since 1967

| S/N | Name of Governors | Year of Tenure | Remarks |
|---|---|---|---|
| 1. | Police Com. Audu Bako | May, 1967 - July, 1975 | Military Regime |
| 2. | Col. Sani Bello | July,1975 - Sept. 1978 | Military Regime |
| 3. | AVM Ishaya Aboi Shekari | Sept. 1978 - Oct. 1979 | Military Regime |
| 4. | Alh. Muhammadu Abubakar Rimi | Oct. 1979 - May, 1983 | Civilian Regime |
| 5. | Alh. Abdu Dawakin-Tofa | May,1983 - Oct. 1983 | Civilian Regime |
| 6. | Alh. Sabo Bakin Zuwo | Oct. 1983 - Dec. 1983 | Civilian Regime |
| 7. | Air Comd. Hamza Abdullahi | Dec.1983 - Aug. 1985 | Military Regime |
| 8. | Brigadier Ahmad Mohammed Daku | Aug.1985- Aug.1986 | Military Regime |
| 9. | Group Captain Muhammed Ndatsu Umaru | Aug.1986- July,1988 | Military Regime |
| 10. | Brigadier Idris Garba | July,1988- June,1992 | Military Regime |
| 11. | Arc. Kabiru Ibrahim Gaya | June,1992- Nov.1993 | Military/Civilian Regime |
| 12. | Brigadier Muhammed Abdullahi Wase | Dec.1993 - June,1995 | Military Regime |
| 13. | Brigadier Dominic O. Oneya | Aug.1995 - Sept. 1998 | Military Regime |
| 14. | Brigadier Aminu Isa Kontagora | Sept. 1998 - May,1999 | Military Regime |
| 15. | Engr. Rabiu Musa Kwankwaso | May 1999 - May 2003 | Civilian Regime |
| 16. | Mal Ibrahim Shekarau | May 2003 - May 2011 | Civilian Regime |
| 17. | Engr. Rabiu Musa Kwankwaso | May 2011 - to date | Civilian Regime |

# INDEX

## A

Abagayawa, 111

Abdulhamid, Adnan, iv, viii, 33

Adamawa, 132, 140, 279

Adamu, Abdallah U, iv, v, ix, xi, xiii, xvi, 62, 64, 68, 69, 70, 71, 72, 73, 76, 79, 80, 93, 107, 108, 111, 117, 122, 147, 158, 159, 161, 163, 166, 167, 172, 173, 303, 308, 318, 321, 323, 330, 349, 350, 351, 357, 358, 362, 493, 503

Adekiya, Oyelawo A, vi, xiv

Afforestation Projects, 57

Agadez, 112

Agalawa floodplain, 27

Agricultural Development Projects, 229

Ahmed, Mohammed, iv, vi, ix, xiii, xv, xvi, 4, 6, 10, 46, 47, 51, 62, 81, 88, 91, 105, 108, 121, 122, 123, 163, 384, 434, 477, 478, 479, 480, 481, 483, 484, 485, 486

Akpan, Otoabasi, ii

Aliyu, Ishaq A., iv, v, vi, ix, x, xiii, 51, 62, 91, 143, 168, 199, 204

Alluvial Channel, 5

almajiri phenomenon, 500

Annual rainfall, 247, 462, 480

Arabic language, 131, 163, 296

## B

Badamasi, Murtala M, iv, v, viii, x, 59, 62

Badawa, 165, 167, 168, 314, 315

Badume, 179, 181, 182

Barau, Aliyu Salisu, iv, ix, 92, 93, 95, 105

Basara Plains, 3

Basement Complex, 1, 3, 6, 23, 24, 25, 26, 30, 33, 35, 36, 209, 211, 225, 227

Bayero University, xvi, 11, 18, 19, 33, 64, 77, 80, 88, 105, 106, 107, 108, 109, 158, 163, 172, 173, 174, 204, 221, 222, 223, 235, 244, 247, 248, 275, 292, 302, 318, 344, 362, 384, 385, 386, 434, 437, 439, 448, 463, 475, 486

Benue valley, 114

biodiversity, xi, 92, 94, 98, 103, 237, 245, 246, 248, 250, 251, 252, 253, 254, 255, 258,

Index | A.I. Tanko and S.B. Momale (Eds.)
Kano: Environment, Society and Development
London & Abuja, Adonis & Abbey Publishers

**505**

Index | A.I. Tanko and S.B. Momale (Eds.)
Kano: Environment, Society and Development
London & Abuja, Adonis & Abbey Publishers

Index | A.I. Tanko and S.B. Momale (Eds.)
Kano: Environment, Society and Development
London & Abuja, Adonis & Abbey Publishers

**507**

Index | A.I. Tanko and S.B. Momale (Eds.)
Kano: Environment, Society and Development
London & Abuja, Adonis & Abbey Publishers

**508**

Index | A.I. Tanko and S.B. Momale (Eds.)
Kano: Environment, Society and Development
London & Abuja, Adonis & Abbey Publishers

**509**

# M

Maconachie, Roy, vi, xiv, xvi, 47, 59, 60, 61, 63, 122
Madatai Community, 69
Magaga River System, 28
Maghreb-al-Aksa, 126
Manchester cottons, 130
Masama, 360
Maulana Sultan Kano,, 137
Medical Geography, xiii, 347, 348
Middle School, 75
Millennium Ecosystem Assessment, 100, 108
Ministries, Departments and Agencies, 78
Mohammed, Salisu, v, vii, xi, xii, xiii, 64, 131, 211, 222, 245, 246, 250, 264, 266, 273, 275, 334, 337, 338, 340, 341, 344, 378, 503
Mohd, Unmi K, iv
Momale, Saleh B., 3, iv, v, xi, 286, 293
Morocco, 112, 126, 127, 129, 136, 149

# N

Naira Magwan Water Restaurant, 119
Nassarawa, 72, 74, 75, 99, 102, 162, 172, 307, 326, 327, 376, 378, 380, 381, 383
National Academy of Sciences, 449
National Economic Empowerment Development Strategy, 392
National Infrastructural Improvement Act, 295
National Policy on Education, 296, 297, 298, 300
National Union of Road Transport Workers, 311, 348
Native Authorities, 49
Natural Vegetation, 44
Niger Republic, 112, 144, 247, 278, 279
Nigerian Conservation Society., 58
Nigerian Environmental Society, 58
Nigerian Meteorological Agency, 456
Nigerian. Relative measure of poverty, 190

Index | A.I. Tanko and S.B. Momale (Eds.)
Kano: Environment, Society and Development
London & Abuja, Adonis & Abbey Publishers

**510**

Index | A.I. Tanko and S.B. Momale (Eds.)
Kano: Environment, Society and Development
London & Abuja, Adonis & Abbey Publishers

**511**

Index | A.I. Tanko and S.B. Momale (Eds.)
Kano: Environment, Society and Development
London & Abuja, Adonis & Abbey Publishers

Index | A.I. Tanko and S.B. Momale (Eds.)
Kano: Environment, Society and Development
London & Abuja, Adonis & Abbey Publishers

**513**

www.ingramcontent.com/pod-product-compliance
Lightning Source LLC
Chambersburg PA
CBHW021805270326
41932CB00007B/61